Life's Questions: and Sma

AN INTRODUCTION TO MORAL PHILOSOPHY

Frederik Kaufman

Mc Graw Hill **Higher Education**

Boston   Burr Ridge, IL   Dubuque, IA   New York   San Francisco   St. Louis
Bangkok   Bogotá   Caracas   Kuala Lumpur   Lisbon   London   Madrid   Mexico City
Milan   Montreal   New Delhi   Santiago   Seoul   Singapore   Sydney   Taipei   Toronto

Higher Education

HARDEST QUESTIONS: BIG AND SMALL
NTRODUCTION TO MORAL PHILOSOPHY

lished by McGraw-Hill, a business unit of The McGraw-Hill Companies, Inc., 1221 Avenue of the
ericas, New York, NY 10020. Copyright © 2010 by The McGraw-Hill Companies, Inc. All rights
served. No part of this publication may be reproduced or distributed in any form or by any means,
r stored in a database or retrieval system, without the prior written consent of The McGraw-Hill
Companies, Inc., including, but not limited to, any network or other electronic storage or transmission,
or broadcast for distance learning.

1   2   3   4   5   6   7   8   9   0   DOC/DOC   0   9

ISBN: 978-0-07-290108-5
MHID: 0-07-290108-X

Editor in Chief: *Michael Ryan*
Editorial Director: *Beth Mejia*
Sponsoring Editor: *Mark Georgiev*
Development Editor: *Nicole C. Bridge*
Editorial Assistant: *Briana Porco*
Marketing Manager: *Pamela Cooper*
Project Manager: *Meghan Durko*
Designer: *Laurie Entringer*
Production Supervisor: *Richard DeVitto*
Compositor: *10/12 Palatino by Laserwords Private Limited*
Printer: *45# New Era Matte Plus by R. R. Donnelley & Sons*

Credits appear on page 429 and constitute an extension of the copyright page.

Library of Congress Cataloging-in-Publication Data

Kaufman, Frederik.
   Life's hardest questions-big and small : An introduction to
moral philosophy / Frederik Kaufman. — 1st ed.
      p. cm.
   ISBN-13: 978-0-07-290108-5 (alk. paper)
   ISBN-10: 0-07-290108-X (alk. paper)
   1. Ethics. I. Title.
BJ1012.K155   2008
170—dc22   2008043966

To Donna

Contents

Preface

The Problem

The most daunting challenge facing instructors in introduction to ethics courses is conveying the centrality of reasoned inquiry to moral deliberation in a convincing manner. Morality is often taken to be just a hazy mixture of personal conviction, religious instruction, gut feeling, and cultural norms, not something amenable to rational inquiry. It is no wonder then that instructors have an uphill struggle even to establish the legitimate role of philosophy in this subject. Add the common thought that we should respect differences of opinion no matter what (since, after all, there are no correct answers), and the stage is set for instructors to be perceived as denying common sense about the nature of ethics throughout the semester. One can be coerced to do philosophical ethics more or less mechanically—utilitarians say this, Kantians say that—but without the proper appreciation for moral philosophy, the entire subject remains abstract and alien, rather than something palpably essential to our lives. *Life's Hardest Questions* is motivated by the Socratic conviction that we are dealing with "no small matter, but how we ought to live" and that our "greatest good" lies in this inquiry. What could be more compelling or important than questions of right and wrong, good and evil, and how we ought to live? These truly are life's hardest questions.

The Solution

In this text I have deliberately aimed to address a wider range of subjects than is normally found in introductory ethics texts. Newcomers to philosophical ethics are understandably curious about the extent of moral inquiry, not just moral theory or contemporary moral problems, important as those areas are. Thus, in addition to classical sources of moral theory (Kant, Mill, Aristotle, Aquinas, Hobbes), and various important contemporary moral issues (abortion, sex, euthanasia, animals, war, capital punishment), there are chapters on non-Western ethics, feminist ethics, global ethics, environmental ethics, metaethics, amoralism, and two rarely discussed topics that nevertheless play a huge role in our personal lives: forgiveness, and toleration.

I have sought to do much more than present primary sources. Beginning with discussions of relativism, religion, and the scope and nature of morality, and after presenting basic moral theories, I have organized subsequent chapters around a series of hard questions—questions that one would likely ask about a range of moral issues. A few examples: Should we tolerate hate speech on campus? What is cruel and unusual punishment? Is war ever the answer? Is killing people wrong? When should we forgive? Should we eat animals? Am I responsible for world poverty? Why be moral? The introductory essays for each chapter are not intended to summarize the reprinted material; they serve instead as models for philosophical inquiry into the topic. This means that they are not scrupulously neutral in the sense of not trying to answer the hard question at hand, for what is the point of asking such difficult questions if we don't try to answer a few of them, even tentatively? I give reasoned and balanced discussions, and though certainly not definitive, in each case I have at least sought to clarify the conceptual landscape surrounding the questions. The introductory essays are accessible and engaging without sacrificing intellectual rigor.

Features

- Appendix includes separate essays on ethics of plagiarism and etiquette.
- Inclusion of topics in non-western ethics.
- Accessible introduction to metaethics.
- Discussions on what we are to make of the fact that there are many different moral theories—how do we decide which one to adopt?

Pedagogical Aids

- Each reprinted reading includes a biographical note.
- Thesis statements precede the readings to provide students with context.
- Critical Reading Questions guide students through reading assignments.

Acknowledgments

I would like to thank the following reviewers, whose suggestions and insights helped improve this text: Richard Askay, Philosophy, University of Portland; Dr. David M. Brahinsky, Social Science, Bucks County Community College; Francis Danquah, History, Southern University at Baton Rouge; Andrea Fiala, Philosophy, CSO Fresno; Dan Frank, Ethics, Purdue University; Frank Macaluso, Philosophy, University of Miami; Mark Packer, Philosophy, USC Upstate; Ann A. Pang-White, Philosophy, University of Scranton.

I hope that students and instructors will find my text useful, stimulating and worthy of the vital subject that it seeks to introduce.

Frederik Kaufman
Ithaca College

CHAPTER 1

What Is Ethics?

Ethics, we might say, consists of our beliefs regarding right and wrong. But it is one thing to hold ideas about right and wrong and another to assess them. Are all ethical beliefs equally good? Perhaps that seems a strange question to ask, since, as the saying goes, "Everyone has his or her own ethics." But it would be strange if our ethical beliefs were *that* different. It is not as though some people think that lying, cheating, and stealing are just fine and others think they are not. So our ethical beliefs probably do not diverge as much as the claim that we each have our own ethics makes it sound.

Where our ethical beliefs *do* differ, is this because of different preferences, akin perhaps to differences of taste—sort of like preferring vanilla ice cream to mint chocolate chip? If ethical beliefs are basically matters of taste or individual preference, then it hardly makes sense to get so worked up about those who do not share our ethical views. But we do get worked up about ethical disagreements, especially those we take to be important. It can be frustrating to meet someone who seems decent and sensible but who disagrees with us on, say, abortion or capital punishment or war—important issues where much is at stake. Of course, we just *know* that our ethical judgments are right, or best, at least for us. Thus, arguing about ethical matters does seem as pointless as arguing about ice cream flavors. Other than expressing our own heartfelt preferences, and perhaps hoping to influence others, there seems to be little more to do.

Our capacity for moral reflection progresses through various stages (we will not distinguish here between the terms *ethical* and *moral*), beginning with an unquestioning and reflexive obedience to rules externally imposed. But this does not satisfy us for very long, and as we mature we seek justification for the restrictions that morality places on us. We want to know why we cannot simply do whatever we want or why we cannot take someone else's property if we desire it or why we should give consideration to the interests of others, especially if doing so is not to our immediate advantage.

To ask these and similar questions is a profound and potentially disturbing step to take, because we may find that what had seemed intuitively obvious, or just "felt right," upon analysis turns out to be unsubstantiated, the result of cultural bias or misguided thinking. Rational inquiry does not regard tradition or authority as justificatory, nor does it take depth of feeling, mere intuition, or sincerity as reasons; and the fact that a particular ethical belief might be part of one's religious orientation makes it unavailable to those outside the faith.

Philosophical reflection on ethics can alienate and confuse people, as Socrates learned over 2500 years ago. In the *Apology* (Plato's account of Socrates' defense of philosophy to the Athenian court that ultimately convicted him), Socrates claimed that "it is the greatest good for a man to discuss virtue every day," because "the unexamined life is not worth living."

Socrates' legacy survives in the capacity to engage in independent and critical moral thought. This capacity can be cultivated, and that is the purpose of this book. We shall explore the main questions and issues that constitute ethics, or moral philosophy, the preeminent quandary of the human condition.

MORAL RELATIVISM

Ethical reflection often involves a kind of cognitive dissociation. As long as we stick to clear, specific cases, passing moral judgment can be easy. We do it all the time. Did I do wrong to steal your wallet, assuming that I simply wanted your money and had no other pressing concerns, such as needing to buy life-saving medicine for my sick child? Yes, of course I did. But when asked to reflect on ethics more broadly, we frequently forget these confident judgments in specific cases and say that ethics is just individual opinion, there being no truth to the matter—that one person's ethical judgment is as good as another's. It is a peculiar state of affairs. Why do we do that? Often it is because we accept a view called moral relativism.

Moral relativism is the view that there are no objectively correct moral beliefs that transcend local customs about right and wrong. Moral judgments are thus relative either to individuals or to cultures, there being no independent or objective fact of the matter. According to the moral relativist, when we make a moral judgment we are not gaining insight into the way things really are, as we are when we judge that the earth is round or that $2 + 2 = 4$. "Real facts" are independent of what we think; that is, the earth retains its shape regardless of what we think about it. If we think it is flat, then we are mistaken; if we think it is spherical, then we are correct. There is an objective reality that our judgments track and to which they correspond when we judge correctly.

None of this, the relativist asserts, holds with moral judgments; there is no objective, independent moral reality to which our moral judgments could correspond. Therefore, people cannot make moral mistakes, and one person's ethical judgment is as good as another person's. Perhaps someone can make a moral "mistake" in the sense that his or her moral beliefs might not correspond to those of the larger society, but those of the larger society do not correspond to anything. It is as though you lived in a society of vanilla ice cream lovers, but you loved chocolate. Your preference would be "wrong" only in the sense that it does not conform to that of others. This is different from thinking that the earth is flat while living in a society that thinks it is round.

Moral relativism raises deep metaphysical questions about the nature of morality, such as whether objective moral facts exist, whether our moral judgments can have a truth value (that is, can be true or false), and whether relativism, if true, extends beyond ethics to include other areas of inquiry such as religion or even science. There can be more and less sophisticated versions of relativism, but let's consider a simplistic version—one that purports to make rational moral inquiry pointless right from the start. We will call it "simple moral relativism." It holds that because there are no objectively correct, independent moral truths, all moral judgments are equally worthy. This type of relativism is often behind remarks such as "Who's to say?" and "According to whose ethics?" and "Right for me, wrong for you."

A moment's reflection reveals the absurdity of simple moral relativism. If all moral beliefs are equally good, then Hitler's moral beliefs are as good as anyone else's. He thinks that it is morally acceptable to exterminate Jews. We disagree, of course, but the disagreement goes no deeper than a disagreement about preferences, like the ice cream flavor preferences mentioned earlier, because if simple moral relativism is true, then it is not as though what Hitler did really is wrong. It is wrong only from our point of view; from his point of view, it is right. There is nothing more to say than that. If simple moral relativism is true, we have no argument to establish the correctness of our view or the incorrectness of his, because all views are equally "correct." To fight against Hitler would be simply a matter of our trying to impose our views on him, there being no basis for opposition other than that we don't like what he does.

Is simple moral relativism true? The mere fact that it has uncomfortable implications does not show that it is false. Maybe morality is as moral relativism says, and all we can do is impose our ethical beliefs on those with whom we disagree. "Impose" is something we do only if we have the power to do so; otherwise, we might try to influence others to see things as we do. But remember, if simple moral relativism is true, and if we do persuade others to see things our way, that is not because our moral beliefs are right; there are *no* correct moral views, according to simple moral relativism. Persuading others to accept our moral beliefs would be analogous to getting them to switch favorite ice cream flavors. We will have prevailed in our opinion, but only because we are passionate or eloquent or charismatic, not because our view is correct.

Despite the problems with simple moral relativism, it remains intuitively and stubbornly obvious to many. When we are asked point blank why we should think that simple moral relativism is an accurate account of the nature of morality, the following argument comes to mind: Because people disagree about ethical matters, there must not be any objectively correct moral beliefs. More than any other feature of our moral lives, disagreement about ethical issues seems to make simple moral relativism a compelling account of the nature of ethics. At this point we need to ask two questions: (1) Is there genuine ethical disagreement? and (2) If there is, does that show that there are no correct moral beliefs?

The first question might seem absurd. Consider the seemingly interminable moral argument about abortion. According to some, abortion is murder; others disagree. Is this a disagreement about ethics or a disagreement about how to interpret uncontested ethical principles? We agree that murder is the wrongful killing of persons, but we disagree about whether fetuses count as persons. Even if fetuses are persons, it is not clear that killing them counts as murder. So what seems to be a disagreement about ethics might turn out instead to be a disagreement about how to interpret widely shared principles, about which principles apply, about which non-moral facts are relevant, and so forth. This is not to say that there are no genuine ethical disagreements, only that we cannot confidently assume that there are, as the argument above for simple moral relativism presupposes.

Let's consider the second question. If there are genuine ethical disagreements, would that show that there are no objectively correct moral beliefs? No. The mere fact that people disagree about something hardly shows that there are no objectively correct answers. Scientists can disagree, but this does not show that there is no fact of the matter. Irrespective of what we are talking about, be it science, religion, economics, or ethics, it does not follow from disagreement alone that there is no objectively correct answer, because the existence of an objectively correct answer is compatible with some people getting it right and others getting it wrong. This is a point about logic, not ethics.

Suppose for a moment that there are objectively correct answers to moral questions. Why should we think that everyone will know what they are? It doesn't work this way in science or in any other area where we think objectively correct judgments can be made. Continents ride on tectonic plates, but does everyone know that? It could be the same in ethics. This is not to say that there are objective moral facts, only that *if* there are, there is no reason to think people will agree on what they are. Ethical disagreement, just like disagreement in other areas, is compatible with objective correctness. Hence, the mere fact of ethical disagreement does not establish simple moral relativism.

But still, one might object, in ethics nothing can be proved. Much depends on what we mean by "prove." If by "prove" we mean "establish as incontrovertible," then outside of mathematics nothing can be proved. Even in science we do not have those standards of proof. Rather than fixating on the idea of proof in ethics, think instead about good reasons. If the store's lights are out and the sign in the window says, "Sorry, We're Closed," does this *prove* that the store is closed? Maybe the owner forgot to turn the sign around or maybe the power went out. But for all that, these are good reasons for thinking that the store is closed, even if they do not conclusively, incontrovertibly establish it.

We operate successfully with good reasons in legal proceedings, literary interpretations, aesthetic judgments, historical analyses, economic forecasts, scientific hypotheses, political predictions, psychological explanations, military strategy, interpersonal relationships, and on and on. These all rely on standards of evidence that fall short of incontrovertible proof. The same holds in ethics. If I stole a friend's wallet because I wanted money to go to the movies, and I lied later about it, and I have done similar things in the past to others, what better reasons could someone want for thinking that I am a bad person? Maybe there is some incredible explanation that will show it is all some sort of terrible misunderstanding, but without some such explanation, these are excellent reasons for thinking that I am a bad person, even though they do not prove it. Once we reject a simple-minded moral relativism that purports to make moral inquiry impossible and get over the idea that moral judgments are somehow defective because they cannot be conclusively proved, we can engage in sensible and productive moral reflection.

THE POINT AND SCOPE OF MORALITY

What is morality about? Moral concepts such as good, bad, right, wrong, commendable, despicable, worthy, and fair are modes of evaluation. But what are we evaluating when we use these terms, and to what end?

Moral evaluation is a particular way of assessing people and their actions. We can morally evaluate governments, policies, laws, and institutions—and even books, strategies, plans, and cultures—but these too reduce to people and their actions. For moral evaluation to be intelligible there must be a rational mind at work, one that can intend, choose, assess, and be responsive to reasons for and against alternative courses of action, and thereby be responsible for its actions. This is the idea of a **moral agent.**

Normal adult human beings are moral agents, but not all human beings, as a biological kind, are moral agents. Young children and mentally damaged human beings, for example, are not (full) moral agents. They are not amenable to reasons, and they cannot deliberate or weigh the consequences of their actions, so their behavior cannot be thought to represent their considered judgment. Not only are their actions immune from moral assessment, but an entire dimension of assessment is unavailable to them. Just as some people are colorblind, such human beings are morally blind.

Like any kind of evaluation, moral evaluation presupposes a point or aim of the evaluation. We evaluate cars because we want cars that are comfortable, fuel-efficient, and safe; we rate them with respect to those criteria. What is the point of moral evaluation and what is a moral reason? Ever since we got ejected from the Garden of Eden, human life has been subject to a host of difficulties. Given our condition and the contingencies of life, there is an inherent tendency for things to go badly for us. We all want security, comfort, enough to eat, and a chance to develop our capacities; we want power, freedom, social stability, and the respect of our peers. But the things necessary for a tolerable human existence do not spontaneously appear. As the great seventeenth-century philosopher Thomas Hobbes (1588–1679) memorably said, the natural human condition is "solitary, poor, nasty, brutish, and short."

Our condition might not be as bleak as Hobbes thought, but it is not all that rosy either. Material scarcity, fear, competition, ignorance, superstition, greed, and limited sympathy all conspire to make our lot less than ideal. A minimal account of morality, then, would involve those rules and precepts that make social living possible. Commonsense prohibitions about lying, cheating, and stealing do just that. No society can function without a presumption of truthfulness, for example; communication and exchanges of any sort would otherwise be impossible. The point of morality, then, in the words of the contemporary Oxford philosopher G. J. Warnock, is to "ameliorate the human predicament."

Given the inherent tendency of things to go badly for us, morality seeks to ameliorate the conditions under which we must live. But it does this in a special way because not all attempts to ameliorate the human predicament count as morality. Seeking to produce more food or working to conquer cancer may also ameliorate the human predicament, but that does not make those activities moral activities. The moral is distinguished by how it seeks to ameliorate our predicament. It opposes our tendency for parochialism—that is, a tendency to be relatively indifferent to the interests and well-being of others. A narrow, short-sighted, uncooperative kind of self-concern is especially damaging to human relations, and ethics seeks to overcome that propensity by cultivating a wider range of concern in us.

Perhaps a tendency to extend our concern to others is as "natural" as our propensity for self-concern; both can easily be part of human nature. But encouraging a proper regard for the well-being of others is the distinctive contribution of ethics to ameliorating the human predicament. Our "other-regarding" capacities can be refined and enlarged by cultivating our moral imagination—that is, our ability to see things from the perspective of someone else. The realization that there are other people relevantly similar to ourselves is the key insight of the ancient injunction to do unto others as you would have them do unto you—the Golden Rule. When we see that there are other people relevantly similar to us, we realize that there is no rational basis to think that our interests automatically ought to be promoted over the similar interests of others. The fact that our interests are ours hardly privileges them. We are thus forced, on pain of irrationality, to acknowledge the legitimacy of the interests of others, if we think ours worthy of attention.

Understanding the point of ethics now raises questions about its scope. If the point of morality is to ameliorate the human predicament, then morality is essentially connected to human well-being. But limiting ethics to human interests might be unjustifiably parochial, since there are nonhuman interests that are relevantly similar to human interests. For example, certain animals share interests with human beings, such as an interest in not suffering. If so, then it is unjustified automatically to prefer human interests in not suffering to an animal's interest in not suffering. Suddenly the scope of morality has expanded to include nonhuman animals, at least the ones that have interests relevantly similar to our own. The moral status of animals is a large issue, one that we will consider further in this book. Whether our sympathies can keep pace with a much-expanded moral community is an important question.

RELIGION AND ETHICS

Religion gives us a comprehensive account of the nature of the world, our purpose in being here, and how we should live, so it seems entirely natural that religion and ethics should be closely connected. Many people do derive their ethical commitments from their religious commitments, or at least this is the order of explanation. Because religion attempts to structure life according to the thoughts, intentions, or authority of a transcendent power, that will be the basis for religiously grounded moral pronouncements. In theory, this is a straightforward approach to ethics: All we have to do is figure out what a higher power intends (perhaps by means of special sacred texts, prayer, intuition, mystical experiences, ritual, religious teachings, or what have you), and we know what we ought to do and how we ought to live.

In a short and eminently readable platonic dialogue called the *Euthyphro,* Socrates considers the relationship between morality and religion. He asks Euthyphro, the main character in the dialogue, a series of deceptively simple questions that have become some of the most famous questions in the history of philosophy. Socrates' questions go to the nerve of an alleged link between morality and religion, and they remain deeply instructive to us even today. Imagine that God (or whatever transcendent force is embraced by a religion) commands and forbids certain things. Let's suppose that God forbids slavery and so, because of God's condemnation, we know that slavery is wrong (in the dialogue Socrates considers piety, not slavery). Socrates asks us to consider these two questions: Is slavery wrong *because* God forbids it? Or does God forbid it *because* it is wrong?

What is the difference between Socrates' two questions? If slavery is wrong simply *because* God forbids it, then God is arbitrary. There is nothing inherently wrong with slavery; God just declares it wrong. On the other hand, if God forbids slavery *because* it is wrong, then God sees that slavery is wrong and communicates that fact to us. On the first question (wrong because God forbids), morality is dependent on God's will; on the second (God forbids because wrong), morality is independent of God's will.

The same point can be made with numbers. Suppose God declares that $2 + 2 = 4$. (Why God would do such a thing is beside the point; remember, from God's point of view, all facts are equally obvious.) Is $2 + 2 = 4$ because God says it is, or does God say $2 + 2 = 4$ because it is so? If $2 + 2 = 4$ simply because God says it is, then God could say that $2 + 2 = 5$ or that $2 + 2 = 80$ and then that would be so. In other words, God's picking 4 as the answer is arbitrary. However, if God says that $2 + 2 = 4$ *because* $2 + 2 = 4$, then that is something God apprehends, not decrees. So either God is arbitrary or morality (like mathematics) is independent of God.

What is the problem with an arbitrary God? An arbitrary God is not worthy of worship, because it makes no sense to praise God for what he does if he would be equally praiseworthy had he done the opposite. If the only reason slavery is wrong is that God says it is, then God could say it is right and it would be right. If one is inclined to object that God would never say that slavery is right; well, why not? Is it because God knows that slavery is wrong and he would not mislead us? Fine, but then God is not determining the wrongness of slavery; the wrongness of slavery is, on the contrary, something that he knows.

What have we learned from Socrates' questions? We now see that ethics is logically independent of God's will. Does this mean that believers can no longer look to God for ethical guidance? No. Since God as traditionally conceived knows all, believers can still regard God's word—however it is received—as absolutely authoritative. It is just that we must understand the relationship between God's word and ethics properly: Rather than determining right and wrong, God would apprehend it. This is a subtle but important difference.

Our powers of comprehension are vastly inferior to God's. Nevertheless, just as we do not need God to tell us that $2 + 2 = 4$, perhaps we do not need

God to tell us that slavery is immoral. We can see that slavery is immoral, and we can see that it is immoral for the same reasons that God has for thinking it immoral (although, given the historical fact of slavery, maybe this hasn't been so clear to us!). Slavery is wrong because we should not treat people as things and that to do so is a terrible violation of a person's dignity. If God's reasons for condemning slavery are utterly different from ours, then we would want to know what they could possibly be.

PHILOSOPHICAL MORAL DELIBERATION

Philosophical moral deliberation is different from what we might have initially thought. It requires a willingness to pursue questions of right and wrong rationally and systematically. Rather than being a simple reflection of what we have been taught by our culture, religion, or friends and family, philosophical moral deliberation demands that we seek good grounds for our beliefs. This does not mean that we must reject our current moral beliefs and start from scratch, but it does require us to look for reasons to justify convictions we may already hold about what is right and what is wrong.

Why is that important? There are many reasons. First, since ethics is action-guiding, we want to make sure that our actions are guided by sound moral reasons. Ethical decisions can involve important matters (such as life, justice, property, reputations, and well-being), and merely feeling a certain way or having a hunch or doing something because that's what we were taught or that's how it has been done in the past are not adequate grounds for proper action, especially when so much is at stake. Big economic decisions are not wisely made on hunches and feelings, so why should it be any different when even more important moral matters are at stake?

Second, a coherent intellectual life requires us to understand why we do what we do. In ethics we wonder about what we ought to do, and it is always legitimate to ask "Why?" This is part of the logic of "ought," because it makes no sense to say that we ought to do something but that there are no reasons why we ought to do it. And once reasons are given, they can be evaluated. Are they good reasons, and why or why not? To justify a course of action as morally correct involves an impersonal appeal to moral principles and a coherent explanation of how the principles legitimize the action.

And third, a rational understanding of ethics is an aspect of human dignity. Rather than being wholly subject to the causal forces that impinge on us from our surroundings, we hope to be moved by reasons. We conceive of ourselves as agents, beings who can deliberate about right and wrong and then act accordingly. Respect for others requires that we see them as similar to ourselves; that is, we must regard them as centers of rational self-awareness too. They are, like ourselves, beings who are capable of acting for the sake of a reason. And since our respect for others is conceptually tied to presenting them with reasons for action, rather than merely manipulating them, so our self-respect is similarly bound to our willingness to explore the rational basis of our own moral beliefs and commitments.

CHAPTER 2

Ethics and Consequences

THE ROLE OF CONSEQUENCES IN ETHICS

When we deliberate about what we ought to do, the consequences of our actions are a natural starting place for moral assessment. But not just any consequences. If we first have an account of what is ultimately good or worthwhile, then we can measure the consequences of our actions with respect to those ends. For if there is an intrinsic good or ultimate value, then it makes sense for that to be the goal of ethics. Right and wrong could then be defined with respect to producing the greatest balance of good over bad on any occasion. This is the intuitive idea behind a moral theory known as utilitarianism. Right actions are those that produce the most good in any situation. But what shall we count as good?

Utilitarianism was systematically expounded by Jeremy Bentham (1748–1832) and John Stuart Mill (1806–1873), both English philosophers and social reformers. Classical utilitarians take pleasure (or happiness)—broadly and deeply understood—as the only good. Right and wrong are thus defined as those actions that maximize the amount of happiness in any given situation. In other words, we are to judge the utility (hence the name *utilitarianism*) of actions according to their consequences in bringing about the greatest balance of happiness over unhappiness.

Why should we think that happiness is the only intrinsic good? This has some plausibility, since all our actions can be seen as ultimately aiming at happiness. When pressed to explain why we undertake one course of action or another, sooner or later we wind up saying that it will make us happy. For example, a student matriculates in college; why? Answer: to get an education. Why does the student want an education? Answer: this will lead to a good job. Why does the student want a good job? Answer: because this will promote happiness. Or consider the person working out at the gym; why is she doing that? Answer: because she wants to stay in shape. But why does she want to stay in shape? Answer: because that will promote health. But why does she want to promote her health? Answer: because that will promote happiness. A similar line of questioning for any intentional activity will lead to happiness—broadly understood—as the ultimate good toward which we aim. Whether happiness can be narrowly construed as pleasure is a separate question. The important consideration for ethics is to see that once we posit happiness as the ultimate good, then it makes sense to think about right and wrong with respect to the only thing that is good in itself.

Whose happiness should we promote? Utilitarians answer that we should strive to bring about the greatest balance of happiness for the greatest number. This is because there is no reason to prefer the happiness of one person over that of another; happiness is happiness. I cannot argue that my happiness is more important than anyone else's and should therefore come ahead of any other's happiness in a particular situation. Utilitarians are thus morally impartial, seeking to promote good (understood as happiness) as the foundational maxim of their moral philosophy.

What could be more obvious? Utilitarianism seems utterly straightforward—even trite—insofar as it recommends trying to bring about the greatest amount of good in any situation. But problems emerge when we think a bit more carefully about what utilitarianism requires. What if we can produce a lot of happiness, but it must come at the expense of a few individuals? Remember, even though utilitarianism is impartial, there is nothing sacrosanct about individual persons; only happiness is ultimately valuable, not individual people. It is true that individual people are the bearers of happiness, but because utilitarianism is an aggregative view, the individuality of people tends to drop out of consideration. We might be in a situation where we can maximize happiness for many but only because we reduce it for a few. Suppose, for example, that we have a promising new drug for a particular disease, but we are unsure of the proper dosage. In order to determine the proper dosage, we decide to test it on people, some of whom will probably be harmed, but we figure that in the long run harming a few people will be outweighed by the good we produce. Or consider automobile design. We could engineer cars so that there would be far fewer fatal accidents; in fact, we could engineer cars so that they would be many times safer than they currently are. Of course, doing so would make them prohibitively expensive. What we seek instead, with car safety design, is some sort of reasonable trade-off between affordability and safety; we figure that it promotes happiness to have more cars that are relatively safe instead of far fewer that are much safer. Evidently, we are willing to sacrifice a few people to achieve affordability for many people. That is, on balance, there will be more happiness overall, even though a few people will be harmed for the greater good.

This is the utilitarian calculation. And utilitarians are inclined to calculate, since if one course of action will lead to more happiness overall than another, then the first is obviously the right thing to do, so we need some way of figuring out which one that is. There are many complications to the utilitarian calculation: Does increasing the happiness of a few a whole lot outweigh minor increases in happiness for a larger number of people? Are all forms of happiness equally valuable, and if not, what kinds of trade-offs can we make among them? Will six units of an especially good form of happiness outweigh twelve of a not-so-worthy kind? And what if we can increase the happiness overall by doing really awful things to a few? What if we could achieve world peace by torturing a small child (as Dostoyevsky would have it in *The Brothers Karamazov*) or more realistically, what if we could maximize happiness by having a slave society? Utilitarians might respond by denying that a slave society could be happiest in the long run—that we would all be happiest in a society that accorded its citizens equal rights and individual liberties, thus subsuming individual rights under utility. Irrespective of whether this reply is adequate, utilitarianism remains worrisome precisely because it allows—indeed, it might require—doing awful things to a few to maximize the general happiness. In this way, utilitarianism is deeply at odds with views that take individual persons as the ultimate source of value. For the utilitarian, individual human rights will always be derivative of more general utilitarian considerations and thus can be overruled by them.

READINGS ON UTILITARIANISM

John Stuart Mill, from *Utilitarianism*

J. S. Mill (1806–1873) was the most influential British philosopher of the nineteenth century. He received a rigorous education from his father, who schooled him in Latin, Greek, and logic at an early age so that the young John Stuart Mill could defend the utilitarian doctrines espoused by an earlier proponent of the view, Jeremy Bentham (1748–1832). But Mill's severe education in the service of utilitarian theory also had an unintended result: He experienced an emotional crisis. "The habit of analysis has a tendency to wear away the feelings: as indeed it has, when no other mental habit is cultivated," Mill observed in his Autobiography.

Reprinted here is a selection from Mill's short but enormously influential book *Utilitarianism*, wherein he describes and defends the utilitarian approach to moral philosophy, something that he maintained in a somewhat modified form throughout his life despite his early bad experience.

To give you a sense of how best to use the critical reading questions that you will find at the beginning of each reading throughout this textbook, for this first selection from Mill, I have provided some reading notes and other commentary that correspond to the critical reading questions.

Critical Reading Questions

1. What does Mill mean by "happiness," and how is that relevant to utilitarianism?
2. How does Mill respond to critics who denigrate utilitarianism as "worthy of swine"?
3. How does Mill argue that some pleasures are better than others?
4. What does Mill mean when he claims that the utilitarian perspective is that of a "benevolent spectator"?

Response to Critical Reading Question 1. By "happiness" Mill means pleasure. This identification forms the core of utilitarianism, since the right thing to do is that action which produces the greatest amount of pleasure, the only intrinsic value. Right action is thus defined with respect to what is good. Hedonism, espoused by the ancient philosopher Epicurus, is the theory that pleasure is the only intrinsic good. Mill is thus a hedonist.

Response to Critical Reading Question 2. Those who criticize utilitarianism as worthy only of swine—because of utilitarianism's embrace of pleasure as the end—sell people short, since it takes more than bodily pleasures to satisfy a person.

Response to Critical Reading Question 3. There must be a quantity/quality distinction with pleasures because there is a quantity/quality distinction for "all other things." And we can tell which pleasures are of higher quality by finding out which pleasures those who are acquainted with all kinds of pleasure prefer, since they and they alone are "the only competent judges."

Response to Critical Reading Question 4. The utilitarian perspective requires the greatest good for the greatest number, so I cannot count my pleasure as more important than anyone else's. I must adopt the view of an impartial and benevolent spectator; my happiness counts as much as yours, and yours counts as much as mine.

UTILITARIANISM

John Stuart Mill

Edited by Oskar Piest

The creed which accepts as the foundation of morals "utility" or the "greatest happiness principle" holds that actions are right in proportion as they tend to promote happiness; wrong as they tend to produce the reverse of happiness. By happiness is intended pleasure and the absence of pain; by unhappiness, pain and the privation of pleasure. To give a clear view of the moral standard set up by the theory, much more requires to be said; in particular, what things it includes in the ideas of pain and pleasure, and to what extent this is left an open question. But these supplementary explanations do not affect the theory of life on which this theory of morality is grounded—namely, that pleasure and freedom from pain are the only things desirable as ends; and that all desirable things (which are as numerous in the utilitarian as in any other scheme) are desirable either for pleasure inherent in themselves or as means to the promotion of pleasure and the prevention of pain.

Now such a theory of life excites in many minds, and among them in some of the most estimable in feeling and purpose, inveterate dislike. To suppose that life has (as they express it) no higher end than pleasure—no better and nobler object of desire and pursuit—they designate as utterly mean and groveling, as a doctrine worthy only of swine, to whom the followers of Epicurus were, at a very early period, contemptuously likened; and modern holders of the doctrine are occasionally made the subject of equally polite comparisons by its German, French, and English assailants.

When thus attacked, the Epicureans have always answered that it is not they, but their accusers, who represent human nature in a degrading light, since the accusation supposes human beings to be capable of no pleasures except those of which swine are capable. If this supposition were true, the charge could not be gainsaid, but would then be no longer an imputation; for if the sources of pleasure were precisely the same to human beings and to swine, the rule of life which is good enough for the one would be good enough for the other. The comparison of the Epicurean life to that of beasts is felt as degrading, precisely because a beast's pleasures do not satisfy a human being's conceptions of happiness. Human beings have faculties more elevated than the animal appetites and, when once made conscious of them, do not regard anything as happiness which does not include their gratification. I do not, indeed, consider the Epicureans to have been by any means faultless in drawing out their scheme of consequences from the utilitarian principle. To do this in any sufficient manner, many Stoic, as well as Christian, elements require to be included. But there is no known Epicurean theory of life which does not assign to the pleasures of the intellect, of the feelings and imagination, and of the moral sentiments a much higher value as pleasures than to those of mere sensation. It must be admitted, however, that utilitarian writers in general have placed the superiority of mental over bodily pleasures chiefly in the greater permanency, safety, uncostliness, etc., of the former—that is, in their circumstantial advantages rather than in their intrinsic nature. And on all these points utilitarians have fully proved their case; but they might have taken the other and, as it may be called, higher ground with entire consistency. It is quite compatible with the principle of utility to recognize the fact that some kinds of pleasure are more desirable and more valuable than others. It would be absurd that, while in estimating all other things quality is considered as well as quantity, the estimation of pleasure should be supposed to depend on quantity alone.

If I am asked what I mean by difference of quality in pleasures, or what makes one pleasure more valuable than another, merely as a pleasure, except its being greater in amount, there is but one possible answer. Of two pleasures, if there be one to which all or almost all who have experience of both give a decided preference, irrespective of any feeling of moral obligation to prefer it, that is the more desirable pleasure. If one of the two is, by those who are competently acquainted with both, placed so far above the other that they prefer it, even though knowing it to be attended with a greater amount of discontent, and would not resign it for any quantity of the other pleasure which their nature is capable of, we are justified in ascribing to the preferred enjoyment a superiority in quality so far outweighing quantity as to render it, in comparison, of small account.

Now it is an unquestionable fact that those who are equally acquainted with and equally capable of appreciating and enjoying both do give a most marked preference to the manner of existence which employs their higher faculties. Few human creatures would consent to be changed into any of the lower animals for a promise of the fullest allowance of a beast's pleasures; no intelligent human being would consent to be a fool, no instructed person would be an ignoramus, no person of feeling and conscience would be selfish and base, even though they should be persuaded that the fool, the dunce, or the rascal is better satisfied with his lot than they are with theirs. They would not resign what they possess more than he for the most complete satisfaction of all the desires which they have in common with him. If they ever fancy they would, it is only in cases of unhappiness so extreme that to escape from it they would exchange their lot for almost any other, however undesirable in their own eyes. A being of higher faculties requires more to make him happy, is capable probably of more

acute suffering, and certainly accessible to it at more points, than one of an inferior type; but in spite of these liabilities, he can never really wish to sink into what he feels to be a lower grade of existence. We may give what explanation we please of this unwillingness; we may attribute it to pride, a name which is given indiscriminately to some of the most and to some of the least estimable feelings of which mankind are capable; we may refer it to the love of liberty and personal independence, an appeal to which was with the Stoics one of the most effective means for the inculcation of it; to the love of power or to the love of excitement, both of which do really enter into and contribute to it; but its most appropriate appellation is a sense of dignity, which all human beings possess in one form or other, and in some, though by no means in exact, proportion to their higher faculties, and which is so essential a part of the happiness of those in whom it is strong that nothing which conflicts with it could be otherwise than momentarily an object of desire to them. Whoever supposes that this preference takes place at a sacrifice of happiness—that the superior being, in anything like equal circumstances, is not happier than the inferior—confounds the two very different ideas of happiness and content. It is indisputable that the being whose capacities of enjoyment are low has the greatest chance of having them fully satisfied; and a highly endowed being will always feel that any happiness which he can look for, as the world is constituted, is imperfect. But he can learn to bear its imperfections, if they are at all bearable; and they will not make him envy the being who is indeed unconscious of the imperfections, but only because he feels not at all the good which those imperfections qualify. It is better to be a human being dissatisfied than a pig satisfied; better to be Socrates dissatisfied than a fool satisfied. And if the fool, or the pig, are of a different opinion, it is because they only know their own side of the question. The other party to the comparison knows both sides.

It may be objected that many who are capable of the higher pleasures occasionally, under the influence of temptation, postpone them to the lower. But this is quite compatible with a full appreciation of the intrinsic superiority of the higher. Men often, from infirmity of character, make their election for the nearer good, though they know it to be the less valuable; and this no less when the choice is between two bodily pleasures than when it is between bodily and mental. They pursue sensual indulgences to the injury of health, though perfectly aware that health is the greater good. It may be further objected that many who begin with youthful enthusiasm for everything noble, as they advance in years, sink into indolence and selfishness. But I do not believe that those who undergo this very common change voluntarily choose the lower description of pleasures in preference to the higher. I believe that, before they devote themselves exclusively to the one, they have already become incapable of the other. Capacity for the nobler feelings is in most natures a very tender plant, easily killed, not only by hostile influences, but by mere want of sustenance; and in the majority of young persons it speedily dies away if the occupations to which their position in life has devoted them, and the society into which it has thrown them, are not favorable to keeping that higher capacity in exercise. Men lose their high aspirations as they lose their intellectual tastes, because they have not time or opportunity for indulging them; and they addict themselves to inferior pleasures, not because they deliberately prefer them, but because they are either the only ones to which they have access or the only ones which they are any longer capable of enjoying. It may be questioned whether anyone who has remained equally susceptible to both classes of pleasures ever knowingly and calmly preferred the lower, though many, in all ages, have broken down in an ineffectual attempt to combine both.

From this verdict of the only competent judges, I apprehend there can be no appeal. On a question which is the best worth having of two pleasures, or which of two modes of existence is the most grateful to the feelings, apart from its moral attributes and from its consequences, the judgment of those who are qualified by knowledge of both, or, if they differ, that of the majority among them, must be admitted as final. And there needs be the less hesitation to accept this judgment respecting the quality of pleasures, since there is no other tribunal to be referred to even on the question of quantity. What means

are there of determining which is the acutest of two pains, or the intensest of two pleasurable sensations, except the general suffrage of those who are familiar with both? Neither pains nor pleasures are homogeneous, and pain is always heterogeneous with pleasure. What is there to decide whether a particular pleasure is worth purchasing at the cost of a particular pain, except the feelings and judgment of the experienced? When, therefore, those feelings and judgment declare the pleasures derived from the higher faculties to be preferable *in kind,* apart from the question of intensity, to those of which the animal nature, disjoined from the higher faculties, is susceptible, they are entitled on this subject to the same regard.

I have dwelt on this point as being a necessary part of a perfectly just conception of utility or happiness considered as the directive rule of human conduct. But it is by no means an indispensable condition to the acceptance of the utilitarian standard; for that standard is not the agent's own greatest happiness, but the greatest amount of happiness altogether; and if it may possibly be doubted whether a noble character is always the happier for its nobleness, there can be no doubt that it makes other people happier, and that the world in general is immensely a gainer by it. Utilitarianism, therefore, could only attain its end by the general cultivation of nobleness of character, even if each individual were only benefited by the nobleness of others, and his own, so far as happiness is concerned, were a sheer deduction from the benefit. But the bare enunciation of such an absurdity as this last renders refutation superfluous.

According to the greatest happiness principle, as above explained, the ultimate end, with reference to and for the sake of which all other things are desirable—whether we are considering our own good or that of other people—is an existence exempt as far as possible from pain, and as rich as possible in enjoyments, both in point of quantity and quality; the test of quality and the rule for measuring it against quantity being the preference felt by those who, in their opportunities of experience, to which must be added their habits of self-consciousness and self-observation, are best furnished with the means of comparison. This, being according to the utilitarian opinion the end of human action, is necessarily also the standard of morality, which may accordingly be defined "the rules and precepts for human conduct," by the observance of which an existence such as has been described might be, to the greatest extent possible, secured to all mankind; and not to them only, but, so far as the nature of things admits, to the whole sentient creation.

. . .

I must again repeat what the assailants of utilitarianism seldom have the justice to acknowledge, that the happiness which forms the utilitarian standard of what is right in conduct is not the agent's own happiness but that of all concerned. As between his own happiness and that of others, utilitarianism requires him to be as strictly impartial as a disinterested and benevolent spectator. In the golden rule of Jesus of Nazareth, we read the complete spirit of the ethics of utility. "To do as you would be done by," and "to love your neighbor as yourself," constitute the ideal perfection of utilitarian morality. As the means of making the nearest approach to this ideal, utility would enjoin, first, that laws and social arrangements should place the happiness or (as, speaking practically, it may be called) the interest of every individual as nearly as possible in harmony with the interest of the whole; and, secondly, that education and opinion, which have so vast a power over human character, should so use that power as to establish in the mind of every individual an indissoluble association between his own happiness and the good of the whole, especially between his own happiness and the practice of such modes of conduct, negative and positive, as regard for the universal happiness prescribes; so that not only he may be unable to conceive the possibility of happiness to himself, consistently with conduct opposed to the general good, but also that a direct impulse to promote the general good may be in every individual one of the habitual motives of action, and the sentiments connected therewith may fill a large and prominent place in every human being's sentient existence. If the impugners of the utilitarian morality represented it to their own minds in this its true character, I know not what recommendation possessed by any other morality they could possibly affirm to be wanting to it; what more beautiful or more exalted developments of human nature any other ethical system can be supposed to foster, or what springs of action, not accessible to the utilitarian, such systems rely on for giving effect to their mandates.

Discussion Questions

1. What is happiness, and is Mill correct to take it as the end toward which everything else is a means?
2. Is Mill correct to claim that "it is quite compatible with the principle of utility to recognize the fact that some kinds of pleasure are more desirable and more valuable than others"?
3. Is it better to be Socrates dissatisfied than a fool satisfied?
4. Is the utilitarian perspective of a "strictly impartial" benevolent spectator a proper one for morality?
5. What might it be like to live in a fully utilitarian society?

CHAPTER 3

Kantian Ethics

THE ROLE OF INTENTIONS IN ETHICS

Consider someone who does the right thing but for the wrong reasons. This person might give money to the poor, but only because he figures that it will impress his friends and help him socially. Or consider someone who devotes herself to community service, but only because she expects to be rewarded for her acts of seeming selflessness, either in this life or the next. Or suppose someone who wants money refrains from robbing the bank, not because he thinks it would be wrong but because he is afraid of getting caught. Really, the only difference between this person and the actual bank robber is that the actual bank robber figures he won't get caught. From the moral point of view they are the same because if the person who wants money refrains from robbing the bank only because he fears getting caught, then if he could be assured that he wouldn't get caught, he would rob the bank. The decision to rob the bank would then be simply a calculation of whether it is worth the risk of apprehension, not whether it is something that morally one ought not to do. If the people described act for the reasons indicated, once this is revealed, then we are reluctant to think that their seemingly praiseworthy actions really have moral worth at all.

Consider, too, a person who devotes herself to helping the poor because she is overcome by compassion at their plight, or the person who acts benevolently because he is so empathic. What shall we say about these and similar cases where someone acts in a morally praiseworthy manner because of a compassionate or empathic nature? The question to pursue is whether these people would still act in the way they did if they were not so empathic or sensitive to the plight of others. If the compassionate person was not so compassionate or the empathic person so empathic, then they might well act other than they did. And this means that their original actions result from accidental features of their psychologies. True, we are relieved that the compassionate person is compassionate and that the empathic person is empathic, but this is just a bit of moral good luck, not something we can regard as morally praiseworthy in itself, because if things had turned out differently, if the people were cold-hearted and not so sensitive by nature, then they would not have done what they did.

It looks as though proper moral motivation requires understanding *why* one is acting, in the sense of understanding the principle or reason for which one acts. The person who refrains from bank robbing because he sees that it is wrong is morally very different from the person who refrains from bank robbing because he figures that he will get caught. And the person who helps others because she thinks that is the right thing to do irrespective of how one feels is morally very different from the person who helps others because of an especially empathic nature. When we act out of our conception of what we ought to do irrespective of how we feel, then our actions have a very different character than when they are merely caused by our desires or are the result of fortuitous circumstances. The capacity to act for the sake of a principle is the core of our moral agency. It was so conceived by the renowned eighteenth-century German philosopher Immanuel Kant. (See the biographical note that accompanies the reading for this chapter.)

Kant's moral philosophy is uncompromising in its insistence that the moral worth of an action lies in its motivation. According to Kant, the only thing that is good without qualification is a good will—roughly, our ability to conceive of the proper principles for whose sake we act when we act as we ought. As Kant famously put it, a good will completely shorn of its ability to effect anything that it intends would nevertheless "sparkle like a jewel in its own right," because it would remain properly motivated regardless of its ability to affect the world.

A properly motivated will is one that acts in accordance with its conception of duty; it does not act out of self-interest, nor does it act because it is overwhelmed by emotion or inclination. Only when the will has a clear conception of the proper principles for the sake of which it acts can it be called unqualifiedly good. But how does a will determine its duty? Kant distinguishes between two sorts of imperatives, or things that one must do: hypothetical imperatives and categorical imperatives. **Hypothetical imperatives** are imperatives that are contingent on our inclinations. So *if* I want to do well in school, then I must study. Note the hypothetical in that statement; I am enjoined to study, provided that I want to do well in school. What if I don't care about doing well in school? In that case the imperative does not apply to me. The defining characteristic of hypothetical imperatives is that one is released from the force of the imperative simply by renouncing the inclination on which it is based.

One of Kant's insights is that the imperatives of morality—the things that morality enjoins us to do or not to do—are not hypothetical, for if they were, then they would be contingent on inclination, and we could be released from the strictures of morality by simply renouncing the relevant inclination. Consider how odd it would be to express moral imperatives hypothetically: If you want people to like you, then you must not lie; or if you want to be respected, you must not commit murder. If morality were composed of hypothetical imperatives, I could lie or commit murder so long as I didn't care what others thought of me. But we cannot escape from the demands of morality so easily!

Kant holds that the imperatives of morality bind us categorically; that is, they hold no matter what our likes, dislikes, wants, preferences, or desires. Morality imposes on us things that we must do . . . *period.*

Kantian morality is thus a system of categorical imperatives, all of which are subsumed under one grand central principle called (appropriately enough) *the* **Categorical Imperative.** Kant states it as follows: "Act only according to that maxim by which you can at the same time will that it should become a universal law." Commentators have been variously interpreting Kant's claim ever since he first announced it. It seems to mean that at root, morality has to do with our acting for the sake of principles (maxims) that can be followed by everyone similarly situated. Just as when mathematicians reason about triangles, they disregard the details of any particular triangle (the dimensions of a triangle and whether it is drawn in chalk or pencil or scratched in sand are irrelevant to triangularity), so we are supposed to abstract from the irrelevant particular features of our individual situations and reason about moral principles that apply to all rational agents. Our particular likes, dislikes, preferences, and emotions are alleged to be irrelevant to what we ought to do in a particular situation. If I ought to help someone or return a borrowed item, for example, the fact that I don't feel like it is beside the point.

A Kantian moral agent is one who abstracts from his or her inclinations and acts for the sake of principles that are binding on anyone similarly situated. One does not make a special exception for oneself; if it is wrong for you to steal, then it is wrong for me to steal; if it is wrong for you to lie, then it is wrong for me to lie. Indeed, it is the height of irrationality for me to think that it is morally acceptable for me to do something that it is not acceptable for you to do if we are similarly situated, because that would mean that similar cases would be treated differently for no good reason. Kant even has a special term for beings who can act according to their conception of their duty; he calls them "persons." Thus not all members of the species *Homo sapiens* are Kantian persons, for not all members of our biological kind are capable of acting according to their conception of their duty. And furthermore, there could be Kantian persons who are not members of our biological kind, such as Martians, if they were rational beings (and if they exist!).

The Kantian universe is thus divided into **persons** and **things.** Things are nonrational entities of any kind, such as plants, animals, and inanimate objects, whereas persons are rational agents (by definition). Persons are different from things by virtue of their rational autonomy—their ability to act for their conception of a principle in accordance with the categorical imperative. That's a pretty hefty requirement; there might be fewer Kantian persons than we thought! Nevertheless, rational autonomy demarks persons as radically different from things and confers on them a special status, indeed for Kant the highest status. For it is by virtue of our rational autonomy that we have dignity. Rather than just being pushed around the world by causal forces that impinge on us, we are able to act for the sake of a principle, something that no thing can do.

It is no wonder, then, that Kant offers us what he claims is a second formulation of the main principle of morality—the categorical imperative—that is centered on persons. Kant tells us, "Act so that you treat humanity whether in your own person or in that of another, always as an end and never as a means only."

Just like his first formulation of the categorical imperative, Kant's cryptic insight about the status of persons has been subject to much interpretation. He seems to be telling us that persons should not be treated as things, that to do so is to violate what is most valuable about them. Think of how you treat a thing—a chair, for instance. You move it around as you wish, you can sell it or destroy it; it is entirely subject to your will. Now think of doing that to a person. It is immediately obvious that you are doing something wrong and Kant can explain why. By manipulating a person as though he or she were a thing, you fail to respect that person's rational autonomy and hence violate the person's dignity (as well as your own).

READINGS ON KANTIAN ETHICS

Immanuel Kant, from *The Foundations of the Metaphysics of Morals*

Immanuel Kant (1724–1804) is one of the most influential philosophers in the history of thought. He has contributed profoundly to all the major areas of philosophy: metaphysics, epistemology, aesthetics, political philosophy, philosophy of religion, philosophy of mind, and ethics. He spent forty years as professor at the university in Königsberg, Prussia; he never married, never traveled much beyond Königsberg, and is said to have had such regular habits that the townspeople would set their watches by the afternoon walks he took at precisely the same time every day.

Among his many works in ethics, Kant's short but formidably titled The Foundations of the Metaphysics of Morals *is perhaps his greatest; it is certainly his most influential. Although his writing is difficult, bristling with technical terms embedded in extremely dense prose, many people find Kant's view deeply compelling. Despite the infelicity of Kant's writing, his ethical ideas are richly rewarding and worthy of our close consideration.*

Critical Reading Questions

1. Why does Kant think that a good will remains good even if it cannot accomplish its purposes?
2. What is Kant's example of the merchant who does not overcharge an inexperienced customer supposed to demonstrate?
3. Why does Kant dismiss actions done from self-interest or inclination as not having moral worth?
4. How does Kant derive the categorical imperative?
5. What four duties does Kant offer as examples of how the categorical imperative functions in moral deliberation?
6. Why does Kant think that persons are intrinsically valuable?
7. What is the "Kingdom of Ends"?

GROUNDING FOR THE METAPHYSICS OF MORALS

Immanuel Kant

TRANSITION FROM THE ORDINARY RATIONAL KNOWLEDGE OF MORALITY TO THE PHILOSOPHICAL

There is no possibility of thinking of anything at all in the world, or even out of it, which can be regarded as good without qualification, except a *good will*. Intelligence, wit, judgment, and whatever talents of the mind one might want to name are doubtless in many respects good and desirable, as are such qualities of temperament as courage, resolution, perseverance. But they can also become extremely bad and harmful if the will, which is to make use of these gifts of nature and which in its special constitution is called character, is not good. The same holds with gifts of fortune; power, riches, honor, even health, and that complete well-being and contentment with one's condition which is called happiness make for pride and often hereby even arrogance, unless there is a good will to correct their influence on the mind and herewith also to rectify the whole principle of action and make it universally conformable to its end. The sight of a being who is not graced by any touch of a pure and good will but who yet enjoys an uninterrupted prosperity can never delight a rational and impartial spectator. Thus a good will seems to constitute the indispensable condition of being even worthy of happiness.

Some qualities are even conducive to this good will itself and can facilitate its work. Nevertheless, they have no intrinsic unconditional worth; but they always presuppose, rather, a good will, which restricts the high esteem in which they are otherwise rightly held, and does not permit them to be regarded as absolutely good. Moderation in emotions and passions, self-control, and calm deliberation are not only good in many respects but even seem to constitute part of the intrinsic worth of a person. But they are far from being rightly called good without qualification (however unconditionally they were commended by the ancients). For without the principles of a good will, they can become extremely bad; the coolness of a villain makes him not only much more dangerous but also immediately more abominable in our eyes than he would have been regarded by us without it.

A good will is good not because of what it effects or accomplishes, nor because of its fitness to attain some proposed end; it is good only through its willing, i.e., it is good in itself. When it is considered in itself, then it is to be esteemed very much higher than anything which it might ever bring about merely in order to favor some inclination, or even the sum total of all inclinations. Even if, by some especially unfortunate fate or by the niggardly provision of stepmotherly nature, this will should be wholly lacking in the power to accomplish its purpose; if with the greatest effort it should yet achieve nothing, and only the good will should remain (not, to be sure, as a mere wish but as the summoning of all the means in our power), yet would it, like a jewel, still shine by its own light as something which has its full value in itself. Its usefulness or fruitlessness can neither augment nor diminish this value. Its usefulness would be, as it were, only the setting to enable us to handle it in ordinary dealings or to attract to it the attention of those who are not yet experts, but not to recommend it to real experts or to determine its value.

But there is something so strange in this idea of the absolute value of a mere will, in which no account is taken of any useful results, that in spite of all the agreement received even from ordinary reason, yet there must arise the suspicion that such an idea may perhaps have as its hidden basis merely some high-flown fancy, and that we may have misunderstood the purpose of nature in assigning to reason the governing of our will. Therefore, this idea will be examined from this point of view.

In the natural constitution of an organized being, i.e., one suitably adapted to the purpose of life, let us take as a principle that in such a being no organ is to be found for any end unless it be the most fit and the best adapted for that end. Now if that being's preservation, welfare, or in a word its happiness, were the real end of nature in the case of a being having reason and will, then nature would have hit upon a very poor arrangement in having the reason of the creature carry out this purpose. For all the actions which such a creature has to perform with this purpose in view, and the whole rule of his conduct would have been prescribed much more exactly by instinct; and the purpose in question could have been attained much more certainly by instinct than it ever can be by reason. And if in addition reason had been imparted to this favored creature, then it would have had to serve him only to contemplate the happy constitution of his nature, to admire that nature, to rejoice in it, and to feel grateful to the cause that bestowed it; but reason would not have served him to subject his faculty of desire to its weak and delusive guidance nor would it have served him to meddle incompetently with the purpose of nature. In a word, nature would have taken care that reason did not strike out into a practical use nor presume, with its weak insight, to think out for itself a plan for happiness and the means for attaining it. Nature would have taken upon herself not only the choice of ends but also that of the means, and would with wise foresight have entrusted both to instinct alone.

And, in fact, we find that the more a cultivated reason devotes itself to the aim of enjoying life and happiness, the further does man get away from true contentment. Because of this there arises in many persons, if only they are candid enough to admit it, a certain degree of misology, i.e., hatred of reason. This is especially so in the case of those who are the most experienced in the use of reason, because after calculating all the advantages they derive, I say not from the invention of all the arts of common luxury, but even from the sciences (which in the end seem to them to be also a luxury of the understanding), they yet find that they have in fact only brought more trouble on their heads than they have gained in happiness. Therefore, they come to envy, rather than despise, the more common run of men who are closer to the guidance of mere natural instinct and who do not allow their reason much influence on their conduct. And we must admit that the judgment of those who would temper, or even reduce below zero, the boastful eulogies on behalf of the advantages which reason is supposed to provide as regards the happiness and contentment of life is by no means morose or ungrateful to the goodness with which the world is governed. There lies at the root of such judgments, rather, the idea that existence has another and much more worthy purpose, for which, and not for happiness, reason is quite properly intended, and which must, therefore, be regarded as the supreme condition to which the private purpose of men must, for the most part, defer.

Reason, however, is not competent enough to guide the will safely as regards its objects and the satisfaction of all our needs (which it in part even multiplies); to this end would an implanted natural instinct have led much more certainly. But inasmuch as reason has been imparted to us as a practical faculty, i.e., as one which is to have influence on the will, its true function must be to produce a will which is not merely good as a means to some further end, but is good in itself. To produce a will good in itself reason was absolutely necessary, inasmuch as nature in distributing her capacities has everywhere gone to work in a purposive manner. While such a will may not indeed be the sole and complete good, it must, nevertheless, be the highest good and the condition of all the rest, even of the desire for happiness. In this case there is nothing inconsistent with the wisdom of nature that the cultivation of reason, which is requisite for the first and unconditioned purpose, may in many ways restrict, at least in this life, the attainment of the second purpose, viz., happiness, which is always conditioned. Indeed happiness can even be reduced to less than nothing, without nature's failing thereby in her purpose; for reason recognizes as its highest practical function the establishment of a good will, whereby in the attainment of this end reason is capable only of its own kind of satisfaction, viz., that of fulfilling a purpose which is in turn determined only by reason, even though such fulfilment were often to interfere with the purposes of inclination.

The concept of a will estimable in itself and good without regard to any further end must now be developed. This concept already dwells in the natural sound understanding and needs not so much to be taught as merely to be elucidated. It always holds first place in estimating the total worth of our actions and constitutes the condition of all the rest. Therefore, we shall take up the concept of *duty,* which includes that of a good will, though with certain subjective restrictions and hindrances, which far from hiding a good will or rendering it unrecognizable, rather bring it out by contrast and make it shine forth more brightly.

I here omit all actions already recognized as contrary to duty, even though they may be useful for this or that end; for in the case of these the question does not arise at all as to whether they might be done from duty, since they even conflict with duty. I also set aside those actions which are really in accordance with duty, yet to which men have no immediate inclination, but perform them because they are impelled thereto by some other inclination. For in this [second] case to decide whether the action which is in accord with duty has been done from duty or from some selfish purpose is easy. This difference is far more difficult to note in the [third] case where the action accords with duty and the subject has in addition an immediate inclination to do the action. For example, that a dealer should not overcharge an inexperienced purchaser certainly accords with duty; and where there is much commerce, the prudent merchant does not overcharge but keeps to a fixed price for everyone in general, so that a child may buy from him just as well as everyone else may. Thus customers are honestly served, but this is not nearly enough for making us believe that the merchant has acted this way from duty and from principles of honesty; his own advantage required him to do it. He cannot, however, be assumed to have in addition [as in the third case] an immediate inclination toward his buyers, causing him, as it were, out of love to give no one as far as price is concerned any advantage over another. Hence the action was done neither from duty nor from immediate inclination, but merely for a selfish purpose.

On the other hand, to preserve one's life is a duty; and, furthermore, everyone has also an immediate inclination to do so. But on this account the often anxious care taken by most men for it has no intrinsic worth, and the maxim of their action has no moral content. They preserve their lives, to be sure, in accordance with duty, but not from duty. On the other hand, if adversity and hopeless sorrow have completely taken away the taste for life, if an unfortunate man, strong in soul and more indignant at his fate than despondent or dejected, wishes for death and yet preserves his life without loving it—not from inclination or fear, but from duty—then his maxim indeed has a moral content.

To be beneficent where one can is a duty; and besides this, there are many persons who are so sympathetically constituted that, without any further motive of vanity or self-interest, they find an inner pleasure in spreading joy around them and can rejoice in the satisfaction of others as their own work. But I maintain that in such a case an action of this kind, however dutiful and amiable it may be, has nevertheless no true moral worth. It is on a level with such actions as arise from other inclinations, e.g., the inclination for honor, which if fortunately directed to what is in fact beneficial and accords with duty and is thus honorable, deserves praise and encouragement, but not esteem; for its maxim lacks the moral content of an action done not from inclination but from duty. Suppose then the mind of this friend of mankind to be clouded over with his own sorrow so that all sympathy with the lot of others is extinguished, and suppose him still to have the power to benefit others in distress, even though he is not touched by their trouble because he is sufficiently absorbed with his own; and now suppose that, even though no inclination moves him any longer, he nevertheless tears himself from this deadly insensibility and performs the action without any inclination at all, but solely from duty—then for the first time his action has genuine moral worth. Further still, if nature has put little sympathy in this or that man's heart, if (while being an honest man in other respects) he is by temperament cold and indifferent to the sufferings of others, perhaps because as regards his own sufferings he is endowed with the special gift of patience and fortitude and expects or even requires that others should have the same; if such a man (who would truly not be nature's worst product) had not been exactly fashioned by her to be a philanthropist, would he not yet find in himself a source from which he might give himself a worth far higher than any that a good-natured temperament might have? By all means, because just here does the worth of the character come out; this worth is moral and incomparably the highest of all, viz., that he is beneficent, not from inclination, but from duty.

To secure one's own happiness is a duty (at least indirectly); for discontent with one's condition under many pressing cares and amid unsatisfied wants might easily become a great temptation to transgress one's duties. But here also do men of themselves already have, irrespective of duty, the strongest and deepest inclination toward happiness, because just in this idea are all inclinations combined into a sum total. But the precept of happiness is often so constituted as greatly to interfere with some inclinations, and yet men cannot form any definite and certain concept of the sum of satisfaction of all inclinations that is called happiness. Hence there is no wonder that a single inclination which is determinate both as to what it promises and as to the time within which it can be satisfied may outweigh a fluctuating idea; and there is no wonder that a man, e.g., a gouty patient, can choose to enjoy what he likes and to suffer what he may, since by his calculation he has here at least not sacrificed the enjoyment of the present moment to some possibly groundless expectations of the good fortune that is supposed to be found in health. But even in this case, if the universal inclination to happiness did not determine his will and if health, at least for him, did not figure as so necessary an element in his calculations; there still remains here, as in all other cases, a law, viz., that he should promote his happiness not from inclination but

from duty, and thereby for the first time does his conduct have real moral worth.

Undoubtedly in this way also are to be understood those passages of Scripture which command us to love our neighbor and even our enemy. For love as an inclination cannot be commanded; but beneficence from duty, when no inclination impels us and even when a natural and unconquerable aversion opposes such beneficence, is practical, and not pathological, love. Such love resides in the will and not in the propensities of feeling, in principles of action and not in tender sympathy; and only this practical love can be commanded.

The second proposition is this: An action done from duty has its moral worth, not in the purpose that is to be attained by it, but in the maxim according to which the action is determined. The moral worth depends, therefore, not on the realization of the object of the action, but merely on the principle of volition according to which, without regard to any objects of the faculty of desire, the action has been done. From what has gone before it is clear that the purposes which we may have in our actions, as well as their effects regarded as ends and incentives of the will, cannot give to actions any unconditioned and moral worth. Where, then, can this worth lie if it is not to be found in the will's relation to the expected effect? Nowhere but in the principle of the will, with no regard to the ends that can be brought about through such action. For the will stands, as it were, at a crossroads between its a priori principle, which is formal, and its a posteriori incentive, which is material; and since it must be determined by something, it must be determined by the formal principle of volition, if the action is done from duty—and in that case every material principle is taken away from it.

The third proposition, which follows from the other two, can be expressed thus: Duty is the necessity of an action done out of respect for the law. I can indeed have an inclination for an object as the effect of my proposed action; but I can never have respect for such an object, just because it is merely an effect and is not an activity of the will. Similarly, I can have no respect for inclination as such, whether my own or that of another. I can at most, if my own inclination, approve it; and, if that of another, even love it, i.e., consider it to be favorable to my own advantage. An object of respect can only be what is connected with my will solely as ground and never as effect—something that does not serve my inclination but, rather, outweighs it, or at least excludes it from consideration when some choice is made—in other words, only the law itself can be an object of respect and hence can be a command. Now an action done from duty must altogether exclude the influence of inclination and therewith every object of the will. Hence there is nothing left which can determine the will except objectively the law and subjectively pure respect for this practical law, i.e., the will can be subjectively determined by the maxim that I should follow such a law even if all my inclinations are thereby thwarted.

Thus the moral worth of an action does not lie in the effect expected from it nor in any principle of action that needs to borrow its motive from this expected effect. For all these effects (agreeableness of one's condition and even the furtherance of other people's happiness) could have been brought about also through other causes and would not have required the will of a rational being, in which the highest and unconditioned good can alone be found. Therefore, the pre-eminent good which is called moral can consist in nothing but the representation of the law in itself, and such a representation can admittedly be found only in a rational being insofar as this representation, and not some expected effect, is the determining ground of the will. This good is already present in the person who acts according to this representation, and such good need not be awaited merely from the effect.

But what sort of law can that be the thought of which must determine the will without reference to any expected effect, so that the will can be called absolutely good without qualification? Since I have deprived the will of every impulse that might arise for it from obeying any particular law, there is nothing left to serve the will as principle except the universal conformity of its actions to law as such, i.e., I should never act except in such a way that I can also will that my maxim should become a universal law. Here mere conformity to law as such (without having as its basis any law determining particular actions) serves the will as principle and must

so serve it if duty is not to be a vain delusion and a chimerical concept. The ordinary reason of mankind in its practical judgments agrees completely with this, and always has in view the aforementioned principle.

For example, take this question. When I am in distress, may I make a promise with the intention of not keeping it? I readily distinguish here the two meanings which the question may have; whether making a false promise conforms with prudence or with duty. Doubtless the former can often be the case. Indeed I clearly see that escape from some present difficulty by means of such a promise is not enough. In addition I must carefully consider whether from this lie there may later arise far greater inconvenience for me than from what I now try to escape. Furthermore, the consequences of my false promise are not easy to forsee, even with all my supposed cunning; loss of confidence in me might prove to be far more disadvantageous than the misfortune which I now try to avoid. The more prudent way might be to act according to a universal maxim and to make it a habit not to promise anything without intending to keep it. But that such a maxim is, nevertheless, always based on nothing but a fear of consequences becomes clear to me at once. To be truthful from duty is, however, quite different from being truthful from fear of disadvantageous consequences; in the first case the concept of the action itself contains a law for me, while in the second I must first look around elsewhere to see what are the results for me that might be connected with the action. For to deviate from the principle of duty is quite certainly bad; but to abandon my maxim of prudence can often be very advantageous for me, though to abide by it is certainly safer. The most direct and infallible way, however, to answer the question as to whether a lying promise accords with duty is to ask myself whether I would really be content if my maxim (of extricating myself from difficulty by means of a false promise) were to hold as a universal law for myself as well as for others, and could I really say to myself that everyone may promise falsely when he finds himself in a difficulty from which he can find no other way to extricate himself. Then I immediately become aware that I can indeed will the lie but can not at all will a universal law to lie. For by such a law there would really be no promises at all, since in vain would my willing future actions be professed to other people who would not believe what I professed, or if they over-hastily did believe, then they would pay me back in like coin. Therefore, my maxim would necessarily destroy itself just as soon as it was made a universal law.

Therefore, I need no far-reaching acuteness to discern what I have to do in order that my will may be morally good. Inexperienced in the course of the world and incapable of being prepared for all its contingencies, I only ask myself whether I can also will that my maxim should become a universal law. If not, then the maxim must be rejected, not because of any disadvantage accruing to me or even to others, but because it cannot be fitting as a principle in a possible legislation of universal law, and reason exacts from me immediate respect for such legislation. Indeed I have as yet no insight into the grounds of such respect (which the philosopher may investigate). But I at least understand that respect is an estimation of a worth that far outweighs any worth of what is recommended by inclination, and that the necessity of acting from pure respect for the practical law is what constitutes duty, to which every other motive must give way because duty is the condition of a will good in itself, whose worth is above all else.

Thus within the moral cognition of ordinary human reason we have arrived at its principle. To be sure, such reason does not think of this principle abstractly in its universal form, but does always have it actually in view and does use it as the standard of judgment.

. . .

This conformity alone is properly what is represented as necessary by the imperative.

Hence there is only one categorical imperative and it is this: Act only according to that maxim whereby you can at the same time will that it should become a universal law.

Now if all imperatives of duty can be derived from this one imperative as their principle, then there can at least be shown what is understood by the concept of duty and what it means, even though there is left undecided whether what is called duty may not be an empty concept.

The universality of law according to which effects are produced constitutes what is properly called nature in the most general sense (as to form), i.e., the existence of things as far as determined by universal laws. Accordingly, the universal imperative of duty may be expressed thus: Act as if the maxim of your action were to become through your will a universal law of nature.

We shall now enumerate some duties, following the usual division of them into duties to ourselves and to others and into perfect and imperfect duties.

1. A man reduced to despair by a series of misfortunes feels sick of life but is still so far in possession of his reason that he can ask himself whether taking his own life would not be contrary to his duty to himself. Now he asks whether the maxim of his action could become a universal law of nature. But his maxim is this: from self-love I make as my principle to shorten my life when its continued duration threatens more evil than it promises satisfaction. There only remains the question as to whether this principle of self-love can become a universal law of nature. One sees at once a contradiction in a system of nature whose law would destroy life by means of the very same feeling that acts so as to stimulate the furtherance of life, and hence there could be no existence as a system of nature. Therefore, such a maxim cannot possibly hold as a universal law of nature and is, consequently, wholly opposed to the supreme principle of all duty.

2. Another man in need finds himself forced to borrow money. He knows well that he won't be able to repay it, but he sees also that he will not get any loan unless he firmly promises to repay it within a fixed time. He wants to make such a promise, but he still has conscience enough to ask himself whether it is not permissible and is contrary to duty to get out of difficulty in this way. Suppose, however, that he decides to do so. The maxim of his action would then be expressed as follows: when I believe myself to be in need of money, I will borrow money and promise to pay it back, although I know that I can never do so. Now this principle of self-love or personal advantage may perhaps be quite compatible with

one's entire future welfare, but the question is now whether it is right. I then transform the requirement of self-love into a universal law and put the question thus: how would things stand if my maxim were to become a universal law? He then sees at once that such a maxim could never hold as a universal law of nature and be consistent with itself, but must necessarily be self-contradictory. For the universality of a law which says that anyone believing himself to be in difficulty could promise whatever he pleases with the intention of not keeping it would make promising itself and the end to be attained thereby quite impossible, inasmuch as no one would believe what was promised him but would merely laugh at all such utterances as being vain pretenses.

3. A third finds in himself a talent whose cultivation could make him a man useful in many respects. But he finds himself in comfortable circumstances and prefers to indulge in pleasure rather than to bother himself about broadening and improving his fortunate natural aptitudes. But he asks himself further whether his maxim of neglecting his natural gifts, besides agreeing of itself with his propensity to indulgence, might agree also with what is called duty. He then sees that a system of nature could indeed always subsist according to such a universal law, even though every man (like South Sea Islanders) should let his talents rust and resolve to devote his life entirely to idleness, indulgence, propagation, and, in a word, to enjoyment. But he cannot possibly will that this should become a universal law of nature or be implanted in us as such a law by a natural instinct. For as a rational being he necessarily wills that all his faculties should be developed, inasmuch as they are given him for all sorts of possible purposes.

4. A fourth man finds things going well for himself but sees others (whom he could help) struggling with great hardships; and he thinks: what does it matter to me? Let everybody be as happy as Heaven wills or as he can make himself; I shall take nothing from him nor even envy him; but I have no desire to contribute anything to his well-being or to his assistance when in need. If such a way of thinking were to become a universal law of nature, the human race admittedly could very well subsist and doubtless

could subsist even better than when everyone prates about sympathy and benevolence and even on occasion exerts himself to practice them but, on the other hand, also cheats when he can, betrays the rights of man, or otherwise violates them. But even though it is possible that a universal law of nature could subsist in accordance with that maxim, still it is impossible to will that such a principle should hold everywhere as a law of nature. For a will which resolved in this way would contradict itself, inasmuch as cases might often arise in which one would have need of the love and sympathy of others and in which he would deprive himself, by such a law of nature springing from his own will, of all hope of the aid he wants for himself.

These are some of the many actual duties, or at least what are taken to be such, whose derivation from the single principle cited above is clear. We must be able to will that a maxim of our action become a universal law; this is the canon for morally estimating any of our actions. Some actions are so constituted that their maxims cannot without contradiction even be thought as a universal law of nature, much less be willed as what should become one. In the case of others this internal impossibility is indeed not found, but there is still no possibility of willing that their maxim should be raised to the universality of a law of nature, because such a will would contradict itself. There is no difficulty in seeing that the former kind of action conflicts with strict or narrow [perfect] (irremissible) duty, while the second kind conflicts only with broad [imperfect] (meritorious) duty. By means of these examples there has thus been fully set forth how all duties depend as regards the kind of obligation (not the object of their action) upon the one principle.

If we now attend to ourselves in any transgression of a duty, we find that we actually do not will that our maxim should become a universal law—because this is impossible for us—but rather that the opposite of this maxim should remain a law universally. We only take the liberty of making an exception to the law for ourselves (or just for this one time) to the advantage of our inclination. Consequently, if we weighed up everything from one and the same standpoint, namely, that of reason, we would find a contradiction in our own will, viz., that a certain principle be objectively necessary as a universal law and yet subjectively not hold universally but should admit of exceptions. But since we at one moment regard our action from the standpoint of a will wholly in accord with reason and then at another moment regard the very same action from the standpoint of a will affected by inclination, there is really no contradiction here. Rather, there is an opposition (*antagonismus*) of inclination to the precept of reason, whereby the universality (*universalitas*) of the principle is changed into a mere generality (*generalitas*) so that the practical principle of reason may meet the maxim halfway. Although this procedure cannot be justified in our own impartial judgment, yet it does show that we actually acknowledge the validity of the categorical imperative and (with all respect for it) merely allow ourselves a few exceptions which, as they seem to us, are unimportant and forced upon us.

We have thus at least shown that if duty is a concept which is to have significance and real legislative authority for our actions, then such duty can be expressed only in categorical imperatives but not at all in hypothetical ones. We have also—and this is already a great deal—exhibited clearly and definitely for every application what is the content of the categorical imperative, which must contain the principle of all duty (if there is such a thing at all). But we have not yet advanced far enough to prove a priori that there actually is an imperative of this kind, that there is a practical law which of itself commands absolutely and without any incentives, and that following this law is duty.

In order to attain this proof there is the utmost importance in being warned that we must not take it into our mind to derive the reality of this principle from the special characteristics of human nature. For duty has to be a practical, unconditioned necessity of action; hence it must hold for all rational beings (to whom alone an imperative is at all applicable) and for this reason only can it also be a law for all human wills. On the other hand, whatever is derived from the special natural condition of humanity, from certain feelings and propensities, or even, if such were possible, from some special tendency peculiar to human reason and not holding necessarily for the will of every rational being—all of this can indeed yield a maxim valid for us, but not a law. This is to say that such can yield a subjective principle according to which we might act if we happen to have the propensity and inclination, but cannot yield an objective principle according to which we would be directed to act even though our every propensity, inclination, and natural tendency were opposed to it. In fact, the sublimity and inner worth of the command are so much the more evident in a duty, the fewer subjective causes there are for it and the more they oppose it; such causes do not in the least weaken the necessitation exerted by the law or take away anything from its validity.

Here philosophy is seen in fact to be put in a precarious position, which should be firm even though there is neither in heaven nor on earth anything upon which it depends or is based. Here philosophy must show its purity as author of its laws, and not as the herald of such laws as are whispered to it by an implanted sense or by who knows what tutelary nature. Such laws may be better than nothing at all, but they can never give us principles dictated by reason. These principles must have an origin that is completely a priori and must at the same time derive from such origin their authority to command. They expect nothing from the inclination of men but, rather, expect everything from the supremacy of the law and from the respect owed to the law. Without the latter expectation, these principles condemn man to self-contempt and inward abhorrence.

Hence everything empirical is not only quite unsuitable as a contribution to the principle of morality, but is even highly detrimental to the purity of morals. For the proper and inestimable worth of an absolutely good will consists precisely in the fact that the principle of action is free of all influences from contingent grounds, which only experience can furnish. This lax or even mean way of thinking which seeks its principle among empirical motives and laws cannot too much or too often be warned against, for human reason in its weariness is glad to rest upon this pillow. In a dream of sweet illusions (in which not Juno but a cloud is embraced) there is substituted for morality some bastard patched up from limbs of quite varied ancestry and looking like anything one wants to see in it but not looking like virtue to him who has once beheld her in her true form.

Therefore, the question is this: is it a necessary law for all rational beings always to judge their actions according to such maxims as they can themselves will that such should serve as universal laws? If there is such a law, then it must already be connected (completely a priori) with the concept of the will of a rational being in general. But in order to discover this connection we must, however reluctantly, take a step into metaphysics, although into a region of it different from speculative philosophy, i.e., we must enter the metaphysics of morals. In practical philosophy the concern is not with accepting grounds for what happens but with accepting laws of what ought to happen, even though it never does happen—that is, the concern is with objectively practical laws. Here there is no need to inquire into the grounds as to why something pleases or displeases, how the pleasure of mere sensation differs from taste, and whether taste differs from a general satisfaction of reason, upon what does the feeling of pleasure and displeasure rest, and how from this feeling desires and inclinations arise, and how, finally, from these there arise maxims through the cooperation of reason. All of this belongs to an empirical psychology, which would constitute the second part of the doctrine of nature, if this doctrine is regarded as the philosophy of nature insofar as this philosophy is grounded on empirical laws. But here the concern is with objectively practical laws, and hence with the relation of a will to itself insofar as it is determined solely by reason. In this case everything related to what is empirical falls away of itself, because if reason entirely by itself determines conduct (and the possibility of such determination we now wish to investigate), then reason must necessarily do so a priori.

The will is thought of as a faculty of determining itself to action in accordance with the representation of certain laws, and such a faculty can be found only in rational beings. Now what serves the will as the objective ground of its self-determination is an end; and if this end is given by reason alone, then it must be equally valid for all rational beings. On the other hand, what contains merely the ground of the possibility of the action, whose effect is an end, is called the means. The subjective ground of desire is the incentive; the objective ground of volition is the motive. Hence there arises the distinction between subjective ends, which rest on incentives, and objective ends, which depend on motives valid for every rational being. Practical principles are formal when they abstract from all subjective ends; they are material, however, when they are founded upon subjective ends, and hence upon certain incentives. The ends which a rational being arbitrarily proposes to himself as effects of this action (material ends) are all merely relative, for only their relation to a specially constituted faculty of desire in the subject gives them their worth. Consequently, such worth cannot provide any universal principles, which are valid and necessary for all rational beings and, furthermore, are valid for every volition, i.e., cannot provide any practical laws. Therefore, all such relative ends can be grounds only for hypothetical imperatives.

But let us suppose that there were something whose existence has in itself an absolute worth, something which as an end in itself could be a ground of determinate laws. In it, and in it alone, would there be the ground of a possible categorical imperative, i.e., of a practical law.

Now I say that man, and in general every rational being, exists as an end in himself and not merely as a means to be arbitrarily used by this or that will. He must in all his actions, whether directed to himself or to other rational beings, always be regarded at the same time as an end. All the objects of inclinations have only a conditioned value; for if there were not these inclinations and the needs founded on them, then their object would be without value. But the inclinations themselves, being sources of needs, are so far from having an absolute value such as to render them desirable for their own sake that the universal wish of every rational being must be, rather, to be wholly free from them. Accordingly, the value of any object obtainable by our action is always conditioned. Beings whose existence depends not on our will but on nature have, nevertheless, if they are not rational beings, only a relative value as means and are therefore called things. On the other hand, rational beings are called persons inasmuch as their nature already marks them out as ends in themselves, i.e., as something which is not to be used merely as means and hence there is imposed thereby a limit on all arbitrary use of such beings, which are thus objects of respect. Persons are, therefore, not merely subjective ends, whose existence as an effect of our actions has a value for us; but such beings are objective ends, i.e., exist as ends in themselves. Such an end is one for which there can be substituted no other end to which such beings should serve merely as means, for otherwise nothing at all of absolute value would be found anywhere. But if all value were conditioned and hence contingent, then no supreme practical principle could be found for reason at all.

If then there is to be a supreme practical principle and, as far as the human will is concerned, a categorical imperative, then it must be such that from the conception of what is necessarily an end for everyone because this end is an end in itself it constitutes an objective principle of the will and can hence serve as a practical law. The ground of such a principle is this: rational nature exists as an end in itself. In this way man necessarily thinks of his own existence; thus far is it a subjective principle of human actions. But in this way also does every other rational being think of his existence on the same rational ground that holds also for me; hence it is at the same time an objective principle, from which, as a supreme practical ground, all laws of the will must be able to be derived. The practical imperative will therefore be the following: Act in such a way that you treat humanity, whether in your own person or in the person of another, always at the same time as an end and never simply as a means.

Discussion Questions

1. Is Kant's division between persons and things a good one?
2. Is Kant successful in showing that we have a duty never to lie? (Or never to commit suicide or to develop our talents or to help the needy?)
3. Is Kant right to think that emotion should play no role in moral deliberation?
4. Could someone actually function as a Kantian? What would that be like?
5. How is Kant's ethical theory non-consequentialist?

CHAPTER 4

Contract Ethics

HOW ETHICS COULD BE CONTRACTUAL

Imagine waking up to find that there is no government: no police, no fire fighters, no court system, no regulatory agencies—no civil authorities of any sort. All have suddenly and mysteriously vanished. It is just you and the people around you. What do you think would happen? Life might carry on in the usual way for a while, but do you think that once people realized they could do whatever they wanted with impunity things would remain as they were when there were civil authorities? People could walk into stores and take anything they wanted without paying for it; if the store owner objected, they could just ignore him. People could drive as fast as they liked, since there would be no traffic police. They could trespass, rob, threaten, rape, or kill as they pleased. They could set fires, settle disputes as they saw fit, vandalize, intimidate, and run unchecked. Do you think that any of these things would happen? It is telling that whenever there is a breakdown of civil authority, people do tend toward anarchy. That is why the National Guard is called out during natural disasters to try to protect people and property against the mayhem that seems always to follow.

Perhaps *you* wouldn't do anything untoward if there were no authority to enforce the rules, but if those around you descended into barbarism, why assume that it would not affect you too? It is pretty clear that even if some are not tempted to take advantage of the situation, many others certainly are, so people would do what they could to protect themselves from one another. They would arm themselves, they would be suspicious and fearful of others, and they would not trust anyone. And so the breakdown in social order—driven by fear of others and concern for one's own safety and ability to get what one needs to survive—would quickly engulf everyone. In the memorable words of the great seventeenth-century English philosopher Thomas Hobbes (see the biographical sketch for the reading in this chapter), life without civil society would be "solitary, poor, nasty, brutish, and short." Hobbes called this miserable condition the "state of nature," and the challenge to humanity is to avoid it at all costs.

We can avoid the state of nature, according to Hobbes, only if we are prepared to surrender some of our freedom to do as we want in exchange for similar agreements by others. I will agree not to try to take your possessions if you agree not to try to take mine; I will agree not to kill you if you agree not to kill me; and so on. Of course, I would prefer that you agree to restrain yourself without my having to agree to restrain myself, but since you are rational too, you would never agree to that. Much as we both dislike having to do so, since we lack the power to do exactly as we wish, we will each grudgingly agree to various mutually beneficial rules that make social living possible. The alternative, the state of nature, is even worse.

But mere agreement is not enough. Once I agree not to steal your possessions on the condition that you agree not to steal mine, I nevertheless start to covet the nice things that you have and so my desires for your things will slowly weaken my resolve. And so for all the other agreements we made. Or perhaps I never really intended to abide by my agreements with you. Agreements, after all, consist of words only. Moreover, even though we each agreed to restrain ourselves in order to make social living possible, I really do not trust you because I know that you are like me and I am not trustworthy. I am not trustworthy because I agreed to restrict myself under duress; had I the power to do whatever I want, I would do so. We each realize this about ourselves and about one another. Therefore, knowing that we will not keep to our agreements on our own, we also agree to establish a "sovereign," a powerful authority created by us to enforce the agreements that we made. We give the sovereign the power of life and death over us, if it comes to that, in order to force us to keep to our agreements. Only thus can we escape the state of nature.

For Hobbes, morality is a purely instrumental compromise position that we reluctantly accept because we lack the power to achieve our ends independently. It is second best—not as bad as the state of nature where there is no morality and our lives are miserable, but not as good as doing as we want with impunity. There is no right or wrong in the state of nature because, according to Hobbes, nothing is inherently so; right and wrong are defined simply by our agreements. The state of nature is an amoral condition, one where killing or being killed, or taking someone else's things, might be good or bad but cannot be right or wrong.

Hobbes's contractarian account of morality is theoretically powerful. It explains the nature of morality simply and clearly: morality is entirely conventional; and it explains why we should be moral: it is to our advantage to obey the rules, provided others do so too. Yet despite its strengths, there is something unsettling about Hobbes's theory. Kant (see Chapter 3) would surely condemn the moral motivation of Hobbesian moral agents, since morality is merely an uneasy compromise necessary for social living. And we could raise questions about the historical fiction of a contract; surely we never actually agreed to anything (As some have noted, the contract isn't worth the paper it was never written on!). Moreover, even if there was some sort of a formal contract in the distant past, how is that relevant to me now? I cannot be bound by something someone else agreed to a long time ago. And if we say that the contract is a hypothetical one to which I *would* agree, then it is hard to see why I should be bound by things to which I would agree without my actually having done so, since hypothetical promises are not real promises.

But most important, we need to ask who is covered by the contract. To enter into a contract, one must be rational and autonomous; nonrational beings cannot make contracts. If morality consists of those rules that rational beings will agree to among themselves for their mutual benefit, then nonrational beings will not be covered by the rules of morality. This means that although I have a moral obligation not to harm you because I agreed not to harm you (because you agreed not to harm me), I cannot have a similar obligation to a dog or a child, and this flies in the face of our ordinary everyday moral sense. It is wrong to cause a dog or a child to suffer pointlessly. Yet it is hard to see why causing pointless suffering to nonrational beings should be wrong if ethics is defined by contracts between rational beings.

Maybe the contract can be patched up somehow to account for our pre-theoretical intuitions about the wrongness of harming nonrational beings; we—that is, rational contracting agents—might agree not to harm one another's children and pets, but even here, my obligation is to you, since I made the agreement with you, not with your pet or child. And in any case, our agreement does not cover nonrational beings in general when there is no rational agent with whom I can bargain. Why should rational agents ever care about the well-being of nonrational beings with whom they have no connection? This cannot be explained on purely contractual grounds. Hence we must either amend a contractual account of ethics to accommodate our everyday moral intuitions regarding the treatment of nonrational beings or abandon our moral intuitions as theoretically spurious.

There is another way to think about contracts and ethics. Rather than being constitutive of ethics, as in Hobbes's conception of morality, the idea of a contract or agreement of some sort could instead be a device used to discover our obligations once we already have a robust understanding of moral value. We might begin with a commitment to the moral equality of persons, as conceived by Kant (see Chapter 3), and then use contracts or bargaining as a way to determine what we owe to one another, how we should behave, and how we should structure social institutions to reflect our moral commitments. This is the path taken by the most renowned political philosopher of the twentieth century, John Rawls (see the biographical sketch for the reading in this chapter).

Rawls imagines persons in the "original position"—a hypothetical state that corresponds to Hobbes's state of nature—bargaining with one another over the rules that will govern their interactions and structure their society. We are each rational and self-interested, but there is a twist: We do not know the particulars of our lives. We do not know whether we are rich, poor, male, female, healthy, sickly, advantaged, or disadvantaged. In short, we are to bargain with one another behind a **veil of ignorance,** a wonderfully vivid conception of the original position that will force us to bargain fairly. Because we do not know what roles we will occupy in society when the veil is lifted and we take our places in life, we will be constrained to bargain in good faith. When the veil is lifted, no matter where the hand of fate places us, we will be living in a just society. We might not be happy, but we cannot complain that our situation is unjust.

What principles would we choose behind the veil of ignorance? To start with, we would *not* choose to be utilitarians, claims Rawls, because there is no reason why any of us "would agree to a principle which may require lesser life prospects for some simply for the sake of a greater sum of advantages enjoyed by others." What we would choose, according to Rawls, are the following two principles of justice:

1. Each person is to have an equal right to the most extensive basic liberty compatible with a similar liberty for others.
2. Social and economic inequalities are to be arranged so that they are both (a) reasonably expected to be to everyone's advantage, and (b) attached to positions and offices open to all.

Everyone should have maximal freedom, compatible with the like freedoms of others. The second principle has two parts; Rawls calls the first the "difference principle." Behind the veil of ignorance, Rawls thinks that you would agree to differences in wealth and social status, provided that they benefited you. You might initially disagree, thinking that an absolutely equal division of economic and social goods would be best. But what if you could do even better by allowing some to have more? If an inequality acts as an incentive for others to produce more that would then benefit you, then that would make even more sense. So you would agree to economic and social inequalities, but only on the condition that you benefit from them more than you would if economic and social goods were equally distributed. The second qualification rules out discrimination, something it is hard to imagine anyone rationally choosing, especially without knowing one's own race, gender, national origin, sexual orientation, and the like.

Is Rawls right about what principles we would choose behind the veil? They are the principles that "mutually disinterested" "free and rational persons concerned to further their own interests would accept in an initial position of equality." Rawls figures that if I am concerned to promote my own interests and I am rational, then I will not elect to allow discrimination or other sorts of treatment that are based on irrelevant features of gender or race, because I might wind up as a person discriminated against when the veil is lifted. But consider: What if the odds of being a slave, say, are very low, and what if the society with slaves would be so much more enjoyable for the non-slaves than it would be without slavery? Why would it then be irrational for me to allow slavery? True, if I wind up as a slave when the veil is lifted, I will be very unhappy, but if the odds are much against it and the benefits copious if I am not a slave, then it does not seem irrational for me to gamble with my life. If my only concern is to promote my own interests and I really don't care about others—we are "mutually disinterested"—then Rawls's account of what principles I will choose seems excessively cautious.

Furthermore, even though Rawls views the original position as "a procedural interpretation of Kant's conception of autonomy and the categorical imperative," it is hard to see how it is truly Kantian (see Chapter 3). Rather than asking us to consider other people as inherently valuable in themselves, behind the veil we are to imagine what would happen if *we* turn out to be on the receiving end of any principles we sanction. The motivation is thus not a direct concern for the worth of others but the worry that one might be adversely affected. In other words, self-interest, a motive for which Kant had particular scorn, seems to animate Rawls's thought experiment.

Whatever problems Rawls's account raises, the veil of ignorance is one of the most famous and intuitively powerful thought experiments in contemporary philosophy. It forces us to consider the implications of something to which we often just give lip service—namely, the moral equality of persons.

READINGS ON CONTRACT ETHICS

Thomas Hobbes, from *The Leviathan*

John Rawls, from *A Theory of Justice*

Thomas Hobbes, from *The Leviathan*

Thomas Hobbes (1588–1679) is one of the world's great philosophers. His masterpiece, Leviathan, *is a powerful and disturbing account of the human condition. According to Hobbes, we are moved by desire for personal gain—we are egoists. And because we all want pretty much the same things and there is never enough to satisfy us, and none of us can emerge victorious in our struggle to dominate and subdue others, we are condemned to compete endlessly and fruitlessly. In this dismal state, "the state of nature," our lives are "solitary, poor, nasty, brutish, and short." The state of nature is so bad that we are willing to sacrifice some of our freedoms to escape it, but only on the condition that others do so as well. Hence the social contract, which for Hobbes is the basis of morality.*

Critical Reading Questions

1. What are the three principal causes of quarrel, according to Hobbes?
2. What does Hobbes mean by a state of war?
3. Why does Hobbes think that the state of nature is amoral?
4. What does Hobbes mean by "Laws of Nature"?
5. How does the sovereign come to be?
6. What powers does the sovereign have?

CHAP. XIII

Of the NATURALL CONDITION *of Mankind, as concerning their Felicity, and Misery*

NATURE hath made men so equall, in the faculties of body, and mind; as that though there bee found one man sometimes manifestly stronger in body, or of quicker mind then another; yet when all is reckoned together, the difference between man, and man, is not so considerable, as that one man can thereupon claim to himselfe any benefit, to which another may not pretend, as well as he. For as to the strength of body, the weakest has strength enough to kill the strongest, either by secret machination, or by confederacy with others, that are in the same danger with himselfe.

And as to the faculties of the mind, (setting aside the arts grounded upon words, and especially that skill of proceeding upon generall, and infallible rules, called Science; which very few have, and but in few things; as being not a native faculty, born with us; nor attained, (as Prudence,) while we look after somewhat els,) I find yet a greater equality amongst men, than that of strength. For Prudence, is but Experience; which equall time, equally bestowes on all men, in those things they equally apply themselves unto. That which may perhaps make such equality incredible, is but a vain conceipt of ones owne wisdome, which almost all men think they have in a greater degree, than the Vulgar; that is, than all men but themselves, and a few others, whom by Fame, or for concurring with themselves, they approve. For such is the nature of men, that howsoever they may acknowledge many others to be more witty, or more eloquent, or more learned; Yet they will hardly believe there be many so wise as themselves: For they see their own wit at hand, and other mens at a distance. But this proveth rather that men are in that point equall, than unequall. For there is not ordinarily a greater signe of the equall distribution of any thing, than that every man is contented with his share.

From this equality of ability, ariseth equality of hope in the attaining of our Ends. And therefore if any two men desire the same thing, which neverthelesse they cannot both enjoy, they become enemies; and in the way to their End, (which is principally their owne conservation, and sometimes their delectation only,) endeavour to destroy, or subdue one an other. And from hence it comes to passe, that where an Invader hath no more to feare, than an other mans single power; if one plant, sow, build, or possesse a convenient Seat, others may probably be expected to come prepared with forces united, to dispossesse, and deprive him, not only of the fruit of his labour, but also of his life, or liberty. And the Invader again is in the like danger of another.

And from this diffidence of one another, there is no way for any man to secure himselfe, so reasonable, as Anticipation; that is, by force, or wiles, to master the persons of all men he can, so long, till he see no other power great enough to endanger him: And this is no more than his own conservation requireth, and is generally allowed. Also because there be some, that taking pleasure in contemplating their own power in the acts of conquest, which they pursue farther than their security requires; if others, that otherwise would be glad to be at ease within modest bounds, should not by invasion increase their power, they would not be able, long time, by standing only on their defence, to subsist. And by consequence, such augmentation of dominion over men, being necessary to a mans conservation, it ought to be allowed him.

Againe, men have no pleasure, (but on the contrary a great deale of griefe) in keeping company, where there is no power able to over-awe them all. For every man looketh that his companion should value him, at the same rate he sets upon himselfe: And upon all signes of contempt, or undervaluing, naturally endeavours, as far as he dares (which amongst them that have no common power to keep them in quiet, is far enough to make them destroy each other,) to extort a greater value from his contemners, by dommage; and from others, by the example.

So that in the nature of man, we find three principall causes of quarrell. First, Competition; Secondly, Diffidence; Thirdly, Glory.

The first, maketh men invade for Gain; the second, for Safety; and the third, for Reputation. The first use Violence, to make themselves Masters of other mens persons, wives, children, and cattell; the second, to defend them; the third, for trifles, as a word, a smile, a different opinion, and any other signe of undervalue, either direct in their Persons, or by reflexion in their Kindred, their Friends, their Nation, their Profession, or their Name.

Hereby it is manifest, that during the time men live without a common Power to keep them all in awe, they are in that condition which is called Warre; and such a warre, as is of every man against every man. For WARRE, consisteth not in Battell onely, or the act of fighting; but in a tract of time, wherein the Will to contend by Battell is sufficiently known: and therefore the notion of *Time,* is to be considered in the nature of Warre; as it is in the nature of Weather. For as the nature of Foule weather, lyeth not in a showre or two of rain; but in an inclination thereto of many dayes together; So the nature of War, consisteth not in actuall fighting; but in the known disposition thereto, during all the time there is no assurance to the contrary. All other time is PEACE.

Whatsoever therefore is consequent to a time of Warre, where every man is Enemy to every man; the same is consequent to the time, wherein men live without other security, than what their own strength, and their own invention shall furnish them withall. In such condition, there is no place for Industry; because the fruit thereof is uncertain: and consequently no Culture of the Earth, no Navigation, nor use of the commodities that may be imported by Sea; no commodious Building; no Instruments of moving, and removing such things as require much force; no Knowledge of the face of the Earth; no account of Time; no Arts; no Letters; no Society; and which is worst of all, continuall feare, and danger of violent death; And the life of man, solitary, poore, nasty, brutish, and short.

It may seem strange to some man, that has not well weighed these things; that Nature should thus dissociate, and render men apt to invade, and destroy one another: and he may therefore, not trusting to this Inference, made from the Passions, desire perhaps to have the same confirmed by Experience. Let him therefore consider with himselfe, when taking a journey, he armes himselfe, and seeks to go well accompanied; when going to sleep, he locks his dores; when even in his house he locks his chests; and this when he knowes there bee

Lawes, and publike Officers, armed, to revenge all injuries shall bee done him; what opinion he has of his fellow subjects, when he rides armed; of his fellow Citizens, when he locks his dores; and of his children, and servants, when he locks his chests. Does he not there as much accuse mankind by his actions, as I do by my words? But neither of us accuse mans nature in it. The Desires, and other Passions of man, are in themselves no Sin. No more are the Actions, that proceed from those Passions, till they know a Law that forbids them: which till Lawes be made they cannot know: nor can any Law be made, till they have agreed upon the Person that shall make it.

It may peradventure be thought, there was never such a time, nor condition of warre as this; and I believe it was never generally so, over all the world: but there are many places, where they live so now. For the savage people in many places of *America,* except the government of small Families, the concord whereof dependeth on naturall lust, have no government at all; and live at this day in that brutish manner, as I said before. Howsoever, it may be perceived what manner of life there would be, where there were no common Power to feare; by the manner of life, which men that have formerly lived under a peacefull government, use to degenerate into, in a civill Warre.

But though there had never been any time, wherein particular men were in a condition of warre one against another; yet in all times, Kings, and Persons of Soveraigne authority, because of their Independency, are in continual jealousies, and in the state and posture of Gladiators; having their weapons pointing, and their eyes fixed on one another; that is, their Forts, Garrisons, and Guns, upon the Frontiers of their Kingdomes; and continuall Spyes upon their neighbours; which is a posture of War. But because they uphold thereby, the Industry of their Subjects; there does not follow from it, that misery, which accompanies the Liberty of particular men.

To this warre of every man against every man, this also is consequent; that nothing can be Unjust. The notions of Right and Wrong, Justice and Injustice have there no place. Where there is no common Power, there is no Law: where no Law, no Injustice. Force, and Fraud, are in warre the two Cardinall vertues. Justice, and Injustice are none of the Faculties neither of the Body, nor Mind. If they were, they might be in a man that were alone in the world, as well as his Senses, and Passions. They are Qualities, that relate to men in Society, not in Solitude. It is consequent also to the same condition, that there be no Propriety, no Dominion, no *Mine* and *Thine* distinct; but onely that to be every mans, that he can get; and for so long, as he can keep it. And thus much for the ill condition, which man by meer Nature is actually placed in; though with a possibility to come out of it, consisting partly in the Passions, partly in his Reason.

The Passions that encline men to Peace, are Feare of Death; Desire of such things as are necessary to commodious living; and a Hope by their Industry to obtain them. And Reason suggesteth convenient Articles of Peace, upon which men may be drawn to agreement. These Articles, are they, which otherwise are called the Lawes of Nature: whereof I shall speak more particularly, in the two following Chapters.

CHAP. XIV

Of the first and second NATURALL LAWES, *and of* CONTRACTS

THE RIGHT OF NATURE, which Writers commonly call *Jus Naturale,* is the Liberty each man hath, to use his own power, as he will himselfe, for the preservation of his own Nature; that is to say, of his own Life; and consequently, of doing any thing, which in his own Judgement, and Reason, hee shall conceive to be the aptest means thereunto.

By LIBERTY, is understood, according to the proper signification of the word, the absence of externall Impediments: which Impediments, may oft take away part of a mans power to do what hee would; but cannot hinder him from using the power left him, according as his judgement, and reason shall dictate to him.

A LAW OF NATURE, (*Lex Naturalis,*) is a Precept, or generall Rule, found out by Reason, by which a man is forbidden to do, that, which is destructive of his life, or taketh away the means of preserving the same; and to omit, that, by which he thinketh it may be best preserved. For though they that speak of this subject, use to confound *Jus,* and *Lex, Right* and *Law;* yet they ought to be distinguished; because RIGHT, consisteth in liberty to do, or to forbeare; Whereas LAW, determineth, and bindeth to one of them: so that Law, and Right, differ as much, as Obligation, and Liberty; which in one and the same matter are inconsistent.

And because the condition of Man, (as hath been declared in the precedent Chapter) is a condition of Warre of every one against every one; in which case every one is governed by his own Reason; and there is nothing he can make use of, that may not be a help unto him, in preserving his life against his enemyes; It followeth, that in such a condition, every man has a Right to every thing; even to one anothers body. And therefore, as long as this naturall Right of every man to every thing endureth, there can be no security to any man, (how strong or wise soever he be,) of living out the time, which Nature ordinarily alloweth men to live. And consequently it is a precept, or generall rule of Reason, *That every man, ought to endeavour Peace, as farre as he has hope of obtaining it; and when he cannot obtain it, that he may seek, and use, all helps, and advantages of Warre.* The first branch of which Rule, containeth the first, and Fundamentall Law of Nature; which is, *to seek Peace, and follow it.* The Second, the summe of the Right of Nature; which is, *By all means we can, to defend our selves.*

From this Fundamentall Law of Nature, by which men are commanded to endeavour Peace, is derived this second Law; *That a man be willing, when others are so too, as farre-forth, as for Peace, and defence of himselfe he shall think it necessary, to lay down this right to all things; and be contented with so much liberty against other men, as he would allow other men against himselfe.* For as long as every man holdeth this Right, of doing any thing he liketh; so long are all men in the condition of Warre. But if other men will not lay down their Right, as well as he; then there is no Reason for any one, to devest himselfe of his: For that were to expose himselfe to Prey, (which no man is bound to) rather than to dispose himselfe to Peace. This is that Law of the Gospell; *Whatsoever you require that others should do to you, that do ye to them.* And that Law of all men, *Quod tibi fieri non vis, alteri ne feceris.*

To *lay downe* a mans *Right* to any thing, is to *devest* himselfe of the *Liberty,* of hindring another of the benefit of his own Right to the same. For he that renounceth, or passeth away his Right, giveth not to any other man a Right which he had not before; because there is nothing to which every man had not Right by Nature: but onely standeth out of his way, that he may enjoy his own originall Right, without hindrance from him; not without hindrance from another. So that the effect which redoundeth to one man, by another mans defect of Right, is but so much diminution of impediments to the use of his own Right originall.

Right is layd aside, either by simply Renouncing it; or by Transferring it to another. By *Simply* Renouncing; when he cares not to whom the benefit thereof redoundeth. By Transferring; when he intendeth the benefit thereof to some certain person, or persons. And when a man hath in either manner abandoned, or granted away his Right; then is he said to be Obliged, or Bound, not to hinder those, to whom such Right is granted, or abandoned, from the benefit of it: and that he *Ought*, and it is his Duty, not to make voyd that voluntary act of his own: and that such hindrance is Injustice, and Injury, as being *Sine Jure;* the Right being before renounced, or transferred. So that *Injury,* or *Injustice,* in the controversies of the world, is somewhat like to that, which in the disputations of Scholers is called *Absurdity.* For as it is there called an Absurdity, to contradict what one maintained in the Beginning: so in the world, it is called Injustice, and Injury, voluntarily to undo that, which from the beginning he had voluntarily done. The way by which a man either simply Renounceth, or Transferreth his Right, is a Declaration, or Signification, by some voluntary and sufficient signe, or signes, that he doth so Renounce, or Transferre; or hath so Renounced, or Transferred the same, to him that accepteth it. And these Signes are either Words onely, or Actions onely; or (as it happeneth most often) both Words, and Actions. And the same are the Bonds, by which men are bound, and obliged: Bonds, that have their strength, not from their own Nature, (for nothing is more easily broken then a mans word,) but from Feare of some evill consequence upon the rupture.

Whensoever a man Transferreth his Right, or Renounceth it; it is either in consideration of some Right reciprocally transferred to himselfe; or for some other good he hopeth for thereby. For it is a voluntary act: and of the voluntary acts of every man, the object is some *Good to himselfe.* And therefore there be some Rights, which no man can be understood by any words, or other signes, to have abandoned, or transferred. As first a man cannot lay down the right of resisting them, that assault him by force, to take away his life; because he cannot be understood to ayme thereby, at any Good to himselfe. The same may be sayd of Wounds, and Chayns, and Imprisonment; both because there is no benefit consequent to such patience; as there is to the patience of suffering another to be wounded, or imprisoned: as also because a man cannot tell, when he seeth men proceed against him by violence, whether they intend his death or not. And lastly the motive, and end for which this renouncing, and transferring of Right is introduced, is nothing else but the security of a mans person, in his life, and in the means of so preserving life, as not to be weary of it. And therefore if a man by words, or other signes, seem to despoyle himselfe of the End, for which those signes were intended; he is not to be understood as if he meant it, or that it was his will; but that he was ignorant of how such words and actions were to be interpreted.

The mutuall transferring of Right, is that which men call Contract.

There is difference, between transferring of Right to the Thing; and transferring, or tradition, that is, delivery of the Thing it selfe. For the Thing may be delivered together with the Translation of the Right; as in buying and selling with ready mony; or exchange of goods, or lands: and it may be delivered some time after.

Again, one of the Contractors, may deliver the Thing contracted for on his part, and leave the other to perform his part at some determinate time after, and in the mean time be trusted; and then the Contract on his part, is called Pact, or Covenant: Or both parts may contract now, to performe hereafter: in which cases, he that is to performe in time to come, being trusted, his performance is called *Keeping of Promise,* or Faith; and the fayling of performance (if it be voluntary) *Violation of Faith.*

When the transferring of Right, is not mutuall; but one of the parties transferreth, in hope to gain thereby friendship, or service from another, or from his friends; or in hope to gain the reputation of Charity, or Magnanimity; or to deliver his mind from the pain of compassion; or in hope of reward in heaven; This is not Contract, but GIFT, FREE-GIFT, GRACE: which words signifie one and the same thing.

Signes of Contract, are either *Expresse,* or *by Inference.* Expresse, are words spoken with understanding of what they signifie: And such words are either of the time *Present,* or *Past;* as, *I Give, I Grant, I have Given, I have Granted, I will that this be yours:* Or of the future; as, *I will Give, I will Grant:* which words of the future, are called PROMISE.

Signes by Inference, are sometimes the consequence of Words; sometimes the consequence of Silence; sometimes the consequence of Actions; sometimes the consequence of Forbearing an Action: and generally a signe by Inference, of any Contract, is whatsoever sufficiently argues the will of the Contractor.

Words alone, if they be of the time to come, and contain a bare promise, are an insufficient signe of a Free-gift and therefore not obligatory. For if they be of the time to Come, as, *To morrow I will Give,* they are a signe I have not given yet, and consequently that my right is not transferred, but remaineth till I transferre it by some other Act. But if the words be of the time Present, or Past, as, *I have given, or do give to be delivered to morrow,* then is my to morrows Right given away to day; and that by the vertue of the words, though there were no other argument of my will. And there is a great difference in the signification of these words, *Volo hoc tuum esse cras,* and *Cras dabo;* that is, between *I will that this be thine to morrow,* and, *I will give it thee to morrow:* For the word *I will,* in the former manner of speech, signifies an act of the will Present; but in the later, it signifies a promise of an act of the will to Come: and therefore the former words, being of the Present, transferre a future right; the later, that be of the Future, transferre nothing. But if there be other signes of the Will to transferre a Right, besides Words; then, though the gift be Free, yet may the Right be understood to passe by words of the future: as if a man propound a Prize to him that comes first to the end of a race, The gift is Free; and though the words be of the Future, yet the Right passeth: for if he

would not have his words so be understood, he should not have let them runne.

In Contracts, the right passeth, not onely where the words are of the time Present, or Past; but also where they are of the Future: because all Contract is mutuall translation, or change of Right; and therefore he that promiseth onely, because he hath already received the benefit for which he promiseth, is to be understood as if he intended the Right should passe: for unlesse he had been content to have his words so understood, the other would not have performed his part first. And for that cause, in buying, and selling, and other acts of Contract, a Promise is equivalent to a Covenant; and therefore obligatory.

He that performeth first in the case of a Contract, is said to MERIT that which he is to receive by the performance of the other; and he hath it as *Due.* Also when a Prize is propounded to many, which is to be given to him onely that winneth; or mony is thrown amongst many, to be enjoyed by them that catch it; though this be a Free gift; yet so to Win, or so to Catch, is to *Merit,* and to have it as DUE. For the Right is transferred in the Propounding of the Prize, and in throwing down the mony; though it be not determined to whom, but by the Event of the contention. But there is between these two sorts of Merit, this difference, that In Contract, I Merit by vertue of my own power, and the Contractors need; but in this case of Free gift, I am enabled to Merit onely by the benignity of the Giver: In Contract, I merit at the Contractors hand that he should depart with his right; In this case of Gift, I Merit not that the giver should part with his right; but that when he has parted with it, it should be mine, rather than anothers. And this I think to be the meaning of that distinction of the Schooles, between *Meritum congrui,* and *Meritum condigni.* For God Almignty, having promised Paradise to those men (hoodwinkt with carnall desires,) that can walk through this world according to the Precepts, and Limits prescribed by him; they say, he that shall so walk, shall Merit Paradise *Ex congruo.* But because no man can demand a right to it, by his own Righteousnesse, or any other power in himselfe, but by the Free Grace of God onely; they say, no man can Merit Paradise *ex condigno.* This I say, I think is the meaning of that distinction; but because Disputers do not agree upon the signification of their own termes of Art, longer than it serves their turn; I will not affirme any thing of their meaning: onely this I say; when a gift is given indefinitely, as a prize to be contended for, he that winneth Meriteth, and may claime the Prize as Due.

If a Covenant be made, wherein neither of the parties performe presently, but trust one another; in the condition of meer Nature, (which is a condition of Warre of every man against every man,) upon any reasonable suspition, it is Voyd: But if there be a common Power set over them both, with right and force sufficient to compell performance; it is not Voyd. For he that performeth first, has no assurance the other will performe after; because the bonds of words are too weak to bridle mens ambition, avarice, anger, and other Passions, without the feare of some coerceive Power; which in the condition of meer Nature, where all men are equall, and judges of the justnesse of their own fears, cannot possibly be supposed. And therefore he which performeth first, does but betray himselfe to his enemy; contrary to the Right (he can never abandon) of defending his life, and means of living.

But in a civill estate, where there is a Power set up to constrain those that would otherwise violate their faith, that feare is no more reasonable; and for that cause, he which by the Covenant is to perform first, is obliged so to do.

The cause of feare, which maketh such a Covenant invalid, must be always something arising after the Covenant made; as some new fact, or other signe of the Will not to performe: else it cannot make the Covenant voyd. For that which could not hinder a man from promising, ought not to be admitted as a hindrance of performing.

He that transferreth any Right, transferreth the Means of enjoying it, as farre as lyeth in his power. As he that selleth Land, is understood to transferre the Herbage, and whatsoever growes upon it; Nor can he that sells a Mill turn away the Stream that drives it. And they that give to a man the Right of government in Soveraignty, are understood to give him the right of levying mony to maintain Souldiers; and of appointing Magistrates for the administration of Justice.

To make Covenants with bruit Beasts, is impossible; because not understanding our speech, they understand not, nor accept of any translation of Right; nor can translate any Right to another: and without mutuall acceptation, there is no Covenant.

To make Covenant with God, is impossible, but by Mediation of such as God speaketh to, either by Revelation supernaturall, or by his Lieutenants that govern under him, and in his Name: For otherwise we know not whether our Covenants be accepted, or not. And therefore they that Vow any thing contrary to any law of Nature, Vow in vain; as being a thing unjust to pay such Vow. And if it be a thing commanded by the Law of Nature, it is not the Vow, but the Law that binds them.

The matter, or subject of a Covenant, is always something that falleth under deliberation; (For to Covenant, is an act of the Will; that is to say an act, and the last act, of deliberation;) and is therefore always understood to be something to come; and which is judged Possible for him that Covenanteth, to performe.

And therefore, to promise that which is known to be Impossible, is no Covenant. But if that prove impossible afterwards, which before was thought possible, the Covenant is valid, and bindeth, (though not to the thing it selfe,) yet to the value; or, if that also be impossible, to the unfeigned endeavour of performing as much as is possible: for to more no man can be obliged.

Men are freed of their Covenants two wayes; by Performing; or by being Forgiven. For Performance, is the naturall end of obligation; and Forgivenesse, the restitution of liberty; as being a re-transferring of that Right, in which the obligation consisted.

Covenants entred into by fear, in the condition of meer Nature, are obligatory. For example, if I Covenant to pay a ransome, or service for my life, to an enemy; I am bound by it. For it is a Contract, wherein one receiveth the benefit of life; the other is to receive mony, or service for it; and consequently, where no other Law (as in the condition, of meer nature) forbiddeth the performance, the Covenant is valid. Therefore Prisoners of warre, if trusted with the payment of their Ransome, are obliged to pay it: And if a weaker Prince, make a disadvantageous peace with a stronger, for feare; he is bound to keep it; unlesse (as hath been sayd before) there ariseth some new, and just cause to feare, to renew the war. And even in Common-wealths, if I be forced to redeem my selfe from a Theefe by promising him mony, I am bound to pay it, till the Civill Law discharge me. For whatsoever I may lawfully do without Obligation, the same I may lawfully Covenant to do through feare: and what I lawfully Covenant, I cannot lawfully break.

A former Covenant makes voyd a later. For a man that hath passed away his Right to one man to day, hath it not to passe to morrow to another: and therefore the later promise passeth no Right, but is null.

A Covenant not to defend my selfe from force, by force, is alwayes voyd. For (as I have shewed before) no man can transferre, or lay down his Right to save himselfe from Death, Wounds, and Imprisonment, (the avoyding whereof is the onely End of laying down any Right, and therefore the promise of not resisting force, in no Covenant transferreth any right; nor is obliging. For though a man may Covenant thus, *Unlesse I do so, or so, kill me;* he cannot Covenant thus, *Unlesse I do so, or so, I will not resist you, when you come to kill me.* For man by nature chooseth the lesser evill, which is danger of death in resisting; rather than the greater, which is certain and present death in not resisting. And this is granted to be true by all men, in that they lead Criminals to Execution, and Prison, with armed men, notwithstanding that such Criminals have consented to the Law, by which they are condemned.

A Covenant to accuse ones selfe, without assurance of pardon, is likewise invalide. For in the condition of Nature, where every man is Judge, there is no place for Accusation: and in the Civil State, the Accusation is followed with Punishment; which being Force, a man is not obliged not to resist. The same is also true, of the Accusation of those, by whose Condemnation a man falls into misery; as of a Father, Wife, or Benefactor.

For the Testimony of such an Accuser, if it be not willingly given, is preasumed to be corrupted by Nature; and therefore not to be received: and where a mans Testimony is not to be credited, he is not bound to give it. Also Accusations upon Torture, are not to be reputed as Testimonies. For Torture is to be used but as means of conjecture, and light, in the further examination, and search of truth: and what is in that case confessed, tendeth to the ease of him that is Tortured; not to the informing of the Torturers: and therefore ought not to have the credit of a sufficient Testimony: for whether he deliver himselfe by true, or false Accusation, he does it by the Right of preserving his own life.

The force of Words, being (as I have formerly noted) too weak to hold men to the performance of their Covenants; there are in mans nature, but two imaginable helps to strengthen it. And those are either a Feare of the consequence of breaking their word; or a Glory, or Pride in appearing not to need to breake it. This later is a Generosity too rarely found to be presumed on, especially in the pursuers of Wealth, Command, or sensuall Pleasure; which are the greatest part of Mankind. The Passion to be reckoned upon, is Fear; whereof there be two very generall Objects: one, The Power of Spirits Invisible; the other, The Power of those men they shall therein Offend. Of these two, though the former be the greater Power, yet the feare of the later is commonly the greater Feare. The Feare of the former is in every man, his own Religion, which hath place in the nature of man before Civill Society. The later hath not so; at least not place enough, to keep men to their promises; because in the condition of meer Nature, the inequality of Power is not discerned, but by the event of Battell. So that before the time of Civill Society, or in the interruption thereof by Warre, there is nothing can strengthen a Covenant of Peace agreed on, against the temptations of Avarice, Ambition, Lust, or other strong desire, but the feare of that Invisible Power, which they every one Worship as God; and Feare as a Revenger of their perfidy. All therefore that can be done between two men not subject to Civill Power, is to put one another to swear by the God he feareth: Which *Swearing,* or OATH, is a *Forme of Speech, added to a Promise; by which he that promiseth, signifieth, that unlesse he performe, he renounceth the mercy of his God, or calleth to him for vengeance on himselfe.* Such was the Heathen Forme, *Let* Jupiter *kill me else, as I kill this Beast.* So is our Forme, *I shall do thus, and thus, so help me God.* And this, with the Rites and

Ceremonies, which every one useth in his own Religion, that the feare of breaking faith might be the greater.

By this it appears, that an Oath taken according to any other Forme, or Rite, then his, that sweareth, is in vain; and no Oath: And that there is no Swearing by any thing which the Swearer thinks not God. For though men have sometimes used to swear by their Kings, for feare, or flattery; yet they would have it thereby understood, they attributed to them Divine honour.

And that Swearing unnecessarily by God, is but prophaning of his name: and Swearing by other things, as men do in common discourse, is not Swearing, but an impious Custome, gotten by too much vehemence of talking.

It appears also, that the Oath addes nothing to the Obligation. For a Covenant, if lawfull, binds in the sight of God, without the Oath, as much as with it: if unlawfull, bindeth not at all; though it be confirmed with an Oath.

Discussion Questions

1. Is Hobbes's account of the state of nature plausible? What is it supposed to show?
2. Is the sovereign trustworthy?
3. Consider some implications of Hobbes's conventionalism in morality.
4. Are there conditions under which you should not obey the sovereign?
5. Is the problem of moral obligations to nonrational beings (see the introductory discussion) a problem for Hobbes's contract account of ethics?

John Rawls, from *A Theory of Justice*

John Rawls (1921–2002) is widely considered one of the most influential moral philosophers of the twentieth century. His work is known by philosophers and nonphilosophers alike. Particularly vivid is his account in A Theory of Justice of what Rawls called the "veil of ignorance," a device whereby abstract persons ignorant of the particular conditions of their lives must choose the principles to govern their interactions. The principles of justice are those principles that rational agents would choose behind the veil of ignorance. It is a matter of some controversy exactly which principles we would choose. Rawls thinks we would choose maximal freedom compatible with like freedoms for all and that we would allow social and economic differences, provided that they benefited everyone, including those who are worse off.

Critical Reading Questions

1. What does Rawls mean by "justice as fairness"?
2. Why, according to Rawls, would we not choose utilitarianism behind the veil of ignorance?
3. What principles would we choose behind the veil of ignorance, according to Rawls?
4. Explain the difference principle.
5. What are people like behind the veil of ignorance?
6. What are primary goods?

A THEORY OF JUSTICE

John Rawls

THE MAIN IDEA OF THE THEORY OF JUSTICE

My aim is to present a conception of justice which generalizes and carries to a higher level of abstraction the familiar theory of the social contract as found, say, in Locke, Rousseau, and Kant.[1] In order to do this we are not to think of the original contract as one to enter a particular society or to set up a particular form of government. Rather, the guiding idea is that the principles of justice for the basic structure of society are the object of the original agreement. They are the principles that free and rational persons concerned to further their own interests would accept in an initial position of equality as defining the fundamental terms of their association. These principles are to regulate all further agreements; they specify the kinds of social cooperation that can be entered into and the forms of government that can be established. This way of regarding the principles of justice I shall call justice as fairness.

Thus we are to imagine that those who engage in social cooperation choose together, in one joint act, the principles which are to assign basic rights and duties and to determine the division of social benefits. Men are to decide in advance how they are to regulate their claims against one another and what is to be the foundation charter of their society. Just as each person must decide by rational reflection what constitutes his good, that is, the system of ends which it is rational for him to pursue, so a group of persons must decide once and for all what is to count among them as just and unjust. The choice which rational men would make in this hypothetical situation of equal liberty, assuming for the present that this choice problem has a solution, determines the principles of justice.

In justice as fairness the original position of equality corresponds to the state of nature in the traditional theory of the social contract. This original position is not, of course, thought of as an actual historical state of affairs, much less as a primitive condition of culture. It is understood as a purely hypothetical situation characterized so as to lead to a certain conception of justice.[2]

[1]As the text suggests, I shall regard Locke's *Second Treatise of Government*, Rousseau's *The Social Contract*, and Kant's ethical works beginning with *The Foundations of the Metaphysics of Morals* as definitive of the contract tradition. For all of its greatness, Hobbe's *Leviathan* raises special problems. A general historical survey is provided by J. W. Gough, *The Social Contract*, 2nd ed. (Oxford, The Clarendon Press, 1957), and Otto Gierke, *Natural Law and the Theory of Society*, trans. with an introduction by Ernest Barker (Cambridge, The University Press, 1934). A presentation of the contract view as primarily an ethical theory is to be found in G. R. Grice, *The Grounds of Moral Judgment* (Cambridge, The University Press, 1967).

[2]Kant is clear that the original agreement is hypothetical. See *The Metaphysics of Morals*, pt. I (*Rechtslehre*), especially 47, 52; and pt. II of the essay "Concerning the Common Saying: This May Be True in Theory but It Does Not Apply in Practice," in *Kant's Political Writings*, ed. Hans Reiss and trans, by H. B. Nisbet (Cambridge, The University Press, 1970), pp. 73–87. See Georges Vlachos, *La Pensée politique de Kant* (Paris, Presses Universitaires de France, 1962), pp. 326–335; and J. G. Murphy, *Kant: The Philosophy of Right* (London, Macmillan, 1970), pp. 109–112, 133–136, for a further discussion.

Among the essential features of this situation is that no one knows his place in society, his class position or social status, nor does any one know his fortune in the distribution of natural assets and abilities, his intelligence, strength, and the like. I shall even assume that the parties do not know their conceptions of the good or their special psychological propensities. The principles of justice are chosen behind a veil of ignorance. This ensures that no one is advantaged or disadvantaged in the choice of principles by the outcome of natural chance or the contingency of social circumstances. Since all are similarly situated and no one is able to design principles to favor his particular condition, the principles of justice are the result of a fair agreement or bargain. For given the circumstances of the original position, the symmetry of everyone's relations to each other, this initial situation is fair between individuals as moral persons, that is, as rational beings with their own ends and capable, I shall assume, of a sense of justice. The original position is, one might say, the appropriate initial status quo, and thus the fundamental agreements reached in it are fair. This explains the propriety of the name "justice as fairness": it conveys the idea that the principles of justice are agreed to in an initial situation that is fair. The name does not mean that the concepts of justice and fairness are the same, any more than the phrase "poetry as metaphor" means that the concepts of poetry and metaphor are the same.

Justice as fairness begins, as I have said, with one of the most general of all choices which persons might make together, namely, with the choice of the first principles of a conception of justice which is to regulate all subsequent criticism and reform of institutions. Then, having chosen a conception of justice, we can suppose that they are to choose a constitution and a legislature to enact laws, and so on, all in accordance with the principles of justice initially agreed upon. Our social situation is just if it is such that by this sequence of hypothetical agreements we would have contracted into the general system of rules which defines it. Moreover, assuming that the original position does determine a set of principles (that is, that a particular conception of justice would be chosen), it will then be true that whenever social institutions satisfy these principles those engaged in them can say to one another that they are cooperating on terms to which they would agree if they were free and equal persons whose relations with respect to one another were fair. They could all view their arrangements as meeting the stipulations which they would acknowledge in an initial situation that embodies widely accepted and reasonable constraints on the choice of principles. The general recognition of this fact would provide the basis for a public acceptance of the corresponding principles of justice. No society can, of course, be a scheme of cooperation which men enter voluntarily in a literal sense; each person finds himself placed at birth in some particular position in some particular society, and the nature of this position materially affects his life prospects. Yet a society satisfying the principles of justice as fairness comes as close as a society can to being a voluntary scheme, for it meets the principles which free and equal persons would assent to under circumstances that are fair. In this sense its members are autonomous and the obligations they recognize self-imposed.

One feature of justice as fairness is to think of the parties in the initial situation as rational and mutually disinterested. This does not mean that the parties are egoists, that is, individuals with only certain kinds of interests, say in wealth, prestige, and domination. But they are conceived as not taking an interest in one another's interests. They are to presume that even their spiritual aims may be opposed, in the way that the aims of those of different religions may be opposed. Moreover, the concept of rationality must be interpreted as far as possible in the narrow sense, standard in economic theory, of taking the most effective means to given ends. I shall modify this concept to some extent . . . but one must try to avoid introducing into it any controversial ethical elements. The initial situation must be characterized by stipulations that are widely accepted.

In working out the conception of justice as fairness one main task clearly is to determine which principles of justice would be chosen in the original position. To do this we must describe this situation in some detail and formulate with care the problem of choice which it presents. . . . It may be observed, however, that once the principles of justice are thought of as arising from an original agreement in a situation of equality, it is an open question whether the principle of utility would be acknowledged. Offhand it hardly seems likely that persons who view themselves as equals, entitled to press their claims upon one another, would agree to a principle which may require lesser life prospects for some simply for the sake of a greater sum of advantages enjoyed by others. Since each desires to protect his interests, his capacity to advance his conception of the good, no one has a reason to acquiesce in an enduring loss for himself in order to bring about a greater net balance of satisfaction. In the absence of strong and lasting benevolent impulses, a rational man would not accept a basic structure merely because it maximized the algebraic sum of advantages irrespective of its permanent effects on his own basic rights and interests. Thus it seems that the principle of utility is incompatible with the conception of social cooperation among equals for mutual advantage. It appears to be inconsistent with the idea of reciprocity implicit in the notion of a well-ordered society. Or, at any rate, so I shall argue.

I shall maintain instead that the persons in the initial situation would choose two rather different principles: the first requires equality in the assignment of basic rights and duties, while the second holds that social and economic inequalities, for example inequalities of wealth and authority, are just only if they result in compensating benefits for everyone, and in particular for the least advantaged members of society. These principles rule out justifying institutions on the grounds that the hardships of some are offset by a greater good in the aggregate. It may be expedient but it is not just that some should have less in order that others may prosper. But there is no injustice in the greater benefits earned by a few provided that the situation of persons not so fortunate is thereby improved. The intuitive idea is that since everyone's well-being depends upon a scheme of cooperation without which no one could have a satisfactory life, the division of advantages should be such as to draw forth the willing cooperation of everyone taking part in it, including those less well situated. Yet this can be expected only if reasonable terms are proposed. The two principles mentioned seem to be a fair agreement on the basis of which those better endowed, or more fortunate in their social position, neither

of which we can be said to deserve, could expect the willing cooperation of others when some workable scheme is a necessary condition of the welfare of all.[3] Once we decide to look for a conception of justice that nullifies the accidents of natural endowment and the contingencies of social circumstance as counters in quest for political and economic advantage, we are led to these principles. They express the result of leaving aside those aspects of the social world that seem arbitrary from a moral point of view.

The problem of the choice of principles, however, is extremely difficult. I do not expect the answer I shall suggest to be convincing to everyone. It is, therefore, worth noting from the outset that justice as fairness, like other contract views, consists of two parts: (1) an interpretation of the initial situation and of the problem of choice posed there, and (2) a set of principles which, it is argued, would be agreed to. One may accept the first part of the theory (or some variant thereof), but not the other, and conversely. The concept of the initial contractual situation may seem reasonable although the particular principles proposed are rejected. To be sure, I want to maintain that the most appropriate conception of this situation does lead to principles of justice contrary to utilitarianism and perfectionism, and therefore that the contract doctrine provides an alternative to these views. . . .

A final remark. Justice as fairness is not a complete contract theory. For it is clear that the contract idea can be extended to the choice of more or less an entire ethical system, that is, to a system including principles for all the virtues and not only for justice. Now for the most part I shall consider only principles of justice and others closely related to them; I make no attempt to discuss the virtues in a systematic way. Obviously if justice as fairness succeeds reasonably well, a next step would be to study the more general view suggested by the name "rightness as fairness." But even this wider theory fails to embrace all moral relationships, since it would seem to include only our relations with other persons and to leave out of account how we are to conduct ourselves toward animals and the rest of nature. I do not contend that the contract notion offers a way to approach these questions

[3]For the formulation of this intuitive idea I am indebted to Allan Gibbard.

which are certainly of the first importance; and I shall have to put them aside. We must recognize the limited scope of justice as fairness and of the general type of view that it exemplifies. How far its conclusions must be revised once these other matters are understood cannot be decided in advance. . . .

TWO PRINCIPLES OF JUSTICE

I shall now state in a provisional form the two principles of justice that I believe would be chosen in the original position. In this section I wish to make only the most general comments, and therefore the first formulation of these principles is tentative. As we go on I shall run through several formulations and approximate step by step the final statement to be given much later. I believe that doing this allows the exposition to proceed in a natural way.

The first statement of the two principles reads as follows.

First: Each person is to have an equal right to the most extensive basic liberty compatible with a similar liberty for others.

Second: Social and economic inequalities are to be arranged so that they are both (a) reasonably expected to be to everyone's advantage, and (b) attached to positions and offices open to all. . . .

By way of general comment, these principles primarily apply, as I have said, to the basic structure of society. They are to govern the assignment of rights and duties and to regulate the distribution of social and economic advantages. As their formulation suggests, these principles presuppose that the social structure can be divided into two more or less distinct parts, the first principle applying to the one, the second to the other. They distinguish between those aspects of the social system that define and secure the equal liberties of citizenship and those that specify and establish social and economic inequalities. The basic liberties of citizens are, roughly speaking, political liberty (the right to vote and to be eligible for public office) together with freedom of speech and assembly; liberty of conscience and freedom of thought; freedom of the person along with the right to hold (personal) property; and freedom from arbitrary arrest and seizure as defined by the concept of the rule of law. These liberties are all required to be equal by the first principle, since citizens of a just society are to have the same basic rights.

The second principle applies, in the first approximation, to the distribution of income and wealth and to the design of organizations that make use of differences in authority and responsibility, or chains of command. While the distribution of wealth and income need not be equal, it must be to everyone's advantage, and at the same time, positions of authority and offices of command must be accessible to all. One applies the second principle by holding positions open, and then, subject to this constraint, arranges social and economic inequalities so that everyone benefits.

These principles are to be arranged in a serial order with the first principle prior to the second. This ordering means that a departure from the institutions of equal liberty required by the first principle cannot be justified by, or compensated for, by greater social and economic advantages. The distribution of wealth and income, and the hierarchies of authority, must be consistent with both the liberties of equal citizenship and equality of opportunity.

It is clear that these principles are rather specific in their content, and their acceptance rests on certain assumptions that I must eventually try to explain and justify. A theory of justice depends upon a theory of society in ways that will become evident as we proceed. For the present, it should be observed that the two principles (and this holds for all formulations) are a special case of a more general conception of justice that can be expressed as follows.

All social values—liberty and opportunity, income and wealth, and the bases of self-respect—are to be distributed equally unless an unequal distribution of any, or all, of these values is to everyone's advantage.

Injustice, then, is simply inequalities that are not to the benefit of all. Of course, this conception is extremely vague and requires interpretation.

As a first step, suppose that the basic structure of society distributes certain primary goods, that is, things that every rational man is presumed to want. These goods normally have a use whatever a person's rational plan of life. For simplicity, assume that the chief primary goods at the disposition of society are rights and liberties, powers and opportunities, income and wealth. . . . These are the social primary goods. Other primary goods such as health and vigor, intelligence and imagination, are natural goods; although their possession is influenced by the basic structure, they are not so directly under its control. Imagine, then, a hypothetical initial arrangement in which all the social primary goods are equally distributed: everyone has similar rights and duties, and income and wealth are evenly shared. This state of affairs provides a benchmark for judging improvements. If certain inequalities of wealth and organizational powers would make everyone better off than in this hypothetical starting situation, then they accord with the general conception.

Now it is possible, at least theoretically, that by giving up some of their fundamental liberties men are sufficiently compensated by the resulting social and economic gains. The general conception of justice imposes no restrictions on what sort of inequalities are permissible; it only requires that everyone's position be improved. We need not suppose anything so drastic as consenting to a condition of slavery. Imagine instead that men forego certain political rights when the economic returns are significant and their capacity to influence the course of policy by the exercise of these rights would be marginal in any case. It is this kind of exchange which the two principles as stated rule out; being arranged in serial order they do not permit exchanges between basic liberties and economic and social gains. The serial ordering of principles expresses an underlying preference among primary social goods. When this preference is rational so likewise is the choice of these principles in this order.

In developing justice as fairness I shall, for the most part, leave aside the general conception of justice and examine instead the special case of the two principles in serial order. The advantage of this procedure is that from the first the matter of priorities is recognized and an effort made to find principles to deal with it. One is led to attend throughout to the conditions under which the acknowledgment of the absolute weight of liberty with respect to social and economic advantages, as defined by the lexical order of the two principles, would be reasonable. Offhand, this ranking appears extreme and too special a case to be of much interest; but there is more justification for it than would appear at first sight. Or at any rate, so I shall maintain. . . . Furthermore, the distinction between fundamental rights and liberties and economic and social benefits marks a difference among primary social goods that one should try to exploit. It suggests an important division in the social system. Of course, the distinctions drawn and the ordering proposed are bound to be at best only approximations. There are surely circumstances in which they fail. But it is essential to depict clearly the main lines of a reasonable conception of justice; and under many conditions anyway, the two principles in serial order may serve well enough. When necessary we can fall back on the more general conception.

The fact that the two principles apply to institutions has certain consequences. Several points illustrate this. First of all, the rights and liberties referred to by these principles are those which are defined by the public rules of the basic structure. Whether men are free is determined by the rights and duties established by the major institutions of society. Liberty is a certain pattern of social forms. The first principle simply requires that certain sorts of rules, those defining basic liberties, apply to everyone equally and that they allow the most extensive liberty compatible with a like liberty for all. The only reason for circumscribing the rights defining liberty and making men's freedom less extensive than it might otherwise be is that these equal rights as institutionally defined would interfere with one another.

Another thing to bear in mind is that when principles mention persons, or require that everyone gain from an inequality, the reference is to representative persons holding the various social positions, or offices, or whatever, established by the basic structure. Thus in applying the second principle I assume that it is possible to assign an expectation of well-being to representative individuals holding these positions. This expectation indicates their life prospects as viewed from their social station. In general, the expectations of representative persons depend upon the distribution of rights and duties throughout the basic structure. When this changes, expectations change.

I assume, then, that expectations are connected: by raising the prospects of the representative man in one position we presumably increase or decrease the prospects of representative men in other positions. Since it applies to institutional forms, the second principle (or rather the first part of it) refers to the expectations of representative individuals. As I shall discuss below, neither principle applies to distributions of particular goods to particular individuals who may be identified by their proper names. The situation where someone is considering how to allocate certain commodities to needy persons who are known to him is not within the scope of the principles. They are meant to regulate basic institutional arrangements. We must not assume that there is much similarity from the standpoint of justice between an administrative allotment of goods to specific persons and the appropriate design of society. Our common sense institutions for the former may be a poor guide to the latter.

Now the second principle insists that each person benefit from permissible inequalities in the basic structure. This means that it must be reasonable for each relevant representative man defined by this structure, when he views it as a going concern, to prefer his prospects with the inequality to his prospects without it. One is not allowed to justify differences in income or organizational powers on the ground that the disadvantages of those in one position are outweighed by the greater advantages of those in another. Much less can infringements of liberty be counterbalanced in this way. Applied to the basic structure, the principle of utility would have us maximize the sum of expectations of representative men (weighed by the number of persons they represent, on the classical view); and this would permit us to compensate for the losses of some by the gains of others. Instead, the two principles require that everyone benefit from economic and social inequalities. It is obvious, however, that there are indefinitely many ways in which all may be advantaged when the initial arrangement of equality is taken as a benchmark. How then are we to choose among these possibilities? The principles must be specified so that they yield a determinate conclusion. I now turn to this problem. . . .

Discussion Questions

1. Is Rawls right about what principles one would choose behind the veil of ignorance?
2. In what respect does Rawls's account of contract ethics differ from that of Hobbes?
3. How well does our society correspond to Rawls's conception of a just society?

CHAPTER 5

Virtue Ethics

THE NATURE OF HAPPINESS: HUMAN EXCELLENCES

Everyone wants to be happy. We want it for ourselves; we wish it for our loved ones. Parents hope their kids will be happy, and happiness is even part of the founding ethos of the United States, a country alleged to be committed to protecting its citizens' rights to "life, liberty, and the pursuit of happiness." Happiness is even taken to be the point or goal of life. We go to school and study hard, we watch our diets and maintain our physical health, we form close relationships with others, travel, develop our talents, and seek work that expresses our values—all in order to be happy. But what is happiness?

We tend to think of happiness as a psychological state and identify it with pleasure. Ordinary language promotes this identification, since pleasure pleases, and to be pleased is to be happy. Recall that this is how the classical utilitarians conceived of it (see Chapter 2). But it is easy to see that although pleasure might be a component of happiness, happiness is more complicated and cannot simply be identified with pleasure. Pleasures are episodic; they come and go. Happiness is not so fleeting. True, someone might be happy today and sad tomorrow, but the happiness of a life can surely endure fluctuations of mood. Moreover, whereas pleasures can often be located somewhere in the body, happiness cannot be similarly located, unless we want to speak of a general sense of well-being. But well-being is an entire state, not a passing sensation; rather than calling it happiness, we might better call it contentment or satisfaction.

Most significantly, if pleasure is what we are seeking in life when we say we want to be happy, then a life of utterly mindless pleasure would be a happy life. Consider a person who plays cards all day or watches television constantly; this person might have a life that is as pleasant as can be. We might even say the person is happy, but only in the sense that it has been a life of ease, diversion, entertainment—a life of pleasure. Or imagine a brain-damaged person who takes great delight in the simplest things, such as a clean diaper, a full stomach, and some colorful toys. This person could lead a pleasant life in the sense that she or he laughs a lot and feels good all the time, but would anyone of ability willingly trade places with this unfortunate individual? The fact that few would choose to do so shows that we ought not simply to equate a happy life with a pleasurable life.

A richer understanding of happiness does not identify it with pleasure or, indeed, with any psychological state whatsoever, even if pleasure and other emotional states are ingredients of happiness. Rather than seeing happiness as purely psychological we will do better to think of it functionally, as a kind of fulfillment or flourishing. Consider an oak tree. What is it for an oak tree to flourish? A flourishing oak tree is one that has realized its potential as an oak tree; that is, its characteristic traits are developed to a high degree. It will be tall, straight, and deeply rooted; it will have strong limbs supporting a broad canopy of leaves that efficiently turn sunlight into food; its bark will be thick and protective; it will produce many acorns. We can say that such an oak tree is flourishing and has reached a fulfillment of its kind.

We can tell a similar story for people. What is it for a person to flourish—not as a mother, an employee, a student, a friend, or a child, but as a person? We need an abstract account of what it is to lead an excellent human life, one where our characteristic traits are fully developed. Such a life would manifest the human excellences and thus be a happy one. *Note:* Manifesting the human excellences would not lead to a flourishing life, it would *be* one; flourishing does not make one happy, flourishing is what it *means* to be happy.

The project of identifying, explaining, and interrelating human excellences is the core of what is now called **virtue ethics.** The word *virtue* sounds somewhat old-fashioned, connoting a Victorian obsession with sexual propriety. But in this context, the term refers to various traits of character; indeed, virtue ethics also can be called character ethics. Its focus is on those traits of character that constitute a good person. It is concerned not so much with what we ought to *do* as with what sorts of people we ought to *be*—that is, with what attitudes and dispositions of character we ought to develop.

Virtue ethics was prominent among the ancients; Socrates, Plato, and Aristotle sought to describe an ideal or appropriate human life. They reasoned that a flourishing human life is one that manifests what is most distinctive about us. It is not surprising that they identified our rational capacities as our distinctive feature. Hence a life where our distinctive feature is fully engaged, refined, exercised, and developed is most appropriate for a person. We can broaden their conception of human flourishing to include obvious and important human capacities that go beyond a narrowly conceived rationality, such as emotional fulfillment, sensitivity to others, and aesthetic appreciation. But the important point, irrespective of how broadly or narrowly we wish to define human flourishing, is that happiness now has an objective basis. It is tied to realizing our distinctive nature as persons. And this means, among other things, that an individual is not the sole determiner of the happiness of his or her life, because happiness is not determined simply by how one feels. A person might think that he or she is happy (in the sense of flourishing) and be mistaken. Regrettably, many people are prone to this mistake about happiness, and as a result they lead misdirected, unhappy lives, regardless of how much pleasure they contain.

Even though it was central among ancient thinkers, virtue ethics lost favor as Christianity came to dominate the Western world. Philosophical concerns about character were supplanted over time by Christianity's preoccupation with absolute obedience to God the law-giver. An indication of the profound shift in orientation from virtue ethics to modern moral theory can be seen in the broad egalitarianism at the center of the moral theories considered in this text: Utilitarianism is committed to the equal consideration of interests; all rational agents are equal members of Kant's Kingdom of Ends; bargainers either in the state of nature or behind the veil of ignorance bargain with one another from positions of equality; and rational beings are equally subject to natural law. All of these moral theories accept some specified account of moral equality.

This commitment to equality is strikingly similar to Christian dogma, wherein all persons are created in the image of God and stand equally before God. We are so accustomed to the idea of human equality that we can scarcely imagine failing to recognize and acknowledge it. But virtue ethics has no such commitment. It would have seemed absurd to the ancients to propose equal moral status for all people simply by dint of their all being human. It would make no more sense to say that all human beings are equally capable of flourishing or equally capable of leading worthy lives than to say it of oak trees. As is true of oak trees, some are defective, some are warped by their environments, and some are just bad specimens of their kind. This is not to say that human equality cannot be a feature of virtue ethics, but it is not an essential feature of the theory.

In an important article entitled "Modern Moral Philosophy," published in 1958, the British philosopher Elizabeth Anscombe argued that contemporary moral concepts governing moral behavior, such as duty and obligation, are intellectually bankrupt because they depend for their meaning on Christianity's conception of our absolute duty to submit to God. And because God no longer dominates everyday life, as in medieval times, those ideas now have no basis. According to Anscombe, "the concepts of obligation, and duty—*moral* obligation and *moral* duty, that is to say—and of what is *morally* right and wrong, and of the *moral* sense of "ought," ought to be jettisoned . . . because they are survivals, or derivatives from survivals, from an earlier conception of ethics which no longer generally survives." In place of modern moral philosophy's focus on duty and obligation, namely, on what we ought to *do*, Anscombe recommended that we return to ancient questions of how we ought to *be* as people, and virtue ethics has experienced a renaissance ever since.

Since ethics is ultimately action-guiding, Anscombe's recommendation seems problematic. It is no help to be told that we should be a certain kind of person when we are wondering what we ought to do. Moreover, if we ask why we should seek to cultivate particular virtues, such as courage or truthfulness, the reasons will look very much like the reasons that ground other moral theories. For example, courage is a virtue because it helps people to overcome adversity and this will maximize their good (consequentialism), and truthfulness is a virtue because truthful people can be trusted and this also has good consequences (or was part of the social contract or is a manifestation of personal dignity, etc.). It is thus questionable whether virtue ethics, important as it is, can be conceived as a form of ethical theory that is independent of action and could supplant it. Contrary to Anscombe, in ethics we *do* need to maintain the concepts of moral obligation and moral duty, precisely because they are action-guiding. Ethics involves both being and doing.

We might even say that Anscombe's criticism commits what is known as the genetic fallacy insofar as she focuses on the origin of our moral concepts rather than their content. The mere historical fact that a distinctively moral "ought" derives from religious commitments that are now largely ignored is no reason to jettison the concept if it can be given a different foundation. And secular moral theories seek to do just that, by grounding moral obligation and duty in good consequences (utilitarianism) or contracts (contract ethics) or autonomy (Kant's ethics). The origin of something need not condemn it.

READINGS ON VIRTUE ETHICS

Aristotle, from *Nicomachean Ethics*

Aristotle (384–322 BCE), along with his teacher Plato, is regarded as one of the founders of Western philosophy. His influence on Western thought is incalculable. St. Thomas Aquinas—the foremost philosopher in the Middle Ages—referred to Aristotle simply as The Philosopher. For Aristotle the universe is teleological (that is, end-oriented); things happen not just for a reason but for a purpose. It rains, for example, not merely because falling temperature precipitates moisture from the air but also because plants need water. Since teleological explanations of events fit nicely with Christianity's view of the universe administered by God, Aristotle's metaphysical framework provided intellectual support for the medieval world view. Teleological explanations are no longer used in science, but Aristotle's ethical thought continues to provide guidance and insight into the human condition.

Aristotle begins the Nicomachean Ethics *with the deceptively simple claim that all intentional activity is aimed at some good. Whenever we act purposively—going to the store, applying to a college, or writing a friend—we aim at some good. Even the bank robber aims at what he conceives to be good; he thinks that it would be good for him to rob the bank. What, asks Aristotle, is the good at which we aim when we act? The good at which we aim at in life, the goal or point of all intentional activity, is happiness, which is the way Aristotle's word* eudiamonia *is usually translated. Our concept of happiness does not capture the richness of this concept, however. Eudaimonia (literally, "good demon or spirit") refers to "living well and doing well," more of what we might mean by flourishing or thriving.*

Aristotle reasons that since "the good and the 'well' is thought to reside in the function" of any object, human happiness—eudiamonia—will reside in our function. And what is our function? It resides in what is distinctive of us. Neither mere biological life nor perception is distinctive of us, claims Aristotle, since plants are alive and animals perceive. Aristotle identifies rational activity as the seat of our proper function. "Human good," he tells us, "turns out to be activity of soul in accordance with virtue." The moral virtues necessary for happiness are the midpoint on a continuum of character traits. Courage, for instance, is midway between rashness and cowardice, and so on for the other moral virtues. Thus can we locate the moral virtues, and happily for us, they can be cultivated by habituation. By acting bravely we become courageous. This means that courage and the other virtues necessary for happiness should be within our grasp.

Critical Reading Questions

1. What does Aristotle mean by the claim that "the good has been well described as that at which everything aims"?
2. How does Aristotle argue that happiness is not pleasure, wealth, or honor?
3. What characterizes good? How do those features lead Aristotle to identify it with happiness?
4. Why does Aristotle think that human beings have a function?
5. How does Aristotle conceive of virtues and how are they acquired?

THE NATURE OF VIRTUE

Aristotle

BOOK I: HAPPINESS

Ends and goods

§1 Every craft and every line of inquiry, and likewise every action and decision, seems to seek some good; that is why some people were right to describe the good as what everything seeks. §2 But the ends [that are sought] appear to differ; some are activities, and others are products apart from the activities. Wherever there are ends apart from the actions, the products are by nature better than the activities.

§3 Since there are many actions, crafts, and sciences, the ends turn out to be many as well; for health is the end of medicine, a boat of boat building, victory of generalship, and wealth of house-hold management. §4 But some of these pursuits are subordinate to some one capacity; for instance, bridle making and every other science producing equipment for horses are subordinate to horsemanship, while this and every action in warfare are, in turn, subordinate to generalship, and in the same way other pursuits are subordinate to further ones. In all such cases, then, the ends of the ruling sciences are more choiceworthy than all the ends subordinate to them, since the lower ends are also pursued for the sake of the higher. §5 Here it does not matter whether the ends of the actions are the activities themselves, or something apart from them, as in the sciences we have mentioned.

The highest good and political science

§1 Suppose, then, that the things achievable by action have some end that we wish for because of itself, and because of which we wish for the other things, and that we do not choose everything because of something else—for if we do, it will go on without limit, so that desire will prove to be empty and futile. Clearly, this end will be the good, that is to say, the best good.

§2 Then surely knowledge of this good also carries great weight for [determining the best] way of life; if we know it, we are more likely, like archers who have a target to aim at, to hit the right mark. §3 If so, we should try to grasp, in outline at any rate, what the good is, and which is its proper science or capacity.

§4 It seems proper to the most controlling science—the highest ruling science. §5 And this appears characteristic of political science. §6 For it is the one that prescribes which of the sciences ought to be studied in cities, and which ones each class in the city should learn, and how far; indeed we see that even the most honored capacities—generalship, household management, and rhetoric, for instance—are subordinate to it. §7 And since it uses the other sciences concerned with action, and moreover legislates what must be done and what avoided, its end will include the ends of the other sciences, and so this will be the human good. §8 For even if the good is the same for a city as for an individual, still the good of the city is apparently a greater and more complete good to acquire and preserve. For while it is satisfactory to acquire and preserve the good even for an individual, it is finer and more divine to acquire and preserve it for a people and for cities. And so, since our line of inquiry seeks these [goods, for an individual and for a community], it is a sort of political science.

The method of political science

§1 Our discussion will be adequate if we make things perspicuous enough to accord with the subject matter; for we would not seek the same degree of exactness in all sorts of arguments alike, any more than in the products of different crafts. §2 Now, fine and just things, which political science examines, differ and vary so much as to seem to rest on convention only, not on nature. §3 But [this is not a good reason, since] goods also vary in the same way, because they result in harm to many people—for some have been destroyed because of their wealth, others because of their bravery. §4 And so, since this is our subject and these are our premises, we shall be satisfied to indicate the truth roughly and in outline; since our subject and our premises are things that hold good usually [but not universally], we shall be satisfied to draw conclusions of the same sort.

Each of our claims, then, ought to be accepted in the same way [as claiming to hold good usually]. For the educated person seeks exactness in each area to the extent that the nature of the subject allows; for apparently it is just as mistaken to demand demonstrations from a rhetorician as to accept [merely] persuasive arguments from a mathematician. §5 Further, each person judges rightly what he knows, and is a good judge about that; hence the good judge in a given area is the person educated in that area, and the unqualifiedly good judge is the person educated in every area.

This is why a youth is not a suitable student of political science; for he lacks experience of the actions in life, which are the subject and premises of our arguments. §6 Moreover, since he tends to follow his feelings, his study will be futile and useless; for the end [of political science] is action, not knowledge. §7 It does not matter whether he is young in years or immature in character, since the deficiency does not depend on age, but results from following his feelings in his life and in a given pursuit; for an immature person, like an incontinent person, gets no benefit from his knowledge. But for those who accord with reason in forming their desires and in their actions, knowledge of political science will be of great benefit.

§8 These are the preliminary points about the student, about the way our claims are to be accepted, and about what we propose to do.

Common beliefs

§1 Let us, then, begin again. Since every sort of knowledge and decision pursues some good, what is the good that we say political science seeks? What, [in other words,] is the highest of all the goods achievable in action?

§2 As far as its name goes, most people virtually agree; for both the many and the cultivated call it happiness, and they suppose that living well and doing well are the same as being happy. But they disagree about what happiness is, and the many do not give the same answer as the wise.

§3 For the many think it is something obvious and evident—for instance, pleasure, wealth, or honor. Some take it to be one thing, others another. Indeed, the same person often changes his mind; for when he has fallen ill, he thinks happiness is health, and when he has fallen into poverty, he thinks it is wealth. And when they are conscious of their own ignorance, they admire anyone who speaks of something grand and above their heads. [Among the wise,] however, some used to think that besides these many goods there is some other good that exists in its own right and that causes all these goods to be goods.

§4 Presumably, then, it is rather futile to examine all these beliefs, and it is enough to examine those that are most current or seem to have some argument for them.

§5 We must notice, however, the difference between arguments from principles and arguments toward principles. For indeed Plato was right to be puzzled about this, when he used to ask if [the argument] set out from the principles or led toward them—just as on a race course the path may go from the starting line to the far end, or back again. For we should certainly begin from things known, but things are known in two ways; for some are known to us, some known without qualification. Presumably, then, *we* ought to begin from things known to *us*.

§6 That is why we need to have been brought up in fine habits if we are to be adequate students of fine and just things, and of political questions generally. §7 For we begin from the [belief] that [something is true]; if this is apparent enough to us, we can begin without also [knowing] why [it is true]. Someone who is well brought up has the beginnings, or can easily acquire them. Someone who neither has them nor can acquire them should listen to Hesiod: 'He who grasps everything himself is best of all; he is noble also who listens to one who has spoken well; but he who neither grasps it himself nor takes to heart what he hears from another is a useless man.'

The three lives

§1 But let us begin again from the point from which we digressed. For, it would seem, people quite reasonably reach their conception of the good, i.e., of happiness, from the lives [they lead]; §2 for there are roughly three most favored lives: the lives of gratification, of political activity, and, third, of study.

The many, the most vulgar, would seem to conceive the good and happiness as pleasure, and hence they also like the life of gratification. §3 In this they appear completely slavish, since the life they decide on is a life for grazing animals. Still, they have some argument in their defense, since many in positions of power feel as Sardanapallus felt, [and also choose this life]. §4 The cultivated people, those active [in politics], conceive the good as honor, since this is more or less the end [normally pursued] in the political life. This, however, appears to be too superficial to be what we are seeking; for it seems to depend more on those who honor than on the one honored, whereas we intuitively believe that the good is something of our own and hard to take from us. §5 Further, it would seem, they pursue honor to convince themselves that they are good; at any rate, they seek to be honored by prudent people, among people who know them, and for virtue. It is clear, then, that—in their view at any rate—virtue is superior [to honor].

§6 Perhaps, indeed, one might conceive virtue more than honor to be the end of the political life. However, this also is apparently too incomplete [to be the good]. For it seems possible for someone to possess virtue but be asleep or inactive throughout his life, and, moreover, to suffer the worst evils and misfortunes. If this is the sort of life he leads, no one would count him happy, except to defend a philosopher's paradox. Enough about this, since it has been adequately discussed in the popular works as well.

§7 The third life is the life of study, which we shall examine in what follows.

§8 The moneymaker's life is in a way forced on him [not chosen for itself]; and clearly wealth is not the good we are seeking, since it is [merely] useful, [choiceworthy only] for some other end. Hence one would be more inclined to suppose that [any of] the goods mentioned earlier is the end, since they are liked for themselves. But apparently they are not [the end] either; and many arguments have been presented against them. Let us, then, dismiss them.

An account of the human good

§1 But let us return once again to the good we are looking for, and consider just what it could be. For it is apparently one thing in one action or craft, and another thing in another; for it is one thing in medicine, another in generalship, and so on for the rest. What, then, is the good of each action or craft? Surely it is that for the sake of which the other things are done; in medicine this is health, in generalship victory, in housebuilding a house, in another case something else, but in every action and decision it is the end, since it is for the sake of the end that everyone does the other actions. And so, if there is some end of everything achievable in action, the good achievable in action will be this end; if there are more ends than one, [the good achievable in action] will be these ends.

§2 Our argument, then, has followed a different route to reach the same conclusion. But we must try to make this still more perspicuous. §3 Since there are apparently many ends, and we choose some of them (for instance, wealth, flutes, and, in general, instruments) because of something else, it is clear that not all ends are complete. But the best good is apparently something complete. And so, if only one end is complete, the good we are looking for will be this end; if more ends than one are complete, it will be the most complete end of these.

§4 We say that an end pursued in its own right is more complete than an end pursued

57

because of something else, and that an end that is never choiceworthy because of something else is more complete than ends that are choiceworthy both in their own right and because of this end. Hence an end that is always choiceworthy in its own right, never because of something else, is complete without qualification.

§5 Now happiness, more than anything else, seems complete without qualification. For we always choose it because of itself, never because of something else. Honor, pleasure, understanding, and every virtue we certainly choose because of themselves, since we would choose each of them even if it had no further result; but we also choose them for the sake of happiness, supposing that through them we shall be happy. Happiness, by contrast, no one ever chooses for their sake, or for the sake of anything else at all.

§6 The same conclusion [that happiness is complete] also appears to follow from self-sufficiency. For the complete good seems to be self-sufficient. What we count as self-sufficient is not what suffices for a solitary person by himself, living an isolated life, but what suffices also for parents, children, wife, and, in general, for friends and fellow citizens, since a human being is a naturally political [animal]. §7 Here, however, we must impose some limit; for if we extend the good to parents' parents and children's children and to friends of friends, we shall go on without limit; but we must examine this another time. Anyhow, we regard something as self-sufficient when all by itself it makes a life choiceworthy and lacking nothing; and that is what we think happiness does.

§8 Moreover, we think happiness is most choiceworthy of all goods, [since] it is not counted as one good among many. [If it were] counted as one among many, then, clearly, we think it would be more choiceworthy if the smallest of goods were added; for the good that is added becomes an extra quantity of goods, and the larger of two goods is always more choiceworthy. Happiness, then, is apparently something complete and selfsufficient, since it is the end of the things achievable in action.

§9 But presumably the remark that the best good is happiness is apparently something [generally] agreed, and we still need a clearer statement of what the best good is. §10 Perhaps, then, we shall find this if we first grasp the function of a human being. For just as the good, i.e., [doing] well, for a flautist, a sculptor, and every craftsman, and, in general, for whatever has a function and [characteristic] action, seems to depend on its function, the same seems to be true for a human being, if a human being has some function.

§11 Then do the carpenter and the leather worker have their functions and actions, but has a human being no function? Is he by nature idle, without any function? Or, just as eye, hand, foot, and, in general, every [bodily] part apparently has its function, may we likewise ascribe to a human being some function apart from all of these?

§12 What, then, could this be? For living is apparently shared with plants, but what we are looking for is the special function of a human being; hence we should set aside the life of nutrition and growth. The life next in order is some sort of life of sense perception; but this too is apparently shared with horse, ox, and every animal.

§13 The remaining possibility, then, is some sort of life of action of the [part of the soul] that has reason. One [part] of it has reason as obeying reason; the other has it as itself having reason and thinking. Moreover, life is also spoken of in two ways [as capacity and as activity], and we must take [a human being's special function to be] life as activity, since this seems to be called life more fully. We have found, then, that the human function is activity of the soul in accord with reason or requiring reason.

§14 Now we say that the function of a [kind of thing]—of a harpist, for instance—is the same in kind as the function of an excellent individual of the kind—of an excellent harpist, for instance. And the same is true without qualification in every case, if we add to the function the superior achievement in accord with the virtue; for the function of a harpist is to play the harp, and the function of a good harpist is to play it well. Moreover, we take the human function to be a certain kind of life, and take this life to be activity and actions of the soul that involve reason; hence the function of the excellent man is to do this well and finely.

§15 Now each function is completed well by being completed in accord with the virtue proper [to that kind of thing]. And so the human good proves to be activity of the soul in accord with virtue, and indeed with the best and most complete virtue, if there are more virtues than one. §16 Moreover, it must be in a complete life. For one swallow does not make a spring, nor does one day; nor, similarly, does one day or a short time make us blessed and happy.

§17 This, then, is a sketch of the good; for, presumably, we must draw the outline first, and fill it in later. If the sketch is good, anyone, it seems, can advance and articulate it, and in such cases time discovers more, or is a good partner in discovery. That is also how the crafts have improved, since anyone can add what is lacking [in the outline].

§18 We must also remember our previous remarks, so that we do not look for the same degree of exactness in all areas, but the degree that accords with a given subject matter and is proper to a given line of inquiry. §19 For the carpenter's and the geometer's inquiries about the right angle are different also; the carpenter restricts himself to what helps his work, but the geometer inquires into what, or what sort of thing, the right angle is, since he studies the truth. We must do the same, then, in other areas too, [seeking the proper degree of exactness], so that digressions do not overwhelm our main task.

§20 Nor should we make the same demand for an explanation in all cases. On the contrary, in some cases it is enough to prove rightly that [something is true, without also explaining why it is true]. This is so, for instance, with principles, where the fact that [something is true] is the first thing, that is to say, the principle.

§21 Some principles are studied by means of induction, some by means of perception, some by means of some sort of habituation, and others by other means. §22 In each case we should try to find them out by means suited to their nature, and work hard to define them rightly. §23 For they carry great weight for what follows; for the principle seems to be more than half the whole, and makes evident the answer to many of our questions.

Defense of the account of the good

§1 We should examine the principle, however, not only from the conclusion and premises [of a deduction], but also from what is said about it; for all the facts harmonize with a true account, whereas the truth soon clashes with a false one.

§2 Goods are divided, then, into three types, some called external, some goods of the soul, others goods of the body. We say that the goods of the soul are goods most fully, and more than the others, and we take actions and activities of the soul to be [goods] of the soul. And so our account [of the good] is right, to judge by this belief anyhow—and it is an ancient belief, and accepted by philosophers.

§3 Our account is also correct in saying that some sort of actions and activities are the end; for in that way the end turns out to be a good of the soul, not an external good.

§4 The belief that the happy person lives well and does well also agrees with our account, since we have virtually said that the end is a sort of living well and doing well.

§5 Further, all the features that people look for in happiness appear to be true of the end described in our account. §6 For to some people happiness seems to be virtue; to others prudence; to others some sort of wisdom; to others again it seems to be these, or one of these, involving pleasure or requiring it to be added; others add in external prosperity as well. §7 Some of these views are traditional, held by many, while others are held by a few men who are widely esteemed. It is reasonable for each group not to be completely wrong, but to be correct on one point at least, or even on most points.

§8 First, our account agrees with those who say happiness is virtue [in general] or some [particular] virtue; for activity in accord with virtue is proper to virtue. §9 Presumably, though, it matters quite a bit whether we suppose that the best good consists in possessing or in using—that is to say, in a state or in an activity [that actualizes the state]. For someone may be in a state that achieves no good—if, for instance, he is asleep or inactive in some other way—but this cannot be true of the activity; for it will necessarily act and act well. And just as Olympic prizes are not for the finest and strongest, but for the contestants—since it is only these who win—the same is true in life; among the fine and good people, only those who act correctly win the prize.

§10 Moreover, the life of these active people is also pleasant in itself. For being pleased is a condition of the soul, [and hence is included in the activity of the soul]. Further, each type of person finds pleasure in whatever he is called a lover of; a horse, for instance, pleases the horse-lover, a spectacle the lover of spectacles. Similarly, what is just pleases the lover of justice, and in general what accords with virtue pleases the lover of virtue.

§11 Now the things that please most people conflict, because they are not pleasant by nature, whereas the things that please lovers of the fine are things pleasant by nature. Actions in accord with virtue are pleasant by nature, so that they both please lovers of the fine and are pleasant in their own right.

§12 Hence these people's life does not need pleasure to be added [to virtuous activity] as some sort of extra decoration; rather, it has its pleasure within itself. For besides the reasons already given, someone who does not enjoy fine actions is not good; for no one would call a person just, for instance, if he did not enjoy doing just actions, or generous if he did not enjoy generous actions, and similarly for the other virtues.

§13 If this is so, actions in accord with the virtues are pleasant in their own right. Moreover, these actions are good and fine as well as pleasant; indeed, they are good, fine, and pleasant more than anything else is, since on this question the excellent person judges rightly, and his judgment agrees with what we have said.

§14 Happiness, then, is best, finest, and most pleasant, and the Delian inscription is wrong to distinguish these things: "What is most just is finest; being healthy is most beneficial; but it is most pleasant to win our heart's desire." For all three features are found in the best activities, and we say happiness is these activities, or [rather] one of them, the best one.

§15 Nonetheless, happiness evidently also needs external goods to be added, as we said, since we cannot, or cannot easily, do fine actions if we lack the resources. For, first of all, in many actions we use friends, wealth, and political power just as we use instruments. §16 Further, deprivation of certain [externals]—for instance, good birth, good children, beauty—mars our blessedness. For we do not altogether have the character of happiness if we look utterly repulsive or are ill-born, solitary, or childless; and we have it even less, presumably, if our children or friends are totally bad, or were good but have died.

§17 And so, as we have said, happiness would seem to need this sort of prosperity added also. That is why some people identify happiness with good fortune, and others identify it with virtue.

How is happiness achieved?

§1 This also leads to a puzzle: Is happiness acquired by learning, or habituation, or by some other form of cultivation? Or is it the result of some divine fate, or even of fortune.

§2 First, then, if the gods give any gift at all to human beings, it is reasonable for them to give us happiness more than any other human good, insofar as it is the best of human goods. §3 Presumably, however, this question is more suitable for a different inquiry.

But even if it is not sent by the gods, but instead results from virtue and some sort of learning or cultivation, happiness appears to be one of the most divine things, since the prize and goal of virtue appears to be the best good, something divine and blessed. §4 Moreover [if happiness comes in this way] it will be widely shared; for anyone who is not deformed [in his capacity] for virtue will be able to achieve happiness through some sort of learning and attention.

§5 And since it is better to be happy in this way than because of fortune, it is reasonable for this to be the way [we become] happy. For whatever is natural is naturally in the finest state possible. §6 The same is true of the products of crafts and of every other cause, especially the best cause; and it would be seriously inappropriate to entrust what is greatest and finest to fortune.

§7 The answer to our question is also evident from our account. For we have said that happiness is a certain sort of activity of the soul in accord with virtue, [and hence not a result of fortune]. Of the other goods, some are necessary conditions of happiness, while others are naturally useful and cooperative as instruments [but are not parts of it].

§8 Further, this conclusion agrees with our opening remarks. For we took the goal of political science to be the best good; and most of its attention is devoted to the character of the citizens, to make them good people who do fine actions.

§9 It is not surprising, then, that we regard neither ox, nor horse, nor any other kind of animal as happy; for none of them can share in this sort of activity. §10 For the same reason a child is not happy either, since his age prevents him from doing these sorts of actions. If he is called happy, he is being congratulated [simply] because of anticipated blessedness; for, as we have said, happiness requires both complete virtue and a complete life.

§11 It needs a complete life because life includes many reversals of fortune, good and bad, and the most prosperous person may fall into a terrible disaster in old age, as the Trojan stories tell us about Priam. If someone has suffered these sorts of misfortunes and comes to a miserable end, no one counts him happy.

Praise and honor

§1 Now that we have determined these points, let us consider whether happiness is something praiseworthy, or instead something honorable; for clearly it is not a capacity [which is neither praiseworthy nor honorable].

§2 Whatever is praiseworthy appears to be praised for its character and its state in relation to something. We praise the just and the brave person, for instance, and in general the good person and virtue, because of their actions and achievements; and we praise the strong person, the good runner, and each of the others because he naturally has a certain character and is in a certain state in relation to something good and excellent. §3 This is clear also from praises of the gods; for these praises appear ridiculous because they are referred to us, but they are referred to us because, as we said, praise depends on such a reference.

§4 If praise is for these sorts of things, then clearly for the best things there is no praise, but something greater and better. And indeed this is how it appears. For the gods and the most godlike of men are [not praised, but] congratulated for their blessedness and happiness. The same is true of goods; for we never praise happiness, as we praise justice, but we count it blessed, as something better and more godlike [than anything that is praised].

§5 Indeed, Eudoxus seems to have used the right sort of argument in defending the supremacy of pleasure. By not praising pleasure, though it is a good, we indicate—so he thought—that it is superior to everything praiseworthy; [only] the god and the good have this superiority since the other goods are [praised] by reference to them.

§6 [Here he seems to have argued correctly.] For praise is given to virtue, since it makes us do fine actions; but celebrations are for achievements, either of body or of soul. §7 But an exact treatment of this is presumably more proper for specialists in celebrations. For us, anyhow, it is clear from what has been said that happiness is something honorable and complete.

§8 A further reason why this would seem to be correct is that happiness is a principle; for [the principle] is what we all aim at in all our other actions; and we take the principle and cause of goods to be something honorable and divine.

Introduction to the virtues

§1 Since happiness is a certain sort of activity of the soul in accord with complete virtue, we must examine virtue; for that will perhaps also be a way to study happiness better. §2 Moreover, the true politician seems to have put more effort into virtue than into anything else, since he wants to make the citizens good and law-abiding. §3 We find an example of this in the Spartan and Cretan legislators and in any others who share their concerns. §4 Since, then, the examination of virtue is proper for political science, the inquiry clearly suits our decision at the beginning.

§5 It is clear that the virtue we must examine is human virtue, since we are also seeking the human good and human happiness. §6 By human virtue we mean virtue of the soul, not of the body, since we also say that happiness is an activity of the soul. §7 If this is so, it is clear that the politician must in some way know about the soul, just as someone setting out to heal the eyes must know about the whole body as well. This is all the more true to the extent that political science is better and more honorable than medicine; even among doctors, the cultivated ones devote a lot of effort to finding out about the body. Hence the politician as well [as the student of nature] must study the soul. §8 But he must study it for his specific purpose, far enough for his inquiry [into virtue]; for a more exact treatment would presumably take more effort than his purpose requires.

§9 [We] have discussed the soul sufficiently [for our purposes] in [our] popular works as well [as our less popular], and we should use this discussion. We have said, for instance, that one [part] of the soul is nonrational, while one has reason. §10 Are these distinguished as parts of a body and everything divisible into parts are? Or are they two [only] in definition, and inseparable by nature, as the convex and the concave are in a surface? It does not matter for present purposes.

§11 Consider the nonrational [part]. One [part] of it, i.e., the cause of nutrition and growth, would seem to be plantlike and shared [with all living things]; for we can ascribe this capacity of the soul to everything that is nourished, including embryos, and the same capacity to full-grown living things, since this is more reasonable than to ascribe another capacity to them.

§12 Hence the virtue of this capacity is apparently shared, not [specifically] human. For this part and this capacity more than others seem to be active in sleep, and here the good and the bad person are least distinct; hence happy people are said to be no better off than miserable people for half their lives. §13 This lack of distinction is not surprising, since sleep is inactivity of the soul insofar as it is called excellent or base, unless to some small extent some movements penetrate [to our awareness], and in this way the decent person comes to have better images [in dreams] than just any random person has. §14 Enough about this, however, and let us leave aside the nutritive part, since by nature it has no share in human virtue.

§15 Another nature in the soul would also seem to be nonrational, though in a way it shares in reason. For in the continent and the incontinent person we praise their reason, that is to say, the [part] of the soul that has reason, because it exhorts them correctly and toward what is best; but they evidently also have in them some other [part] that is by nature something apart from reason, clashing and struggling with reason. For just as paralyzed parts of a body, when we decide to move them to the right, do the contrary and move off to the left, the same is true of the soul; for incontinent people have impulses in contrary directions. §16 In bodies, admittedly, we see the part go astray, whereas we do not see it in the soul; nonetheless, presumably, we should suppose that the soul also has something apart from

reason, countering and opposing reason. The [precise] way it is different does not matter.

§17 However, this [part] as well [as the rational part] appears, as we said, to share in reason. At any rate, in the continent person it obeys reason; and in the temperate and the brave person it presumably listens still better to reason, since there it agrees with reason in everything.

§18 The nonrational [part], then, as well [as the whole soul] apparently has two parts. For while the plantlike [part] shares in reason not at all, the [part] with appetites and in general desires shares in reason and obeys it. This is the way in which we are said to "listen to reason" from father or friends, as opposed to the way in which [we "give the reason"] in mathematics. The nonrational part also [obeys and] is persuaded in some way by reason, as is shown by correction, and by every sort of reproof and exhortation.

§19 If, then, we ought to say that this [part] also has reason, then the [part] that has reason, as well [as the nonrational part], will have two parts. One will have reason fully, by having it within itself; the other will have reason by listening to reason as to a father.

The division between virtues accords with this difference. For some virtues are called virtues of thought, others virtues of character; wisdom, comprehension, and prudence are called virtues of thought, generosity and temperance virtues of character. For when we speak of someone's character we do not say that he is wise or has good comprehension, but that he is gentle or temperate. And yet, we also praise the wise person for his state, and the states that are praiseworthy are the ones we call virtues.

BOOK II [VIRTUE OF CHARACTER]

How a virtue of character is acquired

§1 Virtue, then, is of two sorts, virtue of thought and virtue of character. Virtue of thought arises and grows mostly from teaching; that is why it needs experience and time. Virtue of character [i.e., of *ethos*] results from habit [*ethos*]; hence its name "ethical", slightly varied from "ethos".

§2 Hence it is also clear that none of the virtues of character arises in us naturally. For if something is by nature in one condition, habituation cannot bring it into another condition.

A stone, for instance, by nature moves downwards, and habituation could not make it move upwards, not even if you threw it up ten thousand times to habituate it; nor could habituation make fire move downwards, or bring anything that is by nature in one condition into another condition. §3 And so the virtues arise in us neither by nature nor against nature. Rather, we are by nature able to acquire them, and we are completed through habit.

§4 Further, if something arises in us by nature, we first have the capacity for it, and later perform the activity. This is clear in the case of the senses; for we did not acquire them by frequent seeing or hearing, but we already had them when we exercised them, and did not get them by exercising them. Virtues, by contrast, we acquire, just as we acquire crafts, by having first activated them. For we learn a craft by producing the same product that we must produce when we have learned it; we become builders, for instance, by building, and we become harpists by playing the harp. Similarly, then, we become just by doing just actions, temperate by doing temperate actions, brave by doing brave actions. . . .

Habituation

§1 Our present discussion does not aim, as our others do, at study; for the purpose of our examination is not to know what virtue is, but to become good, since otherwise the inquiry would be of no benefit to us. And so we must examine the right ways of acting; for, as we have said, the actions also control the sorts of states we acquire.

§2 First, then, actions should accord with the correct reason. That is a common [belief], and let us assume it. We shall discuss it later, and say what the correct reason is and how it is related to the other virtues.

§3 But let us take it as agreed in advance that every account of the actions we must do has to be stated in outline, not exactly. As we also said at the beginning, the type of accounts we demand should accord with the subject matter; and questions about actions and expediency, like questions about health, have no fixed answers.

§4 While this is the character of our general account, the account of particular cases is still more inexact. For these fall under no craft or profession; the agents themselves must consider in each case what the opportune action is, as doctors and navigators do. §5 The account we offer, then, in our present inquiry is of this inexact sort; still, we must try to offer help.

§6 First, then, we should observe that these sorts of states naturally tend to be ruined by excess and deficiency. We see this happen with strength and health—for we must use evident cases [such as these] as witnesses to things that are not evident. For both excessive and deficient exercise ruin bodily strength, and, similarly, too much or too little eating or drinking ruins health, whereas the proportionate amount produces, increases, and preserves it.

§7 The same is true, then, of temperance, bravery, and the other virtues. For if, for instance, someone avoids and is afraid of everything, standing firm against nothing, he becomes cowardly; if he is afraid of nothing at all and goes to face everything, he becomes rash. Similarly, if he gratifies himself with every pleasure and abstains from none, he becomes intemperate; if he avoids them all, as boors do, he becomes some sort of insensible person. Temperance and bravery, then, are ruined by excess and deficiency, but preserved by the mean.

§8 But these actions are not only the sources and causes both of the emergence and growth of virtues and of their ruin; the activities of the virtues [once we have acquired them] also consist in these same actions. For this is also true of more evident cases; strength, for instance, arises from eating a lot and from withstanding much hard labor, and it is the strong person who is most capable of these very actions. §9 It is the same with the virtues. For abstaining from pleasures makes us become temperate, and once we have become temperate we are most capable of abstaining from pleasures. It is similar with bravery; habituation in disdain for frightening situations and in standing firm against them makes us become brave, and once we have become brave we shall be most capable of standing firm.

The importance of pleasure and pain

§1 But we must take someone's pleasure or pain following on his actions to be a sign of his state. For if someone who abstains from bodily pleasures enjoys the abstinence itself, he is temperate; if he is grieved by it, he is intemperate. Again, if he stands firm against terrifying situations and enjoys it, or at least does not find it painful, he is brave; if he finds it painful, he is cowardly. For virtue of character is about pleasures and pains.

For pleasure causes us to do base actions, and pain causes us to abstain from fine ones. §2 That is why we need to have had the appropriate upbringing—right from early youth, as Plato says—to make us find enjoyment or pain in the right things; for this is the correct education. . . .

§6 We assume, then, that virtue is the sort of state that does the best actions concerning pleasures and pains, and that vice is the contrary state. . . .

§11 To sum up: Virtue is about pleasures and pains; the actions that are its sources also increase it or, if they are done badly, ruin it; and its activity is about the same actions as those that are its sources.

Virtuous actions versus virtuous character

§1 Someone might be puzzled, however, about what we mean by saying that we become just by doing just actions and become temperate by doing temperate actions. For [one might suppose that] if we do grammatical or musical actions, we are grammarians or musicians, and, similarly, if we do just or temperate actions, we are thereby just or temperate.

§2 But surely actions are not enough, even in the case of crafts; for it is possible to produce a grammatical result by chance, or by following someone else's instructions. To be grammarians, then, we must both produce a grammatical result and produce it grammatically—that is to say, produce it in accord with the grammatical knowledge in us.

§3 Moreover, in any case, what is true of crafts is not true of virtues. For the products of a craft determine by their own qualities whether they have been produced well; and so it suffices that they have the right qualities when they have been produced. But for actions in accord with the virtues to be done temperately or justly it does not suffice that they themselves have the right qualities. Rather, the agent must also be

in the right state when he does them. First, he must know [that he is doing virtuous actions]; second, he must decide on them, and decide on them for themselves; and, third, he must also do them from a firm and unchanging state. . . .

§4 Hence actions are called just or temperate when they are the sort that a just or temperate person would do. But the just and temperate person is not the one who [merely] does these actions, but the one who also does them in the way in which just or temperate people do them.

§5 It is right, then, to say that a person comes to be just from doing just actions and temperate from doing temperate actions; for no one has the least prospect of becoming good from failing to do them. . . .

Virtue of character: its genus

§1 Next we must examine what virtue is. Since there are three conditions arising in the soul—feelings, capacities, and states—virtue must be one of these. . . .

§3 First, then, neither virtues nor vices are feelings. For we are called excellent or base insofar as we have virtues or vices, not insofar as we have feelings. Further, we are neither praised nor blamed insofar as we have feelings; for we do not praise the angry or the frightened person, and do not blame the person who is simply angry, but only the person who is angry in a particular way. We are praised or blamed, however, insofar as we have virtues or vices. . . .

§5 For these reasons the virtues are not capacities either; for we are neither called good nor called bad, nor are we praised or blamed, insofar as we are simply capable of feelings. . . .

§6 If, then, the virtues are neither feelings nor capacities, the remaining possibility is that they are states. And so we have said what the genus of virtue is.

Virtue of character: its differentia

§1 But we must say not only, as we already have, that it is a state, but also what sort of state it is.

§2 It should be said, then, that every virtue causes its possessors to be in a good state and to perform their functions well. The virtue of eyes, for instance, makes the eyes and their functioning excellent, because it makes us see well; and similarly, the virtue of a horse makes the horse excellent, and thereby good at galloping, at carrying its rider, and at standing steady in the face of the enemy. §3 If this is true in every case, the virtue of a human being will likewise be the state that makes a human being good and makes him perform his function well.

§4 We have already said how this will be true, and it will also be evident from our next remarks, if we consider the sort of nature that virtue has.

In everything continuous and divisible we can take more, less, and equal, and each of them either in the object itself or relative to us; and the equal is some intermediate between excess and deficiency. §5 By the intermediate in the object I mean what is equidistant from each extremity; this is one and the same for all. But relative to us the intermediate is what is neither superfluous nor deficient; this is not one, and is not the same for all.

§6 If, for instance, ten are many and two are few, we take six as intermediate in the object, since it exceeds [two] and is exceeded [by ten] by an equal amount, [four]. §7 This is what is intermediate by numerical proportion. But that is not how we must take the intermediate that is relative to us. For if ten pounds [of food], for instance, are a lot for someone to eat, and two pounds a little, it does not follow that the trainer will prescribe six, since this might also be either a little or a lot for the person who is to take it— for Milo [the athlete] a little, but for the beginner in gymnastics a lot; and the same is true for running and wrestling. §8 In this way every scientific expert avoids excess and deficiency and seeks and chooses what is intermediate—but intermediate relative to us, not in the object. . . .

§10 By virtue I mean virtue of character; for this is about feelings and actions, and these admit of excess, deficiency, and an intermediate condition. We can be afraid, for instance, or be confident, or have appetites, or get angry, or feel pity, and in general have pleasure or pain, both too much and too little, and in both ways not well. §11 But having these feelings at the right times, about the right things, toward the right people, for the right end, and in the right way, is the intermediate and best condition, and this is proper to virtue. §12 Similarly, actions also

admit of excess, deficiency, and an intermediate condition.

Now virtue is about feelings and actions, in which excess and deficiency are in error and incur blame, whereas the intermediate condition is correct and wins praise, which are both proper to virtue. §13 Virtue, then, is a mean, insofar as it aims at what is intermediate. . . .

§15 Virtue, then, is a state that decides, consisting in a mean, the mean relative to us, which is defined by reference to reason, that is to say, to the reason by reference to which the prudent person would define it. It is a mean between two vices, one of excess and one of deficiency.

§16 It is a mean for this reason also: Some vices miss what is right because they are deficient, others because they are excessive, in feelings or in actions, whereas virtue finds and chooses what is intermediate.

§17 That is why virtue, as far as its essence and the account stating what it is are concerned, is a mean, but, as far as the best [condition] and the good [result] are concerned, it is an extremity.

§18 Now not every action or feeling admits of the mean. For the names of some automatically include baseness—for instance, spite, shamelessness, envy [among feelings], and adultery, theft, murder, among actions. For all of these and similar things are called by these names because they themselves, not their excesses or deficiencies, are base. Hence in doing these things we can never be correct, but must invariably be in error. We cannot do them well or not well—by committing adultery, for instance, with the right woman at the right time in the right way. On the contrary, it is true without qualification that to do any of them is to be in error.

§19 [To think these admit of a mean], therefore, is like thinking that unjust or cowardly or intemperate action also admits of a mean, an excess and a deficiency. If it did, there would be a mean of excess, a mean of deficiency, an excess of excess and a deficiency of deficiency. §20 On the contrary, just as there is no excess or deficiency of temperance or of bravery (since the intermediate is a sort of extreme), so also there is no mean of these vicious actions either, but whatever way anyone does them, he is in error. For in general there is no mean of excess or of deficiency, and no excess or deficiency of a mean.

The particular virtues of character

§1 However, we must not only state this general account but also apply it to the particular cases. For among accounts concerning actions, though the general ones are common to more cases, the specific ones are truer, since actions are about particular cases, and our account must accord with these. Let us, then, find these from the chart.

§2 First, then, in feelings of fear and confidence the mean is bravery. The excessively fearless person is nameless (indeed many cases are nameless), and the one who is excessively confident is rash. The one who is excessive in fear and deficient in confidence is cowardly.

§3 In pleasures and pains—though not in all types, and in pains less than in pleasures—the mean is temperance and the excess intemperance. People deficient in pleasure are not often found, which is why they also lack even a name; let us call them insensible.

§4 In giving and taking money the mean is generosity, the excess wastefulness and the deficiency ungenerosity. Here the vicious people have contrary excesses and defects; for the wasteful person is excessive in spending and deficient in taking, whereas the ungenerous person is excessive in taking and deficient in spending. §5 At the moment we are speaking in outline and summary, and that is enough; later we shall define these things more exactly.

Relations between mean and extreme states

§1 Among these three conditions, then, two are vices—one of excess, one of deficiency—and one, the mean, is virtue. In a way, each of them is opposed to each of the others, since each extreme is contrary both to the intermediate condition and to the other extreme, while the intermediate is contrary to the extremes.

§2 For, just as the equal is greater in comparison to the smaller, and smaller in comparison to the greater, so also the intermediate states are excessive in comparison to the deficiencies and deficient in comparison to the excesses—both in feelings and in actions. For the brave person, for instance, appears rash in comparison to the coward, and cowardly in comparison to the rash person; the temperate person appears intemperate in comparison to the insensible person, and insensible in comparison with the intemperate person; and the generous person appears wasteful in comparison to the ungenerous, and ungenerous in comparison to the wasteful person. §3 That is why each of the extreme people tries to push the intermediate person to the other extreme, so that the coward, for instance, calls the brave person rash, and the rash person calls him a coward, and similarly in the other cases.

§4 Since these conditions of soul are opposed to each other in these ways, the extremes are more contrary to each other than to the intermediate. For they are further from each other than from the intermediate, just as the large is further from the small, and the small from the large, than either is from the equal.

§5 Further, sometimes one extreme—rashness or wastefulness, for instance—appears somewhat like the intermediate state, bravery or generosity. But the extremes are most unlike one another; and the things that are furthest apart from each other are defined as contraries. And so the things that are further apart are more contrary.

§6 In some cases the deficiency, in others the excess, is more opposed to the intermediate condition. For instance, cowardice, the deficiency, not rashness, the excess, is more opposed to bravery, whereas intemperance, the excess, not insensibility, the deficiency, is more opposed to temperance.

§7 This happens for two reasons: One reason is derived from the object itself. Since sometimes one extreme is closer and more similar to the intermediate condition, we oppose the contrary extreme, more than this closer one, to the intermediate condition. Since rashness, for instance, seems to be closer and more similar to bravery, and cowardice less similar, we oppose cowardice, more than rashness, to bravery; for what is further from the intermediate condition seems to be more contrary to it. This, then, is one reason, derived from the object itself.

§8 The other reason is derived from ourselves. For when we ourselves have some natural tendency to one extreme more than to the other, this extreme appears more opposed to the intermediate condition. Since, for instance, we have more of a natural tendency to pleasure, we drift more easily toward intemperance than toward orderliness. Hence we say that an extreme is more contrary if we naturally develop more in that direction; and this is why intemperance is more contrary to temperance, since it is the excess [of pleasure].

How can we reach the mean?

§1 We have said enough, then, to show that virtue of character is a mean and what sort of mean it is; that it is a mean between two vices, one of excess and one of deficiency; and that it is a mean because it aims at the intermediate condition in feelings and actions.

§2 That is why it is also hard work to be excellent. For in each case it is hard work to find the intermediate; for instance, not everyone, but only one who knows, finds the midpoint in a circle. So also getting angry, or giving and spending money, is easy and everyone can do it; but doing it to the right person, in the right amount, at the right time, for the right end, and in the right way is no longer easy, nor can everyone do it. Hence doing these things well is rare, praiseworthy, and fine.

§3 That is why anyone who aims at the intermediate condition must first of all steer clear of the more contrary extreme, following the advice that Calypso also gives: 'Hold the ship outside the spray and surge.' For one extreme is more in error, the other less. §4 Since, therefore, it is hard to hit the intermediate extremely accurately, the secondbest tack, as they say, is to take the lesser of the evils. We shall succeed best in this by the method we describe.

We must also examine what we ourselves drift into easily. For different people have different natural tendencies toward different goals, and we shall come to know our own tendencies from the pleasure or pain that arises in us. §5 We must drag ourselves off in the contrary direction; for if we pull far away from error, as they do in straightening bent wood, we shall reach the intermediate condition.

§6 And in everything we must beware above all of pleasure and its sources; for we are already biased in its favor when we come to judge it. Hence we must react to it as the elders reacted to Helen, and on each occasion repeat what they said; for if we do this, and send it off, we shall be less in error.

§7 In summary, then, if we do these things we shall best be able to reach the intermediate condition. But presumably this is difficult, especially in particular cases, since it is not easy to define the way we should be angry, with whom, about what, for how long. For sometimes, indeed, we ourselves praise deficient people and call them mild, and sometimes praise quarrelsome people and call them manly.

§8 Still, we are not blamed if we deviate a little in excess or deficiency from doing well, but only if we deviate a long way, since then we are easily noticed. But how great and how serious a deviation receives blame is not easy to define in an account; for nothing else perceptible is easily defined either. Such things are among particulars, and the judgment depends on perception.

§9 This is enough, then, to make it clear that in every case the intermediate state is praised, but we must sometimes incline toward the excess, sometimes toward the deficiency; for that is the easiest way to hit the intermediate and good condition.

Discussion Questions

1. Is Aristotle right that all intentional activity aims at some good?
2. How many virtues can you identify as a midpoint between deficiency and excess? Consider, for example, toleration, industriousness, civility, temperance, wisdom, courteousness, sensitivity, kindness, generosity, fairness, friendliness, loyalty, thoughtfulness, and any others you can come up with.
3. How is virtue ethics different from the other ethical theories considered in this text? What are its strengths? What are its weaknesses?
4. Why should we strive to develop the virtues? What would the other moral theories say about why we should develop the virtues?

CHAPTER 6

Natural Law Ethics

THE NATURAL LAW TRADITION

The idea of natural law has a long, complicated history. In a very general sense, natural law consists of standards governing human behavior that are thought to be beyond or "higher" than mere convention. These standards, defined with respect to human good, apply to all, and we are all capable of knowing them, provided that we think about matters properly. The notion of objective moral standards independent of culture is the basic intuition behind human rights and crimes against humanity, and in the American experience it is a foundational principle of democracy. People everywhere (not just Americans) are supposedly endowed by our creator with self-evident and inalienable rights—rights that merit respect regardless of where one lives. According to the natural law tradition, morality is not simply up to us to decide.

Natural law is "law" because these standards of conduct are alleged to be universal, binding on everyone, and it is "natural" because the standards reflect our nature as rational beings. Many have taken our nature to be essentially rational, so acting in a manner that reflects our nature is to act rationally. Ancient Greek and early Roman thinkers called Stoics (from *stoa*, the porch where teachings were originally held) thought that the universe is ordered by a divine force called *logos*, or rationality. As a portion of the universe, we also have rationality within us, so a good human life consists in living in accordance with our nature, or *logos*. The idea that our essential nature is rationality, so to act naturally is to act rationally, is the key intuition underlying natural law. Acting rationally is most fitting because it reflects our essential nature.

There are numerous sources for natural law, but scholars trace its first explicit statement to the Roman Stoic philosopher and statesman Cicero (106–43 BCE). In *The Republic* (modeled after Plato's dialogue on the same topic), Cicero writes,

True law is right reason in agreement with nature; it is of universal application, unchanging and everlasting; it summons to duty by its commands, and averts from wrongdoing by its prohibitions. And it does not lay its commands or prohibitions upon good men in vain, though neither have any effect on the wicked. It is a sin to try to alter this law, nor is it allowable to attempt to repeal any part of it, and it is impossible to abolish it entirely. We cannot be freed from its obligations by senate or people, and we need not look outside ourselves for an expounder or interpreter of it. And there will not be different laws at Rome and at Athens, or different laws now and in the future, but one eternal and unchangeable law will be valid for all nations and all times, and there will be one master and ruler, that is, God, over us all, for he is the author of this law, its promulgator, and its enforcing judge. Whoever is disobedient is fleeing from himself and denying his human nature, and by reason of this very fact he will suffer the worst penalties, even if he escapes what is commonly considered punishment.

Here we see an appeal to objective eternal universal standards of rational conduct referred to as "law" because of its authority over us and our corresponding obligation to obey, in the sense of our obligation to be rational, which we flout at our peril. God, the universal rational mind, is regarded as the supreme legislator, so when we act rationally, we share (however fleetingly) in the divine essence, for we conform to God.

Natural law thinking was given its definitive expression by the great medieval philosopher and theologian St. Thomas Aquinas (1225–1274) in his magisterial *Summa Theologica*. Most contemporary natural law theorists trace their lineage to Aquinas, so if we can get a good understanding of Aquinas's conception of natural law, we will grasp the fundamentals of the theory. Moreover, if we take Aquinas's account of natural law as paradigm, we can see the extent to which a theory can be "natural law–like" if it rejects or modifies elements of Aquinas's account.

For Aquinas, law, in the sense of something to which we are bound, is "an ordinance of reason for the common good made by the authority who has care of the community and promulgated." This abstract definition is supposed to hold for law of any sort, whether humanly constructed positive law (from *posit*) or natural law. Aquinas claims that law as such must be rational; it must not be incoherent, nor can it be senselessly arbitrary. Thus, for example, any positive "law" that sanctions discrimination is not really law because discrimination is senselessly arbitrary. Furthermore, law must be for the common good (otherwise, there is no reason why one should be bound by it), and it must be promulgated—that is, made known to all (otherwise one cannot be expected to follow it)—by the authority who has care of the community. Not just anyone can proclaim law; only those authorized may issue rational dictates for the common good. This authority can be an assembly, as in the legislative branch of government.

"Law," says Aquinas, "is nothing other than a decree of reason." The precepts of natural law are thus allegedly self-evident. That is, one who reflects on them will see that they are true. They are not derived from other principles, nor are they known by intuition. They are straightforwardly apprehended as aspects of *the* fundamental rule of practical deliberation, which is that "good ought to be pursued."

It is self-evident, claims Aquinas, that if something is good, then it ought to be pursued. This is part of the very meaning of *good*, since it makes no sense to say that something is good but it ought not to be pursued (other things being equal). If "ought to be pursued" is analytically part of *good*, then "good ought to be pursued" is self-evident in the same way that "triangles have three sides" is self-evident. Someone who knows what triangles are, sees that they have three sides. Since not everyone knows what triangles are, however, this suggests two accounts of self-evidence: Self-evident could mean known by everyone or it could mean known only to "the wise." This will be an important point to bear in mind in debates about whether particular practices, such as euthanasia or contraception, flout natural law. It might be claimed that this is self-evident only to some, the wise.

Good ought to be pursued, but what is good? If we can determine that, then our practical reasoning will have some content. Aquinas tells us that "A thing is good if it is an end that we have a natural inclination to desire." Aquinas holds that God created us with certain "natural inclinations" as reasons for action; we are naturally inclined to pursue that which constitutes our good. Indeed, it would be a perverse god who instilled in his creatures a propensity to do otherwise. What ends are we naturally inclined to pursue? Aquinas lists life, sexual union of man and woman and the creation of family, knowledge (including knowledge of God), and social life. These, he claims, are the ends toward which we are naturally inclined; the fulfillment of these ends therefore constitutes our good, and practical reason determines how best to achieve them.

Natural law ethics is the official moral philosophy of the Catholic Church (and Aquinas one of its most revered philosophers). It is now easy to understand why the Church has traditionally opposed practices that (they argue) violate natural law. Abortion is destructive of life, so are capital punishment and euthanasia; non-procreative sex (such as contraception, masturbation, and oral sex) allegedly thwarts the natural inclination to procreate, and, of course, so does homosexuality. The Church's long and distinguished commitment to social justice and education also flows from a natural law conception of our good.

One might augment Aquinas's list of fundamental human goods, but for natural law theorists there will still be some relatively small set of such goods. The goods are fundamental in the sense that they are not derived from more basic goods, nor can they be reduced to each other. This means they are incommensurable, and *this* means there will be acceptable and unacceptable ways of seeking to realize human good. If all basic human goods are equally basic and equally good, then we may not trade one off against another, for that would arbitrarily deny one good at the expense of another. For example, it would be illegitimate to pursue social good or knowledge at the expense of individual lives (hence natural law is opposed to utilitarianism). Proponents of natural law have developed elaborate ways to adapt natural law thinking to everyday life, where it seems that we often face situations in which we are asked to trade one basic human good for another.

Outside of Catholic thought, natural law is not very well regarded. Professional philosophers frequently claim that it violates "Hume's dictum," a principle named for the famous Scottish philosopher David Hume (1711–1776), who argued that one cannot validly derive "ought" statements from "is" statements. For example, if taking a wallet is stealing, it does not follow merely as a matter of logic that one ought not to do it, unless we add the premise that one ought not to steal. Critics of natural law sometimes think that its proponents view moral standards as somehow read off nature and thus seek to deduce "ought" from "is." However, at least for Aquinas, this common charge seems false, since the precepts of natural law are all alleged to be aspects of the fundamental, self-evident principle of practical reason that good ought to be done. Aquinas seeks to specify what ought to be from a purportedly self-evident abstract account of good. For Aquinas, to say that something is good just means, in part that it ought to be. So it is debatable whether he violate's Hume's dictum.

Natural law's questionable reputation is probably a function of its association with religion, for outside the realm of religious philosophy, Aquinas's entire system is currently out of favor. This is not to say that it is incorrect, only that the contemporary philosophical mind is not motivated by concerns about God in the way the medieval mind was. But is God essential to natural law? Aquinas's account of practical reason (that good ought to be pursued) can be accepted independent of God, and so can the idea that various human goods are fundamental. It is thus possible to develop secular versions of natural law ethics; natural law's historical association with religion is not crucial to it. All that is necessary is an account of fundamental human good and the self-evident principle that good ought to be pursued. For example, if human life, properly understood, is a fundamental good, then actions that promote human life ought to be pursued.

READINGS ON NATURAL LAW ETHICS

St. Thomas Aquinas, from *Summa Theologica*

St. Thomas Aquinas (1224–1274) is widely regarded as the most important philosopher of the Middle Ages. He achieved a grand synthesis of Aristotle's teleological conception of reality within a Christian world view. Aquinas's moral philosophy is an official doctrine of the Catholic Church, whereby the key question to ask is whether a practice is compatible or incompatible with natural law. (See the introductory discussion above for an account of natural law ethics.) The Summa Theologica *is divided into a series of chapters that seek to answer particular questions. Each question is further divided into articles wherein Aquinas states several objections to the thesis at issue. His response often begins by citing an authority, and then he offers his own view and responds to each objection.*

Critical Reading Questions

1. What does Aquinas think is essential to law?
2. What is the difference between eternal law and natural law?
3. What is the fundamental principle of practical reasoning?
4. What is good?

SUMMA THEOLOGICA

St. Thomas Aquinas

WHETHER THERE IS IN US A NATURAL LAW?

. . . A Gloss on Rom. ii. 14 (*When the Gentiles, who have not the law, do by nature those things that are of the law*) comments as follows: *Although they have no written law, yet they have the natural law, whereby each one knows, and is conscious of, what is good and what is evil.*

I answer that, As we have stated above, law, being a rule and measure, can be in a person in two ways: in one way, as in him that rules and measures; in another way, as in that which is ruled and measured, since a thing is ruled and measured in so far as it partakes of the rule or measure. Therefore, since all things subject to divine providence are ruled and measured by the eternal law, as was stated above, it is evident that all things partake in some way in the eternal law, in so far as, namely, from its being imprinted on them, they derive their respective inclinations to their proper acts and ends. Now among all others, the rational creature is subject to divine providence in a more excellent way, in so far as it itself partakes of a share of providence, by being provident both for itself and for others. Therefore it has a share of the eternal reason, whereby it has a natural inclination to its proper act and end; and this participation of the eternal law in the rational creature is called the natural law. Hence the Psalmist, after saying (*Ps. iv. 6*): *Offer up the sacrifice of justice,* as though someone asked what the works of justice are, adds: *Many say, Who showeth us good things?* in answer to which question he says: *The light of Thy countenance, O Lord, is signed upon us.* He thus implies that the light of natural reason, whereby we discern what is good and what is evil, which is the function of the natural law, is nothing else than an imprint on us of the divine light. It is therefore evident that the natural law is nothing else than the rational creature's participation of the eternal law. . . .

WHETHER THERE IS HUMAN LAW?

. . . Now it is to be observed that the same procedure takes place in the practical and in the speculative reason, for each proceeds from principles to conclusions, as was stated above. Accordingly, we conclude that, just as in the speculative reason, from naturally known indemonstrable principles we draw the conclusions of the various sciences, the knowledge of which is not imparted to us by nature, but acquired by the efforts of reason, so too it is that from the precepts of the natural law, as from common and indemonstrable principles, the human reason needs to proceed to the more particular determination of certain matters. These particular determinations, devised by human reason, are called human laws, provided that the other essential conditions of law be observed, as was stated above. . . .

WHETHER THE NATURAL LAW CONTAINS SEVERAL PRECEPTS, OR ONLY ONE?

. . . As was stated above, the precepts of the natural law are to the practical reason what the first principles of demonstrations are to the speculative reason, because both are self-evident principles. Now a thing is said to be self-evident in two ways: first, in itself; secondly, in relation to us. Any proposition is said to be self-evident in itself, if its predicate is contained in the notion of the subject; even though it may happen that to one who does not know the definition of the subject, such a proposition is not self-evident. For instance, this proposition, *Man is a rational being,* is, in its very nature, self-evident, since he who says *man,* says *a rational being;* and yet to one who does not know what a man is, this proposition is not self-evident. Hence it is that, as Boethius says, certain axioms or propositions are universally self-evident to all; and such are the propositions whose terms are known to all, as, *Every whole is greater than its part,* and, *Things equal to one and the same are equal to one another.* But some propositions are self-evident only to the wise, who understand the meaning of the terms of such propositions. Thus to one who understands that an angel is not a body, it is self-evident that an angel is not circumscriptively in a place. But this is not evident to the unlearned, for they cannot grasp it.

Now a certain order is to be found in those things that are apprehended by men. For that which first falls under apprehension is *being,* the understanding of which is included in all things whatsoever a man apprehends. Therefore the first indemonstrable principle is that *the same thing cannot be affirmed and denied at the same time,* which is based on the notion of *being* and *not-being:* and on this principle all others are based, as is stated in *Metaph.* iv. Now as *being* is the first thing that falls under the apprehension absolutely, so *good* is the first thing that falls under the apprehension of the practical reason, which is directed to action (since every agent acts for an end, which has the nature of good). Consequently, the first principle in the practical reason is one founded on the nature of good, viz., that *good is that which all things seek after.* Hence this is the first precept of law, that *good is to be done and promoted, and evil is to be avoided.* All other precepts of the natural law

are based upon this; so that all the things which the practical reason naturally apprehends as man's good belong to the precepts of the natural law under the form of things to be done or avoided.

Since, however, good has the nature of an end, and evil, the nature of the contrary, hence it is that all those things to which man has a natural inclination are naturally apprehended by reason as being good, and consequently as objects of pursuit, and their contraries as evil, and objects of avoidance. Therefore, the order of the precepts of the natural law is according to the order of natural inclinations. For there is in man, first of all, an inclination to good in accordance with the nature which he has in common with all substances, inasmuch, namely, as every substance seeks the preservation of its own being, according to its nature; and by reason of this inclination, whatever is a means of preserving human life, and of warding off its obstacles, belongs to the natural law. Secondly, there is in man an inclination to things that pertain to him more specially, according to that nature which he has in common with other animals; and in virtue of this inclination, those things are said to belong to the natural law *which nature has taught to all animals,* such as sexual intercourse, the education of offspring and so forth. Thirdly, there is in man an inclination to good according to the nature of his reason, which nature is proper to him. Thus man has a natural inclination to know the truth about God, and to live in society; and in this respect, whatever pertains to this inclination belongs to the natural law: e.g., to shun ignorance, to avoid offending those among whom one has to live, and other such things regarding the above inclination.

Discussion Questions

1. Is Aquinas right about the relationship between our natural inclinations and good? Can we be naturally inclined toward evil?
2. Is God the only explanation for our natural inclinations?
3. What does it mean to say that something is "natural"? What does Aquinas mean by saying that something is natural?
4. Is Aquinas right that good ought to be pursued? If he is, does this commit us to natural law ethics?
5. Are any goods self-evidently so?

Reflections on Theoretical Disunity in Ethics

Ethics is supposed to be practical, but how can moral theory help us decide what to do when there are so many different theories? What if the theories disagree about a particular issue? For example, natural law ethics often condemns homosexuality, but for contract ethics, sexual practices among consenting adults are not an issue; Kant's view endorses capital punishment on retributive grounds, whereas utilitarianism is not sure that the benefits of capital punishment outweigh the harms. Different theories can yield different answers for many of our most pressing practical moral questions, so how can studying moral theories help us resolve those issues?

We should not distort the extent of theoretical disunity, for different moral theories can yield convergent answers in many cases. No plausible theory can be too far out of step with our considered moral intuitions; otherwise we would have more reason to doubt the theory than to abandon our intuitions for the sake of the theory. All of the moral theories we have studied agree in condemning obvious cases of wrong-doing. One then wonders why we need the theory in the first place, if its adequacy is confirmed only by coinciding with our pretheoretical intuitions.

Even when there is convergence among the theories regarding a particular action, it is often for radically different reasons. All the theories condemn slavery, for example, but the Kantian explanation for why slavery is wrong differs from the utilitarian, the virtue ethics account from the natural law view. So even with practical unanimity, explanatory disunity remains. We could simply choose one theory and approach all ethical questions from the perspective of that theory, but why choose one theory over another? Furthermore, moral theories seem to play no role in actual moral decision making. People do not ordinarily say, "Well, since I'm a utilitarian (or a Kantian, or whatever), this is the right thing to do." Rather than appealing to a moral theory in our quotidian moral deliberations, we consider such mundane facts as whether what we do will harm someone or whether we have treated someone fairly. So once again, moral theories seem beside the point. It might be interesting to know what philosophers have thought about morality, but the theories seem utterly remote from the day-to-day practicality of morality.

This is a strong indictment of moral theory. For a newcomer to moral philosophy, the range of moral theories must be especially bewildering, so some defense of our study of moral theory is warranted. First, we should not hastily assume that all moral theories are in fact equally good, so that we are being asked to make what amount to arbitrary choices among equally plausible theories. The philosophers we studied in this section obviously favor one theory over another, but disagreement is no obstacle to there being a best (or worst) theory.

Here are some issues to keep in mind as we reflect on the moral theories. First, each theory rests on assumptions about human nature that may or may not be warranted. Moreover, there is no reason to assume that the moral theories are all equally coherent or equally comprehensive, or that they all have the same explanatory power or conceptual resources in the face of objections. We cannot here enter into the debate about which theory emerges as more comprehensive or explanatorily powerful (or which emerges as least plausible). But we should realize that the fact that there are several moral theories does not imply that they are all equally acceptable. So adopting a general theoretical orientation in ethics need not be an arbitrary choice, as perhaps it seemed at first. As moral deliberators, each of us has a responsibility to try to come to some general understanding about the nature of morality.

Second, different moral theories each bring a range of considerations to bear on moral deliberation. Moral issues are complex and multidimensional; it is simplistic to think that focusing on only one dimension is the proper way to understand a moral issue. Focusing on rights ignores consequences, thinking about contractual obligations ignores other possible bases for obligations, considering only one form of human good diminishes others, and exclusive concern about action ignores the characters of agents. Responsible moral deliberation requires us to be sensitive to a full range of considerations, as supplied by the different moral theories, where principled considerations are articulated and systematically interrelated.

Third, moral reflection is not a mechanical process whereby we feed some initial conditions into our favorite theory and out pops a moral recommendation. Sure, utilitarians tend to see things one way and Kantians another, but in the end what we want to know is what we should do. So rather than being driven by theory, perhaps we should proceed more elliptically by first trying to make sense of an issue in its own terms and only then seeing where we wind up theoretically. In this "bottom-up" approach to moral thinking, we find ourselves with a theoretical orientation only after we have sifted through the details of a particular moral problem, rather than starting with a theory that we use as a generic approach to all moral questions. Moral theories can help us to organize our thinking after the fact rather than driving it initially.

The "bottom-up" approach might allow us to see how one theory emerges as the most plausible if we find ourselves thinking in its terms throughout a range of practical moral problems. Suppose that after careful reflection on abortion, war, sexuality, and global issues, we find that the most plausible solutions are, say, broadly consequentialist in nature. This would increase our confidence in consequentialism. Of course, if we began as consequentialists, it would be no wonder that this view emerged as the most plausible. But if we proceed thoughtfully and independently through a range of issues, one broad theoretical orientation could emerge as the most insightful and explanatorily powerful one.

Alternatively, it could turn out that different theoretical approaches are more illuminating for different kinds of questions. Moral theories might be attuned to phenomena of different scales. Perhaps intimate human relations are best understood by character ethics, everyday societal interactions are best understood by rights-based theories, and mass human endeavors (such as war or dealing with poverty and epidemics) are best understood by consequentialist thinking. This would mean that the different theories are something like different tools; when we are dealing with a problem of a certain sort, then we reach for a particular theory. A natural fit between type of moral theory and type of problem is a possibility that we cannot discount, even though it would mean conceptual chaos, because there would be no overarching conception of morality. But there is no *a priori* reason to think that morality must be theoretically univocal, much as we might prefer it to be so.

Another way to think about theoretical disunity in ethics is to imagine that the different theories are all somehow part of a larger coherent moral theory that we haven't yet figured out. Each theory gets something right about morality—but then goes wrong by trying to make that feature the whole of morality. Consider the main points from each theory and their importance for moral thought. For example, it is difficult to imagine carrying on moral deliberation without considering the consequences of our actions. Sensitivity to how what we do affects others is the hallmark of the ethical. The important interests of people can be seen as natural in some sense, and protecting and promoting those interests can provide the ultimate grounds for rights. And persons attuned to the effects of their behavior on the important interests of others will have characters of a certain kind. They will act with reciprocity. This compilation covers utilitarianism (consequences), virtue ethics (character), Kantian ethics (rights), natural law ethics (interests), and contract ethics (reciprocity). Perhaps someday we will have a unified theoretical structure that will incorporate what now seem like different individual theories.

As we leave the theory section of this text and enter the world of practical morality, we should remain alert to the differing ways in which moral theories can help us understand the relevant factors in these issues. After working through the hard questions that arise for practical ethics, you may find that your ethical orientation tends toward one theory or another. But being more comfortable with one theory or another is no reason to think that it is the correct or best theory, for now begins the hard work of rationally defending a comprehensive moral outlook. Welcome to moral philosophy!

CHAPTER 7

Abortion

HARD QUESTION: IS ABORTION A MORAL ISSUE?

Nothing provokes moral disagreement quite like abortion. Before entering the debate, however, it is worth asking what makes abortion a moral issue in the first place. This is not to ask whether abortion is morally permissible or morally impermissible; rather, it is to ask by virtue of what abortion is a moral issue at all. The natural response is to say that abortion is a moral issue because fetuses have some sort of moral status. If fetuses have moral status, then they have interests that will be affected by what we do. If fetuses have no moral significance, this means that they have no morally important interests. Terminating pregnancies would then not be a moral issue, at least not in the sense that fetuses could be directly wronged by being aborted.

The morality of abortion does not turn on the moral significance of fetuses alone, as though the women who carry them are an afterthought. But what women may permissibly do to fetuses does depend on the latters' moral status. For if fetuses are morally significant to one degree or another, then that will affect what women may permissibly do to them. Abortion might still be morally permissible, all things considered, but if fetuses are morally significant to any degree at all, then that is a factor that must be outweighed by other considerations in order for abortion to be morally permissible. There is also no reason to suppose that the moral significance of fetuses (if they have any) remains fixed throughout pregnancy. As fetuses develop, their moral status could change too, such that more stringent reasons would be needed to justify a late-term abortion than one performed in an early stage of pregnancy.

It is common to refer to prenatal human organisms at any time during pregnancy as fetuses, but strictly speaking, *fetus* is a medical term properly used only after eight weeks of development. Prior to that is the embryo, and earlier still is the zygote, a fertilized egg. Unless it is important to specify otherwise, however, we will use the term *fetus* incorrectly but conveniently to refer to any stage of *in utero* development.

To return to our initial question, why should we think that fetuses have any moral status at all? We will consider four common grounds for thinking that fetuses are morally significant: fetuses are alive, fetuses are sentient, fetuses are persons, fetuses are potential persons.

1. Fetuses have moral status because they are alive. Fetuses are indisputably alive in a purely biological sense. There is cellular activity and all the other indications of a living organism are manifest. So the tired question "When does human life begin?" is not very illuminating. If we want to know when the life of an identifiable human organism begins, meaning when its biological existence is established, it seems that the only possible answer is conception, the time when egg and sperm unite, cellular division begins, and the various life processes of an individual biological entity commence. (Because of twinning, this might not be strictly correct, but it is good enough for our purposes.) But if fetuses are morally significant simply because they are biologically alive, then any living thing is morally significant too. Since all organisms are equally alive—trees are not more alive than cats—this suggests that the moral status of fetuses would be minimal. Moreover, we need an account of why merely being alive confers moral status, however minimal.

At this point we might be reminded that human fetuses are *human* life, as though the qualifier *human* made all the difference. But why should the fact that some life is human, meaning biologically of the species *Homo sapiens,* matter? Human cancer cells are biologically of the species *Homo sapiens* and no one accords them special moral status. Typically, reference to "human life" is supposed to mean more than mere biology, but exactly what more is intended needs explanation.

2. Fetuses have moral status because they are sentient. Sentience means the ability to feel—perhaps most important, the ability to feel pain. Sentience thus presupposes some minimal level of consciousness. Fetal sentience at even a rudimentary level is possible only after a nervous system is formed, around the eighth week, although when human fetuses can experience pain remains a matter of controversy. According to some experts, sentience is possible at twenty weeks. Minimally, early fetuses (zygotes and embryos) are not sentient. So if moral status depends on sentience, then early fetuses have no moral status. Once sentient, fetuses would then have whatever moral status any creature with that degree of sentience has, if moral status is a function of sentence.

3. Fetuses have moral status because they are persons. If we are indisputably persons, what makes us so? Our personhood is typically taken to reside somehow in our mentality: our consciousness, self-awareness, emotional complexity, and rational autonomy. This is what makes us persons and trees not. Our mentality is a causal consequence of our biology. This means that our personhood results from our biology. But it also means that one could be a person with a different biology. Superman and Santa Claus, if they existed, would be persons too because of their developed mentality, irrespective of the biology that underlies and makes their personhood possible. Furthermore, if consciousness is a function of biological structure, then replacing biological structure with functionally equivalent components made out of some other material should also yield consciousness. There is thus no theoretical barrier to full persons made of nonbiological material. Science fiction is full of conscious machines; though far-fetched, they do not strike us as *conceptually* impossible.

If some constellation of higher-order mental traits is constitutive of personhood, then fetuses are not persons. Perhaps late-stage fetuses have enough mentality to count as minimal persons, but early fetuses will not count as persons because early fetuses have no mentality. One worry with this account of personhood is that neither infants nor mentally defective individuals will count as persons either. Perhaps the term *person* could be reserved for creatures with full moral status in virtue of their fully developed mentality. It is hard to see how we could separate mentality entirely from the idea of personhood without losing our grip on the concept altogether. Could rocks be persons? So fetuses, at best, might be minimal sorts of persons because of their minimal awareness. But this also means that their moral status as minimal persons is the same as that of any other creature with that degree of awareness. Dogs would be persons in this minimal sense too. The term *person* is thus a stand-in for anything that exhibits the person-making properties to one degree or another, and because the person-making properties come in degrees, so does personhood.

Someone who disputes this account of personhood owes us an explanation of how an early fetus, something that we may need a microscope to see, is a person in the same sense in which any one of us is a person. Talk of invisible souls is not helpful, because it presupposes religious or metaphysical views that are at least as doubtful as the claim about persons.

4. Fetuses have moral status because they are potential persons. When we talk about the moral significance of fetuses, often we have in mind the intuitively powerful idea that fetuses become persons. If fetuses did not become persons, then it would be hard to see why there is such intense debate about them. It is worth noting that fetuses do not grow into persons organically, like tomatoes on a vine. To get a being like one of us—a full person as a rational deliberator—requires a lot of work once an infant is born. The infant must be nurtured, taught a language, educated, and socialized. Nevertheless, since persons are morally significant, it seems that potential persons should also have some degree of moral significance by virtue of that fact alone.

It will not do, however, to argue that because fetuses have the potential to become persons, they are persons now. Caterpillars are not butterflies just because they have the potential to become butterflies. If something has the potential to become something else, then this presupposes that it is not now a thing of the sort it has the potential to become. Otherwise, it would not be a potential one of those things, but an actual one.

Potential persons are not already a kind of person, as a short person is already a person. How and to what degree potential personhood confers moral status on fetuses are important matters for discussion. But even if potential personhood does confer some degree of moral significance, it is hard to see how potential persons, since they are not yet actual persons, could have anything like the moral status of actual persons. This will have implications for the moral permissibility of abortion.

Even if fetuses have full moral status as persons with a right to life, it still does not follow that abortion is impermissible. Having a right to life does not mean that one may never be killed; otherwise, it would not be possible to kill an attacker in self-defense. Nor does having a right to life mean that one has a right to whatever one needs to stay alive. What if I need your kidneys to stay alive? A right to life means, roughly, having a right not to be unjustifiably killed. So even if fetuses have a full right to life, as is often asserted in abortion debates, it does not follow that killing them violates that right. It is worth emphasizing this point: Killing something with a right to life does not entail violating that right. If one person kills another person, it does not *follow* that the right to life was violated. Perhaps the killing was self-defense, or perhaps it was euthanasia. But perhaps it was murder, an unjustified killing. We cannot tell from the bare fact that one person killed another. Similarly, in any particular abortion, we need to know whether killing the fetus was an unjustified killing. Whatever rights or moral significance we want to accord fetuses must be considered in light of the fact that fetuses are inside pregnant women. Pregnant women have rights and prerogatives that we must not ignore when we contemplate the moral status of fetuses.

TWO CONCEPTUAL ISSUES IN ABORTION: MURDER AND MOTHER

Opponents of abortion frequently claim that abortion is murder. This is a very serious charge, for if abortion is murder, then it would be seriously wrong, and that would be an excellent reason to make it illegal. Not that all immoral things should be illegal, but some immoral things—and murder is among them—are illegal precisely because they are so immoral. Note, too, that the standard "pro-choice" rhetoric fails to engage the accusation properly: One cannot respond to the charge of murder by claiming to have a choice in the matter.

Murder is a concept that applies only to the killing of persons. Anything living can be killed, but only persons can be murdered. To commit murder is to kill a person unjustifiably; it is a wrongful killing. So although all murders necessarily involve the killing of persons, not all killings of persons count as murder. Killing an attacker in self-defense, for example, is not murder, and many argue that mercy killing of the terminally ill is not murder (see Chapter 9). Thus when an opponent of abortion claims that abortion is murder, a lot has been assumed, namely, that a person is killed, and that that person is unjustifiably killed. This is not to say that arguments for those assumptions cannot be given, but the important point is to realize that they are substantive claims for which reasons must be given. Otherwise, the charge of murder is mere rhetoric.

A similar point holds for the frequent use of the term *mother* in abortion discussions. It has become so commonplace to refer to the pregnant woman as the mother that we scarcely bat an eye. But think about it for a minute. If a pregnant woman can correctly be called a mother, then that presupposes that the fetus is a child, since a woman cannot be a mother without her having produced a child. If we refer to pregnant women as mothers, then the moral status of fetuses is already established by implication—they are children. And this begs the question, because the moral status of fetuses is what we are trying to determine. We cannot argue that fetuses must be children because pregnant women are mothers. The question is whether we can legitimately refer to pregnant women as mothers in the first place.

READINGS ON THE MORALITY OF ABORTION

Judith Jarvis Thomson, "A Defense of Abortion"

Judith Jarvis Thomson is currently a professor emerita of philosophy at MIT, where she taught for many years. Her celebrated article "A Defense of Abortion," published in 1971, is the most widely reprinted article in contemporary moral philosophy. It is a vivid and deft discussion—moral philosophy at its best. Thomson begins by supposing just for the sake of argument that fetuses are persons. She supposes this in order to assess the strength of the anti-abortion position. Even if fetuses have full moral status, Thomson argues, there is still conceptual room to defend the moral permissibility of abortion.

Critical Reading Questions

1. How is the famous violinist story relevant to moral questions about abortion?
2. On what grounds does Thomson argue that the "extreme anti-abortion" position is mistaken?
3. What does it mean to have a right to life, according to Thomson?
4. What does the box of chocolates example show?
5. How is the example of the Good Samaritan relevant to abortion?

A DEFENSE OF ABORTION

Judith Jarvis Thomson

Most opposition to abortion relies on the premise that the fetus is a human being, a person, from the moment of conception. The premise is argued for, but, as I think, not well. Take, for example, the most common argument. We are asked to notice that the development of a human being from conception through birth into childhood is continuous; then it is said that to draw a line, to choose a point in this development and say "before this point the thing is not a person, after this point it is a person" is to make an arbitrary choice, a choice for which in the nature of things no good reason can be given. It is concluded that the fetus is, or anyway we had better say it is, a person from the moment of conception. But this conclusion does not follow. Similar things might be said about the development of an acorn into an oak tree, and it does not follow that acorns are oak trees or that we had better say they are. Arguments of this form are sometimes called "slippery slope arguments"—the phrase is perhaps self-explanatory—and it is dismaying that opponents of abortion rely on them so heavily and uncritically.

I am inclined to agree, however, that the prospects for "drawing a line" in the development of the fetus look dim. I am inclined to think also that we shall probably have to agree that the fetus has already become a human person well before birth. Indeed, it comes as a surprise when one first learns how early in its life it begins to acquire human characteristics. By the tenth week, for example, it already has a face, arms and legs, fingers and toes; it has internal organs, and brain activity is detectable.[1] On the other hand, I think that the premise is false, that the fetus is not a person from the moment of conception. A newly fertilized ovum, a newly implanted clump of cells, is no more a person than an acorn is an oak tree. But I shall not discuss any of this. For it seems to me to be of great interest to ask what happens if, for the sake of argument, we allow the premise. How, precisely, are we supposed to get from there to the conclusion that abortion is morally impermissible? Opponents of abortion commonly spend most of their time establishing that the fetus is a person, and hardly any time explaining the step from there to the impermissibility of abortion. Perhaps they think the step too simple and obvious to require much comment. Or perhaps instead they are simply being economical in argument. Many of those who defend abortion rely on the premise that the fetus is not a person, but only a bit of tissue that will become a person at birth; and why pay out more arguments than you have to? Whatever the explanation, I suggest that the step they take is neither easy nor obvious, that it calls for closer examination than it is commonly given, and that when we do give it this closer examination we shall feel inclined to reject it.

I propose, then, that we grant that the fetus is a person from the moment of conception. How does the argument go from here? Something like this, I take it. Every person has a right to life. So the fetus has a right to life. No doubt the mother has a right to decide what shall happen in and to her body; everyone would grant that. But surely a person's right to life is stronger and more stringent than the mother's right to decide what happens in and to her body, and so outweighs it. So the fetus may not be killed; an abortion may not be performed.

It sounds plausible. But now let me ask you to imagine this. You wake up in the morning and find yourself back to back in bed with an unconscious violinist. A famous unconscious violinist. He has been found to have a fatal kidney ailment, and the Society of Music Lovers has canvassed all the available medical records and found that you alone have the right blood type to help. They have therefore kidnapped you, and last night the violinist's circulatory system was plugged into yours, so that your kidneys can be used to extract poisons from his blood as well as your own. The director of the hospital now tells you, "Look, we're sorry the Society of Music Lovers did this to you— we would never have permitted it if we had known. But still, they did it, and the violinist now is plugged into you. To unplug you would be to kill him. But never mind, it's only for nine months. By then he will have recovered from his ailment, and can safely be unplugged from you." Is it morally incumbent on you to accede to this situation? No doubt it would be very nice of you if you did, a great kindness. But do you *have* to accede to it? What if it were not nine months, but nine years? Or longer still? What if the director of the hospital says, "Tough luck, I agree, but you've now got to stay in bed, with the violinist plugged into you, for the rest of your life. Because remember this. All persons have a right to life, and violinists are persons. Granted you have a right to decide what happens in and to your body, but a person's right to life outweighs your right to decide what happens in and to your body. So you cannot ever be unplugged from him." I imagine you would regard this as outrageous, which suggests that something really is wrong with that plausible-sounding argument I mentioned a moment ago.

In this case, of course, you were kidnapped; you didn't volunteer for the operation that plugged the violinist into your kidneys. Can those who oppose abortion on the ground I mentioned make an exception for a pregnancy due to rape? Certainly. They can say that persons have a right to life only if they didn't come into existence because of rape; or they can say that all persons have a right to life, but that some have less of a right to life than others, in particular, that those who came into existence

because of rape have less. But these statements have a rather unpleasant sound. Surely the question of whether you have a right to life at all, or how much of it you have, shouldn't turn on the question of whether or not you are the product of a rape. And in fact the people who oppose abortion on the ground I mentioned do not make this distinction, and hence do not make an exception in case of rape.

Nor do they make an exception for a case in which the mother has to spend the nine months of her pregnancy in bed. They would agree that would be a great pity, and hard on the mother; but all the same, all persons have a right to life, the fetus is a person, and so on. I suspect, in fact, that they would not make an exception for a case in which, miraculously enough, the pregnancy went on for nine years, or even the rest of the mother's life.

Some won't even make an exception for a case in which continuation of the pregnancy is likely to shorten the mother's life; they regard abortion as impermissible even to save the mother's life. Such cases are nowadays very rare, and many opponents of abortion do not accept this extreme view. All the same, it is a good place to begin: a number of points of interest come out in respect to it.

1. Let us call the view that abortion is impermissible even to save the mother's life "the extreme view." I want to suggest first that it does not issue from the argument I mentioned earlier without the addition of some fairly powerful premises. Suppose a woman has become pregnant, and now learns that she has a cardiac condition such that she will die if she carries the baby to term. What may be done for her? The fetus, being a person, has a right to life, but as the mother is a person too, so has she a right to life. Presumably they have an equal right to life. How is it supposed to come out that an abortion may not be performed? If mother and child have an equal right to life, shouldn't we perhaps flip a coin? Or should we add to the mother's right to life her right to decide what happens in and to her body, which everybody seems to be ready to grant—the sum of her rights now outweighing the fetus's right to life?

The most familiar argument here is the following. We are told that performing the abortion would be directly killing[2] the child, whereas doing nothing would not be killing the mother, but only letting her die. Moreover, in killing the child, one would be killing an innocent person, for the child has committed no crime, and is not aiming at his mother's death. And then there are a variety of ways in which this might be continued. (1) But as directly killing an innocent person is always and absolutely impermissible, an abortion may not be performed. Or, (2) as directly killing an innocent person is murder, and murder is always and absolutely impermissible, an abortion may not be performed.[3] Or, (3) as one's duty to refrain from directly killing an innocent person is more stringent than one's duty to keep a person from dying, an abortion may not be performed. Or, (4) if one's only options are directly killing an innocent person or letting a person die, one must prefer letting the person die, and thus an abortion may not be performed.[4]

Some people seem to have thought that these are not further premises which must be added if the conclusion is to be reached, but that they follow from the very fact that an innocent person has a right to life.[5] But this seems to me to be a mistake, and perhaps the simplest way to show this is to bring out that while we must certainly grant that innocent persons have a right to life, the theses in (1) through (4) are all false. Take (2), for example. If directly killing an innocent person is murder, and thus is impermissible, then the mother's directly killing the innocent person inside her is murder, and thus is impermissible. But it cannot seriously be thought to be murder if the mother performs an abortion on herself to save her life. It cannot seriously be said that she *must* refrain, that she *must* sit passively by and wait for her death. Let us look again at the case of you and the violinist. There you are, in bed with the violinist, and the director of the hospital says to you, "It's all most distressing, and I deeply sympathize, but you see this is putting an additional strain on your kidneys, and you'll be dead within the month. But you *have* to stay where you are all the same. Because unplugging you would be directly killing an innocent violinist, and that's murder, and that's impermissible." If anything in the world is true, it is that you do not commit murder, you do not do what is impermissible, if you reach around to your back and unplug yourself from that violinist to save your life.

The main focus of attention in writings on abortion has been on what a third party may or may not do in answer to a request from a woman for an abortion. This is in a way understandable. Things being as they are, there isn't much a woman can safely do to abort herself. So the question asked is what a third party may do; and what the mother may do, if it is mentioned at all, is deduced, almost as an afterthought, from what it is concluded that the third parties may do. But it seems to me that to treat the matter in this way is to refuse to grant to the mother that very status of person which is so firmly insisted on for the fetus. For we cannot simply read off what a person may do from what a third party may do. Suppose you find yourself trapped in a tiny house with a growing child. I mean a very tiny house, and a rapidly growing child—you are already up against the wall of the house and in a few minutes you'll be crushed to death. The child on the other hand won't be crushed to death; if nothing is done to stop him from growing he'll be hurt, but in the end he'll simply burst open the house and walk out a free man. Now I could well understand it if a bystander were to say, "There's nothing we can do for you. We cannot choose between your life and his, we cannot be the ones to decide who is to live, we cannot intervene." But it cannot be concluded that you too can do nothing, that you cannot attack it to save your life. However innocent the child may be, you do not have to wait passively while it crushes you to death. Perhaps a pregnant woman is vaguely felt to have the status of a house, to which we don't allow the right of self-defense. But if the woman houses the child, it should be remembered that she is a person who houses it.

I should perhaps stop to say explicitly that I am not claiming that people have a right to do anything whatever to save their lives. I think, rather, that there are drastic limits to the right of self-defense. If someone threatens you with death unless you torture someone else to death, I think you have not the right, even to save your life, to do so. But the case under consideration here is very different. In our case there are only two people involved, one whose life is threatened, and one who threatens it.

84

Both are innocent: the one who is threatened is not threatened because of any fault, the one who threatens does not threaten because of any fault. For this reason we may feel that we bystanders cannot intervene. But the person threatened can.

In sum, a woman surely can defend her life against the threat to it posed by the unborn child, even if doing so involves its death. And this shows not merely that the theses in (1) through (4) are false; it shows also that the extreme view of abortion is false, and so we need not canvass any other possible ways of arriving at it from the argument I mentioned at the outset.

2. The extreme view could of course be weakened to say that while abortion is permissible to save the mother's life, it may not be performed by a third party, but only by the mother herself. But this cannot be right either. For what we have to keep in mind is that the mother and the unborn child are not like two tenants in a small house which has, by an unfortunate mistake, been rented to both: the mother *owns* the house. The fact that she does adds to the offensiveness of deducing that the mother can do nothing from the supposition that third parties can do nothing. But it does more than this: it casts a bright light on the supposition that third parties can do nothing. Certainly it lets us see that a third party who says "I cannot choose between you" is fooling himself if he thinks this is impartiality. If Jones has found and fastened on a certain coat, which he needs to keep him from freezing, but which Smith also needs to keep him from freezing, then it is not impartiality that says "I cannot choose between you" when Smith owns the coat. Women have said again and again "This body is *my* body!" and they have reason to feel angry, reason to feel that it has been like shouting into the wind. Smith, after all, is hardly likely to bless us if we say to him, "Of course it's your coat, anybody would grant that it is. But no one may choose between you and Jones who is to have it. . .".

3. Where the mother's life is not at stake, the argument I mentioned at the outset seems to have a much stronger pull. "Everyone has a right to life, so the unborn person has a right to life." And isn't the child's right to life weightier than anything other than the mother's own right to life, which she might put forward as ground for an abortion?

This argument treats the right to life as if it were unproblematic. It is not, and this seems to me to be precisely the source of the mistake.

For we should now, at long last, ask what it comes to, to have a right to life. In some views having a right to life includes having a right to be given at least the bare minimum one needs for continued life. But suppose that what in fact *is* the bare minimum a man needs for continued life is something he has no right at all to be given? If I am sick unto death, and the only thing that will save my life is the touch of Henry Fonda's cool hand on my fevered brow, then all the same, I have no right to be given the touch of Henry Fonda's cool hand on my fevered brow. It would be frightfully nice of him to fly in from the West Coast to provide it. It would be less nice, though no doubt well meant, if my friends flew out to the West Coast and carried Henry Fonda back with them. But I have no right at all against anybody that he should do this for me. Or again, to return to the story I told earlier, the fact that for continued life that violinist needs the continued use of your kidneys does not establish that he has a right to be given the continued use of your kidneys. He certainly has no right against you that *you* should give him continued use of your kidneys. For nobody has any right to use your kidneys unless you give him such a right; and nobody has the right against you that you shall give him this right—if you do allow him to go on using your kidneys, this is a kindness on your part, and not something he can claim from you as his due. Nor has he any right against anybody else that *they* should give him continued use of your kidneys. Certainly he had no right against the Society of Music Lovers that they should plug him into you in the first place. And if you now start to unplug yourself, having learned that you will otherwise have to spend nine years in bed with him, there is nobody in the world who must try to prevent you, in order to see to it that he is given something he has a right to be given.

Some people are rather stricter about the right to life. In their view, it does not include the right to be given anything, but amounts to, and only to, the right not to be killed by anybody. But here a related difficulty arises. If everybody is to refrain from killing that violinist, then everybody must refrain from doing a great many different sorts of things. Everybody must refrain from slitting his throat, everybody must refrain from shooting him—and everybody must refrain from unplugging you from him. But does he have a right against everybody that they shall refrain from unplugging you from him? To refrain from doing this is to allow him to continue to use your kidneys. It could be argued that he has a right against us that *we* should allow him to continue to use your kidneys. That is, while he had no right against us that we should give him the use of your kidneys, it might be argued that he anyway has a right against us that we shall not now intervene and deprive him of the use of your kidneys. I shall come back to third-party interventions later. But certainly the violinist has no right against you that *you* shall allow him to continue to use your kidneys. As I said, if you do allow him to use them, it is a kindness on your part, and not something you owe him.

The difficulty I point to here is not peculiar to the right to life. It reappears in connection with all the other natural rights; and it is something which an adequate account of rights must deal with. For present purposes it is enough just to draw attention to it. But I would stress that I am not arguing that people do not have a right to life—quite to the contrary, it seems to me that the primary control we must place on the acceptability of an account of rights is that it should turn out in that account to be a truth that all persons have a right to life. I am arguing only that having a right to life does not guarantee having either a right to be given the use of or a right to be allowed continued use of another person's body—even if one needs it for life itself. So the right to life will not serve the opponents of abortion in the very simple and clear way in which they seem to have thought it would.

4. There is another way to bring out the difficulty. In the most ordinary sort of case, to deprive someone of what he has a right to is to treat him unjustly. Suppose a boy and his small brother are jointly given a box of chocolates for Christmas. If the older boy takes the box and refuses to give his brother any of the chocolates, he is unjust to him, for the brother has been given a right to half of them. But suppose that, having learned that otherwise it means nine years in bed with that violinist, you unplug yourself from him. You surely are not being unjust to him, for you gave him no right to use your kidneys, and no one else can have given him any such right. But we have to notice that in unplugging yourself, you are killing him; and violinists, like everybody else, have a right to life, and thus in the view we were considering just now, the right not to be killed.

So here you do what he supposedly has a right you shall not do, but you do not act unjustly to him in doing it.

The emendation which may be made at this point is this: the right to life consists not in the right not to be killed, but rather in the right not to be killed unjustly. This runs a risk of circularity, but never mind: it would enable us to square the fact that the violinist has a right to life with the fact that you do not act unjustly toward him in unplugging yourself, thereby killing him. For if you do not kill him unjustly, you do not violate his right to life, and so it is no wonder you do him no injustice.

But if this emendation is accepted, the gap in the argument against abortion stares us plainly in the face: it is by no means enough to show that the fetus is a person, and to remind us that all persons have a right to life—we need to be shown also that killing the fetus violates its right to life, i.e., that abortion is unjust killing. And is it?

I suppose we may take it as a datum that in a case of pregnancy due to rape the mother has not given the unborn person a right to the use of her body for food and shelter. Indeed, in what pregnancy could it be supposed that the mother has given the unborn person such a right? It is not as if there were unborn persons drifting about the world, to whom a woman who wants a child says "I invite you in."

But it might be argued that there are other ways one can have acquired a right to the use of another person's body than by having been invited to use it by that person. Suppose a woman voluntarily indulges in intercourse, knowing of the chance it will issue in pregnancy, and then she does become pregnant; is she not in part responsible for the presence, in fact the very existence, of the unborn person inside her? No doubt she did not invite it in. But doesn't her partial responsibility for its being there itself give it a right to the use of her body? If so, then her aborting it would be more like the boy's taking away the chocolates, and less like your unplugging yourself from the violinist—doing so would be depriving it of what it does have a right to, and thus would be doing it an injustice.

And then, too, it might be asked whether or not she can kill it even to save her own life: If she voluntarily called it into existence, how can she now kill it, even in self-defense?

The first thing to be said about this is that it is something new. Opponents of abortion have been so concerned to make out the independence of the fetus, in order to establish that it has a right to life, just as its mother does, that they have tended to overlook the possible support they might gain from making out that the fetus is *dependent* on the mother, in order to establish that she has a special kind of responsibility for it, a responsibility that gives it rights against her which are not possessed by any independent person—such as an ailing violinist who is a stranger to her.

On the other hand, this argument would give the unborn person a right to its mother's body only if her pregnancy resulted from a voluntary act, undertaken in full knowledge of the chance a pregnancy might result from it. It would leave out entirely the unborn person whose existence is due to rape. Pending the availability of some further argument, then, we would be left with the conclusion that unborn persons whose existence is due to rape have no right to the use of their mothers' bodies, and thus that aborting them is not depriving them of anything they have a right to and hence is not unjust killing.

And we should also notice that it is not at all plain that this argument really does go even as far as it purports to. For there are cases and cases, and the details make a difference. If the room is stuffy, and I therefore open a window to air it, and a burglar climbs in, it would be absurd to say, "Ah, now he can stay, she's given him a right to the use of her house—for she is partially responsible for his presence there, having voluntarily done what enabled him to get in, in full knowledge that there are such things

as burglars, and that burglars burgle." It would be still more absurd to say this if I had had bars installed outside my windows, precisely to prevent burglars from getting in, and a burglar got in only because of a defect in the bars. It remains equally absurd if we imagine it is not a burglar who climbs in, but an innocent person who blunders or falls in. Again, suppose it were like this: people-seeds drift about in the air like pollen, and if you open your windows, one may drift in and take root in your carpets or upholstery. You don't want children, so you fix up your windows with fine mesh screens, the very best you can buy. As can happen, however, and on very, very rare occasions does happen, one of the screens is defective; and a seed drifts in and takes root. Does the person-plant who now develops have a right to the use of your house? Surely not—despite the fact that you voluntarily opened your windows, you knowingly kept carpets and upholstered furniture, and you knew that screens were sometimes defective. Someone may argue that you are responsible for its rooting, that it does have a right to your house, because after all you *could* have lived out your life with bare floors and furniture, or with sealed windows and doors. But this won't do—for by the same token anyone can avoid a pregnancy due to rape by having a hysterectomy, or anyway by never leaving home without a (reliable!) army.

It seems to me that the argument we are looking at can establish at most that there are *some* cases in which the unborn person has a right to the use of its mother's body, and therefore *some* cases in which abortion is unjust killing. There is room for much discussion and argument as to precisely which, if any. But I think we should sidestep this issue and leave it open, for at any rate the argument certainly does not establish that all abortion is unjust killing.

5. There is room for yet another argument here, however. We surely must all grant that there may be cases in which it would be morally indecent to detach a person from your body at the cost of his life. Suppose you learn that what the violinist needs is not nine years of your life, but only one hour: all you need do to save his life is to spend one hour in that bed with him. Suppose also that letting him use your kidneys for

that one hour would not affect your health in the slightest. Admittedly you were kidnapped. Admittedly you did not give anyone permission to plug him into you. Nevertheless it seems to me plain you *ought* to allow him to use your kidneys for that hour—it would be indecent to refuse.

Again, suppose pregnancy lasted only an hour, and constituted no threat to life or health. And suppose that a woman becomes pregnant as a result of rape. Admittedly she did not voluntarily do anything to bring about the existence of a child. Admittedly she did nothing at all which would give the unborn person a right to the use of her body. All the same it might well be said, as in the newly emended violinist story, that she *ought* to allow it to remain for that hour—that it would be indecent in her to refuse.

Now some people are inclined to use the term "right" in such a way that it follows from the fact that you ought to allow a person to use your body for the hour he needs, that he has a right to use your body for the hour he needs, even though he has not been given that right by any person or act. They may say that it follows also that if you refuse, you act unjustly toward him. This use of the term is perhaps so common that it cannot be called wrong; nevertheless it seems to me to be an unfortunate loosening of what we would do better to keep a tight rein on. Suppose that box of chocolates I mentioned earlier had not been given to both boys jointly, but was given only to the older boy. There he sits, stolidly eating his way through the box, his small brother watching enviously. Here we are likely to say "You ought not to be so mean. You ought to give your brother some of those chocolates." My own view is that it just does not follow from the truth of this that the brother has any right to any of the chocolates. If the boy refuses to give his brother any, he is greedy, stingy, callous—but not unjust. I suppose that the people I have in mind will say it does follow that the brother has a right to some of the chocolates, and thus that the boy does act unjustly if he refuses to give his brother any. But the effect of saying this is to obscure what we should keep distinct, namely the difference between the boy's refusal in this case and the boy's refusal

in the earlier case, in which the box was given to both boys jointly, and in which the small brother thus had what was from any point of view clear title to half.

A further objection to so using the term "right" that from the fact that A ought to do a thing for B, it follows that B has a right against A that A do it for him, is that it is going to make the question of whether or not a man has a right to a thing turn on how easy it is to provide him with it; and this seems not merely unfortunate, but morally unacceptable. Take the case of Henry Fonda again. I said earlier that I had no right to the touch of his cool hand on my fevered brow, even though I needed it to save my life. I said it would be frightfully nice of him to fly in from the West Coast to provide me with it, but that I had no right against him that he should do so. But suppose he isn't on the West Coast. Suppose he has only to walk across the room, place a hand briefly on my brow—and lo, my life is saved. Then surely he ought to do it, it would be indecent to refuse. Is it to be said "Ah, well, it follows that in this case she has a right to the touch of his hand on her brow, and so it would be an injustice in him to refuse"? So that I have a right to it when it is easy for him to provide it, though no right when it's hard? It's rather a shocking idea that anyone's rights should fade away and disappear as it gets harder and harder to accord them to him.

So my own view is that even though you ought to let the violinist use your kidneys for the one hour he needs, we should not conclude that he has a right to do so—we should say that if you refuse, you are, like the boy who owns all the chocolates and will give none away, self-centered and callous, indecent in fact, but not unjust. And similarly, that even supposing a case in which a woman pregnant due to rape ought to allow the unborn person to use her body for the hour he needs, we should not conclude that he has a right to do so; we should conclude that she is self-centered, callous, indecent, but not unjust, if she refuses. The complaints are no less grave; they are just different. However, there is no need to insist on this point. If anyone does wish to deduce "he has a right" from "you ought," then all the same he must surely grant that there are cases in which it is not morally required of you that you allow that violinist to use your kidneys, and in which he does not have a right to use them, and in which you do not do him injustice if you refuse. And so also for mother and unborn child. Except in such cases as where the unborn person has a right to demand it—and we were leaving open the possibility that there may be such cases—nobody is morally *required* to make large sacrifices, of health, of all other interests and concerns, of all other duties and commitments, for nine years, or even for nine months, in order to keep another person alive. . . .

6. My argument will be found unsatisfactory on two counts by many of those who want to regard abortion as morally permissible. First, while I do argue that abortion is not impermissible, I do not argue that it is always permissible. I am inclined to think it a merit of my account precisely that it does *not* give a general yes or a general no. It allows for and supports our sense that, for example, a sick and desperately frightened fourteen-year-old schoolgirl, pregnant due to rape, may *of course* choose abortion, and that any law which rules this out is an insane law. And it also allows for and supports our sense that in other cases resort to abortion is even positively indecent. It would be indecent in the woman to request an abortion, and indecent in a doctor to perform it, if she is in her seventh month, and wants the abortion just to avoid the nuisance of postponing a trip abroad. The very fact that the arguments I have been drawing attention to treat all cases of abortion, or even all cases of abortion in which the mother's life is not at stake, as morally on a par ought to have made them suspect at the outset.

Secondly, while I am arguing for the permissibility of abortion in some cases, I am not arguing for the right to secure the death of the unborn child. It is easy to confuse these two things in that up to a certain point in the life of the fetus it is not able to survive outside the mother's body; hence removing it from her body guarantees its death. But they are importantly different. I have argued that you are not morally required to spend nine months in bed, sustaining the life of that violinist; but to say this is by no means to say that if, when you unplug yourself, there is a miracle and he survives, you then have a

right to turn round and slit his throat. You may detach yourself even if this costs him his life; you have no right to be guaranteed his death, by some other means, if unplugging yourself does not kill him. There are some people who will feel dissatisfied by this feature of my argument. A woman may be utterly devastated by the thought of a child, a bit of herself, put out for adoption and never seen or heard of again. She may therefore want not merely that the child be detached from her, but more, that it die. Some opponents of abortion are inclined to regard this as beneath contempt—thereby showing insensitivity to what is surely a powerful source of despair. All the same, I agree that the desire for the child's death is not one which anybody may gratify, should it turn out to be possible to detach the child alive.

At this place, however, it should be remembered that we have only been pretending throughout that the fetus is a human being from the moment of conception. A very early abortion is surely not the killing of a person, and so is not dealt with by anything I have said here.

NOTES

1. Daniel Callahan, *Abortion: Law, Choice and Morality* (New York, 1970), p. 373. This book gives a fascinating survey of the available information on abortion. The Jewish tradition is surveyed in David M. Feldman, *Birth Control in Jewish Law* (New York, 1968), Part 5; the Catholic tradition in John T. Noonan, Jr, "An Almost Absolute Value in History," in *The Morality of Abortion*, ed. John T. Noonan, Jr (Cambridge, Mass., 1970).

2. The term "direct" in the arguments I refer to is a technical one. Roughly, what is meant by "direct killing" is either killing as an end in itself, or killing as a means to some end, for example, the end of saving someone else's life. See note 5, below, for an example of its use.

3. Cf. *Encyclical Letter of Pope Pius XI on Christian Marriage*, St Paul Editions (Boston, n.d.), p. 32: "however much we may pity the mother whose health and even life is gravely imperiled in the performance of the duty allotted to her by nature, nevertheless what could ever be a sufficient reason for excusing in any way the direct murder of the innocent? This is precisely what we are dealing with here." Noonan (*The Morality of Abortion*, p. 43) reads this as follows: "What cause can ever avail to excuse in any way the direct killing of the innocent? For it is a question of that."

4. The thesis in (4) is in an interesting way weaker than those in (1), (2), and (3): they rule out abortion even in cases in which both mother *and* child will die if the abortion is not

performed. By contrast, one who held the view expressed in (4) could consistently say that one needn't prefer letting two persons die to killing one.

5. Cf. the following passage from Pius XII, *Address to the Italian Catholic Society of Midwives:* "The baby in the maternal breast has the right to life immediately from God.—Hence there is no man, no human authority, no science, no medical, eugenic, social, economic or moral 'indication' which can establish or grant a valid juridical ground for a direct deliberate disposition of an innocent human life, that is a disposition which looks to its destruction either as an end or as a means to another end perhaps in itself not illicit.— The baby, still not born, is a man in the same degree and for the same reason as the mother" (quoted in Noonan, *The Morality of Abortion*, p. 45).

Discussion Questions

1. What are the limits of self-defense? Does it count as self-defense to kill an innocent person who is threatening you simply because of unfortunate circumstances?
2. Under what circumstances might one person acquire the right to use another person's body in order to stay alive?
3. How much are we morally required to do for one another?

Don Marquis, "Why Abortion Is Immoral"

Don Marquis is a professor of philosophy at the University of Kansas. He publishes in ethics and medical ethics. "Why Abortion Is Immoral" is a model of philosophical clarity and presents a profound challenge to the pro-choice view. In contrast to many antiabortion positions, however, Marquis makes no religious suppositions, nor does he assume that fetuses are persons. He argues that what makes it wrong to kill one of us applies to fetuses too, so if it is wrong to kill us, then it will be wrong to kill fetuses for the same reason.

Critical Reading Questions

1. According to Marquis, what impasse is reached by both the pro-choice and the pro-life positions?
2. Why is it wrong to kill one of us, according to Marquis?
3. How does Marquis support the deprivation account of the wrongness of killing?
4. How does Marquis argue against the desire account of the wrongness of killing?
5. How does Marquis argue that his view does not apply to contraception?

AN ARGUMENT THAT ABORTION IS WRONG

Don Marquis

The purpose of this essay is to set out an argument for the claim that abortion, except perhaps in rare instances, is seriously wrong.[1] One reason for these exceptions is to eliminate from consideration cases whose ethical analysis should be controversial and detailed for clear-headed opponents of abortion. Such cases include abortion after rape and abortion during the first fourteen days after conception when there is an argument that the fetus is not definitely an individual. Another reason for making these exceptions is to allow for those cases in which the permissibility of abortion is compatible with the argument of this essay. Such cases include abortion when continuation of a pregnancy endangers a woman's life and abortion when the fetus is anencephalic. When I speak of the wrongness of abortion in this essay, a reader should presume the above qualifications. I mean by an abortion an action intended to bring about the death of a fetus for the sake of the woman who carries it. (Thus, as is standard on the literature on this subject, I eliminate spontaneous abortions from consideration.) I mean by a fetus a developing human being from the time of conception to the time of birth. (Thus, as is standard, I call embryos and zygotes, fetuses.)

The argument of this essay will establish that abortion is wrong for the same reason as killing a reader of this essay is wrong. I shall just assume, rather than establish, that killing you is seriously wrong. I shall make no attempt to offer a complete ethics of killing. Finally, I shall make no attempt to resolve some very fundamental and difficult general philosophical issues into which this analysis of the ethics of abortion might lead.

WHY THE DEBATE OVER ABORTION SEEMS INTRACTABLE

Symmetries that emerge from the analysis of the major arguments on either side of the abortion debate may explain why the abortion debate seems intractable. Consider the following standard anti-abortion argument: Fetuses are both human and alive. Humans have the right to life. Therefore, fetuses have the right to life. Of course, women have the right to control their own bodies, but the right to life overrides the right of a woman to control her own body. Therefore, abortion is wrong.

Thomson's view

Judith Thomson (1971) has argued that even if one grants (for the sake of argument only) that fetuses have the right to life, this argument fails. Thomson invites you to imagine that you have been connected while sleeping, bloodstream to bloodstream, to a famous violinist. The violinist, who suffers from a rare blood disease, will die if disconnected. Thomson argues that you surely have the right to disconnect yourself. She appeals to our intuition that having to lie in bed with a violinist for an indefinite period is too much for morality to demand. She supports this claim by nothing that the body being used is *your* body, not the violinist's body. She distinguishes the right to life, which the violinist clearly has, from the right to use someone else's body when necessary to preserve one's life, which it is not at all obvious the violinist has. Because the case of pregnancy is like the case of the violinist, one is no more morally obligated to remain attached to a fetus than to remain attached to the violinist.

It is widely conceded that one can generate from Thomson's vivid case the conclusion that abortion is morally permissible when a pregnancy is due to rape (Warren, 1973, p. 49; and Steinbock, 1992, p. 79). But this is hardly a general right to abortion. Do Thomson's more general theses generate a more general right to an abortion? Thomson draws our attention to the fact that in a pregnancy, although a fetus uses a woman's body as a life-support system, a pregnant woman does not use a fetus's body as a life-support system. However, an opponent of abortion might draw our attention to the fact that in an abortion the life that is lost is the fetus's, not the woman's. This symmetry seems to leave us with a stand-off.

Thomson points out that a fetus's right to life does not entail its right to use someone else's body to preserve its life. However, an opponent of abortion might point out that a woman's right to use her own body does not entail her right to end someone else's life in order to do what she wants with her body. In reply, one might argue that a pregnant woman's right to control her own body doesn't come to much if it is wrong for her to take any action that ends the life of the fetus within her. However, an opponent of abortion can argue that the fetus's right to life doesn't come to much if a pregnant woman can end it when she chooses. The consequence of all of these symmetries seems to be a stand-off. But if we have the stand-off, then one might argue that we are left with a conflict of rights: a fetal right to life versus the right of a woman to control her own body. One might then argue that the right to life seems to be a stronger right than the right to control one's own body in the case of abortion because the loss of one's life is a greater loss than the loss of the right to control one's own body in one respect for nine months. Therefore, the right to life overrides the right to control one's own body and abortion is wrong. Considerations like these have suggested to both opponents of abortion and supporters of choice that a Thomsonian strategy for defending a general right to abortion will not succeed (Tooley, 1972; Warren, 1973; and Steinbock, 1992). In fairness, one must note that Thomson did not intend her strategy to generate a general moral permissibility of abortion.

Do fetuses have the right to life?

The above considerations suggest that whether abortion is morally permissible boils down to the question of whether fetuses have the right to life. An argument that fetuses either have or lack the right to life must be based upon some general criterion for having or lacking the right to life. Opponents of abortion, on the one hand, look around for the broadest possible plausible criterion, so that fetuses will fall under it. This explains why classic arguments against abortion appeal to the criterion of being human (Noonan, 1970; Beckwith, 1993). This criterion appears plausible: The claim that all humans, whatever their race, gender, religion or *age*, have the right to life seems evident enough. In addition, because the fetuses we are concerned with do not, after all, belong to another species, they are clearly human. Thus, the syllogism that generates the conclusion that fetuses have the right to life is apparently sound.

On the other hand, those who believe abortion is morally permissible wish to find a narrow, but plausible, criterion for possession of the right to life so that fetuses will fall outside of it. This explains, in part, why the standard pro-choice arguments in the philosophical literature appeal to the criterion of being a person (Feinberg, 1986; Tooley, 1972; Warren, 1973; Benn, 1973; Engelhardt, 1986). This criterion appears plausible: The claim that only persons have the right to life seems evident enough. Furthermore, because fetuses neither are rational nor possess the capacity to communicate in complex ways nor possess a concept of self that continues through time, no fetus is a person. Thus, the syllogism needed to generate the conclusion that no fetus possesses the right to life is apparently sound. Given that no fetus possesses the right to life, a woman's right to control her own body easily generates the general right to abortion. The existence of two apparently defensible syllogisms which support contrary conclusions helps to explain why partisans on both sides of the abortion dispute often regard their opponents as either morally depraved or mentally deficient.

Which syllogism should we reject? The anti-abortion syllogism is usually attacked by attacking its major premise: the claim that whatever is biologically human has the right to life. This premise is subject to scope problems because the class of the biologically human includes too much: human cancer-cell cultures are biologically human, but they do not have the right to life. Moreover, this premise also is subject to moral-relevance problems: the connection between the biological and the moral is merely assumed. It is hard to think of a good *argument* for such a connection. If one wishes to consider the category of "human" a moral category, as some people find it plausible to do in other contexts, then one is left with no way of showing that the fetus is fully human without begging the question. Thus, the classic anti-abortion argument appears subject to fatal difficulties.

These difficulties with the classic anti-abortion argument are well known and thought by many to be conclusive. The symmetrical difficulties with the classic pro-choice syllogism are not as well recognized. The pro-choice syllogism can be attacked by attacking its major premise: Only persons have the right to life. This premise is subject to scope problems because the class of persons includes too little: infants, the severely retarded, and some of the mentally ill seem to fall outside the class of persons as the supporter of choice understands the concept. The premise is also subject to moral-relevance problems: Being a person is understood by the pro-choicer as having certain psychological attributes. If the prochoicer questions the connection between the biological and the moral, the opponent of abortion can question the connection between the psychological and the moral. If one wishes to consider "person" a moral category, as is often done, then one is left with no way of showing that the fetus is not a person without begging the question.

Pro-choicers appear to have resources for dealing with their difficulties that opponents of abortion lack. Consider their moral-relevance problem. A pro-choicer might argue that morality rests on contractual foundations and that only those who have the psychological attributes of persons are capable of entering into the moral contract and, as a consequence, being a member of the moral community. [This is essentially Engelhardt's (1986) view.] The great advantage of this contractarian approach to morality is that it seems far more plausible than any approach the anti-abortionist can provide. The great disadvantage of this contractarian approach to morality is that it adds to our earlier scope problems by leaving it unclear how we can have the duty not to inflict pain and suffering on animals.

Contractarians have tried to deal with their scope problems by arguing that duties to some individuals who are not persons can be justified even though those individuals are not contracting members of the moral community. For example, Kant argued that, although we do not have direct duties to animals, we "must practice kindness towards animals, for he who is cruel to animals becomes hard also in his dealings with men" (Kant, 1963, p. 240). Feinberg argues that infanticide is wrong, not because infants have the right to life, but because our society's protection of infants has social utility. If we do not treat infants with tenderness and consideration, then when they are persons they will be worse off and we will be worse off also (Feinberg, 1986, p. 271).

These moves only stave off the difficulties with the pro-choice view; they do not resolve them. Consider Kant's account of our obligations to animals. Kantians certainly know the difference between persons and animals. Therefore, no true Kantian would treat persons as she would treat animals. Thus, Kant's defense of our duties to animals fails to show that Kantians have a duty not to be cruel to animals. Consider Feinberg's attempt to show that infanticide is wrong even though no infant is a person. All Feinberg really shows is that it is a good idea to treat with care and consideration the infants we intend to keep. That is quite compatible with killing the infants we intend to discard. This point can be supported by an analogy with which any pro-choicer will agree. There are plainly good reasons to treat with care and consideration the fetuses we intend to keep. This is quite compatible with aborting those fetuses we intend to discard. Thus, Feinberg's account of the wrongness of infanticide is inadequate.

Accordingly, we can see that a contractarian defense of the pro-choice personhood syllogism fails. The problem arises because the contractarian cannot account for our duties to individuals who are not persons, whether these individuals are animals or infants. Because the pro-choicer wishes to adopt a narrow criterion for the right to life so that fetuses will not be included, the scope of her major premise is too narrow. Her problem is the opposite of the problem the classic opponent of abortion faces.

The argument of this section has attempted to establish, albeit briefly, that the classic anti-abortion argument and the pro-choice argument favored by most philosophers both face problems that are mirror images of one another. A stand-off results. The abortion debate requires a different strategy.

THE "FUTURE LIKE OURS" ACCOUNT OF THE WRONGNESS OF KILLING

Why do the standard arguments in the abortion debate fail to resolve the issue? The general principles to which partisans in the debate appeal are either truisms most persons would affirm in the absence of much reflection, or very general moral theories. All are subject to major problems. A different approach is needed.

Opponents of abortion claim that abortion is wrong because abortion involves killing someone like us, a human being who just happens to be very young. Supporters of choice claim that ending the life of a fetus is not in the same moral category as ending the life of an adult human being. Surely this controversy cannot be resolved in the absence of an account of what it is about killing us that makes killing us wrong. On the one hand, if we know what property we possess that makes killing us wrong, then we can ask whether fetuses have the same property. On the other hand, suppose that we do not know what it is about us that makes killing us wrong. If this is so, we do not understand even easy cases in which killing is wrong. Surely, we will not understand the ethics of killing fetuses, for if we do not understand easy cases, then we will not understand hard cases. Both pro-choicer and anti-abortionist agree that it is obvious that it is wrong to kill us. Thus, a discussion of what it is about us that makes killing us not only wrong, but seriously wrong, seems to be the right place to begin a discussion of the abortion issue.

Who is primarily wronged by a killing? The wrong of killing is not primarily explained in terms of the loss to the family and friends of the victim. Perhaps the victim is a hermit. Perhaps one's friends find it easy to make new friends. The wrong of killing is not primarily explained in terms of the brutalization of the killer. The great wrong to the victim explains the brutalization, not the other way around. The wrongness of killing us is understood in terms of what killing does to us. Killing us imposes on us the misfortune of premature death. That misfortune underlies the wrongness.

Premature death is a misfortune because when one is dead, one has been deprived of life. This misfortune can be more precisely specified. Premature death cannot deprive me of my past life. That part of my life is already gone. If I die tomorrow or if I live thirty more years my past life will be no different. It has occurred on either alternative. Rather than my past, my death deprives me of my future, of the life that I would have lived if I had lived out my natural life span.

The loss of a future biological life does not explain the misfortune of death. Compare two scenarios: In the former I now fall into a coma from which I do not recover until my death in thirty years. In the latter I die now. The latter scenario does not seem to describe a greater misfortune than the former.

The loss of our future conscious life is what underlies the misfortune of premature death. Not any future conscious life qualifies, however. Suppose that I am terminally ill with cancer. Suppose also that pain and suffering would dominate my future conscious life. If so, then death would not be a misfortune for me.

Thus, the misfortune of premature death consists of the loss to us of the future goods of consciousness. What are these goods? Much can be said about this issue, but a simple answer will do for the purposes of this essay. The goods of life are whatever we get out of life. The goods of life are those items toward which we take a "pro" attitude. They are completed projects of which we are proud, the pursuit of our goals, aesthetic enjoyments, friendships, intellectual pursuits, and physical pleasures of various sorts. The goods of life are what makes life worth living. In general, what makes life worth living for one person will not be the same as what makes life worth living for another. Nevertheless, the list of goods in each of our lives will overlap. The lists are usually different in different stages of our lives.

What makes the goods of my future good for me? One possible, but wrong, answer is my desire for those goods now. This answer does not account for those aspects of my future life that I now believe I will later value, but about which I am wrong. Neither does it account for those aspects of my future that I will come to value, but which I don't value now. What is valuable to the young may not be valuable to the middle-aged. What is valuable to the middle-aged may not be valuable to the old. Some of life's values for the elderly are best appreciated by the elderly. Thus it is wrong to say that the value of my future to me is just what I value now. What makes my future valuable to me are those aspects of my future that I will (or would) value when I will (or would) experience them, whether I value them now or not.

It follows that a person can believe that she will have a valuable future and be wrong. Furthermore, a person can believe that he will not have a valuable future and also be wrong. This is confirmed by our attitude toward many of the suicidal. We attempt to save the lives of the suicidal and to convince them that they have made an error in judgment. This does not mean that the future of an individual obtains value from the value that others confer on it. It means that, in some cases, others can make a clearer judgment of the value of a person's future *to that person* than the person herself. This often happens when one's judgment concerning the value of one's own future is clouded by personal tragedy. (Compare the views of McInerney, 1990, and Shirley, 1995.)

Thus, what is sufficient to make killing us wrong, in general, is that it causes premature death. Premature death is a misfortune. Premature death is a misfortune, in general, because it deprives an individual of a future of value. An individual's future will be valuable to that individual if that individual will come, or would come, to value it. We know that killing us is wrong. What makes killing us wrong, in general, is that it deprives us of a future of value. Thus, killing someone is wrong, in general,

when it deprives her of a future like ours. I shall call this "an FLO."

ARGUMENTS IN FAVOR OF THE FLO THEORY

At least four arguments support this FLO account of the wrongness of killing.

The considered judgment argument

The FLO account of the wrongness of killing is correct because it fits with our considered judgment concerning the nature of the misfortune of death. The analysis of the previous section is an exposition of the nature of this considered judgment. This judgment can be confirmed. If one were to ask individuals with AIDS or with incurable cancer about the nature of their misfortune, I believe that they would say or imply that their impending loss of an FLO makes their premature death a misfortune. If they would not, then the FLO account would plainly be wrong.

The worst of crimes argument

The FLO account of the wrongness of killing is correct because it explains why we believe that killing is one of the worst of crimes. My being killed deprives me of more than does my being robbed or beaten or harmed in some other way because my being killed deprives me of all of the value of my future, not merely part of it. This explains why we make the penalty for murder greater than the penalty for other crimes.

As a corollary the FLO account of the wrongness of killing also explains why killing an adult human being is justified only in the most extreme circumstances, only in circumstances in which the loss of life to an individual is outweighed by a worse outcome if that life is not taken. Thus, we are willing to justify killing in self-defense, killing in order to save one's own life, because one's loss if one does not kill in that situation is so very great. We justify killing in a just war for similar reasons. We believe that capital punishment would be justified if, by having such an institution, fewer premature deaths would occur. The FLO account of the wrongness of killing does not entail that killing is always wrong. Nevertheless, the FLO account explains both why killing is one of the worst of crimes and, as a corollary, why the exceptions to the wrongness of killing are so very rare. A correct theory of the wrongness of killing should have these features.

The appeal to cases argument

The FLO account of the wrongness of killing is correct because it yields the correct answers in many life-and-death cases that arise in medicine and have interested philosophers.

Consider medicine first. Most people believe that it is not wrong deliberately to end the life of a person who is permanently unconscious. Thus we believe that it is not wrong to remove a feeding tube or a ventilator from a permanently comatose patient, knowing that such a removal will cause death. The FLO account of the wrongness of killing explains why this is so. A patient who is permanently unconscious cannot have a future that she would come to value, whatever her values. Therefore, according to the FLO theory of the wrongness of killing, death could not, *ceteris paribus,* be a misfortune to her. Therefore, removing the feeding tube or ventilator does not wrong her.

By contrast, almost all people believe that it is wrong, *ceteris paribus,* to withdraw medical treatment from patients who are temporarily unconscious. The FLO account of the wrongness of killing also explains why this is so. Furthermore, these two unconsciousness cases explain why the FLO account of the wrongness of killing does not include present consciousness as a necessary condition for the wrongness of killing.

Consider now the issue of the morality of legalizing active euthanasia. Proponents of active euthanasia argue that if a patient faces a future of intractable pain and wants to die; then, *ceteris paribus,* it would not be wrong for a physician to give him medicine that she knows would result in his death. This view is so universally accepted that even the strongest *opponents* of active euthanasia hold it. The official Vatican view (Sacred Congregation, 1980) is that it is permissible for a physician to administer to a patient morphine sufficient (although no more than sufficient) to control his pain even if

she foresees that the morphine will result in his death. Notice how nicely the FLO account of the wrongness of killing explains this unanimity of opinion. A patient known to be in severe intractable pain is presumed to have a future without positive value. Accordingly, death would not be a misfortune for him and an action that would (foreseeably) end his life would not be wrong.

Contrast this with the standard emergency medical treatment of the suicidal. Even though the suicidal have indicated that they want to die, medical personnel will act to save their lives. This supports the view that it is not the mere *desire* to enjoy an FLO which is crucial to our understanding of the wrongness of killing. *Having* an FLO is what is crucial in the account, although one would, of course, want to make an exception in the case of fully autonomous people who refuse life-saving medical treatment. Opponents of abortion can, of course, be willing to make an exception for fully autonomous fetuses who refuse life support.

The FLO theory of the wrongness of killing also deals correctly with issues that have concerned philosophers. It implies that it would be wrong to kill (peaceful) persons from outer space who come to visit our planet even though they are biologically utterly unlike us. Presumably, if they are persons, then they will have futures that are sufficiently like ours so that it would be wrong to kill them. The FLO account of the wrongness of killing shares this feature with the personhood views of the supporters of choice. Classical opponents of abortion who locate the wrongness of abortion somehow in the biological humanity of a fetus cannot explain this.

The FLO account does not entail that there is another species of animals whose members ought not to be killed. Neither does it entail that it is permissible to kill any non-human animal. On the one hand, a supporter of animals' rights might argue that since some non-human animals have a future of value, it is wrong to kill them also, or at least it is wrong to kill them without a far better reason than we usually have for killing non-human animals. On the other hand, one might argue that the futures of non-human animals are not sufficiently like ours for the FLO account to entail that it is wrong to kill them. Since the FLO account does not specify which properties a future of another individual must possess so that killing that individual is wrong, the FLO account is indeterminate with respect to this issue. The fact that the FLO account of the wrongness of killing does not give a determinate answer to this question is not a flaw in the theory. A sound ethical account should yield the right answers in the obvious cases; it should not be required to resolve every disputed question.

A major respect in which the FLO account is superior to accounts that appeal to the concept of person is the explanation the FLO account provides of the wrongness of killing infants. There was a class of infants who had futures that included a class of events that were identical to the futures of the readers of this essay. Thus, reader, the FLO account explains why it was as wrong to kill you when you were an infant as it is to kill you now. This account can be generalized to almost all infants. Notice that the wrongness of killing infants can be explained in the absence of an account of what makes the future of an individual sufficiently valuable so that it is wrong to kill that individual. The absence of such an account explains why the FLO account is indeterminate with respect to the wrongness of killing non-human animals.

If the FLO account is the correct theory of the wrongness of killing, then because abortion involves killing fetuses and fetuses have FLOs for exactly the same reasons that infants have FLOs, abortion is presumptively seriously immoral. This inference lays the necessary groundwork for a fourth argument in favor of the FLO account that shows that abortion is wrong.

The analogy with animals argument

Why do we believe it is wrong to cause animals suffering? We believe that, in our own case and in the case of other adults and children, suffering is a misfortune. It would be as morally arbitrary to refuse to acknowledge that animal suffering is wrong as it would be to refuse to acknowledge that the suffering of persons of another race is wrong. It is, on reflection, suffering that is a misfortune, not the suffering of white males or the suffering of humans. Therefore, infliction of suffering is presumptively wrong no matter on whom it is inflicted and whether it is inflicted on persons or nonpersons. Arbitrary restrictions on the wrongness of suffering count as racism or speciesism. Not only is this argument convincing on its own, but it is the only way of justifying the wrongness of animal cruelty. Cruelty toward animals is clearly wrong. (This famous argument is due to Singer, 1979.)

The FLO account of the wrongness of abortion is analogous. We believe that, in our own case and the cases of other adults and children, the loss of a future of value is a misfortune. It would be as morally arbitrary to refuse to acknowledge that the loss of a future of value to a fetus is wrong as to refuse to acknowledge that the loss of a future of value to Jews (to take a relevant twentieth-century example) is wrong. It is, on reflection, the loss of a future of value that is a misfortune; not the loss of a future of value to adults or loss of a future of value to non-Jews. To deprive someone of a future of value is wrong no matter on whom the deprivation is inflicted and no matter whether the deprivation is inflicted on persons or nonpersons. Arbitrary restrictions on the wrongness of this deprivation count as racism, genocide or ageism. Therefore, abortion is wrong. This argument that abortion is wrong should be convincing because it has the same form as the argument for the claim that causing pain and suffering to non-human animals is wrong. Since the latter argument is convincing, the former argument should be also. Thus, an analogy with animals supports the thesis that abortion is wrong.

REPLIES TO OBJECTIONS

The four arguments in the previous section establish that abortion is, except in rare cases, seriously immoral. Not surprisingly, there are objections to this view. There are replies to the four most important objections to the FLO argument for the immorality of abortion.

The potentiality objection

The FLO account of the wrongness of abortion is a potentiality argument. To claim that a fetus *has* an FLO is to claim that a fetus now has the potential to be in a state of a certain kind in the future. It is not to claim that all ordinary fetuses *will* have FLOs. Fetuses who are aborted, of course, will not. To say that a standard fetus has an FLO is to say that a standard fetus either will have or would have a life it will or would value. To say that a standard fetus would have a life it would value is to say that it will have a life it will value if it does not die prematurely. The truth of this conditional is based upon the nature of fetuses (including the fact that they naturally age) and this nature concerns their potential.

Some appeals to potentiality in the abortion debate rest on unsound inferences. For example, one may try to generate an argument against abortion by arguing that because persons have the right to life, potential persons also have the right to life. Such an argument is plainly invalid as it stands. The premise one needs to add to make it valid would have to be something like: "If Xs have the right to Y, then potential Xs have the right to Y." This premise is plainly false. Potential presidents don't have the rights of the presidency; potential voters don't have the right to vote.

In the FLO argument potentiality is not used in order to bridge the gap between adults and fetuses as is done in the argument in the above paragraph. The FLO theory of the wrongness of killing adults is based upon the adult's potentiality to have a future of value. Potentiality is in the argument from the very beginning. Thus, the plainly false premise is not required. Accordingly, the use of potentiality in the FLO theory is not a sign of an illegitimate inference.

The argument from interests

A second objection to the FLO account of the immorality of abortion involves arguing that even though fetuses have FLOs, nonsentient fetuses do not meet the minimum conditions for having any moral standing at all because they lack interests. Steinbock (1992, p. 5) has presented this argument clearly:

Beings that have moral status must be capable of caring about what is done to them. They must be capable of being made, if only in a rudimentary sense, happy or miserable, comfortable or distressed. Whatever reasons we may have for preserving or protecting nonsentient beings, these reasons do not refer to their own interests. For without conscious awareness, beings cannot have interests. Without interests, they cannot have a welfare of their own. Without a welfare of their own, nothing can be done for their sake. Hence, they lack moral standing or status.

Medical researchers have argued that fetuses do not become sentient until after 22 weeks of gestation (Steinbock, 1992, p. 50). If they are correct, and if Steinbock's argument is sound, then we have both an objection to the FLO account of the wrongness of abortion and a basis for a view on abortion minimally acceptable to most supporters of choice.

Steinbock's conclusion conflicts with our settled moral beliefs. Temporarily unconscious human beings are nonsentient, yet no one believes that they lack either interests or moral standing. Accordingly, neither conscious awareness nor the capacity for conscious awareness is a necessary condition for having interests.

The counter-example of the temporarily unconscious human being shows that there is something internally wrong with Steinbock's argument. The difficulty stems from an ambiguity. One cannot *take* an interest in something without being capable of caring about what is done to it. However, something can be *in* someone's interest without that individual being capable of caring about it, or about anything. Thus, life support can be *in* the interests of a temporarily unconscious patient even though the temporarily unconscious patient is incapable of *taking* an interest in that life support. If this can be so for the temporarily unconscious patient, then it is hard to see why it cannot be so for the temporarily unconscious (that is, nonsentient) fetus who requires placental life support. Thus the objection based on interests fails.

The problem of equality

The FLO account of the wrongness of killing seems to imply that the degree of wrongness associated with each killing varies inversely with the victim's age. Thus, the FLO account of the wrongness of killing seems to suggest that it is far worse to kill a five-year-old than an 89-year-old because the former is deprived of far more than the latter. However, we believe that all persons have an equal right to life.

Thus, it appears that the FLO account of the wrongness of killing entails an obviously false view (Paske, 1994).

However, the FLO account of the wrongness of killing does not, strictly speaking, imply that it is worse to kill younger people than older people. The FLO account provides an explanation of the wrongness of killing that is sufficient to account for the serious presumptive wrongness of killing. It does not follow that killings cannot be wrong in other ways. For example, one might hold, as does Feldman (1992, p. 184), that in addition to the wrongness of killing that has its basis in the future life of which the victim is deprived, killing an individual is also made wrong by the admirability of an individual's past behavior. Now the amount of admirability will presumably vary directly with age, whereas the amount of deprivation will vary inversely with age. This tends to equalize the wrongness of murder.

However, even if, *ceteris paribus*, it is worse to kill younger persons than older persons, there are good reasons for adopting a doctrine of the legal equality of murder. Suppose that we tried to estimate the seriousness of a crime of murder by appraising the value of the FLO of which the victim had been deprived. How would one go about doing this? In the first place, one would be confronted by the old problem of interpersonal comparisons of utility. In the second place, estimation of the value of a future would involve putting oneself, not into the shoes of the victim at the time she was killed, but rather into the shoes the victim would have worn had the victim survived, and then estimating from that perspective the worth of that person's future. This task seems difficult, if not impossible. Accordingly, there are reasons to adopt a convention that murders are equally wrong.

Furthermore, the FLO theory, in a way, explains why we do adopt the doctrine of the legal equality of murder. The FLO theory explains why we regard murder as one of the worst of crimes, since depriving someone of a future like ours deprives her of more than depriving her of anything else. This gives us a reason for making the punishment for murder very harsh, as harsh as is compatible with civilized society. One should not make the punishment for younger victims harsher than that. Thus, the doctrine of the equal legal right to life does not seem to be incompatible with the FLO theory.

The contraception objection

The strongest objection to the FLO argument for the immorality of abortion is based on the claim that, because contraception results in one less FLO, the FLO argument entails that contraception, indeed, abstention from sex when conception is possible, is immoral. Because neither contraception nor abstention from sex when conception is possible is immoral, the FLO account is flawed.

There is a cogent reply to this objection. If the argument of the early part of this essay is correct, then the central issue concerning the morality of abortion is the problem of whether fetuses are individuals who are members of the class of individuals whom it is seriously presumptively wrong to kill. The properties of being human and alive, of being a person, and of having an FLO are criteria that participants in the abortion debate have offered to mark off the relevant class of individuals. The central claim of this essay is that having an FLO marks off the relevant class of individuals. A defender of the FLO view could, therefore, reply that since, at the time of contraception, there is no individual to have an FLO, the FLO account does not entail that contraception is wrong. The wrong of killing is primarily a wrong to the individual who is killed; at the time of contraception there is no individual to be wronged.

However, someone who presses the contraception objection might have an answer to this reply. She might say that the sperm and egg are the individuals deprived of an FLO at the time of contraception. Thus, there are individuals whom contraception deprives of an FLO and if depriving an individual of an FLO is what makes killing wrong, then the FLO theory entails that contraception is wrong.

There is also a reply to this move. In the case of abortion, an objectively determinate individual is the subject of harm caused by the loss of an FLO. This individual is a fetus. In the case of contraception, there are far more candidates (see Norcross, 1990). Let us consider some possible candidates in order of the increasing number of individuals harmed: (1) The single harmed individual might be the combination of the particular sperm and the particular egg that would have united to form a zygote if contraception had not been used. (2) The two harmed individuals might be the particular sperm itself, and, in addition, the ovum itself that would have physically combined to form the zygote. (This is modeled on the double homicide of two persons who would otherwise in a short time fuse. (1) is modeled on harm to a single entity some of whose parts are not physically contiguous, such as a university.) (3) The many harmed individuals might be the millions of *combinations* of sperm and the released ovum whose (small) chances of having an FLO were reduced by the successful contraception. (4) The even larger class of harmed individuals (larger by one) might be the class consisting of all of the individual sperm in an ejaculate and, in addition, the individual ovum released at the time of the successful contraception. (1) through (4) are all candidates for being the subject(s) of harm in the case of successful contraception or abstinence from sex. Which should be chosen? Should we hold a lottery? There seems to be no non-arbitrarily determinate subject of harm in the case of successful contraception. But if there is no such subject of harm, then no determinate thing was harmed. If no determinate thing was harmed, then (in the case of contraception) no wrong has been done. Thus, the FLO account of the wrongness of abortion does not entail that contraception is wrong.

CONCLUSION

This essay contains an argument for the view that, except in unusual circumstances, abortion is seriously wrong. Deprivation of an FLO explains why killing adults and children is wrong. Abortion deprives fetuses of FLOs. Therefore, abortion is wrong. This argument is based on an account of the wrongness of killing that is a result of our considered judgment of the nature of the misfortune of premature death. It accounts for why we regard killing as one of the worst of crimes. It is superior to alternative accounts of the wrongness of killing that are intended to provide insight into the ethics of abortion. This account of the wrongness of killing is supported by the way it handles cases in which our moral judgments are settled. This account has an analogue in the most plausible account of the wrongness of causing animals to suffer. This account makes no appeal to religion. Therefore, the FLO account shows that abortion, except in rare instances, is seriously wrong.

NOTE

1. This essay is an updated version of a view that first appeared in the *Journal of Philosophy* (1989). This essay incorporates attempts to deal with the objections of McInerney (1990), Norcross (1990), Shirley (1995), Steinbock (1992), and Paske (1994) to the original version of the view.

Discussion Questions

1. Is the deprivation account of the wrongness of killing correct?
2. Why is it wrong (other things being equal) to deprive people of their lives?
3. Do fetuses have the same relationship to their futures that we have to ours? What implications does this have for Marquis's argument?
4. Does Marquis's argument apply to contraception?

CHAPTER 8

Sex and Pornography

HARD QUESTION: IS PORNOGRAPHY IMMORAL?

The term *pornography* derives from the Greek word *porne,* which means "prostitute," so its literal meaning is "writing about prostitutes." Pornography thus has something to do with sexual arousal and is usually understood as sexually explicit material intended to achieve that end, even though it might fail miserably. Pornography is everywhere. It saturates the Internet, it is widely available in magazines and on specialty TV, and whole sections of stores that rent films are devoted to adult entertainment. Pornography is big business—billions of dollars yearly—and so is the business of trying to regulate and control it. Despite its ubiquity (or perhaps because of it), pornography raises difficult moral and legal questions. Before we consider a few of them, we need to consider a prior question: What is pornography? Defining pornography is more difficult than it might seem. As an exasperated Justice Stewart famously quipped in a 1972 Supreme Court case, even though he was unable to define pornography, he knew it when he saw it!

If pornography is sexually explicit material created with the intention to arouse sexually, then, contrary to Justice Stewart, we cannot tell simply by looking whether the material is pornography. To make that determination, we would have to know the intentions of the person who produced it. Intention is often clear enough, but imagine some sexually explicit material produced by accident (maybe a photographer forgot to shut off his camera when his girlfriend visited). Would that be pornography? It could arouse viewers sexually and be virtually indistinguishable from material created with that intention.

Is sexual explicitness necessary for something to count as pornography? We can easily imagine material that functions as pornography without being sexually explicit. Among shoe fetishists, for example, glossy photographs of shoes might be produced with the intention of sexual arousal, but there is nothing sexually explicit in such images. Would this be pornography? Perhaps in a whole society of shoe fetishists it would be pornography, but we would not count it as such. With purely functional accounts of pornography, anything that functions as pornography, that is, material intended to arouse sexually, is pornography. In ordinary contexts and given the normal range of sexual desires, varieties of sexual explicitness tend to arouse. But as the example of the shoe fetishist shows, understanding pornography functionally means that explicit sexual content drops out as conceptually necessary. Suppose that in some strange society, we find depictions of tennis balls functioning as pornography functions in our society. People are sexually aroused at the sight of tennis balls; a whole industry emerges that deals with depictions of tennis balls, access to those depictions is restricted for minors, and various civil groups worry about the influence of tennis ball depictions on society. Imagine further that sexually explicit material that we would regard as pornography is unremarkable to them. Such a story might be coherent, but it distorts the concept of pornography by straying too far from our understanding of sexuality. Therefore, a purely functional account of pornography will not yield a useful understanding of the concept. In theory, people might become sexually aroused by depictions of anything, but in reality, it is explicit sexual content that typically has this effect. This means that we should preserve sexual explicitness as a necessary component for something to count as pornography. The shoe fetishist might be aroused when looking at shoe catalogues, but the pictures of shoes do not count as pornography, even if they are created to arouse shoe fetishists.

Another question is whether the concept of pornography is an evaluative one. "Murder" is not just a killing, it is a *wrongful* killing; weeds are not just any kind of plant, they are *undesirable* ones. Is the concept of pornography similarly evaluative? If it is, then there is no point in morally evaluating pornography, for that would already have been done by definition. For example, pornography is sometimes understood as sexually explicit material designed to appeal to prurient interests, and prurient interests are those that are lewd or lascivious. Since prurient or lewd interests are bad, pornography is bad by definition. Or pornography is sometimes identified with obscenity, understood as what is shocking to prevailing community standards of decency. Because obscenity is wrong or bad, then so is pornography—again, by definition. But should we identify pornography with obscenity? This hardly seems correct because there can be things that are obscene but not pornographic, a claim some people make about flag burning or desecrating graves or certain forms of speech.

Instead of identifying pornography with obscenity, we might understand pornography as a subclass within the obscene: specifically, the sexually obscene. This would also make pornography objectionable by definition, but then the problem lies in distinguishing pornography from erotica, which we can understand as pornography that is not obscene. Unless one is a complete prude (evaluative term!) and has a problem with any material designed to arouse sexually, it will be important to distinguish between pornography and erotica, both of which are sexually explicit material intended to arouse sexually.

The problem of evaluative definition emerges in the definition of pornography proposed by Catherine McKinnon, an important legal scholar and feminist. She defines pornography as "the graphic sexually explicit subordination of women," allowing that there can be homosexual and other kinds of pornography, provided that there is sexually explicit subordination. Sexually explicit subordination is morally objectionable because subordination is morally objectionable, so a moral evaluation is part of her definition of pornography. But what counts as sexually explicit subordination? This seems highly subjective.

Let us waive the difficulties in trying to define pornography for a moment; maybe Justice Stewart was right after all. Let us ask instead about the morality of pornography, for there would not be such a big legal fuss about pornography if there were no moral questions at stake. What considerations bear on a moral assessment of pornography? McKinnon and others claim that pornography causes oppression of women by cultivating negative attitudes and expectations about sexuality for both men and woman. This is a huge empirical claim, one where the evidence is very much in dispute. But if pornography (whatever it is!) has this effect, then that would be a good reason to condemn it morally and perhaps to restrict it legally, for it would cause unjustified harm to others.

In *On Liberty*, J. S. Mill (see his biographical note in Chapter 2) tells us that the only justified ground for state coercion of an individual is prevention of harm to others, and that "his own good, either physical or moral, is not a sufficient warrant." This is known as the harm principle. To apply it we must know what harms an activity causes and whether they are sufficient to warrant state restriction, given what else is at stake. Not all harms caused to others merit state coercion of the individuals causing them, although they might still be morally condemnable. So even if the use of pornography does harm others and can be morally condemned on those grounds, there remain difficult questions of whether state restriction is justified, for whatever harms are caused might be outweighed by other values, such as free speech. This is a vast and controversial area that we will only mention in passing.

There are also questions about the effects of producing pornography on the actors themselves. If the actors are coerced or exploited, that is morally problematic, but the production of pornography does not require coercion or exploitation. Some forms of pornography might be degrading to the actors involved, and this would be good grounds for moral condemnation, because people ought not to treat one another in ways that affront their essential dignity. But unless we stipulate it to be so, as in McKinnon's definition, degradation is not necessary to pornography.

We should also consider effects on the consumer of pornography. Surely it degrades one to enjoy seeing other people degraded; this suggests that fascination with certain forms of pornography does not fulfill an obligation to one's self (see Kant in Chapter 3 for obligations to one's self). Moreover, if one's sex life is dominated by pornography, this cannot contribute to a flourishing existence, as Aristotle would have it.

Because there are various forms of pornography, it will be hard to make a blanket claim about the morality of pornography as such. Some forms will involve morally objectionable elements, others not. But it should be apparent that the morality of a form of pornography is not just a matter of how we react emotionally. One person might be disgusted or repulsed and someone else amused or titillated, but we should not assume that our emotions are determinative of its morality. For that we must reach a reasoned and principled conclusion.

What can ethics tell us about sex? It is incontestable that some sex acts are morally wrong. But are they wrong because of the kind of sex or are they wrong for some other reason? For example, it is obvious that rape is seriously morally wrong, but is rape wrong because of the sex itself or because rape is a reprehensible violation of a person's integrity? If rape is morally wrong because it is unconscionable mistreatment of a person, then any unconscionable mistreatment of a person is morally wrong, and the fact that rape involves sex organs adds nothing special to its moral seriousness. A similar analysis might be given for the wrongness of pedophilia; pedophilia is wrong because it traumatizes and scars a child for life. But anything intentionally done that traumatizes and scars a child for life is deeply and inexcusably wrong, such as torturing a child or forcing a child to kill his or her parents.

On this understanding of sexual ethics, the sexual is just another context in which we apply common moral principles, assess our duties, evaluate consequences, and respect (or violate) rights. There is no more a sexual ethics as an independent area for moral reflection than there is a sports ethics or a culinary ethics. In any area of human activity, our fundamental duties and responsibilities remain the same. The morality of a particular kind of activity will reflect how our ordinary moral principles apply to that activity.

Alternatively, one could claim that some sexual acts are morally wrong because of the sex itself, not for a reason external to it. This is often what is intended when a kind of sex is called perverted. Perverted sex is alleged to be morally wrong simply by virtue of its being perverted. But this raises numerous questions: What is perverted sex, how is it different from non-perverted sex, and what makes perverted sex morally wrong?

Perverted sex is necessarily sex that deviates from some norm. But how do we establish the norm? We must distinguish between a statistical and an ideal norm. A **statistical norm** is discovered empirically. We simply look at what people do and determine what sexual practices are most common. However, anything could be the statistical norm, and such a norm carries no evaluation with it, moral or otherwise. All we know from a statistical norm is that a practice is common—that most people do it. We cannot deduce from the fact that a sexual practice is common whether it is good or whether it ought to be accepted or condoned. Stealing might be common, but that is no reason to condone or tolerate it.

An **ideal norm,** by contrast, sets out an ideal—a way in which things are supposed to be, irrespective of how they are. When we consider an ideal norm the fact that certain sexual practices are common is irrelevant to our evaluation of them, although we may lament that what is common is not ideal. Can an ideal norm for sex be established? This will depend on an account of human nature, one that tells us where our proper sexual function or well-being lies. Deviations from an ideal sexual norm will thus be defects, by definition.

It is important to be clear about the difference between moral and nonmoral evaluations. A car can be good or bad, but this has no moral significance. Similarly, we can evaluate people non-morally. Someone who is blind or missing a limb or is suffering from a disease has a defect, something that is amiss; the person is not functioning according to the ideal norm, but no moral evaluation follows from that fact. The same can hold for sexual practices; a form of sex might be defective, but no moral evaluation need follow from that fact alone. This means that if there are such things as sexual perversions—defective sexual practices—we cannot infer anything about their morality, unless those practices are morally wrong on other grounds. The shoe fetishist is a sexual pervert if anyone is, but this defect has no moral significance since whatever one does to shoes is without moral significance, whereas the pedophile, also a sexual pervert, does something morally wrong because he harms children.

It is common enough to think that ideal or proper sex is reproductive sex, since sex is for reproduction. Non-reproductive sex is then suspect, and sexual perversions can all be seen as deviations from the reproductive function of sex. Homosexuality and garden variety sexual perversions (such as pedophilia, coprophilia, bestiality, necrophilia, voyeurism, and fetishism) can all be condemned for failing to meet the proper form of human sexuality. Even something as commonplace as masturbation is, in the words of the Catholic Church, "seriously disordered." But we should consider carefully whether reproductive sex ought to be taken as proper or ideal sex.

A common objection to taking reproductive sex as ideal or proper sex is that ordinary heterosexual intercourse among sterile people or old people should then be condemned too. Since that is absurd, reproductive sex must not be ideal. But this response misconstrues the original claim about ideal sex as reproductive sex. According to proponents of reproductive sex as ideal sex, the issue is the *form* of the sex, not whether the sex actually causes impregnation. Homosexual sex, masturbation, fetishism, and other sexual perversions lack the proper form, claims the proponent of reproductive sex as the ideal. Even though no offspring result, heterosexual sex among sterile or old people is of the ideal form "reproductive sex." Consider an analogy: Hammers are for driving nails, but using one to strike something else is still the right form of hammer use, whereas eating with a hammer is not.

Should we concede that proper or ideal sex is reproductive sex? No. What does sex have to do with reproduction? It is true that sex sometimes causes pregnancy and that sometimes people have sex in order to become pregnant, but much—perhaps most—sex is not intended to result in pregnancy. Our reasons for having sex need not reflect its biological purpose. Consider another analogy: The biological purpose of eating is nutrition, but much of our eating is not for nutrition. We snack because we are nervous, we eat junk food because we are manipulated by advertising, we dine for social intimacy, we create elaborate meals to impress others, and so forth; our purpose in eating is often not for nutrition and is sometimes inimical to it. In sex, too, our purposes need not match its biological purpose. Biologically, sex is for reproduction (actually, it is just for impregnation, since reproduction broadly understood requires a whole lot more), but that is not the only reason why we do it. We also do it for intimacy, pleasure, and all the other emotions that motivate people sexually. So without a background theory that links proper human activity to biological purposes only, the connection often alleged between proper sexuality and reproduction remains dubious.

Ann Garry, "Sex, Lies, and Pornography"

Ann Garry is a professor of philosophy at California State University, Los Angeles. She specializes in feminist philosophy, philosophy of law, and bioethics. She has written many influential articles, and her book Women, Knowledge, and Reality: Explorations in Feminist Philosophy *(edited with Marilyn Pearsall in 1996) is a well-regarded contribution to "analytic feminism." Analytic feminists believe that the conceptual clarity and argumentative rigor found in analytic philosophy will ultimately best serve feminism. In "Sex, Lies, and Pornography," Garry evaluates the moral argument that pornography is objectionable because it degrades people. She argues that even though much pornography is morally objectionable because it degrades, degradation is not a necessary feature of pornography.*

Critical Reading Questions

1. How does Garry define pornography, and how is her definition different from that of other feminists?
2. What is the argument from degradation?
3. On what grounds does Garry object to treating women as sex objects?
4. What is the link between sex and harm, according to Garry?
5. Under what conditions could there be morally acceptable pornography, according to Garry?

SEX, LIES, AND PORNOGRAPHY

Ann Garry

In the last third of the twentieth century pornography became much more widely available, but the moral and political issues surrounding it remain unresolved. In the 1960s the United States, for example, was barely past the era of banning books; courts had begun to grapple with obscenity cases.[1] Visual pornography could be seen in certain public theatres, and some people, mainly men, had private collections. Keep in mind that there were no video stores on the corner renting pornographic tapes for home VCR use, no cable channels showing it, and no internet to provide a panoply of sites for every erotic taste. When I first started thinking about pornography as a young feminist philosopher in the early 1970s, writing in the public arena concerning the topic came primarily from two groups of (mostly male) writers: "conservatives" who seemed to assume that sex was evil and "liberal" aficionados of the "sexual revolution," who had no clue what feminists meant when we demanded not to be treated as "sex objects." Pornography was also an object of political concern and academic study; for example, then President Nixon appointed a Commission on Obscenity and Pornography (and subsequently disregarded its results).

Where did this leave a feminist philosopher in the 1970s? Torn, conflicted, and unhappy with the level of discussion. On the one hand, I had been inclined to think that pornography was innocuous and to dismiss "moral" arguments for censoring it because many such arguments rested on an assumption I did not share—that sex is an evil to be controlled. On the other

hand, I believed that it was wrong to exploit or degrade human beings, particularly women and others who are especially susceptible. So if pornography degrades human beings, then even if I would oppose its censorship, I surely could not find it morally innocuous. In order to think about the issues further, I wrote "Pornography and Respect for Women"—offering a moral argument that would ground a feminist objection to pornography, but avoid a negative view of sex.[2]

The public and academic debates about pornography have subsequently become much richer, and alliances and divisions have shifted in unusual ways. North American feminists became deeply divided over pornography—debating whether pornography should be censored or in some other way controlled, and analyzing pornography's positive or negative value in moral, legal and political terms reflecting a wide variety of women's experiences. Some of the feminists most vehemently opposed to pornography found themselves allied with other foes of pornography—religious political conservatives with whom they had very little else in common. All the while, the mainstream "culture wars" pitted many of these same conservatives against a variety of people, including feminists, who choose "alternative" life styles or advocate significant social change. The picture I am sketching of the debates should look complex and frequently shifting. Yet this picture is no more complex and variegated than pornography itself has come to be. Although the central argument of this essay focuses on fairly tame and widespread heterosexual pornography, there is pornography available today for any conceivable taste and orientation. Where there's a market, there's pornography for it.

In this paper I first sketch very briefly some feminist positions concerning the law, politics, and morality of pornography. In the next section I offer a moral argument for maintaining that pornography degrades (or exploits or dehumanizes) women in ways or to an extent that it does not degrade men. In the final section, I argue that although much current pornography does degrade women, it is possible to have non-degrading, nonsexist pornography. However, this possibility rests on our making certain fundamental changes in our conceptions of gender roles and of sex. At a number of points throughout the paper I compare my position to those of other feminists.

I

Although some feminists find (some) pornography liberating, many feminists oppose (much) pornography for a variety of reasons.[3] Let's look at some who oppose it. Catharine MacKinnon and Andrea Dworkin drafted civil ordinances that categorize pornography as a form of sex-discrimination; they were passed in Indianapolis, Indiana, and Minneapolis, Minnesota, but subsequently overturned in the courts. In the ordinances they use the definition below.

Pornography is the graphic sexually explicit subordination of women, whether in pictures or in words that includes one of more of the following:. . . women are presented dehumanized as sexual objects, things or commodities; or . . . as sexual objects who enjoy pain or humiliation . . . or . . . who experience sexual pleasure in being raped . . . tied up or cut up or mutilated or bruised or physically hurt [the definition continues through five more long, graphic clauses before noting that men, children or transsexuals can be used in the place of women].[4]

Although in my way of thinking of morality, this definition already incorporates moral objections to pornography within it, MacKinnon has argued that pornography is not a moral issue but a political one. By a political issue, she means that pornography is about the distribution of power, about domination and subordination. Pornography sexualizes the domination and subordination of women. It makes sexually exciting and attractive the state of affairs in which women, both in body and spirit, are under the control of men. In pornography men define what women want and who we are: we want to be taken, used, and humiliated. Pornography is not about harmless fantasy and sexual liberation. I'll return to MacKinnon and Dworkin from time to time in this paper as examples of "anti-pornography" feminists.[5]

Other feminists claim that pornography is a form of hate speech/literature or that it lies about or defames women. Eva Kittay uses the analogy with racist hate literature that justifies the abuse of people on the basis of their racial characteristics to argue that pornography "justifies the abuse of women on the basis of their sexual characteristics."[6] Helen Longino defines pornography as "material that explicitly represents or describes degrading and abusive sexual behavior so as to endorse and/or recommend the behavior as described."[7] She argues that pornography defames and libels women by its deep and vicious lies, and supports and reinforces oppression of women by the distorted view of women that it portrays. Susan Brownmiller's classic statement is also worth noting: "Pornography, like rape, is a male invention, designed to dehumanize women, to reduce the female to an object of sexual access, not to free sensuality from moralistic or parental inhibition. . . . Pornography is the undiluted essence of anti-female propaganda."[8]

In order to understand how my view overlaps with, but differs from the feminist positions just described, we need to note some differences in our terminology and in our legal interests. The authors above build the objectionable character of pornography into their definitions of it. Sometimes those who do this want to reserve 'erotica' for explicit sexual material lacking those characteristics (though MacKinnon and Dworkin evidence little interest in this). Other times a negatively-value-laden definition is part of a legal strategy aimed at controlling pornography. I take a different approach to defining pornography, one that stems from ordinary usage and does not bias from the start any discussion of whether pornography is morally objectionable. I use "pornography" simply to label those explicit sexual materials intended to arouse the reader, listener, or viewer sexually. There is probably no sharp line that divides pornographic from nonpornographic material. I do not see this as a problem because I am not interested here in legal strategies that require a sharp distinction. In addition, I am focusing on obvious cases that would be uncontroversially pornographic—sleazy material that no one would ever dream has serious literary, artistic, political, or scientific merit.

I should say a little more about legal matters to clarify a difference between my interests and those of MacKinnon and Dworkin. They are interested in concrete legal strategies and believe that their proposed civil ordinances do not constitute censorship. My primary concern here is with neither a civil ordinance nor censorship, but with the basis for objecting to pornography on moral grounds. Nevertheless, it is important for me to state my belief that even if moral objections to pornography exist, there is no simple inference from "pornography is immoral" to "pornography should be censored" or to "pornography should be controlled by means of a civil ordinance that allows women to sue for harms based on sex-discrimination." Consider censorship. An argument to censor pornography requires us to balance a number of competing values: self-determination and freedom of expression (of both the users of pornography and those depicted in it or silenced by it), the nature of the moral and political problems with pornography (including its harms or potential harms to individuals and to communities), and so forth. Although there are fascinating issues here, there is no fast move from "immoral" to "illegal."

II

I want to take a step back from the feminist positions sketched above that assume the morally objectionable character of pornography within the definition. I want to evaluate the moral argument that pornography is objectionable because it degrades people. To degrade someone in this context is to lower her or his status in humanity—behavior incompatible with showing respect for a person. Of the many kinds of degradation and exploitation possible in the production of pornography, I focus only on the *content of the pornographic work.*[9] The argument is that

pornography itself exemplifies and recommends behavior that violates the moral principle to respect persons. It treats women as mere sex objects to be exploited and manipulated and degrades the role and status of women.

In order to evaluate this argument, I will first clarify what it would mean for pornography itself to treat someone as a sex object in a degrading manner. I will then deal with three issues central to the discussion of pornography and respect for women: how "losing respect" for a woman is connected with treating her as a sex object; what is wrong with treating someone as a sex object; and why it is worse to treat women rather than men as sex objects. I will argue that the current content of pornography sometimes violates the moral principle to respect persons. Then, in Part III of this paper, I will suggest that pornography need not violate this principle if certain fundamental attitude changes were to occur. Morally objectionable content is thus not necessary to pornography.

First, the simple claim that pornography treats people as sex objects is not likely to be controversial. It is pornography after all. Let's ask instead whether the content of pornography or pornography itself *degrades* people as it treats them as sex objects. It is not difficult to find examples of degrading content in which women are treated as sex objects. All we need to do is look at examples in MacKinnon and Dworkin's definition of pornography. Some pornography conveys the message that women really want to be raped, beaten or mutilated, that their resisting struggle is not to be believed. By portraying women in this manner, the content of the movie degrades women. Degrading women is morally objectionable. Even if seeing the movie does not cause anyone to imitate the behavior shown, we can call the content degrading to women because of the character of the behavior and attitudes it recommends. The same kind of point can be made about films, books, and TV commercials with other kinds of degrading, thus morally objectionable, content—for example, racist or homophobic messages.

The next step in the argument might be to infer that, because the content or message of pornography is morally objectionable, we can call pornography itself morally objectionable. Support for this step can be found in an analogy. If a person takes every opportunity to recommend that men force sex on women, we would think not only that his recommendation is immoral but that he is immoral too. In the case of pornography, the objection to making an inference from recommended behavior to the person who recommends it is that we ascribe predicates such as "immoral" differently to people than to films or books. A film vehicle for an objectionable message is still an object independent of its message, its director, its producer, those who act in it, and those who respond to it. Hence one cannot make an unsupported inference from "the content of the film is morally objectionable" to "the film is morally objectionable." In fact, I am not clear what support would work well here. Because the central points in this paper do not depend on whether pornography itself (in addition to its content) is morally objectionable, I will not pursue the issue further. Certainly one appropriate way to evaluate pornography is in terms of the moral features of its content. If a pornographic film exemplifies and recommends morally objectionable attitudes or behavior, then its content is morally objectionable.

Let us now turn to the first of our three questions about sex objects and respect: What is the connection between losing respect for a woman and treating her as a sex object? Some people who have lived through the era in which women were taught to worry about men "losing respect" for them if they engaged in sex in inappropriate circumstances have found it troublesome (or at least amusing) that feminists—supposedly "liberated" women—are outraged at being treated as sex objects, either by pornography or in any other way. The apparent alignment between feminists and traditionally "proper" women need not surprise us when we look at it more closely.

The "respect" that men have traditionally believed they have for women—hence a respect they can lose—is not a general respect for persons as autonomous beings; nor is it respect that is earned because of one's personal merits or achievements. It is respect that is an outgrowth of the traditional "double standard"—a standard that has certainly diminished in North America, but has not fully disappeared (and is especially tenacious in some ethnic and religious communities). Traditionally, women are

to be respected because they are more pure, delicate, and fragile than men, have more refined sensibilities, and so on.[10] Because some women clearly do not have these qualities, thus do not deserve respect, women must be divided into two groups—the good ones on the pedestal and the bad ones who have fallen from it. The appropriate behavior by which to express respect for good women would be, for example, not swearing or telling dirty jokes in front of them, giving them seats on buses, and other "chivalrous" acts. This kind of "respect" for good women is the same sort that adolescent boys in the back seats of cars used to "promise" not to lose. Note that men define, display, and lose this kind of respect. If women lose respect for women, it is not typically a loss of respect for (other) women as a class, but a loss of self-respect.

It has now become commonplace to acknowledge that, although a place on the pedestal might have advantages over a place in the gutter beneath it, a place on the pedestal is not at all equal to the place occupied by other people (i.e., men). "Respect" for those on the pedestal was not respect for whole, full-fledged people but for a special class of inferior beings.

If a person makes two traditional assumptions—that (at least some) sex is dirty and that women fall into two classes, good and bad—it is easy to see how that person might think that pornography could lead people to lose respect for women or that pornography is itself disrespectful to women. Pornography describes or shows women engaging in activities inappropriate for good women to engage in—or at least inappropriate for them to be seen by strangers engaging in. If one sees these women as symbolic representatives of all women, then all women fall from grace with these women. This fall is possible, I believe, because the traditional "respect" that men have had for women is not genuine, wholehearted respect for full-fledged human beings but half-hearted respect for lesser beings, some of whom they feel the need to glorify and purify. It is easy to fall from a pedestal. We cannot imagine half the population of the US answering "yes" to the question, "Do movies showing men engaging in violent acts lead people to lose respect for men?" Yet this has been the response to surveys concerning the analogous question for women in pornography.[11]

Two interesting asymmetries appear. The first is that losing respect for men as a class (men with power, typically Anglo men) is more difficult than losing respect for women or ethnic minorities as a class. Anglo men whose behavior warrants disrespect are more likely to be seen as exceptional cases than are women or minorities (whose "transgressions" may be far less serious). Think of the following: women are temptresses; Arabs are terrorists; Blacks cheat the welfare system; Italians are gangsters; however, Bill Clinton and the men of the Nixon and Reagan administrations are exceptions—Anglo men as a class did not lose respect because of, respectively, womanizing, Watergate, and the Iran-Contra scandals.

The second asymmetry looks at first to concern the active and passive roles of the sexes. Men are seen in the active role. If men lose respect for women because of something "evil" done by women (such as appearing in pornography), the fear is that men will then do harm to women—not that women will do harm to men. Whereas if women lose respect for some male politicians because of Watergate, Iran-Contra or womanizing, the fear is still that male politicians will do harm, not that women will do harm to male politicians. This asymmetry might be a result of one way in which our society thinks of sex as bad—as harm that men do to women (or to the person playing a female role, as in homosexual rape). Robert Baker calls attention to this point in " 'Pricks' and 'Chicks': A Plea for 'Persons'."[12] Our slang words for sexual intercourse— "fuck," "screw," or older words such as "take" or "have"—not only can mean harm but also have traditionally taken a male subject and a female object. The active male screws (harms) the female. A "bad" woman only tempts men to hurt her further. An interesting twist here is that the harmer/harmed distinction in sex does not depend on *actual* active or passive behavior. A woman who is sexually active, even aggressive, can still be seen as the one harmed by sex. And even now that it is more common to say that a woman can fuck a man, the notion of harm remains in the terms ("The bank screwed me with excessive ATM charges").

It is easy to understand why one's traditionally proper grandmother would not want men to see pornography or lose respect for women.

But feminists reject these "proper" assumptions: good and bad classes of women do not exist; and sex is not dirty (though some people believe it is). Why then are feminists angry at the treatment of women as sex objects, and why are some feminists opposed to pornography?

The answer is that feminists as well as proper grandparents are concerned with respect. However, there are differences. A feminist's distinction between treating a woman as a full-fledged person and treating her as merely a sex object does not correspond to the good-bad woman distinction. In the latter distinction, "good" and "bad" are properties applicable to groups of women. In the feminist view, all women are full-fledged people; however, some are treated as sex objects and perhaps think of themselves as sex objects. A further difference is that, although "bad" women correspond to those thought to deserve treatment as sex objects, good women have not corresponded to full-fledged people; only men have been full-fledged people. Given the feminist's distinction, she has no difficulty whatever in saying that pornography treats women as sex objects, not as full-fledged people. She can morally object to pornography or anything else that treats women as sex objects.

One might wonder whether any objection to treatment as a sex object implies that the person objecting still believes, deep down, that sex is dirty. I don't think so. Several other possibilities emerge. First, even if I believe intellectually and emotionally that sex is healthy, I might object to being treated *only* as a sex object. In the same spirit, I would object to being treated only as a maker of chocolate chip cookies or *only* as a tennis partner, because only one of my talents is being valued. Second, perhaps I feel that sex is healthy, but since it is apparent to me that you think sex is dirty, I don't want you to treat me as a sex object. Third, being treated as any kind of object, not just as a sex object, is unappealing. I would rather be a partner (sexual or otherwise) than an object. Fourth, and more plausible than the first three possibilities, is Robert Baker's view mentioned above. Both (i) our traditional double standard of sexual behavior for men and women and (ii) the linguistic evidence that we connect the concept of sex with the concept of harm point to what is wrong with treating women as sex objects. As I said earlier, the traditional uses of "fuck" and "screw" have taken a male subject, a female object, and have had at least two meanings: harm and have sexual intercourse with. (In addition, a prick is a man who harms people ruthlessly; and a motherfucker is so low that he would do something very harmful to his own dear mother.)[13]

Because in our culture we have connected sex with harm that men do to women, and because we have thought of the female role in sex as that of harmed object, we can see that to treat a woman as a sex object is automatically to treat her as less than fully human. To say this does not imply that healthy sexual relationships are impossible; nor does it say anything about individual men's conscious intentions to degrade women by desiring them sexually (though no doubt some men have these intentions). It is merely to make a point about the concepts embodied in our language.[14]

Psychoanalytic support for the connection between sex and harm comes from Robert J. Stoller. He thinks that sexual excitement is linked with a wish to harm someone (and with at least a whisper of hostility). The key process of sexual excitement can be seen as dehumanization (fetishization) in fantasy of the desired person. He speculates that this is true in some degree of everyone, both men and women, with "normal" or "perverted" activities and fantasies.[15]

Thinking of sex objects as harmed objects enables us to explain some of the reasons why one wouldn't want to be treated as a sex object: (1) I may object to being treated only as a tennis partner, but being a tennis partner is not connected in our culture with being a harmed object; and (2) I may not think that sex is dirty and that I would be a harmed object; I may not know what your view is; but what bothers me is that this is the view embodied in our language and culture.

Awareness of the connection between sex and harm helps explain other interesting points. Women are angry about being treated as sex objects in situations or roles in which they do not intend to be regarded in that manner—for example, while serving on a committee or participating in a discussion. It is not merely that a sexual role is inappropriate for the circumstances; it is thought to be a less fully human role than the one in which they intended to function.

Finally, the sex-harm connection allows us to acknowledge that pornography treats both women and men as sex objects and at the same time understand why it is worse to treat women as sex objects than to treat men as sex objects, and why some men have had difficulty understanding women's anger about the matter. It is more difficult for heterosexual men than for women to assume the role of "harmed object" in sex, for men have the self-concept of sexual agents, not of objects. This is also related to my earlier point concerning the difference in the solidity of respect for men and for women; respect for women is more fragile. Men and women have grown up with different patterns of self-respect and expectations regarding the extent to which they deserve and will receive respect or degradation. The man who doesn't understand why women do not want to be treated as sex objects (because he'd sure like to be) is not likely to think of himself as being harmed by that treatment; a woman might. (In fact, if one were to try to degrade a man sexually a promising strategy would be to make him feel like a non-man—a person who is either incapable of having sex at all or functioning only in the place of a woman.)[16]

Having seen that the connection between sex and harm helps explain both what is wrong with treating someone as a sex object and why it is worse to treat a woman in this way, let's keep in mind the views of anti-pornography feminists as we think about the range of pornography that exists today. Although an anti-pornography feminist need not claim that a pornographer has a *conscious intent* to degrade, to subordinate, or to lie about women's sexuality, some have said precisely this—remember Susan Brownmiller's claim cited in section I that pornography is designed to dehumanize women. The feminist who is not willing to attribute a "design" in pornography (beyond an intent to arouse and to earn a profit) can still find it deplorable that it is an empirical fact that degrading or subordinating women arouses quite a few men. After all, it is a pretty sorry state of affairs that this material sells well.

Suppose now we were to rate the content of all pornography from most morally objectionable to least morally objectionable. Among the most objectionable would be the most degrading—for example, "snuff" films and movies that recommend that men rape and mutilate women, molest children and animals, and treat nonmasochists very sadistically. The clauses in MacKinnon and Dworkin's definition of "pornography" again come to mind; one clause not yet cited is, "Women are presented in scenarios of degradation, injury, torture, shown as filthy or inferior, bleeding, bruised, or hurt in a context that makes these conditions sexual."[17]

Moving along the spectrum, we would find a large amount of material (perhaps most pornography) not quite so blatantly objectionable. With this material it is relevant to use the analysis of sex objects given above. As long as sex is connected with harm done to women, it will be very difficult not to see pornography as degrading to women. We can agree that pornography treats men as sex objects, too, but maintain that this is only pseudoequality: such treatment is still more degrading to women.

In addition, pornography often overtly exemplifies either the active/passive or the harmer/harmed object roles. Because much pornography today is male-oriented and is supposed to make a profit, the content is designed to appeal to male fantasies. Judging from the content of much pornography, male fantasies often still run along the lines of stereotypical gender roles—and, if Stoller is right, include elements of hostility. In much pornography the women's purpose is to cater to male desires, to service the man or men, and to be dependent on a man for her pleasure (except in the lesbian scenes in heterosexual pornography—which, too, are there for male excitement). Even if women are idealized rather than specifically degraded, women's complex humanity is taken away: the idealized women and the idealized sexual acts are in the service of the male viewer. Real women are not nearly so pliable for male fantasies. In addition, women are clearly made into passive objects in still photographs showing only close-ups of their genitals. Although many kinds of specialty magazines, films and videos are gauged for different sexual tastes, much material exemplifies the range of traditional sex roles of male heterosexual fantasies. There is no widespread attempt to replace the harmer/harmed distinction with anything more positive and healthy.[18]

The cases in this part of the spectrum would be included in the anti-pornography feminists' scope, too. MacKinnon and Dworkin's point that pornography makes domination and subordination sexually exciting is relevant here as well as in the more extreme cases. In fact, other clauses in their definition cover much "regular" pornography: "women are presented in postures of sexual submission, servility or display; . . . women's body parts, including but not limited to vaginas, breasts, and buttocks—are exhibited, such that women are reduced to those parts."[19] Whether or not "regular," corner-video-store pornography is consciously designed to degrade or subordinate women, the fact that it does both degrade women and produce sexual excitement in men is sufficient to make MacKinnon and Dworkin's point.

What would cases toward the least objectionable end of the spectrum be like? They would be increasingly less degrading and sexist. The genuinely nonobjectionable cases would be nonsexist and nondegrading. The question is: Does or could any pornography have nonsexist, non-degrading content?

III

To consider the possibility of nonsexist, morally acceptable pornography, imagine the following situation. Two fairly conventional heterosexuals who love each other try to have an egalitarian relationship. In addition, they enjoy playing tennis, beach volleyball and bridge together, cooking good food together, and having sex together. In these activities they are partners—free from hang-ups, guilt, and tendencies to dominate or objectify each other. These two people like to watch tennis and beach volleyball matches, cooking shows, and old romantic movies on TV, like to read the bridge column and food sections in the newspaper, and like to watch pornographic videos. Imagine further that this couple is not at all uncommon in society and that nonsexist pornography is as common as this kind of nonsexist sexual relationship. This situation sounds morally and psychologically acceptable to me. I see no reason to think that an interest in pornography would disappear in these circumstances.[20] People seem to enjoy watching others experience or do (especially do well) what they enjoy experiencing, doing, or wish they could do themselves. We do not morally object to the content of TV programs showing cooking, tennis or beach volleyball or to people watching them. I have no reason to object to our hypothetical people watching nonsexist pornography.

What kinds of changes are needed to move from the situation today to the situation just imagined? One key factor in moving to nonsexist pornography would be to break the connection between sex and harm. If Stoller is right, this task may be impossible without changing the scenarios of our sexual lives—scenarios that we have been writing since early childhood, but that we can revise. But whatever the individual complexities of changing our sexual scenarios, the sex–harm connection is deeply entrenched and has widespread implications. What is needed is a thorough change in people's deep-seated attitudes and feelings about gender roles in general, as well as about sex and roles in sex. Feminists have been advocating just such changes for a few decades now. Does it make sense to try to change pornography in order to help to bring about the kinds of changes that feminists advocate? Or would we have to wait until after these changes have taken place to consider the possibility of nonsexist pornography? First, it is necessary to acknowledge how difficult and complex a process it is to change deeply held attitudes, beliefs and feelings about gender and sex (and how complex our feelings about gender and sex are). However, if we were looking for avenues to promote these changes, it would probably be more fruitful to look to television, children's educational material, nonpornographic movies, magazines and novels than to focus on pornography. On the other hand, we might not want to take the chance that pornography is working against changes in feelings and attitudes. So we might try to change pornography along with all the other, more important media.

Before sketching some ideas along these lines, let's return briefly to MacKinnon and Dworkin—feminists who would be very skeptical of any such plan. Their view of human sexuality is that it is "a social construct, gendered to the ground."[21] There is no essential sexual being or sexual substratum that has been corrupted by male dominance. Sexuality as we know it simply is male defined. Pornography, therefore, does not distort sexuality; pornography constitutes sexual reality. Even if MacKinnon and Dworkin were to grant me my more inclusive definition of pornography, they would find it bizarre to entertain the possibility of making pornography neutral, not to mention using it as an "ally" for social change.

However, bear with me. If sexual reality is socially constructed, it can be constructed differently. If sexuality is male defined, it can be defined differently—by women who can obtain enough power to overcome our silence and by men who are our allies. Dworkin herself advocates changing our concept of sexuality. It probably makes more sense to speak of constructing *sexualities* in any case—to acknowledge the variety of sexualities human beings are likely to construct.

So let's suppose that we want to make changes to pornography that would help us with the deep social changes needed to break the sex–harm connection and to make gender roles more equitable in sexual and nonsexual contexts. When I thought about this subject in the 1970s, I sketched out a few plot lines, partly in jest, involving women in positions of respect—urologists, high-ranking female Army officers, long-distance truck drivers—as well as a few ideas for egalitarian sex scenes.[22] However, in the intervening decades while I was standing around teaching philosophy, the pornography industry far surpassed my wildest plot dreams. There is pornography now made by feminists and (thanks to the women who pick up videos at the corner video store as they do more than their fair share of the errands), some pornography that is more appealing to women—feminist or not.[23]

One might still wonder whether any current pornography is different "enough" to be nonsexist and to start to change attitudes and feelings. This is a difficult call to make, but I think we should err on the side of keeping an open mind. For, after all, if we are to attempt to use pornography as a tool to change the attitudes of male pornography viewers (along with their willing and not-so-willing female partners), any changes would have to be fairly subtle at first; the fantasies in nonsexist pornography must become familiar enough to sell and be watched. New symbols and fantasies need to be introduced with care, perhaps incrementally.

Of course, realistically, we would need to realize that any positive "educational value" that nonsexist pornography might have may well be as short-lived as most of the other effects of pornography. But given these limitations, feminist pornographers could still try (and do try).

There are additional problems, however. Our world is not the world imagined at the beginning of section III for the couple watching tennis, beach volleyball and pornography; in their world nonsexist pornography can be appreciated in the proper spirit. Under these conditions the content of our new pornography could be nonsexist and morally acceptable. But could the content of the same pornography be morally acceptable if shown to men with sexist attitudes today? It might seem strange for us to change our moral evaluation of the content on the basis of a different audience, but I have trouble avoiding this conclusion. There is nothing to prevent men who really do enjoy degrading women from undermining the most well-intentioned plot about, say, a respected, powerful woman filmmaker—even a plot filled with sex scenes with egalitarian detail, "respectful" camera angles and lighting, and so on. Men whose restricted vision of women makes it impossible to absorb the film as intended could still see the powerful filmmaker as a demeaned plaything or kinky prostitute, even if a feminist's intention in making and showing the film is to undermine this view. The effect is that, although the content of the film seems morally acceptable and our intention in showing it is morally flawless, women are still degraded. The importance of the audience's attitude makes one wary of giving wholehearted approval to much pornography seen today.

The fact that good intentions and content are insufficient does not imply that feminists' efforts toward change would be entirely in vain. Of course, I could not deny that anyone who tries to change an institution from within faces serious difficulties. This is particularly evident when one is trying to change both pornography and a whole set of related attitudes, feelings, and institutions concerning gender roles and sex. But in conjunction with other attempts to change this set of attitudes, it seems preferable to try to change pornography instead of closing one's eyes in the hope that it will go away. For it seems realistic to expect that pornography is here to stay.[24]

NOTES

I would like to thank Talia Bettcher and David Ashen-Garry for very helpful comments and references.

1. Some of the key first amendment/obscenity cases are: *Roth* v. *US* 354 U.S. 476 (1957), *Paris Adult Theatre* I v. *Slaton* 413 U.S. 49 (1973), *Miller* v. *State of California* 413 U.S. 15 (1973); a recent internet case is Reno v. American Civil Liberties Union 117 S. Ct. 2329 (1997). It is easy to find cases at *www.FindLaw.com* or other legal internet sites.

2. Ann Garry, "Pornography and Respect for Women," *Social Theory and Practice* 4 (1978): 395–421, and published at approximately the same time in *Philosophy and Women*, ed. Sharon Bishop and Marjorie Weinzweig (Belmont, CA: Wadsworth, 1979). Sections II–III of the present paper use some of the central arguments from Parts III–IV of the earlier paper.

3. Examples of feminists works that are pro-pornography or anthologies of pro- and anti-pornography writings include Nadine Strossen, *Defending Pornography* (New York: Scribner, 1995), Diana E. H. Russell, ed., *Making Violence Sexy: Feminist Views on Pornography* (Buckingham, UK: Open University Press, 1993), Lynn Segal and Mary McIntosh, eds., *Sex Exposed: Sexuality and the Pornography Debate* (New Brunswick, NJ: Rutgers University Press, 1992), Pamela Church Gibson and Roma Gibson, eds., *Dirty Looks: Women, Pornography, Power* (London: BFI Press, 1993), Susan Dwyer, ed., *The Problem of Pornography* (Belmont, CA: Wadsworth, 1995). Several other anti-pornography references are in subsequent footnotes.

4. Catharine MacKinnon, *Feminism Unmodified* (Cambridge, MA: Harvard University Press, 1987), p. 146, n.1. The Indianapolis case is American Bookseller Association v. Hudnut 771F. 2d 323 (1985). A more recent work of MacKinnon's is *Only Words* (Cambridge, MA: Harvard University Press, 1993).

5. First, readers should not confuse the position of Andrea Dworkin with that of Ronald Dworkin (see ch. 36, pp. 356–63, this volume).

Second, concerning whether pornography is a moral or political issue: MacKinnon and Dworkin associate "moral arguments" against pornography with the liberal ideology they reject in their political and legal strategies. MacKinnon rejects arguments such as mine, among other reasons, because they use concepts associated with the liberal intellectual tradition—respect, degrade, dehumanize, etc. She claims that pornography dehumanizes women in "culturally specific and empirically descriptive—not liberal moral–sense" (*Feminism Unmodified*, p. 159). My take on it is different. I find MacKinnon's political argument to be a moral argument as well—it is morally wrong to subordinate women.

Third, Rae Langton discusses the MacKinnon/Dworkin claims that pornography subordinates and silences women in the context of philosophy of language: "Speech Acts and Unspeakable Acts," *Philosophy and Public Affairs* 22 (1993): 293–330, revised as "Pornography, Speech Acts, and Silence," in *Ethics in Practice*, ed. Hugh LaFollette (Cambridge, MA: Blackwell, 1997).

6. Eva Feder Kittay, "Pornography and the Erotics of Domination," in *Beyond Domination*, ed. Carol Gould (Totowa, NJ: Rowman and Allanheld, 1983), pp. 156–7. Of course, sometimes pornography is both sexist and racist—it utilizes many negative racial/ethnic stereotypes in its fantasy-women (and men) and degrades in culturally specific ways. See Tracey Gardner, "Racism in Pornography and the Women's Movement," in *Take Back the Night*, ed. Laura Lederer (New York: Bantam, 1982). Gloria Cowan and Robin R. Campbell, "Racism and Sexism in Interracial Pornography: A Content Analysis," *Psychology of Women Quarterly* 18 (1994): 323–38.

7. Helen Longino, "Pornography, Oppression and Freedom: A Closer Look," in *Take Back the Night*, ed. Laura Lederer (New York: Bantam, 1982), p. 31.

8. Brownmiller, *Against Our Will: Men, Women and Rape* (New York: Simon Schuster, 1975), p. 394.

9. By focusing on the content of pornography I exclude many important kinds of degradation and exploitation: (i) the ways in which pornographic film makers might exploit people in making a film, distributing it, and charging too much to see it or buy it; (ii) the likelihood that actors, actresses, or technicians will be exploited, underpaid, or made to lose self-respect or self-esteem; and (iii) the exploitation and degradation involved in prostitution and crime that often accompany urban centers of pornography.

It is obvious that I am also excluding many other moral grounds for objecting to pornography: The US Supreme Court has held that pornography invades our privacy, hurts the moral tone of the community, and so on. There are also important and complex empirical questions whether pornography in fact increases violence against women or leads men to treat women in degrading ways (and leads women to be more likely to accept this treatment). I dealt with some early social science literature on the last topic in "Pornography and Respect for Women," but the length limitations of the present paper do not permit an update. Once you leave the empirical correlation between the use of pornography and masturbation, very little is simple to prove. Summaries of and references to social science work can be found in Edward Donnerstein, et al., *The Question of Pornography: Research Findings and Policy Implications* (New York: Free Press, 1987), Neil Malamuth and Daniel Ling, *Pornography* (Newbury Park, CA: Sage Publications, 1993), Marcia Palley, *Sex and Sensibility: Reflections on Hidden Mirrors and the Will to Censor* (Hopewell, NJ: Ecco Press, 1994), and Neil Malamuth and Edward Donnerstein, eds., *Pornography and Sexual Aggression* (Orlando, FL: Academic Press, 1984).

10. The question of what is required to be a "good" woman varies greatly by ethnicity, class, age, religion, politics, and so on. For example, many secular North Americans would no longer require virginity (after a certain age), but might well expect some degree of restraint or judgment with respect to sexual activity.

12. In Robert Baker and Frederick Elliston, eds., *Philosophy and Sex* (2nd edn.) (Buffalo, NY: Prometheus Books, 1984), p. 264.

13. Ibid.

14. A fuller treatment of sex objectification would need to be set in a more general context of objectification. Martha Nussbaum writes about both. See her "Objectification," *Philosophy and Public Affairs* 24 (1995): 249–91.

15. Robert J. Stoller, "Sexual Excitement," *Archives of General Psychiatry* 33 (1976): 899–909, especially p. 903. Reprinted in Stoller, *Sexual Excitement: Dynamics of Erotic Life* (Washington: American Psychiatric Press, 1979). The extent to which Stoller sees men and women in different positions with respect to harm and hostility is not clear. He often treats men and women alike, but in *Perversion: The Erotic Form of Hatred* (New York: Pantheon, 1975), pp. 89–91, he calls attention to differences between men and women especially regarding their responses to pornography and lack of understanding by men of women's sexuality. These themes are elaborated in his later books, *Porn: Myths for the Twentieth Century* (New Haven: Yale University Press, 1991) and Stoller and I. S. Levine, *Coming Attractions: The Making of an X-Rated Video* (New Haven: Yale University Press, 1993).

16. Three points: First, generalizations are always risky. It is important to remember that people's expectations of respect and their ability to be degraded can differ significantly by their race/ethnicity, sexual orientation, class, and individual psychological makeup. So although men's and women's expectations of respect or degradation are constructed differently within any given group, e.g., an ethnic group, the specifics of their expectations may well vary.

Second, heterosexual men have developed more sensitivity to being treated as sex objects (even if not as "harmed" objects) as women have become more sexually aggressive. In addition, heterosexual male worries about sex objectification surface readily in discussions of openly gay men serving in the military; there is far less worry about openly lesbian military personnel.

Third, although objectification of men working in the pornography industry is beyond the scope of this paper, Susan Faludi writes interestingly about it in "The Money Shot," *The New Yorker*, October 30, 1995, pp. 64–87. Stoller's interviews in *Porn* and *Coming Attractions* are also relevant, see n. 15.

17. MacKinnon, *Feminism Unmodified*, p. 146, n.1.

18. There is a whole array of sadomasochistic pornography (including women treating men sadistically) that I have not addressed in this discussion. There have been intense, multilayered controversies among feminists (both heterosexual and lesbian) about consenting sadomasochistic practices and pornography. See Samois, *Coming to Power: Writings and Graphics on Lesbian S/M* (Boston: Alyson Publications, 1987), Robin Linden, et al., eds., *Against Sadomasochism: A Radical Feminist Analysis* (East Palo Alto, CA: Frog in the Well, 1982), and Patrick D. Hopkins, "Rethinking Sadomasochism: Feminism, Interpretation, and Simulation," *Hypatia* 9 (1994), pp. 116–51, reprinted in Alan Soble, ed., *The Philosophy of Sex* (3rd edn.) (Lanham, MD: 1997).

19. MacKinnon, *Feminism Unmodified*, p. 146, n.1.

20. First, one might wonder whether Stoller's connection between hostility and sex negates the possibility or likelihood of "healthy" pornography. I think not, for although Stoller maintains that hostility is an element of sexual excitement generally, he thinks it important to distinguish degrees of hostility both in sex and in pornography. In his

1990s work specifically on pornography he makes this clear; see, e.g., references above in n.15, especially *Porn*, pp. 223–6. He also realizes that pornographers must know quite a bit about human sexual excitement in order to stay in business; so if sexual excitement requires increasingly less hostility, smart pornographers (even anti-feminists!) will reflect this change very quickly in their work.

Second, would the voyeurism required in pornography make it immoral? Again, I think not. Since the "voyeurism" in pornography invades no one's privacy, indeed, is intended and desired, I have trouble finding grounds for immorality.

21. MacKinnon, *Feminism Unmodified*, p. 149. See also Andrea Dworkin, *Pornography: Men Possessing Women* (New York: E.P. Dutton, 1981, with introduction written in 1989).

22. Garry, pp. 413–16. Examples of the kinds of egalitarian features I had in mind are: an absence of suggestions of dominance or conquest, changes in control over the circumstances of and positions in sex (women's preferences and desires would be shown to count equally with men's), no pseudo- enjoyed pain or violence, no great inequality between men and women in states of dress or undress or types and angles of bodily exposure, a decrease in the amount of "penis worship," a positive attempt to set a woman's sexual being within a more fully human context, and so on.

23. Among the best known feminists in the pornography industry are Candida Royalle, Nina Hartley, and (now performance artist) Annie Sprinkle.

Discussion Questions

1. How should pornography be defined?
2. Is there a distinction between pornography and erotica?
3. Do you agree with Garry about a link between sex and harm?

Burton Leiser, "Homosexuality and the 'Unnaturalness Argument'"

Burton Leiser is retired professor of philosophy from Pace University. He has published widely in social and legal philosophy. In "Homosexuality and the 'Unnaturalness Argument,'" Leiser examines the argument that homosexuality is immoral because it is unnatural. Natural *and* unnatural *can mean many things, and Leiser shows just how difficult it is to attach a meaning to the term* unnatural *so that it leads to the conclusion that homosexuality is immoral because it is unnatural. Leiser concludes that "without some more satisfactory explanation of the connection between the wrongfulness of homosexuality and its alleged unnaturalness, the argument must be rejected."*

Critical Reading Questions

1. What senses of *natural* and *unnatural* does Leiser discuss? Can you list them?
2. How does Leiser argue that unnatural in the sense of "uncommon" does not have moral import?
3. How does Leiser address the argument that sex organs are for reproduction?
4. How does Leiser argue that "unnaturalness" and "wrongfulness" are different concepts?

HOMOSEXUALITY AND THE "UNNATURALNESS ARGUMENT"

Burton M. Leiser

[The alleged "unnaturalness" of homosexuality] raises the question of the meaning of *nature, natural,* and similar terms. Theologians and other moralists have said that [homosexual acts] violate the "natural law," and that they are therefore immoral and ought to be prohibited by the state.

The word *nature* has a built-in ambiguity that can lead to serious misunderstandings. When something is said to be "natural" or in conformity with "natural law" or the "law of nature," this may mean either (1) that it is in conformity with the descriptive laws of nature, or (2) that it is not artificial, that man has not imposed his will or his devices upon events or conditions as they exist or would have existed without such interference.

1. The descriptive laws of nature. The laws of nature, as these are understood by the scientist, differ from the laws of man. The former are purely descriptive, whereas the latter are prescriptive. When a scientist says that water boils at 212° Fahrenheit or that the volume of a gas varies directly with the heat that is applied to it and inversely with the pressure, he means merely that as a matter of recorded and observable fact, pure water under standard conditions always boils at precisely 212° Fahrenheit and that as a matter of observed fact, the volume of a gas rises as it is heated and falls as pressure is applied to it. These "laws" merely *describe* the manner in which physical substances *actually behave.* They differ from municipal and federal laws in that they *do not prescribe behavior.* Unlike manmade laws, natural laws are not passed by any legislator or group of legislators; they are

not proclaimed or announced; they impose no obligation upon anyone or anything; their "violation" entails no penalty, and there is no reward for "following" them or "abiding by" them. When a scientist says that the air in a tire "obeys" the laws of nature that "govern" gases, he does *not* mean that the air, having been informed that it *ought* to behave in a certain way, behaves appropriately under the right conditions. He means, rather, that as a matter of fact, the air in a tire *will* behave like all other gases. In saying that Boyle's law "governs" the behavior of gases, he means merely that gases do, as a matter of fact, behave in accordance with Boyle's law, and that Boyle's law enables one to predict accurately what will happen to a given quantity of a gas as its pressure is raised; he does *not* mean to suggest that some heavenly voice has proclaimed that all gases should henceforth behave in accordance with the terms of Boyle's law and that a ghostly policeman patrols the world, ready to mete out punishments to any gases that "violate" the heavenly decree. In fact, according to the scientist, it does not make sense to speak of a natural law being violated. For if there were a true exception to a so-called law of nature, the exception would require a change in the description of those phenomena, and the "law" would have been shown to be no law at all. The laws of nature are revised as scientists discover new phenomena that require new refinements in their descriptions of the way things actually happen. In this respect they differ fundamentally from human laws, which are revised periodically by legislators who are not so interested in *describing* human behavior as they are in *prescribing* what human behavior *should* be.

2. *The artificial as a form of the unnatural.* On occasion when we say that something is not natural, we mean that it is a product of human artifice. My typewriter is not a natural object, in this sense, for the substances of which it is composed have been removed from their natural state—the state in which they existed before men came along—and have been transformed by a series of chemical and physical and mechanical processes into other substances. They have been rearranged into a whole that is quite different from anything found in nature. In short, my typewriter is an artificial object. In this sense, the clothing that I wear as I lecture before my students is not natural, for it has been transformed considerably from the state in which it was found in nature; and my wearing of clothing as I lecture before my students is also not natural, in this sense, for in my natural state, before the application of anything artificial, before any human interference with things as they are, I am quite naked. Human laws, being artificial conventions designed to exercise a degree of control over the natural inclinations and propensities of men, may in this sense be considered to be unnatural.

Now when theologians and moralists speak of homosexuality, contraception, abortion, and other forms of human behavior as being unnatural, and say that for that reason such behavior must be considered to be wrong, in what sense are they using the word *unnatural?* Are they saying that homosexual behavior and the use of contraceptives are contrary to the scientific laws of nature, are they saying that they are artificial forms of behavior, or are they using the terms *natural* and *unnatural* in some third sense?

They cannot mean that homosexual behavior (to stick to the subject presently under discussion) violates the laws of nature in the first sense, for, as we have pointed out, in *that* sense it is impossible to violate the laws of nature. Those laws, being merely descriptive of what actually does happen, would have to *include* homosexual behavior if such behavior does actually take place. Even if the defenders of the theological view that homosexuality is unnatural were to appeal to a statistical analysis by pointing out that such behavior is not normal from a statistical point of view, and

therefore not what the laws of nature require, it would be open to their critics to reply that any descriptive law of nature must account for and incorporate all statistical deviations, and that the laws of nature, in this sense, do not *require* anything. These critics might also note that the best statistics available reveal that about half of all American males engage in homosexual activity at some time in their lives, and that a very large percentage of American males have exclusively homosexual relations for a fairly extensive period of time; from which it would follow that such behavior is natural, for them, at any rate, in this sense of the word *natural.*

If those who say that homosexual behavior is unnatural are using the term *unnatural* in the second sense, it is difficult to see why they should be fussing over it. Certainly nothing is intrinsically wrong with going against nature (if that is how it should be put) in this sense. That which is artificial is often far better than what is natural. Artificial homes seem, at any rate, to be more suited to human habitation and more conducive to longer life and better health than caves and other natural shelters. There are distinct advantages to the use of such unnatural (i.e. artificial) amenities as clothes, furniture, and books. Although we may dream of an idyllic return to nature in our more wistful moments, we would soon discover, as Thoreau did in his attempt to escape from the artificiality of civilization, that needles and thread, knives and matches, ploughs and nails, and countless other products of human artifice are essential to human life. We would discover, as Plato pointed out in the *Republic,* that no man can be truly self-sufficient. Some of the by-products of industry are less than desirable; but neither industry itself, nor the products of industry, are intrinsically evil, even though both are unnatural in this sense of the word.

Interference with nature is not evil in itself. Nature, as some writers have put it, must be tamed. In some respects man must look upon it as an enemy to be conquered. If nature were left to its own devices, without the intervention of human artifice, men would be consumed with disease, they would be plagued by insects, they would be chained to the places where they were born with no means of swift communication or transport, and they would suffer the discomforts and the torments of wind and weather and flood and fire with no practical means of combating any of them.

Interfering with nature, doing battle with nature, using human will and reason and skill to thwart what might otherwise follow from the conditions that prevail in the world, is a peculiarly human enterprise, one that can hardly be condemned merely because it does what is not natural.

Homosexual behavior can hardly be considered to be unnatural in this sense. There is nothing "artificial" about such behavior. On the contrary, it is quite natural, in this sense, to those who engage in it. And even if it were not, even if it were quite artificial, this is not in itself a ground for condemning it.

It would seem, then, that those who condemn homosexuality as an unnatural form of behavior must mean something else by the word *unnatural,* something not covered by either of the preceding definitions. A third possibility is this:

3. *Anything uncommon or abnormal is unnatural.* If this is what is meant by those who condemn homosexuality on the ground that it is unnatural, it is quite obvious that their condemnation cannot be accepted without further argument. For the fact that a given form of behavior is uncommon provides no justification for condemning it. Playing viola in a string quartet is no doubt an uncommon form of human behavior. I do not know what percentage of the human race engages in such behavior, or what percentage of his life any given violist devotes to such behavior, but I suspect that the number of such people must be very small indeed, and that the total number of man-hours spent in such activity would justify our calling that form of activity uncommon, abnormal (in the sense that it is statistically not the kind of thing that people are ordinarily inclined to do), and therefore unnatural, in this sense of the word. Yet there is no reason to suppose that such uncommon, abnormal behavior is, by virtue of its uncommonness, deserving of condemnation or ethically or morally wrong. On the contrary, many forms of behavior are praised precisely because they are so uncommon. Great artists, poets, musicians, and scientists are "abnormal" in this sense; but clearly the world is better off for having them, and it would be absurd to condemn them or their activities for their failure to be common and normal. If homosexual behavior is wrong, then, it must be for some reason other than its "unnaturalness" in this sense of the word.

4. *Any use of an organ or an instrument that is contrary to its principal purpose or function is unnatural.* Every organ and every instrument—perhaps even every creature—has a function to perform, one for which it is particularly designed. Any use of those instruments and organs that is consonant with their purposes is natural and proper, but any use that is inconsistent with their principal functions is unnatural and improper, and to that extent, evil or harmful. Human teeth, for example, are admirably designed for their principal functions—biting and chewing the kinds of food suitable for human consumption. But they are not particularly well suited for prying the caps from beer bottles. If they are used for the latter purpose, which is not natural to them, they are liable to crack or break under the strain. The abuse of one's teeth leads to their destruction and to a consequent deterioration in one's overall health. If they are used only for their proper function, however, they may continue to serve well for many years. Similarly, a given drug may have a proper function. If used in the furtherance of that end, it can preserve life and restore health. But if it is abused, and employed for purposes for which it was never intended, it may cause serious harm and even death. The natural uses of things are good and proper, but their unnatural uses are bad and harmful.

What we must do, then, is to find the proper use, or the true purpose, of each organ in our bodies. Once we have discovered that, we will know what constitutes the natural use of each organ, and what constitutes an unnatural, abusive, and potentially harmful employment of the various parts of our bodies. If we are rational, we will be careful to confine our behavior to our proper functions and to refrain from unnatural behavior. According to those philosophers who follow this line of reasoning, the way to discover the "proper" use of any organ is to determine what it is peculiarly suited to do. The eye is suited for seeing, the ear for hearing, the nerves for transmitting impulses from one part of the body to another, and so on.

What are the sex organs peculiarly suited to do? Obviously, they are peculiarly suited to enable men and women to reproduce their own kind. No other organ in the body is capable of fulfilling that function. It follows, according to those who follow the natural-law line, that the "proper" or "natural" function of the sex organs is reproduction, and that strictly speaking, any use of those organs for other purposes is unnatural, abusive, potentially harmful, and therefore wrong. The sex organs have been given to us in order to enable us to maintain the continued existence of mankind on this earth. All perversions—including masturbation, homosexual behavior, and heterosexual intercourse that deliberately frustrates the design of the sexual organs—are unnatural and bad. As Pope Pius XI once said, "Private individuals have no other power over the members of their bodies than that which pertains to their natural ends."

But the problem is not so easily resolved. Is it true that every organ has one and only one proper function? A hammer may have been designed to pound nails, and it may perform that particular job best. But it is not sinful to employ a hammer to crack nuts if I have no other more suitable tool immediately available. The hammer, being a relatively versatile tool, may be employed in a number of ways. It has no one "proper" or "natural" function. A woman's eyes are well adapted to seeing, it is true. But they seem also to be well adapted to flirting. Is a woman's use of her eyes for the latter purpose sinful merely because she is not using them, at that moment, for their "primary" purpose of seeing? Our sexual organs are uniquely adapted for procreation, but that is obviously not the only function for which they are adapted. Human beings may—and do—use those organs for a great many other purposes, and it is difficult to see why any *one* use should be considered to be the only proper one. The sex organs, for one thing, seem to be particularly well adapted to give their owners and others intense sensations of pleasure. Unless one believes that pleasure itself is bad, there seems to be little reason to believe that the use of the sex organs for the production of pleasure in oneself or in others is evil. In view of the peculiar design of these organs, with their great concentration of nerve endings, it would seem that they were designed (if they *were* designed) with that very goal in mind, and that their use for such purposes would be no more unnatural than their use for the purpose of procreation.

Nor should we overlook the fact that human sex organs may be and are used to express, in the deepest and most intimate way open to man, the love of one person for another. Even the most ardent opponents of "unfruitful" intercourse admit that sex does serve this function. They have accordingly conceded that a man and his wife may have intercourse even though she is pregnant, or past the age of child bearing, or in the infertile period of her menstrual cycle.

Human beings are remarkably complex and adaptable creatures. Neither they nor their organs can properly be compared to hammers or to other tools. The analogy quickly breaks down. The generalization that a given organ or instrument has one and only one proper function does not hold up, even with regard to the simplest manufactured tools, for, as we have seen, a tool may be used for more than one purpose—less effectively than one especially designed for a given task, perhaps, but "properly" and certainly not *sinfully.* A woman may use her eyes not only to see and to flirt, but also to earn money—if she is, for example, an actress or a model. Though neither of the latter functions seems to have been a part of the original "design," if one may speak sensibly of *design* in this context, of the eye, it is difficult to see why such a use of the eyes of a woman should be considered sinful, perverse, or unnatural. Her sex organs have the unique capacity of producing ova and nurturing human embryos, under the right conditions; but why should any other use of those organs, including their use to bring pleasure to their owner or to someone else, or to manifest love to another person, or even, perhaps, to earn money, be regarded as perverse, sinful, or unnatural? Similarly, a man's sexual organs possess the unique capacity of causing the generation of another human being, but if a man chooses to use them for pleasure, or for the expression of love, or for some other purpose—so long as he does not interfere with the rights of some other person—the fact that his sex organs do have their unique capabilities does not constitute a convincing justification for condemning their other uses as being perverse, sinful, unnatural, or criminal. If a man "perverts" himself by wiggling his ears for the entertainment of his neighbors instead of using them exclusively for their "natural" function of hearing, no one thinks of consigning him to prison. If he abuses his teeth by using them to pull staples from memos—a function for which teeth were clearly not designed—he is not accused of being immoral, degraded, and degenerate. The fact that people *are* condemned for using their sex organs for their own pleasure or profit, or for that of others, may be more revealing about the prejudices and taboos of our society than it is about our perception of the true nature or purpose or "end" (whatever that might be) of our bodies.

To sum up, then, the proposition that any use of an organ that is contrary to its principal purpose or function is unnatural assumes that organs *have* a principal purpose or function, but this may be denied on the ground that the purpose or function of a given organ may vary according to the needs or desires of its owner. It may be denied on the ground that a given organ may have more than one principal purpose or function, and any attempt to call one use or another the only natural one seems to be arbitrary, if not question-begging. Also, the proposition suggests that what is unnatural is evil or depraved. This goes beyond the pure description of things, and enters into the problem of the evaluation of human behavior, which leads us to the fifth meaning of "natural."

5. *That which is natural is good, and whatever is unnatural is bad.* When one condemns homosexuality or masturbation or the use of contraceptives on the ground that it is unnatural, one implies that whatever is unnatural is bad, wrongful, or perverse. But as we have seen, in some senses of the word, the unnatural (i.e., the artificial) is often very good, whereas that which is natural (i.e., that which has not been subjected to human artifice or improvement) may be very bad indeed. Of course, interference with nature may be bad. Ecologists have made us more aware than we have ever been of the dangers of unplanned and uninformed interference with nature. But this is not to say that *all* interference with nature is bad. Every time a man cuts down a tree to make room for a home for himself, or catches a fish to feed himself or his family, he is interfering with nature. If men did not interfere with nature, they would have no homes, they could eat no fish, and, in fact, they could not survive. What, then, can be meant by those who say that whatever is natural is good and whatever is unnatural is bad? Clearly, they cannot have intended merely to reduce the word *natural* to a synonym of *good, right,* and *proper,* and

unnatural to a synonym of *evil, wrong, improper, corrupt,* and *depraved.* If that were all they had intended to do, there would be very little to discuss as to whether a given form of behavior might be proper even though it is not in strict conformity with someone's views of what is natural; for *good* and *natural* being synonyms, it would follow inevitably that whatever is good must be natural, and vice versa, by definition. This is certainly not what the opponents of homosexuality have been saying when they claim that homosexuality, being unnatural, is evil. For if it were, their claim would be quite empty. They would be saying merely that homosexuality, being evil, is evil—a redundancy that could as easily be reduced to the simpler assertion that homosexuality is evil. This assertion, however, is not an argument. Those who oppose homosexuality and other sexual "perversions" on the ground that they are "unnatural" are saying that there is some objectively identifiable quality in such behavior that is unnatural; and that that quality, once it has been identified by some kind of scientific observation, can be seen to be detrimental to those who engage in such behavior, or to those around them; and that *because* of the harm (physical, mental, moral, or spiritual) that results from engaging in any behavior possessing the attribute of unnaturalness, such behavior must be considered to be wrongful, and should be discouraged by society. "Unnaturalness" and "wrongfulness" are not synonyms, then, but different concepts. The problem with which we are wrestling is that we are unable to find a meaning for *unnatural* that enables us to arrive at the conclusion that homosexuality is unnatural or that if homosexuality is unnatural, it is therefore wrongful behavior. We have examined four common meanings of *natural* and *unnatural,* and have seen that none of them performs the task that it must perform if the advocates of this argument are to prevail. Without some more satisfactory explanation of the connection between the wrongfulness of homosexuality and its alleged unnaturalness, the argument must be rejected.

Discussion Questions

1. What do people mean when they say homosexuality is unnatural?
2. Should same-sex marriage be legally permitted? Are there any moral arguments against same-sex marriage?
3. Is homosexuality a moral issue? Why or why not?

CHAPTER 9

Euthanasia

HARD QUESTION: IS KILLING PEOPLE WRONG?

"Thou shalt not kill" is about as uncontroversial a principle as we are likely to find in ethics. But even here there are difficult questions. What are we enjoined from killing? Since anything alive can be killed, such as plants or animals, most plausibly the principle refers to persons; we should not kill persons. But what are persons? As we saw in Kant's ethics (see Chapter 3), Kant holds that persons are by definition rational agents, so not all members of the species *Homo sapiens* count as persons, at least in Kant's sense of the term. Coma victims and patients with Alzheimer's, for example, are not Kantian persons because these individuals lack rational agency. Even if we restrict the injunction against killing to Kantian persons, are there no circumstances when it is morally permissible to kill persons? What about self-defense, capital punishment (see Chapter 10), or a just war (see Chapter 11)?

We might amend the principle to say that what is enjoined is not killing but *murder,* the unjustified or wrongful killing of persons. Of course, now the principle is vacuous, since to tell us that we should not kill persons wrongfully is to say that we should not do what it is wrong to do. And, in any case, we still want to know when we are justified or unjustified in killing someone: What makes killing a person a murder? Perhaps we can fix things up by adding the qualification that we should not kill *innocent* persons. That can handle cases where a morally culpable person is killed. For example, killing a malicious and unprovoked attacker in self-defense is not killing an innocent person; it is justified killing and thus not murder. So what the injunction against killing persons really means is that we should not kill innocent people. It might be morally acceptable to kill non-innocent persons in certain circumstances, but according to the moral principle, under no circumstances may we intentionally kill innocent persons.

Is there a good reason why we should not kill innocent people? When we do moral philosophy we should seek rational justification for even the most intuitively obvious claims, for without rational grounds we can never be sure that what seems intuitively correct is in fact correct. Our intuitions are subject to all sorts of cultural biases and irrational prejudices, so the mere fact that something just seems right is no guarantee that we should accept it. At one time it seemed obvious to many people in America that blacks should be slaves, so intuition alone is no sure guide to morality. Can we explain the intuitive obviousness of why it is wrong to kill innocent people?

The primary explanation for why it is wrong to kill innocent people is the effect that killing has on the victim. Friends and family might be sad, but the effects on others are not why killing someone is wrong, when it is wrong. It is wrong because of the effect on the person who is killed—it makes the person dead. But why is it wrong to bring about an innocent person's death? It is wrong to kill an innocent person because ordinarily death is a harm, and it is wrong to inflict an unjustified harm on someone. So the wrongness of killing innocent people rests on the idea that death is bad.

Is death bad, an evil? This is a strange and surprisingly difficult question, but one plausible answer is that when death is an evil, it is an evil because it deprives the victim of life. Think of all the good things that make life worth living: conscious enjoyment of daily activities, emotional fulfillment, development of one's talents, enjoyment of friendships, engaging in meaningful projects, and so on. Death is bad, when it is bad, because it deprives one of all of that. Were it not for death, one would have experienced a worthwhile existence. So it is wrong to kill innocent people, when it is wrong to kill them, because it deprives them of the goods of life.

Because the practice of euthanasia seeks the deaths of innocent people, it may initially seem to impose the harm of death on them. But a key question is whether death is evil in the circumstances where euthanasia is a possibility. The term means "good death" (*eu* = good, *thanatos* = death), so euthanasia makes sense only when someone's continued existence is worse than death, such that death is good for the person who dies. In ordinary circumstances, because death deprives a person of the goods of life, death is rightly seen as a bad thing. But if death is good for someone, then the usual reasons against hastening a person's death do not apply.

It is important to be clear about this. In euthanasia, death must be good for the person who dies; otherwise, hastening that person's death cannot count as euthanasia. The judgment that death would be better than continued existence (and hence good for the person) must be correct for euthanasia to be conceptually possible. If one is mistaken that death would be better than continued existence, hastening that person's death might be failed euthanasia or attempted euthanasia, but not euthanasia.

If we assume that under some circumstances death would be better than continued existence, who decides that? Clearly, the preferences of the person whose life is at stake should carry significant weight, but those preferences are not automatically determinative that one's life is no longer worth living. Whether a life is worth living is a complex judgment involving one's values and commitments as well as objective features of human existence. It is the sort of thing about which one could be mistaken. Given what is at stake, it is not a decision reached lightly.

What does it mean to be alive and what makes life valuable? One way of understanding life is simply as a biological concept. To be alive means that respiration, digestion, and other metabolic processes occur within an organism—indeed, they constitute being an organism. But it is hard to see how biological life is more than instrumentally valuable for what matters in human life: having a biographical existence, not just a biological one. To have a biographical life means that one is consciously aware of oneself; one's experiences are organized into the trajectory and development of a self, unified by memory and anticipating the future. This is what makes life valuable, for biological life without biographical life is worthless. It is easy to see this if we imagine having to choose between dying now or falling into an irreversible comma for ten years and then dying. For most people there is no intrinsic reason to prefer one over the other; they are experiential blanks in either case. We rightly value conscious life, our biographical lives. Euthanasia becomes an issue when our biographical lives are over even if our biological lives are not.

Depending on who does what, there can be several forms of euthanasia. We shall limit ourselves to situations where the question of euthanasia normally arises—namely, with grievously ill or mortally injured patients. It is common to distinguish between active and passive euthanasia. **Passive euthanasia** occurs when medical care can do no more for someone and that person is left to die, whereas in **active euthanasia** the patient is directly killed by, say, a lethal injection because of the hopelessness of her or his underlying condition. In both cases, death is intended to benefit the patient.

If the patient requests death, that is **voluntary euthanasia;** when someone else decides that death would be good for the patient because the patient cannot decide for himself or herself what would be good, that is **nonvoluntary euthanasia.** Someone in an irreversible comma, for example, cannot make decisions about whether to live or die. The decision whether that person will continue to exist, even only as an unconscious body, must be made by someone else. (**Involuntary euthanasia**—that is, killing people against their wishes—is deeply morally problematic, even if the individual would in fact be better off dead. For killing people against their wishes is a spectacular violation of their autonomy.)

Thus we can generate four forms of euthanasia:

	Voluntary	Nonvoluntary
Active	1	2
Passive	3	4

Passive voluntary euthanasia is the most morally acceptable form for many people, because here the doctor simply lets her patient die at the patient's request, assuming that the patient is competent to make such a decision (something that is not always easy to determine). Passive nonvoluntary euthanasia is more problematic because someone else decides for a person unable to decide for herself or himself that death is better than life. But in neither form of passive euthanasia is someone actively killed; a person is merely let die. Whether that is morally preferable to active euthanasia, where a person is killed, is a point of deep controversy about the morality of euthanasia. Active euthanasia allegedly violates the principle that one ought not to kill innocent people, even if it is done with their consent. However, as we have seen, the usual reason why one ought not to kill innocent people—that it imposes the evil of death—does not apply to someone for whom death is not an evil but a good. It is easy to lose sight of this point because we are accustomed to think that we should not kill innocent people. But when we reflect on *why* we should not kill innocent people, we see that there are reasonable exceptions even to this intuitively basic principle.

SUICIDE AND EUTHANASIA

Questions about the morality of euthanasia are inextricably linked to questions about the morality of suicide. If people should never kill themselves, then others should not do it for them. By **suicide** we shall understand intentionally bringing about one's own death. Because with suicide one's own death is intended, simply killing oneself by, say, unthinkingly digging around in the toaster with a fork is not suicide. And the soldier who throws himself on a hand grenade to spare his fellows does not commit suicide, since if he miraculously survives, none of his plans are thwarted. Acting in a way that one foresees will bring about one's death is not suicide if death is not part of one's intention. Typically the smoker knows that smoking will cause his death, but that is not what he seeks; his plans are not thwarted if he reaches old age having smoked all his life. However, the plans of the person who is serious about committing suicide are thwarted if he or she wakes up the next day.

Many people who commit suicide are deeply disturbed or they make rash and unfortunate judgments about the value of their lives in the heat of crisis. But this is not necessarily so. If it is possible for a life to be not worth living, that life could be one's own and one could have an accurate understanding of that dismal fact. Under these circumstances, it would seem that suicide is a rational option. We tend to think of suicide as actively killing oneself, but the active/passive distinction applies to suicide too. One can commit suicide passively by, say, refusing to eat and starving to death. How one brings about one's own death is subordinate to the fact that one intends it, and it is the intention of death that makes it a suicide.

Imagine a patient in the final stages of a terminal illness; there is no hope for recovery, and medical care is simply protracting a humiliating and painful death. The patient realizes this and concludes that what little remains of life is not worth living. If the patient would be justified in removing the catheters and medical equipment that sustains him and passively dying, then the physician should also be permitted to remove them at the patient's request. We have just moved from the rational permissibility of passive suicide to the rational permissibility of what we might call passive physician-assisted suicide. Indeed, physician-assisted suicide is one form of voluntary euthanasia. The role of the physician is morally incidental, there being no intrinsic moral difference between passive voluntary physician-assisted suicide and a passive voluntary suicide assisted by accountants or professors.

Voluntary passive physician-assisted suicide gives way pretty quickly to voluntary active physician-assisted suicide, because if it would be permissible for me to actively kill myself, why should it matter whether I do it or someone else (the physician, typically) assists me? By virtue of their medical knowledge, physicians know how to bring about death painlessly and effectively. But with physician-assisted suicide, the physician still acts as the agent of the person committing suicide.

Consider the notorious crusader for euthanasia, Dr. Jack Kevorkian, also known as Dr. Death. Dr. Kevorkian's "thanatron," or death machine, is a crude contraption that allows his clients to push a button to release poison into their systems. Dr. Kevorkian evaded legal sanctions for years because he maintained that *he* did not kill his "patients" (some of whom he knew only briefly); he just made it possible for terminally ill people to kill themselves. Let's not focus on Kevorkian's attention-seeking tactics or his inexcusably unprofessional handling of his patients (some of whom were evidently not terminally ill, for example). Let's focus instead on what finally got him arrested for murder. One patient was too incapacitated to push the button on the thanatron, so Dr. Kevorkian pushed it for him. Because Dr. Kevorkian killed the patient, he was arrested and sent to jail for murder. Perhaps this was the only way the state could stop his macabre shenanigans, but it is hard to see the big moral difference between the patient pushing the button and Dr. Kevorkian pushing it for him. It is true that Dr. Kevorkian killed the patient, but if death in this case was a good, one that the patient very much wanted, then killing the patient was no harm. It is hard to see why it would be impermissible for someone to assist me in doing what it is permissible for me to do myself, at least in standard sorts of cases. This suggests that the moral permissibility of suicide pushes one to accept the moral permissibility of active voluntary euthanasia.

Once we reach this point, it seems that other pressures force us to accept active nonvoluntary euthanasia as well—that is, killing people without their consent. And indeed there is a case to be made for that. Why should release from pain and humiliation be reserved only for the autonomous, those who are competent and capable of forming an opinion about their continued existence? Only the competent can rationally commit suicide, but there is no reason to think that if death is a good, that good is limited to those capable of intending it. It is arbitrary to restrict active euthanasia to the competent, so it looks as though the permissibility of active voluntary euthanasia gives way to active nonvoluntary euthanasia. This is called a "slippery slope" argument; the idea is that once we start a practice, it will lead to disastrous results, so we should not take the first step on the slope. When thinking about slippery slope arguments we need to consider two things: How slippery is the slope and is what's at the bottom so bad?

If permitting active voluntary euthanasia drives us to accept active non-voluntary euthanasia, will we next find ourselves killing thousands of people with dementia in nursing homes? Furthermore, how can we justifiably restrict active nonvoluntary euthanasia to the terminally ill, since some non-terminally ill people have lives that are not worth living? And how do we determine when a life is not worth living? The Nazi program of "euthanasia" is often brought up as the sort of thing that can happen once we allow active forms of euthanasia. But calling the Nazis' "final solution" euthanasia is a twisted misnomer, a grotesque euphemism, since death was not good for their victims (nor was it intended to be). It was simply mass murder driven by eugenic fantasies. Nevertheless, the range of individuals who might be killed if active nonvoluntary euthanasia were practiced should give us pause.

There are other concerns. We've seen how the moral permissibility of rational suicide drives us to accept different forms of euthanasia. Perhaps we should examine the claim that suicide is ever morally permissible. For if it is not, then euthanasia would not be morally permissible because of the moral permissibility of rational suicide (however, it might still be permissible on other grounds). Kant (see Chapter 3) was deeply opposed to suicide. In *The Foundations of the Metaphysics of Morals*, he famously proclaims,

> The person who is contemplating suicide will ask himself, whether his act can coexist together with the idea of mankind *as an end in itself*. If he destroys himself in order to escape from a burdensome situation he uses a person merely as a *means* to maintain a tolerable condition up to the end of his life. However, man is not a thing and therefore not something that may be used as a means only, but in all his actions he must be considered as an end in itself. Consequently I can make no disposition of the man in my own person to mutilate, destroy or kill him.

According to Kant, suicide is incompatible with one's dignity as a person, for in committing suicide, one uses oneself merely as a means of avoiding a "burdensome situation." Whether this is so will depend on how we interpret matters, for it seems possible that one could commit suicide out of respect for one's personhood. If one foresaw that a terminal condition would compromise one's dignity, then self-respect might require that one not let oneself disintegrate. Perhaps Kant does not rule out suicide categorically, but only suicides that are incompatible with one's worth as a person. Much depends on one's motivation.

READINGS ON EUTHANASIA

James Rachels, "Active and Passive Euthanasia"

James Rachels (1941–2003) was an influential contemporary moral philosopher. He had an unusual ability for expressing the most complicated matters in deceptively simply, everyday language that often made one wonder what the learned fuss was all about. His famous article "Active and Passive Euthanasia" was originally published in The New England Journal of Medicine, *where it reached a wide audience among doctors and health policy experts. This article also brought euthanasia to the attention of philosophers, among whom it continues to exert considerable influence.*

Rachels argues that if we accept passive euthanasia, then we should also accept active euthanasia, because the humanitarian impulse that inclined us to accept passive euthanasia in the first place is better achieved by active euthanasia. Rachels goes on to argue that the bare difference between killing and letting die (the basis of the distinction between passive and active euthanasia) is not morally significant. If Rachels is right that killing, in itself, is no worse than letting die, then there is no good moral reason to allow passive but not active euthanasia.

Critical Reading Questions

1. How, according to Rachels, can passive euthanasia cause needless suffering?
2. How does Rachels argue that allowing only passive euthanasia leads to irrational decisions about the life and death of infants with Down syndrome?
3. Explain the case of Smith and Jones. What does Rachels think it shows?
4. Why, according to Rachels, are we inclined to think that killing is worse than letting die?

ACTIVE AND PASSIVE EUTHANASIA

James Rachels

The distinction between active and passive euthanasia is thought to be crucial for medical ethics. The idea is that it is permissible, at least in some cases, to withhold treatment and allow a patient to die, but it is never permissible to take any direct action designed to kill the patient. This doctrine seems to be accepted by most doctors, and it is endorsed in a statement adopted by the House of Delegates of the American Medical Association on December 4, 1973:

The intentional termination of the life of one human being by another—mercy killing—is contrary to that for which the medical profession stands and is contrary to the policy of the American Medical Association.

The cessation of the employment of extraordinary means to prolong the life of the body when there is irrefutable evidence that biological death is imminent is the decision of the patient and/or his immediate family. The advice and judgment of the physician should be freely available to the patient and/or his immediate family.

However, a strong case can be made against this doctrine. In what follows, I will set out some of the relevant arguments, and urge doctors to reconsider their views on this matter.

To begin with a familiar type of situation, a patient who is dying of incurable cancer of the throat is in terrible pain, which can no longer be satisfactorily alleviated. He is certain to die within a few days, even if present treatment is continued, but he does not want to go on living for those days since the pain is unbearable. So he asks the doctor for an end to it, and his family joins in the request.

Suppose the doctor agrees to withhold treatment, as the conventional doctrine says he may.

The justification for his doing so is that the patient is in terrible agony, and since he is going to die anyway, it would be wrong to prolong his suffering needlessly. But now notice this. If one simply withholds treatment, it may take the patient longer to die, and so he may suffer more than he would if more direct action were taken and a lethal injection given. This fact provides strong reason for thinking that, once the initial decision not to prolong his agony has been made, active euthanasia is actually preferable to passive euthanasia, rather than the reverse. To say otherwise is to endorse the option that leads to more suffering rather than less, and is contrary to the humanitarian impulse that prompts the decision not to prolong his life in the first place.

Part of my point is that the process of being "allowed to die" can be relatively slow and painful, whereas being given a lethal injection is relatively quick and painless. Let me give a different sort of example. In the United States about one in 600 babies is born with Down's syndrome. Most of these babies are otherwise healthy—that is, with only the usual pediatric care, they will proceed to an otherwise normal infancy. Some, however, are born with congenital defects such as intestinal obstructions that require operations if they are to live. Sometimes, the parents and the doctor will decide not to operate, and let the infant die. Anthony Shaw describes what happens then:

... When surgery is denied [the doctor] must try to keep the infant from suffering while natural forces sap the baby's life away. As a surgeon whose natural inclination is to use the scalpel to fight off death, standing by and watching a salvageable baby die is the most emotionally exhausting experience I know. It is easy at a conference, in a theoretical discussion, to decide that such infants should be allowed to die. It is altogether different to stand by in the nursery and watch as dehydration and infection wither a tiny being over hours and days. This is a terrible ordeal for me and the hospital staff—much more so than for the parents who never set foot in the nursery.[1]

I can understand why some people are opposed to all euthanasia, and insist that such infants must be allowed to live. I think I can also understand why other people favor destroying these babies quickly and painlessly. But why should anyone favor letting "dehydration and infection wither a tiny being over hours and days"? The doctrine that says that a baby may be allowed to dehydrate and wither, but may not be given an injection that would end its life without suffering, seems so patently cruel as to require no further refutation. The strong language is not intended to offend, but only to put the point in the clearest possible way.

My second argument is that the conventional doctrine leads to decisions concerning life and death made on irrelevant grounds.

Consider again the case of the infants with Down's syndrome who need operations for congenital defects unrelated to the syndrome to live. Sometimes, there is no operation, and the baby dies, but when there is no such defect, the baby lives on. Now, an operation such as that to remove an intestinal obstruction is not prohibitively difficult. The reason why such operations are not performed in these cases is, clearly, that the child has Down's syndrome and the parents and doctor judge that because of that fact it is better for the child to die.

But notice that this situation is absurd, no matter what view one takes of the lives and potentials of such babies. If the life of such an infant is worth preserving, what does it matter if it needs a simple operation? Or, if one thinks it better that such a baby should not live on, what difference does it make that it happens to have an unobstructed intestinal tract? In either case, the matter of life and death is being decided on irrelevant grounds. It is the Down's syndrome, and not the intestines, that is the issue. The matter should be decided, if at all, on that basis, and not be allowed to depend on the essentially

irrelevant question of whether the intestinal tract is blocked.

What makes this situation possible, of course, is the idea that when there is an intestinal blockage, one can "let the baby die," but when there is no such defect there is nothing that can be done, for one must not "kill" it. The fact that this idea leads to such results as deciding life or death on irrelevant grounds is another good reason why the doctrine should be rejected.

One reason why so many people think that there is an important moral difference between active and passive euthanasia is that they think killing someone is morally worse than letting someone die. But is it? Is killing, in itself, worse than letting die? To investigate this issue, two cases may be considered that are exactly alike except that one involves killing whereas the other involves letting someone die. Then, it can be asked whether this difference makes any difference to the moral assessments. It is important that the cases be exactly alike, except for this one difference, since otherwise one cannot be confident that it is this difference and not some other that accounts for any variation in the assessments of the two cases. So, let us consider this pair of cases:

In the first, Smith stands to gain a large inheritance if anything should happen to his six-year-old cousin. One evening while the child is taking his bath, Smith sneaks into the bathroom and drowns the child, and then arranges things so that it will look like an accident.

In the second, Jones also stands to gain if anything should happen to his six-year-old cousin. Like Smith, Jones sneaks in planning to drown the child in his bath. However, just as he enters the bathroom Jones sees the child slip and hit his head, and fall face down in the water. Jones is delighted; he stands by, ready to push the child's head back under if it is necessary, but it is not necessary. With only a little thrashing about the child drowns all by himself, "accidentally," as Jones watches and does nothing.

Now Smith killed the child, whereas Jones "merely" let the child die. That is the only difference between them. Did either man behave better, from a moral point of view? If the difference between killing and letting die were in itself a morally important matter, one should say that Jones's behavior was less reprehensible than Smith's. But does one really want to say that?

I think not. In the first place, both men acted from the same motive, personal gain, and both had exactly the same end in view when they acted. It may be inferred from Smith's conduct that he is a bad man, although that judgment may be withdrawn or modified if certain further facts are learned about him—for example, that he is mentally deranged. But would not the very same thing be inferred about Jones from his conduct? And would not the same further considerations also be relevant to any modification of this judgment? Moreover, suppose Jones pleaded, in his own defense, "After all, I didn't do anything except just stand there and watch the child drown. I didn't kill him; I only let him die." Again, if letting die were in itself less bad than killing, this defense should have at least some weight. But it does not. Such a "defense" can only be regarded as a grotesque perversion of moral reasoning. Morally speaking, it is no defense at all.

Now, it may be pointed out, quite properly, that the cases of euthanasia with which doctors are concerned are not like this at all. They do not involve personal gain or the destruction of normally healthy children. Doctors are concerned only with cases in which the patient's life is of no further use to him, or in which the patient's life has become or will soon become a terrible burden. However, the point is the same in these cases: the bare difference between killing and letting die does not, in itself, make a moral difference. If a doctor lets a patient die, for humane reasons, he is in the same moral position as if he had given the patient a lethal injection for humane reasons. If his decision was wrong—if, for example, the patient's illness was in fact curable—the decision would be equally regrettable no matter which method was used to carry it out. And if the doctor's decision was the right one, the method used is not in itself important.

The AMA policy statement isolates the crucial issue very well; the crucial issue is "the intentional termination of the life of one human being by another." But after identifying this issue, and forbidding "mercy killing," the statement goes on to deny that the cessation of treatment is the intentional termination of a life. This is where the mistake comes in, for what is the cessation of treatment, in these circumstances, if it is not "the intentional termination of the life of one human being by another"? Of course, it is exactly that, and if it were not, there would be no point to it.

Many people will find this judgment hard to accept. One reason, I think, is that it is very easy to conflate the question of whether killing is, in itself, worse than letting die, with the very different question of whether most actual cases of killing are more reprehensible than most actual cases of letting die. Most actual cases of killing are clearly terrible (think, for example, of all the murders reported in the newspapers), and one hears of such cases every day. On the other hand, one hardly ever hears of a case of letting die, except for the actions of doctors who are motivated by humanitarian reasons. So one learns to think of killing in a much worse light than of letting die. But this does not mean that there is something about killing that makes it in itself worse than letting die, for it is not the bare difference between killing and letting die that makes the difference in these cases. Rather, the other factors—the murderer's motive of personal gain, for example, contrasted with the doctor's humanitarian motivation—account for different reactions to the different cases.

I have argued that killing is not in itself any worse than letting die; if my contention is right, it follows that active euthanasia is not any worse than passive euthanasia. What arguments can be given on the other side? The most common, I believe, is the following:

"The important difference between active and passive euthanasia is that, in passive euthanasia, the doctor does not do anything to bring about the patient's death. The doctor does nothing, and the patient dies of whatever ills already afflict him. In active euthanasia, however, the doctor does something to bring about the patient's death: he kills him. The doctor who gives the patient with cancer a lethal injection has himself caused his patient's death; whereas if he merely ceases treatment, the cancer is the cause of the death."

A number of points need to be made here. The first is that it is not exactly correct to say that in passive euthanasia the doctor does nothing, for he does do one thing that is very important: he lets the patient die. "Letting someone die" is certainly different, in some respects, from other types of action—mainly in that it is a kind of action that one may perform by way of not performing certain other actions. For example, one may let a patient die by way of not giving medication, just as one may insult someone by way of not shaking his hand. But for any purpose of moral assessment, it is a type of action nonetheless. The decision to let a patient die is subject to moral appraisal in the same way that a decision to kill him would be subject to moral appraisal: it may be assessed as wise or unwise, compassionate or sadistic, right or wrong. If a doctor deliberately let a patient die who was suffering from a routinely curable illness, the doctor would certainly be to blame for what he had done, just as he would be to blame if he had needlessly killed the patient. Charges against him would then be appropriate. If so, it would be no defense at all for him to insist that he didn't "do anything." He would have done something very serious indeed, for he let his patient die.

Fixing the cause of death may be very important from a legal point of view, for it may determine whether criminal charges are brought against the doctor. But I do not think that this notion can be used to show a moral difference between active and passive euthanasia. The reason why it is considered bad to be the cause of someone's death is that death is regarded as a great evil—and so it is. However, if it has been decided that euthanasia—even passive euthanasia—is desirable in a given case, it has also been decided that in this instance death is no greater an evil than the patient's continued existence. And if this is true, the usual reason for not wanting to be the cause of someone's death simply does not apply.

Finally, doctors may think that all of this is only of academic interest—the sort of thing that philosophers may worry about but that has no practical bearing on their own work. After all, doctors must be concerned about the legal consequences of what they do, and active euthanasia is clearly forbidden by the law. But even so, doctors should also be concerned with the fact that the law is forcing upon them a moral doctrine that may well be indefensible, and has a considerable effect on their practices. Of course, most doctors are not now in the position of being coerced in this matter, for they do not regard themselves as merely going along with what the law requires. Rather, in statements such as the AMA policy statement that I have quoted, they are endorsing this doctrine as a central point of medical ethics. In that statement, active euthanasia is condemned not merely as illegal but as "contrary to that for which the medical profession stands," whereas passive euthanasia is approved. However, the preceding considerations suggest that there is really no moral difference between the two, considered in themselves (there may be important moral differences in some cases in their *consequences,* but, as I pointed out, these differences may make active euthanasia, and not passive euthanasia, the morally preferable option). So, whereas doctors may have to discriminate between active and passive euthanasia to satisfy the law, they should not do any more than that. In particular, they should not give the distinction any added authority and weight by writing it into official statements of medical ethics.

NOTE

1. A. Shaw: "Doctor, Do We Have a Choice?" *The New York Times Magazine,* Jan. 30, 1972, p. 54.

Discussion Questions

1. Do you agree with Rachels that the bare difference between killing and letting die is not morally significant?
2. Consider the "slippery slope" criticism of allowing active euthanasia. Is this a good reason to prohibit it?
3. What sorts of abuses can you imagine arising if all forms of euthanasia were permitted? Can you come up with ways of minimizing those abuses?
4. Would *you* like to have euthanasia available as an option?

David Velleman, "A Right to Self-Termination?"

David Velleman is a professor of philosophy at New York University. He works in the areas of ethics and metaethics, where his writings have received a good deal of attention. In "A Right to Self-Termination?" Velleman develops Kantian ideas to question whether and under what circumstances people have a right to self-termination. If we have no right of self-termination, then suicide and assisted suicide will be morally problematic. Velleman distinguishes between what is good for a person and a person's value, arguing that a person's good presupposes an interest-independent value. "A value of this kind, which a person has in himself but not for anyone, is the basis of Kantian moral theory. Kant's term for this value is 'dignity,' and he attributes dignity to all persons in virtue of their rational nature. What morality requires of us, according to Kant, is that we respect the dignity of persons." Velleman goes on to claim, "I don't deny that there are circumstances under which it would be better for one's life to end and permissible to hasten its ending. What I deny is that one may end one's life simply because one isn't getting enough out of it. One has to consider whether one is doing justice to it."

Critical Reading Questions

1. What does his example of the smoker show, according to Velleman?
2. Why ought we to defer to a person's assessment of whether his or her own life is worth living?
3. Why does Velleman deny that a person has a right to end his life "solely on the grounds of the benefits he will thereby obtain or the harms he will avoid"?
4. Why, according to Velleman, is it not paternalistic to challenge a person's judgment about his dignity?
5. What does Velleman mean when he makes the following claim: "[T]he dignity of a person isn't something that he can accept or decline, since it isn't a value *for* him; it's a value *in* him, which he can only violate or respect."
6. When and under what circumstances might suicide or assisted suicide be morally permissible, according to Velleman?

A RIGHT OF SELF-TERMINATION?[*]

J. David Velleman

Getting cancer changed my feelings about people who smoke.

I remember hearing a fellow philosopher expound, with a wave of his cigarette, on his right to choose whether to live and die smoking, or to quit and merely survive. I was just beginning a year of chemotherapy, and mere survival sounded pretty good to me. But I was the visiting speaker, and my hosts were unaware of my diagnosis. Several of them lit up after dinner as we listened to their colleague's disquisition—they with amused familiarity, I with an outrage that surprised even me and would have baffled them, if I had dared to express it. That I didn't dare is a cause for regret even now, ten years after the fact.

One objection was already clear to me at the time. A few months with cancer had taught me that a tumor rarely invades a region smaller than an extended family.

[*]Work on this article was supported by a fellowship from the National Endowment for the Humanities, and by a sabbatical leave from the College of Literature, Science, and the Arts, University of Michigan. An earlier and very different version was presented to the philosophy department and the Center for Ethics and Humanities in the Life Sciences at Michigan State University. I received helpful comments on that version from Elizabeth Anderson and Stephen Darwall, both of whom have also contributed significantly to my thinking on this subject through their published work. I also received comments from Bette Crigger and an anonymous referee for the *Hastings Center Report*. For comments on the present version, I am grateful to Sally Haslanger, Connie Rosati, Tamar Schapiro, and Brian Slattery.

Ethics 109 (April 1999): 606–628

Physically, the cancer was confined to my body, but even in that respect it was difficult to regard as mine. The tumor cells were growing in my bone marrow, which didn't live up to its poetic billing as the core of my being. The marrow in my bones, I discovered, was as foreign to me as the far side of the moon: it was, in a sense, *my* far side—unseen, insensate—its depth inside me being a measure of remoteness rather than intimacy. Of course, this fertile gunk in my pelvis and skull was also my sole source of blood cells, and my life depended on it. But so did the life of my sons' father, my wife's husband, my parents' son, my brothers' brother, and I was never sure who among us would suffer the greater harm if that life ran out of gunk.

Listening to my host laugh at his future cancer, I wondered whether he realized how many others would share it. What I would have said on their behalf, however, wouldn't have expressed my strongest feelings, which were felt on my own behalf, in a sense that I couldn't articulate. I was somehow offended, insulted. Watching smoke curl from the lips of people unmindful of my mortality, I felt as I probably would feel listening to anti-Semitic remarks directed at another person by a speaker unaware that I, too, was a Jew. I was witnessing an insult to a group of which I was also a member.

This symposium isn't about the right to smoke, of course; it's about the right to die. Not surprisingly, however, these rights tend to be articulated in the same terms. A person claiming either right might describe it, for instance, as a right "to live and die in the light of . . . his own convictions about why his life is valuable and where its value lies."

I can't recall whether the speaker in my story used these exact words, but I seemed to hear his voice again when I read them in the *New York Review of Books*, under the title "The Philosophers' Brief."[1] This brief had been submitted to the U.S. Supreme Court in support of a challenge to statutes outlawing physician-assisted suicide. Reading it, I once again felt a collective slight, and this time I couldn't miss which group was being slighted.

So I think that I can now explain why I was once offended by one philosopher's defense of smoking, and the explanation leads me to reject The Philosophers' defense of assisted suicide as well. As for assisted suicide itself, however, I don't know what to think. The complexities of the issue have thus far defeated my attempts to arrive at a settled position. On the policy question posed by this symposium, then, I am neither Pro nor Con. I'm, like, Not So Fast.

The principle quoted above, which would settle the issue quickly, can be derived from two broader principles. The first principle is that a person has the right to make his own life shorter in order to make it better—to make it shorter, that is, if doing so is a necessary means or consequence of making it a better life on the whole for him. The second principle is that there is a presumption in favor of deferring to a person's judgment on the subject of his own good. Together, these principles imply that a person has the right to live and die, in particular, by his own convictions about which life would be better for him.

For the smoker in my story, of course, shortening his life was not a means of making it better but rather a likely consequence of an activity that made it better, in his opinion, despite making it shorter, too. But in most of the cases for which assisted suicide is advocated, shortening

a patient's life is intended as a means of making it better, because the continuation of the patient's life would detract from its overall value for him.[2] When the first principle is confined to this latter context, it can be rephrased as the assertion of a patient's right to end his life on the grounds that it is no longer worth living.

I think that this principle is mistaken. Before I criticize it, however, I should speak briefly to the second principle stated above, which I can accept. I think that a person's considered judgment about his good is a judgment to which we generally ought to defer.

More specifically, then, I think that we generally ought to defer to a person on the question whether his life is worth living, since the living-worthiness of a life measures the extent to which the continuation of that life would be good for the person living it. The person living a life is the best judge of the value that its continuation would afford him—not an infallible judge, of course, but usually more reliable than anyone else is likely to be. Indeed, his judgment of this value is to some extent self-fulfilling, since his merely liking or disliking aspects of his life can to some extent make them good or bad for him.

The reasons for deferring to a person's judgment about his good go beyond his reliability as a judge. Respect for a person's autonomy may require that we defer to his considered judgment about his good even when we have reason to regard that judgment as mistaken. Letting him live his own life may sometimes entail letting him make his own mistakes about what's good for him—including, perhaps, mistakes about whether it would be good for him to go on living. Forbidding a person to make such mistakes can be objectionably paternalistic, because it would usurp his role as the primary agent of his own affairs.

Thus, if a person had the right to end his life on the grounds that it wasn't worth living (in accordance with the first principle, above), then he would have the right to be guided by his own judgment on that score (in accordance with the second principle). But I reject the principle that a person has the right to end his life solely

[1]Ronald Dworkin et al., "Assisted Suicide: The Philosophers' Brief," *New York Review of Books* 44 (March 27, 1997): 41–47. The brief was submitted in the case of Washington et al. v. Glucksberg et al. Links to briefs and opinions in this case can be found on the World Wide Web at http://ethics.acusd.edu/euthanasia.html.

[2]I discuss evaluations of this kind in "Well-Being and Time," *Pacific Philosophical Quarterly* 72 (1991): 48–77.

on the grounds of the benefits he will thereby obtain or the harms he will avoid.

One reason for rejecting this principle is that a life confers benefits and harms on people other than the person living it. Does a person have the right to deprive his children of a parent simply because life isn't worth enough to him?

I want to set aside this question, however, because it tacitly concedes the assumption that the values at stake in life-or-death decisions are relative to personal interests; it merely invites us to consider a wider circle of potential beneficiaries. The values that we need to consider, in my view, aren't relative to personal interests and consequently have no beneficiaries.

One might insist that values must have beneficiaries, because they wouldn't exist if there weren't someone who could appreciate them: nothing would be good or bad in a universe devoid of sentient beings.[3] But the fact that values wouldn't exist without potential valuers does not entail that they must accrue to someone.

Values are relative to potential valuers because they are normative, in the first instance, for valuation.[4] That is, for something to be valuable just is for it to be such as ought to be valued in some way—respected, loved, admired, wanted, treasured, or the like. The very concept of value therefore contains the concept of a valuer, actual or potential.

The experience of valuing something can be beneficial, as in the case of appreciating the aesthetic value in a work of art. But the concept of value, in positing a potential valuer, doesn't necessarily require that he would benefit from the experience. Things can be venerable, for example, whether or not there is any benefit in venerating them; and they can be awesome whether or not one would gain by holding them in awe. So the fact that value must be capable of registering with someone, who would thus appreciate it, does not mean that it must be capable of accruing to someone, who would thus gain by it. Value requires a potential valuer but not a potential beneficiary.

In fact, our appreciation of values that are relative to the interest of a beneficiary may depend on a prior appreciation of a value that is not relational in this sense. This dependence emerges when we try to explicate the concept of interest-relative value, or what is good for a person.

The concept of what is good for a person turns out to be fairly resistant to explication. We might initially think to equate what's good for a person with whatever would be rational for him to care about. But this equation would end up implying that all rational concerns are self-interested, by definition. In order to allow for the possibility of rational selflessness, we have to acknowledge that not everything that would be rational for someone to care about is necessarily in his interest.

Various philosophers have therefore attempted to define what's good for a person as a proper subset of the things that would be rational for him to care about, such as the subset including only those things which require his existence. It may or may not be a drawback in these definitions that they would exclude from a person's good such things as posthumous fame. In any case, these definitions are still too inclusive, since the things involving a person's existence that are rational for him to care about include, for example, particular sacrifices that he can make for other people.

The only convincing analysis of a person's good, to my knowledge, is one recently proposed by Stephen Darwall, who argues that what's good for a person is what's rational to want *for his sake*.[5] 'For the sake of' is a phrase that marks the subordination of one concern to another: to care about one thing for the sake of something else is to care about the former out of concern for the latter. To want something for the sake of a person is thus to want it out of concern for the person himself. Darwall's analysis says that a person's good is what would be rational to want out of concern for that person.

Darwall argues—convincingly, to my mind— that a person's good is a rational object of desire

[3]See Peter Railton, "Facts and Values," *Philosophical Topics* 14 (1986): 5–31.

[4]See Elizabeth Anderson, *Value in Ethics and Economics* (Cambridge, Mass.: Harvard University Press, 1993).

[5]Stephen Darwall, "Self-Interest and Self-Concern," *Social Philosophy and Policy* 14 (1997): 158–78, reprinted in *Self-Interest*, ed. Ellen Paul (Cambridge: Cambridge University Press, 1997). This article is also the source for my statement of the problem in the preceding section.

for anyone who cares about that person. By the same token, he argues that even the person himself is rationally obliged to care about his good only insofar as he cares about the person whose good it is—that is, himself.[6]

Think here of the familiar connection between how you feel about yourself and how you feel about your good. Sometimes when you realize that you have done something mean spirited or shameful, you come to feel worthless as a person; you may even hate yourself; and one symptom of self-hatred is a loss of concern for your own welfare. It no longer seems to matter whether life treats you well or badly, because you yourself seem to be no good. Your desire for your good thus depends on your concern for yourself—and rationally so, according to Darwall's analysis.

Note that self-loathing isn't the feeling that you are worthless *to* yourself. Indeed, the value that things afford to you is precisely what no longer seems to matter, and so your having no value for yourself wouldn't seem to matter, either. The reason why value accruing to you no longer seems to matter, however, is just that *you* don't seem to matter, period. You have lost your appreciation for the value that things have in relation to your interest because you have lost a sense of embodying value in yourself.

Now, things could still be good for you, in Darwall's analysis, even if you didn't embody any value; since they could still be such as *would* be rational for someone to want *if* he cared about you, however baseless the latter concern might be. But things that were good for you would not actually merit concern unless you merited concern; and if you didn't, then despite their being good for you, they wouldn't ultimately be worth wanting, after all. As I put it a moment ago, what's good for you wouldn't matter if you didn't matter.

This account of a person's good therefore implies—rightly, again, in my opinion—that what's good for a person is not a categorical value, any more than what's good for a purpose. What's good for a purpose is worth caring about only out of concern for the purpose, and hence only insofar as the purpose is worth caring about. Similarly, what's good for a person

is worth caring about only out of concern for the person, and hence only insofar as he is worth caring about. A person's good has only hypothetical or conditional value, which depends on the value of the person himself.[7]

Of course, we assume that a person's good does matter. But we make this assumption only because we assume that people matter—that everyone has a value that makes him worth caring about. Darwall's analysis of a person's good reveals how our appreciation of value that accrues to someone depends on a prior appreciation of a value inhering in him.

The latter value cannot be relative to personal interests, on pain of setting off a problematic regress. If this value were relative to someone's interest, then it would matter only to the same extent as that beneficiary. This regress of values would continue until it reached a value that was not relative to anyone's interest and that consequently mattered for its own sake. In fact, however, the regress never gets started, because we assume that every person already matters for his own sake, because of embodying an interest-independent value.

A value of this kind, which a person has *in* himself but not *for* anyone, is the basis of Kantian moral theory. Kant's term for this value is 'dignity', and he attributes dignity to all persons in virtue of their rational nature. What morality requires of us, according to Kant, is that we respect the dignity of persons.[8]

The dignity of a person is a value that differs in kind from his interest. Unlike his interest, for example, his dignity is a value on which his opinion carries no more weight than anyone else's. Because this value does not accrue to him, he is in no better position to judge it than others.

Similarly, respect for a person's autonomy does not require deference to him on questions of his dignity, as it does on questions of his good. On the contrary, respect for a person's

---

[6]The points made here and in the following paragraph appear in Anderson, p. 26.

[7]This point, too, is made by Anderson.

[8]Here I am making a leap that requires more justification than I can provide in the present context. I am equating the value that we appreciate in caring about a person with the value that we appreciate, somewhat differently, in respecting that person in the Kantian sense. I defend this equation in "Love as a Moral Emotion," *Ethics* 109 (1999): 338–74.

autonomy just is an appreciation of a value in him that amounts to a dignity, in Kant's sense of the term, precisely because it commands respect. If a person denies embodying such a value, he can hardly claim that we should defer to him out of an appreciation for a value such as he denies. He cannot claim, in other words, that out of respect for his autonomy we should defer to his judgment that he possesses nothing worthy of our respect.

Nor is it paternalistic to challenge a person's judgment about his dignity, as it is in the case of his good. Challenging a person's judgment about his good is objectionable because it undermines his role as the agent of his own affairs; but his value as a person is not just his affair. Although his good is a value that accrues to him alone, in the first instance, his value as a person inheres in him among other persons. It's a value that he possesses by virtue of being one of us, and the value of being one of us is not his alone to assess or defend. The value of being a person is therefore something larger than any particular person who embodies it.

That's what I miss in so many discussions of euthanasia and assisted suicide: a sense of something in each of us that is larger than any of us, something that makes human life more than just an exchange of costs for benefits, more than just a job or a trip to the mall. I miss the sense of a value in us that makes a claim on us—a value that we must *live up to*.

I don't deny that there are circumstances under which it would be better for one's life to end and permissible to hasten its ending. What I deny is that one may end one's life simply because one isn't getting enough *out* of it. One has to consider whether one is doing justice *to* it.

If a person possesses no value that he must live up to, or do justice to, then his life becomes a mere instrument, to be used or discarded according to whether it serves his interest. His moral claim to his own life then looks something like this:

[A] patient's right to life includes a right not to be killed. But that right gives [him] a protected option whether to live or die, an option with which others cannot legitimately interfere; it does not give [him] a duty to live. If a patient decides to die, he is waiving his right to live. By waiving his right, he releases others (perhaps a specific other person) from a duty not to kill him.

This can't be right. It portrays morality as protecting a person's options without protecting the person himself, except insofar as his own existence is one of his options. Surely, however, options are worth protecting, not for their own sake, but for the sake of the person whose options they are. So how can morality treat the person as worth protecting only for the sake of protecting one of his options? If he doesn't already merit protection, how can they?

The quotation above is drawn from a recent essay by Frances Kamm, who goes on to answer Kantian objections as follows:[9]

Suppose life involves such unbearable pain that one's whole life is focused on that pain. In such circumstances, one could, I believe, decline the honor of being a person. . . . We might acknowledge the great (and normally overriding) value of being a person . . . [and yet] allow that some bad conditions may overshadow its very great value.

Here Kamm is claiming that someone can view life as a mere option even while accepting the Kantian view of his value as a person. The problem with this passage is that it misstates the Kantian view.

When Kamm says that the value of a person normally "overrides" the value of other goods, but can be "overshadowed" by conditions that are exceptionally bad, she implies that it can be balanced against the person's interest. And when she goes on to speak of this value as an "honor" that the person can decline, she implies that it is actually part of a person's interest, since an honor accrues to a particular person, whose role as its beneficiary entitles him to accept or decline it.

But the dignity of a person isn't something that he can accept or decline, since it isn't a value *for* him; it's a value *in* him, which he can only violate or respect. Nor can it be weighed against what is good or bad for the person. As I have argued, value *for* a person stands to value *in* the person roughly as the value of means stands to that of the end: in each case, the former merits concern only on the basis of concern for the latter. And conditional values cannot be weighed against

[9]Frances Kamm, "A Right to Choose Death?" *Boston Review* 22 (1997): 20–23.

the unconditional values on which they depend. The value of means to an end cannot overshadow or be overshadowed by the value of the end, because it already is only a shadow of that value, in the sense of being dependent upon it. Similarly, the value of what's good for a person is only a shadow of the value inhering in the person, and cannot overshadow or be overshadowed by it.

These are abstract considerations, but they are concretely illustrated by the story with which I began. When my host claimed that he benefited more from the pleasures of smoking than he would be harmed by an early death, my first thought was that he had failed to consider harms and benefits to people other than himself. On second thought, however, I resented his assumption that harms and benefits were the only values at stake.

My host's remarks implied that an early death, of the sort he was risking and I was hoping to forestall, would be a loss to him that could be offset by sufficient gains. But what would it matter how much I lost or gained if I myself would be no loss? My gains or losses would merit concern only on the basis of concern for me—which, being the basis of concern for them, could not then be offset by that concern. Hence my gains or losses wouldn't matter unless I had a value that could not be offset by theirs.

My host was implicitly denying the existence of such a value. For he claimed that death was worth worrying about only in respects for which he could be compensated by the pleasures of smoking. He was thus implicitly denying the interest-independent value of a person, without which it couldn't really matter whether I lived or died.

Of course, he was denying the existence of this value in his own case, not in mine; but our cases were indistinguishable on this score. By implicitly denying his own interest-independent value, my host was somehow trivializing or denigrating himself as a person. Sometimes people's self-denigrating remarks just embarrass us, but in other instances they can be sufficiently principled to give offense. Recall my earlier reference to anti-Semitism. Anti-Semitism can manifest itself in self-denigrating remarks, if it is the anti-Semitism of a self-hating Jew. My host's disregard for his own value as a person offended me as another person, just as someone's denigrating himself as a Jew would offend me as another Jew.

I think Kant was right to say that trading one's person in exchange for benefits, or relief from harms, denigrates the value of personhood, respect for which is a criterion of morality (Kant would say, *the* criterion). That's why I think that smoking is a vice—at least, when practiced for the reasons offered by my host. It's also why I think that suicide is immoral when committed on the grounds that life isn't worth living.

Mind you, I don't go around snatching cigarettes out of people's mouths. And I'm not sure that I would forcibly try to stop someone from committing suicide solely because it would be immorally self-destructive. The impermissibility of someone else's conduct doesn't necessarily give me permission to interfere with it. By the same token, however, I think that encouraging or assisting others in impermissible conduct is itself impermissible. That's why I think that the tobacco industry is engaged in an immoral enterprise. And it's why I think the same of Dr. Kevorkian, who has done more than anyone to help people die by their own convictions.

Note that these moral judgments distinguish between self-destruction and mere self-harm. As I have said, I believe that people are sometimes entitled to act on mistaken judgments about their own interest; and to this extent, at least, they are entitled to harm themselves. But the behaviors that I have criticized don't merely damage the agents interests at all, if the agents are right about the costs and benefits involved. These behaviors are to be criticized, in my view, because they are premised on a disregard for the value of the agents themselves.

The same criticism would apply, for example, to agents who put up their own freedom as collateral in order to obtain loans. People have no right to sell themselves into slavery, no matter what their convictions, but the reason is not that they would thereby be harming themselves; the reason is that they would be violating their own personhood.

These moral judgments depend, of course, on my belief that a person has an interest-independent value; and they may consequently seem to impose my Kantian values even on people who don't believe in them. Don't people have the right to live and die by their own convictions as to the value of their lives?

If the question is whether people are morally permitted to end their existence solely because they find it unrewarding, then I have already answered in the negative, on the grounds that they would then be violating their own interest-independent value as persons. But of course the present question is meant to be taken differently, as suggesting that we defer to people's judgments about whether they have an interest-independent value, in the first place. Under this interpretation, the question is not whether people are permitted to violate their own dignity but whether they are entitled to be believed when they insist that they have none. I have answered in the negative to this latter version of the question as well. The reasons for deferring to people about values relative to their interests do not apply in the case of interest-independent value.

This answer may seem to beg the question, since it presupposes the existence of the very interest-independent value that is at issue. What I have now argued, however, is that we cannot avoid presupposing the existence of this value anyway, since it's needed to account for the importance of interest-relative values. We cannot justify someone's death on the grounds that it's good for him, while also denying the existence of another value, embodied in him. For if he were himself a cipher, evaluatively speaking, then what's good for him would be, in the same manner of speaking, good for nothing.

I admit that talk of someone's value as a person sounds like religion rather than philosophy. Such talk is a secular version of religious talk about the sanctity of human life.

Historically speaking, however, most moral discourse has religious sources. The question for secular ethics is whether we can rationally accept the values bequeathed to us by religion while being skeptical of their theological basis. A question that's equally pressing, though less widely acknowledged, is whether we can selectively accept some of these values while discarding others. My view is that our values will be incoherent so long as they lack a counterpart to the sanctity of human life.

This view will immediately seem to entail reactionary consequences, such as a rejection of euthanasia and abortion in any form. But a secular value that corresponds to the sanctity of human life needn't be exactly the same value or yield exactly the same consequences. In particular, it need not attach to biological life or biological humanity per se; and so it needn't rule out abortion, for example, simply because the fetus is both alive and human. What secular morality must regard as sacrosanct, I have suggested, is not the human organism but the person, and a fetus may embody one but not the other.

Recognizing the interest-independent value of a person wouldn't necessarily rule out euthanasia or suicide, either. On the contrary, recognizing such a value is essential to one familiar argument in favor of these practices—namely, the argument for dying with dignity.

The idea that dignity can justify a person's death may seem incompatible with the Kantian conception of dignity as a value inhering in the person. Wouldn't a person's value always militate in favor of saving his life?

This apparent conflict is due, however, to a confusion about the normative implications of dignity. Dignity is what Kant called a "self-existent" value—a value to which we are obliged to respond only when it already exists, and then only by paying it reverence or respect. The value of persons does not oblige us to maximize the number of people in existence; it obliges us only to respect the people who do exist. And respecting these people is not necessarily a matter of keeping them in existence; it is rather a matter of treating them in the way that is required by their personhood—whatever way that is.[10]

The Kantian objection to suicide, then, is not that it destroys something of value. The objection is not even to suicide per se, but to suicide committed for a particular kind of reason—that is, in order to obtain benefits or escape harms. And the objection to suicide committed for this reason is that it denigrates the person's dignity, by trading his person for interest-relative goods, as if it were one of them. This interpretation of the objection to suicide leaves open the

[10]The interpretation of Kant expressed in this paragraph is not uncontroversial. I defend it at length in "Love as a Moral Emotion."

possibility that a person's dignity may justify suicide in other contexts, if suicide would constitute an appropriate expression of respect for one's person. Kantianism would then be able to endorse the notion of dying with dignity.[11]

Actually, the phrase 'dying with dignity' is potentially misleading. We don't think that a person's death is morally acceptable so long as he can carry it off with dignity. Rather, we think that a person's death is acceptable if he can no longer live with dignity. The operative concept is undignified life, not dignified death.

When a person cannot sustain both life and dignity, his death may indeed be morally justified. One is sometimes permitted, even obligated, to destroy objects of dignity if they would otherwise deteriorate in ways that would offend against that value. The moral obligation to bury or burn a corpse, for example, is an obligation not to let it become an affront to what it once was. Librarians have similar practices for destroying tattered books—and honor guards, for destroying tattered flags—out of respect for the dignity inherent in these objects.

Of course, the value inhering in mere things, such as books or flags, must be different from that inhering in persons by virtue of their rational nature. But all of these values belong together as a class, the class of dignity values, whose defining characteristic is that they call for reverence or respect.[12]

These examples suggest that dignity can require not only the preservation of what possesses it but also the destruction of what is losing it, if the loss would be irretrievable.[13]

Dignity, unlike well-being, does not come in degrees that we are obliged to maximize; as we have seen, it is not a value whose existence we are obliged to promote at all. To treat a dignity value as capable of degrees, all of them worth preserving, would be to treat it like an ordinary good—which would in fact be disrespectful. Respect for an object of dignity can sometimes require its destruction.

The question, then, is what constitutes the loss of dignity for a person. The dignity in question has nothing to do with being dignified, with keeping up appearances, or with sustaining any particular social status. It has nothing to do with what people ought to admire or esteem in one another, or with what they actually respect. It is rather what they ought to respect, in the way that they can manifest only by treating one another morally. According to Kant, what people ought to respect in this way is one another's rational nature.

Ironically, Kant's view is borne out by Kamm's example, in which "life involves such unbearable pain that one's whole life is focused on that pain." Kamm assumes that this case invites us to weigh the disvalue of pain against the value of being a rational agent. In fact, however, Kamm has described a case in which pain is more than painful, since it not only hurts the patient but also becomes the sole focus of his life. Pain that tyrannizes the patient in this fashion undermines his rational agency, by preventing him from choosing any ends for himself other than relief. It reduces the patient to the psychological hedonist's image of a person—a pleasure-seeking, pain-fleeing animal—which is undignified indeed. And Kamm is clearly envisioning that this severely reduced condition of the patient can be ended only by his death.

I suspect, then, that if euthanasia seems justified in Kamm's example, the reason is not that relieving the patient's pain is more important

---

[11]For a Kantian argument along these lines, see Thomas E. Hill, Jr., "Self-Regarding Suicide: A Modified Kantian View," in his *Autonomy and Self-Respect* (Cambridge: Cambridge University Press, 1991), pp. 85–103.

[12]Actually, I am inclined to think that the dignity of books or flags is borrowed from the dignity of personhood; but this question is beyond the scope of the present article.

[13]I believe that this feature of dignity values explains why the permissibility of euthanasia and assisted suicide is limited mainly to cases of terminal illness. Felicia Ackerman has recently claimed that such a restricted permission is unstable ("Assisted Suicide, Terminal Illness, Severe Disability, and the Double Standard," in *Physician-Assisted Suicide: Expanding the Debate*, ed. M. Pabst Battin et al. [New York: Routledge, 1998], pp. 149–61). She argues that assistance in dying must be permissible either for all competent adults or

for none. I agree with Ackerman that the arguments usually offered in favor of assistance in dying cannot be restricted to cases of terminal illness, although their proponents often adopt that restriction anyway, without justification. As Ackerman shows, e.g., the arguments of "The Philosophers' Brief" support assisted suicide for everyone if they support it for anyone. But I think that the Kantian view can justify the restriction and that its ability to do so counts in its favor.

than his dignity as a person; the reason is rather that pain has already undermined the patient's dignity, and irretrievably so. The example thus supports dying for the sake of dignity, not for the sake of self-interest.

I often wonder whether proponents of assisted suicide don't overstate the moral significance of pain. Pain is a bad thing, of course, but I doubt whether it can justify anything close to euthanasia or suicide unless it is (as Kamm calls it) unbearable. And then what justifies death is the unbearableness of the pain rather than the painfulness.

What do we mean in calling pain unbearable? What is it *not to bear* pain? It certainly isn't a matter of refusing to feel the pain, of shutting one's eyes to it, as one might to an unbearable sight, or of walking away from it, as one might from an unbearable situation. Not to bear pain is somehow to fall apart in the face of it, to disintegrate as a person. To find pain unbearable is to find it thus destructive not just of one's well-being but of oneself.

But then we make a mistake if we describe the patient in unbearable pain as if he were his rational old self, weighing the harm of pain against the benefits of existence. If his pain is truly unbearable, then he isn't his rational self any longer: he is falling apart in pain. Even if he enjoys some moments of relief and clarity, he is still falling apart diachronically, a temporally scattered person at best.

I don't think that we serve the patient well, in these circumstances, by claiming broad rights of self-determination in his name. He may indeed be entitled to help in dying, and he will certainly have to participate in the relevant decisions. But let us keep in mind that these decisions would be premature if the patient were not already in the twilight of his autonomy, where self-determination is more of a shadowy presumption than a clear fact.

I do not know how to frame a public policy or law that would distinguish between the cases in which I think that euthanasia or suicide is morally permissible and the cases in which I think it is not. Of course, the law would not have to follow the moral vicissitudes of the practice so closely if they were covered by a right of self-determination. If there were a broad class of cases in which the patient had the right to decide for himself whether death was justified, then we could legalize euthanasia or assisted suicide in those cases, even though it might not be justified in all of them. If a patient then opted for death when it wasn't justified, he would still be acting within his rights, which the law would have been justified in protecting.

But I do not believe that a person has the right, in general, to choose between life and death; nor do I believe that a person's rights suddenly expand when he becomes terminally ill. So I don't see how a case for legalization can be founded on rights of self-determination, and I am once again faced with the difficulty of legalizing death for the sake of dignity without also legalizing it for the sake of self-interest.

I certainly don't think that the law should forbid activities simply because they have the potential of being self-destructive in some circumstances. I don't think that mountain climbing should be outlawed—or smoking, for that matter. The problem is that killing, unlike mountain climbing or smoking, impinges on the dignity of persons essentially and not just in some unfortunate circumstances or cases. The result is that the law on killing, like the law on slavery, unavoidably expresses our collective valuation of personhood itself.

Supporters of euthanasia and assisted suicide sometimes liken them to the other intrinsically injurious treatments to which a patient may consent for his greater good—the cutting and stabbing and drugging and poisoning that are the physician's stock in trade. Then they ask: what's so special about killing?[14] Isn't killing just another medical intervention to which a patient should be allowed to submit when it serves his interest?

My inclination is to answer this question with another: what's so special about slavery? Isn't enslavement just another cost that a person should be allowed to risk in pursuit of his interests?

[14]Kamm asks this question in sec. 4 of "A Right to Choose Death?"

Surely, there is something special about slavery. Though we may indeed have a right to live and die in light of our own convictions, it doesn't extend to convictions about the price for which our freedom would be worth selling. Nor does it extend, in my view, to convictions about the price for which our lives would be worth ending.

Discussion Questions

1. Should assisted suicide be illegal? Why or why not?
2. Is active euthanasia incompatible with the dignity of persons?
3. What is "death with dignity"?
4. Might one have a duty to die? What would Velleman say?

CHAPTER 10

Capital Punishment

HARD QUESTION: WHAT IS CRUEL AND UNUSUAL PUNISHMENT?

"Excessive bail shall not be required, nor excessive fines imposed, nor cruel and unusual punishments inflicted."

—Article VIII, Constitution of the United States of America, 1787

"That excessive bail ought not to be required, nor excessive fines imposed, nor cruel and unusual punishments inflicted."

—English Bill of Rights, 1689

People have long opposed cruel and unusual punishment; indeed, it is hard to see how anyone could approve of a punishment with that description. But what counts as cruel and unusual punishment? Clearly, standards change on this matter because judicial punishment in seventeenth- and eighteenth-century America and England allowed for whipping, branding, scalding, pillorying, drawing and quartering, burning at the stake, dunking, pressing, hanging, disemboweling, and other forms of ghastly corporal punishment that would shock and deeply offend modern sensibility.

Before we consider whether capital punishment is or is not cruel and unusual, we should spend some time reflecting on what it means to say that a form of punishment is cruel and unusual. In the abstract, a cruel punishment would be one that is somehow excessive, one that imposes more suffering than is warranted to achieve its end. Conceptually, punishment requires intentionally imposing something undesirable or evil on an offender with the aim of rehabilitation, deterrence, or retribution. A great deal more can be said about the ends of punishment, but any punishment that imposes more evil than necessary to achieve its end is excessive and therefore cruel, because the "extra" evil is pointless. Pointlessly imposing evil on someone, typically pain and suffering, is what it means to be cruel. Inflicting physical pain is not necessary for punishment; loss of freedom, loss of money, loss of public standing—theoretically, anything bad or undesirable—can be the evil imposed for purposes of punishment.

It seems, too, that a punishment can be cruel even if it is not excessive. A punishment that effectively achieves its ends might still be cruel if it is incompatible with human dignity. Suppose people had their heads shaved or were spanked for parking violations. That might effectively achieve whatever goals of punishment we have in mind, but the humiliation involved is cruel. More significantly, branding, torturing, or beheading people for especially heinous crimes might effectively achieve deterrence or retribution, but that would be shockingly cruel nonetheless, because those forms of punishment are incompatible with human dignity—something we must not sink to in punishment, for our sake as well as for the sake of the offender.

Perhaps such bizarre punishments would count as unusual instead of cruel. In this context, *unusual* cannot mean just infrequently used, for otherwise we could avoid the charge simply by using the type of punishment at issue more frequently. *Unusual* refers most plausibly to the kind of punishment, the relationship between the crime and the punishment, and the manner in which the punishment is imposed. If it is imposed on convicted criminals arbitrarily, for example (some getting it and others not, for no good reason), that would probably make it unusual. It might also make it cruel because it is unfairly imposed.

What about capital punishment? Is it cruel and unusual and therefore unconstitutional? We must remember that constitutionality is one question, morality another; capital punishment could be constitutional and still immoral, or it could be morally permissible and still unconstitutional. So settling its constitutionality does not settle its morality. But looking at debates about the constitutionality of capital punishment is a good place to begin.

In the 1970s capital punishment came under intense legal scrutiny in a series of landmark cases. *Furman v. Georgia* (1972) was particularly significant because the U.S. Supreme Court found capital punishment, at least as it was administered at the time, to be cruel and unusual, thus halting executions nationwide. Apparently, sentencing guidelines were so vague that the death penalty was being imposed in an "arbitrary and capricious" manner. This prompted many states to revise their death penalty procedures. Then, in *Gregg v. Georgia* (1976), the Court reversed itself and declared capital punishment to be constitutional provided that certain guidelines were followed in sentencing people to death.

Of particular interest to us is Justice Brennan's philosophically rich opinion in *Furman*, where he proposed a test to determine whether a form of punishment is cruel and unusual. A punishment, he claimed, is cruel and unusual "if it does not comport with human dignity." Torture, for example, clearly violates the "primary principle" that "a punishment must not by its severity be degrading to human dignity." More specifically, Brennan maintained,

If a punishment is unusually severe, if there is a strong probability that it is inflicted arbitrarily, if it is substantially rejected by contemporary society, and if there is no reason to believe that it serves any penal purpose more effectively than some less severe punishment, then the continued infliction of that punishment violates the command of the clause that the State may not inflict inhuman and uncivilized punishments upon those convicted of crimes.

Capital punishment, Brennan argued, violates all of those conditions, which makes it cruel and unusual and therefore an unconstitutional form of punishment. Let's consider each condition more closely: unusual severity, arbitrary infliction, social unacceptability, not uniquely effective as a penal method.

1. Is capital punishment unusually severe? Capital punishment is *supposed* to be unusually severe; it is by definition the most severe punishment that we may legally impose. Obviously more severe punishments are possible, but they would not pass constitutional review. According to Brennan, capital punishment is "unusual in its pain, in its finality, and in its enormity. No other existing punishment is comparable to death in terms of physical and mental suffering." Since painless death is theoretically possible, executions do not have to be painful. Death, not pain before death, is the punishment. Methods of execution should therefore be as humane as possible. Before lethal injection became the standard method of execution, electric chairs sometimes caused great suffering, especially when they did not work properly, as occasionally happened. There is now considerable controversy about how much suffering lethal injection causes. The dark art of execution will always have practical problems in killing people, but unless pain before death becomes a declared part of the punishment—something difficult to justify morally or constitutionally—painless execution should be the goal.

Mental anguish while waiting to be executed must be excruciating, but perhaps that varies from case to case. The mental anguish of those on death row might be less than the anguish of those who spend their life in prison, though again, that can vary from case to case. So Brennan's observations about the mental and physical suffering caused by executing people do not count decisively against the practice.

Brennan is obviously correct to note that the death penalty is unusual in its finality and enormity. Other legal punishments do not come close. The death penalty truly "is in a class by itself." But this is not clearly an objection, because again, capital punishment (conceptually distinct from the death penalty) is just the most severe punishment judicially available. The finality of the death penalty, however, should give pause, because mistakes are possible, and innocent people can be (indeed, have been) executed. The State can at least try to compensate people wrongly imprisoned; no compensation is possible for innocent people wrongly executed. This is a real worry, not one to be blithely offset by whatever advantages the death penalty has, since it is hard to imagine a greater injustice done by the State.

2. Is the death penalty arbitrarily inflicted? Brennan argued that its infrequent use (some 50 executions per year for over 4000 death-penalty-eligible murderers) strongly suggests that it is being arbitrarily imposed (out of over approximately 22,000 criminal homicides each year). Since it is extremely unlikely that the convicted criminals actually executed are truly the worst of the worst, the death penalty does appear to be arbitrarily imposed on those who suffer it. We could, of course, execute more death-penalty-eligible criminals than we do now; we could kill thousands per year. Would we tolerate that?

It would be interesting to compare data for other serious crimes, such as rape or armed robbery, to see whether a similar gap obtains between conviction rates and punishment. It could turn out that even if capital punishment is arbitrarily imposed on convicted criminals, it is no more arbitrarily imposed than other forms of punishment. This would have to be a tricky comparison, since the death penalty does not come in degrees where as other criminals can receive more or less sentences, but it should still be possible somehow to assess the extent to which punishment is arbitrarily imposed for noncapital offenses.

3. Is the death penalty socially unacceptable? Brennan remarked that our understanding of cruel and unusual punishment "must draw its meaning from the evolving standards of decency that mark the progress of a maturing society." This begs the question against death penalty supporters, since it presupposes that progressively evolving standards of decency will come to condemn the death penalty. However, it is a striking fact that the United States is virtually alone among developed countries that still impose the death penalty. In any case, if something violates human dignity, as the death penalty is alleged to do, we should be able to argue directly for that claim independent of social awareness. Do we want to say that slavery did not violate human dignity until people thought it did? Social attitude about capital punishment is still a good point for Brennan to bring up, because it will be hard for the State to impose a form of punishment that is socially unacceptable. But might society think it is morally acceptable just because it is used? We have to wonder about the effect that capital punishment could have on our attitudes toward it. Currently, only about 52 percent of U.S. citizens support the death penalty. (See the Death Penalty Information Center at www.deathpenaltyinfo.org for lots of facts and information about the death penalty.)

4. Last, does the death penalty serve "any penal purpose more effectively than some less severe punishment"? We will consider the purposes of punishment in more detail below, but the issue is crucial. Capital punishment must be shown to be uniquely effective in achieving its ends, for if those same ends can be achieved with a less severe punishment, such as life in prison, then capital punishment is excessive. What ends might capital punishment serve? Death penalty advocates typically claim that it deters others from committing similar crimes and that it is just retribution for evil acts. As Brennan deftly notes, "the question, however, is not whether death serves these supposed purposes of punishment, but whether death serves them more effectively than imprisonment." There is no evidence that it does.

There is a reasonable but not overwhelming case that capital punishment is unconstitutional because it is cruel and unusual. However, as other justices have noted, the Constitution does not explicitly rule out capital punishment, which was an acceptable form of punishment when the Constitution was drafted. More important than its constitutionality is the question of whether capital punishment is immoral. Here we must turn to moral philosophy.

THEORIES OF PUNISHMENT

Since punishment of any sort intentionally inflicts harm, it must be justified, because intentionally harming someone must be justified. Theories of punishment try to justify that harm; they are not sociological or psychological but moral theories, purporting to explain how offenders ought to be treated. (We will focus on judicial punishment, not punishment meted out by parents on their children or by teachers on their students.) There are two basic types of moral theories of punishment: forward-looking and backward-looking. Forward-looking theories, which are broadly utilitarian because they look forward to the consequences of punishment, justify harming criminals on grounds of deterrence. People who otherwise might commit a similar offense now refrain from doing so because the offender has been made an example; the offender is also deterred from committing that crime again and, in this sense, is rehabilitated. It is thus no accident that prisons are called correctional facilities. That is where one goes to get corrected, at least in theory.

Does punishment deter? The data are open to debate and sociologists and criminologists debate them constantly. But worse, utilitarian theories of punishment are subject to serious objections even if, or especially if, punishment deters. Why, for example, should we punish only the guilty? Apart from Kantian worries about using people as a means of social control, why not punish the innocent if that will also deter crime? Actual guilt is not necessary for punishment to deter; presumed guilt will do just as well. To reply that punishing the innocent is bad policy because if the truth ever got out there would be even bigger problems might be true, but that is the wrong kind of reason why we shouldn't punish innocent people. We ordinarily think that punishing innocent people is wrong not because bigger problems will follow if it is detected, but because it is unjust. (As we saw in Chapter 2, utilitarianism has difficulties with justice.)

Here's another problem with forward-looking accounts of punishment: Why should punishment fit the crime? If punishment deters, more severe punishments should deter even better. Executing someone for a parking violation would deter a lot of people from parking illegally! Why not engage in horrendous punishments if they deter better than more humane punishments? Public executions, beheadings, torture—nothing is beyond the pale if we look only to the social consequences of punishment. Adverse public reactions to such brutal punishments would have to be weighed, but for forward-looking theories nothing is initially "off the table," because punishment is justified on the basis of its consequences alone.

Backward-looking, or retributive, theories justify punishment by referring to the past actions of the offender. Because the offender is morally responsible for his actions, he now *deserves* punishment. And punishment should vary according to the severity of the crime; more serious crimes deserve more severe punishments. In this way, retributive accounts of punishment seek to fit the punishment to the crime. This is the ancient doctrine of *lex talionis* (Latin for "law of retaliation"), an eye for an eye, a tooth for a tooth, whereby punishment exacts from an offender precisely what was taken from an innocent victim. This is why death can seem to be the naturally appropriate punishment for murder.

A moment's reflection shows, however, that *lex talionis* is deeply flawed, since we cannot rape rapists or hijack hijackers or embezzle from embezzlers. And what do we do to serial murderers? If we try to proportion punishment exactly to crime, we will find ourselves doing the same ghastly, inhumane things to criminals that they did to their victims. If we say instead that the most serious crimes deserve the most serious punishments, then we still have to determine what the most serious punishment should be. It is not obvious that the *capital* punishment should be death; maybe it should be life in prison.

Because purely retributive accounts of punishment focus only on what offenders deserve, not on the social utility of punishment, they also have to explain why the State should be in the business of making criminals suffer by punishing them. If the State's obligation is only to protect its citizens, then unless causing criminals to suffer protects citizens by reforming criminals or by deterring potential criminals, the state has no special reason to give criminals what they deserve.

Worse still is the possibility that certain forms of punishment, such as the death penalty, might actually cause more crime. Perhaps capital punishment brutalizes society, or maybe unstable people will seek the notoriety that inevitably surrounds capital cases, spawning "copycat" crimes. If that possibility is ever shown to be true, then retributive accounts of punishment, and the death penalty in particular, would be perversely self-defeating, for giving criminals "what they deserve" creates more criminals.

This objection applies to forward-looking justifications of capital punishment too, but those theories can easily abandon capital punishment if the social consequences are bad, whereas purely backward-looking reasons are blind to future consequences. Hence a plausible retributive account of capital punishment (or punishment in general) cannot be purely backward-looking; forward-looking considerations will always be relevant for any sensible account of punishment. Perhaps best is some sort of mixed view that combines forward- and backward-looking considerations in a theoretically insightful manner.

Our readings explore the interplay between forward- and backward-looking reasons for and against capital punishment.

READINGS ON CAPITAL PUNISHMENT

Hugo Adam Bedau, "An Abolitionist's Survey of the Death Penalty in America Today"

Professor Bedau taught philosophy for many years at Tufts University. Through a widely influential series of books and articles, Bedau has established his reputation as one of the nation's leading opponents of the death penalty. The article reprinted here is, as the title suggests, a survey of the death penalty in America. In addition to interesting facts about the death penalty, Bedau offers what "I [Bedau] now think is the best argument against the death penalty." This argument turns on the "Minimal Invasion principle," the idea that "invasions by the government of an individual's privacy, liberty, and autonomy are justified only if no less invasive practice is sufficient to achieve an important social good." The death penalty, Bedau argues, violates that principle.

Critical Reading Questions

1. What reforms in the history of the death penalty in America does Bedau list?
2. How, according to Bedau, might reforms in sentencing and executing criminals entrench the death penalty?
3. How is the "Minimal Invasion" argument against the death penalty unlike most arguments against the death penalty?
4. How does Bedau support each premise in the Minimal Invasion argument?
5. What does Bedau say in response to the claim that the death penalty deters?
6. What does Bedau say in response to the claim that murderers deserve to die?
7. What does Bedau say about the execution of Timothy McVeigh?

AN ABOLITIONIST'S SURVEY OF THE DEATH PENALTY IN AMERICA TODAY

Hugo Adam Bedau

Lest there be any doubt in the reader's mind, let me declare at the outset that I strongly oppose the death penalty no matter what the crime or the criminal. This will be evident enough later as this essay unfolds and especially when I offer an argument against capital punishment. My position to the side, perhaps the best place to begin this discussion of the death penalty in America and the controversies it has provoked is by summarizing its history in our country. That history is largely a story of efforts to limit and abolish it.

I

The first European colonist whose execution on these shores has been recorded is George Kendall, in Virginia's Jamestown colony. He was hanged in 1608 for the crime of "spying for the Spanish." In the subsequent four centuries an uncounted number—perhaps twenty thousand or more—of convicted murderers, rapists, horse thieves, spies, witches, and kidnappers, among others, have met a similar fate. No one should be surprised that the colonists embraced the death penalty (along with other corporal punishments, such as flogging, branding, and the pillory); the Mother Country itself put extensive reliance on such punishments to control an unruly public.

During the Revolutionary era, historian Louis Masur tells us, "a diverse group of Americans considered the death penalty morally and politically repugnant." So they did. Benjamin Rush of Philadelphia—physician, friend of Benjamin Franklin, and one of the Founding Fathers—was second to none as an outspoken opponent of the hangman. In 1797 he published a lecture attacking public executions under the title "Considerations on the Injustice and Impolicy of Punishing Murder by Death"; printed as a pamphlet, it was widely circulated. Rush argued that "The Punishment of Murder by Death is contrary to *reason,* and to the order and happiness of society [as well as] contrary to divine revelation." Rush's lectures and essays mark the beginning of the abolition movement in this country. During the next century and a half—roughly from the 1780s to the 1950s—several developments in the law affecting the death penalty were pioneered in various state legislatures or, in more recent decades, decreed by the Supreme Court. . . .

II

What lessons can be learned from this brief history? Contemplating the record, some extremist friends of the death penalty are bound to feel frustrated and discouraged. Just look at what they are denied! Nasty and protracted methods of carrying out the death penalty. Mandatory death penalties for murder. A wide variety of nonhomicidal capital crimes. Infliction of the death penalty in public for all to see. Capital punishment flanked by other lawful modes of corporal punishment. Using a method of execution more appropriate than lethal injection to the brutality and horror of the crime. Swift execution after conviction and sentencing, without procedural delays at both the state and federal levels.

The changes wrought by these developments show that the death penalty in America today is but a shadow of its former self; abolitionists are not the only ones likely to believe there is no serious prospect of breathing much life into the practice of capital punishment in the future. As historian Thomas Laqueur has remarked, "The death penalty as it is carried into practice today is like an endangered species brought back from the brink of extinction, a creature from an earlier age making its way in a very different time from when it ruled the earth." Thus it should not be surprising that when abolitionists look at this same record, they draw support from what they see and remain confident that it is just a matter of time before the death penalty in this country is completely abolished.

But is that true? One might equally well argue that the lesson to be drawn from history is rather this: *Each of these reforms has entrenched ever deeper what remains of the death penalty,* which makes what remains of it more resistant to complete repeal. Reform legislation does this by making those who are sentenced to death under its authority seem more deserving of such a penalty. Every step toward greater fairness in death penalty sentencing makes it just that much harder to dismantle what's left. For example, lethal injection surely qualifies as a humane way to put a human being to death. If so, then this method of carrying out lawful executions is all but immune from attack. Of all possible capital crimes, first-degree murder is at the head of everyone's list of crimes that "deserve" the death penalty. Repealing or allowing to fall into desuetude nonhomicidal capital statutes leaves the capital crime of murder standing virtually alone. Shielding from risk of the death penalty all offenders other than those convicted of first-degree murder effectively defines the class of those guilty of the worst crime and so deserving of the severest punishment. (The capital statutes enacted by Congress in the mid-1990s are, with very few exceptions, defined by reference to some form of homicide, e.g., killing a federal witness.) Allowing the death sentence to be issued not by a trial judge but by a fairly drawn panel of ordinary citizens with the discretionary power to sentence the offender to life in prison is democracy in action. Ending the execution of juveniles and of the mentally retarded (rejected by the Supreme Court in 2002) makes executing ordinary adults all the

more acceptable, despite evidence that "almost all murderers . . . studied show evidence of brain damage." Eliminating the racist aspects of the death penalty would do no more than make capital punishment an equal opportunity destroyer.

For the past few years, the abolition movement has devoted considerable energy to obtaining a nationwide moratorium on executions. The ostensible purpose has been to make possible a careful study of the practices and procedures governing the administration of the death penalty, with an eye to reducing the risk of error and introducing greater fairness throughout the system. So far the movement has succeeded only in one capital jurisdiction—Illinois—although it claims endorsement from nearly 2,000 organizations and half a hundred city and county jurisdictions. What is it reasonable to expect from the moratorium movement? For one thing, Illinois is unique in the nation in having more persons on death row exonerated in recent years than it has executed. No other state has such an incentive for reform. Second, the judicially imposed moratorium from 1967 through 1976 enabled the Supreme Court to evaluate the constitutional status of the death penalty and to support major changes in the administration of this punishment. But the moratorium had little or no effect in bringing the public closer to embracing abolition. Third, supporters of the death penalty tend to see the moratorium movement as a stalking horse for abolition. They argue that the proponents of the moratorium are not really interested in improving the administration of the death penalty. Most of the agitation to create a moratorium comes from those who are really interested in using it as a tactic to advance the cause of abolition, and so their efforts are really disingenuous. Finally and most troubling, a widespread moratorium might succeed—that is, end up by introducing various procedural reforms that would give an even more convincing seal of approval to whatever death sentences and executions were imposed under their aegis. (The same problem haunts the Innocence Protection Act, pending in Congress.) Only time will tell whether the friends or the opponents of the death penalty will be happier with the way the moratorium movement unfolds.

III

So much by way of history and its lessons. Let us turn now to look at the current death penalty in the context of our criminal justice system. What we need to see can be neatly described by means of the following set of seven numbers.

1. 22,000
2. 15,000
3. 13,500
4. 10,000
5. 2–4,000
6. 300
7. 55

Each of these numbers is an average annual estimate for the decade of the 1990s. The first is the number of *criminal homicides* reported by the FBI in its category of "murder and non-negligent manslaughter." In the past decade, something more than twenty thousand "murders and non-negligent manslaughters" were recorded each year by the nation's police forces. The second is the number of *arrests* reported by the police of persons charged with criminal homicide. Notice the attrition, from 22,000 to 15,000. (Criminal homicide has always had the highest arrest rate of any felony, yet that rate is only about 65 percent.) The third number estimates the volume of *homicide cases actually prosecuted,* which according to the FBI is about 90 percent of all those arrested for this crime. The fourth number is an estimate of the number of *homicide convictions,* again about two-thirds of those arrested and nearly three-fourths of those prosecuted. The fifth number—2–4,000—is a rough estimate of the so-called *death-eligible defendants,* that is, all and only the offenders convicted of first-degree murder who are at risk of a death sentence because their crime in a death penalty jurisdiction involved one or more "aggravating circumstances" on which the jury could decide to rest its decision to impose a death sentence. Here the attrition is considerable, a drop of about two-thirds of the remaining cases at the higher end of the rough estimate (80 percent at the lower end). The sixth number, the average of *death sentences* annually, is about one-tenth of the death-eligible defendants. In other words, nine out of ten convicted defendants who are death-eligible do not get sentenced to death. And the final number is the average number of *executions* per year. At this point the attrition is nothing short of remarkable: Out of more than twenty thousand criminal homicides per year (assuming roughly one victim for each offender), only 300 perpetrators are sentenced to death and only 55 are actually executed.

With these numbers before us, let us ask how they might be interpreted by friends and opponents of the death penalty.

The friends divide into two groups. The angrier and more vindictive see these figures and argue: We must reduce the number of those murdered, and the best way to do that is to use the death penalty more frequently, much more frequently. For of course there will be little or no special deterrent effect with such a tiny fraction of murderers executed—only one out of about 500. Likewise, we must protect society and express our horror at murder by executing as many of the death-eligible defendants as we can. The two aspects of prevention—individual incapacitation and general deterrence—require no less. And for the same reasons we must increase the number of arrests, the number prosecuted, the number convicted, and especially the number sentenced to death—now, only one out of about 70.

To put it bluntly, these desires are doomed to frustration. For a variety of reasons, the criminal justice system is not capable of making the kinds of changes these extreme friends of the death penalty would like. Only those with little or no familiarity with death penalty jurisprudence can hold out hopes for such a complete reversal of present practice. I note with satisfaction that Judge Kozinski himself has pointed this out in recent writings on the subject.

Those in the other group favoring the death penalty—I think it includes Judge Kozinski, Judge Cassell, and prosecutor Marquis—look at these numbers very differently. They argue: The death penalty was never intended to apply to *all* murderers, but only to the worst. What these numbers and their attrition show is that the criminal justice system is winnowing out the worst from the bad. Three hundred or so of the worst murderers are sentenced to death each year on average—that sounds about right. Half a hundred are executed on average each year—that, too, looks about right (give or take adding another dozen or so). And we know that these are the worst murderers because in every case since the mid-1970s the death sentence rests on the jury's having found one or more "aggravating" circumstances, as defined by statute, and no "mitigating" circumstances (or at least none weightier). Complacent defenders of the death penalty see little if any reason for introducing extensive or fundamental changes in the system; they recognize the insuperable obstacles to significant reduction in the attrition at each step of the way. Probably most defenders of the death penalty today in America hold views more or less like those portrayed here.

Death penalty supporters of this sort are also bound to be disappointed, if they confront political reality candidly. Absolutely essential to their argument is the belief that the system really does segregate the worst from the bad and that it does so in a manner that respects fundamental justice for the accused offender and the convicted prisoner. Yet no one acquainted with the facts can rest comfortably in such a belief. This is especially true where racial factors enter, as they typically do in the Death Belt firmly buckled across the South. On this subject I refer and defer again to my colleagues in this symposium, Bright and Stevenson. Here, I will add only three observations.

First, some states—Texas in particular—base a death sentence (to quote from the Texas statute) on the jury's decision that "the defendant would commit criminal acts of violence that would constitute a continuing threat to society." How a jury is able to make such a prediction, on which their choice of punishment depends, is a mystery. Making reliable predictions of future dangerousness is all but impossible, if we can believe several decades of social science research. (The late law professor Charles Black, Jr., made the difficulty of doing so abundantly clear a generation ago in his superb monograph, *Capital Punishment: The Inevitability of Caprice and Mistake* [1981]). And isn't the whole idea—punishing someone not for what he has done but for what a dozen laypersons predict he will do—morally objectionable? Second, in a few states—Florida is the prime example—the jury's sentencing decision is only advisory; and the trial judge is empowered to decide the sentence by reference to whatever considerations he deems appropriate regardless of whether they are defined by statute as aggravating circumstances. More than a few convicts whom the jury wanted sentenced to life in prison were instead sentenced to death by the arbitrary authority of the trial judge. Third, most death penalty jurisdictions cite as an aggravating circumstance that the murder was "heinous, depraved, and cruel"—a vague criterion that almost any murder could be said to satisfy. The truth is, as the extensive research conducted by the Capital Jury Project has shown, that the statutory guidelines enacted since *Furman* and ratified in *Gregg* are seldom fully understood by the trial jury; even when they are, the jurors often disregard them and sentence the defendant to death or to prison for whatever reasons they find compelling.

Let us turn now to see how abolitionists view the set of seven numbers cited above. They, too, divide into two classes.

One group believes that the elusive goal of complete abolition is out of reach at present but will soon be grasped. In their view the moratorium movement is a vehicle through which friends and nominal supporters of the death penalty will see the error of their ways, as they discover the virtual impossibility of the task they have undertaken to satisfy the mandate of the moratorium. These opponents of the death penalty are cheered by the knowledge that the rest of the civilized world openly and increasingly condemns our death penalty practices, pointing out that such practices violate international human rights law. They notice the unsavory company we keep in continuing to use the death penalty—China, Iran, Saudi Arabia, the Democratic Republic of the Congo—nations whose human rights record leaves much to be desired. These critics note with approval the way foreign countries refuse to extradite persons accused in the United States of a capital crime unless there is prior assurance that the prosecution will not seek the death penalty. They note with satisfaction the steady progress made in persuading the states and federal government to prohibit execution of the mentally retarded and of persons who were juveniles (under 18) at the time of their crime. In their view, support for abolition is growing in the nation's religious communities, especially in the Roman Catholic

Church, where the papal encyclical, *Evangelium Vitae* (1995), strongly argues for ending executions. Finally, they believe that the general public has absorbed the message that our death penalty system is bound to make errors, not all of them caught in time, some of them fatal, and that the marginal gains of a death penalty system—if any—are outweighed by the risks.

Others who also oppose the death penalty (I include myself here) are less optimistic. We see the posture of the current Supreme Court as a massive and virtually insurmountable obstacle. We believe that nationwide repeal of the death penalty depends on the Court, since neither the executive nor the legislative branch of the federal government has the authority to overturn state death penalty legislation. We believe that it's bad enough that the Court should tolerate the procedural abuses and disregard for equal protection so well described by Bright and Stevenson (see their remarks later in this volume). It is even worse that the Court should embrace the idea (as it did in *Gregg*) that there is no substantive objection to the death penalty on constitutional grounds because this form of punishment is not "cruel and unusual" in the sense of those words as used in the Constitution. Nationwide abolition is simply inconceivable without a change of heart and mind (and personnel) on the Court. As for the recent shift of public opinion on the death penalty, the drop in 2001 from nearly 80 percent support to 63 percent is surely welcome, but it is too recent to be a clear-cut trend. Finally, the death penalty is deeply entrenched in Texas, Florida, and other states of the Old Confederacy, where lynching was once the preferred way to deal with black men accused of the murder or rape of a white female. No one has any idea how the death penalty in these states—where the vast proportion of all death sentences and executions in the United States takes place—is to be ended or even seriously reduced in the near future.

The anti-death penalty movement led by the lawyers in the mid-1960s was a direct product of the civil rights movement of the late 1950s and early 1960s. Perhaps there is further affinity between the two. After the Supreme Court ruled in *Plessy v. Ferguson* (1896) that "separate but equal" was constitutionally permissible, it took half a century before the Court reversed itself in *Brown v. Board of Education* (1954), with the argument that separate was "inherently" unequal. If abolition of the death penalty by the Supreme Court is on a similar schedule, perhaps we abolitionists can hope for a favorable ruling from the Court, overturning the decision in *Gregg* and allied cases (1976) in another two or three decades.

IV

Abolitionists attacking the death penalty typically employ a wide variety of moral arguments. The value of human life, respect for human life—these norms play a decisive role for some. Others object on the ground that the state has no right to kill any of its prisoners. Some oppose it because they regard it as an affront to human dignity. Many others object on the ground that the death penalty violates the offender's right to life. Some will insist that it is the unfair administration of the death penalty, and the impossibility of making it fair, that warrants abolishing it. Still others insist that the risk of executing the innocent outweighs whatever alleged benefits the death penalty provides, or that, all things considered, a policy of selective death sentences has less overall social utility—in particular, it squanders scarce resources—than does a policy of no death sentencing. Or (to borrow language from the Supreme Court) "evolving standards of decency" condemn the death penalty today, even if they did not a century ago. Some oppose the death penalty not so much for what it does to the offender as for what it reveals about *us* in tolerating, not to say advocating, such killings. These and perhaps other moral concerns can be connected in various ways; they show that there is much to think about from the moral point of view in evaluating and criticizing the death penalty.

This occasion does not present the opportunity to develop an adequate review and critique of all the arguments implied by these varied moral norms. For that reason I propose to present and discuss only one argument—the one I now think is the best argument against the death penalty. Its lineage can be traced back to the little book by Cesare Beccaria, *An Essay on Crimes and Punishments* (1764), the tract usually credited with inspiring the abolition movement during the period of the Enlightenment in Europe and a version of which reappears in the recent papal encyclical, *Evangelium Vitae*. The argument rests on a fundamental principle that neither Beccaria nor the Pope explicitly formulated: Given a compelling state interest in some goal or purpose, the government in a constitutional democracy built on the principle of equal freedom and human rights for all must use the least restrictive means sufficient to achieve that goal or purpose. More expansively, the principle (a near-neighbor to what students of constitutional law would recognize as the principle of "substantive due process") holds that if individual privacy, liberty, and autonomy (or other fundamental values) are to be invaded and deliberately violated, it must be because the end to be achieved is of undeniable importance to society, and no less severe interference will suffice. For convenience of reference, let us henceforth call this the Minimal Invasion argument against the death penalty and the principle that generates it the Minimal Invasion principle.

The Minimal Invasion argument is unlike most arguments against the death penalty in two important respects. First, it does not rely on such familiar values as the right to life, values that either are not widely shared or are widely shared but at the cost of excessive vagueness. Second, the argument (with the exception of the debate over deterrence) does not hinge on establishing the usual faults that plague this form of punishment as actually administered. Thus, this argument sidesteps worries about the risk of executing the innocent, the arbitrariness of death sentencing and executions, the demonstrable effects of racial bias (especially in the South), the evident vulnerability of the poor, the unavoidable economic costs that exceed those of imprisonment. Opponents of the death penalty are often challenged to declare where they would stand were these flaws to be corrected. Despite the current interest in reforming our several systems of capital punishment, it is doubtful whether all or even most of the reforms so far proposed will be adopted. In any case, the Minimal Invasion argument does not depend on such contingencies. While it is a far cry from a philosopher's a priori argument, it comes close to sharing with such arguments immunity to a wide variety of factual considerations.

If an argument against the death penalty is to be constructed around the Minimal Invasion principle, at least three further propositions must be accepted. First, punishment for crime must be judged to be a legitimate practice in society under a constitution such as ours. Second, the death penalty by its very nature must be judged to be more severe, invasive, and irremediable than the alternative of some form of long-term imprisonment. Third, the death penalty must be judged not to play a necessary role in securing public safety either by way of general deterrence or specific incapacitation. If these three propositions are true, as I think they are, then in conjunction with the principle with which we began they lead to the conclusion that we ought to abolish the death penalty for all crimes and all offenders. Restating this argument in semi-formal style, this is what we get:

The principle. Invasions by the government of an individual's privacy, liberty, and autonomy (or other fundamental value) are justified only if no less invasive practice is sufficient to achieve an important social goal.

1. Punishment is justified only if it is necessary as a means to some socially valid end.
2. The death penalty is more severe—more invasive—than long-term imprisonment.
3. Long-term imprisonment is sufficient as an invasion of individual liberty, privacy, and autonomy (and other fundamental values) to achieve valid social goals.
4. Society ought to abolish any lawful practice that imposes more violation of individual liberty, privacy, or autonomy (or other fundamental value) when it is known that a less invasive practice is available and is sufficient.

The conclusion. Society ought to abolish the death penalty.

There's the argument. What can be said on behalf of the truth of each of its premises? Consider first the Minimal Invasion principle (and its corollary, step [4]). How much defense does it require? Surely it is clear that only extreme socialists, fascists, theocrats, or other totalitarians who for various reasons want to extend state power and intervention into the lives of citizens as far as possible will quarrel with this principle. Liberals and conservatives alike, who accept the basic tenets of constitutional democracy and believe in human rights, should readily embrace it. The only issue calling for further discussion among these supporters is whether this principle might ever conflict with other principles worthier of respect in certain cases, so that it must yield to them. What might such an incompatible but superior principle be? What sort of case might arise where such a conflict occurs? A fuller account of the rationale behind this principle would require us to connect it with more fundamental principles of social justice, a topic that cannot be pursued here. As for the three other steps in the argument, each warrants a closer look.

The first premise. Affirming the legitimacy of a system of punishment poses no problem for supporters of the death penalty nor for any but a few of its opponents. No one disputes that public security—protection against criminal victimization—is a salient value and that intervention by government into the behavior of its citizens to achieve that goal is warranted. But pursuit of such a goal is subject to constraints. Not every imaginable weapon to fight crime is morally permissible. Principles of various sorts (e.g., due process of law) restrict the tactics of intervention. These constraints to the side, as things stand, society needs recourse to punitive methods as a necessary condition of public safety.

This is not, however, because punishment is an end in itself; it is because we know of no less invasive responses to individual behavior sufficient as a means to achieve the purpose. If we did, then it would be difficult and perhaps impossible to defend punishment as a morally permissible practice. After all, punishment by its very nature involves deliberately inflicting deprivations and hardships on persons that, if inflicted by private citizens, would be crimes. So punishment needs to be justified, and the only justification available is that it is a necessary means to a fundamental social goal. For present purposes, then, we can say that there is little dispute over the truth of the first proposition.

The second premise. Few will deny the greater brutality and violence of the death penalty when compared to imprisonment. From time to time one hears a friend of the death penalty—and even on occasion some of its enemies—claiming that life in prison is a much more severe punishment than death. Beccaria and his English admirer, Jeremy Bentham (1748–1832), both pioneering abolitionists, believed that life in prison involved more suffering than a few moments on the gallows. I think it is sufficient by way of a reply to point out that those in the best position to know behave in a manner that suggests otherwise.

Few death row prisoners try to commit suicide and fewer succeed. Few death row prisoners insist that all appeals on their behalf be dropped. Few convicted murderers sentenced to life in prison declare years later that they wish they had been sentenced instead to death and executed. Few if any death row prisoners refuse clemency if it is offered to them. No doubt prison life can be made unbearable and hideous; no doubt death row can be managed by the authorities in an inhumane fashion. But none of this is necessary. No doubt not all life-term prisoners find ways to make their imprisonment something more than an inhumane endurance test. So it should hardly come as a surprise that the vast majority of friends of the death penalty as well as its opponents believe that death is worse than imprisonment. This is why its opponents want to abolish it—and why its supporters want to keep it. So we can accept the second proposition without further ado.

The third premise. The third proposition affirms that whatever the legitimate purposes of punishment are, imprisonment serves them as well as or better than the death penalty. This proposition rests on a variety of kinds of empirical evidence, ranging from statistical research on deterrence, the behavior in prison and on parole of convicted murderers not sentenced to death and executed, and above all on the experience of jurisdictions such as Michigan that have gone without the death penalty for decades.

Here is what the record shows: There is no evidence that prison officials, guards, or visitors in prisons where there is no death penalty are more at risk than are their counterparts in the death penalty states. There is no evidence that residents of abolition jurisdictions are at greater risk of murderous victimization than are residents in the death penalty jurisdictions. (The District of Columbia in recent years has had a very high homicide rate and is an abolition jurisdiction; but there is no research that connects the one fact with the other. Most other abolition jurisdictions have a noticeably lower homicide rate than do neighboring death penalty jurisdictions.) To be sure, some convicted murderers commit another murder while in prison or after release—the U.S. Bureau of Justice Statistics reports that 9 percent of those currently on death row had a previous homicide conviction. But not all of these recidivist murderers were guilty in their first homicide of a death-eligible murder. For these murderers, their second homicide could not have been prevented by inflicting the death penalty on them for the first homicide, since their first homicide was not death-eligible. Furthermore, there is no way to predict in advance which convicted murderers are likely to recidivate; the predictions of future dangerousness are plagued with false positives. If we could make accurate and reliable predictions of which prisoners would be dangerous in the future, these offenders could be kept under confinement, just as a typhoid carrier may be quarantined as a public health menace. The only way to prevent such recidivism would be to execute *every* convicted murderer—a policy that is politically unavailable and morally indefensible. Today's defenders of the death penalty must accept a pick-and-choose system of death sentences and executions, with all the adverse effects—as they see it—that such a system has on prevention and retribution.

It is also true that opponents of the death penalty who want to rest their case on the argument under discussion would be vulnerable to evidence—if there were any—showing that the death penalty is a better deterrent than imprisonment. Were there such evidence, opponents would have to rely on some other argument. (I have not claimed that the Minimal Invasion argument is the only argument for abolition; I claim only that I find it the most persuasive.) But since there is so little reason to suppose that the death penalty is ever a marginally superior deterrent over imprisonment, or that such superiority (if any) can be detected by the currently available methods of social science, this "what-if" counterargument can be put to the side and disregarded. (Below, I return to the issue of deterrence.)

With worries about prevention, deterrence, and incapacitation behind us (for the moment), what might we reasonably expect to be the public response in quarters where the death penalty currently has wide support? Is there reason to believe that if the death penalty were abolished, the police would take to administering curbstone justice and the public would revolt? Would the clamor of surviving family members of murder victims force the authorities to restore the death penalty? Would outspoken abolitionists become targets for violent rage, as have some doctors in abortion clinics? Nothing of the sort has happened in any current abolition jurisdiction. However, given the utter lack of political leadership on all aspects of the death penalty in states in the Deep South, where the death penalty has been so conspicuously used, I must admit to some uneasiness over what might happen if Texas were told—say, by a Supreme Court ruling—that it could no longer use the death penalty. The heirs of those who plastered the South in the 1950s with billboards shouting "Impeach Earl Warren" would rise to the occasion and denounce whatever political leadership brought about abolition. Fundamentalist Christians, Mormons, and others who have persuaded themselves that the Bible decrees the death penalty for murder pose a somewhat different problem. How members of these religious groups—clergy and laity, concentrated in (but by no means confined to) the Bible Belt across the South—would behave is far from obvious.

The upshot is that the third premise in the argument under discussion is reasonably supported by the available facts; and that suffices to prove the conclusion. . . .

VII

Unquestionably, the killers who most trouble us and who are first and foremost believed to deserve the death penalty are those who commit recidivist murder (such as Gary Gilmore, executed in Utah in 1977), or serial murder (such as John Wayne Gacy, executed in Illinois in 1994), or multiple murder (such as Timothy McVeigh, executed in 2001, having killed 168 people in Oklahoma). Cases such as these pose the greatest challenge to abolitionists. On occasion I have said that if it were up to me, I would be willing to let defenders of the death penalty execute killers of this stripe, provided they were willing to have resentenced to life imprisonment all other death row convicts. This would mean in the United States today that out of some 3,700 prisoners currently on our death rows, all but a tiny fraction, perhaps no more than 2 percent, would evade the executioner's summons. I would consider that a major gain, even though I favor complete abolition. My point in this hypothetical concession is to bring out how unusual the recidivist, serial, or multiple murderer is and to that extent how unreasonable it is to focus argument over the death penalty on such cases; the vast majority of death row convicts present a very different picture—as the sample of cases recounted by Bright and Stevenson show. It is as absurd as trying to shed light on the merits of the death penalty in the United States by insisting that the convicted Nazi war criminals at Nuremberg in 1945 deserved to be executed (as many of them were); there are no Hitlers or Görings or Himmlers on America's death rows. Nevertheless, something needs to be said here about the McVeigh case and others (*horribile dictu*) that could arise to present a similar challenge.

What can a dedicated abolitionist say about the death sentence and execution of McVeigh? Surely, there is something to the comment made by many, including Judge Kozinski, that McVeigh is a poster boy for the death penalty. Yet those who favor complete abolition are unwilling to make an exception for McVeigh or for others like him—notably terrorists of the sort who destroyed the World Trade Center and damaged the Pentagon on 9/11/01. On what grounds can abolitionists argue against their execution? What good would it do to fail to execute such offenders and instead to confine them behind bars for the rest of their lives?

Let us put aside a variety of lesser considerations that came to the surface in the McVeigh case: the inequity of sentencing McVeigh to death and his co-defendant to life in prison; the lost opportunity to learn from McVeigh, had he been sentenced to prison, more about how he committed the crime, his motivation, and his associates; the denial to the defense of a mass of documents in the government's custody bearing on the case; the millions of dollars spent on prosecuting this federal death penalty case; and the transformation of his execution in the federal prison at Terre Haute, Indiana, into a multimedia entertainment event. (Similar considerations apply to other terrorists whom we might arrest, try, and convict.)

Instead, let us notice first the harm that his execution did. McVeigh's execution is a perfect example of a violation of the Minimal Invasion principle. If that principle is sound and thus deserves our respectful compliance, then this execution is a thumb in the eye. There is no reason to doubt that McVeigh could have been kept in safe confinement indefinitely had the government wanted to do that. There is also no reason to believe that other violent ideologues will refrain from using weapons of mass violence because they have been deterred by the example of McVeigh's execution. There is no argument to support that killing McVeigh provides adequate retribution—how could killing him possibly serve as adequate retribution for his murdering scores and severely injuring dozens more? Retribution, incapacitation, deterrence—none was fostered by executing McVeigh. The harm that executing him did in the face of these facts is the harm of miseducating the public, obscuring the truth, cultivating a violent outlet for public anger, and fostering a pattern of official government conduct that climaxes in deliberately inflicting death without necessity.

Those who favored the execution of McVeigh, including Attorney General John Ashcroft, pointed to the "closure" the execution would give the hundreds of bereaved survivors, a consolation and assuagement for them that lifelong imprisonment for McVeigh (they believe) could never provide. May I suggest that the evidence shows that closure sought by this route is rarely found? Carroll L. Pickett, chaplain to death row prisoners in Huntsville, Texas, informs us that his encounters with survivors seeking closure convinced him that "almost without exception . . . the feeling of relief so long anticipated was not realized." The same lesson is taught in vivid detail by Sister Helen Prejean, in her powerful book, *Dead Man Walking* (1993). She recounted to journalist Garry Wills the way prosecutors urge surviving family members to attend the trial: "They learn new details of the crime, and with each new turn of the trial and its aftermath the media call them to get a reaction." Wills commented sardonically, "This is less like healing than like tearing scabs open again and again." In her book, Prejean relates the experience of one victim's father who witnessed the execution of Robert Willie in Louisiana in 1984. "He had walked away from the execution chamber with his rage satisfied but his heart empty." Hardly a lesson in closure of the sort anyone would seriously recommend.

What is so distinctive about the McVeigh case is not just the magnitude of the harm he caused; the publicity surrounding the crime and the way it was motivated by McVeigh's antigovernmental ideology helped make it a crime unlike others. His death at the hands of the government he professed to despise could in time make him a martyr to the cause, another feature of this case that illustrates how atypical it was. Of course no one knows the consequences that will accrue from McVeigh's execution, but it is a sobering thought that by executing McVeigh, the government could have helped turn a poster boy for the death penalty into a poster boy for the thousands of his ideological companions on the violent anarchist fringe who seek a role model.

What good, then, could have come from not executing McVeigh? Abstractly, the abolitionist can say that it is the good of doing the right thing. That it *is* the right thing to do is presumably settled on other grounds, such as those offered in the Minimal Invasion argument. Concretely, however, it is quite difficult to specify with precision any good that might come out of sparing McVeigh (and the few others who might be said to be like him) from death. Murderers serving a life term in prison have been known to make major contributions to educating other prisoners, helping them draft legal documents, cooling racial tensions, and so forth. Is it reasonable to have hoped that McVeigh behind bars might have made comparable contributions to the welfare of others? I do not know enough about him or the prison conditions that might have been imposed on him to speak to the point, but I do know that it is impossible to rule out all such future developments. Were such good things to take place, would they make amends for the harm done? Of course not. Good deeds do not cancel out evil deeds in any such tit-for-tat fashion. McVeigh was a person, as we are, even if he is unlike us in having committed a terrible and unforgivable crime. And being a person, he ought to be treated by us not solely in light of his awful crime. He may not deserve better from us, but even so we ought not to be guided solely—in this case or others—by reference to what punishment we think he deserves for his crime.

Desert, in any case, is not the only morally relevant consideration in determining how we ought to treat others. To conclude that we had to execute McVeigh because that is what he deserved requires us to show that there were no other weighty moral considerations against giving him what he deserved. But supporters of deserved death rarely if ever even try to show this; it is a conspicuous piece of argument missing from the usual philosophies of punishment. If abolitionists invoke the Minimal Invasion argument at this point, they will say that retribution is not an essential feature of the purposes or goals of a system of punishment—except in the uncontroversial sense of the term noted earlier, to the effect that all punishments are retributive. The punishment that McVeigh or others like him *deserve* does not tell us how we *ought* to punish him. We learn that—what we ought to do to him by way of punishment—by figuring out what is the minimally invasive punishment sufficient to achieve the goal of public safety. Killing killers is not minimally invasive.

Questions for Discussion

1. Should executions be as humane as possible?
2. Is Bedau's Minimal Invasion argument successful?
3. Should death be reserved as punishment only for the most severe crimes, such as multiple murders? Should crimes other than murder be punishable by death?

Louis P. Pojman, "Why the Death Penalty Is Morally Permissible"

Louis Pojman taught philosophy at the U.S. Military Academy at West Point for many years (he died in 2005). He was an extraordinarily prolific philosopher, having edited or authored over thirty books and eighty articles. In the article reprinted here Pojman defends the death penalty, arguing in fact for its expansion. "If the death penalty is an appropriate punishment for those who commit treason," he writes, "it is applicable to business executives who violate the public trust and undermine faith in our economic system." He defends the important "Best Bet" argument: Given our ignorance about whether the death penalty for convicted murderers deters potential murderers better than life in prison, the "best bet" is to use it and hope that it does; otherwise, we are allowing innocent people to be murdered whose murderers would have been deterred if we had used the death penalty. The murderers would have remained "potential" murderers instead of becoming actual murderers.

Critical Reading Questions

1. Why does Pojman think the death penalty should be used for certain "white-collar" crimes?
2. What is the difference between retribution and revenge, according to Pojman?
3. What does the example of "cosmic retribution" show?
4. What commonsense evidence do we have that the death penalty is a better deterrent than prison sentences, according to Pojman?
5. What is the "Best Bet" argument? How does Pojman defend it?
6. How does Pojman respond to two objections to capital punishment: execution of the innocent and discriminatory imposition of the death penalty?

WHY THE DEATH PENALTY IS MORALLY PERMISSIBLE[*]

Louis P. Pojman

The death penalty as punishment for the most serious crimes is morally justified. Honest people and philosophers may disagree on these matters, but I will present my reasons for supporting the retention of this practice. I have no illusions about my ability to change the minds of my ardent abolitionist opponents, but I can hope to clear the air of misperceptions and help those with an open mind come to an informed judgment of this crucial matter. . . .

A DEFENSE OF THE DEATH PENALTY

Who so sheddeth man's blood, by man shall his blood be shed. (Genesis 9:6)

There is an ancient tradition, going back to biblical times, but endorsed by the mainstream of philosophers, from Plato to Thomas Aquinas, from Thomas Hobbes to Immanuel Kant, Thomas Jefferson, John Stuart Mill, and C. S. Lewis, that a fitting punishment for murder is the execution of the murderer. One prong of this tradition, the *backward-looking* or deontological position, epitomized in Aquinas and Kant, holds that because human beings, as rational agents, have dignity, one who with malice aforethought kills a human being forfeits his right to life and deserves to die. The other, the *forward-looking* or consequentialist, tradition, exemplified by Jeremy Bentham, Mill, and

*Some of the material in the section on deterrence is adapted from my essay "For the Death Penalty" in *The Death Penalty: For and Against* by Louis P. Pojman and Jeffrey Reiman (Rowman & Littlefield, 1998). That book contains a defense of the theory of punishment discussed in this essay. It also includes a fuller defense of my theory of desert. I am indebted to Stephen Kershnar and Michel Levin for comments on an earlier draft of this essay.

Ernest van den Haag, holds that punishment ought to serve as a deterrent, and that capital punishment is an adequate deterrent to prospective murderers. Abolitionists like Bedau and Jeffrey Reiman deny both prongs of the traditional case for the death penalty. They hold that long prison sentences are a sufficient retributive response to murder and that the death penalty probably does not serve as a deterrent or is no better deterrent than other forms of punishment. I will argue that both traditional defenses are sound and together they make a strong case for retaining the death penalty. That is, I hold a combined theory of punishment. A backward-looking judgment that the criminal has committed a heinous crime plus a forward-looking judgment that a harsh punishment will deter would-be murderers is sufficient to justify the death penalty. I turn first to the retributivist theory in favor of capital punishment.

RETRIBUTION

The small crowd that gathered outside the prison to protest the execution of Steven Judy softly sang, "We Shall Overcome" . . . But it didn't seem quite the same hearing it sung out of concern for someone who, on finding a woman with a flat tire, raped and murdered her and drowned her three small children, then said that he hadn't been "losing any sleep" over his crimes. . . .

I remember the grocer's wife. She was a plump, happy woman who enjoyed the long workday she shared with her husband in their ma-and-pa store. One evening, two young men came in and showed guns, and the grocer gave them everything in the cash register.

For no reason, almost as an afterthought, one of the men shot the grocer in the face. The woman stood only a few feet from her husband when he was turned into a dead, bloody mess.

She was about 50 when it happened. In a few years her mind was almost gone, and she looked 80. They might as well have killed her too.

Then there was the woman I got to know after her daughter was killed by a wolfpack gang during a motoring trip. The mother called me occasionally, but nothing that I said could ease her torment. It ended when she took her own life.

A couple of years ago I spent a long evening with the husband, sister and parents of a fine young woman who had been forced into the trunk of a car in a hospital parking lot. The degenerate who kidnapped her kept her in the trunk, like an ant in a jar, until he got tired of the game. Then he killed her.

Human beings have dignity as self-conscious rational agents who are able to act morally. One could maintain that it is precisely their moral goodness or innocence that bestows dignity and a right to life on them. Intentionally taking the life of an innocent human being is so evil that absent mitigating circumstances, the perpetrator forfeits his own right to life. He or she deserves to die.

The retributivist holds three propositions: (1) that all the guilty deserve to be punished; (2) that only the guilty deserve to be punished; and (3) that the guilty deserve to be punished in proportion to the severity of their crime. Thomas Jefferson supported such a system of proportionality of punishment to crime:

> Whosoever shall be guilty of rape, polygamy, sodomy with man or woman, shall be punished, if a man, by castration, if a woman by cutting through the cartilage of her nose a hole of one half inch in diameter at the least. [And] whosoever shall maim another, or shall disfigure him . . . shall be maimed, or disfigured in the like sort: or if that cannot be, for want of some part, then as nearly as may be, in some other part of at least equal value.

Criminals like Steven Judy, Jeffrey Dahmer, Timothy McVeigh, Ted Bundy (who is reported to have raped and murdered over 100 women), John Mohammed and John Lee Malvo, who murdered 12 people in the killing spree of 2002, and the two men who gunned down the grocer (mentioned in the quotation by Royko, above) have committed capital offenses and deserve nothing less than capital punishment. No doubt malicious acts like the ones committed by these criminals deserve worse punishment than death, and I would be open to suggestions of torture (why not?), but at a minimum, the death penalty seems warranted.

People often confuse *retribution* with *revenge*. Governor George Ryan, who recently commuted the sentences of all the prisoners on death row in the State of Illinois, in his essay in this volume quotes a letter from the Reverend Desmond Tutu that "to take a life when a life has been lost is revenge, it is not justice." This is simply false. While moral people will feel outrage at acts of heinous crimes, such as those described above by Mike Royko, the moral justification of punishment is not *vengeance*, but *desert*. Vengeance signifies inflicting harm on the offender out of anger because of what he has done. Retribution is the rationally supported theory that the criminal deserves a punishment fitting the gravity of his crime.

The nineteenth-century British philosopher James Fitzjames Stephens thought vengeance was a justification for punishment, arguing that punishment should be inflicted "for the sake of ratifying the feeling of hatred—call it revenge, resentment, or what you will—which the contemplation of such [offensive] conduct excites in healthily constituted minds." But retributivism is not based on hatred for the criminal (though a feeling of vengeance may accompany the punishment). Retributivism is the theory that the criminal *deserves* to be punished and deserves to be punished in proportion to the gravity of his or her crime, whether or not the victim or anyone else desires it. We may all deeply regret having to carry out the punishment, but consider it warranted.

On the other hand, people do have a sense of outrage and passion for revenge directed at criminals for their crimes. Imagine that someone in your family was on the receiving end of Stephen Judy's violent acts. Stephens was correct in asserting that "[t]he criminal law stands to the passion for revenge in much the same relation as marriage to the sexual appetite." Failure to punish would no more lessen our sense of vengeance than the elimination of marriage would lessen our sexual appetite. When a society fails to punish criminals in a way thought to be proportionate to the gravity of the crime, the danger arises that the public would take the law into its own hands, resulting in vigilante justice, lynch mobs, and private acts of retribution.

The outcome is likely to be an anarchistic, insecure state of injustice. As such, legal retribution stands as a safeguard for an orderly application of punitive desert.

Our natural instinct is for *vengeance*, but civilization demands that we restrain our anger and go through a legal process, letting the outcome determine whether and to what degree to punish the accused. Civilization demands that we not take the law into our own hands, but it should also satisfy our deepest instincts when they are consonant with reason. Our instincts tell us that some crimes, like McVeigh's, Judy's, and Bundy's, should be severely punished, but we refrain from personally carrying out those punishments, committing ourselves to the legal processes. The death penalty is supported by our gut animal instincts as well as our sense of justice as desert.

The death penalty reminds us that there are consequences to our actions, that we are responsible for what we do, so that dire consequences for immoral actions are eminently appropriate. The death penalty is such a fitting response to evil.

DETERRENCE

The second tradition justifying the death penalty is the utilitarian theory of deterrence. This holds that by executing convicted murderers we will deter would-be murderers from killing innocent people. The evidence for deterrence is controversial. Some scholars, like Thornstein Sellin and Bedau, argue that the death penalty is not a deterrent of homicides superior to long-term imprisonment. Others, such as Isaac Ehrlich, make a case for the death penalty as a significant deterrent. Granted that the evidence is ambiguous, and honest scholars can differ on the results. However, one often hears abolitionists claiming the evidence shows that the death penalty fails to deter homicide. This is too strong a claim. The sociological evidence doesn't show either that the death penalty deters or that it fails to deter. The evidence is simply inconclusive. But a commonsense case can be made for deterrence.

Imagine that every time someone intentionally killed an innocent person he was immediately struck down by lightning. When mugger Mike slashed his knife into the neck of the elderly pensioner, lightning struck, killing Mike. His fellow muggers witnessed the sequence of events. When burglar Bob pulled his pistol out and shot the bank teller through her breast, a bolt leveled Bob, his compatriots beholding the spectacle. Soon men with their guns lying next to them were found all across the world in proximity to the corpses of their presumed victims. Do you think that the evidence of cosmic retribution would go unheeded?

We can imagine the murder rate in the United States and everywhere else plummeting. The close correlation between murder and cosmic ~~retribution~~ would serve as a deterrent to would-be murderers. If this thought experiment is sound, we have a prima facie argument for the deterrent effect of capital punishment. In its ideal, prompt performance, the death penalty would likely deter <u>most rational</u> criminally minded from committing murder. The question then becomes how do we institute the death penalty so as to have the maximal deterrent effect without violating the rights of the accused.

We would have to bring the accused to trial more quickly and limit the appeals process of those found guilty "beyond reasonable doubt." Having DNA evidence should make this more feasible than hitherto. Furthermore, public executions of the convicted murderer would serve as a reminder that crime does not pay. Public executions of criminals seem an efficient way to communicate the message that if you shed innocent blood, you will pay a high price. Bedau cites Nat Hentoff's advocacy of a public execution of Timothy McVeigh in terms of being accountable for such actions (p. 4). I agree with Hentoff on the matter of accountability but also believe such publicity would serve to deter homicide.

Abolitionists like Stephen Nathanson argue that because the statistical evidence in favor of the deterrent effect of capital punishment is indecisive, we have no basis for concluding that it is a better deterrent than long prison sentences. If I understand these opponents, their argument presents us with an exclusive disjunct: Either we must have conclusive statistical evidence (i.e., a proof) for the deterrent effect of the death penalty, or we have no grounds for supposing that the death penalty deters. Many people accept this argument. Recently, a colleague said to me, "There is no statistical evidence that the death penalty deters," as if to dismiss the argument from deterrence altogether. This is premature judgment, for the argument commits the fallacy of supposing that only two opposites are possible. There is a middle position that holds that while we cannot prove conclusively that the death penalty deters, the weight of evidence supports its deterrence. Furthermore, I think there are too many variables to hold constant for us to prove via statistics the deterrence hypothesis, and even if the requisite statistics were available, we could question whether they were cases of mere correlation versus causation. On the other hand, commonsense or anecdotal evidence may provide insight into the psychology of human motivation, providing evidence that fear of the death penalty deters some types of would-be criminals from committing murder. Granted, people are sometimes deceived about their motivation. But usually they are not deceived, and, as a rule, we should presume they know their motives until we have evidence to the contrary. The general commonsense argument goes like this:

1. What people (including potential criminals) fear more will have a greater deterrent effect on them.
2. People (including potential criminals) fear death more than they do any other humane punishment.
3. The death penalty is a humane punishment.
4. Therefore, people (including criminals) will be deterred more by the death penalty than by any other humane punishment.

Since the purpose of this argument is to show that the death penalty very likely deters more than long-term prison sentences, I am assuming it is *humane*—that is, acceptable to the moral sensitivities of the majority in our society. Torture might deter even more, but it is not considered humane. I will say more about the significance of humaneness with regard to the death penalty below.

Common sense informs us that most people would prefer to remain out of jail, that the threat of public humiliation is enough to deter some people, that a sentence of 20 years will deter most people more than a sentence of two years, that a life sentence will deter most

would-be criminals more than a sentence of 20 years. I think that we have commonsense evidence that the death penalty is a better deterrent than prison sentences. For one thing, as Richard Herrnstein and James Q. Wilson have argued in *Crime and Human Nature*, a great deal of crime is committed on a cost-benefit schema, wherein the criminal engages in some form of risk assessment as to his or her chances of getting caught and punished in some manner. If he or she estimates the punishment mild, the crime becomes inversely attractive, and vice versa. The fact that those who are condemned to death do everything in their power to get their sentences postponed or reduced to long-term prison sentences, in the way *lifers* do not, shows that they fear death more than life in prison.

The point is this: Imprisonment constitutes one evil, the loss of freedom, but the death penalty imposes a more severe loss, that of life itself. If you lock me up, I may work for a parole or pardon, I may learn to live stoically with diminished freedom, and I can plan for the day my freedom will be restored. But if I believe that my crime may lead to death, or loss of freedom followed by death, then I have more to fear than mere imprisonment. I am faced with a great evil plus an even greater evil. I fear death more than imprisonment because it alone takes from me all future possibility.

I am not claiming that the fear of legal punishment is all that keeps us from criminal behavior. Moral character, good habit, fear of being shamed, peer pressure, fear of authority, or the fear of divine retribution may have a greater influence on some people. However, many people will be deterred from crime, including murder, by the threat of severe punishment. The abolitionist points out that many would-be murderers simply do not believe they will be caught. Perhaps this is true for some. While the fantastic egoist has delusions of getting away with his crime, many would-be criminals are not so bold or delusionary.

Former Prosecuting Attorney for the State of Florida, Richard Gernstein, has set forth the commonsense case for deterrence. First of all, he claims, the death penalty certainly deters the murderer from any further murders, including those he or she might commit within the prison where he is confined. Second, statistics cannot tell us how many potential criminals have refrained from taking another's life through fear of the death penalty. He quotes Judge Hyman Barshay of New York: "The death penalty is a warning, just like a lighthouse throwing its beams out to sea. We hear about shipwrecks, but we do not hear about the ships the lighthouse guides safely on their way. We do not have proof of the number of ships it saves, but we do not tear the lighthouse down."

Some of the commonsense evidence is anecdotal, as the following quotation shows. British member of Parliament Arthur Lewis explains how he was converted from an abolitionist to a supporter of the death penalty:

One reason that has stuck in my mind, and which has proved [deterrence] to me beyond question, is that there was once a professional burglar in [my] constituency who consistently boasted of the fact that he had spent about one-third of his life in prison. . . . He said to me "I am a professional burglar. Before we go out on a job we plan it down to every detail. Before we go into the boozer to have a drink we say 'Don't forget, no shooters'—shooters being guns." He adds "We did our job and didn't have shooters because at that time there was capital punishment. Our wives, girlfriends and our mums said, 'Whatever you do, do not carry a shooter because if you are caught you might be topped [executed].' If you do away with capital punishment they will all be carrying shooters."

It is difficult to know how widespread this reasoning is. My own experience corroborates this testimony. Growing up in the infamous Cicero, Illinois, home of Al Capone and the Mafia, I had friends who went into crime, mainly burglary and larceny. It was common knowledge that one stopped short of killing in the act of robbery. A prison sentence could be dealt with—especially with a good lawyer—but being convicted of murder, which at that time included a reasonable chance of being electrocuted, was an altogether different matter. No doubt exists in my mind that the threat of the electric chair saved the lives of some of those who were robbed in my town. No doubt some crimes are committed in the heat of passion or by the temporally (or permanently) insane, but some are committed through a process of risk assessment. Burglars, kidnappers, traitors and vindictive people will sometimes be restrained by the threat of death. We simply don't know how much capital punishment deters, but this sort of commonsense, anecdotal evidence must be taken into account in assessing the institution of capital punishment.

John Stuart Mill admitted that capital punishment does not inspire terror in hardened criminals, but it may well make an impression on prospective murderers. "As for what is called the failure of the death punishment, who is able to judge of that? We partly know who those are whom it has not deterred; but who is there who knows whom it has deterred, or how many human beings it has saved who would have lived to be murderers if that awful association had not been thrown round the idea of murder from their earliest infancy?" Mill's points are well taken: (1) Not everyone will be deterred by the death penalty, but some will; (2) the potential criminal need not consciously calculate a cost-benefit analysis regarding his crime to be deterred by the threat. The idea of the threat may have become a subconscious datum "from their earliest infancy." The repeated announcement and regular exercise of capital punishment may have deep causal influence.

Gernstein quotes the British Royal Commission on Capital Punishment (1949–53), which is one of the most thorough studies on the subject and which concluded that there was evidence that the death penalty has some deterrent effect on normal human beings. Some of its evidence in favor of the deterrence effect includes these points:

1. Criminals who have committed an offense punishable by life imprisonment, when faced with capture, refrained from killing their captor though by killing, escape seemed probable. When asked why they refrained from the homicide, quick responses indicated a willingness to serve life sentence, but not risk the death penalty.
2. Criminals about to commit certain offenses refrained from carrying deadly weapons. Upon apprehension, answers to questions concerning absence of such weapons indicated a desire to avoid more serious punishment by carrying a deadly weapon, and also to avoid use of the weapon which could result in imposition of the death penalty.

3. Victims have been removed from a capital punishment State to a non-capital punishment State to allow the murderer opportunity for homicide without threat to his own life. This in itself demonstrates that the death penalty is considered by some would-be-killers.

Gernstein then quotes former District Attorney of New York, Frank S. Hogan, representing himself and his associates:

We are satisfied from our experience that the deterrent effect is both real and substantial . . . for example, from time to time accomplices in felony murder state with apparent truthfulness that in the planning of the 'felony they strongly urged the killer not to resort to violence. From the context of these utterances, it is apparent that they were led to these warnings to the killer by fear of the death penalty which they realized might follow the taking of life. Moreover, victims of hold-ups have occasionally reported that one of the robbers expressed a desire to kill them and was dissuaded from so doing by a confederate. Once again, we think it not unreasonable to suggest that fear of the death penalty played a role in some of these intercessions.

On a number of occasions, defendants being questioned in connection with homicide have shown a striking terror of the death penalty. While these persons have in fact perpetrated homicide, we think that their terror of the death penalty must be symptomatic of the attitude of many others of their type, as a result of which many lives have been spared.

It seems likely that the death penalty does not deter as much as it could due to its inconsistent and rare use. For example, out of an estimated 23,370 cases of murder, nonnegligent manslaughter, and rape in 1949, only 119 executions were carried out in the United States. In 1953, only 62 executions out of 27,000 cases for those crimes took place. Few executions were carried out in the 1960s and none at all from 1967 to 1977. Gernstein points out that at that rate a criminal's chances of escaping execution are better than 100 to 1. Actually, since Gernstein's report, the figures have become even more weighted against the chances of the death sentence. In 1993, there were 24,526 cases of murder and nonnegligent manslaughter and only 56 executions; and in 1994, there were 23,305 cases of murder and nonnegligent manslaughter and only 31 executions—for a ratio of better than 750 to 1. The average length of stay for a prisoner executed in 1994 was 10 years and two months.

If potential murderers perceived the death penalty as a highly probable outcome of murder, would they not be more reluctant to kill? Gernstein notes:

The commissioner of Police of London, England, in his evidence before the Royal Commission on Capital Punishment, told of a gang of armed robbers who continued operations after one of their members was sentenced to death and his sentence commuted to penal servitude, but the same gang disbanded and disappeared when, on a later occasion, two others were convicted of murder and hanged.

Gernstein sums up his data: "Surely it is a common sense argument, based on what is known of human nature, that the death penalty has a deterrent effect particularly for certain kinds of murderers. Furthermore, as the Royal Commission opined, the death penalty helps to educate the conscience of the whole community, and it arouses among many people a quasi-religious sense of awe. In the mind of the public there remains a strong association between murder and the penalty of death. Certainly one of the factors which restrains some people from murder is fear of punishment and surely, since people fear death more than anything else, the death penalty is the most effective deterrent."

I should also point out that *given the retributivist argument* for the death penalty, based on desert, the retentionist does not have to prove that the death penalty deters *better* than long prison sentences, but if the death penalty is deemed at least as effective as its major alternative, it would be justified. If evidence existed that life imprisonment were a *more effective* deterrent, the retentionist might be hard pressed to defend it on retributivist lines alone. My view is that the desert argument plus the common-sense evidence—being bolstered by the following argument, the Best Bet Argument, strongly supports retention of the death penalty.

The late Ernest van den Haag has set forth what he called the Best Bet Argument. He argued that even though we don't know for certain whether the death penalty deters or prevents other murders, we should bet that it does. Indeed, due to our ignorance, any social policy we take is a gamble. Not to choose capital punishment for first-degree murder is as much a bet that capital punishment doesn't deter as choosing the policy is a bet that it does. There is a significant difference in the betting, however, in that to bet against capital punishment is to bet against the innocent and for the murderer, while to bet for it is to bet against the murderer and for the innocent.

The point is this: We are accountable for what we let happen, as well as for what we actually do. If I fail to bring up my children properly so that they are a menace to society, I am to some extent responsible for their bad behavior. I could have caused it to be somewhat better. If I have good evidence that a bomb will blow up the building you are working in and fail to notify you (assuming I can); I am partly responsible for your death, if and when the bomb explodes. So we are responsible for what we omit doing, as well as for what we do. Purposefully to refrain from a lesser evil which we know will allow a greater evil to occur is to be at least partially responsible for the greater evil. This responsibility for our omissions underlies van den Haag's argument, to which we now return.

Suppose that we choose a policy of capital punishment for capital crimes. In this case we are betting that the death of some murderers will be more than compensated for by the lives of some innocents not being murdered (either by these murderers or others who would have murdered). If we're right, we have saved the lives of the innocent. If we're wrong, unfortunately, we've sacrificed the lives of some murderers. But say we choose not to have a social policy of capital punishment. If capital punishment doesn't work as a deterrent, we've come out ahead, but if it does work, then we've missed an opportunity to save innocent lives. If we value the saving of innocent lives more highly than the loss of the guilty, then to bet on a policy of capital punishment turns out to be rational. Since the innocent have a greater right to life than the guilty, it is our moral duty to adopt a policy that has a chance of protecting them from potential murderers.

It is noteworthy that prominent abolitionists, such as Charles Black, Hugo Adam Bedau, Ramsey Clark, and Henry Schwartzchild, have admitted to Ernest van den Haag that even if every execution were to deter a hundred murders, they would oppose it, from which van den Haag concludes, "To these abolitionist leaders,

the life of every murderer is more valuable than the lives of a hundred prospective victims, for these abolitionists would spare the murderer, even if doing so will cost a hundred future victims their lives." Black and Bedau said they would favor abolishing the death penalty even if they knew that doing so would increase the homicide rate 1,000 percent. This response of abolitionists is puzzling, since one of Bedau's arguments against the death penalty is that it doesn't bring back the dead. "We cannot do anything for the dead victims of crime. (How many of those who oppose the death penalty would continue to do so if, *mirabile dictu,* executing the murderer might bring the victim back to life?)" Apparently, he would support the death penalty if it brought a dead victim back to life, but not if it prevented a hundred innocent victims from being murdered.

If the Best Bet Argument is sound, or if the death penalty does deter would-be murderers, as common sense suggests, then we should support some uses of the death penalty. It should be used for those who commit first-degree murder, for whom no mitigating factors are present, and especially for those who murder police officers, prison guards, and political leaders. Many states rightly favor it for those who murder while committing another crime, such as burglary or rape. It should be used in cases of treason and terrorist bombings. It should also be considered for the perpetrators of egregious white collar crimes such as bank managers embezzling the savings of the public. The savings and loan scandals of the 1980s, involving wealthy bank officials absconding with the investments of elderly pensioners and others, ruined the lives of many people. This gross violation of the public trust warrants the electric chair. Such punishment would meet the two conditions set forth in this paper. The punishment would be deserved and it would likely deter future crimes by people in the public trust. It would also make the death penalty more egalitarian, applicable to the rich as well as the poor.

Let me consider two objections often made to the implementation of the death penalty: that it sometimes leads to the death of innocents and that it discriminates against blacks.

Objection 1: Miscarriages of justice occur. Capital punishment is to be rejected because of human fallibility in convicting innocent parties

169

and sentencing them to death. In a survey done in 1985 Hugo Adam Bedau and Michael Radelet found that of the 7,000 persons executed in the United States between 1900 and 1985, 25 were innocent of capital crimes. While some compensation is available to those unjustly imprisoned, the death sentence is irrevocable. We can't compensate the dead. As John Maxton, a member of the British Parliament puts it, "If we allow one innocent person to be executed, morally we are committing the same, or, in some ways, a worse crime than the person who committed the murder."

Response: Mr. Maxton is incorrect in saying that mistaken judicial execution is morally the same as or worse than murder, for a deliberate intention to kill the innocent occurs in a murder, whereas no such intention occurs in wrongful capital punishment.

Sometimes the objection is framed this way: It is better to let ten criminals go free than to execute one innocent person. If this dictum is a call for safeguards, then it is well taken; but somewhere there seems to be a limit on the tolerance of society toward capital offenses. Would these abolitionists argue that it is better that 50 or 100 or 1,000 murderers go free than that one innocent person be executed? Society has a right to protect itself from capital offenses even if this means taking a finite chance of executing an innocent person. If the basic activity or process is justified, then it is regrettable, but morally acceptable, that some mistakes are made. Fire trucks occasionally kill innocent pedestrians while racing to fires, but we accept these losses as justified by the greater good of the activity of using fire trucks. We judge the use of automobiles to be acceptable even though such use causes an average of 50,000 traffic fatalities each year. We accept the morality of a defensive war even though it will result in our troops accidentally or mistakenly killing innocent people.

The fact that we can err in applying the death penalty should give us pause and cause us to build a better appeals process into the judicial system. Such a process is already in most places in the American and British legal systems. That an occasional error may be made, regrettable though this is, is not a sufficient reason for us to refuse to use the death penalty, if on balance it serves a just and useful function.

Furthermore, abolitionists are simply misguided in thinking that prison sentences are a satisfactory alternative here. It's not clear that we can always or typically compensate innocent parties who waste away in prison. Jacques Barzun has argued that a prison sentence can be worse than death and carries all the problems that the death penalty does regarding the impossibility of compensation:

In the preface of his useful volume of cases, *Hanged in Error,* Mr. Leslie Hale refers to the tardy recognition of a minor miscarriage of justice—one year in jail: "The prisoner emerged to find that his wife had died and that his children and his aged parents had been removed to the workhouse. By the time a small payment had been assessed as 'compensation' the victim was incurably insane." So far we are as indignant with the law as Mr. Hale. But what comes next? He cites the famous Evans case, in which it is very probable that the wrong man was hanged, and he exclaims: "While such mistakes are possible, should society impose an irrevocable sentence?" Does Mr. Hale really ask us to believe that the sentence passed on the first man, whose wife died and who went insane, was in any sense *revocable*? Would not any man rather be Evans dead than that other wretch "emerging" with his small compensation and his reason for living gone?

The abolitionist is incorrect in arguing that death is different from long-term prison sentences because it is irrevocable. Imprisonment also takes good things away from us that may never be returned. We cannot restore to the inmate the freedom or opportunities he or she lost. Suppose an innocent 25-year-old man is given a life sentence for murder. Thirty years later the error is discovered and he is set free. Suppose he values three years of freedom to every one year of life. That is, he would rather live 10 years as a free man than 30 as a prisoner. Given this man's values, the criminal justice system has taken the equivalent of 10 years of life from him. If he lives until he is 65, he has, as far as his estimation is concerned, lost 10 years, so that he may be said to have lived only 55 years.

The numbers in this example are arbitrary, but the basic point is sound. Most of us would prefer a shorter life of higher quality to a longer one of low quality. Death prevents all subsequent quality, but imprisonment also irrevocably harms one by diminishing the quality of life of the prisoner.

Objection 2: The second objection of ten made against the death penalty is that it is unjust because it discriminates against the poor and minorities, particularly African Americans, over rich people and whites. Stephen B. Bright makes this objection in his chapter. Former Supreme Court Justice William Douglas wrote that "a law which reaches that [discriminatory] result in practice has no more sanctity than a law, which in terms provides the same." Nathanson argues that "in many cases, whether one is treated justly or not depends not only on what one deserves but on how other people are treated." He offers the example of unequal justice in a plagiarism case. "I tell the students in my class that anyone who plagiarizes will fail the course. Three students plagiarize papers, but I give only one a failing grade. The other two, in describing their motivation, win my sympathy, and I give them passing grades." Arguing that this is patently unjust, he likens this case to the imposition of the death penalty and concludes that it too is unjust.

Response: First of all, it is not true that a law that is applied in a discriminatory manner is unjust. Unequal justice is no less justice, however uneven its application. The discriminatory application, not the law itself, is unjust. A just law is still just even if it is not applied consistently. For example, a friend once got two speeding tickets during a 100-mile trip (having borrowed my car). He complained to the police officer who gave him his second ticket that many drivers were driving faster than he was at the time. They had escaped detection, he argued, so it wasn't fair for him to get two tickets on one trip. The officer acknowledged the imperfections of the system but, justifiably, had no qualms about giving him the second ticket. Unequal justice is still justice, however regrettable. So Justice Douglas is wrong in asserting that discriminatory results invalidate the law itself. Discriminatory practices should be reformed, and in many cases they can be. But imperfect practices in themselves do not entail that the laws engendering these practices themselves are unjust.

With regard to Nathanson's analogy with the plagiarism case, two things should be said against it. First, if the teacher is convinced that the motivational factors are mitigating factors,

then he or she may be justified in passing two of the plagiarizing students. Suppose that the one student did no work whatsoever, showed no interest (Nathanson's motivation factor) in learning, and exhibited no remorse in cheating, whereas the other two spent long hours seriously studying the material and, upon apprehension, showed genuine remorse for their misdeeds. To be sure, they yielded to temptation at certain—though limited—sections of their long papers, but the vast majority of their papers represented their own diligent work. Suppose, as well, that all three had C averages at this point. The teacher gives the unremorseful, gross plagiarizer an F but relents and gives the other two D's. Her actions parallel the judge's use of mitigating circumstances and cannot be construed as arbitrary, let alone unjust.

The second problem with Nathanson's analogy is that it would have disastrous consequences for all law and benevolent practices alike. If we concluded that we should abolish a rule or practice, unless we treated everyone exactly by the same rules all the time, we would have to abolish, for example, traffic laws and laws against imprisonment for rape, theft, and even murder. Carried to its logical limits, we would also have to refrain from saving drowning victims if a number of people were drowning but we could only save a few of them. Imperfect justice is the best that we humans can attain. We should reform our practices as much as possible to eradicate unjust discrimination wherever we can, but if we are not allowed to have a law without perfect application, we will be forced to have no laws at all.

Nathanson acknowledges this latter response but argues that the case of death is different. "Because of its finality and extreme severity of the death penalty, we need to be more scrupulous in applying it as punishment than is necessary with any other punishment" (p. 67). The retentionist agrees that the death penalty is a severe punishment and that we need to be scrupulous in applying it. The difference between the abolitionist and the retentionist seems to lie in whether we are wise and committed enough as a nation to reform our institutions so that they approximate fairness. Apparently, Nathanson is pessimistic here, whereas I have faith in our ability to learn from our mistakes and reform our systems. If we can't reform our legal system, what hope is there for us?

More specifically, the charge that a higher percentage of blacks than whites are executed was once true but is no longer so. Many states have made significant changes in sentencing procedures, with the result that currently whites convicted of first-degree murder are sentenced to death at a higher rate than blacks.

One must be careful in reading too much into these statistics. While great disparities in statistics should cause us to examine our judicial procedures, they do not in themselves prove injustice. For example, more males than females are convicted of violent crimes (almost 90% of those convicted of violent crimes are males—a virtually universal statistic), but this is not strong evidence that the law is unfair, for there are biological/psychological explanations for the disparity in convictions. Males are on average and by nature more aggressive (usually tied to testosterone) than females. Simply having a Y chromosome predisposes them to greater violence. Nevertheless, we hold male criminals responsible for their violence and expect them to control themselves. Likewise, there may be good explanations why people of one ethnic group commit more crimes than those of other groups, explanations that do not impugn the processes of the judicial system nor absolve rational people of their moral responsibility.

Recently, Governor George Ryan of Illinois, the state of my childhood and youth, commuted the sentences of over 150 death row inmates. Apparently, some of those convicted were convicted on insufficient evidence. If so, their sentences should have been commuted and the prisoners compensated. Such decisions should be done on a case-by-case basis. If capital punishment is justified, its application should be confined to clear cases in which the guilt of the criminal is "beyond reasonable doubt." But to overthrow the whole system because of a few possible miscarriages is as unwarranted as it is a loss of faith in our system of criminal justice. No one would abolish the use of fire engines and ambulances because occasionally they kill innocent pedestrians while carrying out their mission.

Abolitionists often make the complaint that only the poor get death sentences for murder. If their trials are fair, then they deserve the death penalty, but rich murderers may be equally deserving. At the moment only first-degree murder and treason are crimes deemed worthy of the death penalty. Perhaps our notion of treason should be expanded to include those who betray the trust of the public: corporation executives who have the trust of ordinary people, but who, through selfish and dishonest practices, ruin their lives. As noted above, my proposal is to consider broadening, not narrowing, the scope of capital punishment, to include business personnel who unfairly harm the public. The executives in the recent corporation scandals who bailed out of sinking corporations with golden, million-dollar lifeboats while the pension plans of thousands of employees went to the bottom of the economic ocean, may deserve severe punishment, and if convicted, they should receive what they deserve. My guess is that the threat of the death sentence would have a deterrent effect here. Whether it is feasible to apply the death penalty for horrendous white-collar crimes is debatable. But there is something to be said in its favor. It would remove the impression that only the poor get executed.

CONCLUSION

While the abolitionist movement is gaining strength due in part to the dedicated eloquence of opponents to the death penalty like Hugo Adam Bedau, Stephen Nathanson, and Jeffrey Reiman, a cogent case can be made for retaining the death penalty for serious crimes, such as first-degree murder and treason. The case primarily rests on a notion of justice as desert but is strengthened by utilitarian arguments involving deterrence. It is not because retentionists disvalue life that we defend the use of the death penalty. Rather, it is because we value human life as highly as we do that we support its continued use. The combined argument based on both backward-looking and forward-looking considerations justifies use of the death penalty. I have suggested that the application of the death penalty include not only first-degree murder but also treason (willful betrayal of one's country), including the treasonous behavior of business executives who violate the public trust.

The abolitionists in this book point out the problems in applying the death penalty. We can concede that there are problems and reform is constantly needed, but since the death penalty is justified in principle, we should seek to improve its application rather than abolish a just institution. We ought not throw out the baby with the dirty bathwater.

Questions for Discussion

1. Is the death penalty morally permissible?
2. Consider the "Best Bet" argument closely. Is it a good reason for us to use the death penalty?
3. What if capital punishment does not deter better than life in prison? What if life in prison does not deter either?
4. Can a case be made for executing murderers but not as punishment?

CHAPTER 11

War

HARD QUESTION: IS WAR EVER THE ANSWER?

It is hard to think about war as a moral issue; it seems instead that war is the suspension of morality. Yet when a nation goes to war, its leaders typically say that the country is doing the right thing. The leaders talk about justice or reparation or self-defense, and they appeal to past wrongs or to religious rights or to the triumph of good over evil. They appeal, in other words, to grand moral concepts and say that it is right or just or correct to go to war. Could such claims ever be true? Or are the leaders just cynically manipulating moral discourse in ways that serve their immediate political interests?

No doubt moral discourse can be cynically manipulated, but moral reasoning has an inherent logic of its own; to appeal to concepts of right and justice and self-defense commits one to certain standards of evidence and forms of argumentation. Merely saying that a cause is just or right does not make it so, even if citizens can sometimes be convinced by duplicitous or ingenuous but misguided political leaders. However, irrespective of what political leaders may say about a particular war, or about war in general, we want to know about the moral reality of war. Is going to war ever morally acceptable? And once a nation is in a war, are there morally acceptable and morally unacceptable ways to fight?

Just war theory embodies a long history of thought about war and morality; it aims to specify when and how it is morally acceptable to fight. The theory of just war is thus at odds with two other views about the morality of war: pacifism, the claim that war is always morally wrong, and what sometimes goes by the name of "**political realism**," the position that war is not a moral issue. We will consider realism first.

According to political realism, war is either the suspension or denial of morality in international relations or it embraces some version of "might makes right" where nations with power simply do as they wish to promote their own interests. According to the realist, the international arena is one of pure egoism as each nation seeks to promote its own interests irrespective of the interests of other nations.

It is hard to see how realism could be rationally defended because it shares the irrationality of egoism, namely, the irrationality of categorically preferring one's own interests over comparable interests of others (see Chapter 1). If nations can have interests that are not simply a shorthand way of talking about the interests of the individuals who compose them, then nations would be big individuals and the political realist must explain why morality holds among individual persons but not among nations conceived as big individuals. Alternatively, if talk of national interest really is just shorthand for talking about the interests of individual persons who compose nations, then international relations are reducible to relations among individuals, and if so, then why the interests of one group of individuals should trump all others requires justification.

When political leaders give moral arguments for going to war, such as appeals to self-defense or retribution or justice, and when ordinary people reflect on war in moral terms, the realist must dismiss this as utterly mistaken. According to the realist position, when otherwise astute people engage in moral reflection about war, they do not understand what they are doing. If the realist is correct, moral deliberation about war mistakenly imports moral concepts into an area where they do not apply, akin to astronomers using moral concepts to talk about stars and galaxies.

Without a compelling background theory to explain why moral deliberation is out of place when we consider war, realism looks implausible. This is because it does not reflect the ways in which most of us actually do think about war. We tend to think about war in moral terms; we often wonder whether it would be fair, right, or just to go to war. At a minimum, the burden of proof is on realists to show that what seems like a comprehensible and appropriate application of moral reasoning is nevertheless deeply flawed.

Because just war theory purports to specify conditions under which war is morally acceptable, it is also opposed to **pacifism,** the position that all wars are morally unacceptable. We might distinguish between absolute and near pacifism. Absolute pacifism holds that no conceivable war could ever be justified, whereas near pacifism holds that even though no actual wars have met that standard, it is conceivable for a war to be just. Like political realism, absolute pacifism requires a powerful background theory to support such an uncompromising position. According to near pacifism, by contrast, no wars that have ever been fought were just, and it is likely that any future wars will also be unjust, although it is at least conceivable that a war be just. In this respect, near pacifism is actually a very strict sort of just war theory.

What would it take to justify going to war? In traditional just war theory, the following conditions must be met: a just cause, last resort, fighting the war must produce more good than evil, and the decision to go to war must be undertaken by the proper authority. All of these conditions except a just cause are self-evident. Since war causes a lot of harm, it should not be undertaken unless all reasonable means to avoid it are exhausted, so fighting must be a last resort. If a war will produce more evil than good, then it obviously should not be undertaken. And the decision to go to war can be made only by the proper authority. In the United States, Congress has the authority to declare war; in other countries it could be the king, the church, an assembly, or some other body vested with authority to declare war. Otherwise, the fighting is not legitimate, according to traditional just war thinking. But each of these conditions makes sense only on the assumption that there is a just case, and what is that?

The most intuitively plausible just cause is national self-defense, alleged to be an extension of the moral legitimacy of individual self-defense. Yet how the legitimacy of individual self-defense gets extended to the national level is unclear. Nations are not people, they are not conscious, they cannot be killed in the way individual people can be killed, and they do not have desires that death can frustrate. If nations are entities at all, they appear to be different sorts of entities than individual persons, so we cannot be confident that whatever we want to say about the moral acceptability of individual self-defense simply transfers to national self-defense. For self-defense to apply to national self-defense, some account of the moral legitimacy and value of a society's way of life must be given—a way of life that is worth defending with force, if necessary. And we cannot simply assume that a society's way of life is worthy of defense. Just as someone robbing a bank cannot claim self-defense when he shoots the guard who reaches for his gun—the robber has lost that right by his wrongful action—so a society that has lost its moral legitimacy cannot properly wage wars in self-defense.

We must distinguish between self-defense and self-preservation, at both the national and individual levels. I am not morally justified in doing absolutely anything whatsoever to save my life. Suppose I must torture ten babies to death; otherwise I will be shot. Doing so merely to preserve my life does not count as self-defense. Thus **self-defense** is morally justified self-preservation, since not all forms of self-preservation are morally permissible.

What makes an act of self-preservation self-defense (and hence morally acceptable)? To justify killing in self-defense, an attack on an innocent person must be unprovoked, immediate, with no other choice except to kill the attacker. Applied at the national level to legitimize a war of self-defense, a nation must be the innocent victim of unjust aggression; it must have no other choice except to fight, and the threat must be immediate. This last condition is especially important given the U.S. war in Iraq. What counts as an immediate threat to justify resorting to lethal force? On an individual level, self-defense is not limited to fighting only after being attacked. If it is evident that another person is about to hit me, I can hit him first. So the person who hits first need not be the aggressor. This idea of a preemptive strike is useful in thinking about war, where a first military strike against an enemy that is preparing to attack can count as a form of self-defense.

For a preemptive strike to count as self-defense, the enemy's attack must be imminent; otherwise a first strike is preventive, not preemptive. There is an important difference between preemption and prevention. As we have just seen, a *preemptive* strike can be legitimate self-defense, but a *preventive* war cannot be construed as self-defense, because it does not meet the immediacy condition for self-defense. A preventive war is not in response to an immediate threat, so there are probably ways of avoiding the use of force, and perhaps there is some mistake interpreting the intentions of another country. Thus preventive war violates the "last resort" criterion set out by just war theory.

The real problem with preventive war (rather than preemptive war) is that preventive war makes wars all too frequent. The heightened suspicions aroused by a policy of preventive military strikes among nations would perversely generate the conditions that justify more war, since each country would be aware that others could justifiably attack it merely on suspicion that it could be attacked. So the first country would arm itself, thus threatening others and thereby ensure that others will attack it. Furthermore, aware that other countries will attack it merely on suspicion of attack, the first country should then attack first to prevent the others from attacking. A policy allowing preventive war thus engenders more war than would otherwise occur, and for this reason it should be viewed with extreme caution internationally, for it unleashes a principle that makes for more war rather than less.

The George W. Bush administration is arguably engaged in a preventive war in Iraq, not a preemptive one, despite the fact that officials have deliberately sought to obscure the difference between preemption and prevention. Since Iraq had no weapons of mass destruction, an attack on the United States or its interests with those weapons was not imminent. Therefore, the war cannot be preemptive. What if Bush and his backers sincerely believed that an attack was imminent? Irrespective of how firmly they believed an attack was forthcoming, they were mistaken. If they argue that an attack could have been forthcoming and that it is better to prevent a distant attack before it becomes imminent, then they confirm the point that a policy of preventive war will result in more war.

We have been addressing the question of when to go to war, now let us consider a related question: Once a nation is in a war, is there a morally acceptable way to fight? According to just war theory, there is: Only proper military targets may be legitimately attacked. What are proper military targets? We can distinguish between things and people, and between civilians and soldiers, and on the basis of just war thinking, only soldiers and their means of war may be legitimately targeted. The problem, of course, is how to draw the line between military and civilian. What do we say about attacking factory workers who produce armaments or farmers who grow food for the army? Distinguishing between combatants—those who may be targeted—and the noncombatants—those who may not be intentionally targeted—is a contested area of just war theory. The distinction is intuitively plausible in theory, but it is very hard to apply.

The essence of morally acceptable fighting, according to just war theory, is that only combatants may fight and kill each other. How can this be? The traditional explanation is that having been trained to fight on command, combatants lose their right to life, so when they are killed (or kill other combatants in a "fair" fight), no combatant rights are violated.

It is not clear, however, that this explanation can adequately ground the moral acceptability of combatants fighting combatants. According to just war theory, combatants on both sides meet as moral equals on the battlefield; both just and unjust combatants have an equal right to try to kill each other. But this hardly seems correct, since combatants on the just side have done nothing wrong, so why should they lose their right to life and why should unjust combatants be able to kill them with impunity? That hardly seems fair.

Just war theory purports to give a comprehensive account of when and how war may be fought within the bounds of morality. It is conceptually situated between political realism (morality does not apply to war, so "anything goes") and pacifism (all war is morally wrong). As we have seen, however, trying to detail the bounds of morally acceptable war gives rise to numerous difficult questions. The challenge for just war theory is to provide actual moral guidance for the conduct of war.

TERRORISM

There is no uniformly accepted definition of terrorism. The term has taken on such rhetorical power that *terrorists* sometimes means merely "fighters one doesn't like." But most definitions of terrorism incorporate the idea of attacking civilians to achieve some political goal. The U.S. Code of Federal Regulations is typical; it defines the term *terrorism* as "the unlawful use of force and violence against persons or property to intimidate or coerce a government, the civilian population, or any segment thereof, in furtherance of political or social objectives."

According to just war theory, it is never legitimate to attack civilians directly, which is precisely what terrorists do. They indiscriminately attack and kill civilians in order to terrorize other civilians. Those attacked are not the true target, for terrorists hope that by killing *these* civilians, they will induce *other* terrorized civilians to urge their government to accede to the terrorists' demands.

Usually we think of terrorists as subnational groups, but there is no reason why states cannot also engage in terrorism. Indeed, the United States has engaged (and arguably continues to engage) in state-sponsored terrorism. The bombing of German cities in World War II and the nuclear destruction of Hiroshima and Nagasaki were direct attacks on civilians in an effort to coerce their governments. It is hard to see how the qualification of lawful as opposed to unlawful use of force, in the definition spelled out in the U.S. Code of Federal Regulations, makes a moral difference, for how does intentionally killing civilians ever become "lawful"?

Is terrorism categorically immoral or can it possibly be justified? If the conceptual core of terrorism is intentionally killing civilians as a means of furthering some political or social goal, the morality of terrorism turns on whether it is ever permissible to do that. Sometimes the term *civilian* is qualified by *innocent*. If the phrase *innocent civilians* is understood to mean morally innocent civilians, then imagine civilians who vigorously support an obviously unjust war. In what sense are they morally innocent? If we are entitled to attack those who are morally liable to attack, then it is not inconceivable that civilians could be targeted. However, in just war theory, *innocent* does not mean "morally innocent." *Innocent* comes from the Latin *nocens*, which means "to harm," so the innocent are those who do not harm. Civilians are thus innocent in the sense that they do not bear arms. They can be morally guilty, but the fact that they pose no threat of harm means that they are not legitimate targets, irrespective of whether their side is justified in fighting.

Whether it is ever permissible to intentionally attack nonmilitary people— civilians—divides just war thinkers. The division turns on moral theory, on whether one is a consequentialist or a moral absolutist. Consequentialists can imagine circumstances when terrorism is permissible; absolutists cannot. One might try to split the difference by adopting a "threshold view" and accept an absolutist conception against terrorism until the consequences of doing so become too great, at which point a threshold is reached where a consequentialist calculation becomes permissible. If, for example, a criminally unjust aggressor is on the verge of militarily defeating a country fighting for its life in self-defense, and if the aggressor will impose morally abhorrent conditions on the defeated country, and if the aggressor can be stopped only by attacking the aggressor nation's civilians, then it is legitimate to attack those civilians, according to some just war thinkers.

READINGS ON WAR AND MORALITY

Jeff McMahan, "Innocence, Self-Defense and Killing in War"

Jeff McMahan is a professor of philosophy at Rutgers University. He is the author of many influential articles in applied ethics, especially on abortion, war, and disability. In the article reprinted here, McMahan argues that a central feature of just war theory—what he calls the Orthodox View—is deeply flawed. It is flawed, according to McMahan, because it accords soldiers who fight unjust wars the same war rights as soldiers who fight justified wars.

Critical Reading Questions

1. What is the Orthodox View?
2. What objections does McMahan raise against the Orthodox View?
3. How does McMahan argue that the Orthodox View does not derive from self-defense?
4. What is an innocent attacker?
5. According to McMahan, what makes one liable to attack?
6. On what grounds does McMahan deny that military service is honorable?
7. How is the morality of war related to the laws of war, according to McMahan?

INNOCENCE, SELF-DEFENSE AND KILLING IN WAR

Jeff McMahan

I. THE ORTHODOX VIEW

Most of us believe that there are conditions in which war is justified and thus that there are conditions in which the individual soldier is morally permitted, and nearly as often morally required, intentionally to attack and even to kill other human beings. Many people, indeed, accept this quite uncritically, often assuming that war is a special condition in which morality, if it applies at all, is radically transformed. But consider the perspective of the morally scrupulous soldier who is ordered to kill. To what considerations may he appeal for justification?[1]

What I will refer to as the *Orthodox View* among moral theorists is that, while it is normally or even always wrong intentionally to attack or kill the innocent, people may, because of what they do, render themselves relevantly noninnocent, thereby losing their moral immunity to intentional attack and instead becoming liable, or morally vulnerable, to attack. To be innocent, on this view, is to be harmless; correspondingly, one ceases to be innocent if one poses an imminent threat of harm to, or is engaged in harming, another person. To the modern mind this may seem a curious understanding of the notions of innocence and noninnocence. Yet there is etymological warrant for the use. To be "innocent" is not to be *nocentes*—a Latin term that refers to one who is harmful or

who injures. To distinguish this sense of innocence from the more familiar notion of moral innocence, some writers have stipulated that a person who is harmless is "materially innocent," while one who is threatening or causing harm is said to be "materially noninnocent."

On the Orthodox View, it is assumed that all those who are, to use Michael Walzer's phrase, "currently engaged in the business of war" are *ipso facto* engaged in causing harm and are therefore relevantly noninnocent.[2] It has therefore been assumed that there is a rough equivalence, in war, between the innocent and noncombatants and between the noninnocent and combatants.[3] From there it has seemed a relatively short step to the conclusion that, while civilians in time of war remain relevantly innocent, all soldiers (except those who have surrendered or been incapacitated) are noninnocent. This, it is claimed, is why it is permissible for soldiers to kill other soldiers.

---

[1]Most combat soldiers have traditionally been, and still are, male. Doubtless this will change but until it does it seems justifiable to use male-gendered pronouns to refer to them.

[2]Michael Walzer, *Just and Unjust Wars* (Harmondsworth: Penguin, 1978), p. 43.

[3]For representative statements of this view, see ibid., pp. 43 and 145–6; Thomas Nagel, "War and Massacre," in Charles R. Beitz et al., eds, *International Ethics* (Princeton: Princeton University Press, 1985), p. 69; Jeffrie Murphy, "The Killing of the Innocent," *The Monist*, 57 (1973), pp. 532 and 536; Robert K. Fullinwider, "War and Innocence," in Beitz, *International Ethics*, p. 94; Philip Devine, *The Ethics of Homicide* (London: Cornell University Press, 1978), p. 152; Anthony Kenny, *The Logic of Deterrence* (London: Firethorn Press, 1985), p. 10; and John Finnis, Joseph M. Boyle, Jr, and Germain Grisez, *Nuclear Deterrence, Morality, and Realism* (Oxford: Oxford University Press, 1987), pp. 86–90.

The presumed equivalence between the materially innocent, noncombatants, and civilians is only approximate, as is that between the materially noninnocent, combatants, and soldiers. In international law, for example, "combatant" is a technical term that refers to a person who wears a distinctive emblem, carries arms openly, and so on.[4] Proponents of the Orthodox View, however, see themselves as articulating the morality of war and not the positive law of war (though they assume that there is a close congruence between the two) and hence use the term in a rather different way. They typically include among combatants certain types of civilian—for example, political leaders, persons who work in war industries, and so on—whose activities contribute directly to the war effort.[5] But, because of the vagueness of such notions as making a contribution to the war effort, the task of drawing the relevant distinctions in a way that is intuitively plausible has been a persistent source of embarrassment to proponents of the View. For it is not obvious why a political leader who orders troops into battle is engaged in causing harm while voters in a democracy who demand that the leader should do so are not; or why drivers who transport arms to the troops count as combatants while the taxpayers who provide the arms by paying for them do not; or why a soldier who is asleep or sitting at a desk well behind the lines can be regarded as threatening or causing harm when a civilian editorialist who stirs support for the war is not; and so forth. I will not labor these objections since they have been well rehearsed elsewhere.[6]

In becoming a soldier, according to the Orthodox View, one gains the right to kill other soldiers but loses one's own immunity to being killed by soldiers of the opposing side. This distribution of rights and liabilites among soldiers is impartial in the sense that no special rights are granted to those who fight in a just cause and no special constraints are imposed on those whose cause is unjust. Thus judgements about the morality of resorting to war (*jus ad bellum*) and judgements about the morality of conduct in war (*jus in bello*) are, in Walzer's words, "logically independent. It is perfectly possible for a just war to be fought unjustly and for an unjust war to be fought in strict accordance with the rules."[7]

It is often supposed that the Orthodox View is grounded in a doctrine that contrasts the legitimacy of intentional killing in self-defense with the doubtful legitimacy of killing in self-preservation.[8] When lethal violence is directed against someone whose action threatens one's own life, one's action counts as self-defensive and is legitimate. But to try to save one's life by directing lethal violence against someone who is not causing the threat to oneself is an act of self-preservation and is at least presumptively wrong. Grounding the Orthodox View in a doctrine of self-defense has various advantages. Among these is that, by discriminating among threats of various degrees of seriousness, the doctrine of self-defense explains why only combatants, and not all people who are engaged in causing harm, however trivial, are vulnerable to lethal attack. Also, if the Orthodox View is supported in this way, then there is no discontinuity between the morality of killing in ordinary life and the morality of killing in war. War is a morally special condition only in that the number of people that it causes to render themselves noninnocent vis-a-vis one another is abnormally large.

II. OBJECTIONS TO THE ORTHODOX VIEW

The Orthodox View is vulnerable to numerous objections. I will begin with one that I believe is answerable but will then advance several that I believe are not.

I. Defense Against Initially Nonlethal Threats

Imagine that the forces of an invading army have crossed one's borders and are moving

---

[4]See Ingrid Detter De Lupis, *The Law of War* (Cambridge: Cambridge University Press, 1987), pp. 106–20.

[5]See, for example, Finnis, Boyle, and Grisez, *Nuclear Deterrence, Morality, and Realism*, pp. 89–90.

[6]A related line of attack is pressed with considerable ingenuity in Noam J. Zohar, "Collective War and Individual Ethics: Against the Conscription of 'Self-Defense'," sections III and IV, forthcoming in *Political Theory*.

[7]Walzer, *Just and Unjust Wars*, p. 21.

[8]See, for example, Fullinwider, "War and Innocence," pp. 92–4.

towards the capital with the avowed aim of annexing one's country to their own. Yet they have announced—and are known to be sincere—that they will not fire their weapons except in self-defense—that is, unless they meet with forcible resistance. It may seem that, since the invading soldiers do not threaten anyone's life, the soldiers of the invaded country have no justification under the Orthodox View for killing members of the invading force. Yet surely it is permissible to resist such an invasion with lethal force.

There are at least two responses to this objection. One is to argue that, even though the invading forces do not directly threaten anyone's life, the threat they pose to the invaded country's political independence is sufficiently serious to warrant a lethal defensive response. While there are, as any theory of self-defense will acknowledge, threats that are insufficiently grave to justify a lethal defensive response, there are also less-than-lethal threats, such as threats of rape, torture, or kidnapping, against which one may defend oneself by lethal means. It is arguable that the political independence of the state is, similarly, a value that the citizens may permissibly defend by lethal means.

The second response appeals to an analogy with private life. Suppose that one discovers a burglar in the process of stealing valuable possessions from one's home. Although this is perhaps controversial, most of us believe that it would not be permissible to kill the burglar to prevent him from taking the possessions; for that would be a disproportionate response to the threat. One is, however, entitled to take certain steps to resist the theft. Suppose, however, that the thief threatens to kill one if one resists. In that case one is permitted to create the conditions of one's own lethal defense. For the thief's threat does not nullify one's right to resist. Indeed, it seems that, as soon as the thief structures the situation in such a way that the attempt to defend one's possessions automatically creates a need for self-defensive killing, one's right to self-defense is immediately activated. One is permitted to kill the thief even without first provoking him to attack by attempting a non-lethal defense of one's possessions.

The logic of this situation seems to apply to the case of the nonviolent invasion. Even if the threat to the invaded country's political independence is not itself sufficiently grave to warrant a lethal defensive response, that threat is backed by a threat to kill in response to resistance and since resistance is justified, the soldiers in effect confront a lethal threat that they may meet with lethal defensive force.

2. Initial Aggression

Let us refer to a soldier who fights in a just war as a *Just Combatant* and to one who fights in an unjust war as an *Unjust Combatant*.[9] (The latter term should not be interpreted to imply culpability. It is possible for a person to fight in an unjust war and yet be morally innocent. I will return to this.) As I noted, the Orthodox View does not discriminate morally between Just and Unjust Combatants; both are permitted to kill enemy combatants, provided that the killing is proportionate to a legitimate military aim it is intended to achieve and inflicts the minimum amount of harm necessary to achieve that aim. Within these constraints, the Orthodox View licenses any killing of one active combatant by another. In war, such an act is never a crime, never an act of murder, never an act for which the agent is culpable or punishable, even if the agent's cause is unjust. Individual soldiers do wrong only when they violate the requirements of *jus in bello*; they are not accountable for violations of *jus ad bellum* (that is, merely for participating in an unjust war).

Yet it is not obvious that the considerations cited by the Orthodox View in support of this claim are in fact sufficient to justify it. As the previous case of the initially nonviolent invasion shows, it is possible to initiate a state of war without attacking anyone except in self-defense against violent acts of resistance. But many wars are initiated in another way: by a surprise attack on the unmobilized forces of the adversary (as occurred, for example, at Pearl Harbor). An act of war of this sort, while directed against military forces and personnel, is not directed against combatants in the sense specified by the Orthodox View. The quiescent,

---

[9] I say "unjust war" rather than "unjust cause" because it is possible to fight an unjust war to achieve a just cause—for example, when war is an unnecessary or disproportionate means of achieving the just cause.

unmobilized forces who are the victims of the surprise attack are not threatening or causing harm. Though they wear uniforms, they are not yet combatants. So how can the Orthodox View simultaneously hold both that in war only combatants are legitimate targets of attack and that individual soldiers who participate in a surprise attack that initiates an unjust war are not guilty of a crime (since they can be held accountable only for violations of *jus in bello* and not simply for participation in an unjust war)?

Assuming that it is possible for a war of aggression (that is, a nondefensive war) to be just, it may be that a surprise attack can be justified even if the targets are not, or not yet, combatants. The Orthodox View makes combatant status a sufficient condition for the loss of immunity; it need not, it seems, make it a necessary condition. In other words, it need not exclude other possible justifications for the use of violence or killing. So it seems compatible with the Orthodox View that participation in a surprise attack that initiates a just war could be justified by reference to considerations other than that the targets of the attack are combatants. Suppose, however, that the war initiated by a surprise attack is unjust because its cause is unjust. In that case, it seems impossible that there could be other considerations that could justify the action of the attacking soldiers. Since it cannot appeal to the claim that the intended targets of the attack are combatants in the relevant sense, the Orthodox View appears to be unable to avoid the conclusion that the Unjust Combatants who participate in a surprise attack that initiates a war are guilty of wrongful, indeed criminal, behavior. Because it denies this conclusion, it appears to be unable to support its own claims.

3. Unjust Wars and the Doctrine of Self-Defense

The foregoing objection is in fact part of a wider criticism of the Orthodox View that challenges its claim to derive from a doctrine of self-defense. Let us say that one who wrongfully and culpably threatens the life of a morally innocent person is a *Culpable Attacker,* while the victim of the Culpable Attacker who then engages in self-defense against the culpable attack is a *Just Attacker.* According to virtually all accounts of the right of individual self-defense, the Culpable

Attacker is not morally permitted to use lethal violence even to defend himself against his initial victim's self-defensive response.[10] Suppose, for example, that a burglar enters a person's home and, discovering that the homeowner is there, fires at her with a gun but misses. If she returns fire, does this activate the burglar's right to self-defense, making it permissible for him to kill her in self-defense? I think clearly not: self-defense against a Just Attacker is wrong.

The application of this conclusion to war should be straightforward. Consider an Unjust Combatant who knows his country's aggressive war is unjust but decides to participate nonetheless, perhaps because he prefers the risks of combat to the obloquy suffered by dissenters in his society. Is it really plausible to suppose that he does no wrong in attacking and killing morally innocent victims of his country's aggression? Is it plausible to suppose that, by justifiably taking up arms to defend themselves and their compatriots against this unjust aggression, these victims thereby lose their moral immunity, making it justifiable for the Unjust Combatant to kill them? I find it impossible to believe that the answer to either of these questions could be "yes," yet that is the answer that the Orthodox View gives. The important point, however, is that the only doctrines of self-defense that support this answer are those that make the right of self-defense absolute, implying, for example, that a murderer may justifiably kill a police officer who attempts to kill him in order to prevent him from committing a further murder. Since, with few exceptions, proponents of the Orthodox View do not accept any such account of the right of self-defense, but instead agree that the right of self-defense is incapable of justifying the killing of a Just Attacker by a Culpable Attacker, they cannot claim that the Orthodox View can be derived from our views about self-defense. If the Unjust Combatant is justified in

[10]The exceptions are certain accounts in the Hobbesian tradition that regard the right of self-defense as absolute. See, for example, Jenny Teichman, *Pacifism and the Just War* (Oxford: Basil Blackwell, 1986), Chapter 8. Notice that there is a distinction between provoking an attack by attacking and other forms of provocation. Only those attacks provoked in the former way are self-defensive and only Culpable Attackers normally forfeit the right of self-defense. Other culpable provocateurs generally retain it.

killing Just Combatants on the opposing side, the justification cannot be simply that he has a right to defend himself against those who threaten him.

Certain theorists, perhaps aware of the doubtful consistency between the Orthodox View and our views about self-defense, have advanced an alternative justification for killing in war that does seem to be a consistent extension of common views about self-defense into the sphere of war. The most prominent of these theorists is G.E.M. Anscombe, who, beginning with the standard assumption that the non-innocent lose their immunity to intentional attack in war, claims that "what is required, for the people attacked to be non-innocent in the relevant sense, is that they should be engaged in an objectively unjust proceeding which the attacker has the right to make his concern; or—the commonest case—should be unjustly attacking him."[11] According to this view, in order for it to be justifiable to attack someone who poses a threat, it must be the case that the one who poses the threat is "objectively" unjustified in doing so. This allows for the permissibility of killing a *morally* innocent person in self-defense provided that the person *would* be culpable for the threat he poses if, contrary to fact, the necessary conditions of moral responsibility obtained. (I will refer to such a person, who is morally innocent but poses a morally unjustifiable threat, as an *Innocent Attacker*.) It does not, however, permit the killing of a person, even in self-defense, if what that person is doing is not "objectively unjust," which of course it will not be if it is morally permissible. Thus Anscombe's view does not permit, and indeed prohibits, the self-defensive killing of a Just Attacker (for example, by a Culpable Attacker).

Despite its apparent success in organizing many of our intuitions about self-defense under a single simple principle, Anscombe's view is vulnerable to objections, not least of which is that it seems to lack any foundation for the implication that it is permissible to kill an Innocent Attacker in self-defense.[12] The point that should be noted here, however, is that Anscombe's view is radically at odds with the Orthodox View. For Unjust Combatants are engaged in an objectively unjust proceeding; therefore the Just Combatants who oppose them are justified in attacking them and, since these Just Combatants are justified in what they do, they retain their innocence; hence it is wrong for Unjust Combatants to attack Just Combatants even in self-defense.[13]

III. THE PRIMACY OF MORAL INNOCENCE AND NONINNOCENCE

Critics of the Orthodox View sometimes challenge the significance of the distinction between combatants and noncombatants in the following way. Suppose that one could advance the just cause of a war by one or the other of two equally effective means. Either one could intentionally attack a member of the adversary's civilian population who is clearly a noncombatant but who bears significant moral responsibility for the wrong the redress of which constitutes the just cause for war (for example, an editorialist and propagandist who is now an invalid in hospital) or one could intentionally attack a pure-hearted but simple-minded conscript who has been manipulated into fighting by means of coercion, deception, and indoctrination. Is it really plausible, the critics ask, to suppose that, while it is impermissible to attack the former because he retains his material innocence, the latter is fair game because he does not? Citing just such a comparison, George Mavrodes asks: "Is it not clear that 'innocence,' as used here, leaves out entirely all of the relevant moral considerations—that it has no moral content

[11]G.E.M. Anscombe, *Collected Philosophical Papers, Volume III: Ethics, Religion, and Politics* (Minneapolis, MN: University of Minnesota Press, 1981), p. 53. Some commentators have mistakenly seen Anscombe as an exponent of the Orthodox View. See, for example, Nagel, "War and Massacre," p. 69, n. 10. A recent theory of the foundations of the right of self-defense that has certain affinities with Anscombe's view can be found in Judith Jarvis Thomson's "Self-Defense," *Philosophy and Public Affairs*, 20 (1991), 283–310.

[12]I advance certain objections to Anscombe's view in "Self-Defense and the Problem of the Innocent Attacker," *Ethics*, 104 (1994).

[13]That Anscombe's view has this implication is noted by Teichman (*Pacifism and the Just War*, p. 65), who, however, appears to find the implication so implausible that she wonders whether Anscombe could have been aware of it.

at all?"[14] Mavrodes concludes that the requirement to distinguish between the innocent and the noninnocent so understood, or between noncombatants and combatants, is merely a convention, like driving on a certain side of the road, that is highly useful for people to agree to observe.

There is, of course, another possibility, which is that there is a deeper morality of war that is not convention-dependent but which does not coincide with the Orthodox View. I believe that there is such a morality and that one of its crucial features is suggested by the contrast between the guilty noncombatant and the morally innocent soldier. Let us consider more closely why that contrast seems to challenge the Orthodox View.

The guilty civilian is an example of what I call a *Culpable Cause*—that is, a person whose culpable action in the past is the cause of a threat that has materialized only now. There are cases—and we are imagining that that of the guilty civilian is one of these—in which, though the Culpable Cause of some present threat does not now himself pose a threat, so that self-defensive violence against him is not even a conceptual possibility, nevertheless attacking or killing him would, for one reason or another, eliminate the threat caused by his previous culpable action. It is, I believe, intuitively plausible to suppose that it is permissible (subject, perhaps, to some suitable proportionality restriction) intentionally to harm the Culpable Cause in order to prevent his own culpable action from now causing harm to the morally innocent. It is, for example, permissible to kill the Culpable Cause to prevent his culpable past action from now causing one's own death. This would be a case of permissible killing in self-preservation.

What the case of the Culpable Cause shows is that moral noninnocence may weaken or nullify a person's immunity to attack even if the person is materially innocent. It is also clear, as is shown by the impermissibility of self-defense against a Just Attacker, that mere material noninnocence (that is, causing harm) is not sufficient for the loss, or even the weakening, of a person's moral immunity to intentional attack. If a person is morally innocent, his being materially noninnocent may have no effect on the moral barriers to harming him. This is why the case of the Unjust Combatant who is morally innocent is disturbing: his moral innocence causes us to doubt whether he has lost his moral immunity and therefore whether it is permissible to attack him, despite his material noninnocence.

The case of the Innocent Attacker is, however, merely disturbing; it does not show that one who is morally innocent but materially noninnocent retains his immunity. For, while some believe that it is wrong, and therefore at most excused, intentionally to harm an Innocent Attacker, even in self-defense, most people believe that self-defense against an Innocent Attacker is permissible.[15] The reason why the case of the Innocent Attacker is nevertheless disturbing is that none of the justifications that have been offered for self-defense against an Innocent Attacker is wholly convincing.[16] The problem, as I see it, is to find a difference between the Innocent Attacker and the Innocent Bystander (someone who bears neither causal nor moral responsibility for a certain threat) that is sufficiently morally important to justify killing the former given our belief that intentionally killing the latter, even in self-preservation, is a paradigm of wrongful action.

According to the Orthodox View, the justification for self-defense against an Innocent Attacker is exactly the same as the justification for self-defense against a Culpable Attacker—namely, that the attacker, by threatening harm, has lost his immunity. This is implausible; if it were true, then whatever restrictions there are on the defensive use of violence against an Innocent Attacker would also apply to self-defense against a Culpable Attacker. But intuitively the restrictions on self-defense against an Innocent Attacker are considerably more stringent. For example, if it is possible to retreat from

---

[14]George I. Mavrodes, "Conventions and the Morality of War," in Beitz et al., *International Ethics*, p. 81.

[15]Those who reject the permissibility of self-defense against an Innocent Attacker include Laurence Alexander, "Justification and Innocent Aggressors," Wayne Law Review, 33 (1987), pp. 1184–9; and Zohar, "Collective War and Individual Ethics."

[16]The various arguments for the permissibility of self-defense against an Innocent Attacker are critically assessed in McMahan, "Self-Defense and the Problem of the Innocent Attacker."

a confrontation with an Innocent Attacker in safety, then one must retreat rather than engage in self-defense. This is true even if one is where one has a right to be—for example, in one's home. One need not, by contrast, flee from a confrontation with a Culpable Attacker. Particularly if one is where one has a right to be, one may stand one's ground, killing the attacker in self-defense even if one could flee in complete safety. Or, to take another example, the proportionality restriction governing self-defense against an Innocent Attacker is in some respects stronger than that governing self-defense against a Culpable Attacker. If, for example, one could be certain of avoiding being killed by an Innocent Attacker by killing him but could alternatively reduce the risk of being killed to an almost negligible level by attempting to incapacitate him with lesser force, one might be required to accept the greater risk to oneself in order to reduce the harm to the attacker. No such requirement would apply if the attacker were a Culpable Attacker. It might, of course, be argued that these examples show only that the combination of moral noninnocence and material noninnocence has a greater effect in weakening a person's immunity than material noninnocence alone. But if—as I believe is true—the restrictions that apply to self-preservative violence against a Culpable Cause are exactly the same as those that apply to self-defense against a Culpable Attacker, then we are entitled to draw a stronger conclusion: namely, that moral noninnocence has a greater effect in weakening a person's immunity than material noninnocence, other things being equal.

We may summarize our results so far as follows. Material innocence does not guarantee moral immunity. Neither is it clear that moral innocence guarantees immunity. On reflection, however, it may seem that the case for self-preservative action against the Culpable Cause is stronger than that for self-defensive action against the Innocent Attacker (as evidenced by the fact that the restrictions that apply in the latter case seem stronger) and thus that moral noninnocence has a stronger effect in weakening a person's immunity than mere material noninnocence. This conclusion is reinforced by the fact that there are cases in which material noninnocence fails to weaken a person's immunity

at all. Moral noninnocence, by contrast, always appears to be a ground for liability.

We can illustrate these rather abstract conclusions by means of an example. Suppose there is a group of your enemies who wish you to be killed, since they will profit from your death. They build a device that can be programmed to transmit irresistible commands to a person through a receiver implanted in his brain. Once programmed and activated, the device requires no further guidance or intervention. Your enemies then kidnap an innocent person, install the implant in his brain, program the controlling device with the command that this innocent person should kill you, and activate the device. You learn what has been done and realize that there are only two things that can be done to save yourself. One is to kill your implacable though morally innocent pursuer. The other is to find the controlling device and deactivate it. Since the police think your tale is pure fantasy, your only recourse, other than killing the innocent pursuer, is to coerce your enemies to deactivate or reveal the location of the device. You soon realize, however, that the only way to do this is to begin killing them, one by one, until one of them is sufficiently intimidated to tell you where the device is located.

Notice that the enemies do not constitute a threat to you. Like the guilty civilian in the earlier example, they may all be helpless invalids. They are Culpable Causes; thus you cannot, as a matter of conceptual necessity, engage in self-defense against them. According to the Orthodox View, therefore, the enemies are innocent and retain their immunity to attack, while the pursuer, who does threaten you, is relevantly noninnocent and has therefore lost his immunity. It is permissible to kill him in self-defense. This, however, is obviously implausible. Assuming that killing the enemies would be equally effective in averting the threat and other things are equal, it is clearly morally preferable to kill the enemies—and to kill as many of them as necessary—rather than to kill the innocent pursuer.

The parallels with war are obvious. Earlier, in Section I, I rehearsed the familiar point that certain types of civilian—more types than the proponent of the Orthodox View would care to admit—may seem to forfeit their immunity in war by causally contributing in various ways to the threat their country poses. The point here is different. It is that, like the enemies in the case of the innocent pursuer, many civilians are Culpable Causes of the unjust threat their country poses. While the Orthodox View declares them immune, it seems clearly morally preferable to attack them rather than to attack innocent soldiers if either option would be equally effective in contributing to the achievement of the just cause of the war.

It is worth noting that, just as the enemies are Culpable Causes of the threat to you, they are also Culpable Causes of the predicament of the innocent pursuer. There is thus an additional reason for attacking the enemies, which is that one would be rescuing the pursuer from the awful and dangerous situation in which they have unjustly placed him. (This assumes, plausibly, that third party intervention against a Culpable Cause is permissible.) This is worth mentioning because an analogous consideration applies in war—namely, that if attacking guilty civilians would be equally effective in promoting the just cause as attacking morally innocent soldiers would be, then one has as an additional reason for attacking the civilians that this would help to free the innocent soldiers from the dangerous and morally repugnant predicament in which they have been unjustly placed.

The case of the innocent pursuer provides vivid support for the central claim of this section: that whether a person is morally innocent or noninnocent has a clearer and stronger effect on that person's immunity to intentional attack than whether he is materially innocent or noninnocent. Depending on what one believes about the permissibility of self-defense against an Innocent Attacker, material noninnocence alone may function to weaken a person's immunity and may therefore have a subordinate role in defining the requirement of discrimination in war. But the principal distinction is between the morally innocent and the morally noninnocent.

The significance of moral innocence and noninnocence is connected with considerations of justice. In some instances a person may, as a matter of justice, *deserve* to suffer a certain harm because of his moral noninnocence. In that case it may be permissible, or even obligatory, for the appropriately authorized person or persons to

inflict that harm even if the alternative would be that no one would be harmed. In other cases a person may be *liable* to suffer harm if, through his own culpable action, he has made it inevitable that *someone* must suffer harm. In such a case, it is permissible, and sometimes even obligatory, to harm the morally guilty person rather than to allow his morally culpable action to cause harm to the morally innocent.[17] The interests of the innocent have priority as a matter of justice.

Given a choice between causing or not causing a certain harm, or between causing or allowing one harm and causing or allowing another, a person is innocent relative to that choice if she has done no wrong that renders her deserving of or liable to being caused or allowed to suffer that harm. The notions of innocence and noninnocence must be relativized, as they are here, to particular choices, since moral guilt renders a person liable only to certain specific harms and not to others. My unjustifiably attacking you makes me liable only to the minimum amount of harm necessary to prevent my harming you, together, perhaps, with any further harm I may deserve as punishment. My immunity is compromised only to that extent; I do not become fair game for any sort of violence that anyone might want to inflict on me for any reason. Thus in war the noninnocent are those who are morally responsible for the offense or crime the prevention or rectification of which constitutes the just cause for war; and they may permissibly be harmed only to the minimum extent necessary to achieve the just cause. I will leave open what constitutes a just cause for war. Thus it is possible that people may be relevantly guilty for offenses other than aggression.

Considerations of moral guilt and innocence may interact in complex ways with other factors to determine the morality of action. Moral guilt is often, however, a morally decisive consideration that can nullify the relevance of factors that would otherwise be significant. It can, for example, nullify the relevance of the distinction between doing and allowing or that of the

<hr>

[17]This claim is developed as an account of the right of individual self-defense in Phillip Montague, "Self-Defense and Choosing Among Lives," *Philosophical Studies*, 40 (1981), 207–19.

distinction between intending and merely foreseeing. If one is being attacked by a Culpable Attacker, there is no reason to save oneself by allowing him to tread on a landmine rather than by shooting him (for example, if there would be a slightly greater risk to oneself in the former case). Nor is there any reason to intend only to incapacitate him rather than to intend to kill him if one knows that what one must do will, either way, in fact kill him. These considerations may have important implications for the morality of war. Some have suggested, for example, that, if certain civilians are morally responsible for the grievance that provides the just cause for war, then this may justify acts of war that foreseeably but unintentionally harm them[18]—or, more significantly, may weaken the stringency of the proportionality restriction on causing them unintended harm. If, however, moral guilt has the significance I have suggested, then a civilian's moral guilt may have the stronger effect of rendering him liable to intentional attack. I will return to this.

IV. IMPLICATIONS FOR THE CONDUCT OF WAR

1. Can Unjust Combatants Permissibly Fight?

The fundamental distinction that determines who is and who is not a permissible target for attack in war is the distinction between the morally guilty and the morally innocent. We may, as an exercise in persuasive definition, refer to this view as the *Moral View*. Since a combatant's moral guilt or innocence may be determined in part by whether or not he is fighting in a just war, the Moral View denies the Orthodox View's claim that *jus in bello* and *jus ad bellum* are logically independent. For the rights and liabilities of Just Combatants may be different from those of Unjust Combatants.

The Orthodox View holds that Unjust Combatants do no wrong provided that they fight within the limits of the conventional rules of engagement. If, however, those against whom they fight are morally innocent, because they fight permissibly for a just cause, then, according to the Moral View, the use of violence by Unjust Combatants is problematic, since the objects of that violence presumably retain their immunity to intentional attack.

We may distinguish between two uses of violence by an Unjust Combatant: violence in the service of the unjust war and violence that is entirely self-defensive. There is, it seems, no justification for the Unjust Combatant's use of violence in the service of the unjust war. If the war lacks a just cause, it follows that the cause it serves is incapable of justifying belligerent action. (This is true whether the aims of the war are inherently unjust or whether they are good or worthy aims that, for whatever reason, are insufficient to justify the resort to war.) And even if there is a just cause, the fact that the war itself is unjust again implies that the cause may not, in the circumstances, be permissibly pursued by belligerent means.

Whether an Unjust Combatant may permissibly use violence in self-defense is a more complicated question, the answer to which may depend on whether he is a Culpable Attacker or an Innocent Attacker. An Unjust Combatant may be morally innocent if he is nonculpably or excusably ignorant of the fact that the war in which he fights is unjust or if, even if he knows or suspects that the war is unjust, he is subject to irresistible coercion that compels him, against his will, to fight. If neither of these conditions applies, so that the Unjust Combatant's participation in an unjust war is not fully excused, then he is a Culpable Attacker whose use of force, even in self-defense, is wrong. If, however, his participation is fully excused, then he is an Innocent Attacker and a case can perhaps be made for the claim that Innocent Attackers, while merely excused for their initial attack, are nevertheless justified in engaging in self-defense against the defensive counterattack by the victims of their initial attack. If it is true that an Innocent Attacker retains the right of self-defense against the victim of his initial attack, then an innocent Unjust Combatant does no wrong if he uses violence purely for the purpose of self-defense. (This in turn implies that the mere material noninnocence of the Just Combatant does indeed weaken his immunity vis-a-vis the innocent Unjust Combatant.) Since it would be absurd to suppose that the

[18]See James Child, "Political Responsibility and Noncombatant Liability," in Kenneth Kipnis and Diana T. Meyers, eds, *Political Realism and International Morality* (Boulder: Westview Press, 1987), esp. p. 64.

innocent Unjust Combatant retains the right of self-defense while the Just Combatant does not, the struggle between the innocent Unjust Combatant and the Just Combatant becomes one in which each party is justified in attempting to kill the other. There are thus conditions in which the implications of the Moral View coincide with those of the Orthodox View (which of course regards all rule-governed struggles between Just and Unjust Combatants as ones in which both parties are justified).

1.1 Is Military Service an Honorable Profession?

Among the reasons for thinking that many of the soldiers who fight in unjust wars are Innocent Attackers are that the reasoning that leads the higher authorities to decide to go to war and to fight the war in a certain way is generally not made accessible to ordinary soldiers, that soldiers are often or even typically lied to about the real purposes of the wars in which they are required to participate, that they are indoctrinated to accept uncritically whatever their superiors in rank tell them, that they are intensively conditioned to obey orders without reflection, and so on. While at least some of these features of military life are in some degree necessary in order for a military force to be able to mobilize quickly and to function smoothly and cohesively, there is also no question that they tend to diminish the autonomy and moral responsibility of individual soldiers. They are therefore among the considerations that might be cited in making a case for the claim that many soldiers who fight in unjust wars are morally innocent.

Persons who join the military are typically aware that this abdication of moral autonomy is a condition of military life; indeed, some join the military in part in order to enjoy the freedom from responsibility. They know, in short, that they are allowing themselves to become instruments of the wills of others. There is, moreover, something else they could know with a little reflection, which is that most wars in which people fight are unjust. This follows from the assumption that a war can be just on at most one side, though it can be unjust on both. Even if this formal assumption is unwarranted, it does seem true as a contingent fact that very

few wars, if any, have been just on both sides, while, as Anscombe puts it, "human pride, malice and cruelty are so usual that . . . wars have mostly been mere wickedness on both sides."[20]

Putting these two points together, we arrive at the conclusion that, in joining the military, one allows oneself to become an instrument for the violent pursuit of purposes that are more than likely to be unjust. How can this possibly be a morally acceptable thing to do? Of course, in many cases, the pressure to join the military may be nearly as strong as the pressure, once one is in the military, to surrender the prerogative of determining for oneself whether or not the war in which one is asked to fight is just. It is only when this is true that there can be a convincing case for regarding an Unjust Combatant as morally innocent. For, otherwise, following one's superiors into an unjust war is roughly analogous to committing a crime while drunk: one may not be responsible for one's action given one's condition at the time, but one's conduct nevertheless remains culpable because of one's responsibility for getting oneself into a condition of diminished responsibility.

This leaves the question how it can be permissible voluntarily to join the military given the knowledge that one is likely to be used as an instrument of injustice. I have no answer to this question, though I offer two observations. First, the problem is most acute in countries, like the US, with a history of extensive use of force abroad. The likelihood that a soldier will be called upon to fight unjustly is much lower in a country, such as Switzerland or Sweden, with a recent record free of external interventions and whose forces are manifestly configured for defensive operations only (though even in these countries there is a risk of being used for unjust purposes internally—or, perhaps, externally in what was once an internal area, as in the case of the Yugoslav army, which was configured for territorial defense but has since supported aggression against areas that were formerly within the territory of Yugoslavia). Second, the problem here is but one instance of the broader problem of reconciling individual moral autonomy with structures of authority, which in turn appear necessary for many valuable forms of collective action. An analogous question is raised, for example, by participation in democratic decision-making procedures. By participating, one acquires a moral commitment—one that is perhaps defeasible but nonetheless real—to abide by the result. If the issue is one of moral importance, one risks being bound to support and perhaps participate in an immoral activity. Non-pacifists may take some comfort in the fact that very few people have been prompted by this reflection to reject democracy in favor of anarchy. For whatever arguments can be marshalled in defense of democracy can presumably be applied, *mutatis mutandis,* to the defense of soldiering.

If, however, it is morally permissible voluntarily to join the military even in conditions in which there is a significant probability that one will then serve as an instrument of injustice, can soldiers who voluntarily join be regarded as Innocent Attackers if they do fight in an unjust war? If one is permitted to place oneself in a situation in which one is likely to act unjustly, does the permission then excuse one's later unjust action? I do not believe that it can; hence one is left with a profound tension between the presumption that voluntary participation in the military is permissible and the claim that participation in an unjust war is both wrong and culpable if the Unjust Combatant freely chose to risk being used in this way.

1.2 The Divergence Between the Morality of War and the Laws of War

The Orthodox View, as I noted, coincides rather closely with the international laws of war. In particular, the laws of war, like the Orthodox View, permit Unjust combatants to attack and kill Just Combatants. According to the Moral View, however, Unjust Combatants are justified in killing Just Combatants only in self-defense and only if they (the Unjust Combatants) are morally innocent. If the Moral View is the correct account of the morality of war, then the laws of war permit forms of action that are immoral. Is this acceptable?

There are compelling reasons why the laws of war cannot treat the use of violence by Unjust Combatants as criminal. The main reason is that we cannot regard ordinary soldiers as liable to punishment simply for having participated in an unjust war. This is not because an Unjust Combatant cannot deserve punishment provided that he fights in accordance with the positive rules of engagement. Rather, some Unjust Combatants may indeed deserve punishment. Others—the morally innocent—do not. But even those who do will be guilty to differing degrees. And there are no impartial institutions competent to determine which soldiers do deserve punishment and how severe a punishment they deserve. In current conditions, for example, even if the victor in a war is the side that fought in a just cause, it could not possibly administer punishment to large numbers of soldiers in an informed and impartial manner. And matters are of course much worse if it is the unjust side that emerges victorious. For victors do not concede that they have been in the wrong, even if they are aware that they have been (which, given the propensity for self-deception, they often are not). Rather, they invariably declare their cause to have been just; thus, if the practice were sanctioned, they would doubtless be moved to seek vengeance, under the guise of punishment, against soldiers who had justifiably resisted their wrongful aggression. Finally, the expectation that ordinary soldiers would face punishment at the hands of their adversaries in the aftermath of war would deter either side from surrendering, thereby prolonging wars well beyond the point at which fighting might otherwise cease.[21]

The laws of war, therefore, have to diverge from the morality of war.[22] But this will be acceptable if their purpose is not necessarily to reflect and to aid in the enforcement of morality. Given a recognition that unjust wars and individual participation in unjust wars cannot, in current conditions, be eliminated by legislation, the function of the laws of war may have to be to make the best of a bad situation by seeking to minimize the human costs of inevitable wrongdoing. The laws of war, in effect, are conventions in Mavrodes's sense that are justified by their utility. Only by permitting what is immoral can they best fulfill their morally sanctioned purpose.

What, then, is the point of arguing about the morality of war if the rules by which international society must attempt to regulate and restrain the conduct of war are to be determined by their utility rather than by their conformity with the requirements of morality? There are many answers to this question. I will briefly note two relevant considerations. First, the morality of war, and not the rules of war, is what should govern the conscience of the individual soldier. In particular, if the individual soldier has reason to believe or suspect that his country's war is unjust, this is equivalent to believing or suspecting that his action as a belligerent in this war is or would be murderous. If he is convinced that the war is unjust, then he must not participate. (Complications arise in the case in which the adversary's war is also unjust. I will not pursue these matters here.) Second, insofar as domestic laws concerning the right of conscientious objection are influenced by the claim of international law (which of course is shared by the Orthodox View) that an individual soldier does no wrong in participating in an unjust war, those laws should be liberalized to take account of the recognition that participation in an unjust war may be an egregious moral crime that the state has no right to coerce an individual to commit.

Questions for Discussion

1. Is it always wrong to attack civilians? What is McMahan's view on the matter? Is he right?
2. What are the conditions for self-defense? Is a defensive war a just war?
3. Is it permissible to kill an innocent attacker in self-defense?
4. May soldiers permissibly fight and kill each other?

Michael Walzer, "Arguing about War"

Michael Walzer is a professor of social science at the Institute for Advanced Study at Princeton. He is one of the world's most distinguished philosophers on war and morality. His acclaimed book, Just and Unjust Wars, *is a modern classic. Unlike most philosophers whose work is read only by other philosophers, Walzer is widely read by all who are interested in moral questions about war. In the article reprinted here, Walzer argues that terrorism is unjustified.*

Critical Reading Questions

1. What excuses for terrorism does Walzer consider?
2. What objections does Walzer raise for each excuse?
3. What danger does Walzer see in trying to resist terrorism?
4. What is the link between terrorism and oppression, according to Walzer?

ARGUING ABOUT WAR

Michael Walzer

TERRORISM: A CRITIQUE OF EXCUSES
(1988)

No one these days advocates terrorism, not even those who regularly practice it. The practice is indefensible now that it has been recognized, like rape and murder, as an attack upon the innocent. In a sense, indeed, terrorism is worse than rape and murder commonly are, for in the latter cases the victim has been chosen for a purpose; he or she is the direct object of attack, and the attack has some reason, however twisted or ugly it may be. The victims of a terrorist attack are third parties, innocent bystanders; there is no special reason for attacking them; anyone else within a large class of (unrelated) people will do as well. The attack is directed indiscriminately against the entire class. Terrorists are like killers on a rampage, except that their rampage is not just expressive of rage or madness; the rage is purposeful and programmatic. It aims at a general vulnerability: Kill these people in order to terrify those. A relatively small number of dead victims makes for a very large number of living and frightened hostages.

This, then, is the peculiar evil of terrorism—not only the killing of innocent people but also the intrusion of fear into everyday life, the violation of private purposes, the insecurity of public spaces, the endless coerciveness of precaution. A crime wave might, I suppose, produce similar effects, but no one plans a crime wave; it is the work of a thousand individual decision-makers, each one independent of the others, brought together only by the invisible hand. Terrorism is the work of visible hands; it

is an organizational project, a strategic choice, a conspiracy to murder and intimidate . . . you and me. No wonder the conspirators have difficulty defending, in public, the strategy they have chosen.

The moral difficulty is the same, obviously, when the conspiracy is directed not against you and me but against *them*—Protestants, say, not Catholics; Israelis, not Italians or Germans; blacks, not whites. These "limits" rarely hold for long; the logic of terrorism steadily expands the range of vulnerability. The more hostages they hold, the stronger the terrorists are. No one is safe once whole populations have been put at risk. Even if the risk were contained, however, the evil would be no different. So far as individual Protestants or Israelis or blacks are concerned, terrorism is random, degrading, and frightening. That is its hallmark, and that, again, is why it cannot be defended.

But when moral justification is ruled out, the way is opened for ideological excuse and apology. We live today in a political culture of excuses. This is far better than a political culture in which terrorism is openly defended and justified, for the excuse at least acknowledges the evil. But the improvement is precarious, hard won, and difficult to sustain. It is not the case, even in this better world, that terrorist organizations are without supporters. The support is indirect but by no means ineffective. It takes the form of apologetic descriptions and explanations, a litany of excuses that steadily undercuts our knowledge of the evil. Today that knowledge is insufficient unless it is supplemented and reinforced by a systematic critique of excuses. That is my purpose here. I take the principle for granted: that every act of terrorism is a wrongful act. The wrongfulness of the excuses, however, cannot be taken for granted; it has to be argued. The excuses themselves are familiar enough, the stuff of contemporary political debate. I shall state them in stereotypical form. There is no need to attribute them to this or that writer, publicist, or commentator; my readers can make their own attributions.[1]

The most common excuse for terrorism is that it is a last resort, chosen only when all else fails. The image is of people who have literally run out of options. One by one, they have tried every legitimate form of political and military action, exhausted every possibility, failed everywhere, until no alternative remains but the evil of terrorism. They must be terrorists or do nothing at all. The easy response is to insist that, given this description of their case, they should do nothing at all; they have indeed exhausted their possibilities. But this response simply reaffirms the principle, ignores the excuse; this response does not attend to the terrorists' desperation. Whatever the cause to which they are committed, we have to recognize that, given the commitment, the one thing they cannot do is "nothing at all."

But the case is badly described. It is not so easy to reach the "last resort." To get there, one must indeed try everything (which is a lot of things) and not just once, as if a political party might organize a single demonstration, fail to win immediate victory, and claim that it was now justified in moving on to murder. Politics is an art of repetition. Activists and citizens learn from experience, that is, by doing the same thing over and over again. It is by no means clear when they run out of options, but even under conditions of oppression and war, citizens have a good run short of that. The same argument applies to state officials who claim that they have tried "everything" and are now compelled to kill hostages or bomb peasant villages. Imagine such people called before a judicial tribunal and required to answer the question, What exactly did you try? Does anyone believe that they could come up with a plausible list? "Last resort" has only a notional finality; the resort to terror is ideologically last, not last in an actual

series of actions, just last for the sake of the excuse. In fact, most state officials and movement militants who recommend a policy of terrorism recommend it as a first resort; they are for it from the beginning, although they may not get their way at the beginning. If they are honest, then, they must make other excuses and give up the pretense of the last resort.

[Would terrorism be justified in a "supreme emergency" as that condition is described in "Emergency Ethics" (Chapter 3)? It might be, but only if the oppression to which the terrorists claimed to be responding was genocidal in character. Against the imminent threat of political and physical extinction, extreme measures can be defended, assuming that they have some chance of success. But this kind of a threat has not been present in any of the recent cases of terrorist activity. Terrorism has not been a means of avoiding disaster but of reaching for political success.]

The second excuse is designed for national liberation movements struggling against established and powerful states. Now the claim is that nothing else is possible, that no other strategy is available except terrorism. This is different from the first excuse because it does not require would-be terrorists to run through all the available options. Or, the second excuse requires terrorists to run through all the options in their heads, not in the world, notional finality is enough. Movement strategists consider their options and conclude that they have no alternative to terrorism. They think that they do not have the political strength to try anything else, and thus they do not try anything else. Weakness is their excuse.

But two very different kinds of weakness are commonly confused here: the weakness of the movement vis-à-vis the opposing state and the movement's weakness vis-à-vis its own people. This second kind of weakness, the inability of the movement to mobilize the nation, makes terrorism the "only" option because it effectively rules out all the others: nonviolent resistance, general strikes, mass demonstrations, unconventional warfare, and so on.

These options are only rarely ruled out by the sheer power of the state, by the pervasiveness and intensity of oppression. Totalitarian states may be immune to nonviolent or guerrilla resistance, but all the evidence suggests that they are also immune to terrorism. Or, more exactly, in totalitarian states state terror dominates every other sort. Where terrorism is a possible strategy for the oppositional movement (in liberal and democratic states, most obviously), other strategies are also possible if the movement has some significant degree of popular support. In the absence of popular support, terrorism may indeed be the one available strategy, but it is hard to see how its evils can then be excused. For it is not weakness alone that makes the excuse, but the claim of the terrorists to represent the weak; and the particular form of weakness that makes terrorism the only option calls that claim into question.

One might avoid this difficulty with a stronger insistence on the actual effectiveness of terrorism. The third excuse is simply that terrorism works (and nothing else does); it achieves the ends of the oppressed even without their participation. "When the act accuses, the result excuses."[2] This is a consequentialist argument, and given a strict understanding of consequentialism, this argument amounts to a justification rather than an excuse. In practice, however, the argument is rarely pushed so far. More often, the argument begins with an acknowledgment of the terrorists' wrongdoing. Their hands are dirty, but we must make a kind of peace with them because they have acted effectively for the sake of people who could not act for themselves. But, in fact, have the terrorists' actions been effective? I doubt that terrorism has ever achieved national liberation—no nation that I know of owes its freedom to a campaign of random murder—although terrorism undoubtedly increases the power of the terrorists within the national liberation movement. Perhaps terrorism is also conducive to the survival and notoriety (the two go together) of the movement, which is now dominated by terrorists. But even if we were to grant some means-end relationship between terror and national liberation, the third excuse does not work unless it can meet the further requirements of a consequentialist argument. It must be possible to say that the desired end could not have been achieved through any other, less wrongful, means. The third excuse depends, then, on the success of

the first or second, and neither of these look likely to be successful.

The fourth excuse avoids this crippling dependency. This excuse does not require the apologist to defend either of the improbable claims that terrorism is the last resort or that it is the only possible resort. The fourth excuse is simply that terrorism is the universal resort. All politics is (really) terrorism. The appearance of innocence and decency is always a piece of deception, more or less convincing in accordance with the relative power of the deceivers. The terrorist who does not bother with appearances is only doing openly what everyone else does secretly.

This argument has the same form as the maxim "All's fair in love and war." Love is always fraudulent, war is always brutal, and political action is always terrorist in character. Political action works (as Thomas Hobbes long ago argued) only by generating fear in innocent men and women. Terrorism is the politics of state officials and movement militants alike. This argument does not justify either the officials or the militants, but it does excuse them all. We hardly can be harsh with people who act the way everyone else acts. Only saints are likely to act differently, and sainthood in politics is supererogatory, a matter of grace, not obligation.

But this fourth excuse relies too heavily on our cynicism about political life, and cynicism only sometimes answers well to experience. In fact, legitimate states do not need to terrorize their citizens, and strongly based movements do not need to terrorize their opponents. Officials and militants who live, as it were, on the margins of legitimacy and strength sometimes choose terrorism and sometimes do not. Living in terror is not a universal experience. The world the terrorists create has its entrances and exits.

If we want to understand the choice of terror, the choice that forces the rest of us through the door, we have to imagine what in fact always occurs, although we often have no satisfactory record of the occurrence: A group of men and women, officials or militants, sits around a table and argues about whether or not to adopt a terrorist strategy. Later on, the litany of excuses obscures the argument. But at the time, around the table, it would have been no use for defenders of terrorism to say, "Everybody does it," because there they would be face to face with people proposing to do something else. Nor is it historically the case that the members of this last group, the opponents of terrorism, always lose the argument. They can win, however, and still not be able to prevent a terrorist campaign; the would-be terrorists (it does not take very many) can always split the movement and go their own way. Or, they can split the bureaucracy or the police or officer corps and act in the shadow of state power. Indeed, terrorism often has its origin in such splits. The first victims are the terrorists' former comrades or colleagues. What reason can we possibly have, then, for equating the two? If we value the politics of the men and women who oppose terrorism, we must reject the excuses of their murderers. Cynicism at such a time is unfair to the victims.

The fourth excuse can also take, often does take, a more restricted form. Oppression, rather than political rule more generally, is always terroristic in character, and thus, we must always excuse the opponents of oppression. When they choose terrorism, they are only reacting to someone else's previous choice, repaying in kind the treatment they have long received. Of course, their terrorism repeats the evil—innocent people are killed, who were never themselves oppressors—but repetition is not the same as initiation. The oppressors set the terms of the struggle. But if the struggle is fought on the oppressors' terms, then the oppressors are likely to win. Or, at least, oppression is likely to win, even if it takes on a new face. The whole point of a liberation movement or a popular mobilization is to change the terms. We have no reason to excuse the terrorism reactively adopted by opponents of oppression unless we are confident of the sincerity of their opposition, the seriousness of their commitment to a nonoppressive politics. But the choice of terrorism undermines that confidence.

We are often asked to distinguish the terrorism of the oppressed from the terrorism of the oppressors. What is it, however, that makes the difference? The message of the terrorist is the same in both cases: a denial of the peoplehood and humanity of the groups among whom he or she finds victims. Terrorism anticipates, when it does not actually enforce, political domination. Does it matter if one dominated group is replaced by another? Imagine a slave revolt whose protagonists dream only of enslaving in their turn the children of their masters. The dream is understandable, but the fervent desire of the children that the revolt be repressed is equally understandable. In neither case does understanding make for excuse—not, at least, after a politics of universal freedom has become possible. Nor does an understanding of oppression excuse the terrorism of the oppressed, once we have grasped the meaning of "liberation."

These are the four general excuses for terror, and each of them fails. They depend upon statements about the world that are false, historical arguments for which there is no evidence, moral claims that turn out to be hollow or dishonest. This is not to say that there might not be more particular excuses that have greater plausibility, extenuating circumstances in particular cases that we would feel compelled to recognize. As with murder, we can tell a story (like the story that Richard Wright tells in *Native Son,* for example) that might lead us, not to justify terrorism, but to excuse this or that individual terrorist. We can provide a personal history, a psychological study, of compassion destroyed by fear, moral reason by hatred and rage, social inhibition by unending violence—the product, an individual driven to kill or readily set on a killing course by his or her political leaders.[3] But the force of this story will not depend on any of the four general excuses, all of which grant what the storyteller will have to deny: that terrorism is the deliberate choice of rational men and women. Whether they conceive it to be one option among others or the only one available, they nevertheless argue and choose. Whether they are acting or reacting, they have made a decision. The human instruments they subsequently find to plant the bomb or shoot the gun may act under some psychological compulsion, but the men and women who choose terror as a policy act "freely." They could not act in any other way, or accept any other description of their action, and still pretend to be the leaders of the movement or the state. We ought never to excuse such leaders.

What follows from the critique of excuses? There is still a great deal of room for argument about the best way of responding to terrorism. Certainly, terrorists should be resisted, and it is not likely that a purely defensive resistance will ever be sufficient. In this sort of struggle, the offense is always ahead. The technology of terror is simple; the weapons are readily produced and easy to deliver. It is virtually impossible to protect people against random and indiscriminate attack. Thus, resistance will have to be supplemented by some combination of repression and retaliation. This is a dangerous business because repression and retaliation so often take terroristic forms and there are a host of apologists ready with excuses that sound remarkably like those of the terrorists themselves. It should be clear by now, however, that counterterrorism cannot be excused merely because it is reactive. Every new actor, terrorist or counterterrorist, claims to be reacting to someone else, standing in a circle and just passing the evil along. But the circle is ideological in character; in fact, every actor is a moral agent and makes an independent decision.

Therefore, repression and retaliation must not repeat the wrongs of terrorism, which is to say that repression and retaliation must be aimed systematically at the terrorists themselves, never at the people for whom the terrorists claim to be acting. That claim is in any case doubtful, even when it is honestly made. The people do not authorize the terrorists to act in their name. Only a tiny number actually participate in terrorist activities; they are far more likely to suffer than to benefit from the terrorist program. Even if they supported the program and hoped to benefit from it, however, they would still be immune from attack—exactly as civilians in time of war who support the war effort but are not themselves part of it are subject to the same immunity. Civilians may be put at risk by attacks on military targets, as by attacks on terrorist targets, but the risk must be kept to a minimum, even at some cost to the attackers. The refusal to make ordinary people into targets, whatever their nationality or even their politics, is the only way to say no to terrorism. Every act of repression and retaliation has to be measured by this standard.

But what if the "only way" to defeat the terrorists is to intimidate their actual or potential supporters? It is important to deny the premise of this question: that terrorism is a politics dependent on mass support. In fact, it is always the politics of an elite, whose members are dedicated and fanatical and more than ready to endure, or to watch others endure, the devastations of a counterterrorist campaign. Indeed, terrorists will welcome counterterrorism; it makes the terrorists' excuses more plausible and is sure to bring them, however many people are killed or wounded, however many are terrorized, the small number of recruits needed to sustain the terrorist activities.

Repression and retaliation are legitimate responses to terrorism only when they are constrained by the same moral principles that rule out terrorism itself. But there is an alternative response that seeks to avoid the violence that these two entail. The alternative is to address directly, ourselves, the oppression the terrorists claim to oppose. Oppression, they say, is the cause of terrorism. But that is merely one more excuse. The real cause of terrorism is the decision to launch a terrorist campaign, a decision made by that group of people sitting around a table whose deliberations I have already described. However, terrorists do exploit oppression, injustice, and human misery generally and look to these at least for their excuses. There can hardly be any doubt that oppression strengthens their hand. Is that a reason for us to come to the defense of the oppressed? It seems to me that we have our own reasons to do that, and do not need this one, or should not, to prod us into action. We might imitate those movement militants who argue against the adoption of a terrorist strategy—although not, as the terrorists say, because these militants are prepared to tolerate oppression. They already are opposed to oppression and now add to that opposition, perhaps for the same reasons, a refusal of terror. So should we have been opposed before, and we should now make the same addition.

But there is an argument, put with some insistence these days, that we should refuse to acknowledge any link at all between terrorism and oppression—as if any defense of oppressed men and women, once a terrorist campaign has been launched, would concede the effectiveness of the campaign. Or, at least, the defense would give terrorism the appearance of effectiveness and so increase the likelihood of terrorist campaigns in the future. Here we have the reverse side of the litany of excuses; we have turned over the record. First oppression is made into an excuse for terrorism, and then terrorism is made into an excuse for oppression. The first is the excuse of the far left; the second is the excuse of the neoconservative right.[4] I doubt that genuine conservatives would think it a good reason for defending the status quo that it is under terrorist attack; they would have independent reasons and would be prepared to defend the status quo against any attack. Similarly, those of us who think that the status quo urgently requires change have our own reasons for thinking so and need not be intimidated by terrorists or, for that matter, antiterrorists.

If one criticizes the first excuse, one should not neglect the second. But I need to state the second more precisely. It is not so much an excuse for oppression as an excuse for doing nothing (now) about oppression. The claim is that the campaign against terrorism has priority over every other political activity. If the people who take the lead in this campaign are the old oppressors, then we must make a kind of peace with them—temporarily, of course, until the terrorists have been beaten. This is a strategy that denies the possibility of a two-front war. So long as the men and women who pretend to lead the fight against oppression are terrorists, we can concede nothing to their demands. Nor can we oppose their opponents.

But why not? It is not likely in any case that terrorists would claim victory in the face of a serious effort to deal with the oppression of the people they claim to be defending. The effort would merely expose the hollowness of their claim, and the nearer it came to success, the more they would escalate their terrorism. They would still have to be defeated, for what they are after is not a solution to the problem but rather the power to impose their own solution. No decent end to the conflict in Ireland, say, or in Lebanon, or in the Middle East generally, is going to look like a victory for terrorism—if only because the different groups of terrorists are each committed, by the strategy they have adopted, to an indecent end.[5] By working for our own ends, we expose the indecency.

It is worth considering at greater length the link between oppression and terror. To pretend that there is no link at all is to ignore the historical record, but the record is more complex than any of the excuses acknowledge. The first thing to be read out of it, however, is simple enough: Oppression is not so much the cause of terrorism as terrorism is one of the primary means of oppression. This was true in ancient times, as Aristotle recognized, and it is still true today. Tyrants rule by terrorizing their subjects; unjust and illegitimate regimes are upheld through a combination of carefully aimed and random violence.[6] If this method works in the state, there is no reason to think that it will not work, or that it does not work, in the liberation movement. Wherever we see terrorism, we should look for tyranny and oppression. Authoritarian states, especially in the moment of their founding, need a terrorist apparatus—secret police with unlimited power, secret prisons into which citizens disappear, death squads in unmarked cars. Even democracies may use terror, not against their own citizens, but at the margins, in their colonies, for example, where colonizers also are likely to rule tyrannically. Oppression is sometimes maintained by a steady and discriminate pressure, sometimes by intermittent and random violence—what we might think of as terrorist melodrama—designed to render the subject population fearful and passive.

This latter policy, especially if it seems successful, invites imitation by opponents of the state. But terrorism does not spread only when it is imitated. If it can be invented by state officials, it can also be invented by movement militants. Neither one need take lessons from the other; the circle has no single or necessary starting point. Wherever it starts, terrorism in the movement is tyrannical and oppressive in exactly the same way as is terrorism in the state. The terrorists aim to rule, and murder is their method. They have their own internal police, death squads, disappearances. They begin by killing or intimidating those comrades who stand in their way, and they proceed to do the same, if they can, among the people they claim to represent. If terrorists are successful, they rule tyrannically, and their people bear, without consent, the costs of the terrorists' rule. (If the terrorists are only partly successful, the costs to the people may be even greater: What they have to bear now is a war between rival terrorist gangs.) But terrorists cannot win the ultimate victory they seek without challenging the established regime or colonial power and the people it claims to represent, and when terrorists do that, they themselves invite imitation. The regime may then respond with its own campaign of aimed and random violence. Terrorist tracks terrorist, each claiming the other as an excuse.

The same violence can also spread to countries where it has not yet been experienced; now terror is reproduced not through temporal succession but through ideological adaptation. State terrorists wage bloody wars against largely imaginary enemies: army colonels, say, hunting down the representatives of "international communism." Or movement terrorists wage bloody wars against enemies with whom, but for the ideology, they could readily negotiate and compromise: nationalist fanatics committed to a permanent irredentism. These wars, even if they are without precedents, are likely enough to become precedents, to start the circle of terror and counterterror, which is endlessly oppressive for the ordinary men and women whom the state calls its citizens and the movement its "people."

The only way to break out of the circle is to refuse to play the terrorist game. Terrorists in the state and the movement warn us, with equal vehemence, that any such refusal is a sign of softness and naiveté. The self-portrait of the terrorists is always the same. They are tough-minded and realistic; they know their enemies (or privately invent them for ideological purposes); and they are ready to do what must be done for victory. Why then do terrorists turn around and around in the same circle? It is true: Movement terrorists win support because they pretend to deal energetically and effectively with the brutality of the state. It also is true: State terrorists win support because they pretend to deal energetically and effectively with the brutality of the movement. Both feed on the fears of brutalized and oppressed people. But there is no way of overcoming brutality with terror. At most, the burden is shifted from these people to those; more likely, new burdens are added for everyone. Genuine liberation can come only through a politics that mobilizes the victims of brutality and takes careful aim at its agents, or by a politics that surrenders the hope of victory and domination and deliberately seeks a compromise settlement. In either case, once tyranny is repudiated, terrorism is no longer an option. For what lies behind all the excuses, of officials and militants alike, is the predilection for a tyrannical politics.

Questions for Discussion

1. What is the difference between an excuse and a justification?
2. Is terrorism ever justified? What does Walzer think?
3. What is Walzer's view on how best to address terrorism?

CHAPTER 12

Toleration

HARD QUESTION: SHOULD WE TOLERATE HATE SPEECH ON CAMPUS?

Many campuses have regulations prohibiting hate speech. My campus, for example, has regulations that prohibit discrimination on the basis of the usual categories of race, gender, religion, marital status, national origin, sexual orientation, and disability. The freedom-from-discrimination provision of those regulations "includes the right of students to pursue academic study and to live in an environment free from bias-based harassment or intimidation." Racist, sexist, homophobic, or ethnically demeaning epithets, when directed toward an individual or a group, presumably constitute bias-based harassment or intimidation and are therefore banned on many campuses, as are other forms of bias-based conduct.

How is conduct deemed to be "bias-based"? Doing so would seem to require understanding the perpetrator's motivation, since the same outward behavior might be caused by bias in one case and by allegiance to principle in another. Imagine, for example, a student who makes derogatory comments about homosexuals because he believes that homosexuality is immoral. Perhaps this student is a committed Catholic and accepts the Church's teaching that homosexuality is "seriously disordered." His condemnation of homosexuality is principled, not the mere expression of unreflective bias. This is not to say that the principles to which he appeals are acceptable, but there is an important difference between opposing homosexuality on moral grounds and opposing it out of sheer bias. Thus not all opposition to homosexuality falls under the category of homophobia, which literally means "fear of homosexuals." And in any case, opposition to homosexuality on either principled grounds or sheer prejudice is still not hate speech.

Hate speech is presumably the expression of hatred. Whether the expression must be directed toward an identifiable person is not clear. Racist graffiti scrawled on a wall with no one in particular as its target would probably count as hate speech. But for an expression to count as hate speech, must the hatred be unjustified? There are some things that we should hate, or at least strongly disapprove of. Imagine a child molester on campus. Is it hate speech to say to that person, "You're a pervert!"? If hate speech as such presupposes the unjustifiability of the hatred, then we must engage the person who thinks he or she has good grounds for hatred. Is the hatred justified or not?

All can agree that expressions of bias or prejudice are inappropriate, but which expressions are biased or prejudiced? To be biased or prejudiced means that one has no reason for one's attitude. Mistakenly thinking that one has good reason is not the same as having no reason. Imagine two cases: (1) negative comments directed to a person's sexuality and motivated by deep principled moral disapproval and (2) similar negative comments motivated by unreflecting prejudice. If we classify both as hate speech—and seek to silence them as such—then in the first case we have failed to acknowledge what purports to be a morally justified position, one that deserves a fair hearing in an academic setting and, if it is mistaken, a thorough refutation. A principled position must withstand rational scrutiny of its principles; mere bias, because it involves no principles, cannot be rationally evaluated. It must simply be exposed as irrational and opposed.

Regulations that prohibit all forms of offensive expression thus violate a central value for any educational institution. Once we deem certain expressions too offensive to be aired, do we put ourselves on a slippery slope of censorship, since the boundary between permitted and impermissible expression will inevitably widen? Given the mission of educational institutions, the burden of proof should always be on those who favor banning expression. They must show that some forms of expression are not to be tolerated or openly and rationally examined by the campus community; instead, they cross some threshold of harm that justifies their suppression. And is mere offensiveness a sufficiently high level of harm? Furthermore, those who seek to ban speech must explain how their remedy—banning certain forms of speech—will effectively address only the targeted forms of expression, rather than expanding to include others.

This requires a principled understanding of where the boundary between permissible and impermissible forms of expression lies. This is a tall order, but perhaps not impossible to meet, since some forms of prohibited speech are quite restricted, such as defamation or slander. Moreover, what effect will the ban have on the attitudes that give rise to those forms of speech? Prohibiting hate speech might not address the underlying prejudices that hate speech expresses. It seems like a superficial fix, not particularly effective in addressing the attitudes themselves. As many have observed, the remedy for hate speech may well be more speech, not censorship. The question, then, is whether we should tolerate all forms of speech on campus or seek to ban certain expressions because they are too offensive.

Why should you tolerate people or practices that you find, well, intolerable? Surely we are not supposed to tolerate murder, dismissing it as something people sometimes do that we disapprove of but should tolerate all the same. Similarly, the racist shouldn't regard himself as merely tolerating members of the race he despises (perhaps congratulating himself for his tolerance). The racist shouldn't hate to begin with, so his tolerance, such as it is, is misplaced. Rather than learning to tolerate certain people he despises, the racist should abandon his unjustified attitude regarding them. Thus tolerance cannot be simply a matter of putting up with practices that we should not tolerate (such as murder) or putting up with practices that we are not justified in opposing in the first place, like the racist who "tolerates" people he otherwise cannot stand. Nor can it be indifference to what someone else does, because then we are not tolerating anything; we simply do not care what the other person does. Indifference is not toleration.

Toleration requires strong disapproval of what someone does, yet one still refrains from interfering with that person's activity or way of life. One thinks the activity is bad, wrong, tasteless, despicable, unworthy, or contemptible—the list of faults continues—and yet toleration requires that the offender not be prohibited from doing or being whatever it is that is so objectionable. Why?

One answer is that we don't want someone else telling *us* what to do or how to live. Freedom to do as we wish requires recognition that others may do as they wish, within limits, even though we may strongly disapprove of what they do. But if we could impose our will on others without fear of their doing it to us in return, then why not do so? After all, what the other person does is wrong, bad, despicable, etc., etc., and if we could just get those other people to be more like us, then the world would be a better place. But, since we lack that power, second best is to gnash our teeth and just tolerate—that is, put up with—whatever it is that is so hateful. So we tolerate others because we don't want them to do to us what we want to do to them. We tolerate what we cannot abide as a matter of practical necessity, not because tolerance has any moral merits on its own. This view of tolerance does not make it sound especially virtuous.

Is there a genuine moral virtue of tolerance? Tolerance obviously contributes to social harmony, especially if the alternative is armed conflict or social disharmony. But one would have thought that there would be more to say about the moral value of tolerance than acknowledging its contribution to social stability, even though social stability is an important consideration. Suppose one could be assured of winning an armed conflict against those with whom one disagrees. Then perhaps the social harmony that results after the "offensive elements" have been vanquished will compensate for the fight. Once again, tolerance seems to reflect a lack of power, rather than being a moral virtue in its own right.

Tolerance can be seen as a moral virtue once we distinguish between a person and that person's beliefs, values, practices, and commitments. We can respect the person—the belief holder—and still condemn the beliefs. This means that we will restrain our desire to impose our way of life on someone else, despite the manifest error of that person's beliefs or practices—within limits, of course. We allow other people to make their own mistakes (real or imagined) without interfering, not simply because we do not want them to interfere in our lives, and not because we lack the power to correct their misconceptions or obnoxious practices, but because we respect their ability to make their own decisions. Tolerance, in other words, has moral content when it is a manifestation of respect for persons. This means that if we *did* have the power to change someone without fear of reprisal, we would still refrain from doing so out of respect for the person. If the odious practice that we oppose is regarded as a manifestation of authentic choice, an expression of that person's best attempt to construct a life, then our restraint is based on moral considerations—specifically, a respect for personal autonomy. Tolerance is thus a moral virtue when it is grounded in respect for persons. In typical Kantian fashion (see Chapter 3), motivation makes all the difference. Tolerating the behavior of others out of fear of reprisal or because one lacks the power to impose one's will on the "offender" is no virtue, whereas toleration motivated by respect for the autonomous choices of a person is morally significant.

READINGS ON TOLERATION

Bernard Williams, "Toleration: An Impossible Virtue?"

Bernard Williams (1929–2003) was one of the most influential philosophers of the twentieth century. He taught at Cambridge University for many years. In addition to contributing penetrating discussions on personal identity and the history of philosophy (most notably an analysis of Descartes), Williams has had a lasting impact on moral philosophy. In this article on toleration, Williams distinguishes between the practice of toleration and the virtue of tolerance, since the reason why one is tolerant might simply be that one lacks the power to suppress what one detests, or perhaps one is afraid to suppress what one detests for fear that others will try to suppress oneself in turn. Thus the practice of tolerance need not result from anything virtuous. As a virtue, tolerance appears quite strange, since it "seemingly required someone to think that a certain belief or practice was thoroughly wrong or bad, and at the same time that there was some intrinsic good to be found in its being allowed to flourish." How can this be? We must grasp the value of autonomy, according to Williams, to appreciate tolerance as a virtue.

Critical Reading Questions

1. What is the difference between the practice of toleration and the virtue of tolerance, according to Williams?
2. What model of society can bear the weight of equal respect, according to Williams?
3. What value does liberal pluralism require of its citizens?
4. Why does toleration appear to be an impossible virtue? Why is it not really one, according to Williams?
5. How is the basis of tolerance as a virtue especially Kantian?

TOLERATION: AN IMPOSSIBLE VIRTUE?

Bernard Williams

The difficulty with toleration is that it seems to be at once necessary and impossible. It is necessary where different groups have conflicting beliefs—moral, political, or religious—and realize that there is no alternative to their living together, that is to say, no alternative except armed conflict, which will not resolve their disagreements and will impose continuous suffering. These are the circumstances in which toleration is necessary. Yet in those same circumstances it may well seem impossible.

If violence and the breakdown of social cooperation are threatened in these circumstances, it is because people find others' beliefs or ways of life deeply unacceptable. In matters of religion, for instance (which, historically, was the first area in which the idea of toleration was used), the need for toleration arises because one of the groups, at least, thinks that the other is blasphemously, disastrously, obscenely wrong. The members of one group may think that the members of the other group need to be helped toward the truth, or that third parties need to be protected against the bad opinions. Most important—and most relevant for the dilemmas of liberal societies—they may think that the leaders or elders of the other group are keeping the young and perhaps the women from enlightenment and liberation. They see it as not merely in the general interest but in the interest of some in the other group that the true religion (as they believe it to be) should prevail. It is because the disagreement goes this deep that the parties to it think that they cannot accept the existence of each other. We need to tolerate other people and their ways of life only in situations that make it very difficult to do so. Toleration, we may say, is required only for the intolerable. That is its basic problem.

We may think of toleration as an attitude that a more powerful group, or a majority, has (or fails to have) toward a less powerful group or a minority. In a country where there are many Christians and few Muslims, there may be a question whether the Christians tolerate the Muslims; the Muslims do not get the choice, so to speak, whether to tolerate the Christians or not. If the proportions of Christians and Muslims are reversed, so will be the direction of toleration. This is how we usually think of toleration, and it is natural to do so, because discussions of toleration have often been discussions of what laws should exist—in particular, laws permitting or forbidding various kinds of religious practice—and the laws have been determined by the attitudes of the more powerful group. But more basically, toleration is a matter of the attitudes of any group to another and does not concern only the relations of the more powerful to the less powerful. It is certainly not just a question of what laws there should be. A group or a creed can rightly be said to be "intolerant" if it would like to suppress or drive out others even if, as a matter of fact, it has no power to do so. The problems of toleration are to be found first at the level of human relations and of the attitude of one way of life toward another. It is not only a question of how the power of the state is to be used, though of course it supports and feeds a problem about that, a problem of political philosophy. However, we should be careful about making the assumption that what underlies a practice or an attitude of toleration must be a personal virtue of toleration. All toleration involves difficulties, but it is the virtue that especially threatens to involve conceptual impossibility.

A practice of toleration means only that one group as a matter of fact puts up with the existence of the other, differing, group. A tolerant attitude (toward this group) is any disposition or outlook that encourages them to do so: it is more likely to be identified as an attitude of toleration if it applies more generally, in their relations to other groups, and in their views of other groups' relations to each other. One possible basis of such an attitude—but only one—is a virtue of toleration, which emphasises the moral good involved in putting up with beliefs one finds offensive. I am going to suggest that this virtue, while it is not (as it may seem) impossible, does have to take a very specific form, which limits the range of people who can possess it. Because of this, it is a serious mistake to think that this virtue is the only, or perhaps the most important, attitude on which to ground practices of toleration.

If there is to be a question of toleration, it is necessary that there should be something to be tolerated; there has to be some belief or practice or way of life that one group thinks (however fanatically or unreasonably) wrong, mistaken, or undesirable. If one group simply hates another, as with a clan vendetta or cases of sheer racism, it is not really toleration that is needed: the people involved need rather to lose their hatred, their prejudice, or their implacable memories. If we are asking people to be tolerant, we are asking for something more complicated than this. They will indeed have to lose something, their desire to suppress or drive out the rival belief; but they will also keep something, their commitment to their own beliefs, which is what gave them that desire in the first place. There is a tension here between one's own commitments, and the acceptance that other people may have other, perhaps quite distasteful commitments: the tension that is typical of toleration, and which makes it so difficult. (In practice, of course, there is often a very thin or vague boundary between mere tribalism or clan loyalty and differences in outlook or conviction.)

Just because it involves some tension between commitment to one's own outlook and putting up with the other's, the attitude of toleration is supposed to be more than mere weariness or indifference. After the European Wars of Religion in the sixteenth and seventeenth centuries had raged for years, people began to think that it must be better for the different Christian churches to coexist. Various attitudes went with this development. Some people became skeptical about the distinctive claims of any church and began to think that there was no truth, or at least no truth discoverable by human beings, about the validity of one church's creed as opposed to another's. Other people began to think that the struggles had helped them to understand God's purposes better: He did not mind how people worshiped, so long as they did so in good faith within certain broad Christian limits. (In more recent times, a similar ecumenical spirit has extended beyond the boundaries of Christianity.)

These two lines of thought, in a certain sense, went in opposite directions. One of them, the skeptical, claimed that there was less to be known about God's designs than the warring parties, each with its particular fanaticism, had supposed. The other line of thought, the broad church view, claimed to have a better insight into God's designs than the warring parties had. But in their relation to the battles of faith, the two lines of thought did nevertheless end up in the same position, with the idea that precise questions of Christian belief did not matter as much as people had supposed, that less was at stake. This leads to toleration as a matter of political *practice*, and that is an extremely important result; but as an attitude, it is less than toleration. If you do not care all that much what anyone believes, you do not need the attitude of toleration, any more than you do with regard to other people's tastes in food.

In many matters, attitudes that are more tolerant in practice do arise for this reason, that people cease to think that a certain kind of behavior is a matter for disapproval or negative judgment at all. This is what is happening, in many parts of the world, with regard to kinds of sexual behavior that were previously discouraged and, in some cases, legally punished. An extramarital relationship or a homosexual ménage may arouse no hostile comment or reaction, as such things did in the past. But once again, though this is toleration as a matter of practice, the attitude it relies on is indifference rather than, strictly speaking, toleration. Indeed, if I and others in the neighborhood said that we were *tolerating* the homosexual relations of the couple next door, our attitude would be thought to be less than liberal.

There are no doubt many conflicts and areas of intolerance for which the solution should indeed be found in this direction, in the increase of indifference. Matters of sexual and social behavior which in smaller and more traditional societies are of great public concern, will come to seem more a private matter, raising in themselves no question of right or wrong. The slide toward indifference may also provide, as it did in Europe, the only solution to some religious disputes. Not all religions, of course, have any desire to convert, let alone coerce, others. They no doubt have some opinion or other (perhaps of the "broad church" type) about the state of truth or error of those who do not share their faith, but at any rate they are content to leave those other people alone. Other creeds, however, are less willing to allow error, as they see it, to flourish, and it may be that with them there is no solution except that which Europe earlier discovered (in religion, at least, if not in politics), a decline in enthusiasm. It is important that a decline in enthusiasm need not take the form of a movement's merely running out of steam. As some Christian sects discovered, a religion can have its own resources for rethinking its relations to others. One relevant idea, which had considerable influence in Europe, is that an expansive religion really wants people to believe in it, but it must recognize that this is not a result that can be achieved by force. The most that force can achieve is acquiescence and outer conformity. As Hegel said of the slave's master, the fanatic is always disappointed: what he wanted was acknowledgment, but all he can get is conformity.

Skepticism, indifference, or broad church views are not the only source of what I am calling toleration as a practice. It can also be secured in a Hobbesian equilibrium, under which the acceptance of one group by the other is the best that either of them can get. This is not, of course, in itself a principled solution, as opposed to the skeptical outlook, which is, in its own way, principled. The Hobbesian solution is also notoriously unstable. A sect that could, just about, enforce conformity might be deterred by the thought of what things would be like if the other party took over. But for this to be a Hobbesian thought, as opposed to a role-reversal argument that, for instance, refers to rights, some instability must be in the offing. The parties who are conscious of such a situation are likely to go in for preemptive strikes, and this is all the more so if they reflect that even if they can hope only for acquiescence and outer conformity in one generation, they can conceivably hope for more in later generations. As a matter of fact, in the modern world, the imposition by force of political creeds and ideologies has not been very effective over time. One lesson that was already obvious in the year 1984 was the falsity in this respect of Orwell's 1984. However, the imposition of ideology over time has certainly worked in the past, and the qualification in the previous statement, "in the modern world," is extremely important. (This is something I come back to at the end of this paper.)

So far, then, toleration as a *value* has barely emerged from the argument. We can have practices of toleration underlaid by skepticism or indifference or, again, by an understood balance of power. Toleration as a value seems to demand more than this. It has been thought by many that this can be expressed in a certain political philosophy, a certain conception of the state.

To some degree, it is possible for people to belong to communities bound together by shared convictions—religious convictions, for instance—and for toleration to be sustained by a distinction between those communities and the state. The state is not identified with any set of such beliefs and does not enforce any of them; equally, it does not allow any of the groups to impose its beliefs on the others, though each of them can of course advocate what it believes. In the United States, for instance, there is a wide consensus that supports the Constitution in allowing no law that enforces or even encourages any particular religion. There are many religious groups, and no doubt many of them have deep convictions, but most of them do not want the state to suppress others or to allow any of them to suppress others.

Many people have hoped that this can serve as a general model of the way in which a modern society can resolve the tensions of toleration.

On the one hand, there are deeply held and differing convictions about moral or religious matters, held by various groups within the society. On the other hand, there is a supposedly impartial state, which affirms the rights of all citizens to equal consideration, including an equal right to form and express their convictions. This is the model of *liberal pluralism*. It can be seen as enacting toleration. It expresses toleration's peculiar combination of conviction and acceptance, by finding a home for people's various convictions in groups or communities less than the state, while the acceptance of diversity is located in the structure of the state itself.

This implies the presence of toleration as more than a mere practice. But how exactly does it identify toleration as a value? Does it identify toleration as a virtue? This turns on the question of the qualities that such a system demands of its citizens. The citizens must have at least a shared belief in the system itself. The model of a society that is held together by a framework of rights and an aspiration toward equal respect, rather than by a shared body of more specific substantive convictions, demands an ideal of citizenship that will be adequate to bear such a weight. The most impressive version of this ideal is perhaps that offered by the tradition of liberal philosophy flowing from Kant, which identifies the dignity of the human being with autonomy. Free persons are those who make their own lives and determine their own convictions, and power must be used to make this possible, not to frustrate it by imposing a given set of convictions.

This is not a purely negative or skeptical ideal. If it were, it could not even hope to have the power to bind together into one society people with strongly differing convictions. Nor could it provide the motive power that all tolerant societies need in order to fight the intolerant when other means fail. This is an ideal associated with many contemporary liberal thinkers, such as Rawls, Nagel, and Dworkin.

Under the philosophy of liberal pluralism, toleration does emerge as a principled doctrine, and it does require of its citizens a belief in a value: perhaps not so much in the value of toleration itself as in a certain more fundamental value, that of autonomy. Because this value is taken to be understood and shared, this account of the role of toleration in liberal pluralism implies a picture of justification. It should provide an argument that could be accepted by those who do find prima facie intolerable certain outlooks that obtain in the society, and which liberalism refuses to deploy the power of the state to suppress. As Nagel has well put it, "Liberalism purports to be a view that justifies religious toleration not only to religious skeptics but to the devout, and sexual toleration not only to libertines but to those who believe extramarital sex is sinful. It distinguishes between the values a person can appeal to in conducting his own life and those he can appeal to in justifying the exercise of political power."[1] No one, including Nagel himself, believes that this will be possible in every case. There must be, on any showing, limits to the extent to which the liberal state can be disengaged on matters of ethical disagreement. There are some questions, such as that of abortion, on which the state will fail to be neutral whatever it does. Its laws may draw distinctions between different circumstances of abortion, but in the end it cannot escape the fact that some people will believe with the deepest conviction that a certain class of acts should be permitted, while other people will believe with equal conviction that those acts should be forbidden. Equally intractable questions will arise with regard to education, where the autonomy of some fundamentalist religious groups, for instance, to bring up their children in their own beliefs will be seen by liberals as standing in conflict with the autonomy of those children to choose what beliefs they will have. (Such problems may be expressed in terms of group rights.) No society can avoid collective and substantive choices on matters of this kind, and in that sense, on those issues, there are limits to toleration, even if people continue to respect one another's opinions.

The fact that there will be some cases that will be impossible in such a way does not necessarily wreck liberal toleration, unless there are too many of them. There is no argument of principle to show that if *A* thinks a certain practice wrong and *B* thinks that practice right, *A* has to think that the state should suppress that practice or that *B* has to think that the state should promote that practice. These are considerations at different levels. Nevertheless, there is a famous argument to the effect that the liberal ideal is in principle impossible. Some critics of liberalism claim that the liberal pluralist state, as the supposed enactment of toleration, does not really exist. What is happening, they say, is that the state is subtly enforcing one set of principles (roughly in favor of individual choice—at least, consumer choice—social cooperation, and business efficiency) while the convictions that people previously held deeply, on matters of religion or sexual behavior or the significance of cultural experience, dwindle into private tastes. On this showing, liberalism will come close to being "just another sectarian doctrine": the phrase that Rawls used precisely in explaining what liberalism had to avoid being.

What is the critic's justification for saying that the liberal state is "subtly enforcing" one set of attitudes rather than another? Nagel distinguishes sharply between *enforcing* something like individualism, on the one hand, and the practices of liberal toleration, on the other, though he honestly and correctly admits that the educational practices, for instance, of the liberal state are not "equal in their effects." This is an important distinction, and it can make some significant difference in practice. Being proselytized or coerced by militant individualism is not the same thing as merely seeing one's traditional religious surroundings eroded by a modern liberal society. The liberal's opponents must concede that there is something in the distinction, but this does not mean that they will be convinced by the use that the liberal makes of it, because it is not a distinction that is neutral in its inspiration. It is asymmetrically skewed in the liberal direction. This is because it makes a lot out of a difference of procedure, whereas what matters to a nonliberal believer is the difference of outcome. I doubt whether we can find an argument of principle that satisfies the purest and strongest aims of the value of liberal toleration, in the sense that it does not rely on skepticism or on the contingencies of power, and also could in principle explain to rational people whose deepest convictions were not in favor of individual autonomy and related values that they should think a state better that let their values decay in preference to enforcing them.

If toleration as a practice is to be defended in terms of its being a value, then it will have to appeal to substantive opinions about the good, in particular the good of individual autonomy, and these opinions will extend to the value and the meaning of personal characteristics and virtues associated with toleration, just as they will to the political activities of imposing or refusing to impose various substantive outlooks. This is not to say that the substantive values of individual autonomy are misguided or baseless. The point is that these values, like others, may be rejected, and to the extent that toleration rests on those values, then toleration will also be rejected. The practice of toleration cannot be based on a value such as individual autonomy and also hope to escape from substantive disagreements about the good. This really is a contradiction, because it is only a substantive view of goods such as autonomy that could yield the value that is expressed by the practices of toleration.

In the light of this, we can now better understand the impossibility or extreme difficulty that was seemingly presented by the personal virtue or attitude of toleration. It appeared impossible because it seemingly required someone to think that a certain belief or practice was thoroughly wrong or bad, and at the same time that there was some intrinsic good to be found in its being allowed to flourish. This does not involve a contradiction if the other good is found not in that belief's continuing but in the other believer's autonomy. People can coherently think that a certain outlook or attitude is deeply wrong and that the flourishing of such an attitude should be tolerated if they also hold another substantive value in favor of the autonomy or independence of other believers. The exercise of toleration as a virtue, then, and in that sense the belief in it as itself a value, does not necessarily involve a contradiction, though in a given situation it may involve that familiar thing, a conflict of goods. However, we cannot combine this account of liberal toleration with the idea that it rises above the battle of values. The account gives rise to the familiar problem that others may not share the liberal view of these various goods; in particular, the people whom the liberal is particularly required to tolerate are precisely those who are unlikely to share the liberal's view of the good of autonomy, which is the basis of the toleration, to the extent that this expresses a value. The liberal has not, in this representation of toleration, given them a reason to value toleration if they do not share his or her other values.

Granted this, it is as well that, as we saw earlier, the practice of toleration does not necessarily rest on any such value at all. It may be supported by Hobbesian considerations about what is possible or desirable in the matter of enforcement, or again by indifference based on skepticism about the issues involved in the disagreement; though with indifference and skepticism, of course, the point will be reached at which nobody is interested enough in the disagreements for there to be anything to put up with, and toleration will not be necessary.

It is important, too, that the demands on toleration do not arise in contexts in which there are no other values or virtues. Appeals to the misery and cruelty and manifest stupidity involved in intolerance may, in favorable circumstances, have some effect with those who are not dedicated to toleration as an intrinsic value or to the respect for autonomy that underlies toleration as a virtue. As a virtue, it provides a special kind of foundation for the practice of toleration, and one that is specially Kantian, not only in its affinities but in what it demands: its worth lies partly in its difficulty, in its requirement that one should rise not only above one's own desires but above one's desire to secure the fullest expression of one's own values.

It may be that the best hopes for toleration as a practice lie not so much in this virtue and its demand that one combine the pure spirit of toleration with one's detestation of what has to be tolerated. Hope may lie rather in modernity itself and in its principal creation, international commercial society. It is still possible to think that the structures of this international order will encourage skepticism about religious and other claims to exclusivity and about the motives of those who impose such claims. Indeed, it can help to encourage restraint within religions themselves. When such skepticism is set against the manifest harms generated by intolerance,

there is a basis for the practice of toleration, a basis that is allied to liberalism but is less ambitious than the pure value of liberal toleration, which rests on the belief in autonomy. It is close to a tradition that can be traced to Montesquieu and to Constant, which the late Judith Shklar called "the liberalism of fear."[2]

It is a good question whether toleration is a temporary problem. Perhaps toleration will prove to have been an interim value, serving a period between a past when no one had heard of it and a future in which no one will need it. At the present moment, in fact, the idea that intolerant outlooks will sink away from the world seems incredible: such outlooks are notably asserting themselves. If they are successful enough, there will once more be not much room for toleration; it will be the tolerant who, hopelessly, will be asking to be tolerated. More probably, we can expect in the medium term some situation in which there will be a standoff between liberal toleration and intolerant outlooks of various kinds. However, as I implied earlier, one thing that the modern international order does make less likely is the self-contained enforcement of opinion in one society over a long time. It will be harder than in the past for a cultural environment of fanatical belief to coincide for a considerable length of time with a center of state power, remaining shielded from external influences. Liberalism and its opponents will probably coexist on closer terms than across tightly controlled national boundaries.

In those circumstances, toleration and its awkward practices are likely to remain both necessary and in some degree possible. If so, it will be all the clearer—clearer than it is if one concentrates on the very special case of the United States—that the practice of toleration has to be sustained not so much by a pure principle resting on a value of autonomy as by a wider and more mixed range of resources. Those resources include an active skepticism against fanaticism and the pretensions of its advocates; conviction about the manifest evils of toleration's absence; and, quite certainly, power, to provide Hobbesian reminders to the more extreme groups that they will have to settle for coexistence.

NOTES

* A shorter version of this paper has been published in the *UNESCO Courier.* June 1992.

1. Thomas Nagel, *Equality and Partiality* (Oxford: Oxford University Press, 1991), p. 156.

2. See her article with that title in *Liberalism and the Moral Life,* ed. Nancy L. Rosenblum (Cambridge: Harvard University Press, 1989).

Discussion Questions

1. Is toleration a virtue?
2. What is the value of toleration?
3. How can limits be established for which things we should and should not tolerate?
4. How, according to Williams, does respect for autonomy underlie toleration as a virtue?

T. M. Scanlon, "The Difficulty of Tolerance"

T. M. Scanlon is Alford Professor of Natural Religion, Moral Philosophy, and Civil Policy at Harvard University. His recent book, What We Owe to Each Other, *argues that morality is basically contractual. In this article on tolerance, Scanlon explores the importance of informal politics for a decent and therefore tolerant society. Tolerance is an important social value because "what tolerance expresses is a recognition of common membership that is deeper than . . . conflicts, a recognition of others as just as entitled as we are to contribute to the definition of our society." Intolerance, by contrast, involves a denial of the full social membership of "the others." We have no right to do this, claims Scanlon, because they are just as much members of our society as we are.*

Critical Reading Questions

1. What does Scanlon mean by the "informal politics of social life"? How is it distinct from the formal politics of social life?
2. Why, according to Scanlon, should we value tolerance?
3. What examples does Scanlon give of his own attitude of intolerance? How is it relevant to the point that he is making about the value of tolerance?
4. What platitude, attributed to Voltaire, emerges as the point of tolerance?

THE DIFFICULTY OF TOLERANCE

T. M. Scanlon

1. WHAT IS TOLERANCE?

Tolerance requires us to accept people and permit their practices even when we strongly disapprove of them. Tolerance thus involves an attitude that is intermediate between wholehearted acceptance and unrestrained opposition.[1] This intermediate status makes tolerance a puzzling attitude. There are certain things, such as murder, that ought not be tolerated. There are limits to what we are able to do to prevent these things from happening, but we need not restrain ourselves out of tolerance for these actions as expressions of the perpetrators' values. In other cases, where our feelings of opposition or disapproval should properly be reined in, it would be better if we were to get rid of these feelings altogether. If we are moved by racial or ethnic prejudice, for example, the preferred remedy is not merely to tolerate those whom we abhor but to stop abhorring people just because they look different or come from a different background.

Perhaps everything would, ideally, fall into one or the other of these two classes. Except where wholehearted disapproval and opposition are appropriate, as in the case of murder, it would be best if the feelings that generate conflict and disagreement could be eliminated altogether. Tolerance, as an attitude that requires us to hold in check certain feelings of opposition and disapproval, would then be just a second best—a way of dealing with attitudes that we would be better off without but that are, unfortunately, ineliminable. To say this would not be to condemn tolerance. Even if it is, in this sense, a second best, the widespread adoption of tolerant attitudes would be a vast improvement over the sectarian bloodshed that we hear of every

day, in many parts of the globe. Stemming this violence would be no mean feat.

Still, it seems to me that there are pure cases of tolerance, in which it is not merely an expedient for dealing with the imperfections of human nature. These would be cases in which persisting conflict and disagreement are to be expected and are, unlike racial prejudice, quite compatible with full respect for those with whom we disagree. But while respect for each other does not require us to abandon our disagreement, it does place limits on how this conflict can be pursued. In this article, I want to investigate the possibility of pure tolerance of this kind, with the aim of better understanding our idea of tolerance and the difficulty of achieving it. Because I particularly want to see more clearly why it is a difficult attitude and practice to sustain, I will try to concentrate on cases in which I myself find tolerance difficult. I begin with the familiar example of religious toleration, which provides the model for most of our thinking about toleration of other kinds.

Widespread acceptance of the idea of religious toleration is, at least in North America and Europe, a historical legacy of the European Wars of Religion. Today, religious toleration is widely acknowledged as an ideal, even though there are many places in the world where, even as we speak, blood is being spilled over what are at least partly religious divisions.

As a person for whom religion is a matter of no personal importance whatever, it seems easy for me, at least at the outset, to endorse religious toleration. At least this is so when toleration is understood in terms of the twin principles of the First Amendment to the Constitution of the United States: "Congress shall make no law respecting an establishment of religion, or prohibiting the free exercise thereof." Accepting these principles seems to be all benefit and no cost from my point of view. Why should I want to interfere with other people's religious practice, provided that they are not able to impose that practice on me? If religious toleration has costs, I am inclined to say, they are borne by others, not by me.

So it seems at first (although I will later argue that this is a mistake) that for me religious toleration lacks the tension I just described: I do not feel the opposition it tells me to hold in check. Why should I want to tell others what religion to practice, or to have one established as our official creed? On the other hand, for those who do want these things, religious toleration seems to demand a great deal: if I thought it terribly important that everyone worship in the correct way, how could I accept toleration except as an uneasy truce, acceptable as an alternative to perpetual bloodshed, but even so a necessity that is to be regretted? Pure toleration seems to have escaped us.

I want to argue that this view of things is mistaken. Tolerance involves costs and dangers for all of us, but it is nonetheless an attitude that we all have reason to value.

2. WHAT DOES TOLERATION REQUIRE?

This is a difficult question to answer, in part because there is more than one equally good answer, in part because any good answer will be vague in important respects. Part of any answer is legal and political. Tolerance requires that people who fall on the "wrong" side of the differences I have mentioned should not, for that reason, be denied legal and political rights: the right to vote, to hold office, to benefit from the central public goods that are otherwise open to all, such as education, public safety, the protections of the legal system, health care, and access to "public accommodations." In addition, it requires that the state not give preference to one group over another in the distribution of privileges and benefits.

It is this part of the answer that seems to me to admit of more than one version. For example, in the United States, the requirement that each religious group is equally entitled to the protections and benefits conferred by the state

is interpreted to mean that the state may not support, financially or otherwise, any religious organization. The main exception, not an insignificant one, is that any religious organization can qualify for tax-exempt status. So even our idea of "nonestablishment" represents a mixed strategy: some forms of support are prohibited for *any* religion, others are allowed provided they are available for *all* religions. This mixture strikes me more as a particular political compromise than as a solution uniquely required by the idea of religious toleration. A society in which there was a religious qualification for holding public office could not be accounted tolerant or just. But I would not say the same about just any form of state support for religious practice. In Great Britain, for example, there is an established church, and the state supports denominational as well as nondenominational schools. In my view, the range of these schools is too narrow to reflect the religious diversity of contemporary Britain, but I do not see that just any system of this kind is to be faulted as lacking in toleration. Even if it would be intolerant to give one religion certain special forms of support, there are many different acceptable mixtures of what is denied to every religion and what is available to all. The particular mixture that is now accepted in the United States is not the only just solution.

This indeterminacy extends even to the area of freedom of expression, which will be particularly important in what follows. Any just and tolerant society must protect freedom of expression. This does not mean merely that censorship is ruled out, but requires as well that individuals and groups have some effective means for bringing their views before the public. There are, however, many ways of doing this.[2] There are, for example, many ways of defining and regulating a "public forum," and no one of these is specifically required. Permitted and protected modes of expression need not be the same everywhere.

Let me now move from the most clearly institutional aspects of toleration to the less institutional and more attitudinal, thereby moving from the indeterminate to the vague. I have said that toleration involves "accepting as equals" those who differ from us. In what I have said so far, this equality has meant equal possession of fundamental legal and political rights, but the ideal of equality that toleration involves goes beyond these particular rights. It might be stated as follows: all members of society are equally entitled to be taken into account in defining what our society is and equally entitled to participate in determining what it will become in the future. This idea is unavoidably vague and difficult to accept. It is difficult to accept insofar as it applies to those who differ from us or disagree with us, and who would make our society something other than what we want it to be. It is vague because of the difficulty of saying exactly what this "equal entitlement" involves. One mode of participation is, of course, through the formal politics of voting, running for office, and trying to enlist votes for the laws and policies that one favors. But what I now want to stress is the way in which the requirements of toleration go beyond this realm of formal politics into what might be called the informal politics of social life.

The competition among religious groups is a clear example of this informal politics, but it is only one example. Other groups and individuals engage in the same political struggle all the time: we set and follow examples, seek to be recognized or have our standard-bearers recognized in every aspect of cultural and popular life. A tolerant society, I want to say, is one that is democratic in its informal politics. This democracy is a matter of law and institutions (a matter, for example, of the regulation of expression). But it is also, importantly and irreducibly, a matter of attitude. Toleration of this kind is not easy to accept—it is risky and frightening—and it is not easy to achieve, even in one's own attitudes, let alone in society as a whole.

To explain what I have in mind, it is easiest to begin with some familiar controversies over freedom of expression and over "the enforcement of morals." The desire to prevent those with whom one disagrees from influencing the evolution of one's society has been a main motive for restricting expression—for example, for restricting religious proselytizing and for restricting the sale of publications dealing with sex, when these are not sold or used in a way that forces others to see them. This motive supports not only censorship but also the kind of regulation of private conduct that raises the issue of "the enforcement of morals." Sexual relations between consenting adults in the privacy of their bedrooms are not "expression," but it is no mistake to see attempts to regulate such conduct and attempts to regulate expression as closely related. In both cases, what the enforcers want is to prevent the spread of certain forms of behavior and attitude both by deterring it and, at least as important, by using the criminal law to make an authoritative statement of social disapproval.

One form of liberal response has been to deny the legitimacy of any interest in "protecting society" from certain forms of change. (The analog of declaring religion to be purely a private matter.) This response seems to me to be mistaken.[3] We all have a profound interest in how prevailing customs and practices evolve. Certainly, I myself have such an interest, and I do not regard it as illegitimate. I do not care whether other people, individually, go swimming in the nude or not, but I do not want my society to become one in which nude bathing becomes so much the norm that I cannot wear a suit without attracting stares and feeling embarrassed. I have no desire to dictate what others, individually, in couples or in groups, do in their bedrooms, but I would much prefer to live in a society in which sexuality and sexual attractiveness, of whatever kind, was given less importance than it is in our society today. I do not care what others read and listen to, but I would like my society to be one in which there are at least a significant number of people who know and admire the same literature and music that I do, so that that music will be generally available, and so that there will be others to share my sense of its value.

Considered in this light, religious toleration has much greater risks for me than I suggested at the beginning of this article: I am content to leave others to the religious practices of their choice provided that they leave me free to enjoy none. But I will be very unhappy if this leads in time to my society becoming one in which almost everyone is, in one way or another, deeply religious, and in which religion plays a central part in all public discourse. Moreover, I would feel this way even if I would continue to enjoy the firm protection of the First Amendment. What I fear is not merely the legal enforcement of religion but its social predominance.

So I see nothing mistaken or illegitimate about at least some of the *concerns* that have moved those who advocate the legal enforcement of morals or who seek to restrict expression in order to prevent what they see as the deterioration of their society. I might disagree with them in substance, but I would not say that concerns of this kind are ones that anyone should or could avoid having. What is objectionable about the "legal enforcement of morals" is the attempt to restrict individuals' personal lives as a way of controlling the evolution of mores. Legal moralism is an example of intolerance, for example, when it uses the criminal law to deny that homosexuals are legitimate participants in the informal politics of society.

I have not tried to say how this informal politics might be regulated. My aims have been, rather, to illustrate what I mean by informal politics, to point out what I take to be its great importance to all of us, and to suggest that for this reason toleration is, for all of us, a risky matter, a practice with high stakes.

3. THE VALUE OF TOLERANCE

Why, then, value tolerance? The answer lies, I believe, in the relation with one's fellow citizens that tolerance makes possible. It is easy to see that a tolerant person and an intolerant one have different attitudes toward those in society with whom they disagree. The tolerant person's attitude is this: "Even though we disagree, they are as fully members of society as I am. They are as entitled as I am to the protections of the law, as entitled as I am to live as they choose to live. In addition (and this is the hard part) neither their way of living nor mine is uniquely *the* way of our society. These are merely two among the potentially many different outlooks that our society can include, each of which is equally entitled to be expressed in living as one mode of life that others can adopt. If one view is at any moment numerically or culturally predominant, this should be determined by, and dependent on, the accumulated choices of individual members of the society at large."

Intolerant individuals deny this. They claim a special place for their own values and way of life. Those who live in a different way—Turks in Germany, for example, Muslims in India, and homosexuals in some parts of the United States—are, in their view, not full members of their society, and the intolerant claim the right to suppress these other ways of living in the name of protecting their society and "its" values. They seek to do this either by the force of criminal law or by denying forms of public support that other groups enjoy, such as public subsidies for the arts.

What I have just provided is description, not argument. But the first way of making the case for tolerance is simply to point out, on the basis of this description, that tolerance involves a more attractive and appealing relation between opposing groups within a society. Any society, no matter how homogeneous, will include people who disagree about how to live and about what they want their society to be like. (And the disagreements within a relatively homogeneous culture can be more intense than those within a society founded on diversity, like the United States.) Given that there must be disagreements, and that those who disagree must somehow live together, is it not better, if possible, to have these disagreements contained within a framework of mutual respect? The alternative, it seems, is to be always in conflict, even at the deepest level, with a large number of one's fellow citizens. The qualification "even at the deepest level" is crucial here. I am assuming that in any society there will over time be conflicts, serious ones, about the nature and direction of the society. What tolerance expresses is a recognition of common membership that is deeper than these conflicts, a recognition of others as just as entitled as we are to contribute to the definition of our society. Without this, we are just rival groups contending over the same territory. The fact that each of us, for good historical and personal reasons, regards it as *our* territory and *our* tradition just makes the conflict all the deeper.

Whether or not one accepts it as sufficient justification for tolerance, the difference that tolerance makes in one's relation to those who are "different" is easy to see. What is less obvious, but at least as important, is the difference tolerance makes in one's relation with those to whom one is closest. One's children provide the clearest case. As my children, they are as fully members of our society as I am. It is their society just as much as it is mine. What one learns as a parent, however, is that there is no guarantee that the society they will want is the same one that I want. Intolerance implies that their right to live as they choose and to influence others to do so is conditional on their agreement with me about what the right way to live is. If I believe that others, insofar as they disagree with me, are not as entitled as I am to shape the mores of our common society, then I must think this of my children as well, should they join this opposition. Perhaps I hold that simply being *my children* gives them special political standing. But this seems to me unlikely. More likely, I think, is that this example brings out the fact that intolerance involves a denial of the full membership of "the others." What is special about one's children is, in this case, just that their membership is impossible to deny. But intolerance forces one to deny it, by making it conditional on substantive agreement with one's own values.

My argument so far is that the case for tolerance lies in the fact that rejecting it involves a form of alienation from one's fellow citizens. It is important to recognize, however, that the strength of this argument depends on the fact that we are talking about membership in "society" as a political unit. This can be brought out by considering how the argument for tolerance would apply within a private association, such as a church or political movement.[4] Disagreements are bound to arise within any such group about how their shared values are to be understood. Is it then intolerant to want to exclude from the group those with divergent views, to deny them the right to participate in meetings and run for office under the party label, to deny them the sacraments, or stop inviting them to meetings? It might be said that this also involves the kind of alienation I have described, by making others' standing as members conditional on agreement with our values. But surely groups of this kind have good reason to exclude those who disagree. Religious groups and political movements would lose their point if they had to include just anyone.

In at least one sense, the ideas of tolerance and intolerance that I have been describing do apply to private associations. As I have said, disagreements are bound to arise within such groups, and when they do it is intolerant to attempt to deny those with whom one disagrees the opportunity to persuade others to adopt their interpretation of the group's values and mission. Tolerance of this kind is required by the very idea of an association founded on a commitment to "shared values." In what sense would these values be "shared" unless there were some process—like the formal and informal politics to which I have referred—through which they evolve and agreement on them is sustained?[5] But there are limits. The very meaning of the goods in question—the sacraments, the party label—requires that they be conditional on certain beliefs. So it is not intolerant for the group as a whole, after due deliberation, to deny these goods to those who clearly lack these beliefs.

Tolerance at the level of political society is a different matter. The goods at stake here, such as the right to vote, to hold office, and to participate in the public forum, do not lose their meaning if they are extended to people with whom we disagree about the kind of society we would like to have, or even to those who reject its most basic tenets. One can become a member of society, hence entitled to these goods, just by being born into it (as well as in other ways), and one is required to obey its laws and institutions as long as one remains within its territory. The argument for tolerance that I have been describing is based on this idea of society and on the idea that the relation of "fellow citizen" that it involves is one we have reason to value. The form of alienation I have mentioned occurs when the terms of this relation are violated: when we deny others, who are just as much members of our society as we are, the right to their part in defining and shaping it.[6]

As I have said, something similar can occur when we deny fellow members of a private association their rightful share in shaping it. But the relation of "fellow member" that is violated is different from the relation of "fellow citizen," and it is to be valued for different reasons. In particular, the reasons for valuing such a relation often entail limits on the range of its application. It would be absurd, for example, for Presbyterians to consider everyone born within the fifty United States a member of their church, and it would therefore not be intolerant to deny some of them the right to participate in the evolution of this institution. But the relation of "fellow citizen" is supposed to link at least everyone born into a society and remaining within its borders. So it does not entail, and is in fact incompatible with, any narrower limits.

4. THE DIFFICULTY OF TOLERANCE

Examples of intolerance are all around us. To cite a few recent examples from the United States, there are the referenda against gay rights in Oregon and Colorado, attempts by Senator Jesse Helms and others to prevent the National Endowment for the Arts and the National Endowment for the Humanities from supporting projects of which they (Helms et al.) disapprove, recent statements by the governor of Mississippi that "America is a Christian nation," and similar statements in the speeches at the 1992 Republican National Convention by representatives of the Christian right.

But it is easy to see intolerance in one's opponents and harder to avoid it oneself. I am thinking here, for example, of my reactions to recurrent controversies in the United States over the teaching of evolution and "creation science" in public schools and to the proposal to amend the Constitution if necessary in order to allow organized prayer in public schools. I firmly believe that "creation science" is bogus and that science classes should not present scientific theory and religious doctrine as alternatives with similar and equal claim to the same kind of assent. I therefore do not think that it is intolerant per se to oppose the creationists. But I confess to feeling a certain sense of partisan zeal in such cases, a sense of superiority over the people who propose such things and a desire not to let them win a point even if it did not cost anyone very much. In the case of science teaching, there is a cost, as there is in the case of school prayer. But I am also inclined to support removing "In God We Trust" from our coinage and to favor discontinuing the practice of prayer at public events.

These changes appeal to me because they would make the official symbolism of our country more thoroughly secular, hence more in line with my own outlook, and I can also claim that they represent a more consistent adherence to the constitutional principle of "nonestablishment" of religion. Others see these two reasons as inconsistent. In their view, I am not simply removing a partisan statement from our official symbolism, but at the same time replacing it with another; I am not making our public practice neutral as between secularism and religiosity but asking for an official step that would further enthrone secularism (which is already "officially endorsed" in many other ways, they would say) as our national outlook. I have to admit that, whatever the right answer to the constitutional question might be (and it might be indeterminate), this response has more than a little truth to it when taken as an account of my motives, which are strongly partisan.

But why should they not be partisan? It might seem that here I am going too far, bending over backwards in the characteristically liberal way. After all, the argument that in asking to have this slogan removed from our money I am asking for the official endorsement of *irre*-ligiosity is at best indirect and not really very persuasive. Whereas the slogan itself does have that aggressively inclusive, hence potentially exclusive "we": "In God *We* Trust." (Who do you mean "we"?)

Does this mean that in a truly tolerant society there could be no public declarations of this kind, no advocacy or enforcement by the state of any particular doctrine? Not even tolerance itself? This seems absurd. Let me consider the matter in stages.

First, is it intolerant to enforce tolerance in behavior and prevent the intolerant from acting on their beliefs? Surely not. The rights of the persecuted demand this protection, and the demand to be tolerated cannot amount to a demand to do whatever one believes one must.

Second, is it intolerant to espouse tolerance as an official doctrine? We could put it on our coins: "In Tolerance We Trust." (Not a bad slogan, I think, although it would have to be pronounced carefully.) Is it intolerant to have tolerance taught in state schools and supported in state-sponsored advertising campaigns? Surely not, and again for the same reasons. The advocacy of tolerance denies no one their rightful place in society. It grants to each person and group as much standing as they can claim while granting the same to others.

Finally, is it contrary to tolerance to deny the intolerant the opportunities that others

215

have to state their views? This would seem to deny them a standing that others have. Yet to demand that we tolerate the intolerant in even this way seems to demand an attitude that is almost unattainable. If a group maintains that I and people like me simply have no place in our society, that we must leave or be eliminated, how can I regard this as a point of view among others that is equally entitled to be heard and considered in our informal (or even formal) politics? To demand this attitude seems to be to demand too much.

If toleration is to make sense, then, we must distinguish between one's attitude toward what is advocated by one's opponents and one's attitude toward those opponents themselves: it is not that their *point of view* is entitled to be represented but that *they* (as fellow citizens, not as holders of that point of view) are entitled to be heard. So I have fought my way to the ringing statement attributed to Voltaire,[7] that is, to a platitude. But in the context of our discussion, I believe that this is not only a platitude but also the location of a difficulty, or several difficulties.

What Voltaire's statement reminds us is that the attitude toward others that tolerance requires must be understood in terms of specific rights and protections. He mentions the right to speak, but this is only one example. The vague recognition of others as equally entitled to contribute to informal politics, as well as to the more formal kind, can be made more definite by listing specific rights to speak, to set an example through one's conduct, to have one's way of life recognized through specific forms of official support. To this we need to add the specification of kinds of support that *no* way of life can demand, such as prohibiting conduct by others simply because one disapproves of it. These specifications give the attitude of tolerance more definite content and make it more tenable. One *can* be asked (or so I believe) to recognize that others have these specific rights no matter how strongly one takes exception to what they say. . . .

5. CONCLUSION

I began by considering the paradigm case of religious toleration, a doctrine that seemed at first to have little cost or risk when viewed from the perspective of a secular liberal with secure constitutional protection against the "establishment" of a religion. I went on to explain why toleration in general, and religious toleration in particular, is a risky policy with high stakes, even within the framework of a stable constitutional democracy. The risks involved lie not so much in the formal politics of laws and constitutions (though there may be risks there as well) but rather in the informal politics through which the nature of a society is constantly redefined. I believe in tolerance despite its risks, because it seems to me that any alternative would put me in an antagonistic and alienated relation to my fellow citizens, friends as well as foes. The attitude of tolerance is nonetheless difficult to sustain. It can be given content only through some specification of the rights of citizens as participants in formal and informal politics. But any such system of rights will be conventional and indeterminate and is bound to be under frequent attack. To sustain and interpret such a system, we need a larger attitude of tolerance and accommodation, an attitude that is itself difficult to maintain.

NOTES

I am grateful to Joshua Cohen and Will Kymlicka for their helpful comments on earlier drafts of this paper.

1. As John Horton points out in his contribution to this volume.
2. More exactly, there are many ways of trying to do it. I believe that our ideas of freedom of expression must be understood in terms of a commitment both to certain goals and to the idea of certain institutional arrangements as crucial means to those goals. But the means are never fully adequate to the goals, which drive their constant evolution. I discuss this "creative instability" in "Content Regulation Reconsidered," in *Democracy and the Mass Media*, ed. J. Lichtenberg (New York: Cambridge University Press, 1991).
3. Here I draw on points made in section 5 of my article, "Freedom of Expression and Categories of Expression," *University of Pittsburgh Law Review* 40 (1979): 479–520.
4. Here I am indebted to very helpful questions raised by Will Kymlicka. I do not know whether he would agree with my way of answering them.
5. As Michael Walzer has written, addressing a similar question, "When people disagree about the meaning of social goods, when understandings are controversial, then justice requires that the society be faithful to the disagreements, providing institutional channels for their expression, adjudicative mechanisms, and alternative distributions." *Spheres of Justice.* (New York: Basic Books, 1984), p. 313.

6. Intolerance can also be manifested when we deny others the opportunity to *become* members on racial or cultural grounds. But it would take me too far afield to discuss here the limits on just immigration and naturalization policies.

7. He is said to have said, "I disapprove of what you say, but I will defend to the death your right to say it."

Discussion Questions

1. Does Scanlon's account of tolerance apply only to "fellow citizens"? Can it be extended to tolerance of people in other countries? Explain.
2. According to Scanlon, why is the charge of intolerance "powerful political coin"? Is he right?
3. Is it intolerant not to tolerate the intolerant?

CHAPTER 13

Forgiveness

HARD QUESTION: WHEN SHOULD WE FORGIVE?

Forgiveness is often thought of as a peculiarly religious virtue. But irrespective of its prominence in Christianity, forgiveness is important in its own right because it is necessary for social living. If every transgression large or small were vigorously pursued in the name of justice or revenge, normal interpersonal relations would be stretched to the breaking point. Social harmony requires that we sometimes forgive. This holds for human relations of every conceivable sort; forgiveness is at least a possibility for transgressions among lovers, families, friends, neighbors, colleagues, citizens, whole peoples, and even nations. Wherever people can wrong one another, forgiveness is a conceivable response to the wrongdoer. It is even possible to forgive oneself, although that might be a special case.

When someone wrongs us, it is perfectly appropriate to feel resentment or hold some other negative attitude toward the wrongdoer. Not to initially have any negative attitudes toward someone who wrongs us can even be a character flaw, if our failure to react shows too little self-regard. When we forgive, we decide to overcome those negative feelings that we are entirely within our rights to hold; we no longer hold the wrongdoer in contempt, nor do we seek retribution or revenge for the wrong done to us. Because being wronged rather than just harmed presupposes moral agency of the wrongdoer, forgiveness presupposes moral agency as well. If a tree falls on my car, I have been harmed, not wronged, but if someone intentionally or negligently causes the tree to fall on my car, I have been wronged. Forgiveness is thus not conceptually possible when the harms are accidental or caused by someone who is not morally responsible, for there is no wrong, and so resentment is not warranted either. How should we decide when to forgive? Are there times when we should forgive? Are there times when we should not?

Sometimes contrition on the wrongdoer's part seems necessary for forgiveness. We expect that the wrongdoer will acknowledge moral responsibility for the wrong, and if the wrongdoer does not, then we should not forgive. But this does not seem correct. Although repentance might make it easier for us to forgive, there is no reason why our forgiveness should be dependent on that. If the person wronged must wait for the wrongdoer to repent as a condition for forgiving, this gives the wrongdoer power over the person wronged. Since forgiveness is something one chooses to do, it should be freely done and therefore ought not to be contingent on whether the wrongdoer decides to repent. To make it otherwise is incompatible with the self-respect of the person wronged.

One's self-respect is also threatened by a willingness to forgive too quickly. Consider the battered wife who readily forgives her abusive husband after each episode. Minimal self-respect requires that she withhold forgiveness. In a case like this, to forgive is to display a character flaw. But stubborn refusal to forgive can also display a character flaw. Imagine the person who refuses to forgive even though the wrongdoer has repented and begged for forgiveness. If the person wronged is holding a grudge, then perhaps he ought to forgive.

Yet refusal to forgive need not show that one holds a grudge. Are some wrongs just too serious to forgive the wrongdoer? Might the victims of unspeakable crimes have an obligation *not* to forgive? Rape victims and genocide survivors might find solace in forgiving so they can get on with their lives, but do they have a duty not to forgive nonetheless? This is the idea of the unforgivable, something so heinous that forgiveness is always wrong. We sometimes talk about unforgivable actions, but we must remember that actions are not forgivable, only persons are. So for a person to do something literally unforgivable means that no amount of repentance or compensation could justify forgiving the person for what he or she did. And since only the person wronged can forgive the wrongdoer (I cannot forgive someone who wrongs you, only you can do that), if the person wronged is dead, forgiveness is not possible. So there are certainly unforgivable crimes in this non-moral sense. But this is not what is at issue when we ask about unforgivable crimes; here the issue is whether one morally *ought* not to forgive. Whether there can be absolutely unforgivable acts—cases where the victims morally should never forgive the wrongdoer even if they could—is an important question for us as we contemplate forgiveness. One way to think about it is to imaginatively put ourselves in the wrongdoer's position: Can we imagine doing something for which we would never want the victim to forgive us? Imaginatively trading places may be psychologically impossible for the victims of horrendous violations, but it is hard to see why that limitation should matter. If we think that our sincere regret and repentance ought not to matter to whether we should be forgiven, then the unforgivable is possible.

THE MORAL LOGIC OF FORGIVENESS

Let's look more closely at forgiveness. According to Bishop Butler, the celebrated eighteenth-century Anglican theologian and philosopher, forgiveness is "the forswearing of resentment, the resolute overcoming of the anger and hatred that are naturally directed toward a person who has done one an unjustified and non-excused moral injury." Note the crucial elements in this succinct account of forgiveness: You have been wronged, and that naturally produces resentment, which you then forswear. If there is no "anger and hatred," then there is nothing to forswear and hence no forgiveness. And the "anger and hatred" has to be a justified response to what the person did to you. That is, someone wronged you, and in forgiveness you forgo the resentment you are naturally entitled to hold.

Forgiveness is thus very different from forgoing resentment (or any other negative attitudes) because you excuse someone for harming you. To excuse means that the offender is not morally responsible; that person was ignorant, preoccupied, sick, or in some other way not culpable for the harm. In forgiveness, the person who wronged you is not excused; that person is fully morally responsible for the wrong, but you nevertheless forgo (or seek to overcome) the resentment that you are perfectly entitled to hold by virtue of the wrong you have suffered. Forgiveness requires not a diminishment in the moral culpability of the transgressor, as when we excuse the transgressor, but a full recognition that the person who wronged you is morally responsible for the wrong. Thus when Jesus famously beseeched God from the cross "to forgive them, for they know not what they do," it cannot be forgiveness Jesus requests if his executioners really do not know what they are doing. (And shouldn't Jesus be the one to forgive his executioners? But this takes us too far from our topic.)

Forgiveness is also not the same as forgetting, as in "forgive and forget," because when you forget you simply erase the transgression from memory. Forgetting might be a psychologically healthy response to a wrong, and it might be good to do for that reason because it helps one to get on with one's life, but it is still not forgiveness. Forgiveness requires that you remember the wrong—indeed, that you hold it clearly in mind as a wrong—and still forgo (or overcome) the resentment you justifiably feel because of it. Nor is forgiveness the same as showing mercy, because someone might show mercy toward a transgressor and still maintain negative attitudes toward that person that are incompatible with forgiveness. In forgiveness, one forgoes the negative attitudes that one is perfectly entitled to hold.

Forgiveness is thus a second-order judgment (a judgement about a judgement) that we make about a natural and wholly justifiable reaction to a wrong we have suffered. When we forgive, we seek to rise above the resentment that it is our right to hold. Why would anyone seek to do that?

One common reason for forgiving is that by "letting go" of our resentment, we feel better. This sort of therapeutic reason for forgiveness is without moral merit, since the question is whether one is morally justified in forgoing resentment. Perhaps one ought not to forgive, even if forgiving would make one happier. Another reason to forgive—not excuse, but forgive—is that the wrongdoer repents. This means that the person who wronged you acknowledges the wrong and is sorry; it is tantamount to admitting guilt and seeking to make amends for the transgression. Our hard feelings are then directed against the transgressor, not the repentant and morally transformed person before us now. Our hard feelings are no longer warranted because they are not properly directed; in a sense, they are directed toward a person who no longer exists, the former transgressor. But this goes too far. It is true that the repentant person has been morally transformed, but the person who repents must regard himself now as the same person who transgressed. Otherwise, why should he now repent? But once the transgressor is repentant, do the hard feelings of the victim still have an appropriate target? If not, then one is no longer justified in holding on to them, so it seems that one ought to forgive. In this case, however, one does not overcome justified resentment, one comes instead to realize that resentment is no longer appropriate, for their proper target has disappeared.

With true forgiveness, one is justifiably resentful and *still* forgoes the resentment. What could ever justify doing that? Theological considerations aside, it seems that forgiveness is warranted when it is compatible with the self-respect of the victim and serves to repair and maintain important human relationships. That is, one gives up something one is entitled to (the resentment or other negative feelings from having been wronged) for the sake of something else of value. Failure to forgive when other significant values are at stake can show that one has not properly assessed those other values.

READINGS ON FORGIVENESS

Jeffrie Murphy, "Forgiveness and Resentment"

Jeffrie Murphy is Regents' Professor of Law and Philosophy at Arizona State University. He has made substantial contributions to moral, political, and legal philosophy. His work on forgiveness is particularly important. Reprinted here is a central chapter from one of his books on forgiveness. Murphy argues that the primary value defended by the resentment essential for forgiveness is self-respect. He goes on to consider various grounds for forgiveness that are compatible with self-respect.

Critical Reading Questions

1. What is resentment and what value does it protect?
2. When, according to Murphy, is forgiveness a virtue and when is it a vice?
3. What is forgiveness, according to Murphy? How is it distinct from excuse, justification, and mercy?
4. What justifies forgiveness, according to Murphy?
5. What, according to Murphy, is the relationship between self-respect and forgiveness?

FORGIVENESS AND RESENTMENT

Jeffrie Murphy

Understand, and forgive, my mother said, and the effort has quite exhausted me. I could do with some anger to energize me, and bring me back to life again. But where can I find that anger? Who is to help me? My friends? I have been understanding and forgiving my friends, my female friends, for as long as I can remember. . . . Understand and forgive. . . . Understand husbands, wives, fathers, mothers. Understand dog-fights above and the charity box below, understand fur-coated women and children without shoes. Understand school—Jonah, Job and the nature of the Deity; understand Hitler and the bank of England and the behavior of Cinderella's sisters. Preach acceptance to wives and tolerance to husbands; patience to parents and compromise to the young. Nothing in this world is perfect; to protest takes the strength needed for survival. Grit your teeth, endure. Understand, forgive, accept, in the light of your own death, your own inevitable corruption. . . .
Oh mother, what you taught me! And what a miserable, crawling, snivelling way to go, the worn-out slippers neatly placed beneath the bed, careful not to give offense.

—Fay Weldon, *Female Friends*

To err is human; to forgive, supine.
—S. J. PERELMAN

I. INTRODUCTION

Forgiveness, Bishop Butler teaches, is the forswearing of resentment—the resolute overcoming of the anger and hatred that are naturally directed toward a person who has done one an unjustified and non-excused moral injury.[1] By

[1]Joseph Butler, *Fifteen Sermons* (London, 1726), Sermon VIII, "Upon Resentment," and Sermon IX, "Upon Forgiveness of Injuries."

his emphasis on the forswearing of resentment, Butler indicates that he quite properly wants to draw a distinction between forgiveness (which may be a virtue and morally commanded) and forgetting (which may just happen). Forgiveness is the sort of thing that one does for a reason, and where there are reasons there is a distinction between good ones and bad ones.

What, then, are the good reasons for forgiveness? Butler has useful things to say in response to this question, but his response is limited by a perspective that strikes me as too consequentialist. Resentment, he argues, can provoke bad consequences—especially such anti-social actions as personal revenge. Forgiveness is thus justified primarily as a way of avoiding such undesirable consequences. Resentment does indeed perform a useful social job—the job of reinforcing the rules of morality and provoking defenses of those rules—but when it is allowed to range beyond this useful function, as human weakness and vanity typically allow it to, it becomes counterproductive and even seriously harmful to the social fabric. Tendencies to forgive thus are to be supported to the degree that they help individuals to overcome or avoid such excesses.

This is surely part of the story, but—as Butler himself sometimes sees—there is considerably more to be told. Butler stresses that the passion of resentment functions in a defensive role—defensive of the rules of morality and of the social fabric those rules define. But he never fleshes out this insight in sufficient detail adequately to highlight central features of the context wherein resentment and forgiveness have their life.

In my view, resentment (in its range from righteous anger to righteous hatred) functions primarily in defense, not of *all* moral values and norms, but rather of certain *values of the self*. Resentment is a response not to general wrongs but to wrongs against oneself; and these resented wrongs can be of two sorts: resentment of direct violations of one's rights (as in assault) *or* resentment that another has taken unfair advantage of one's sacrifices by free riding on a mutually beneficial scheme of reciprocal cooperation. Only the immediate victim of crime is in a position to resent a criminal in the first way; all the law-abiding citizens, however, may be in a position to resent the criminal (and thus be secondary victims) in the second way—at least on Herbert Morris's well-known theory of such matters.[2]

I am, in short, suggesting that the primary value defended by the passion of resentment is *self-respect*, that proper self-respect is essentially tied to the passion of resentment, and that a person who does not resent moral injuries done to him (of either of the above sorts) is almost necessarily a person lacking in self-respect. Thus some of the primary reasons justifying forgiveness will be found, not in general social utility, but in reasons directly tied to an individual's self-respect or self-esteem, his perception of his own worth, of what he is owed. In some limited sense, then, I side with Stephen: Resentment (perhaps even some hatred) is a good thing, for it is essentially tied to a non-controversially good thing—self-respect. Let me elaborate on this a bit.

As noted by thinkers as otherwise diverse as Butler and Nietzsche, resentment has a very unattractive—even dangerous and unhealthy—dimension. This is something I would not want to deny. In addition to many of its other disadvantages, resentment can stand as a fatal obstacle to the restoration of equal moral relations among persons, and thus it cannot always be the final "bottom line" as the response we take to those who have wronged us. Forgiveness heals and restores; and, without it, resentment would remain as an obstacle to many human relationships we value. This can be seen most clearly in such intimate relationships as love and friendship. The people with whom we are most intimate are those who can harm us the most, for they are the persons to whom we have let down our guard and exposed our vulnerabilities. Because of the nature of intimacy, moral injuries here tend to be not just ordinary injustices but also *betrayals*. Thus resentment here can be deep and nearly intractable—as revealed in the quip of Cosmus, Duke of Florence: "You shall read that we are commanded to forgive our enemies; but you never read that we are commanded to forgive our friends."[3] Deep as these hurts of intimacy may be, however, what would be the consequence of never forgiving any of them? Surely it would be this: the impossibility of ever having the kind of intimate relationships that are one of the crowning delights of human existence. The person who cannot forgive is the person who cannot have friends or lovers.

For this reason, it is easy to see why forgiveness is typically regarded as a virtue. Forgiveness is not always a virtue, however. Indeed, if I am correct in linking resentment to self-respect, a too ready tendency to forgive may properly be regarded as a *vice* because it may be a sign that one lacks respect for oneself. Not to have what Peter Strawson calls the "reactive attitude" of resentment when our rights are violated is to convey—emotionally—either that we do not think we have rights or that we do not take our rights very seriously.[4] Forgiveness may indeed restore relationships, but to seek restoration at all cost—even at the cost of one's very human dignity—can hardly be a virtue. And, in intimate relationships, it can hardly be true love or friendship either—the kind of love and friendship that Aristotle claimed is an essential part of the virtuous life. When we are willing to be doormats for others, we have, not love, but rather what the psychiatrist Karen Horney calls "morbid dependency."[5] If I count morally as much as anyone else (as surely I do), a failure to resent moral injuries done to me is a failure to care about the moral value incarnate in my own person (that I am, in Kantian language, an

[2]Herbert Morris, "Persons and Punishment," *The Monist*, 52 (October 1968); reprinted in his collection of essays *Guilt and Innocence* (Berkeley: University of California Press, 1976).

[3]Quoted in Francis Bacon's essay "Of Revenge" (1597).

[4]Peter Strawson, "Freedom and Resentment," *Proceedings of the British Academy*, 1962.

[5]Karen Horney, *Neurosis and Human Growth* (New York: Norton, 1950).

end in myself) and thus a failure to care about the very rules of morality.[6] To put the point in yet another way: If it is proper to feel *indignation* when I see third parties morally wronged, must it not be equally proper to feel *resentment* when I experience the moral wrong done to myself? Morality is not simply something to be believed in; it is something to be *cared* about. This caring includes concern about those persons (including oneself) who are the proper objects of moral attention.

Interestingly enough, a hasty readiness to forgive—or even a refusal to display resentment initially—may reveal a lack of respect, not just for oneself, but for others as well. The Nietzschean view, for example, is sometimes portrayed (perhaps unfairly) as this: There is no need for forgiveness, because a truly strong person will never feel resentment in the first place. Why? Because he is not so weak as to think that other people—even those who harm him— matter enough to have any impact on his self-respect. We do not resent the insect that stings us (we simply *deal* with it), and neither should we resent the human who wrongs us.[7]

Although there is something attractive and worth discussing about this view, most of us would probably want to reject it as too demeaning of other human beings and our moral relations with them. I shall thus for the present assume the following: Forgiveness is acceptable only in cases where it is consistent with self-respect, respect for others as responsible moral agents, and allegiance to the rules of morality (i.e., forgiveness must not involve complicity or acquiescence in wrongdoing).[8]

II. THE NATURE AND JUSTIFICATION OF FORGIVENESS

Enough by way of introduction. Having presented an overview of the problem of forgiveness, let me now move to a more detailed consideration of the two basic questions concerning forgiveness: (1) What is forgiveness; that is, how is the concept to be analyzed and distinguished from other concepts with which it may be confused? and (2) when, if at all, is forgiveness justified? (If it is never justified, then a tendency to bestow it can surely not be a virtue.)

First the question of meaning. I have already indicated, following Butler, that forgiveness essentially involves an attempt to overcome resentment. This feature allows us to distinguish forgiveness from three other concepts with which it is often confused: *excuse, justification,* and *mercy.* To excuse is to say this: What was done was morally wrong; but, because of certain factors about the agent (e.g., insanity), it would be unfair to hold the wrongdoer responsible or blame him for the wrong action. To justify is to say this: What was done was *prima facie* wrong; but, because of other morally relevant factors, the action was—*all* morally relevant factors considered—the right thing to do. And why is neither of these forgiveness? Because we

[6]See Thomas E. Hill, Jr., "Servility and Self-Respect," *The Monist,* 57 (January 1973), pp. 87–104.

[7]"To be incapable of taking one's enemies, one's accidents, even one's misdeeds seriously for very long—that is the sign of strong, full natures in whom there is an excess of the power to form, to mold, to recuperate and to forget. . . . Such a man shakes off with a single shrug many vermin that eat deep into others." Friedrich Nietzsche, *On the Genealogy of Morals,* Essay I, Section 10 (p. 39 of the Walter Kaufmann translation; New York: Random House, 1967).

According to Paul Lauritzen, a similar indifference to injury by others (a refusal to view it as genuine injury) can be found in some strands of Christianity. If one believes that the Kingdom of God is imminent, interests and well-being become radically redefined; and, since earthly injury is no longer counted as harm, there is no occasion for resentment. See Paul Lauritzen, "Forgiveness: Moral Prerogative or Religious Duty?" *Journal of Religious Ethics,* 15 (Fall 1987), pp. 141–54. Socrates also poses an interesting case here. On his stated view (in *Apology,* for example) a good person cannot be harmed or injured. Thus, if one regards oneself as a good person, then one—though positively brimming over with self-respect—will presumably never have occasion to resent, because one will never regard oneself as having been injured in any morally relevant way. Given the degree to which Socrates dealt with his enemies with ridicule and sarcasm, it is by no means clear that he actually practiced what he preached in this regard. Neither is it clear that the view he advocated is unambiguously desirable—even as an ideal. Could this level of insulation from others be compatible

with true love or friendship or meaningful membership in any human relationship or community, for example? For an exploration of some of these issues, see my "Violence and the Socratic Theory of Legal Fidelity," in my collection *Retribution, Justice, and Therapy: Essays in the Philosophy of Law* (Dordrecht: Reidel, 1979), pp. 40–57.

[8]For a discussion of the ways in which forgiveness may involve complicity in wrongdoing, see Aurel Kolnai's "Forgiveness," *Proceedings of the Aristotelian Society,* 1973–4; reprinted in his collection of essays *Ethics, Value, and Reality* (Indianapolis: Hackett, 1978).

may forgive only what it is initially proper to resent; and, if a person has done nothing wrong or was not responsible for what he did, there is *nothing to resent* (though perhaps much to be sad about). Resentment—and thus forgiveness—is directed toward *responsible wrongdoing;* and therefore, if forgiveness and resentment are to have an arena, it must be where such wrongdoing remains intact—i.e., neither excused nor justified. ("Father forgive them for they know not what they do" would go better as "Father *excuse* them for they know not what they do.")

Forgiveness is also not mercy. To be merciful is to treat a person less harshly than, given certain rules, one has a right to treat that person. For example, the rules of chivalry give me the right to kill you under certain circumstances of combat. If you beg for mercy, you are begging that I do something less severe than kill you. When Portia advises Shylock to show mercy, she is asking that he accept a payment less harsh than the one that, given the terms of his bargain, he has a right to demand. Three things are present in such cases: some notion of just or rightful authority, some notion of the supplicant's having fallen afoul of certain public rules, and the consideration of a certain external action (a killing, a payment of a "pound of flesh"). None of these is necessarily involved in forgiveness. Forgiveness is primarily a matter of how I *feel* about you (not how I treat you), and thus I may forgive you in my heart of hearts or even after you are dead. (I cannot show you mercy in my heart of hearts or after you are dead, however.) I may think I have forgiven you; but, when old resentments rise up again, I may say, "I was wrong—I really have not forgiven you after all." But if I have shown you mercy, this has been done—once and for all. Also, with respect to mercy, it is not necessary that I—in showing it—must be the one wronged or injured by your wrongful conduct. (It is not even necessary that anyone be wronged.) All that is required is that you stand under certain rules and that I have authority to treat you in a certain harsh way because of those rules. But the matter is different with forgiveness. To use a legal term, I do not have *standing* to resent or forgive you unless I have myself been the victim of your wrongdoing. I may forgive you for embezzling my funds; but it would be ludicrous for me, for example,

to claim that I had decided to forgive Hitler for what he did to the Jews. I lack the proper standing for this. Thus, I may legitimately resent (and hence consider forgiving) only wrong done *to me.*[9] If I forgive, this will primarily be a matter of my forswearing my resentment toward the person who has wronged me—a change of attitude quite compatible with my still demanding certain harsh public consequences for the wrongdoer. My forgiving you for embezzling my funds is not, for example, incompatible with a demand that you return my funds or even with a demand that you suffer just legal punishment for what you have done. Neither does my forgiveness entail that I must trust you with my money in the future. Forgiveness restores moral equality but not necessarily equality in every respect—for example, equality of trust. Some harsh treatment would, of course, be incompatible with forgiveness—namely, harsh treatment the very point of which would be to show you how much I hate and resent you. But when the harsh treatment is based on other factors (e.g., a concern with legal justice), forgiveness need pose no obstacle to such treatment.

Having become clearer on what forgiveness is not, let us return to Butler's account of what it is: the forswearing of resentment. Butler's puzzle was this: How could a loving God who commanded that we love our neighbor implant in us so unloving a passion as resentment? Is not this attitude unambiguously bad and any actions or practices based on it (retributive punishment perhaps) also bad? In answering *no* to this question, Butler suggests that resentment understandably arouses suspicion because it is often inappropriate (e.g., directed toward trivial affronts instead of real injuries) and sometimes provokes excessive behavior (e.g., vigilante activity). As Butler sees, however, it would be a

---

[9]In "Rebellion" (Dostoevsky, *The Brothers Karamazov*), Ivan considers the suffering of innocents—especially children—and is outraged at the thought that anyone except the children (or perhaps their mothers) could forgive the injuries suffered.

Sometimes, of course, I will psychologically identify with some persons and will see injuries to them as in some sense injuries to me. I may feel this way, for example, about my children. Here resentment does have a life. There is enormous individual variation, of course, in the degree to which people are psychologically identified with others—even strangers.

mistake to condemn a passion simply because it admits of pathological or irrational extensions. (What passion does not?) Resentment expresses respect for the demands of morality (particularly, as I have argued, for the demands for *self-respect*) and is thus—when so described—consistent, in Butler's view, with any reasonable interpretation of a gospel of love. (Butler has no patience with attempts to view the Christian ethic as irrational sentimentality.) What is not consistent with a gospel of love is being dominated by the passion of resentment or acting unjustly on the basis of that passion; and thus Butler sees forgiveness as a virtue that functions to check resentment and keep it within proper bounds.

Is forgiveness then nothing but the overcoming (or attempt at overcoming) of resentment? Is every instance where resentment is overcome a case of the virtue of forgiveness? I (agreeing, I believe, with Butler) think not; and two sorts of cases will aid in establishing this negative answer. First, consider the case of *forgetting*. Sometimes we lose a vivid memory of old wrongs, become bored with our resentments, and simply forget. But this just *happens* to us; that is, it is totally non-voluntary. As such, it seems too removed from agency to count as a moral virtue—though it still might be a desirable disposition of character to possess. Thus, to the extent that forgiveness is properly regarded as a moral virtue, it strikes me as a mistake to identify forgiving with forgetting. We tend to use the phrase "forgive and forget," and I do not believe the phrase is redundant.[10]

Or consider this second case: You have wronged me deeply, and I deeply resent you for it. The resentment eats away at my peace of mind—I lose sleep, snap at my friends, become less effective at my work, and so on. In short, my resentment so dominates my mental life that I am being made miserable. In order to regain my peace of mind, I go to a behavior-modification therapist to have my resentment extinguished. (Let us suppose there are such techniques.) Have I forgiven you? Surely not—at least not in any sense where forgiveness is supposed to be a moral virtue. For my motivation here was not moral at all; it was purely *selfish*: the desire to promote my own mental health.

What is starting to emerge from this discussion is this: The question "What is forgiveness?" cannot after all be sharply distinguished from the question "How is forgiveness justified?" As the foregoing cases show, not all instances of ceasing to resent will be ones of forgiveness—for example, forgetting is not. We cannot define forgiveness and *then* ask what moral reasons make it appropriate; because, I suggest, my ceasing to resent will not constitute forgiveness unless it is *done for a moral reason*. Forgiveness is not the overcoming of resentment *simpliciter*; it is rather this: forswearing resentment on moral grounds.

What, then, are the moral grounds; that is, what sorts of reasons justify or at least render appropriate an act of forgiveness? Let me start to answer this question simply by listing five reasons that are, in ordinary life and discourse, those most often given as grounds for forgiveness. We will then consider if this is just a laundry list or if some rational principle unites them or some set of them. The reasons are these:

I will forgive the person who has willfully wronged me, because

1. he repented or had a change of heart *or*
2. he meant well (his motives were good)[11] *or*
3. he has suffered enough *or*
4. he has undergone humiliation (perhaps some ritual humiliation, e.g., the apology ritual of "I beg forgiveness") *or*
5. of old times' sake (e.g., "He has been a good and loyal friend to me in the past").

Let me say something about what these reasons tend to have in common and then say something in detail about each one. But first recall the background here: Acceptable grounds for forgiveness must be compatible with self-respect,

[10]Although I am not here able to pursue the matter in any depth, I should at least note that forgetting is in fact more complex than this account suggests. As both Nietzsche and Freud have taught us, some cases that appear to involve mere non-voluntary forgetting might, when analyzed in depth, prove to be complex (though unconscious) rational strategies—strategies for which an individual might legitimately be held accountable. Here cases that initially look like mere forgetting might merit reclassification as forgetting of a more complex sort or even as forgiving.

[11]This point is stressed by Elizabeth Beardsley in her "Understanding and Forgiveness" in *The Philosophy of Brand Blanshard*, ed. Paul Arthur Schilpp (La Salle, Ill.: Open Court, 1981).

respect for others as moral agents, and respect for the rules of morality or the moral order. Can forgiveness ever be consistent with such constraints? I think that it can be for cases where we can draw a distinction between the immoral *act* and the immoral *agent;* for then we can follow Saint Augustine's counsel and "hate the sin but not the sinner." It is, of course, impossible to hate the sin and not the sinner if the sinner is intimately identified with his sin—if the wrongdoer is intimately identified with his wrongdoing. But to the extent that the agent is separated from his evil act, forgiveness *of him* is possible without a tacit approval of his evil act. A similar divorce of act from agent will also help to square forgiveness with self-respect. One reason we so deeply resent moral injuries done to us is not simply that they hurt us in some tangible or sensible way; it is because such injuries are also *messages*—symbolic communications. They are ways a wrongdoer has of saying to us, "I count but you do not," "I can use you for my purposes," or "I am here up high and you are there down below." Intentional wrongdoing *insults* us and attempts (sometimes successfully) to *degrade* us—and thus it involves a kind of injury that is not merely tangible and sensible. It is moral injury, and we care about such injuries. (As Justice Holmes observed, even a dog notices and cares about the difference between being tripped over accidentally and being kicked intentionally.) Most of us tend to care about what others (at least *some* others, some significant group whose good opinion we value) think about us—how much they think we matter. Our self-respect is *social* in at least this sense, and it is simply part of the human condition that we are weak and vulnerable in these ways. And thus when we are treated with contempt by others it attacks us in profound and deeply threatening ways. We resent (or worse) those who so attack us, and want to separate ourselves from them—to harm them in turn or at least to banish them from the realm of those whose well-being should be our concern.

But what if they come to separate or divorce themselves from their own evil act? (True repentance is a clear way of doing this.) Then the insulting message is no longer present—no longer endorsed by the wrongdoer. We can then join the wrongdoer in condemning the very act from which he now stands emotionally separated. Thus to the degree that the items on the preceding list represent ways in which an agent can be divorced from his evil act, they represent grounds for forgiveness that are compatible with self-respect and respect for the rules of the moral order. To explore this idea of "divorce of act from agent," let us now look a bit more closely at each of the five listed reasons.

1. Repentance. This is surely the clearest way in which a wrongdoer can sever himself from his past wrong. In having a sincere change of heart, he is withdrawing his endorsement from his own immoral past behavior; he is saying, "I no longer stand behind the wrongdoing, and I want to be separated from it. I stand with you in condemning it." Of such a person it cannot be said that he is *now* conveying the message that he holds me in contempt. Thus I can relate to him now, through forgiveness, without fearing my own acquiescence in immorality or in judgments that I lack worth. I forgive him for what he now is.

2. Good motives. Sometimes people wrong us without meaning to convey that they hold us in contempt or think we are of less worth than they are. Paternalism is a good example to illustrate this point. A person who interferes with my liberty for what he thinks is my own good is, in my judgment, acting wrongly; that is, he is interfering in my "moral space" in a way he has no right to. His grounds for interfering, however, are well meaning (i.e., he seeks to do me good) even if his actions are misguided and morally insensitive. (Perhaps he is overattentive to utilitarian considerations at the expense of considerations of rights and justice.) It is hard to view the friend who locks my liquor cabinet because he knows I drink too much as on exactly the same moral level as the person who embezzles my funds for his own benefit—even though both are violating my rights. Thus the case for forgiving the former (at least the first time) strikes me as having some merit.

3. Enough suffering. The claim "He has suffered enough" as grounds for forgiveness may understandably be viewed with suspicion; for example, we may think it was involved in such controversial events as President Gerald Ford's pardon of Richard Nixon on the grounds that Nixon, disgraced and forced to resign as president, had suffered enough. But two cautions are relevant here. First, Nixon was not simply forgiven (if he was forgiven at all); he was treated with *mercy*. To pardon someone is not to change the way one feels about him but is to let him avoid what may well be his just deserts. Second, just because *some* suffering may be relevant to forgiveness, it does not follow that *any* suffering is. The suffering occasioned by falling from a position that (as one's wrongful actions demonstrate) one had no right to occupy in the first place hardly seems relevant from the moral point of view.[12]

But what would relevant suffering be? I am not sure, actually, and some part of me wants to throw this consideration out entirely as simply confusion or even superstition. And yet some other part of me cannot quite do this. There is the thought, widespread in our culture, that *suffering is redemptive*. (One thinks, for example, of the old Oedipus in *Oedipus at Colonus*.) This connection between suffering and redemption could, of course, simply be a kind of empirical claim—e.g., the claim that suffering tends to provoke repentance. If so, then the intelligible content of "He has suffered enough" is redundant, collapsing into point 1 above. So too if the suffering is simply guilt or other pangs of conscience. Perhaps there is something in this thought: Wrongdoers attempt to *degrade* us, to bring us low—lower than themselves. We will find it difficult to forgive and restore relations with them in this posture without acquiescing in our own lowered status—something that any self-respecting person is loath to do. But suffering tends to bring people low, to reduce them, to humble them. If so, then enough equality may be restored in order to forgive them consistent with self-respect. They may not have severed themselves from their own evil acts, but there is perhaps a sense in which they have been severed. Given the hurt and sadness that may come to be present in a person's life, it may be difficult and improper to retain, as one's *primary* view of that person, the sense that he is essentially "the one who has wronged me." Perhaps he does and should become in one's mind simply "that poor bastard."

4. Humiliation. What I want to say about humiliation continues the preceding thought about suffering and involves the role of *ritual* in our moral life. We tend to think that rituals are practices that primitive savages have, and that we civilized folks have outgrown this sort of thing. But we are deeply mistaken when we think this. Philosophers have not, I think, paid sufficient attention to the role of ritual in moral relations—a role that illuminates certain aspects of forgiveness.[13] As I mentioned before, wrongdoers attempt (sometimes successfully) to degrade or insult us; to bring us low; to say, "I am on high while you are down there below." As a result, we in a real sense *lose face* when done a moral injury—one reason why easy forgiveness tends to compromise self-esteem. But our moral relations provide for a ritual whereby the wrongdoer can symbolically bring himself low (or raise us up—I am not sure which metaphor best captures the point)—in other words, the humbling ritual of *apology,* the language of which is often that of *begging* for forgiveness. The posture of begging is not very exalted, of course, and thus some symbolic equality—necessary if forgiveness is to proceed consistently with self-respect—is now present. Sometimes, of course, the apology is more than mere ritual; indeed, in the best of cases it is likely to be a way of manifesting repentance. Here it will collapse into point 1. At other times we will settle simply for the ritual—so long as it is not transparently insincere.[14]

5. Old times' sake. As with repentance, we have here a clear case of divorce of act from agent. When you are repentant, I forgive you for what you *now* are. When I forgive you for old times'

---

[12]See *U.S. v. Bergman,* United States District Court, S.D.N.Y., 1976, 416 F. Supp. 496. Rabbi Bergman was convicted of criminal fraud in connection with the operation of some of his nursing homes. He tried to avoid a prison sentence by arguing that he had been disgraced and had thus suffered enough. Judge Frankel was underwhelmed by this argument and suggested that, as Bergman's crimes demonstrated, he was "suffering from loss of public esteem . . . that had been, at least in some measure, wrongly bestowed and enjoyed."

[13]One philosopher who has appreciated the role of ritual in our moral life is Gareth Matthews. See his "Ritual and the Religious Feelings," in *Explaining Emotions,* ed. Amelie Oksenberg Rorty (Berkeley: University of California Press, 1980), pp. 339–53.

[14]On the role of humiliation ("humbling of the will"), see Herbert Fingarette's presidential address in *Proceedings of the American Philosophical Association,* 1977.

sake, I forgive you for what you *once were.* Much of our forgiveness of old friends and parents, for example, is of this sort.

The upshot of what I have argued thus far is this: Forgiveness of a wrongdoer on the basis of any of the preceding grounds (grounds which in various ways divorce act from agent) may be consistent with self-respect, respect for others, and respect for the rules of the moral order. All this shows, of course, is that forgiveness—when directed (for example) toward a truly repentant wrongdoer—is permissible, not wrong because not inconsistent with self-respect. But if forgiveness is a virtue, then it must be that sometimes it is not merely permissible that I forgive but that I *ought* to forgive and can be properly criticized if I do not. Perhaps nobody has a *right* to be forgiven (imposing on others a perfect duty to forgive him), but surely forgiveness—if a virtue—must be like charity in at least this way: Just as charity requires that I sometimes ought to assist those having no right to my assistance, so does forgiveness require that I sometimes ought to forgive those having no right to my forgiveness.

How might one argue for this stronger view? One argument has been latent in what I have said thus far. Although repentance does not give one a right to be forgiven, there is a sense in which it may make resentment *inappropriate*—for why should I resent you now for holding me in contempt when your sincere repentance makes it clear that you do not now hold me in contempt? There is a clear sense in which it is simply not *rational* to continue holding attitudes when I have come to see their inappropriateness and thus—as a rational being—I ought to forswear those attitudes. Just as rational beings value true beliefs, so they should, I think, value appropriate attitudes—attitudes fitting to their objects. This is why rational beings will seek to root out such things as phobias and other neurotic emotions from their psychologies; and so too, I should think, for inappropriate attitudes of resentment. This then is one argument for why we sometimes *ought* to forgive others—why forgiveness is sometimes more than merely permissible, why forgiveness is—in short—sometimes a virtue.

But there are other arguments as well. Two of them I associate particularly with the Christian tradition; and, since neither relies on the divorce

between act and agent that I have made central, it will be worth exploring them briefly to see if they add a significant new dimension to the understanding of forgiveness. The arguments are these:

1. We should forgive in order to reform the wrongdoer; i.e., we should forgive, not because the wrongdoer has repented, but as a step toward bringing his repentance about, making it at least easier for him.
2. We should forgive because we ourselves need to be forgiven. (This, I take it, is the point of the parable of the unforgiving servant in Matt. 18:21–35.)

These grounds for forgiveness may be what prompted Feuerbach and others to suggest that forgiveness cannot be accounted for in ordinary moral and secular terms—that it takes us beyond morality and into a religious dimension that transcends or suspends the ordinarily ethical.[15] I know that some people value obscurity and mystery for their own sake, but I am myself inclined to resist these leaps into special realms. Sometimes we can mine these religious traditions for nuggets of secular value—i.e., values we can recognize even if we do not accept the theological views in which they were originally embedded. Thus we can sometimes avoid leaps into the mysterious and edifying if we will simply think about the matter a bit more. Point 1 above, for example, could be a kind of empirical prediction—almost therapeutic in nature—about what is likely to produce repentance and reform; and, as such, this ground for forgiveness is surely compatible with one's own self-respect. Less clear, however, is the degree to which it is compatible with respect for the wrongdoer. Suppose you had wronged someone. How would you like it if that person assumed that you could not come to repentance on your own but required the aid of his ministry of forgiveness? Might you not feel patronized—condescended to? Forgiveness can be an act of weakness, but it can also be an act of arrogance. Seeing it this way, the wrongdoer might well resent the forgiveness. "Who do you think you

---

[15]For a discussion of Feuerbach and others on this matter, see Chapter 6 of Allen Wood's *Kant's Moral Religion* (Ithaca, N.Y.: Cornell University Press, 1970).

are to forgive me?" he might respond to such well-meaning meddling.

But what about point 2—the need we all have for being forgiven? Recall the parable of the unforgiving servant: A lord had decided to punish and generally ruin his servant's life because that servant had not paid a debt that he owed to the lord. The servant prostrated himself and begged piteously, however, and the lord was moved by compassion and forgave him his debt. Shortly after this, that very servant called in a debt owed to him by one of his underlings. He was unmoved by the pleas of his debtor, however. He refused to forgive the debt and consigned his debtor to prison. The lord, learning of this, called the servant in. Telling the servant that he should have showed compassion comparable to the compassion he received, the lord withdrew his forgiveness of the servant and "delivered him to the tormentors." Jesus concludes the parable by saying: "So likewise shall my heavenly Father do also unto you, if ye from your hearts forgive not every one his brother their trespasses."

What exactly is the argument in favor of forgiveness that is being given here? On one interpretation, the whole appeal looks pretty dreadful—of the kind that Nietzsche liked to note when arguing that Christianity is simply sublimated *ressentiment*. For on the surface the parable looks like nothing but an appeal to our baser instincts of *fear*: If you do not forgive others, then God will not forgive you and then you are in for it. One might reject this appeal either because one does not believe in God or because one will try to resist, on grounds of moral integrity, being bullied by appeals to one's lesser nature. How, in short, can an act of forgiveness exemplify a moral virtue if it is motivated simply by a fear of what some supernatural sorehead will do if one fails to forgive?[16]

But such a rejection would, I think, be too quick. As is often the case with religious parables, there is deep moral insight waiting to be discovered if one will simply explore them with

some patience. And the insight in the present parable (which can surely be granted by the most secular or even atheistic reader) is to be seen in its character as a parable on *moral humility*. Each of us, if honest, will admit two things about ourselves: (1) We will within the course of our lives wrong others—even others about whom we care deeply; and (2) because we care so deeply about these others and our relationships with them, we will want to be forgiven by them for our wrongdoings. In this sense we do all need and desire forgiveness and would not want to live in a world where the disposition to forgive was not present and regarded as a healing and restoring virtue. Given that this is the sort of world we all need and want, is it not then incumbent upon each of us to cultivate the disposition to forgive—not the flabby sentimentality of forgiving every wrong, no matter how deep or unrepented, but at least the willingness to be open to the possibility of forgiveness with hope and some trust? Only a person so arrogant as to believe that he will never wrong others or need to be forgiven by them could (in Kantian language) consistently will membership in a world without forgiveness. To see that none of us is such a person is a lesson in moral humility and is, at least in part, the message of the parable.

Suppose one accepts all of this. To what degree can the virtue of forgiveness, so conceived, be relevant to the law? It surely has at least this relevance: To the degree that Stephen is correct in his view that the law institutionalizes resentment, then to that same degree the law has a reason to go easy on those persons who have been forgiven or for whom forgiveness is appropriate. To the degree that the law does more than institutionalize resentment, however, forgiveness is without relevance to legal response. And surely the law does more—considerably more—than merely institutionalize resentment. As Hobbes taught us, for example, law functions to maintain obedience to rules without which civilized life would be impossible; and if one believed that the punishment of an individual was required to maintain these rules, one could consistently advocate such punishment even if one had forgiven the individual to be punished. To forgive a wrongdoer involves a change of heart toward that

[16]For an argument that this characterization of the response to divine commands may be superficial, see my "Kantian Autonomy and Divine Commands," *Faith and Philosophy*, 4 (July 1987), pp. 276–81. See also Peter Geach's "The Moral Law and the Law of God" in his collection of essays *God and the Soul* (London: Routledge & Kegan Paul, 1969).

person (the overcoming of resentment toward him), but this is not necessarily a change in one's view on how that wrongdoer is to be treated. Because I have ceased to hate the person who has wronged me it does not follow that I act inconsistently if I still advocate his being forced to pay compensation for the harm he has done or his being forced to undergo punishment for his wrongdoing—that he, in short, get his just deserts.[17]

[17]Why, then, should the beneficiary of forgiveness care that he is forgiven if he must still face harsh consequences? Surely he will care for the same reason that the victim of his original injustice cared about the intangible harm he received. Normal human beings, in normal human relations, simply care deeply about the attitudes that (some) other people have toward them—about the messages of respect or lack of respect that are conveyed. Thus most of us can easily imagine a case where, although repentant, we are justly punished yet forgiven (even loved) and another case where we are justly punished and not forgiven (even hated). The punishment will hurt the same in both cases, and yet who would not prefer the former to the latter? Recall Melville's *Billy Budd* and how deeply both Billy and Captain Vere cared—independently of the legal consequences that each knew were inevitable—about how each *felt* about the other. Is there anything at all puzzling about this?

The arena of resentment and forgiveness is individual and personal in a way that legal guilt and responsibility are not. I have the proper standing to forgive injuries done to me, but I do not have the proper standing to let people off the hook for all of their legal accountability. To do the latter is to show *mercy* and is necessarily to *act* (and not just to feel) in a certain way. Forgiveness and mercy are often confused, but they should not be. (Some of Butler's remarks about the social and legal dimensions of forgiveness, for example, might more clearly apply to the topic of mercy.) There is a sense, however, in which mercy may be the legal analogue of forgiveness with this difference: Forgiveness involves the *overcoming* of certain passions (resentment, hatred) when they are inappropriate, whereas mercy involves acting in a certain way *because* of certain passions (love, compassion). Both may be virtues, but they are different virtues and operate in different sorts of context—a topic to be explored in more detail in Chapter 5.

Discussion Questions

1. Do you agree with Murphy that sometimes forgiveness is not compatible with self-respect?
2. Must the wrongdoer repent in order for the victim to forgive?
3. Can a person do something unforgivable?

Norvin Richards, "Forgiveness"

Norvin Richards is a professor of philosophy at the University of Alabama. He works in ethics and legal philosophy. His article "Forgiveness," reprinted here, is an influential and especially clear discussion of forgiveness. Richards argues, among other things, that the traditional definition of forgiveness focuses too narrowly on resentment as the proper attitude to try to overcome.

Critical Reading Questions

1. What objections to the traditional definition of forgiveness does Richards raise?
2. According to Richards, what determines whether forgiveness (or failure to forgive) enacts a virtue or a defect of character?
3. How does repentance make forgiveness possible, according to Richards?

FORGIVENESS[*]

Norvin Richards

What is it to forgive someone? What would be a good reason to do so? Could the reason be so good that one would be wrong not to forgive, or is forgiveness a gift one is always free to withhold?

The first section of this paper criticizes the standard definition of forgiveness and offers a replacement. The second sets out an approach to the moral questions. The third considers the place this approach finds for the usual reasons to forgive—repentance, old times' sake, and so on—and for some less usual reasons as well. A final section offers an overview and replies to two objections.

I

In the following passage, Jeffrie Murphy opts for the account of forgiveness favored by most writers on the topic: "I shall . . . argue (following Bishop Butler) that forgiveness is the foreswearing of *resentment*—where resentment is a negative feeling (anger, hatred) directed toward another who has done one moral injury."[1] This

conception ably distinguishes forgiving someone from merely forgetting what he did. And, since it makes forgiving a matter of controlling powerful emotions, it also explains why this can be a lengthy, effortful process, imperfectly successful or entirely beyond one's powers. Even so, I want to argue against it.

Notice, first, that it precludes forgiving anyone you do not first resent. Suppose that someone's especially treacherous behavior made you not resentful but contemptuous of her. Contempt is an abiding attitude, no less than resentment, but quite a different one: contempt is dismissive, in a way anger and hatred are not.[2] Since contempt is not resentment, if forgiving is *foreswearing* resentment it is impossible for you to forgive such a person. Of course, she might entreat you to view her differently, speaking perhaps of how sorry she was to have acted as she did, and her plea might move you. But it could not be forgiveness to which it moved you, according to the definition.

Similarly, it is possible for mistreatment to make one not angry or contemptuous but just very sad, if it is mistreatment at the hands of a loved one. Imagine, for example, that your grown son had badly let you down. This might make you angry, of course, but it might also make you feel deeply disappointed in him, instead. You are hurt that he should act in this way, not angry, not moved to hatred. Accordingly, if you were to abandon these feelings you would not

[*]I am greatly indebted to Scott Hestevold for many helpful discussions of this topic. This work was supported by University of Alabama research grant 1328.

[1]Jeffrie Murphy, "Forgiveness and Resentment," *Midwest Studies in Philosophy,* vol. 7, ed. Peter French, Theodore Uehling, and Howard Wettstein (Minneapolis: University of Minnesota Press, 1982), p. 504. See also R. J. O'Shaughnessy, "Forgiveness," *Philosophy* 42 (1967): 344; H. J. N. Horsbrugh, "Forgiveness," *Canadian Journal of Philosophy* 4 (1974): 271; Aurel Kolnai, "Forgiveness," *Proceedings of the Aristotelian Society* 74 (1973–74): 93 ff. (but see also p. 104, where forgiveness is defined as "re-acceptance"); Elizabeth Beardsley, "Understanding and Forgiveness," in *The Philosophy of Brand Blanshard,* ed. P. A. Schilpp (LaSalle, Ill.: Open Court, 1981), pp. 249–50, 252; Martin P. Golding, "Forgiveness and Regret," *Philosophical Forum* 16 (1984–85): 134.

[2]Certainly Murphy himself would accept the distinction. See, in particular, his agreement with Nietzsche that having contempt for someone is incompatible with resenting him (Murphy, "Forgiveness and Resentment," p. 505).

Ethics 99 (October 1988): 77–97

be forgiving your son, on the definition in question, no matter how natural you and he might find it to say that you were, since you would not be abandoning an attitude of the specified kind. Again, the limitation seems arbitrary. It should also count as forgiveness to abandon negative feelings of these other kinds.

Finally, imagine a woman whose husband frequently belittles her in public. Most recently, he has done this in the company of some new acquaintances whose opinion was especially important to her. The episode has made her furious, and the anger has stayed with her. She seethes at the sight of her husband, entertains thoughts of violent revenge, and so on. However, such feelings and thoughts themselves distress her, for she believes we should always forgive those who wrong us, lest the Lord not forgive us our own misdeeds. So, she does her best to forgive her husband, and she does manage a certain shift in her emotions: she no longer wants to hit the man or to wring his neck. However, she can't seem to get any further than this. Now, the thought of him makes her laugh scornfully—and, sometimes, a little ruefully at herself as well, for putting up with such treatment all these years. "What a contemptible pair!" she says to herself, and resolves to leave the man as a first act of self-respect.

Is this woman *forgiving* her husband? She does qualify under the definition, since she has foresworn hatred and anger, abandoning resentment through an act of will. But I doubt he would think he was being forgiven, as she ridiculed his urgings that things should return to "normal" and went on packing her bags. And I doubt that *she* should consider that she had forgiven him, either. After all, her efforts to do so were founded in the hope that God would later do for her as she did for her husband. Surely she does not hope the Lord will merely move from hating her to holding her in icy contempt? She wants an embrace, not a different kind of rejection.

Evidently, then, abandoning resentment does not constitute forgiving, because a person can stop resenting and still have a hostile attitude of another kind: here, the dismissive one of contempt. The earlier examples suggested that neither must it be resentment that one is

foreswearing: it should also count as forgiveness to abandon contempt for someone or disappointment in him. Taken together, these suggest that to forgive someone for having wronged one is to abandon all negative feelings toward this person, of whatever kind, insofar as such feelings are based on the episode in question.

One might have other reasons to take a dim view of him, of course. To forgive him for having done X is not to forgive him for everything he has done. So, we are not here equating forgiving with "re-accepting," as Kolnai is sometimes inclined to do.[3]

A broader difficulty with seeing forgiveness as reacceptance is that some wrongdoers were not "accepted" to begin with: there is no relationship to reestablish. Consider the stranger whose car drenches you with mud. Having seen this in her mirror, she stops to apologize, insists on paying your cleaning bill, and so on. Surely it is possible to forgive this woman, just as it would be if she were an equally repentant friend. But to call this "reaccepting" her or "reestablishing our relationship" is rather strained: there was no relationship, and there is none after she drives away.

This is not to deny that when, say, a husband wants his wife to forgive him he wants their relationship restored, wants things to be as if he had never misbehaved, and doesn't feel forgiven if they are not. Since there was a warm relationship prior to the misdeed, there will be many reasons for his wife to treat him with affection. If she is cool and distant instead, this will show that she has not forgiven him. For, if there really were no vestiges of the hard feelings founded on his one misstep, her behavior would be more affectionate. This is not because forgiveness is reacceptance, though, but because it amounts to abandoning all hard feelings founded on the incident, and her coolness shows she has not done that.

Thus far, we have widened the range of negative attitudes one can banish in an act of forgiveness but have put no restrictions on one's reasons for changing one's attitude. Regardless of why I change my attitude toward you, it will count as forgiving you. This is not quite right. Suppose that I do so as an act of mental

[3]Kolnai, p. 104.

hygiene. I am sick and tired of being so angry that my sleep is restless and my stomach upset. I resolve not to endure another day of it, and I manage, with professional help, to end this disruptive state of mind. Am I extending forgiveness to you in this instance?

It seems not, precisely because the process is so entirely self-absorbed. When we forgive we are concerned with other people, or with a more appropriate response to what they did. So we forgive them because they are genuinely sorry, or because we realize they were not malicious but only careless, or for the sake of the children, and so on. To change one's attitude entirely out of self-interest might be (sensibly) to forget what someone did, but it is not to forgive him for having done it.[4]

II

What about the moral questions concerning this banishing of hard feelings? When should one do this? When should one not? And, how strong are these "shoulds"?

My answers turn on viewing acts of forgiveness and refusals to forgive as displays of character. I follow the lead of ordinary practice here, as when we think a person hard for refusing to forgive a particular supplicant, or weak for continuing to forgive someone who continues quite relentlessly to mistreat him. My idea is to take this apparently natural approach much further.

It will turn out that some acts of forgiveness (and, some failures to forgive) do enact flaws of character, just as we think. That is important, since it is always at least prima facie wrong to enact a flaw of character, whether the flaw is cowardice, or arrogance, or something with no simple name. This is not the only thing that can be wrong with an action, of course, nor is it always the worst thing.[5] Still, that behavior is, for instance, *arrogant* is a serious mark against it, and in lieu of unusual circumstances

it is simply wrong to act arrogantly. In the same way, it is wrong to refuse to forgive when that enacts arrogance or some other flaw of character. And it is wrong to extend forgiveness when *that* does so.

On other occasions forgiving someone expresses a highly admirable trait of character, not a defect. Obviously, forgiving is not then wrong in the way described. But, neither would it be wrong *not* to forgive on such an occasion, just as it would not be wrong to fail to perform a rescue which demanded a true hero, for example. There are good reasons to do such deeds, and a person of a certain disposition will find them compelling, but no one is obliged to do them, no one acts wrongly in failing to do them. In the same way as the heroism is beyond duty, when forgiving requires a positive virtue it is admirable to do but not wrong to omit.

What determines whether forgiving (or failing to forgive) would enact a virtue or a defect of character? As we have seen, to forgive someone for something is to abandon all the hard feelings one bases on this particular episode. Were this positive effort not made, the feelings would continue. Their presence, and their precise tendency to continue, is itself an expression of one's character. It is because of the sort of person you are that you are *this* angry with me for having done *that* to you.

Now, to forgive is to overrule this part of your character. The overruling expresses a different part of one's character: you are not only a person who will be this angry with me for having done that, you are also a person who will abandon such feelings in light of certain considerations (or, a person who will not). This second-level, self-regulatory part of one's character is what is in play in acts of forgiveness and refusals to forgive. When forgiving enacts a (self-regulatory) flaw of character, it is wrong to forgive; when it does not, it is not wrong to forgive. Similarly, a refusal to forgive is wrong if it enacts a flaw at this second, self-regulatory level, *not* wrong if it enacts a virtue or a neutral trait.

These matters will turn on what sort of character one would be overruling (or failing to overrule). There appear to be three possibilities.

1. It might be that in forgiving, you would overrule a flaw in your character. For example,

---

[4]This may be Jeffrie Murphy's point in following a similar example with this stipulation: "Forgiveness is not the overcoming of resentment *simpliciter*; it is rather this: to foreswear resentment on moral grounds" ("Forgiveness and Resentment," p. 506). I am grateful to Gary Watson for convincing me of the need for some such restriction.

[5]A model for combining an action's several moral credentials is offered in Norvin Richards, "Moral Symptoms," *Mind* 89 (1980): 49–66.

perhaps your still hating me for the careless remark I made years ago expresses an intolerance for weakness in others, or a deep suspicion that people secretly dislike you, or some other trait without which your life would be a far happier one. The countertendency to overrule that unfortunate trait would at least diminish its impact, if not lead to your eventual reform. Thus the countertendency, expressed in forgiving, is itself a good trait. So, it would not be wrong to forgive on such an occasion—that is, to forgive would not enact a flaw of character.

What about refusing to forgive in such a case? This would amount to a disinclination to check what is (by hypothesis) a flaw in your character, either failing to see it as a flaw or being quite content to remain flawed in this particular way. That is itself a defect of character at a second level, it seems to me, at least where the first-level flaw is a relatively serious one. For one thing, it perpetuates the first-level flaw, increasing thereby its negative contributions to one's life. For another, to be blind to your serious flaws (or, content with them) adds an extra offensiveness of its own: an arrogance, a self-centeredness which is hard to swallow. In short, to refuse to overrule a (relatively serious) flaw is to enact a second flaw. That makes the refusal wrong: it is wrong not to forgive, when forgiving would abandon feelings which themselves express a (relatively serious) defect of character.

2. Alternatively, forgiving could overrule not a defect in one's character but something perfectly in order. Perhaps, for example, there is nothing at all wrong with taking remarks of the kind I once made as seriously as you do: we are not dealing with intolerance or paranoia on your part, but with a perfectly acceptable level of self-respect. If you were to have no tendency to overrule such feelings, that would hardly be a flaw in your character. It would serve to perpetuate, not a defect, but something perfectly acceptable. In short, to refuse to forgive would not be wrong in a case of this kind.

On the other hand, although it is not a flaw to be content with an acceptable feature of one's character, neither must it be a flaw to be dissatisfied with such a feature. Perhaps you aspire to be more than merely acceptably kind, or more generous than a person need be to rise above the miserly. Such aspirations need not collapse

into narcissism or involve ignoring traits in a greater need of attention. Thus, the inclination to overrule an acceptable feature of character need not be a flaw. It needn't be wrong to forgive, then, when this overrules feelings is perfectly acceptable to have. Nor, as noted earlier, is it wrong to decline to forgive, under those circumstances.

3. Finally, suppose that forgiveness would overrule a trait which is not merely acceptable but is essential to decent character: something it would be a defect to be without. Perhaps, for example, to feel no anger toward someone who had just swindled your aged mother out of her life's savings is like this. It is not merely "perfectly acceptable" to be angry at the swindler, that is: there is something wrong with you if you are not.

The inclination to banish feelings without which one would not be a decent human being can hardly be a virtue. It fosters bad character, no less than being satisfied with bad traits one already has. Enacting such an inclination is enacting a flaw in one's character. In short, it is wrong to forgive, when doing so overrules a trait which it would be bad character to lack.

I believe that each of these categories has instances, and thus that it is sometimes wrong to forgive, sometimes wrong not to forgive, and sometimes admirable to forgive but acceptable not to do so. There is a powerful tradition which denies this, however, teaching that one is never wrong to forgive, and, indeed, always wrong not to do so. I will close this section by explaining why I do not find that view compelling.

The point in dispute is not whether people of good character should be repelled by immoral behavior: both sides will agree that they should. Moral wrongs themselves are rather evanescent, however; they cease to exist once they are done. Hard feelings toward the wrongdoer serve to express one's feelings about the (now completed) wrong. In my view, there is nothing inappropriate about this. On the opposing view, there is: one should always hate the sin, but never the sinner.

Why not? Well, such feelings do have costs. They can be distressing, they can preclude certain close relationships, and they can dominate a person's life. However, it would be a mistake to conclude that they *must* be costly on balance.

For one thing, there simply are people against whom it is better to be on one's guard, and there are pairs of people who seem to bring out the worst in each other if they attempt a close relationship. For another, it is a considerable exaggeration to think that unless we forgive we must burn with resentment, our lives consumed by bitter feelings and angry schemes. Resentment is a disposition which varies considerably in its intensity and in the length of its natural tenure. And, as Bishop Butler pointed out, some levels of resentment are perfectly compatible with a general good will toward the wrongdoer.[6] (Think here of the parent who is angry at a child for disobeying, but is certainly not transformed into a spiteful, single-minded avenger unless moved to forgiveness.)

Notice too that when we do hate the sinner, as well as the sin, we are not indulging some isolated quirk but are implementing a broad feature of human psychology. If you had been assaulted, you would feel differently not only about the person who assaulted you but also about the place in which the assault occurred and, perhaps, about a particular instrument your assailant used. The park where you loved to ramble would become a place you dreaded. Similarly, suppose you had been attacked in your own home, with your own kitchen knife. You would scarcely return it to the drawer with the others as just the thing for carving this year's turkey. Instead, the very sight of it would distress you, and the idea of using it would be repugnant. Are we only wrong to change our feelings toward wrongdoers, on the view that we must always forgive, or are we also wrong to feel differently about places and instruments? Neither answer seems particularly attractive.

Instead, how strongly you are repelled by the places, instruments, and agents of a harm is one measure of how bad a thing it was for you. How long such feelings last is another. There is a basis here for speaking of such feelings as in keeping with what happened, or as out of proportion to it. That would provide a way of speaking about

your character, of judging that you take deeds of the kind in question as a person of good character would, or, that you do not. Such judgments make important points about us, it seems to me: points that are lost in thinking that good character simply requires immediate forgiveness on every occasion.

III

What place have the various standard reasons for forgiving, if we take the approach I have suggested? The pleas commonly offered are strikingly different. Some invoke special features of the misbehavior: it wasn't meant to turn out as it did; or, the wrongdoer had no idea it would mean so much to you; or, it was intentional but really only a rather minor misdeed; and so on. Other reasons ask that the deed be taken in a certain context: it was bad behavior, but she's your oldest friend; or, you've treated her this way yourself, quite often; and so on. Still others emphasize new developments: the wrongdoer is now very distressed over the way she acted, despises herself for it, and hopes you'll forgive her.

Often, the person seeking forgiveness is able to offer several of these reasons at once. Certain of them go together in a way, strengthening each other: *since* she's an old friend she probably is *genuinely* sorry for what she's done . . . But the more basic question is why each is itself a reason to forgive. So, it will be better to consider each in turn, as if it were the only consideration put forward.

A. Excuses and Good Intentions

In his sermon, "Upon Forgiveness of Injuries," Bishop Butler maintains that we very seldom injure each other out of malice. Nearly, always, says he, the harm is not done purposely but through ignorance or inadvertence.[7] Perhaps he is right about this. What is of current interest, though, is that he regards these excuses as reasons to forgive: he thinks the fact that you were wronged inadvertently or through a misunderstanding ought to change your feelings about the wrongdoer.

It might be replied that although such discoveries could call for a change in one's feelings,

---

[6]Joseph Butler, "Upon Forgiveness of Injuries," in *The Works of the Right Reverend Father in God, Joseph Butler, D.C.L., Late Bishop of Durham*, ed. Samuel Halifax (New York: Carter, 1846), pp. 106–7. See also William R. Neblett, "Forgiveness and Ideals," *Mind* 73 (1974): 270.

[7]Butler, p. 111.

they could not call for forgiveness. The argument would run as follows. Excuses fall into two categories. Some are so good as to mean the 'wrongdoer' was not at all responsible for what befell the victim. In that case, there is nothing for the 'victim' to forgive this particular person. Such excuses are not reasons to forgive, exactly, but reasons to stop acting as if one had been wronged.

Jeffrie Murphy writes as if all excuses were of this kind: "To excuse is to say this: What was done was morally wrong; but, because of certain factors about the agent (e.g., insanity), it would be unfair to hold the wrongdoer responsible or blame him for the wrong action . . . we may forgive only that which it is initially proper to resent; and, if a person . . . was not responsible for what he did, there is *nothing to resent* (though perhaps much to be sad about)."[8] But, although the insanity excuse perhaps does erase all responsibility, not every excuse is so powerful. Commonly, excuses do not exonerate but only mitigate by showing that one acted less badly than it appears. Since they do leave one having acted somewhat badly, could they perhaps be the reasons to forgive which Butler thought they were?

Again, it might be argued that they could not. To forgive someone for having wronged one is not merely to reduce the intensity of one's hard feelings but to abandon such feelings altogether (insofar as they are based on the incident in question). As we just noted, the excuse leaves it the case that the agent did wrong the person. But if so, the argument continues, hard feelings of *some* intensity are called for: to abandon them would be both a poor defense against repetitions and a display of inadequate aversion to what was done. In short, only someone of bad character fails to resent a wrongdoer, and a wrongdoer with the common sort of excuse is still a wrongdoer. So, the argument concludes, the common sort of excuse cannot be a reason to forgive, any more than the exonerating excuse could be.

The flaw in this argument, I believe, is the premise that only someone of bad character fails to resent a wrongdoer. That is certainly a contention Murphy would advance, and it

seems to appeal to R. S. Downie as well.[9] However, although perhaps it is tautological that one should be averse to any wrong, no matter how minor, it does not follow that this aversion should always find expression in sustained hard feelings toward the source of the wrong. Compare here the man who dislikes the beach because that is where he dropped his ice cream cone in the sand. There is certainly nothing wrong with his regretting having lost his cone, but these feelings about the beach could show that he takes its loss too seriously. Certainly, there is no appeal whatever in the idea that unless he continues to hate the beach, he does not take the loss of the cone as seriously as he should.

Similarly, suppose our man dropped his cone not because a bully viciously twisted his arm but because he was jostled by a careless teenager. The jostling is mistreatment, and one should be averse to being mistreated. But it does not follow that our man will exhibit bad character unless he continues to harbor bad feelings toward the teenager—unless he refuses to forgive him, that is.

The idea is that even if, as Murphy and Downie would urge, good character does require being averse to all forms of mistreatment, it might not require sustained hard feelings toward the sources of the minor kinds. Conceivably, an excuse could show that a misdeed was a very minor one. It would thereby provide a reason to abandon those unwarranted hard feelings without contradicting the intuition that one should always be averse to mistreatment.

We can add to this Bishop Butler's own ideas concerning why excuses are reasons to forgive. Mistake, inadvertence, and so forth "we ought all to be disposed to excuse in others, *from experiencing so much of them in ourselves.*"[10] Tu quoque: but, why should this be a reason to forgive when the deed is done to me? Well, either I am also hard on myself for this same behavior, or I am not. To be hard on myself (as well as on others) over even minor mistakes and inadvertencies amounts to a broad intolerance of human

[8]Murphy, "Forgiveness and Resentment," p. 506.

[9]Ibid., p. 505; R. S. Downie, "Forgiveness," *Philosophical Quarterly*, vol. 15 (1965).

[10]Butler, p. 111 (emphasis added).

limitations. No one can meet my expectations, since I expect perfection, and this must make me a very impatient, frustrated, and generally objectionable fellow.

Alternatively, suppose I am not hard on myself for minor bungles, but only on others. This suggests that I am not actually averse to the wrong as such but to my being wronged (however slightly) myself. Here I am flawed in a different way. I take myself too seriously, and I draw in my own favor a distinction without a relevant difference.

In short, not to forgive minor misbehavior to which one is oneself prone exhibits either a general intolerance of human frailty or an unwarranted exaltation of oneself. It is wrong to enact either trait, for both are flaws of character. Thus, it is wrong not to forgive a person whose excuse makes the misdeed a minor one of a kind to which one is prone oneself.

Let me note that although this argument makes use of Bishop Butler's thinking concerning excuses, it does not reach as sweeping a conclusion as he did. He believed we should always forgive those who had excuses for wronging us (which, in his view, covered virtually everyone who did so). However, not all excuses do reduce the wrong done to a minor misstep of a kind to which one is prone oneself. Some only reduce murder to manslaughter, for example. Unlike Bishop Butler, then, my argument takes only some excuses to be reasons to forgive.

The fact that the wrongdoer had your best interest at heart appears to function in the same way. His good intentions can reduce the behavior to something trivial and familiar, and then they are a reason to forgive. But they can also fail to effect such a reduction, and then they provide no reason to forgive. Murphy, in contrast, sharply distinguishes excuses (which he believes cannot be reasons to forgive) from paternalistic motives (which he believes can be). His discussion of paternalistic motives, however, supports the idea that they are reasons to forgive only insofar as they effect the reduction I have described:

A person who interferes with my liberty for what he thinks is my own good is, in my judgment, acting wrongly. . . . His grounds for interfering, however, are well-meaning (i.e., he seeks to do me good) even if his actions are misguided and morally insensitive. . . . It is hard to view the friend who locks up my liquor cabinet because he knows I drink too much as on the same moral level as the person who embezzles my funds for his own benefit; and thus the case for forgiving the former may have some merit.[11]

Again, just as not all excuses make misbehavior sufficiently minor that it ought to be forgiven, neither do all realizations that the behavior was only "misguided and morally insensitive" paternalism. Some acts of paternalism remain sufficiently serious mistreatments that it is certainly not bad character to take them sufficiently seriously to hold them against their perpetrators. So, it will not always be wrong not to be moved to forgiveness by the news that a certain person meant to be acting in your own best interest.

On the other hand, neither must it be bad character to accept another's effort to look after one. A fierce independence is hardly the only alternative to spinelessness. So, it can also reflect perfectly acceptable character to forgive someone who (after all) only meant to help.

B. Repentance

So far, we have been focusing on pleas that one's behavior was not really bad enough to merit the victim's attitude. It is a different move altogether to agree that the behavior was very bad and ask to be forgiven because one now *repents*. Repentance is perhaps the most familiar of the grounds for forgiveness. The question is, why should it work? What is it about the wrongdoer's repenting that justifies (or even mandates) forgiving him?

Actually, I think, repentance can present appeals of two distinct kinds. At least some forms of repentance involve a change in the wrongdoer from someone who saw nothing wrong with mistreating you in a certain way to someone who joins you in condemning that behavior. This alone might seem to make hard feelings against him rather pointless and forgiveness the only reasonable course.

Murphy and Kolnai both testify to the attractiveness of this line of thinking, though neither accepts it in the end.[12] There are two good

[11]Murphy, "Forgiveness and Resentment," p. 509.

[12]Ibid., p. 511; Kolnai, pp. 101–2.

reasons not to. First, repentance does not guarantee that there will be no future misbehavior. It is always possible that the wrongdoer will revert to his earlier views, or be vulnerable to temptations to violate his new ones. There might also be forms of behavior which his new view does not condemn but against which a general vigilance would provide a defense. (Think here of someone who now agrees that it was wrong to lie to you as he did but still has nothing against a very broad range of deceptive practices.) Since repentance thus does not obviate the need for defensive postures, it does not mandate forgiveness.

Second, the question whether to forgive does not turn entirely on whether defenses against repetition are needed. If it did, one would always be wrong not to forgive a villain who had passed out of one's life: the rapist who was killed while escaping, for example, or the embezzler using your funds to dwell happily in Brazil. Such people are no future threat to you. But, the fact remains that they have done you wrong, and that issues its own call for hard feelings against them.

Wouldn't the same be true of the wrongdoer who was very much at hand, but now repentant? Just like the rapist and the embezzler, even if such a person poses no future threat, he remains someone who did you wrong. That is a second reason to resent him, which is not erased by his repentance. Thus the change undergone in repenting does not render hard feelings pointless after all and does not mandate forgiveness.

It does accomplish something less dramatic, however. It provides a reason to forgive repenters who have changed in the way described. It makes forgiving them an option appealing to persons with one sort of good character: it makes forgiveness morally permissible. How it does this requires a bit of explanation.

First, to repent in the way I have been discussing it is not merely to have newly negative feelings about what one has done, but to have these feelings as part of a change in one's moral views. To know all along that one is misbehaving and only have misgivings about it the next day does not qualify. Rather, we are speaking here of the person who has "seen the light," who has come to disapprove of a kind of behavior which she had thought of as perfectly permissible. A new moral principle is acquired, or there is a new realization that her old principles are inconsistent and that her behavior violated the more important of them.

Now, in such a case, the wrongdoer's permissive former principles are one reason why she acted as she did: she did it, in part, because she did not think it wrong to do. So, a change in her views would be a change in something which was partly responsible for the wrong. Her repentance is thus like repairing that part of a house which contributed to an accident. The child took a nasty fall right here, in part because the steps were uneven, but now I have fixed them; I shouted at the secretary in part because I did not think there was anything wrong with shouting at secretaries, but now I realize that there is.

Despite the change, this is still the house where the child fell and I am still the person who shouted at the secretary. So, there is still a question whether the victims ought not to have hard feelings in both cases. However, there has been a change in them qua source of suffering; there has been a replacement of (part of) what was responsible for the suffering with something which promises to be harmless. Accordingly, there would be nothing amiss in the association being broken—in the child feeling good about the house again, or in the secretary dropping her resentment of me now that I am (clearly) more respectful of her. Forgiveness has become a permissible option with appeal to persons of perfectly good character, rather than something which shows a failure to take the episode as seriously as one should, because the wrongdoer has changed something about himself which contributed to the wrong.

On the other hand, neither would there be anything amiss in the hard feelings continuing, despite the repairs to the stairs and to the wrongdoer's moral views. For one thing, it might not be so clear that the flaw has been repaired, particularly where this consists in reforming one's moral views. (Hence the significance of the allegedly repentant person's apologies, efforts to "make up for it," to be on especially good behavior, and so on.) For another, it might be that the harm was too serious for the change to relieve one's other associations between this person (that face, those hands, that smirk) and what she did to you, despite those features having not even partly caused the harm. So, there needn't be a flaw of character in being unmoved by the change in the repentant person, any more than there must be one in being so moved. On the view I am offering, it is permissible either to forgive or not to do so.

That brings us to the second way in which someone's repentance might provide a good reason to extend forgiveness: a way which applies not only to those who have undergone moral reformation but also to those who knew all along they were misbehaving, and whose repentance consists in their later feeling very sorry. Part of both scenes is emotional: remorse over what was done before the change occurred. In the classic description the repentant wrongdoer is contrite, or "bruised in the heart."

Exactly why the victim's forgiveness should relieve the pain of remorse is somewhat curious, especially if one takes the view that wrongdoing is an offense not just against its most obvious victim but against an abstract moral order and/or against all who refrain from the misbehavior.[13] Perhaps what bothers us about having done wrong is not the abstract fact that we have done it, but the fact that a particular person has suffered a wrong at our hands.

At any rate, the fact is that repentant wrongdoers are pained by their victims' hard feelings toward them. They are unhappy, sometimes deeply so, in a way which the victim could relieve by extending forgiveness. That is a reason to grant the forgiveness: an appeal to the victim's compassion for someone he can rescue from unhappiness. Of course, sometimes the rescue is enormously difficult, because the offense was deeply aversive to the victim and occurred quite recently. Moreover, sometimes the forgiveness seems unlikely to do the wrongdoer all that much good. Perhaps his unhappiness over the

misdeed is genuine but not terribly deep, and seems likely to pass of its own accord before too long; and, perhaps it would do him good to suffer over this a bit longer. So there are surely times when there would be nothing wrong with being unmoved by the appeal the repentant person makes to one's compassion.

By the same token, however, generally speaking there are also times when there *is* something wrong with being unmoved by an appeal to one's compassion. Imagine that it would be quite easy to relieve considerable suffering, as when a single word from you would save the postman from a vicious dog. Wouldn't you be very wrong not to say the word? Shall we say that you would also be wrong not to forgive whenever a single word from you would rescue the wrongdoer from agonies of remorse?

I think not. The postman is simply an object of compassion. The wrongdoer is something more: a wrongdoer. The postman's troubles befell him through no fault of his. The wrongdoer is suffering because he did you wrong. You have thereby a reason not to be compassionate toward him, which you do not have regarding the poor postman.

That is enough, I think, to justify rejecting the idea that it is simply heartless to withhold forgiveness from anyone who is genuinely repentant. The reply is that it is not heartless to resist their appeal to one's compassion because they are not simply objects of compassion. However, it is worth considering more closely why their past behavior does make them so different and why compassion should not simply overrule this further consideration.

There is one (ultimately mistaken) account of this with considerable initial appeal. According to it, the key difference between the postman and the wrongdoer is that the latter deserves his current unhappiness. To leave him to stew in his own juice will not be simply uncompassionate but will be an exercise of your sense of justice. As Butler urged, it is absolutely vital that we have a firm sense of justice to supplement our tender feelings of compassion.[14]

However, there is a certain awkwardness in thinking of hard feelings as penalties one

[13]See, e.g., J. Finnis, "The Restoration of Retribution," *Analysis* 32 (1972): 131–35 (Finnis attributes the view to Thomas Aquinas, as well as advancing it himself); Herbert Morris, "Persons and Punishment," reprinted in *Punishment and Rehabilitation*, ed. Jeffrie Murphy (Belmont, Calif.: Wadsworth, 1973), esp. pp. 43 ff.; Herbert Morris, *Guilt and Innocence* (Berkeley: University of California Press, 1976), esp. pp. 33–34; M. P. Golding, *Philosophy of Law* (Englewood Cliffs, N.J.: Prentice-Hall, 1975), p. 92; Jeffrie Murphy, "Three Mistakes about Retributivism," reprinted in his *Retribution, Justice, and Therapy* (Dordrecht: Reidel, 1979).

[14]Butler, "Upon Resentment," in *The Works of the Right Reverend Father in God*, pp. 99–100.

imposes in the interests of justice, on the same order as fines and imprisonments. They seem instead to be natural consequences of the misbehavior. The victim's resentment is rather like the sore muscles and occasional scratches which a mugger might find to be occupational hazards. Certainly we feel no sympathy for the thug who gets sore or scratched in the process of mugging, and we might express that by saying he "had it coming," or that it was "no worse than he deserved," just as we say such things about the victim's hating him. There's even something satisfying about his having come by these aches and pains in the process of his wrongdoing. But, this is not to say such things are part of what a person deserves for mugging. We are not in the least inclined to have scratches and soreness imposed on muggers who do not suffer these in plying their trade, or to reduce the sentences of other muggers on the ground that (after all) they are scratched and sore. Rather, we treat these as extra misfortunes which we are not sorry the mugger suffers. It is just so, I am suggesting, with any regrets he suffers over his victim's hard feelings for him.

If we do stop thinking of the hard feelings as deserved penalties, however, how will we explain why the wrongdoer's having wronged us matters? How will we explain, that is, why his misbehavior distinguishes him from the simple object of compassion, such as the mailman whom it would be wrong not to save from the vicious dog?

The explanation I want to develop begins from the premise that we are right to be averse to what happens to us when we are wronged and, when the wrong is not trivial, to express this aversion in hard feelings toward its source. The fact is that there is a degree of incompatibility between having hard feelings toward someone and being moved by that person's suffering to go to his or her aid. If I hate a certain man, the news that he is having some minor misfortune does not make me unhappy and might even provide a certain satisfaction. I need not be proud of this—I might wish to be kinder or more generous. Still, part of hating him is wanting him not to flourish, just as part of liking someone is wanting that person to fare well. One measure of the strength of my hatred is the point at which I begin to sympathize instead. Another

is the point at which my sympathies are sufficiently strong that I will exert myself to relieve this person's plight, despite disliking him.

Now, suppose that my hard feelings are not merely present, but are called for by his having wronged me, and that my imperviousness to his plight expresses those hard feelings. Then, that imperviousness is also not just present, but called for. His having wronged me is a reason not to go to his aid—it makes him not simply an object of compassion, like the postman under attack from the dog.

Of course, this does not collapse into saying that his having wronged me means I should never be moved by his troubles, no matter how grave they are or what form his mistreatment of me took. The claim is only that to be victimized by someone creates a perfectly proper obstacle to compassion toward that person. How substantial an obstacle it *should* create would largely depend on how grave the mistreatment was. (I think it would also depend, to some extent, on how recently the wrong was committed: at least some feelings should lessen in intensity as time passes.) How substantial an obstacle it *would* create would depend instead on how aversive the event was for the victim, which is quite another thing. It is obviously possible to take something more seriously than one should, and thus to be impervious to suffering that should move one.

I have argued that even though a repentant wrongdoer does make an appeal to compassion, it is not necessarily a flaw of character to be unmoved to forgiveness, even if it would be easy for you to forgive and a great relief to him. Depending on how badly he acted and how recently, it might be a flaw of character if you *were* moved. Thus, there are times when it would be wrong to forgive such people, but this is not because even repentant wrongdoers deserve to suffer one's wrath. It is because even repentant wrongdoers are wrongdoers, hard feelings are called for toward wrongdoers as sources of wrong, and hard feelings are incompatible with a certain degree of compassion.

Although it is thus sometimes wrong to respond sympathetically to the repentant wrongdoer, by the same reasoning it is also sometimes wrong not to. Suppose the wrong was done long ago and was not extremely serious, and it is quite plain by now that the wrongdoer has undergone a change of character and that your forgiveness would be a considerable relief to him. As Murphy urges, it is possible to take too lightly oneself and the wrong done to one; but, it seems to me, it must also be possible to take these too seriously. I have just sketched what would be involved in doing so.

Between these extremes lies the broad range of cases in which the wrong was neither dreadful nor trivial and happened neither a few minutes nor a few years ago, and over which the (apparently) repentant wrongdoer is remorseful but not devastated. Within this range it is neither wrong to forgive nor wrong not to do so. As Kolnai so nicely puts it, here forgiveness is "a venture of trust"—a venture not always equal in its risks.

C. Old Times' Sake

I will forgive the person who has willfully wronged me because . . . of old time's sake (e.g., "He has been a good and loyal friend to me in the past").[15]

Old Time's Sake. As with repentance we have here a clear case of divorce of act from agent. When you are repentant, I forgive you for what you *now are*. When I forgive you for old time's sake, I forgive you for what you *once were*. Much of our forgiveness of old friends and parents, for example, is of this sort.[16]

Although Murphy says here that we can properly forgive people for old times' sake, for what they once were to us, he does virtually nothing to explain why. Why should your having "been a good and loyal friend to me in the past" be a reason to forgive you for wronging me, rather than something which deepens the hurt? Does it matter whether you had been my friend at least until this episode, or are only someone to whom I was once close, long ago? What, if anything, is it about past or present friendly relationships that provides a reason to forgive?

Suppose we begin with the current friend. Such a person is entitled to have her actions interpreted with a certain generosity, it seems to me. It isn't only that one should not be positively suspicious of one's friends, expecting the worst of

them. More than that, they should have the benefit of the doubt. Even when it does appear they have mistreated you, your inclination should be to disbelieve the appearances. To regard someone as a friend is to trust that this person wishes you well and thus would not have acted as it seems. To be incapable of such trust, of regarding people as friends, is a serious failing.

In my view, this means it is sometimes morally wrong not to disbelieve the evidence that a certain person has mistreated you. That is not a point about forgiving friends, however, but one about assuming that there is nothing to forgive. Your friend is entitled to the assumption that she has not wronged you—but that differs from her being entitled to your forgiveness when, in fact, you know that she has wronged you.

Perhaps we can bring the two together in the following fashion. Part of someone's being your friend is her wishing you well. Part of that is being especially averse to doing you ill. If such a person has wronged you, it is safe to assume there must have been some powerful reason for it, or that she did not fully understand what she was doing. And, it is also safe to assume that she is now quite unhappy over what she has done, in a way you could relieve by extending your forgiveness.

In short, her being a friend is a reason to suppose that you have one of the *other* reasons to forgive her. That is not the same as "old times' sake" being a reason in itself, of course. And, it is less compelling for the merely former friend than for the current one. Still, evidently someone's being your friend can be indirectly a reason to extend forgiveness, and that is at least a role for old times to play.

Consider next this stronger argument. Throughout, I have contended that a person ought to be averse not only to wrongs but to the sources of (nontrivial) wrongs. It seems equally plausible to hold that one should have positive feelings toward morally good actions and toward the sources of such actions, at least insofar as the actions are beyond minimally good behavior. Friendships involve many such actions—the doing of favors, small and sometimes large sacrifices of self-interest, and so on. Hence, one ought to have good will toward a friend, by virtue of the events constituting the friendship, just as one ought to have hard feelings toward

[15]Murphy, "Forgiveness and Resentment," p. 508.

[16]Ibid., p. 510.

a villain, as an expression of one's aversion to what the villain has done to one.

Earlier, it was suggested that hard feelings are incompatible with being easily moved to sympathy. By the same token, wouldn't warm feelings be incompatible with being easily moved to hostility? If so, a part of the good will which a past friendly relationship should have engendered would call for not taking offense at a certain range of wrongs. You simply would not be resentful over such matters if your friends meant what they should to you.

On finding that you *were* resentful, your proper course would be to strive to banish such feelings straightaway—to extend forgiveness, that is. Anyone who did not do this would show an inability to appreciate friends for their kindness and affection—an inability which would surely impoverish life in many ways. In other words, it would be bad character not to forgive a friend a certain range of small wrongs, just because he or she was your friend.

This is certainly not an argument that one should forgive a friend everything. The idea is that friendship is incompatible with being easily provoked to hostility, which suggests that the deeper the friendship, the more tolerant one should be. That does not deny that there is behavior so egregious that one's warm feelings should be overcome.

Discussion Questions

1. Is forgiveness a virtue?
2. What is the difference between forgiving for moral reasons and forgiving for purely psychological reasons?
3. Should we try to overcome negative feelings toward those who have wronged us?

CHAPTER 14

Animals

HARD QUESTION: SHOULD WE EAT ANIMALS?

Eating is imbued with moral significance. We distinguish carefully not only between the edible and the inedible—tomatoes are edible, rocks are not—but also between what it is morally acceptable to eat and what is not. We make moral judgments (usually, but not always, negative) regarding the consumption of human flesh, for instance. We can also make moral judgments about eating animals. Animals are edible, but ought we to eat them? Here the moral terrain is much more controversial than it is for eating people. *Vegetarianism,* as a term for someone who abstains from eating animals, has been around only since 1847 when the Vegetarian Society was founded in Great Britain. Prior to that, abstaining from eating animals was known as the "Pythagorean diet" because the ancient Greek philosopher Pythagoras (570?–495? BCE) recommended it to his followers.

Vegetarianism is often associated with fringe elements of society and seems to be popular among young people, artists, and celebrities. Vegetarians are purported to be compassionate and other-worldly, an impression perhaps cultivated by its original association with the enigmatic and reclusive Pythagoreans. However, one of the most cruel and ruthless people in history, Adolf Hitler, was a vegetarian. Famous vegetarians in the history of thought include Thoreau, Benjamin Franklin (for a while, at least), Leonardo da Vinci, Tolstoy, Voltaire, Shelly, Shaw, Plutarch, and possibly Plato. According to Daniel Dombroski, "That the Republic [Plato's ideal state] was to be a vegetarian city is one of the best-kept secrets in the history of philosophy" (*The Philosophy of Vegetarianism,* p. 62).

Contemporary grounds for vegetarianism are primarily health, environmental concerns, and ethics. Increasingly compelling evidence from multiple sources shows that animal flesh is hardly essential for good health and may even be inimical to it, at least in the quantities that Americans tend to consume. Environmental concerns often focus on how staggeringly inefficient it is to raise animals for food. For example, to produce 1 pound of animal protein requires, on average, 7 pounds of vegetable protein. It is astonishing to realize that the bulk of our agricultural effort is spent growing grain that will be fed to livestock; this is food that we could consume directly rather than wasting most of it by converting it into meat. Apparently, we enjoy consuming animal flesh so much that we will tolerate such inefficiencies.

We shall focus on ethical reasons for vegetarianism. Because moral considerations trump other kinds of considerations, if vegetarianism can be given a principled moral basis, then all moral agents must acknowledge it. Unlike reasons of health or efficiency, one cannot simply dismiss ethical considerations in favor of custom or dietary preference. Imagine, by analogy, trying to assess slavery by appealing only to efficiency, environmental impact, or personal preference. The economic advantages of slavery are perversely irrelevant to the morality of slavery. The ethical vegetarian is making a moral claim, one alleged to apply to everyone because moral reasons are binding on all rational deliberators. But is the ethical vegetarian correct?

By virtue of animals' psychological similarity to ourselves, the ethical vegetarian will assert either that animal interests cannot rationally be ignored in our quest for a tasty meal or that animals have rights, among them the right to be treated with respect, which is incompatible with our rearing them for food. Different versions of ethical vegetarianism are thus possible. One might object primarily to the suffering inflicted on animals by modern methods of factory farming, accepting, perhaps, the painless slaughter of free-ranging, "happy" animals as morally inconsequential. Of course, rearing animals in a humane manner would drive up the price of meat significantly, making it more of a luxury than a staple of our diets. Such a position is basically reformist, since it is not opposed to eating animals *per se* but, rather, objects to the current manner of production, one that is insufficiently sensitive to their suffering.

Alternatively, the ethical vegetarian might argue that even if we could reform our practices so that animals raised for food did not suffer, this misses the main point. The core moral issue in rearing animals for food, one might claim, turns on our willingness to view animals in wholly instrumental terms. According to this version of ethical vegetarianism, animals should be seen as intrinsically valuable in the same way people are intrinsically valuable.

If our intrinsic value is in some way a function of our mental capacities, then the ethical vegetarian will insist that animals with those same mental capacities should also have intrinsic value. What exactly those mental capacities are is a matter for debate. Here is a delicate point exploited by the ethical vegetarian: If we narrowly define the key mental attributes by virtue of which we claim intrinsic value for ourselves, such as consciousness or rationality or self-awareness, then various categories of human beings will fail to be intrinsically valuable: infants, the mentally defective, the insane, and the senile, for example. If, on the other hand, we relax our understanding of the core mental capacities requisite for intrinsic value, seeking instead a lowest common denominator in terms of which all human beings have intrinsic value, then some animals will inevitably qualify as well, for they will meet whatever minimal standards of rationality or consciousness or self-awareness we set for ourselves as a basis for our intrinsic value. In short, claims the ethical vegetarian, there does not seem to be a way to discriminate sharply between the moral status of human beings and that of animals. Either some animals share the moral status of human beings or some human beings share the moral status of animals.

ANIMALS AND MORALITY

It is worth contemplating the nature of animals. We can begin by thinking about the (live) animals with which we are most likely to have everyday contact, such as dogs and cats. What are these animals like? We have a shameless propensity to anthropomorphize our pets (that is, to construe them as human); we fill their heads with our own thoughts and concerns, turning them into furry four-legged people. When asked we deny that our pets are really just like us, but our behavior suggests we think otherwise; we continue to treat our pets as something akin to a person. Is this just plain silly on our part or is there something to it?

Think of the range of mental and emotional states you are completely comfortable ascribing to dogs and cats: consciousness, curiosity, happiness, fear, contentment, jealousy, memory, love, intentionality, anxiety, hate, playfulness, generosity, kindness, depression, joy, courage, loyalty, determination, sensitivity, excitement, cunning, and so on. None of this seems particularly remarkable until we remind ourselves that we are talking about nonhuman animals. We are talking about creatures that, in broad respects, are apparently very much like ourselves. The various mental attributes may not be as sophisticated as they are in normal human beings, but that dogs and cats have these traits to one degree or another is beyond doubt. Moreover, you ascribe these emotional and mental states to dogs and cats easily and without the sense of absurdity you would have in trying to talk about a tree or a table that way. It is, we might say, completely "natural" to see dogs and cats and, indeed, a range of other animals as having complex mental and emotional lives that we can comprehend by using the same mental concepts that we apply to ourselves. In *The Descent of Man,* Charles Darwin claims, "There is no fundamental difference between man and the higher mammals."

One needs a very powerful theory to deny what seems so obvious—namely, that animals are conscious and that mental attributions to animals such as dogs and cats (for example) are perfectly sensible. Since we are dealing with creatures that are broadly similar to ourselves, moral questions about how we should deal with animals are inescapable; we cannot admit that another creature is similar to ourselves but deny that its interests ought to figure into our moral deliberations. To do so would violate a fundamental principle of rationality, the idea that we are to treat similar cases similarly.

Do any animal interests merit equal consideration to our own interests when the "treat likes alike" principle is applied? Consider one interest we share with animals: an interest in not suffering. Since (some) animals can feel pain, and thereby suffer, they have an interest in not suffering for the same reason we have an interest in not suffering. Our interest in not suffering is based on the evil of pain. If we focus simply on the pain, we can ask whether human pain, *because* it is human pain, is morally different from, say, dog pain. If we think it is, then we have to explain why species membership in itself is a morally relevant difference. And unless we can show that species membership in itself is a morally significant difference between human pain and dog pain, we will run afoul of the requirement to treat likes alike.

The view that human suffering, simply because it is human suffering, is morally more significant than nonhuman suffering is called **speciesism,** by analogy with other forms of discrimination such as racism and sexism. If there is no good reason to hold human suffering to be morally significant in a way that nonhuman suffering is not, then the preference for human over nonhuman suffering would reflect an irrational bias, for we would not be treating likes alike. But is dog suffering comparable to human suffering? Let us suppose that sticking the dog with the pin hurts it as much as it hurts a person. Might there still be good reasons to prefer causing the dog to experience that pain instead of the person? Certainly. We can consider the impact on the person's life compared to the impact on the dog's life, the dread of anticipation, the humiliation experienced over and above the pain from the pin prick, recurrent memories of that humiliation, and lots of other ways in which the event could ramify throughout the person's life. Because the negative effects of the pain and the total experience arguably would have a greater effect on the person than on the dog, it might be better, all things considered, to inflict the pain on the dog than on the person.

What do we say, however, in a case where the human being and the dog are mentally and emotionally equivalent? Sadly, some human beings with brain damage are able to function only at the cognitive and emotional level of a normal dog. Their condition will never change. Now consider sticking each with the pin. Is there a basis on which to insist that the human suffering is morally more important—that if we have to choose, it is morally better to cause the dog to experience the pain than the human being? We might say that the brain-damaged human being's loved ones will be upset, but we can always revise the example so that there are people who care more about the dog than the human being. Such examples present a significant challenge to the view that human suffering, because it is *human* suffering, is morally more important than animal suffering. Perhaps it seems that this example is completely unrealistic, we would never have to make such a choice. But painful medical experiments are routinely performed on dogs, and we would never even consider using brain-damaged human beings for those same experiments. Is that choice justified?

ANIMAL RIGHTS

The topic of animal rights is as emotion-laden as abortion (see Chapter 11), which makes calm, reasonable philosophical exploration all the more difficult. Talk of rights can get out of hand pretty fast—people are quick to assert or deny rights in heated moral disputes—so we need to be clear about the nature of the rights at issue. Let's begin by noting the difference between legal (or conventional) rights and moral rights. You have all sorts of **legal (or conventional) rights;** these are the rights that the law or some authoritative body recognizes. For example, if you are a student at a university, you have the right to check books out of the library or the right to swim in the pool (provided you meet whatever other conditions are imposed by the university). This is a right that not everyone has; you have it solely by virtue of your association with your university. Your legal rights are similarly contingent on your citizenship in this country. We can go to the county courthouse and inspect the law books to see what legal rights you actually have. But, it is alleged, not all rights rest upon institutions or conventions. Some rights stand apart from convention, legal systems, and institutions. These are **moral rights**—rights that *ought* to be recognized, whether or not they appear in a legal code. Moral rights can be conceived as legitimate claims that are supported by morality independent of the institutions with which you are associated, the legal system, or the conventions of your society. Indeed, your legal and conventional rights are most plausibly seen as resting upon your moral rights; at least that would be the order of explanation. You have a particular legal right *because* of some underlying moral right that we could articulate if the inquiry were pushed far enough.

We are sometimes apt to think of rights as a special sort of "thing" that one either has or does not have. But that is to misconstrue the issue. It is not as though careful inspection of a person will enable us to detect whether he or she really has rights. Rather, attributing rights is a way of conceiving what our moral obligations are toward one another. Rights are not just arbitrarily bestowed, for it makes sense to attribute rights only where there is some interest that the rights serve to protect. You have a right to liberty, for instance, because you have an interest in functioning autonomously, and you have a right to life because you have an interest in living.

Appeal to rights is thus a dimension of our moral discourse; it is yet another way for us to conceive of what we ought or ought not to be doing. Conceiving of our duties in terms of rights does, however, have a logic of its own. If you have a right to something, then that claim has moral force, for it will impose on others an obligation to respect that right. In other words, your having a particular right implies that others ought either to do or to forbear from doing something with regard to your right. If you have a right to peaceful enjoyment of your property, for example, then that imposes a moral obligation on others not to play loud music. In other words, rights can be understood with respect to the obligations they imply. Part of what we mean by asserting a right is that there are attendant obligations that correspond to the right. No wonder people are quick to cast moral controversies in terms of rights! Rights are very powerful "moral currency," when properly used.

Do rights apply only to people? Can animals, plants, or other natural objects have rights? This is a difficult question that cannot be answered all at once here, because it turns on reaching a settled account of the nature of rights, something we do not have. But if rights are construed as legitimate claims, then it seems at least possible for some nonhumans to have rights, because the idea of having a claim is not obviously limited to human beings. You don't have to be able actually to *make* a claim in order to have one. Incompetent human beings, for example, are not physically able to make claims themselves, but we still think that they have rights because they have a sake, a well-being, an interest, for which we can act. Similarly, if a case can be made for a nonhuman having a legitimate claim—a sake for which we can act—then, yes, it looks as though it at least makes sense to speak of things other than people having rights.

READINGS ON ANIMALS

Peter Singer, from *Animal Liberation*

Peter Singer is one of the best-known contemporary philosophers in the world. He is currently director of the Institute for Bioethics at Princeton University. Animal Liberation, *his influential book from which our selection was taken, was original published over a generation ago, in 1975, and continues both to inspire and to infuriate today. Singer argues that the moral principle of equal consideration applies to animals in a simple and straightforward manner. Moreover, our failure to extend equal consideration to animals constitutes a kind of discrimination that he calls speciesism. According to Singer, speciesism is evident in our eating animals and in our willingness to perform experiments on them that we would never dream of doing on a human being.*

Critical Reading Questions

1. What is the principle of equality?
2. How, according to Singer, does the principle of equality apply to other members of our species?
3. Why, according to Singer, does the principle of equality apply to other species?
4. What is "speciesism," and why is it morally wrong, according to Singer?
5. Why does Singer think animals have interests?
6. Why does the rejection of speciesism not imply that all lives are equally valuable, according to Singer?
7. Why are animals used as subjects in experimentation? What dilemma does this pose for the researcher, according to Singer?
8. Under what circumstances does Singer think animal experimentation is morally acceptable?

ANIMAL LIBERATION

Peter Singer

ALL ANIMALS ARE EQUAL . . .

or why supporters of liberation for Blacks and Women should support Animal Liberation too.

"Animal Liberation" may sound more like a parody of other liberation movements than a serious objective. The idea of "The Rights of Animals" actually was once used to parody the case for women's rights. When Mary Wollstonecraft, a forerunner of today's feminists, published her *Vindication of the Rights of Women* in 1792, her views were widely regarded as absurd, and before long an anonymous publication appeared entitled *A Vindication of the Rights of Brutes.* The author of this satirical work (now known to have been Thomas Taylor, a distinguished Cambridge philosopher) tried to refute Mary Wollstonecraft's arguments by showing that they could be carried one stage further. If the argument for equality was sound when applied to women, why should it not be applied to dogs, cats, and horses? The reasoning seemed to hold for these "brutes" too; yet to hold that brutes had rights was manifestly absurd; therefore the reasoning by which this conclusion had been reached must be unsound, and if unsound when applied to brutes, it must also be unsound when applied to women, since the very same arguments had been used in each case.

In order to explain the basis of the case for the equality of animals, it will be helpful to start with an examination of the case for the equality of women. Let us assume that we wish to defend the case for women's rights against the attack by Thomas Taylor. How should we reply?

One way in which we might reply is by saying that the case for equality between men and women cannot validly be extended to nonhuman animals. Women have a right to vote, for instance, because they are just as capable of making rational decisions about the future as men are; dogs, on the other hand, are incapable of understanding the significance of voting, so they cannot have the right to vote. There are many other obvious ways in which men and women resemble each other closely, while humans and animals differ greatly. So, it might be said, men and women are similar beings and should have similar rights, while humans and nonhumans are different and should not have equal rights.

The reasoning behind this reply to Taylor's analogy is correct up to a point, but it does not go far enough. There *are* important differences between humans and other animals, and these differences must give rise to *some* differences in the rights that each have. Recognizing this obvious fact, however, is no barrier to the case for extending the basic principle of equality to nonhuman animals. The differences that exist between men and women are equally undeniable, and the supporters of Women's Liberation are aware that these differences may give rise to different rights. Many feminists hold that women have the right to an abortion on request. It does not follow that since these same feminists are campaigning for equality between men and women they must support the right of men to have abortions too. Since a man cannot have an abortion, it is meaningless to talk of his right to have one. Since a dog can't vote, it is meaningless to talk of its right to vote. There is no reason why either Women's Liberation or Animal Liberation should get involved in such nonsense. The extension of the basic principle of equality from one group to another does not imply that we must treat both groups in exactly the same way, or grant exactly the same rights to both groups. Whether we should do so will depend on the nature of the members of the two groups. The basic principle of equality does not require equal or identical *treatment;* it requires equal *consideration.* Equal consideration for different beings may lead to different treatment and different rights.

So there is a different way of replying to Taylor's attempt to parody the case for women's rights, a way that does not deny the obvious differences between humans and nonhumans but goes more deeply into the question of equality and concludes by finding nothing absurd in the idea that the basic principle of equality applies to so-called "brutes." At this point such a conclusion may appear odd; but if we examine more deeply the basis on which our opposition to discrimination on grounds of race or sex ultimately rests, we will see that we would be on shaky ground if we were to demand equality for blacks, women, and other groups of oppressed humans while denying equal consideration to nonhumans. To make this clear we need to see, first, exactly why racism and sexism are wrong.

When we say that all human beings, whatever their race, creed, or sex, are equal, what is it that we are asserting? Those who wish to defend hierarchical, inegalitarian societies have often pointed out that by whatever test we choose it simply is not true that all humans are equal. Like it or not we must face the fact that humans come in different shapes and sizes; they come with different moral capacities, different intellectual abilities, different amounts of benevolent feeling and sensitivity to the needs of others, different abilities to communicate effectively, and different capacities to experience pleasure and pain. In short, if the demand for equality were based on the actual equality of all human beings, we would have to stop demanding equality.

Still, one might cling to the view that the demand for equality among human beings is based on the actual equality of the different races and sexes. Although, it may be said, humans differ as individuals there are no differences between the races and sexes *as such.* From the mere fact that a person is black or a woman we cannot infer anything about that person's intellectual or moral capacities. This, it may be said, is why racism and sexism are wrong. The white racist claims that whites are superior to blacks, but this is false—although there are differences among individuals, some blacks are superior to some whites in all of the capacities and abilities that could conceivably be relevant. The opponent of sexism would say the same: a person's sex is no guide to his or her abilities, and this is why it is unjustifiable to discriminate on the basis of sex.

The existence of individual variations that cut across the lines of race or sex, however, provides us with no defense at all against a more sophisticated opponent of equality, one who proposes that, say, the interests of all those with IQ scores below 100 be given less consideration than the interests of those with ratings over 100. Perhaps those scoring below the mark would, in this society, be made the slaves of those scoring higher. Would a hierarchical society of this sort really be so much better than one based on race or sex? I think not. But if we tie the moral principle of equality to the factual equality of the different races or sexes, taken as a whole, our opposition to racism and sexism does not provide us with any basis for objecting to this kind of inegalitarianism.

There is a second important reason why we ought not to base our opposition to racism and sexism on any kind of actual equality, even the limited kind that asserts that variations in capacities and abilities are spread evenly between the different races and sexes: we can have no absolute guarantee that these capacities and abilities really are distributed evenly, without regard to race or sex, among human beings. So far as actual abilities are concerned there do seem to be certain measurable differences between both races and sexes. These differences do not, of course, appear in each case, but only when averages are taken. More important still, we do not yet know how much of these differences is really due to the different genetic endowments of the different races and sexes, and how much is due to poor schools, poor housing, and other factors that are the result of past and continuing discrimination. Perhaps all of the important differences will eventually prove to be environmental rather than genetic. Anyone opposed to racism and sexism will certainly hope that this will be so, for it will make the task of ending discrimination a lot easier; nevertheless it would be dangerous to rest the case against racism and sexism on the belief that all significant differences are environmental in origin. The opponent of, say, racism who takes this line will be unable to avoid conceding that *if* differences in ability do after all prove to have some genetic connection with race, racism would in some way be defensible.

Fortunately there is no need to pin the case for equality to one particular outcome of a scientific investigation. The appropriate response to those who claim to have found evidence of genetically based differences in ability between the races or sexes is not to stick to the belief that the genetic explanation must be wrong, whatever evidence to the contrary may turn up: instead we should make it quite clear that the claim to equality does not depend on intelligence, moral capacity, physical strength, or similar matters of fact. Equality is a moral idea, not an assertion of fact. There is no logically compelling reason for assuming that a factual difference in ability between two people justifies any difference in the amount of consideration we give to their needs and interests. *The principle of the equality of human beings is not a description of an alleged actual equality among humans: it is a prescription of how we should treat humans.*

Jeremy Bentham, the founder of the reforming utilitarian school of moral philosophy, incorporated the essential basis of moral equality into his system of ethics by means of the formula: "Each to count for one and none for more than one." In other words, the interests of every being affected by an action are to be taken into account and given the same weight as the like interests of any other being. A later utilitarian, Henry Sidgwick, put the point in this way: "The good of any one individual is of no more importance, from the point of view (if I may say so) of the Universe, than the good of any other." More recently the leading figures in contemporary moral philosophy have shown a great deal of agreement in specifying as a fundamental presupposition of their moral theories some similar requirement which operates so as to give everyone's interests equal consideration—although these writers generally cannot agree on how this requirement is best formulated.[1]

It is an implication of this principle of equality that our concern for others and our readiness to consider their interests ought not to depend on what they are like or on what abilities they may possess. Precisely what this concern or consideration requires us to do may vary according to the characteristics of those affected by what we do: concern for the well-being of a child growing up in America would require that we teach him to read; concern for the well-being of a pig may require no more than that we leave him alone with other pigs in a place where there is adequate food and room to run freely. But the basic element—the taking into account of the interests of the being, whatever those interests may be— must, according to the principle of equality, be extended to all beings, black or white, masculine or feminine, human or nonhuman.

Thomas Jefferson, who was responsible for writing the principle of the equality of men into the American Declaration of Independence, saw this point. It led him to oppose slavery even though he was unable to free himself fully from his slaveholding background. He wrote in a letter to the author of a book that emphasized the notable intellectual achievements of Negroes in order to refute the then common view that they had limited intellectual capacities:

Be assured that no person living wishes more sincerely than I do, to see a complete refutation of the doubts I have myself entertained and expressed on the grade of understanding allotted to them by nature, and to find that they are on a par with ourselves . . . but whatever be their degree of talent it is no measure of their rights. Because Sir Isaac Newton was superior to others in understanding, he was not therefore lord of the property or person of others.[2]

Similarly when in the 1850s the call for women's rights was raised in the United States a remarkable black feminist named Sojourner Truth made the same point in more robust terms at a feminist convention:

. . . they talk about this thing in the head; what do they call it? ["Intellect," whispered someone near by.] That's it. What's that got to do with women's rights or Negroes' rights? If my cup won't hold but a pint and yours holds a quart, wouldn't you be mean not to let me have my little half-measure full?[3]

It is on this basis that the case against racism and the case against sexism must both ultimately rest; and it is in accordance with this principle that the attitude that we may call "speciesism," by analogy with racism, must also be condemned. Speciesism—the word is not an attractive one, but I can think of no better term—is a prejudice or attitude of bias toward the interests of members of one's own species and against those of members of other species. It should be obvious that the fundamental objections to racism and sexism made by Thomas Jefferson and Sojourner Truth apply equally to speciesism. If possessing a higher degree of intelligence does not entitle one human to use another for his own ends, how can it entitle humans to exploit nonhumans for the same purpose?[4]

Many philosophers and other writers have proposed the principle of equal consideration of interests, in some form or other, as a basic moral principle; but not many of them have recognized that this principle applies to members of other species as well as to our own. Jeremy Bentham was one of the few who did realize this. In a forward-looking passage written at a time when black slaves had been freed by the French but in the British dominions were still being treated in the way we now treat animals, Bentham wrote:

The day *may* come when the rest of the animal creation may acquire those rights which never could have been withholden from them but by the hand of tyranny. The French have already discovered that the blackness of the skin is no reason why a human being should be abandoned without redress to the caprice of a tormentor. It may one day come to be recognized that the number of the legs, the villosity of the skin, or the termination of the *os sacrum* are reasons equally insufficient for abandoning a sensitive being to the same fate. What else is it that should trace the insuperable line? Is it the faculty of reason, or perhaps the faculty of discourse? But a full-grown horse or dog is beyond comparison a more rational, as well as a more conversable animal, than an infant of a day or a week or even a month, old. But suppose they were otherwise, what would it avail? The question is not, Can they *reason?* nor Can they *talk?* but, *Can they suffer?*[5]

In this passage Bentham points to the capacity for suffering as the vital characteristic that gives a being the right to equal consideration. The capacity for suffering—or more strictly, for suffering and/or enjoyment or happiness—is not just another characteristic like the capacity for language or higher mathematics. Bentham is not saying that those who try to mark "the insuperable line" that determines whether the interests of a being should be considered happen to have chosen the wrong characteristic. By saying that we must consider the interests of all beings with the capacity for suffering or enjoyment Bentham does not arbitrarily exclude from consideration any interests at all—as those who draw the line with reference to the possession of reason or language do. The capacity for suffering and enjoyment is *a prerequisite for having interests at all,* a condition that must be satisfied before we can speak of interests in a meaningful way. It would be nonsense to say that it was not in the interests of a stone to be kicked along the road by a schoolboy. A stone does not have interests because it cannot suffer. Nothing that we can do to it could possibly make any difference to its welfare. A mouse, on the other hand, does have an interest in not being kicked along the road, because it will suffer if it is.

If a being suffers there can be no moral justification for refusing to take that suffering into consideration. No matter what the nature of the being, the principle of equality requires that its suffering be counted equally with the like suffering—in so far as rough comparisons can be made—of any other being. If a being is not capable of suffering, or of experiencing enjoyment or happiness, there is nothing to be taken into account. So the limit of sentience (using the term as a convenient if not strictly accurate shorthand for the capacity to suffer and/or experience enjoyment) is the only defensible boundary of concern for the interests of others. To mark this boundary by some other characteristic like intelligence or rationality would be to mark it in an arbitrary manner. Why not choose some other characteristic, like skin color?

The racist violates the principle of equality by giving greater weight to the interests of members of his own race when there is a clash between their interests and the interests of those of another race. The sexist violates the principle of equality by favoring the interests of his own sex. Similarly the speciesist allows the interests of his own species to override the greater interests of members of other species. The pattern is identical in each case. . . .

Animals can feel pain. As we saw earlier, there can be no moral justification for regarding the pain (or pleasure) that animals feel as less important than the same amount of pain (or pleasure) felt by humans. But what exactly does this mean, in practical terms? To prevent misunderstanding I shall spell out what I mean a little more fully.

If I give a horse a hard slap across its rump with my open hand, the horse may start, but it presumably feels little pain. Its skin is thick enough to protect it against a mere slap. If I slap a baby in the same way, however, the baby will cry and presumably does feel pain, for its skin is more sensitive. So it is worse to slap a baby than a horse, if both slaps are administered with equal force. But there must be some kind of blow—I don't know exactly what it would be, but perhaps a blow with a heavy stick—that would cause the horse as much pain as we cause a baby by slapping it with our hand. That is what I mean by "the same amount of pain" and if we consider it wrong to inflict that much pain on a baby for no good reason then we must, unless we are speciesists, consider it equally wrong to inflict the same amount of pain on a horse for no good reason.

There are other differences between humans and animals that cause other complications. Normal adult human beings have mental capacities which will, in certain circumstances, lead them to suffer more than animals would in the same circumstances. If, for instance, we decided to perform extremely painful or lethal scientific experiments on normal adult humans, kidnaped at random from public parks for this purpose, every adult who entered a park would become fearful that he would be kidnaped. The resultant terror would be a form of suffering additional to the pain of the experiment. The same experiments performed on nonhuman animals would cause less suffering since the animals would not have the anticipatory dread of being kidnaped and experimented upon. This does not mean, of course, that it would be right to perform the experiment on animals, but only that there is a reason, which is *not* speciesist, for preferring to use animals rather than normal adult humans, if the experiment is to be done at all. It should be noted, however, that this same argument gives us a reason for preferring to use human infants—orphans perhaps—or retarded humans for experiments, rather than adults, since infants and retarded humans would also have no idea of what was going to happen to them. So far as this argument is concerned nonhuman animals and infants and retarded humans are in the same category; and if we use this argument to justify experiments on nonhuman animals we have to ask ourselves whether we are also prepared to allow experiments on human infants and retarded adults; and if we make a distinction between animals and these humans, on what basis can we do it, other than a bare-faced—and morally indefensible—preference for members of our own species?

There are many areas in which the superior mental powers of normal adult humans make a difference: anticipation, more detailed memory, greater knowledge of what is happening, and so on. Yet these differences do not all point to greater suffering on the part of the normal human being. Sometimes an animal may suffer more because of his more limited understanding. If, for instance, we are taking prisoners in wartime we can explain to them that while they must submit to capture, search, and confinement they will not otherwise be harmed and will be set free at the conclusion of hostilities. If we capture a wild animal, however, we cannot explain that we are not threatening its life. A wild animal cannot distinguish an attempt to overpower and confine from an attempt to kill; the one causes as much terror as the other.

It may be objected that comparisons of the sufferings of different species are impossible to make, and that for this reason when the interests of animals and humans clash the principle of equality gives no guidance. It is probably true that comparisons of suffering between members of different species cannot be made precisely, but precision is not essential. Even if we were to prevent the infliction of suffering on animals only when it is quite certain that the interests of humans will not be affected to anything like the extent that animals are affected, we would be forced to make radical changes in our treatment of animals that would involve our diet, the farming methods we use, experimental procedures in many fields of science, our approach to wildlife and to hunting, trapping and the wearing of furs, and areas of entertainment like circuses, rodeos, and zoos. As a result, a vast amount of suffering would be avoided.

So far I have said a lot about the infliction of suffering on animals, but nothing about killing them. This omission has been deliberate. The application of the principle of equality to the infliction of suffering is, in theory at least, fairly straightforward. Pain and suffering are bad and should be prevented or minimized, irrespective of the race, sex, or species of the being that suffers. How bad a pain is depends on how intense it is and how long it lasts, but pains of the same intensity and duration are equally bad whether felt by humans or animals.

The wrongness of killing a being is more complicated. I have kept, and shall continue to keep, the question of killing in the background because in the present state of human tyranny over other species the more simple, straight-forward principle of equal consideration of pain or pleasure is a sufficient basis for identifying and protesting against all the major abuses of animals that humans practice. Nevertheless, it is necessary to say something about killing.

Just as most humans are speciesists in their readiness to cause pain to animals when they would not cause a similar pain to humans for the same reason, so most humans are speciesists in their readiness to kill other animals when they would not kill humans. We need to proceed more cautiously here, however, because people hold widely differing views about when it is legitimate to kill humans, as the continuing debates over abortion and euthanasia attest. Nor have moral philosophers been able to agree on exactly what it is that makes it wrong to kill humans, and under what circumstances killing a human being may be justifiable.

Let us consider first the view that it is always wrong to take an innocent human life. We may call this the "sanctity of life" view. People who take this view oppose abortion and euthanasia. They do not usually, however, oppose the killing of nonhumans—so perhaps it would be more accurate to describe this view as the "sanctity of *human* life" view.

The belief that human life, and only human life, is sacrosanct is a form of speciesism. To see this, consider the following example.

Assume that, as sometimes happens, an infant has been born with massive and irreparable brain damage. The damage is so severe that the infant can never be any more than a "human vegetable," unable to talk, recognize other people, act independently of others, or develop a sense of self-awareness. The parents of the infant, realizing that they cannot hope for any improvement in their child's condition and being in any case unwilling to spend, or ask the state to spend, the thousands of dollars that would be needed annually for proper care of the infant, ask the doctor to kill the infant painlessly.

Should the doctor do what the parents ask? Legally, he should not, and in this respect the law reflects the sanctity of life view. The life of every human being is sacred. Yet people who would say this about the infant do not object to the killing of nonhuman animals. How can they justify their different judgments? Adult chimpanzees, dogs, pigs, and many other species far surpass the brain-damaged infant in their ability to relate to others, act independently, be self-aware, and any other capacity that could reasonably be said to give value to life. With the most intensive care possible, there are retarded infants who can never achieve the intelligence level of a dog. Nor can we appeal to the concern of the infant's parents, since they themselves, in this imaginary example (and in some actual cases), do not want the infant kept alive.

The only thing that distinguishes the infant from the animal, in the eyes of those who claim it has a "right to life," is that it is, biologically, a member of the species Homo sapiens, whereas chimpanzees, dogs, and pigs are not. But to use *this* difference as the basis for granting a right to life to the infant and not to the other animals is, of course, pure speciesism.* It is exactly the kind of arbitrary difference that the most crude and

---

* I am here putting aside religious views, for example the doctrine that all and only humans have immortal souls, or are made in the image of God. Historically these views have been very important, and no doubt are partly responsible for the idea that human life has a special sanctity. (For further historical discussion see Chapter 5.) Logically, however, these religious views are unsatisfactory, since a reasoned explanation of why it should be that all humans and no nonhumans have immortal souls is not offered. This belief too, therefore, comes under suspicion as a form of speciesism. In any case, defenders of the "sanctity of life" view are generally reluctant to base their position on purely religious doctrines, since these doctrines are no longer as widely accepted as they once were.

overt kind of racist uses in attempting to justify racial discrimination.

This does not mean that to avoid speciesism we must hold that it is as wrong to kill a dog as it is to kill a normal human being. The only position that is irredeemably speciesist is the one that tries to make the boundary of the right to life run exactly parallel to the boundary of our own species. Those who hold the sanctity of life view do this because while distinguishing sharply between humans and other animals they allow no distinctions to be made within our own species, objecting to the killing of the severely retarded and the hopelessly senile as strongly as they object to the killing of normal adults.

To avoid speciesism we must allow that beings which are similar in all relevant respects have a similar right to life—and mere membership in our own biological species cannot be a morally relevant criterion for this right. Within these limits we could still hold that, for instance, it is worse to kill a normal adult human, with a capacity for self-awareness, and the ability to plan for the future and have meaningful relations with others, than it is to kill a mouse, which presumably does not share all of these characteristics; or we might appeal to the close family and other personal ties which humans have but mice do not have to the same degree; or we might think that it is the consequences for other humans, who will be put in fear of their own lives, that makes the crucial difference; or we might think it is some combination of these factors, or other factors altogether.

Whatever criteria we choose, however, we will have to admit that they do not follow precisely the boundary of our own species. We may legitimately hold that there are some features of certain beings which make their lives more valuable than those of other beings; but there will surely be some nonhuman animals whose lives, by any standards, are more valuable than the lives of some humans. A chimpanzee, dog, or pig, for instance, will have a higher degree of self-awareness and a greater capacity for meaningful relations with others than a severely retarded infant or someone in a state of advanced senility. So if we base the right to life on these characteristics we must grant these animals a right to life as good as, or better than, such retarded or senile humans.

Now this argument cuts both ways. It could be taken as showing that chimpanzees, dogs, and pigs, along with some other species, have a right to life and we commit a grave moral offense whenever we kill them, even when they are old and suffering and our intention is to put them out of their misery. Alternatively one could take the argument as showing that the severely retarded and hopelessly senile have no right to life and may be killed for quite trivial reasons, as we now kill animals.

Since the focus of this book is on ethical questions concerning animals and not on the morality of euthanasia I shall not attempt to settle this issue finally. I think it is reasonably clear, though, that while both of the positions just described avoid speciesism, neither is entirely satisfactory. What we need is some middle position which would avoid speciesism but would not make the lives of the retarded and senile as cheap as the lives of pigs and dogs now are, nor make the lives of pigs and dogs so sacrosanct that we think it wrong to put them out of hopeless misery. What we must do is bring nonhuman animals within our sphere of moral concern and cease to treat their lives as expendable for whatever trivial purposes we may have. At the same time, once we realize that the fact that a being is a member of our own species is not in itself enough to make it always wrong to kill that being, we may come to reconsider our policy of preserving human lives at all costs, even when there is no prospect of a meaningful life or of existence without terrible pain.

I conclude, then, that a rejection of speciesism does not imply that all lives are of equal worth. While self-awareness, intelligence, the capacity for meaningful relations with others, and so on are not relevant to the question of inflicting pain—since pain is pain, whatever other capacities, beyond the capacity to feel pain, the being may have—these capacities may be relevant to the question of taking life. It is not arbitrary to hold that the life of a self-aware being, capable of abstract thought, of planning for the future, of complex acts of communication, and so on, is more valuable than the life of a being without these capacities. To see the difference between the issues of inflicting pain and taking life, consider how we would choose within our own species. If we had to choose to save the life of a normal human or a mentally defective human, we would probably choose to save the life of the normal human; but if we had to choose between preventing pain in the normal human or the mental defective—imagine that both have received painful but superficial injuries, and we only have enough painkiller for one of them—it is not nearly so clear how we ought to choose. The same is true when we consider other species. The evil of pain is, in itself, unaffected by the other characteristics of the being that feels the pain; the value of life is affected by these other characteristics.

Normally this will mean that if we have to choose between the life of a human being and the life of another animal we should choose to save the life of the human; but there may be special cases in which the reverse holds true, because the human being in question does not have the capacities of a normal human being.

So this view is not speciesist, although it may appear to be at first glance. The preference, in normal cases, for saving a human life over the life of an animal when a choice *has* to be made is a preference based on the characteristics that normal humans have, and not on the mere fact that they are members of our own species. This is why when we consider members of our own species who lack the characteristics of normal humans we can no longer say that their lives are always to be preferred to those of other animals. This issue comes up in a practical way in the following chapter. In general, though, the question of when it is wrong to kill (painlessly) an animal is one to which we need give no precise answer. As long as we remember that we should give the same respect to the lives of animals as we give to the lives of those humans at a similar mental level, we shall not go far wrong.

Questions for Discussion

1. Is speciesism appropriately compared to racism or sexism? Why or why not?
2. Is Singer correct to claim that the principle of equality applies beyond the bounds of our own species?
3. Singer asserts that "mere membership in our own biological species cannot be a morally relevant criterion for [the right to life]." Is he correct?
4. Is it as morally wrong to conduct painful medical experiments on brain-damaged human infants as on chimpanzees? Why or why not? Is Singer correct to search for "some middle position that would avoid speciesism but would not make the lives of the retarded and senile as cheap as the lives of pigs and dogs now are." Why or why not?
5. Singer thinks that not all lives, including human lives, are of equal worth. Do you agree? How shall we go about determining which human lives are more worthy and which less worthy? Is your life worth more than a dog's life? Why? Is any human life worth more than any nonhuman life?
6. Singer claims that "the ethical question of the justification of animal experimentation cannot be settled by pointing to its benefits for us, no matter how persuasive the evidence in favor of such benefits may be." Is this claim correct? Is it consistent with Singer's utilitarianism? Can a utilitarian argue that animal experimentation is justified?

Carl Cohen, "A Critique of the Alleged Moral Basis of Vegetarianism"

Carl Cohen is a professor of philosophy at the University of Michigan. He has published widely in moral and political philosophy. He is sharply critical of contemporary arguments that purport to show that animals have significant moral status. In this article, Cohen argues that animals cannot have moral rights because "the concept of right is essentially human; *it is rooted in the human moral world and has force and applicability only within that world." If Cohen is correct, then killing animals for food and using them in other ways cannot violate any rights, for they have none to violate.*

Critical Reading Questions

1. Why does Cohen think we are reluctant to deny that animals can have rights?
2. What does Cohen mean by an alleged "symmetrical reciprocity" between rights and obligations? How is that relevant to whether animals can have rights?
3. Why does Cohen think animals cannot have rights?
4. What is Cohen's example of the squirrel in the road show? How does it compare to the child in the road story?
5. What does Cohen mean when he claims that "the capacity for moral judgment that distinguishes humans from animals is not a test to be administered to human beings one by one. Persons who, because of some disability, are unable to perform the full moral functions natural to human beings are not for that reason ejected from the human community."

A CRITIQUE OF THE ALLEGED MORAL BASIS OF VEGETARIANISM

Carl Cohen

There is no obligation to eat meat. But neither is there any obligation to refrain from doing so. The oft-alleged obligation to restrict oneself to a vegetarian diet is commonly grounded on the supposition that animals have moral rights. If they do have such rights then they surely have the right to live, and therefore (it is supposed) killing and devouring them must wrongfully violate their rights.[1] This argument is without merit because, in fact, animals do not have rights.

We care about animals, of course. Most of us care a great deal about them, and we very much want not to be thought uncaring. But there is widespread fear that one who denies that animals have rights is likely to be thought callous or even cruel; this results in a general reluctance to express a moral truth that everyone grasps intuitively: rights, which are central in the moral lives of humans, are not possessed by animals; animals do not have rights. *Why* they do not have them is explained below.

Before turning to that, however, I emphasize one consequence of this moral truth: We may conclude with confidence that opposition to the eating of meat is ungrounded insofar as that opposition is based upon claimed rights that are in fact illusory. Animals cannot be deprived of rights they do not have.

The reluctance to deny that animals have rights lies in a common confusion about the relation between our *obligations* to animals and the claim that they possess *rights*. Humans do have many obligations to animals, of course, as all

decent persons will agree. Many go on to suppose that since such obligations are genuine, animals must have rights because if those rights were to be denied, the obligations owed to animals (not seriously in question) would need to be denied as well. This is a frequent and unfortunate mistake. Denying the reality of animal rights does *not* entail the denial of our obligations to animals. Most certainly it does not. I explain.

Reflect for a moment upon the obligations we humans owe to others. Some of these obligations may be traced to the fact that we are the targets of their rights. My obligation to repay the money I borrowed from you is the obverse of the right that you have to my payment of the debt. So, plainly, *some* of my obligations do arise from the rights of others against me. But that is by no means true of all obligations. A correct understanding of the true relation between rights and obligations is absolutely essential for sound moral judgments.

The common readiness to assent to the proposition that animals have rights is mainly a result of the hasty supposition that if we have obligations to them (which we surely do) they must have rights against us. But this is not so. Recognizing (correctly) that we are not morally free to do anything we please to animals, it is inferred (incorrectly) that they must therefore have "rights"—and that inference yields a defense of vegetarianism on moral grounds.

The premise that underlies such reasoning is the supposition of the *symmetrical reciprocity* of obligations and rights. It is a false premise, and its falsity is easy to discern. Between rights and obligations the relations are not symmetrical. Rights do entail obligations upon the targets of

This essay is a revised version of "Why Animals Do Not Have Rights," in *The Animal Rights Debate*, ed. Carl Cohen and Tom Regan (Lanham, MD: Rowman and Littlefield Publishers, 2001), chap. 5.

those rights, of course, as earlier noted. If you have a right to the return of money you lent me, I have the obligation to return that money, and so on. But we may not correctly infer from the fact that all rights impose obligations upon their targets that all obligations owed arise because one is the target of the rights of another.

A logical confusion underlies the mistake. From the true proposition that all dogs are mammals we certainly may not infer that all mammals are dogs. Universal affirmative propositions of the form "all dogs are mammals" or "all rights entail obligations," cannot be *converted simply* and retain their truth. *Some* mammals are dogs, yes, and *some* obligations do arise from rights. But it is a confusion of mind to conclude, from the fact that all dogs are mammals, that all mammals are dogs. It is no less a confusion of mind to conclude that because all rights entail obligations, all obligations are entailed by rights.

Very many of the moral obligations borne by each of us are owed to other persons or other beings who have no *rights* against us; reflection on everyday experience confirms this quickly. Our obligations arise from a great variety of circumstances and relations, of which being the target of another's right is but one. Illustrations of this rich and important variety are everywhere to be found; here are some:

a) Obligations arise from *commitments* freely made by a moral agent. As a college professor I promise my students explicitly that I will comment at length on the papers they submit, and from this express commitment obligations flow, of course. But my students understand that they have not the right to demand that I provide such comment.
b) Obligations arise from *the possession of authority.* Civil servants are obliged to be courteous to members of the public; presiding officers at a public forum ought to call upon representatives of different points of view in alternation; judges have the obligation to listen patiently to the arguments of parties disputing before them—but such obligations are not grounded in rights.
c) Obligations arise as a consequence of *special relations*; hosts have an obligation to be cordial to their guests, but guests may not demand cordiality as a right.

d) *Faithful service* may engender obligations: shepherds have obligations to their dogs, and cowboys to their horses, none of which flow from the *rights* of those dogs or those horses.
e) My son, eleven years old as I write this, may someday wish to study veterinary medicine as my father did. I will then have the obligation to help him as I can, and with pride I shall—but he has not the authority to demand such help as a matter of right. *Family connections* may give rise to obligations without concomitant rights.
f) My dog has no right to daily exercise and veterinary care, but I do have the obligation to provide these things for him. *Duties of care* freely taken on may bind one even though those to whom the care is given have not got a right to demand it. Recognizing that a beloved pet is suffering great pain, we may be obliged to put it out of its misery, but the tormented animal has no claim of right that that be done.
g) An act of *spontaneous kindness* done may leave us with the obligation to acknowledge and perhaps return that gift, but the benefactor to whom we are thus obliged has no claim of *right* against us.

And so on and on. The circumstances giving rise to obligations are so many and so varied that they cannot all be cataloged. It is nevertheless certain and plainly seen that it is *not only* from the rights of others that our obligations arise.

How then are rights and obligations related? When looked at from the viewpoint of one who holds a right and addresses the target of that right, they appear correlative. But they are plainly not correlative when looked at from the viewpoint of one who recognizes an obligation on himself, an obligation that does not stem from the rights of another. Your right to the money I owe you creates my obligation to pay it, of course. But many of my obligations to the needy, to my neighbors, to sentient creatures of every sort, have no foundation in their rights. The premise that rights and obligations are *reciprocals*, that *every* obligation flows from another's right, is utterly false. It is inconsistent with our intuitive understanding of the difference between what we believe we *ought* to do and what others can justly *demand* that we do.

This lack of symmetry is of enormous importance. It helps to explain how it can be true that, although animals do not have rights, it does not follow from this fact that one is free to treat them with callous disregard. It is silly to think of rats as the holders of moral rights, but it is by no means silly to recognize that rats can feel pain and that it is our obligation to refrain from torturing them because they are beings having that capacity. The obligation to act humanely *we owe to them* even though the concept of a right cannot possibly apply to them. We are obliged to apply to animals the moral principles that govern *us* regarding the gratuitous imposition of pain and suffering. We are the moral agents in this arena, not the rats. Act toward lesser creatures, as the saying goes, "not merely according to their deserts, but according to your dignities." We are restrained by moral principles in this way, but being so restrained does not suggest or suppose that the animals to whom we owe humane regard are the possessors of rights.

. . .

Animals cannot be the bearers of rights because the concept of right is *essentially human;* it is rooted in the human moral world and has force and applicability only within that world. Humans must deal with rats—all too frequently in some parts of the world—and must refrain from cruelty in dealing with them. But a rat can no more be said to have rights than a table can be said to have ambition, or a rock to exhibit remorse. To say of a pig or a fish that it has rights is to confuse categories, to apply to its world a moral category that can have content only in the human moral world.

Try this thought experiment: Imagine, on the Serengeti Plain in East Africa, a lioness hunting to feed her cubs. A baby zebra, momentarily left unattended by its mother, becomes her prey; the lioness snatches it, rips open its throat, tears out chunks of its flesh, and departs. The mother zebra is driven nearly out of her wits when at first she cannot locate her baby; finding its carcass at last, she will not leave its remains for days. The scene may cause you to shudder, but it is perfectly ordinary and common in the world of nature. If that baby zebra had any

rights at all it certainly had the right to live; of all rights that is surely the most fundamental and the one presupposed by all others. So, if in that incident of natural predation, the prey has rights and the predator infringes those rights, we humans ought to intervene in defense of the zebra's rights, if doing so were within our power. But we do not intervene in such matters even when it is in our power; we do not dream of doing so. On the other hand, if we saw (or even suspected) that the lioness was about to attack an unprotected human baby playing at the edge of the forest, we would respond with alacrity, protecting the baby in every way within our power.

What accounts for the moral difference between those cases? Not convenience merely; protecting the baby may be dangerous, while intervening to save the baby zebra may be easy and safe. Humans are often in a position to intervene to avoid predatory killing, yet we deliberately refrain. Our responses to threatened humans differ fundamentally from our responses to threatened zebras. But why? No doubt we have greater empathy for the endangered human. But we also recognize, consciously or subconsciously, that between the moral status of the baby zebra and the moral status of the baby human there are profound differences. The human baby, we might say if later asked, has a right not to be eaten alive, and it has that right because it is a *human* being.

Do you believe the baby zebra has the *right* not to be slaughtered? Or that the lioness has the *right* to kill that baby zebra to feed her cubs? Perhaps you are inclined to say, when confronted by such natural rapacity (duplicated in various forms millions of times each day on planet earth) that *neither* is right or wrong, that neither zebra nor lioness has a right against the other. Then I am on your side. Rights are pivotal in the moral realm and must be taken seriously, yes; but zebras and lions and rats do not live in a moral realm; their lives are totally amoral. There *is* no morality for them; animals do no moral wrong, ever. In their world there are no wrongs and there are no rights.

One contemporary philosopher who has thought a good deal about animals puts this point in terms of the ability to formulate principles. Referring to animals as "moral patients" [that is, beings *upon* whom moral agents like ourselves may act], he writes:

A moral patient [an animal] lacks the ability to formulate, let alone bring to bear, principles in deliberating about which one among a number of possible acts it would be right or proper to perform. Moral patients, in a word, cannot do what is right, nor can they do what is wrong. . . . [E]ven when a moral patient causes significant harm to another, the moral patient has not done what is wrong. Only moral agents can do what is wrong.

Just so. The concepts of wrong, and of right, are totally foreign to animals, not conceivably within their ken or applicable to them, as the author of that passage clearly sees. He is the noted advocate of animal rights, Tom Regan.[2]

Here is yet another thought experiment that illuminates our intuitive judgments about the moral status of animals: Imagine that, as you were driving to work the other day, a squirrel suddenly reversed its course and ran in front of your car. It being impossible for you to avoid hitting it, you clenched your teeth as you heard the telltale thump from beneath the automobile. Pained by the thought that the squirrel had been needlessly killed by your car, you silently express to yourself the hope that, if indeed it was killed, it was caused no great suffering and you drive on. But now suppose that it was not a squirrel but a human toddler who ran into the path of your car and whom you hit through absolutely no fault of your own. Swerving in panic, we will suppose, you avoid a killing blow, but you cannot avoid hitting the child and it becomes plain that she has been badly injured by the impact. Anguish, fear, *horror* overwhelm you. Most assuredly you do not drive on, but stop in wretched torment, to do what can be done for the injured child. You rush it to medical care; its parents you contact at the earliest possible moment, imploring their understanding. Nothing you could possibly have done would have avoided the terrible accident, you explain—and yet you express tearfully your profound regret. At the first opportunity you arrange to visit the recuperating child; you bring it a present, wish it well; her injury and her recovery will be forever on your mind. And so on.

What accounts for the enormous difference between the response you make to the death of a squirrel, and to the injury of a human child,

you being the cause of both, and in both cases entirely innocent of fault? Does that difference not spring from your intuitive grasp of the difference in the moral status of the two, your recognition that the one has rights, which you would not for all the world have deliberately infringed, while the other, although sentient and perhaps endearing, has no rights that you could possibly infringe?

Those who rely on animals for food, like medical investigators who use animals in research to advance human well-being, do not violate the rights of animals by their conduct because, to be blunt, animals have no rights. Rights do not apply to them.

Humans, on the other hand, certainly do have rights. How is this difference to be accounted for? Rabbits are mammals and we are mammals, both inhabiting a natural world. The reality of the moral rights that we possess (and that they do not possess) we do not doubt, and the importance of this great difference between them and us is equally certain. But we are unsure of the ground of these rights of ours. Where do they come from? We are a natural species too, a product of evolution as all animals are. How then can we be so very different from the zebras and the rats? Why are we not crudely primitive creatures, as they are, for whom the concept of moral right is a fiction?

Philosophers and theologians have long struggled, and struggle still, to explain the foundations of natural human rights. I do not propose to offer here the resolution of the deepest questions confronting human beings. But the sharp divide between the moral status of animals and that of humans we can say something more about.

It will be helpful to reflect upon the *kinds* of explanations of human rights that have been given by the greatest of moral philosophers. What has been generally held to account for the fact that humans, unlike animals, do have rights?

(1) Many have thought that the moral understanding of right and duty, by humans, is a *divine gift*, a grasp of the eternal law for which we have been peculiarly equipped by God. So thought St. Thomas of Aquinas, who argued tightly in defense of that view in the thirteenth century. All things, said he,

are ruled and measured by the eternal law. . . . Now among all others, the rational creature is subject to divine providence in the most excellent way, in so far as it partakes of a share of providence. . . . Wherefore it has a share of the eternal reason, whereby it has a natural inclination to its proper act and end: and this participation of the eternal law in the rational creature is called the natural law. Hence the Psalmist after saying . . . "Many say, Who showeth us good things?" in answer to which question he says: "The light of Thy countenance, O Lord, is signed upon us.[3]

He thus implies that the light of natural reason, whereby we discern what is good and what is evil, which is the function of the natural law, is nothing else than an imprint on us of the divine light.[4] The power to grasp the binding power of moral law, and therefore the capacity to understand human rights, and to respect them, is on this account divinely endowed. No one has put this view more cogently than St. Thomas. The account he gave was not new in his day, nor has it lost its authority for many today.

Long before St. Thomas marshaled such arguments, other fathers of the Church, perhaps St. Augustine most profoundly, had pointed out that if God has made us in his own image, as we are taught, and therefore with a will that is truly free and "knowing good and evil,"[5] we, unlike all other creatures, must choose between good and evil, between right and wrong.[6]

(2) Philosophers have very commonly distrusted such theological reasoning. Many accounts of the moral dimension of human experience have been offered that do not rely upon inspired texts or supernatural gifts. Of the most influential philosophers, many have held that human morality is grounded not in the divine but in the human moral community. "I am morally realized," wrote the great English idealist, F. H. Bradley, "not until my personal self has utterly ceased to be my exclusive self, is no more a will which is outside others' wills, but finds in the world of others nothing but self." What Bradley called "the organic moral community" is, he thought, the only context in which there can be right. "Realize yourself as the self-conscious member of an infinite whole, by realizing that whole in yourself."[7]

Before him, the great German idealist G. W. F. Hegel accounted for human rights as a consequence of the self-conscious participation of human beings in "an objective ethical order."[8] And there have been many other such accounts of rights, accounts that center upon human interrelations, upon a moral fabric within which human beings must always act, but within which animals never act and never can *possibly* act.

(3) Such reasoning is exceedingly abstract, and for that reason many find it unsatisfying. A better account of rights, an account more concrete and more true to their own experience, some think to be that given by ethical intuitionists and realists who rely upon the immediate moral experience of ordinary people. Human moral conduct must be governed, said the leading intuitionist H. A. Prichard, by the "underivative, intuitive cognition of the rightness of an action."[9] Would you know how we can be sure that humans have rights? Ask yourself how you know that you have rights. You have no doubt about it. There are some fundamental truths, on this view, for which no argument need be given. In that same spirit Sir David Ross explained our grasp of human rights as our recognition of moral "suitability": "fitness, in a certain specific and unanalyzable way, to a certain situation."[10] And that was the view of my teacher and my friend of happy memory, Professor C. D. Broad. Rights surely are possessed by humans, he thought, by humans but never by animals. The knowledge of right is immediately and certainly possessed.

(4) For those who seek a more naturalistic account of ethical concepts, there are, among others, the writings of Marx and his followers who explicitly repudiated all moral views claiming to have their foundation in some supernatural sphere. "The animal," Marx wrote, "is one with its life activity. It does not distinguish the activity from itself. It is its activity. But man makes his life activity itself an object of his will and consciousness. . . . His own life is an object for him. . . . Conscious life activity distinguishes man from the life activity of the animals."

Hence humans can concern themselves with human*kind*, and humans alone can understand their species; humans, unlike animals, make judgments that can be "universal and consequently free."[11] Moral judgments are typically universal in this sense. That is why, Lenin later wrote, "There is no such thing as morality taken outside of human society."[12] Every conception of moral right, on this view, is a reflection of the concrete conditions of life, but always the conditions of *human* life.

A more sophisticated ethical naturalism was presented by the American pragmatists John Dewey and George Herbert Mead, who shared the view that morality arises only in human community, but who emphasized the development of self within that community. We humans create our selves, selves that develop and become moral, Mead wrote, only through "the consciousness of other moral selves."[13]

Which among all these families of moral positions is most nearly true? Readers will decide for themselves. Differing ethical systems have been very briefly recapitulated here only to underscore the fact that, however much great thinkers have disagreed about fundamental principles, *the essentially human locus of the concept of right* has never been seriously doubted. Of the finest moral philosophers from antiquity to the present not one would deny—as the animal rights movement does seek now to deny—that there is a most profound difference between the moral stature of humans and that of animals, and that rights pertain only to the former.

. . .

The claim that there is no fundamental moral difference between animals and humans is the essential mark of what is loosely called the animal rights movement. "There is no rational basis," says Ingrid Newkirk, of People for the Ethical Treatment of Animals (PETA), "for saying that a human being has special rights." But in this she is profoundly mistaken; there *is* a rational basis for this distinction, a distinction of the deepest importance. The failure to grasp and respect that distinction leads some zealots to interfere with medical research, and others to insist that eating meat is a moral wrong. Reflect upon what it is that differentiates acts by humans from the acts of cows or rabbits. With Immanuel Kant we may say that critical reason reveals at the core of *human* action a uniquely moral will. There is, in humans, a unique capacity to formulate moral *principles* for the direction of our conduct, and we have a direct and immediate understanding of that capacity. Human beings can grasp the maxim of the principles we devise, and by applying those principles to ourselves as well as to others,

we exhibit the autonomy of the human will. Humans, but never cows, confront choices that are purely moral. Humans, but certainly not pigs or chickens, lay down rules, moral imperatives, by which all moral agents are thought to be rightly governed, ourselves along with all others. Human beings are *self*-legislative, morally *auto*nomous.

To be a moral agent is to be able to grasp the generality of moral restrictions upon our will. Humans understand that there are some acts that may be in our interest and yet must not be willed because they are simply wrong. This capacity for moral judgment does not arise in the animal world; rats can neither exercise nor respond to moral claims. My dog knows that there are certain things he must not do, but he knows this only as the outcome of his learning about his interests, the pains he may suffer if he does what he's been taught is forbidden. He does not know, he *cannot* know (as Tom Regan agrees)[14] that any conduct is *wrong*. The proposition : "It would be highly advantageous to act in such-and-such a way, but I may not do so because it would be morally wrong" is one that no dog or bunny rabbit, however sweet and endearing, however loyal or loving or intelligent, can ever entertain, or intend, or begin to grasp. *Right is not in their world.* But right and wrong are the very stuff of human moral life, the ever-present awareness of human beings who *can* do wrong, and who by seeking (often but not always) to avoid wrong conduct prove themselves members of a moral community in which rights may be exercised and must be respected.

Every day humans confront actual or potential conflicts between what is in their own interest and what is just. We restrain ourselves (or at least we can do so) on purely moral grounds. In such a community the concept of a right makes very good sense, of course. Some riches that do not belong to us would please us, no doubt, but we *may* not take them; we refrain from stealing not only because we fear punishment if caught. Even if we knew that the detection of our wrongdoing were impossible, we understand that to deprive others of what is theirs by right is conduct forbidden *by our own moral rules.* We return lost property belonging to others even when keeping it might be much to our advantage; such return is the act that our moral principles call for. Only in a community of that kind, a community constituted by beings capable of self-restricting moral judgments, can the concept of a *right* be intelligibly invoked.

Humans have such moral capacities. They are in this sense self-legislative, members of moral communities governed by moral rules; humans possess rights and recognize the rights of others. Animals do not have such capacities. They cannot exhibit moral autonomy in this sense, cannot possibly be members of a truly moral community. They may be the objects of our moral concern because they are sentient, of course, but they cannot possibly possess rights. People who eat animals do not violate the rights of those animals because, to be plain, they have none to violate.

I repeat one caveat for emphasis: It does not follow from the fact that animals have no rights that we are free to do anything we please to them. Most assuredly not. We do have obligations to animals, weighty obligations—but those obligations do not, because they cannot, arise out of animal rights.

. . .

There is an objection sometimes raised to this view that deserves response and deserves also to be permanently put aside. It cannot be, the critic says, that having rights requires the ability to make moral claims, or to grasp and apply moral laws, because, if that were true, many human beings—the brain-damaged, the comatose, infants, and the senile—who plainly lack those capacities must be without rights. But that is absurd. This proves, the critic concludes, that rights do not depend on the presence of moral capacities.[15]

Objections of this kind arise from a misunderstanding of what it means to say that the moral world is a human world. Children, like elderly adults, have rights *because they are human.* Morality is an essential feature of human life; all humans are moral creatures, infants and the senile included. Rights are not doled out to this individual person or that one by somehow establishing the presence in them of some special capacity. This mistaken vision would result in the selective award of rights to some individuals but not others, and the cancellation of rights when capacities fail.

On the contrary, rights are *universally* human, apply to humans generally. This criticism thus errs by treating the essentially moral feature of humanity as though it were a screen for sorting individual humans, which it most certainly is not. The capacity for moral judgment that distinguishes humans from animals is not a test to be administered to human beings one by one. Persons who, because of some disability, are unable to perform the full moral functions natural to human beings are not for that reason ejected from the human community. The critical distinction is one of kind. Humans are of such a kind that rights pertain to them *as humans*; humans live lives that will be, or have been, or remain *essentially* moral. It is silly to suppose that human rights might fluctuate with an individual's health, or dissipate with an individual's decline. The rights involved are human rights. On the other hand, animals are of such a kind that rights never pertain to them; what humans retain when disabled, rats never had.

The contrast between these two very different moral conditions is highlighted in the world of medical experimentation. Humans must *choose* to allow themselves to be the instruments of scientific research, and because humans have moral authority over their own bodies, we insist that humans may be the subject of scientific experiments only with their informed and freely given consent. Investigators who withhold information from potential subjects, or who deceive potential subjects, thereby making it impossible for them to give genuinely voluntary consent to what is done, will be condemned and punished, rightly. But this consent, which we think absolutely essential in the case of human subjects, is *impossible* for animals to give. The reason is not merely that we cannot communicate with them, or explain to them or inquire of them, but that the kind of moral choice involved in giving consent is totally out of the question for a chicken or a cow.

. . .

An objection of a different kind is raised by some advocates of animal rights. It goes like this:

Animals have internal lives far more rich and complicated than most people realize; many animals are, as Tom Regan points out, "psychologically complex" beings. Therefore, the effort to distinguish the world of humans from the world of animals by pointing to some special capacity of humans cannot succeed. Although in lesser degree than humans, animals do have the capacities we commonly associate with humanity. Humans are rational, but animals can reason too; animals communicate with one another, not with languages like ours of course, but very effectively nonetheless. Animals, like humans, care passionately for their young; animals, like humans, exhibit desires and preferences. And so on and on. So there is no genuine moral distinction to be drawn.[16]

This objection has much popular appeal but it fails because it relies upon a mistaken assumption. *Cognitive* abilities, the ability to communicate or to reason, are simply not at issue. My dog certainly reasons, and he communicates rather well. Nor is it *affective* capacities that are at issue; many animals plainly exhibit fear, love, and anger, care for one another and for their offspring, and so on. Nor is it the exhibition of *preference,* or memory, or aversion that marks the critical divide; no one doubts that a squirrel may recall where it buried a nut, or that a dog would rather go on a walk than remain in the car. Remarkable behaviors are often exhibited by animals, as we all know. Conditioning, fear, instinct, and intelligence all contribute to individual success and to species survival.

Nor is the capacity to suffer sufficient to justify the claim that animals have rights. They surely can suffer; it is obvious that they feel pain. And because they are sentient in that way, they are properly a concern of morally sensitive humans; they are, we may say, morally "considerable." Of course. And that is why the moral principles that govern us oblige us to act thoughtfully, humanely, in our use of them.

But with all the varied capacities of animals granted, it remains absolutely impossible for them to act *morally,* to be members of a moral community. Emphasizing similarities between human families and those of monkeys, or between human communities and those of wolves, and the like, cannot ground the moral equality of species; it serves only to obscure what is truly critical. A being subject to genuinely moral judgment must be capable of grasping the *maxim* of an act, and capable, too, of grasping the *generality* of an ethical premise in a moral argument. Similarities between animal conduct and human conduct cannot refute, cannot even address, the profound moral differences between humans and the lower animals.

Because humans do have rights, and these rights can be violated by other humans, we all understand that humans can and sometimes do commit *crimes.* Whether a crime has been committed, however, depends utterly upon the actor's moral state of mind. If I take your coat from the closet honestly believing that it was mine, I do not steal it. A genuine crime is an act in which the guilty deed, the *actus reus*, is accompanied by a guilty state of mind, a mens rea. Humans can commit crimes not merely because we realize that we may be punished for acting thus-and-so, but because we recognize that there are duties that govern us; to speak of such recognition in the world of cows and horses is literally nonsensical. In primitive times cows and horses were sometimes punished at the bar of human justice. We chuckle now as we look back upon that practice, realizing that to accuse a cow of a crime marks the accuser as inane, confused about the applicability of moral concepts. Animals never can be criminals, obviously— not because they are always law-abiding, but because "law-abiding" has no sense in this context; moral appraisals do not intelligibly apply to them. And that is why it is not true, and never can be true, that animals have moral rights.

The fundamental mistake is one in which a concept (in this case, moral right) that makes very good sense in one context, is applied in another context in which it makes no sense at all. It may be helpful to reflect upon other spheres, very distant from morality, in which mistakes of the same general kind have been commonly made at great cost.

The world of metaphysical thinking is riddled with mistakes of that kind. In his *Critique of Pure Reason*, Immanuel Kant explains at length the metaphysical blunders into which we are led when we apply concepts fundamentally important in one sphere in another sphere in which those concepts can have no grip. In our human experience (for example), the concepts of time and space, the relations of cause and effect, of subject and attribute, and others, are fundamental and inescapable. But these are concepts arising only within the world of our human experience and are bound to it. When we forget that bond we may be misled into asking: "Was the world caused, or is it uncaused?" "Did the world have a beginning in time, or did it not?" Kant explains, in one of the most brilliant long passages in all philosophical literature, why it *makes no sense* to ask such questions.[17] "Causation" is a concept that applies to phenomena we humans encounter; it is a category of our experience and cannot apply to the world as a whole. "Time" is the sequential condition of our experience, the way we experience things, not a container within which the world could have begun. In his discussion of the *paralogisms* of pure reason, and following his analyses of the *antinomies* of pure reason, Kant patiently exhibits the many confusions arising from the *misapplication* of the categories of experience. Whatever our judgment of his conclusions about the limits of reason, his larger lesson in these passages is powerful and deep. The misapplication of concepts leads to fundamental mistakes, to nonsense.

So it is also when we mistakenly transfer the concept of a right from the human moral world where it is rightly applied to the status of humans, to the animal world where it has no possible applicability, and wrongly applied to the status of animals. To say that rats have rights is to apply to the world of rats a concept that makes very good sense when applied to humans, but makes no sense at all when applied to rats. That is why chickens, like rats and cows, *cannot* have rights. The claim that eating them deprives them of their rights, therefore, is nonsensical, and cannot be the ground of a moral defense of vegetarianism.

NOTES

1. Tom Regan, a leading proponent of the view that animals have rights, presents one version of this argument in "The Moral Basis of Vegetarianism," in *All That Dwell Therein: Animal Rights and Environmental Ethics* (Berkeley: University of California Press, 1982).

2. Tom Regan, *The Case for Animal Rights* (Berkeley: University of California Press, 1983), pp. 152–53.

3. The reference by St. Thomas is to Psalm 4, line 6.

4. St. Thomas Aquinas, *Summa Theologica*. First Part of the Second Part, Question 91, Second Article.

5. Genesis 3:22.

6. St. Augustine, *Confessions*, Book Seven, 397 CE.

7. Francis Herbert Bradley, "Why Should I Be Moral?" in *Ethical Studies* (Oxford: Clarendon Press, 1927).

8. Georg Wilhelm Friedrich Hegel, *Philosophy of Right*, 1821.

9. H. A. Prichard, "Does Moral Philosophy Rest on a Mistake?" in *Moral Obligation* (Oxford: Oxford University Press, 1949).

10. Sir David Ross, *The Foundations of Ethics* (Oxford: Clarendon Press, 1939), chap. 3.

11. Karl Marx, *Economic and Philosophical Manuscripts*, 1844.

12. V. I. Lenin, "The Tasks of the Youth Leagues," 1920, reprinted in *The Strategy and Tactics of World Communism*, supp. I (Washington, DC: U.S. Government Printing Office, 1948).

13. George Herbert Mead, "The Genesis of the Self and Social Control," in *Selected Writings*, ed. A. J. Reck (Indianapolis: Bobbs-Merrill, 1964).

14. Tom Regan, *The Case for Animal Rights*.

15. Tom Regan makes this objection explicitly in "The Moral Basis of Vegetarianism." Evelyn Pluhar develops the same argument in her contribution to this volume.

16. Objections of this kind are registered by Dale Jamieson, "Killing Persons and Other Beings," in *Ethics and Animals*, ed. H. B. Miller and W. H. Williams (Clifton, NJ: Humana Press, 1983), and by C. Hoff, "Immoral and Moral Uses of Animals," *New England Journal of Medicine* 302 (1980): 115–18.

17. The analysis of these mistakes is given in what Kant calls the Transcendental Dialectic, which is the Second Division of the Second Part (Transcendental Logic) of the Transcendental Doctrine of Elements. The position Kant is defending is deep and difficult—but the general point he makes in the Transcendental Dialectic is readily accessible. Confusions and errors resulting from the misapplication of concepts in thinking about our *selves* he treats in a chapter called "The Paralogisms of Pure Reason"; confusions and errors resulting from the misapplication of concepts in thinking about *the world as a whole* he treats in a chapter called "The Antinomy of Pure Reason"; confusions and errors resulting from the misapplication of concepts in thinking about *God* he treats in a chapter called "The Ideal of Pure Reason." In all three spheres the categories (of which causation is only one example) that make sense only when applied to phenomena in our direct experience cannot be rationally employed. His analyses are penetrating and telling; the metaphysical blunders he exposes result in every case from the attempt to use categories having applicability in only one sphere in a very different sphere where they can have no applicability whatever.

Discussion Questions

1. Has Cohen shown that animals cannot have rights?
2. Even if animals cannot have rights, might our obligations to them make eating meat impermissible?
3. Should we agree with Cohen that "persons who, because of some disability, are unable to perform the full moral functions natural to human beings are not for that reason ejected from the human community"? Should species membership be morally relevant? What about intelligent aliens?

CHAPTER 15

Environmental Ethics

HARD QUESTION: OUGHT WE TO RESPECT NATURE?

Nature has been a topic of philosophical reflection for a long time, but with environmental degradation now an inescapable reality affecting our well-being if not our survival, philosophers have begun to consider our relationship to the natural world in earnest. Philosophical discussions about the environment center on the question of whether we are justified in taking a purely instrumental approach to nature. Many environmental philosophers think that restricting moral concern to people is a particular kind of unjustified human-centeredness called **anthropocentrism.** If true, this is a challenge to our unreflective ideas about the natural world, how we ought to regard it, and our presumed superiority to it. Most moral philosophy is uncritically anthropocentric, almost by definition. In Chapter 1 we saw that the point of morality is to "ameliorate the *human* predicament." The thought that natural objects such as rocks or trees should figure into our moral deliberations seems preposterous . . . at first.

Suppose that I dump my used motor oil into the nearest lake. Do I do anything wrong? Many people would be horrified at my action, but what, exactly, is wrong with it? One explanation might go like this: I did wrong because I unjustifiably harmed others. People living along the lake will be adversely affected by my pollution. They can't go fishing or swimming, the water stinks, and their property values will decrease because of the ugly mess that I made. Note that this sort of explanation involves only human welfare. If our explanation stops here, then it is anthropocentric because it concerns only the well-being of people. The central claim of many environmental philosophers is that there are other "moral patients" whose well-being ought to figure into our moral assessments, such as individual animals, plants, whole species, and even entire ecosystems. These nonhuman entities merit moral consideration not because our well-being is connected to theirs but, it is argued, because their well-being is worthy of respect in its own right.

Human beings might be the only beings who are able to reflect on morality (actually just a subset of human beings—the moral agents), but it does not follow that only human beings have moral worth. What is moral worth? Discussing moral worth is another way of talking about intrinsic value. If we can make sense of intrinsic, or non-instrumental, value in nature, then it will be impermissible to take a wholly instrumental attitude toward those natural entities that have such value—and for the same reason that it is impermissible to take a wholly instrumental approach to persons. If the lake into which I dumped my used motor oil or the organisms living in it are intrinsically valuable, then not only do I wrong the people harmed by my action, but I wrong the environment too. This is a revolutionary thought because, as we have seen morality is traditionally focused almost exclusively on human welfare. Is there intrinsic value in nature that we have somehow overlooked in our moral deliberations?

INTRINSIC VALUE AND THE NATURAL WORLD

It sounds so high-minded to say that nature or some aspect of it has intrinsic value, but without more this is mere rhetoric. It also sounds mysterious, as if there is a spooky aspect of nature to which only a few people have access. (See J. L. Mackie's discussion of the "queerness" of objective values in Chapter 18.) How could disagreements about whether a tree or a river is intrinsically valuable ever be settled? Moreover, the usual explanations for why people have intrinsic value seem irrelevant to whether natural entities are intrinsically valuable, because mountains are not rational, rivers are not autonomous, trees have no wills, and ecosystems are not morally responsible. So on what possible basis could someone claim non-instrumental value in nature?

If we think of intrinsic value as a sophisticated kind of projection—a way of looking, rather than a structural component of reality—then it might not be so hard to understand how there can be intrinsic value in nature. Think of colors. Are the apples in your refrigerator still red when the door is closed? Physical objects have color not simply when they reflect light, but when the reflected light causes creatures with color vision to experience color. If all creatures were color blind, would the apples still be red? Color is best construed as a kind of response in the minds of creatures capable of reacting to various wavelengths of light. The famous seventeenth-century philosopher John Locke said that colors, tastes, sounds, and the like are secondary properties. That is, they are properties we attribute to objects because of the powers of their real, or primary, properties (such as shape, density, and composition) to produce various experiences in us. It is only because the molecules that compose the apple's skin reflect certain wavelengths of light that the apple appears red to us. Intrinsic value might be similar to such secondary qualities as color: not exactly an objective feature of the world, but something that we are nevertheless caused to recognize by other features and are inclined to attribute, like color, to objects in the world.

Rather than something mysterious, intrinsic value is actually quite ordinary and central to understanding ourselves as persons. Think about the importance you attach to your own concerns, aspirations, well-being, and life choices. Do you think that your value as a person is exhausted by your usefulness to others or to society? To see oneself exclusively in instrumental terms would involve extinguishing one's personhood. One would have to conceive of oneself as a pure thing, and this is impossible because that means one would have no rational autonomy, no will at all. To be a person necessarily involves seeing oneself in non-instrumental terms. As we saw in Chapter 3, Kant captured this sense of non-instrumental value by which we each conceive our own personhood, claiming that persons are intrinsically valuable.

If the operation of our own wills requires us to see ourselves as intrinsically valuable, then the same should hold when we reflect on the operation of other wills. I can't say that I am intrinsically valuable, but not you. The intrinsic value that we each recognize in ourselves can be generalized to explain why we see intrinsic value beyond ourselves, not only in other people but also in certain things that people do. For example, many people consider great art intrinsically valuable. They regard its destruction as a desecration and are willing to pay to protect art they may never see. Recall the world's reaction to the looting of Bhagdad's art museums in the chaotic aftermath of the U.S. invasion of Iraq. Although most people never intended to visit those museums, their destruction was contemptible because the world lost something that could never be replaced. This is the proper response to the destruction of intrinsic value.

Great art's intrinsic value is not simply a function of appearance; otherwise, forgeries would be as valuable as originals. We admire great art as the expression of genius—a powerful, perceptive, and exquisitely sensitive mind at work. By revering great art we actually revere the creative powers of the people who invested so much of themselves in it. A similar account can be given for the intrinsic value many people see in cultural artifacts. Again, museums display the daily implements of aboriginal and ancient cultures, and they are widely thought to be intrinsically valuable. Why? These artifacts represent an entire way of life, the sum total of a culture's creative powers to forge a life in harsh or unusual circumstances and thereby express a view of their world and of themselves. We recognize a deep investment of time, effort, and creative power expressed in artifacts, just as in art. We see both as intrinsically valuable because we can appreciate and in some sense identify with what it took to produce them. Seeing such things as intrinsically valuable is an irresistible response to the manifestations of the inspiring and ingenious creative powers of others.

Understanding intrinsic value this way can also explain why many people see intrinsic value in nature. Despite the efforts of science to explain the world mechanistically, we remain stubbornly committed to regarding nature in human terms. We see intentionality, purpose, and will in nature, rather than just the blind and pointless workings of cause and effect. And like art and other creative expressions of human will, nature seemingly invests time and creative power to produce stupendous works of "art," such as landscapes, mountains, species, and forests. Cave formations, for example, are legally protected; people marvel at their exquisite shapes and delicacy, produced over so many thousands of years, drop by drop. To smash a rare and stunningly beautiful stalagmite for no reason is just as much a desecration as wantonly destroying a piece of great art, because both acts would show a lack of respect for the creative powers that invested so much time and effort, be those powers the artist's or nature's. We personify and romanticize nature, so it is hardly surprising that we should also infuse it with something of ourselves—indeed the most important part, our intrinsic value. A ruthlessly scientific account makes no room for intrinsic value in nature, but it erases *our* intrinsic value too because on a thoroughgoing scientific account of humanity, we become causal mechanisms. We do what we do because of prior events, rather than because we rationally and freely decide to do it. So is there really intrinsic value in nature? Well, no more than there really is intrinsic value in us.

To many environmental philosophers, the standard moral theories, such as we have studied in this text, are irremediably anthropocentric. It is easy to see how this might be so. For Kant, rational autonomy and *only* rational autonomy is intrinsically valuable. That is what distinguishes people from the rest of nature and sets us above it. Nature and all non-persons are things, and to talk about intrinsic value in non-persons is, for Kant, a deep failure to understand the moral significance of persons, for it perverts what is of supreme value. Kant would probably also regard it as a deep failure to comprehend the nature of things, because things cannot, by definition, be intrinsically valuable. Utilitarianism is not so straightforwardly anthropocentric, since it explicitly applies to all sentient beings. Thus sentient animals fall within its scope. But no non-sentient entities can have direct moral significance. And since many natural objects of environmental concern (such as mountains, rivers, forests, species, and ecosystems) are not sentient, utilitarianism cannot accord them the moral status that many environmental philosophers think they ought to have. Contract ethics is woefully incapable of generating a robust environmental ethic, because the central idea of a contract presupposes rational bargainers, and we can't make deals with mountains or trees. Contract ethics is anthropocentric with a vengeance. And despite its name, natural law ethics is also heavily anthropocentric: We are made in god's image and thus fundamentally different from the natural world, which is made *for* us. Therefore the value of nature is purely instrumental. Virtue ethics has some potential as an environmental ethic, even though its focus is on the human excellences. A proper human character might be sensitive to the natural world, respond to its beauty, and find in it an endless source of wonder and delight, but in the end, virtue ethics cannot infuse the natural world with value of its own.

READINGS ON ENVIRONMENTAL ETHICS

J. Baird Callicott, "The Conceptual Foundations of the Land Ethic"

J. Baird Callicott, a professor of philosophy at the University of North Texas, is one of the founders of environmental philosophy. His work is widely read and influential among philosophers and non-philosophers alike. In our selection, "The Conceptual Foundations of the Land Ethic," Callicott shows how the thought of the visionary naturalist Aldo Leopold forms a coherent revolutionary moral outlook, one that conceives of ecosystems as inherently valuable. Callicott seeks to answer the charge that the intrinsic value of ecosystems is inconsistent with human flourishing, leading some to charge that an "eco-centric" ethics is tantamount to environmental fascism.

Critical Reading Questions

1. What does Callicott see as central to a biological account of ethics?
2. According to Callicott, what role does community play in ethics? (Consider here his quote from Darwin on "savage" morality.)
3. Explain what Callicott means when he writes, "The simplest reason, to paraphrase Darwin, should, therefore, tell each individual that he or she ought to extend his or her social instincts and sympathies to all members of the biotic community though different from him or her in appearance of habits."
4. Sketch the Humean account of ethics that, according to Callicott, so influenced Leopold.
5. What does Callicott mean when he says that moral communities develop more like the rings of a tree than like a balloon, which expands without leaving a trace of where it was before?

THE CONCEPTUAL FOUNDATIONS
OF THE LAND ETHIC

J. Baird Callicott

The two great cultural advances of the past century were the Darwinian theory and the development of geology. . . . Just as important, however, as the origin of plants, animals, and soil is the question of how they operate as a community. That task has fallen to the new science of ecology, which is daily uncovering a web of interdependencies so intricate as to amaze—were he here—even Darwin himself, who, of all men, should have least cause to tremble before the veil.

> Aldo Leopold, Fragment 6B16,
> No. 36, Leopold Papers,
> University of Wisconsin—Madison Archives

I

As Wallace Stegner observes, *A Sand County Almanac* is considered "almost a holy book in conservation circles," and Aldo Leopold a prophet, "an American Isaiah." And as Curt Meine points out, "The Land Ethic" is the climactic essay of *Sand County*, "the upshot of 'The Upshot.'" One might, therefore, fairly say that the recommendation and justification of moral obligations on the part of people to nature is what the prophetic *A Sand County Almanac* is all about.

But, with few exceptions, "The Land Ethic" has not been favorably received by contemporary academic philosophers. Most have ignored it. Of those who have not, most have been either nonplussed or hostile. Distinguished Australian philosopher John Passmore dismissed it out of hand, in the first book-length academic discussion of the new philosophical subdiscipline called "environmental ethics." In

a more recent and more deliberate discussion, the equally distinguished Australian philosopher H. J. McCloskey patronized Aldo Leopold and saddled "The Land Ethic" with various far-fetched "interpretations." He concludes that "there is a real problem in attributing a coherent meaning to Leopold's statements, one that exhibits his land ethic as representing a major advance in ethics rather than a retrogression to a morality of a kind held by various primitive peoples." Echoing McCloskey, English philosopher Robin Attfield went out of his way to impugn the philosophical respectability of "The Land Ethic." And Canadian philosopher L. W. Sumner has called it "dangerous nonsense." Among those philosophers more favorably disposed, "The Land Ethic" has usually been simply quoted, as if it were little more than a noble, but naive, moral plea, altogether lacking a supporting theoretical framework—that is, foundational principles and premises which lead, by compelling argument, to ethical precepts.

The professional neglect, confusion, and (in some cases) contempt for "The Land Ethic" may, in my judgment, be attributed to three things: (1) Leopold's extremely condensed prose style in which an entire conceptual complex may be conveyed in a few sentences, or even in a phrase or two; (2) his departure from the assumptions and paradigms of contemporary philosophical ethics; and (3) the unsettling practical implications to which a land ethic appears to lead. "The Land Ethic," in short, is, from a philosophical point of view, abbreviated, unfamiliar, and radical.

Here I first examine and elaborate the compactly expressed abstract elements of the land ethic and expose the "logic" which binds them into a proper, but revolutionary, moral theory. I then discuss the controversial features of the land ethic and defend them against actual and potential criticism. I hope to show that the land ethic cannot be ignored as merely the groundless emotive exhortations of a moonstruck conservationist or dismissed as entailing wildly untoward practical consequences. It poses, rather, a serious intellectual challenge to business-as-usual moral philosophy.

II

"The Land Ethic" opens with a charming and poetic evocation of Homer's Greece, the point of which is to suggest that today land is just as routinely and remorselessly enslaved as human beings then were. A panoramic glance backward to our most distant cultural origins, Leopold suggests, reveals a slow but steady moral development over three millennia. More of our relationships and activities ("fields of conduct") have fallen under the aegis of moral principles ("ethical criteria") as civilization has grown and matured. If moral growth and development continue, as not only a synoptic review of history, but recent past experience suggest that it will, future generations will censure today's casual and universal environmental bondage as today we censure the casual and universal human bondage of three thousand years ago.

A cynically inclined critic might scoff at Leopold's sanguine portrayal of human history. Slavery survived as an institution in the "civilized" West, more particularly in the morally self-congratulatory United States, until a mere generation before Leopold's own birth. And Western history from imperial Athens and Rome to the Spanish Inquisition and the Third Reich has been a disgraceful series of wars, persecutions, tyrannies, pogroms, and other atrocities.

The history of moral practice, however, is not identical with the history of moral consciousness. Morality is not descriptive; it is prescriptive or normative. In light of this distinction, it is clear that today, despite rising rates of violent crime in the United States and institutional abuses of human rights in Iran, Chile, Ethiopia, Guatemala, South Africa, and many other places, and despite persistent organized social injustice and oppression in still others, moral consciousness is expanding more rapidly now than ever before. Civil rights, human rights, women's liberation, children's liberation, animal liberation, and so forth, all indicate, as expressions of newly emergent moral ideals, that ethical consciousness (as distinct from practice) has if anything recently accelerated—thus confirming Leopold's historical observation.

III

Leopold next points out that "this extension of ethics, so far studied only by philosophers"—and therefore, the implication is clear, not very satisfactorily studied "is actually a process in ecological evolution" (p. 202). What Leopold is saying here, simply, is that we may understand the history of ethics, fancifully alluded to by means of the Odysseus vignette, in biological as well as philosophical terms. From a biological point of view, an ethic is "a limitation on freedom of action in the struggle for existence" (p. 202). . . .

Let me put the problem in perspective. How, . . . did ethics originate and, once in existence, grow in scope and complexity?

The oldest answer in living human memory is theological. God (or the gods) imposes morality on people. And God (or the gods) sanctions it. A most vivid and graphic example of this kind of account occurs in the Bible when Moses goes up on Mount Sinai to receive the Ten Commandments directly from God. That text also clearly illustrates the divine sanctions (plagues, pestilences, droughts, military defeats, and so forth) for moral disobedience. Ongoing revelation of the divine will, of course, as handily and as simply explains subsequent moral growth and development.

Western philosophy, on the other hand, is almost unanimous in the opinion that the origin of ethics in human experience has somehow to do with human reason. Reason figures centrally and pivotally in the "social contract theory" of the origin and nature of morals in all its ancient, modern, and contemporary expressions from Protagoras, to Hobbes, to Rawls. Reason is the wellspring of virtue, according to both Plato and Aristotle, and of categorical imperatives, according to Kant. In short, the weight of

Western philosophy inclines to the view that we are moral beings because we are rational beings. The ongoing sophistication of reason and the progressive illumination it sheds upon the good and the right explain "the ethical sequence," the historical growth and development of morality, noticed by Leopold.

An evolutionary natural historian, however, cannot be satisfied with either of these general accounts of the origin and development of ethics. The idea that God gave morals to man is ruled out in principle—as any supernatural explanation of a natural phenomenon is ruled out in principle in natural science. And while morality might *in principle* be a function of human reason (as, say, mathematical calculation clearly is), to suppose that it is so *in fact* would be to put the cart before the horse. Reason appears to be a delicate, variable, and recently emerged faculty. It cannot, under any circumstances, be supposed to have evolved in the absence of complex linguistic capabilities which depend, in turn, for their evolution upon a highly developed social matrix. But we cannot have become social beings unless we assumed limitations on freedom of action in the struggle for existence. Hence we must have become ethical before we became rational.

Darwin, probably in consequence of reflections somewhat like these, turned to a minority tradition of modern philosophy for a moral psychology consistent with and useful to a general evolutionary account of ethical phenomena. A century earlier, Scottish philosophers David Hume and Adam Smith had argued that ethics rest upon feelings or "sentiments"—which, to be sure, may be both amplified and informed by reason. And since in the animal kingdom feelings or sentiments are arguably far more common or widespread than reason, they would be a far more likely starting point for an evolutionary account of the origin and growth of ethics.

Darwin's account, to which Leopold unmistakably (if elliptically) alludes in "The Land Ethic," begins with the parental and filial affections common, perhaps, to all mammals. Bonds of affection and sympathy between parents and offspring permitted the formation of small, closely knit social groups, Darwin argued. Should the parental and familial affections bonding family members chance to extend to less closely related individuals, that would permit an enlargement of the family group. And should the newly extended community more successfully defend itself and/or more efficiently provision itself, the inclusive fitness of its members severally would be increased, Darwin reasoned. Thus the more diffuse familial affections, which Darwin (echoing Hume and Smith) calls the "social sentiments" would be spread throughout a population.

Morality, properly speaking—that is, morality as opposed to mere altruistic instinct—requires, in Darwin's terms, "intellectual powers" sufficient to recall the past and imagine the future, "the power of language" sufficient to express "common opinion," and "habituation" to patterns of behavior deemed, by common opinion, to be socially acceptable and beneficial. Even so, ethics proper, in Darwin's account, remains firmly rooted in moral feelings or social sentiments which were—no less than physical faculties, he expressly avers—naturally selected, by the advantages for survival and especially for successful reproduction, afforded by society.

The protosociobiological perspective on ethical phenomena, to which Leopold as a natural historian was heir, leads him to a generalization which is remarkably explicit in his condensed and often merely resonant rendering of Darwin's more deliberate and extended paradigm: Since "the thing [ethics] has its origin in the tendency of interdependent individuals or groups to evolve modes of co-operation, . . . all ethics so far evolved rest upon a single premise: that the individual is a member of a community of interdependent parts" (pp. 202–3).

Hence, we may expect to find that the scope and specific content of ethics will reflect both the perceived boundaries and actual structure or organization of a cooperative community or society. *Ethics and society or community are correlative.* This single, simple principle constitutes a powerful tool for the analysis of moral natural history, for the anticipation of future moral development (including, ultimately, the land ethic), and for systematically deriving the specific precepts, the prescriptions and proscriptions, of an emergent and culturally unprecedented ethic like a land or environmental ethic.

Anthropological studies of ethics reveal that in fact the boundaries of the moral community are generally coextensive with the perceived boundaries of society. And the peculiar (and, from the urbane point of view, sometimes inverted) representation of virtue and vice in tribal society—the virtue, for example, of sharing to the point of personal destitution and the vice of privacy and private property—reflects and fosters the life way of tribal peoples. Darwin, in his leisurely, anecdotal discussion, paints a vivid picture of the intensity, peculiarity, and sharp circumscription of "savage" mores: "A savage will risk his life to save that of a member of the same community, but will be wholly indifferent about a stranger." As Darwin portrays them, tribespeople are at once paragons of virtue "within the limits of the same tribe" and enthusiastic thieves, manslaughterers, and torturers without.

For purposes of more effective defense against common enemies, or because of increased population density, or in response to innovations in subsistence methods and technologies, or for some mix of these or other forces, human societies have grown in extent or scope and changed in form or structure. Nations—like the Iroquois nation or the Sioux nation—came into being upon the merger of previously separate and mutually hostile tribes. Animals and plants were domesticated and erstwhile hunter-gatherers became herders and farmers. Permanent habitations were established. Trade, craft, and (later) industry flourished. With each change in society came corresponding and correlative changes in ethics. The moral community expanded to become co-extensive with the newly drawn boundaries of societies and the representation of virtue and vice, right and wrong, good and evil, changed to accommodate, foster, and preserve the economic and institutional organization of emergent social orders.

Today we are witnessing the painful birth of a human supercommunity, global in scope. Modern transportation and communication technologies, international economic interdependencies, international economic entities, and nuclear arms have brought into being a "global village." It has not yet become fully formed and it is at tension—a very dangerous tension—with its predecessor, the nation-state. Its eventual institutional structure, a global federalism or whatever it may turn out to be, is at this point completely unpredictable. Interestingly, however, a corresponding global human ethic—the "human rights" ethic, as it is popularly called—has been more definitely articulated.

Most educated people today pay lip service at least to the ethical precept that all members of the human species, regardless of race, creed, or national origin, are endowed with certain fundamental rights which it is wrong not to respect. According to the evolutionary scenario set out by Darwin, the contemporary moral ideal of human rights is a response to a perception—however vague and indefinite—that mankind worldwide is united into one society, one community, however indeterminate or yet institutionally unorganized. As Darwin presciently wrote:

As man advances in civilization, and small tribes are united into larger communities, the simplest reason would tell each individual that he ought to extend his social instincts and sympathies to all the members of the same nation, though personally unknown to him. This point being once reached, there is only an artificial barrier to prevent his sympathies extending to the men of all nations and races. If, indeed, such men are separated from him by great differences of appearance or habits, experience unfortunately shows us how long it is, before we look at them as our fellow-creatures.

According to Leopold, the next step in this sequence beyond the still incomplete ethic of universal humanity, a step that is clearly discernible on the horizon, is the land ethic. The "community concept" has, so far, propelled the development of ethics from the savage clan to the family of man. "The land ethic simply enlarges the boundary of the community to include soils, water, plants, and animals, or collectively: the land" (p. 204).

As the foreword to *Sand County* makes plain, the overarching thematic principle of the book is the inculcation of the idea—through narrative description, discursive exposition, abstractive generalization, and occasional preachment—"that land is a community" (viii). The community concept is "the basic concept of ecology" (viii). Once land is popularly perceived as a biotic community—as it is professionally perceived in ecology—a correlative land ethic will emerge in the collective cultural consciousness.

V

Although anticipated as far back as the mid-eighteenth century—in the notion of an "economy of nature"—the concept of the biotic community was more fully and deliberately developed as a working model or paradigm for ecology by Charles Elton in the 1920s. The natural world is organized as an intricate corporate society in which plants and animals occupy "niches," or as Elton alternatively called them, "roles" or "professions," in the economy of nature. As in a feudal community, little or no socioeconomic mobility (upward or otherwise) exists in the biotic community. One is born to one's trade.

Human society, Leopold argues, is founded, in large part, upon mutual security and economic interdependency and preserved only by limitations on freedom of action in the struggle for existence—that is, by ethical constraints. Since the biotic community exhibits, as modern ecology reveals, an analogous structure, it too can be preserved, given the newly amplified impact of "mechanized man," only by analogous limitations on freedom of action—that is, by a land ethic (viii). A land ethic, furthermore, is not only "an ecological necessity," but an "evolutionary possibility" because a moral response to the natural environment—Darwin's social sympathies, sentiments, and instincts translated and codified into a body of principles and precepts—would be automatically triggered in human beings by ecology's social representation of nature (p. 203).

Therefore, the key to the emergence of a land ethic is, simply, universal ecological literacy.

VI

The land ethic rests upon three scientific cornerstones: (1) evolutionary and (2) ecological biology set in a background of (3) Copernican astronomy. Evolutionary theory provides the conceptual link between ethics and social organization and development. It provides a sense of "kinship with fellow-creatures" as well, "fellow-voyagers" with us in the "odyssey of evolution" (p. 109). It establishes a diachronic link between people and nonhuman nature.

Ecological theory provides a synchronic link—the community concept—a sense of social integration of human and nonhuman nature. Human beings, plants, animals, soils, and waters are "all interlocked in one humming community of cooperations and competitions, one biota." The simplest reason, to paraphrase Darwin, should, therefore, tell each individual that he or she ought to extend his or her social instincts and sympathies to all the members of the biotic community though different from him or her in appearance or habits.

And although Leopold never directly mentions it in *A Sand County Almanac*, the Copernican perspective, the perception of the earth as "a small planet" in an immense and utterly hostile universe beyond, contributes, perhaps subconsciously, but nevertheless very powerfully, to our sense of kinship, community, and interdependence with fellow denizens of the earth household. It scales the earth down to something like a cozy island paradise in a desert ocean.

Here in outline, then, are the conceptual and logical foundations of the land ethic: Its conceptual elements are a Copernican cosmology, a Darwinian protosociobiological natural history of ethics, Darwinian ties of kinship among all forms of life on earth, and an Eltonian model of the structure of biocenoses all overlaid on a Humean–Smithian moral psychology. Its logic is that natural selection has endowed human beings with an affective moral response to perceived bonds of kinship and community membership and identity; that today the natural environment, the land, is represented as a community, the biotic community; and that, therefore, an environmental or land ethic is both possible—the biopsychological and cognitive conditions are in place—and necessary, since human beings collectively have acquired the power to destroy the integrity, diversity, and stability of the environing and supporting economy of nature. In the remainder of this essay I discuss special features and problems of the land ethic germane to moral philosophy.

The most salient feature of Leopold's land ethic is its provision of what Kenneth Goodpaster has carefully called "moral considerability" for the biotic community per se, not just for fellow members of the biotic community.

In short, a land ethic changes the role of *Homo sapiens* from conqueror of the land-community to plain member and citizen of it. It implies respect for his fellow-members, *and also respect for the community as such.* (p. 204, emphasis added)

The land ethic, thus, has a holistic as well as an individualistic cast.

Indeed, as "The Land Ethic" develops, the focus of moral concern shifts gradually away from plants, animals, soils, and waters severally to the biotic community collectively. Toward the middle, in the subsection called "Substitutes for a Land Ethic," Leopold invokes the "biotic rights" of *species*—as the context indicates—of wildflowers, songbirds, and predators. In "The Outlook," the climactic section of "The Land Ethic," nonhuman natural entities, first appearing as fellow members, then considered in profile as species, are not so much as mentioned in what might be called the "summary moral maxim" of the land ethic: "A thing is right when it tends to preserve the integrity, stability, and beauty of the biotic community. It is wrong when it tends otherwise" (pp. 224–25).

By this measure of right and wrong, not only would it be wrong for a farmer, in the interest of higher profits, to clear the woods off a 75 percent slope, turn his cows into the clearing and dump its rainfall, rocks, and soil into the community creek, it would also be wrong for the federal fish and wildlife agency, in the interest of individual animal welfare, to permit populations of deer, rabbits, feral burros, or whatever to increase unchecked and thus to threaten the integrity, stability, and beauty of the biotic communities of which they are members. The land ethic not only provides moral considerability for the biotic community per se, but ethical consideration of its individual members is preempted by concern for the preservation of the integrity, stability, and beauty of the biotic community. The land ethic, thus, not only has a holistic aspect; it is holistic with a vengeance.

The holism of the land ethic, more than any other feature, sets it apart from the predominant paradigm of modern moral philosophy. It is, therefore, the feature of the land ethic which requires the most patient theoretical analysis and the most sensitive practical interpretation.

VII

As Kenneth Goodpaster pointed out, mainstream modern ethical philosophy has taken egoism as its point of departure and reached a wider circle of moral entitlement by a process of generalization: I am sure that *I*, the enveloped ego, am intrinsically or inherently valuable and thus that *my* interests ought to be considered, taken into account, by "others" when their actions may substantively affect *me*. My own claim to moral consideration, according to the conventional wisdom, ultimately rests upon a psychological capacity—rationality or sentiency were the classical candidates of Kant and Bentham, respectively—which is arguably valuable in itself and which thus qualifies *me* for moral standing. However, then I am forced grudgingly to grant the same moral consideration I demand from others, on this basis, to those others who can also claim to possess the same general psychological characteristic.

A criterion of moral value and consideration is thus identified. Goodpaster convincingly argues that mainstream moral theory is based, when all the learned dust has settled, on this simple paradigm of ethical justification and logic exemplified by the Benthamic and Kantian prototypes. If the criterion of moral values and consideration is pitched low enough—as it is in Bentham's criterion of sentiency—a wide variety of animals are admitted to moral entitlement. If the criterion of moral value and consideration is pushed lower still—as it is in Albert Schweitzer's reverence-for-life ethic—all minimally conative things (plants as well as animals) would be extended moral considerability. The contemporary animal liberation/rights, and reverence-for-life/life-principle ethics are, at bottom, simply direct applications of the modern classical paradigm of moral argument. But this standard modern model of ethical theory provides no possibility whatever for the moral consideration of wholes—of threatened population of animals and plants, or of endemic, rare, or endangered species, or of biotic communities, or most expansively, of the biosphere in its totality—since wholes per se have no psychological experience of any kind. Because mainstream modern moral theory has been "psychocentric," it has been radically and intractably individualistic or "atomistic" in its fundamental theoretical orientation.

278

Hume, Smith, and Darwin diverged from the prevailing theoretical model by recognizing that altruism is as fundamental and autochthonous in human nature as is egoism. According to their analysis, moral value is not identified with a natural quality objectively present in morally considerable beings—as reason and/or sentiency is objectively present in people and/or animals—it is, as it were, projected by valuing subjects.

Hume and Darwin, furthermore, recognize inborn moral sentiments which have society as such as their natural object. Hume insists that "we must renounce the theory which accounts for every moral sentiment by the principle of self-love. We must adopt a more *publick affection* and allow that the *interests of society* are not, *even on their own account,* entirely indifferent to us." And Darwin, somewhat ironically (since "Darwinian evolution" very often means natural selection operating exclusively with respect to individuals), sometimes writes as if morality had no other object than the commonweal, the welfare of the community as a corporate entity:

We have now seen that actions are regardéd by savages, and were probably so regarded by primeval man, as good or bad, solely as they obviously affect the welfare of the tribe,—not that of the species, nor that of the individual member of the tribe. This conclusion agrees well with the belief that the so called moral sense is aboriginally derived from social instincts, for both relate at first exclusively to the community.

Theoretically then, the biotic community owns what Leopold, in the lead paragraph of "The Outlook," calls "value in the philosophical sense"—that is, direct moral considerability—because it is a newly discovered proper object of a specially evolved "publick affection" or "moral sense" which all psychologically normal human beings have inherited from a long line of ancestral social primates (p. 223).

VIII

In the land ethic, as in all earlier stages of social–ethical evolution, there exists a tension between the good of the community as a whole and the "rights" of its individual members considered severally. . . .

In any case, the conceptual foundations of the land ethic provide a well-informed, self-consistent theoretical basis for including both fellow members of the biotic community and the biotic community itself (considered as a corporate entity) within the purview of morals. The preemptive emphasis, however, on the welfare of the community as a whole, in Leopold's articulation of the land ethic, while certainly consistent with its Humean–Darwinian theoretical foundations, is not determined by them alone. The overriding holism of the land ethic results, rather, more from the way our moral sensibilities are informed by ecology.

IX

Ecological thought, historically, has tended to be holistic in outlook. Ecology is the study of the relationships of organisms to one another and to the elemental environment. These relationships bind the *relata*—plants, animals, soils, and waters—into a seamless fabric. The ontological primacy of objects and the ontological subordination of relationships characteristic of classical Western science is, in fact, reversed in ecology. Ecological relationships determine the nature of organisms rather than the other way around. A species is what it is because it has adapted to a niche in the ecosystem. The whole, the system itself, thus, literally and quite straightforwardly shapes and forms its component species.

Antedating Charles Elton's community model of ecology was F. E. Clements and S. A. Forbes's organism model. Plants and animals, soils and waters, according to this paradigm, are integrated into one superorganism. Species are, as it were, its organs; specimens its cells. Although Elton's community paradigm (later modified, as we shall see, by Arthur Tansley's ecosystem idea) is the principal and morally fertile ecological concept of "The Land Ethic," the more radically holistic superorganism paradigm of Clements and Forbes resonates in "The Land Ethic" as an audible overtone. In the peroration of "Land Health and the A-B Cleavage," for example, which immediately precedes "The Outlook," Leopold insists that

in all these cleavages, we see repeated the same basic paradoxes: man the conqueror *versus* man the biotic citizen; science the sharpener of his sword *versus* science the searchlight on his universe; land the slave and servant *versus* land the collective organism. (p. 223)

And on more than one occasion Leopold, in the latter quarter of "The Land Ethic," talks about the "health" and "disease" of the land—terms which are at once descriptive and normative and which, taken literally, characterize only organisms proper.

In an early essay, "Some Fundamentals of Conservation in the Southwest," Leopold speculatively flirted with the intensely holistic superorganism model of the environment as a paradigm pregnant with moral implications. . . .

Had Leopold retained this overall theoretical approach in "The Land Ethic," the land ethic would doubtless have enjoyed more critical attention from philosophers. The moral foundations of a land or, as he might then have called it, "earth" ethic would rest upon the hypothesis that the Earth is alive and ensouled—possessing inherent psychological characteristics, logically parallel to reason and sentiency. This notion of a conative whole earth could plausibly have served as a general criterion of intrinsic worth and moral considerability, in the familiar format of mainstream moral thought.

Part of the reason, therefore, that "The Land Ethic" emphasizes more and more the integrity, stability, and beauty of the environment as a whole, and less and less the biotic right of individual plants and animals to life, liberty, and the pursuit of happiness, is that the superorganism ecological paradigm invites one, much more than does the community paradigm, to hypostatize, to reify the whole, and to subordinate its individual members.

In any case, as we see, rereading "The Land Ethic" in light of "Some Fundamentals," the whole Earth organism image of nature is vestigially present in Leopold's later thinking. Leopold may have abandoned the "earth ethic" because ecology had abandoned the organism analogy in favor of the community analogy as a working theoretical paradigm. And the community model was more suitably given moral implications by the social/sentimental ethical natural history of Hume and Darwin.

Meanwhile, the biotic community ecological paradigm itself had acquired, by the late thirties and forties, a more holistic cast of its own. In 1935 British ecologist Arthur Tansley pointed out that from the perspective of physics the "currency" of the "economy of nature" is energy. Tansley suggested that Elton's qualitative and descriptive food chains, food webs, trophic niches, and biosocial professions could be quantitatively expressed by means of a thermodynamic flow model. It is Tansley's state-of-the-art thermodynamic paradigm of the environment that Leopold explicitly sets out as a "mental image of land" in relation to which "we can be ethical" (p. 214). And it is the ecosystemic model of land which informs the cardinal practical precepts of the land ethic.

"The Land Pyramid" is the pivotal section of "The Land Ethic"—the section which effects a complete transition from concern for "fellow-members" to the "community as such." It is also its longest and most technical section. A description of the "ecosystem" (Tansley's deliberately nonmetaphorical term) begins with the sun. Solar energy "flows through a circuit called the biota" (p. 215). It enters the biota through the leaves of green plants and courses through plant-eating animals, and then on to omnivores and carnivores. At last the tiny fraction of solar energy converted to biomass by green plants remaining in the corpse of a predator, animal feces, plant detritus, or other dead organic material is garnered by decomposers—worms, fungi, and bacteria. They recycle the participating elements and degrade into entropic equilibrium any remaining energy. According to this paradigm

land, then, is not merely soil; it is a fountain of energy flowing through a circuit of soils, plants, and animals. Food chains are the living channels which conduct energy upward; death and decay return it to the soil. The circuit is not closed; . . . but it is a sustained circuit, like a slowly augmented revolving fund of life. (p. 216)

In this exceedingly abstract (albeit poetically expressed) model of nature, process precedes substance and energy is more fundamental than matter. Individual plants and animals become less autonomous beings than ephemeral structures in a patterned flux of energy. According to Yale biophysicist Harold Morowitz,

viewed from the point of view of modern [ecology], each living thing . . . is a dissipative structure, that is it does not endure in and of itself but only as a result of the continual flow of energy in the system. An example might be instructive. Consider a vortex in a stream of flowing water. The vortex is a structure made of an ever-changing group of water molecules. It does not exist as an entity in the classical Western sense; it exists only because of the flow of water through the stream. In the same sense, the structures out of which biological entities are made are transient, unstable entities with constantly changing molecules, dependent on a constant flow of energy from food in order to maintain form and structure.

From this point of view the reality of individuals is problematic because they do not exist per se but only as local perturbations in this universal flow.

Though less bluntly stated and made more palatable by the unfailing charm of his prose, Leopold's proffered mental image of land is just as expansive, systemic, and distanced as Morowitz's. The maintenance of "the complex structure of the land and its smooth functioning as an energy unit" emerges in "The Land Pyramid" as the *summum bonum* of the land ethic (p. 216).

X

From this good Leopold derives several practical principles slightly less general, and therefore more substantive, than the summary moral maxim of the land ethic distilled in "The Outlook." "The trend of evolution [not its "goal," since evolution is ateleological] is to elaborate and diversify the biota" (p. 216). Hence, among our cardinal duties is the duty to preserve what species we can, especially those at the apex of the pyramid—the top carnivores. "In the beginning, the pyramid of life was low and squat; the food chains short and simple. Evolution has added layer after layer, link after link" (pp. 215–16). Human activities today, especially those like systematic deforestation in the tropics, resulting in abrupt massive extinctions of species, are in effect "devolutionary"; they flatten the biotic pyramid; they choke off some of the channels and gorge others (those which terminate in our own species).

The land ethic does not enshrine the ecological status quo and devalue the dynamic dimension of nature. Leopold explains that "evolution is a long series of self-induced changes, the net result of which has been to elaborate the flow mechanism and to lengthen the circuit. Evolutionary changes, however, are usually slow and local. Man's invention of tools has enabled him to make changes of unprecedented violence, rapidity, and scope" (pp. 216–17). "Natural" species extinction, that is, species extinction in the normal course of evolution, occurs when a species is replaced by competitive exclusion or evolves into another form. Normally speciation outpaces extinction. Mankind inherited a richer, more diverse world than had ever existed before in the 3.5 billion-year odyssey of life on Earth. What is wrong with anthropogenic species extirpation and extinction is the *rate* at which it is occurring and the *result:* biological impoverishment instead of enrichment.

Leopold goes on here to condemn, in terms of its impact on the eco-system, "the world-wide pooling of faunas and floras," that is, the indiscriminate introduction of exotic and domestic species and the dislocation of native and endemic species, mining the soil for its stored biotic energy, leading ultimately to diminished fertility and to erosion; and polluting and damming water courses (p. 217).

According to the land ethic, therefore: Thou shalt not extirpate or render species extinct; thou shalt exercise great caution in introducing exotic and domestic species into local exosystems, in exacting energy from the soil and releasing it into the biota, and in damming or polluting water courses; and thou shalt be especially solicitous of predatory birds and mammals. Here in brief are the express moral precepts of the land ethic. They are all explicitly informed—not to say derived—from the energy circuit model of the environment.

XI

The living channels—food chains—through which energy courses are composed of individual plants and animals. A central, stark fact lies at the heart of ecological processes: Energy, the currency of the economy nature, passes from one organism to another, not from hand to hand, like coined money, but, so to speak, from stomach to stomach. Eating *and being eaten,* living *and dying* are what make the biotic community hum.

The precepts of the land ethic, like those of all previous accretions, reflect and reinforce the structure of the community to which it is correlative. Trophic asymmetries constitute the kernel of the biotic community. It seems unjust, unfair. But that is how the economy of nature is organized (and has been for thousands of millions of years). The land ethic, thus, affirms as good, and strives to preserve, the very inequities in nature whose social counterparts in human communities are condemned as bad and would be eradicated by familiar social ethics, especially by the more recent Christian and secular egalitarian exemplars. A "right to life" for individual members is not consistent with the structure of the biotic community and hence is not mandated by the land ethic. This disparity between the land ethic and its more familiar social precedents contributes to the apparent devaluation of individual members of the biotic community and augments and reinforces the tendency of the land ethic, driven by the systemic vision of ecology, toward a more holistic or community-per-se orientation.

Of the few moral philosophers who have given the land ethic a moment's serious thought, most have regarded it with horror because of its emphasis on the good of the community and its deemphasis on the welfare of individual members of the community. Not only are other sentient creatures members of the biotic community and subordinate to its integrity, beauty, and stability; so are *we*. Thus, if it is not only morally permissible, from the point of view of the land ethic, but morally required, that members of certain species be abandoned to predation and other vicissitudes of wild life or even deliberately culled (as in the case of alert and sentient whitetail deer) for the sake of the integrity, stability, and beauty of the biotic community, how can we consistently exempt ourselves from a similar draconian regime? We too are only "plain members and citizens" of the biotic community. And our global population is growing unchecked. According to William Aiken, from the point of view of the land ethic, therefore, "massive human diebacks would be good. It is our duty to cause them. It is our species' duty, relative to the whole, to eliminate 90 percent of our numbers." Thus, according to Tom Regan, the land ethic is a clear case of "environmental fascism."

Of course Leopold never intended the land ethic to have either inhumane or antihumanitarian implications or consequences. But whether he intended them or not, a logically consistent deduction from the theoretical premises of the land ethic might force such untoward conclusions. And given their magnitude and monstrosity, these derivations would constitute a *reductio ad absurdum* of the whole land ethic enterprise and entrench and reinforce our current human chauvinism and moral alienation from nature. If this is what membership in the biotic community entails, then all but the most radical misanthropes would surely want to opt out.

XII

The land ethic, happily, implies neither inhumane nor inhuman consequences. That some philosophers think it must follows more from their own theoretical presuppositions than from the theoretical elements of the land ethic itself. Conventional modern ethical theory rests moral entitlement, as I earlier pointed out, on a criterion or qualification. If a candidate meets the criterion—rationality or sentiency are the most commonly posited—he, she, or it is entitled to equal moral standing with others who possess the same qualification in equal degree. Hence, reasoning in this philosophically orthodox way, and forcing Leopold's theory to conform: if human beings are, with other animals, plants, soils, and waters, equally members of the biotic community, and if community membership is the criterion of equal moral consideration, then not only do animals, plants, soils, and waters have equal (highly attenuated) "rights," but human beings are equally subject to the same subordination of individual welfare and rights in respect to the good of the community as a whole.

But the land ethic, as I have been at pains to point out, is heir to a line of moral analysis different from that institutionalized in contemporary moral philosophy. From the biosocial evolutionary analysis of ethics upon which Leopold builds the land ethic, it (the land ethic) neither replaces nor overrides previous accretions. Prior moral sensibilities and obligations attendant upon and correlative to prior strata of social involvement remain operative and preemptive.

Being citizens of the United States, or the United Kingdom, or the Soviet Union, or Venezuela, or some other nation-state, and therefore having national obligations and patriotic duties, does not mean that we are not also members of smaller communities or social groups—cities or townships, neighborhoods, and families—or that we are relieved of the peculiar moral responsibilities attendant upon and correlative to these memberships as well. Similarly, our recognition of the biotic community and our immersion in it does not imply that we do not also remain members of the human community—the "family of man" or "global village"—or that we are relieved of the attendant and correlative moral responsibilities of that membership, among them to respect universal human rights and uphold the principles of individual human worth and dignity. The biosocial development of morality does not grow in extent like an expanding balloon, leaving no trace of its previous boundaries, so much like the circumference of a tree. Each emergent, and larger, social unit is layered over the more primitive, and intimate, ones.

Moreover, *as a general rule,* the duties correlative in the inner social circles to which we belong *eclipse* these correlative to the rings farther from the heart-wood when conflicts arise. Consider our moral revulsion when zealous ideological nationalists encourage children to turn their parents in to the authorities if their parents dissent from the political or economic doctrines of the ruling party. A zealous environmentalist who advocated visiting war, famine, or pestilence on human populations (those existing somewhere else, of course) in the name of the integrity, beauty, and stability of the biotic community would be similarly perverse. Family obligations in general come before nationalistic duties and humanitarian obligations in general come before environmental duties. The land ethic, therefore, is not draconian or fascist. It does not cancel human morality. The land ethic may, however, as with any new accretion, demand choices which affect, in turn, the demands of the more interior social–ethical circles. Taxes and the military draft may conflict with family-level obligations. While the land ethic, certainly, does not cancel human morality, neither does it leave it unaffected.

Nor is the land ethic inhumane. Nonhuman fellow members of the biotic community have no "human rights," because they are not, by definition, members of the human community.

As fellow members of the biotic community, however, they deserve respect.

How exactly to express or manifest respect, while at the same time abandoning our fellow members of the biotic community to their several fates or even actively consuming them for our own needs (and wants), or deliberately making them casualties of wildlife management for ecological integrity, is a difficult and delicate question.

Fortunately, American Indian and other traditional patterns of human–nature interaction provide rich and detailed models. Algonkian woodland peoples, for instance, represented animals, plants, birds, waters, and minerals as other-than-human persons engaged in reciprocal, mutually beneficial socioeconomic intercourse with human beings. Tokens of payment, together with expressions of apology, were routinely offered to the beings whom it was necessary for these Indians to exploit. Care not to waste the usable parts and care in the disposal of unusable animal and plant remains were also an aspect of the respectful, albeit necessarily consumptive, Algonquian relationship with fellow members of the land community. As I have more fully argued elsewhere, the Algonquian portrayal of human–nature relationships is, indeed, although certainly different in specifics, identical in abstract form to that recommended by Leopold in the land ethic. . . . Is the land ethic prudential or deontological? Is the land ethic, in other words, a matter of enlightened (collective, human) self-interest, or does it genuinely admit nonhuman natural entities and nature as a whole to true moral standing?

The conceptual foundations of the land ethic, as I have here set them out, and much of Leopold's hortatory rhetoric, would certainly indicate that the land ethic is deontological (or duty oriented) rather than prudential. In the section significantly titled "The Ecological Conscience," Leopold complains that the then-current conservation philosophy is inadequate because "it defines no right or wrong, assigns no obligation, calls for no sacrifice, implies no change in the current philosophy of values. In respect of land-use, it urges *only* enlightened self-interest" (pp. 207–8, emphasis added). Clearly, Leopold himself thinks that the land ethic goes beyond prudence. In this section he disparages mere "self-interest" two more times, and concludes that "obligations have no meaning without conscience, and the problem we face is the extension of the social conscience from people to land" (p. 209).

In the next section, "Substitutes for a Land Ethic," he mentions rights twice—the "biotic right" of birds to continuance and the absence of a right on the part of human special interest to exterminate predators.

Finally, the first sentences of "The Outlook" read: "It is inconceivable to me that an ethical relation to land can exist without love, respect, and admiration for land, and a high regard for its value. By value, I of course mean something far broader than mere economic value; I mean value in the philosophical sense" (p. 223). By "value in the philosophical sense," Leopold can only mean what philosophers more technically call "intrinsic value" or "inherent worth." Something that has intrinsic value or inherent worth is valuable in and of itself, not because of what it can do for us. "Obligation," "sacrifice," "a conscience," "respect," the ascription of rights, and intrinsic value—all of these are consistently opposed to self-interest and seem to indicate decisively that the land ethic is of the deontological type.

Some philosophers, however, have seen it differently. Scott Lehmann, for example, writes,

Although Leopold claims for communities of plants and animals a "right to continued existence," his argument is homocentric, appealing to the human stake in preservation. Basically it is an argument from enlightened self-interest, where the self in question is not an individual human being but humanity—present and future—as a whole.

Lehmann's claim has some merits, even though it flies in the face of Leopold's express commitments. Leopold does frequently lapse into the language of (collective, long-range, human) self-interest. Early on, for example, he remarks, "in human history, we have learned (I hope) that the conqueror role is eventually *self*-defeating" (p. 204, emphasis added). And later, of the 95 percent of Wisconsin species which cannot be "sold, fed, eaten, or otherwise put to economic use," Leopold reminds us that "these creatures are members of the biotic community, and if (as I believe) its stability depends on its integrity, they are entitled to continuance" (p. 210). The implication is clear: the economic 5 percent cannot survive if a significant portion

of the uneconomic 95 percent are extirpated; nor may *we*, it goes without saying, survive without these "resources."

Leopold, in fact, seems to be consciously aware of this moral paradox. Consistent with the biosocial foundations of his theory, he expresses it in sociobiological terms:

An ethic may be regarded as a mode of guidance for meeting ecological situations so new or intricate, or involving such deferred reactions, that the path of social expediency is not discernible to the average individual. Animal instincts are modes of guidance for the individual in meeting such situations. Ethics are possibly a kind of community instinct in-the-making. (p. 203)

From an objective, descriptive sociobiological point of view, ethics evolve because they contribute to the inclusive fitness of their carriers (or, more reductively still, to the multiplication of their carriers' genes); they are expedient. However, the path to self-interest (or to the self-interest of the selfish gene) is not discernible to the participating individuals (nor, certainly, to their genes). Hence, ethics are grounded in instinctive feeling—love, sympathy, respect—not in self-conscious calculating intelligence. Somewhat like the paradox of hedonism—the notion that one cannot achieve happiness if one directly pursues happiness per se and not other things—one can only secure self-interest by putting the interests of others on a par with one's own (in this case long-range collective human self-interest and the interest of other forms of life and of the biotic community per se).

So, is the land ethic deontological or prudential, after all? It is both—self-consistently both—depending upon one's point of view. From the inside, from the lived, felt point of view of the community member with evolved moral sensibilities, it is deontological. It involves an affective–cognitive posture of genuine love, respect, admiration, obligation, self-sacrifice, conscience, duty, and the ascription of intrinsic value and biotic rights. From the outside, from the objective and analytic scientific point of view, it is prudential. "There is no other way for land to survive the impact of mechanized man," nor, therefore, for mechanized man to survive his own impact upon the land (p. viii).

1. Consider Callicott's explanation for the evolution of ethics. Does it seem plausible to you? Why or why not?
2. What does Callicott mean by claiming that the land ethic is based in sentiment? Could ethics be based in sentiment?
3. Is Callicott's defense of the land ethic against charges of environmental fascism adequate? Does adopting the land ethic require the elimination of most people?

William Baxter, "The Case for Optimal Pollution"

William Baxter, who died in 1998, was a widely respected law professor at Stanford University. As assistant attorney general during the Reagan administration, he was the architect of several important government antitrust measures, such as the breakup of AT&T in the early 1990s. Baxter takes a no-nonsense approach to environmental regulation. He is unapologetically anthropocentric, largely because, as he says, no other approach "corresponds to reality." According to Baxter, nature should be conceived as a means for human well-being; he thus argues for a level of pollution that maximizes our good. He acknowledges, however, that an optimal level of pollution might be different from what we think.

Critical Reading Questions

1. Why, according to Baxter, should we stop using DDT?
2. How does Baxter defend his anthropocentrism? (What are his six reasons?)
3. On what grounds does Baxter argue that nature has no normative connotations? (By normative connotations, Baxter means "moral." So Baxter is arguing that nature is without moral significance. How does he try to show this?)
4. What, according to Baxter, follows from abandoning a normative definition of "the natural state"?
5. What is the optimal state of pollution, according to Baxter?
6. How are the costs of pollution best expressed, according to Baxter?

THE CASE FOR OPTIMAL POLLUTION

William Baxter

I start with the modest proposition that, in dealing with pollution, or indeed with any problem, it is helpful to know what one is attempting to accomplish. Agreement on how and whether to pursue a particular objective, such as pollution control, is not possible unless some more general objective has been identified and stated with reasonable precision. We talk loosely of having clean air and clean water, of preserving our wilderness areas, and so forth. But none of these is a sufficiently general objective: Each is more accurately viewed as a means rather than as an end.

With regard to clean air, for example, one may ask, "how clean?" and "what does clean mean?" It is even reasonable to ask, "why have clean air?" Each of these questions is an implicit demand that a more general community goal be stated—a goal sufficiently general in its scope and enjoying sufficiently general assent among the community of actors that such "why" questions no longer seem admissible with respect to that goal.

If, for example, one states as a goal the proposition that "every person should be free to do whatever he wishes in contexts where his actions do not interfere with the interests of other human beings," the speaker is unlikely to be met with a response of "why." The goal may be criticized as uncertain in its implications or difficult to implement, but it is so basic a tenet of our civilization—it reflects a cultural value so broadly shared, at least in the abstract—that the question "why" is seen as impertinent or imponderable or both.

I do not mean to suggest that everyone would agree with the "spheres of freedom" objective just stated. Still less do I mean to suggest that a society could subscribe to four or five such general objectives that would be adequate in their coverage to serve as testing criteria by which all other disagreements might be measured. One difficulty in the attempt to construct such a list is that each new goal added will conflict, in certain applications, with each prior goal listed; and thus each goal serves as a limited qualification on prior goals.

Without any expectation of obtaining unanimous consent to them, let me set forth four goals that I generally use as ultimate testing criteria in attempting to frame solutions to problems of human organization. My position regarding pollution stems from these four criteria. If the criteria appeal to you and any part of what appears hereafter does not, our disagreement will have a helpful focus: which of us is correct, analytically, in supposing that his position on pollution would better serve these general goals. If the criteria do not seem acceptable to you, then it is to be expected that our more particular judgments will differ, and the task will then be yours to identify the basic set of criteria upon which your particular judgments rest.

My criteria are as follows:

1. The spheres of freedom criterion stated above.
2. Waste is a bad thing. The dominant feature of human existence is scarcity—our available resources, our aggregate labors, and our skill in employing both have always been, and will continue for some time to be, inadequate to yield to every man all the tangible and intangible satisfactions he would like

to have. Hence, none of those resources, or labors, or skills, should be wasted—that is, employed so as to yield less than they might yield in human satisfactions.

3. Every human being should be regarded as an end rather than as a means to be used for the betterment of another. Each should be afforded dignity and regarded as having an absolute claim to an evenhanded application of such rules as the community may adopt for its governance.

4. Both the incentive and the opportunity to improve his share of satisfactions should be preserved to every individual. Preservation of incentive is dictated by the "no-waste" criterion and enjoins against the continuous, totally egalitarian redistribution of satisfactions, or wealth; but subject to that constraint, everyone should receive, by continuous redistribution if necessary, some minimal share of aggregate wealth so as to avoid a level of privation from which the opportunity to improve his situation becomes illusory.

The relationship of these highly general goals to the more specific environmental issues at hand may not be readily apparent, and I am not yet ready to demonstrate their pervasive implications. But let me give one indication of their implications. Recently scientists have informed us that use of DDT in food production is causing damage to the penguin population. For the present purposes let us accept that assertion as an indisputable scientific fact. The scientific fact is often asserted as if the correct implication—that we must stop agricultural use of DDT—followed from the mere statement of the fact of penguin damage. But plainly it does not follow if my criteria are employed.

My criteria are oriented to people, not penguins. Damage to penguins, or sugar pines, or geological marvels is, without more, simply irrelevant. One must go further, by my criteria, and say: Penguins are important because people enjoy seeing them walk about rocks; and furthermore, the well-being of people would be less impaired by halting use of DDT than by giving up penguins. In short, my observations about environmental problems will be people-oriented, as are my criteria. I have no interest in preserving penguins for their own sake.

It may be said by way of objection to this position, that it is very selfish of people to act as if each person represented one unit of importance and nothing else was of any importance. It is undeniably selfish. Nevertheless I think it is the only tenable starting place for analysis for several reasons. First, no other position corresponds to the way most people really think and act—i.e., corresponds to reality.

Second, this attitude does not portend any massive destruction of nonhuman flora and fauna, for people depend on them in many obvious ways, and they will be preserved because and to the degree that humans do depend on them.

Third, what is good for humans is, in many respects, good for penguins and pine trees—clean air for example. So that humans are, in these respects, surrogates for plant and animal life.

Fourth, I do not know how we could administer any other system. Our decisions are either private or collective. Insofar as Mr. Jones is free to act privately, he may give such preferences as he wishes to other forms of life: He may feed birds in winter and do with less himself, and he may even decline to resist an advancing polar bear on the ground that the bear's appetite is more important than those portions of himself that the bear may choose to eat. In short my basic premise does not rule out private altruism to competing life-forms. It does rule out, however, Mr. Jones' inclination to feed Mr. Smith to the bear, however hungry the bear, however despicable Mr. Smith.

Insofar as we act collectively on the other hand, only humans can be afforded an opportunity to participate in the collective decisions. Penguins cannot vote now and are unlikely subjects for the franchise—pine trees more unlikely still. Again each individual is free to cast his vote so as to benefit sugar pines if that is his inclination. But many of the more extreme assertions that one hears from some conservationists amount to tacit assertions that they are specially appointed representatives of sugar pines, and hence that their preferences should be weighted more heavily than the preferences of other humans who do not enjoy equal rapport with "nature." The simplistic assertion that agricultural use of DDT must stop at once because it is harmful to penguins is of that type.

Fifth, if polar bears or pine trees or penguins, like men, are to be regarded as ends rather than means, if they are to count in our calculus of social organization, someone must tell me how much each one counts, and someone must tell me how these life-forms are to be permitted to express their preferences, for I do not know either answer. If the answer is that certain people are to hold their proxies, then I want to know how those proxy-holders are to be selected: self-appointment does not seem workable to me.

Sixth, and by way of summary of all the foregoing, let me point out that the set of environmental issues under discussion—although they raise very complex technical questions of how to achieve any objective—ultimately raise a normative question: what *ought* we to do? Questions of *ought* are unique to the human mind and world—they are meaningless as applied to a nonhuman situation.

I reject the proposition that we *ought* to respect the "balance of nature" or to "preserve the environment" unless the reason for doing so, express or implied, is the benefit of man.

I reject the idea that there is a "right" or "morally correct" state of nature to which we should return. The word "nature" has no normative connotation. Was it "right" or "wrong" for the earth's crust to heave in contortion and create mountains and seas? Was it "right" for the first amphibian to crawl up out of the primordial ooze? Was it "wrong" for plants to reproduce themselves and alter the atmospheric composition in favor of oxygen? For animals to alter the atmosphere in favor of carbon dioxide both by breathing oxygen and eating plants? No answers can be given to these questions because they are meaningless questions.

All this may seem obvious to the point of being tedious, but much of the present controversy over environment and pollution rests on tacit normative assumptions about just such nonnormative phenomena: that it is "wrong" to impair penguins with DDT, but not to slaughter cattle for prime rib roasts. That it is wrong to kill stands of sugar pines with industrial fumes, but not to cut sugar pines and build housing for the poor. Every man is entitled to his own preferred definition of Walden Pond, but there is no definition that has any moral superiority over another, except by reference to the selfish needs of the human race.

From the fact that there is no normative definition of the natural state, it follows that there is no normative definition of clean air or pure water—hence no definition of polluted air—or of pollution—except by reference to the needs of man. The "right" composition of the atmosphere is one which has some dust in it and some lead in it and some hydrogen sulfide in it—just those amounts that attend a sensibly organized society thoughtfully and knowledgeably pursuing the greatest possible satisfaction for its human members.

The first and most fundamental step toward solution of our environmental problems is a clear recognition that our objective is not pure air or water but rather some optimal state of pollution. That step immediately suggests the question: How do we define and attain the level of pollution that will yield the maximum possible amount of human satisfaction?

Low levels of pollution contribute to human satisfaction but so do food and shelter and education and music. To attain ever lower levels of pollution, we must pay the cost of having less of these other things. I contrast that view of the cost of pollution control with the more popular statement that pollution control will "cost" very large numbers of dollars. The popular statement is true in some senses, false in others; sorting out the true and false senses is of some importance. The first step in that sorting process is to achieve a clear understanding of the difference between dollars and resources. Resources are the wealth of our nation; dollars are merely claim checks upon those resources. Resources are of vital importance; dollars are comparatively trivial.

Four categories of resources are sufficient for our purposes: At any given time a nation, or a planet if you prefer, has a stock of labor, of technological skill, of capital goods, and of natural resources (such as mineral deposits, timber, water, land, etc.). These resources can be used in various combinations to yield goods and services of all kinds—in some limited quantity. The quantity will be larger if they are combined efficiently, smaller if combined inefficiently. But in either event the resource stock is limited, the goods and services that they can be made to yield are limited; even the most efficient use of them will yield less than our population, in the aggregate, would like to have.

If one considers building a new dam, it is appropriate to say that it will be costly in the sense that it will require x hours of labor, y tons of steel and concrete, and z amount of capital goods. If these resources are devoted to the dam, then they cannot be used to build hospitals, fishing rods, schools, or electric can openers. That is the meaningful sense in which the dam is costly.

Quite apart from the very important question of how wisely we can combine our resources to produce goods and services is the very different question of how they get distributed—who gets how many goods? Dollars constitute the claim checks which are distributed among people and which control their share of national output. Dollars are nearly valueless pieces of paper except to the extent that they do represent claim checks to some fraction of the output of goods and services. Viewed as claim checks, all the dollars outstanding during any period of time are worth, in the aggregate, the goods and services that are available to be claimed with them during that period—neither more nor less.

It is far easier to increase the supply of dollars than to increase the production of goods and services—printing dollars is easy. But printing more dollars doesn't help because each dollar then simply becomes a claim to fewer goods, i.e., becomes worth less.

The point is this: Many people fall into error upon hearing the statement that the decision to build a dam, or to clean up a river, will cost $X million. It is regrettably easy to say: "It's only money. This is a wealthy country, and we have lots of money." But you cannot build a dam or clean a river with $X million—unless you also have a match, you can't even make a fire. One builds a dam or cleans a river by diverting labor and steel and trucks and factories from making one kind of goods to making another. The cost in dollars is merely a shorthand way of describing the extent of the diversion necessary. If we build a dam for $X million, then we must recognize that we will have $X million less housing and food and medical care and electric can openers as a result.

Similarly, the costs of controlling pollution are best expressed in terms of the other goods we will have to give up to do the job. This is not to say the job should not be done. Badly as we need more housing, more medical care, and more can openers, and more symphony orchestras, we could do with somewhat less of them, in my judgment at least, in exchange for somewhat cleaner air and rivers. But that is the nature of the trade-off, and analysis of the problem is advanced if that unpleasant reality is kept in mind. Once the trade-off relationship is clearly perceived, it is possible to state in a very general way what the optimal level of pollution is. I would state it as follows:

People enjoy watching penguins. They enjoy relatively clean air and smog-free vistas. Their health is improved by relatively clean water and air. Each of these benefits is a type of good or service. As a society we would be well advised to give up one washing machine if the resources that would have gone into that washing machine can yield greater human satisfaction when diverted into pollution control. We should give up one hospital if the resources hereby freed would yield more human satisfaction when devoted to elimination of noise in our cities. And so on, trade-off by trade-off, we should divert our productive capacities from the production of existing goods and services to the production of a cleaner, quieter, more pastoral nation up to—and no further than—the point at which we value more highly the next washing machine or hospital that we would have to do without than we value the next unit of environmental improvement that the diverted resources would create.

Now this proposition seems to me unassailable but so general and abstract as to be unhelpful—at least unadministerable in the form stated. It assumes we can measure in some way the incremental units of human satisfaction yielded by very different types of goods. The proposition must remain a pious abstraction until I can explain how this measurement process can occur . . .

But I insist that the proposition stated describes the result for which we should be striving—and again, that it is always useful to know what your target is even if your weapons are too crude to score a bull's-eye.

Discussion Questions

1. Do you think Baxter has shown that anthropocentrism is justified?
2. Is there a moral difference between human beings polluting the atmosphere with, say, sulfur dioxide and a similar amount being released into the atmosphere by a volcano? What would Baxter say?
3. What is pollution?
4. Do you agree with Baxter's claim that the natural world has no moral significance?
5. Does Baxter's view portend the destruction of nature, or is his view compatible with enlightened anthropocentrism?

CHAPTER 16

Global Ethics

HARD QUESTION: AM I RESPONSIBLE FOR WORLD POVERTY?

Raw data about global inequity in income and the life prospects of those mired in poverty are hard to comprehend. Half the world—roughly 3 billion people—live on less than two dollars per day. The world's 3 richest people have more money than the gross domestic product of the poorest 48 nations (about a quarter of the world's countries). About half of the world's children live in poverty. In 2003, 10.6 million children died before they turned 5. Some 44 percent of the world's population consumes only 1.3 percent of the global product, whereas the wealthy countries, with only 955 million people (out of the world's 6.3 billion), consume about 81 percent of the global product. Nearly 1 billion people entered the twenty-first century unable to read or sign their name. Information about world poverty is widely available online and throughout the media but is seemingly ignored. In some ill-defined sense, we are all aware of global poverty; we know that it exists and we know that it is bad, but it persists. Are we addressing it?

According to the United Nations, if the world's wealthy counties managed to donate just 0.7 percent of their national income, this would eliminate world poverty. But we cannot achieve even that modest amount of aid. The United States gives about 0.01 percent, the lowest among developed nations. With a few exceptions, such as Norway, Sweden, and Denmark, most other developed nations still fall well short of giving the UN's target of seven-tenths of 1 percent of their national income to eliminate world poverty.

Are we in the affluent world morally obligated to donate money to help those in need? If donations would do no good or make the problem worse, then we could not be obligated to donate money because it would not help. But is this the case? Let us assume that professionals who study world poverty understand how to address it and that donated money would be effectively used to bring safe water, basic health care, minimal nutrition, adequate housing, rudimentary education, and a more dignified life for the vast majority of those targeted by the aid. As in any massive undertaking, there is bound to be some inefficiency, corruption, and abuse. But let us assume that these problems are minimized. Under these conditions, ought we to donate money to relief agencies?

When it is put like this, most people in the affluent world would agree that they ought to donate at least something. If there are relief agencies willing and able to channel our money effectively to assist those most in need around the world, then what excuse would we have not to give? Very little. Perhaps we think that the problem is already being adequately addressed through government aid or that world poverty is not as bad as portrayed or that whatever we give will not help or that those in need are somehow responsible for their sad plight. Each of these reasons for not donating requires close scrutiny, but in the end it will be hard to maintain that we have no obligations to the needy of the world. If these reasons not to donate are valid, perhaps our obligations are not as extensive as some maintain, or maybe our obligations are to one kind of aid rather than another—to support birth control and women's education instead of direct food aid, for example. But aid in some form remains an obligation on the assumption that we can help those in need. If we can help, it seems we ought to help.

How much should we give? This is a matter of debate, but when we contemplate all our luxuries (our many vehicles, big houses, expensive vacations, stylish clothes, exotic foods, consumer items, and frivolous forms of entertainment focused on self-gratification), then it is clear that we could give much more than we do without sacrificing anything of comparable moral significance—comparable, that is, to the lives of the impoverished whose well-being could be improved. Certainly, if the tables were turned and we found ourselves living in the sort of poverty that much of the world endures, poverty that could be eliminated if the wealthy gave just a tiny fraction of their wealth, we would find their lack of aid morally incomprehensible.

This much seems clear: Under the conditions of ordinary middle-class life, it is wrong not to contribute at all to alleviate world poverty, since we cannot sensibly argue that our general way of life is justified in the face of such overwhelming suffering and our ability to do something about it. After working through some modest calculations, Peter Singer observed in his recent book *One World* (see Singer's biographical note in Chapter 14) that "a 1 percent donation of annual income to overcome world poverty is the minimum that one must do to lead a morally decent life. To give that amount requires no moral heroics. To fail to give shows indifference to the indefinite continuation of dire poverty and avoidable, poverty-related deaths."

This means that contributing aid to assist the world's poor is not charity; it is instead a moral obligation. The difference is between something that it is good if you do it, but not wrong if you do not, and something that it is wrong not to do. If contributing to the world's needy is an obligation, then you deserve no praise for contributing, since you act as you ought. Rather, you should be morally condemned for not contributing, for you will have failed to meet your obligations. International relief agencies understandably cultivate the impression that you deserve praise for assisting; you are thanked and made to feel good when you contribute. But if donating is an obligation, then this is the wrong attitude for relief organizations to adopt and for you to expect from them. In fact, since they make it easy for you to fulfill your moral obligations, the appreciation should flow in the other direction!

There is another way to think about our obligations to the impoverished of the world: What if we are causally responsible for their suffering? This may seem preposterous at first, but consider: the demeaning legacy of colonialism is as discernible today internationally as are the lingering and now structural effects of slavery in our own country. Patterns of exploitation and dependency are not magically erased by the political decision of a colonial power to vacate a former colony. A radically transformed culture is left behind, one that is rarely better for having been colonized. Political independence hardly translates into social or economic independence; former colonies—many of them poor and undeveloped—remain tethered to the affluent world by their cash crops, cheap labor, natural resources, and corrupt leaders who exploit their own countries as ruthlessly as any colonial power. And we benefit from these gross inequalities and patterns of dependency that now structure international relations. We depend on cheap raw materials from around the world to maintain our extravagant way of life; we import oil, gold, food, clothing, minerals, lumber, and manufactured goods of all kinds. How are these things procured in their places of origin? And what unsavory governments do we support in order to maintain our access to them?

Remember, we are not dealing just with other developed nations like ourselves under conditions of fair trade among the economically sophisticated. The causal history of a particular shirt, gallon of gas, teak chair, computer chip, banana, or wedding ring could not be told without mentioning the legions of repressive, incompetent, or corrupt leaders and government officials in many of the countries where we negotiate lopsided trade agreements and shower money on those who enable us to procure raw materials. Our purchases support tyrants who, in turn, maintain brutal internal security forces and equip their armies as they oversee or otherwise make possible the selling of their country's natural resources or productive capacities, thereby enriching themselves and consolidating their power. Very little if any of the money they receive from us (via multinational corporations or local companies that supply raw materials or finished goods for the affluent world) is used to alleviate poverty in the countries from which we obtain so much of what we consume.

This is a far darker story concerning our way of life. It is not just that we have so much while the impoverished have so little; rather, it is an account of how our having so much *causes* others to have so little. It is an account of how our way of life actually inflicts the harm of poverty on others. And if we are causally responsible for the harm of impoverishment, then our obligation to help the needy has a different foundation altogether. It is based on justice, not compassion or our general obligation to lessen the suffering of others. If this darker story is substantially true, then at a minimum we should stop the harm we cause, since it is wrong knowingly to inflict undeserved harm on people. We would be obligated to help the impoverished because of the harm we have imposed on them. It seems, then, that to the extent that the darker story is true, ordinary life in the affluent world is more costly than we might care to imagine.

MORALITY AND GLOBALIZATION

In 1848, Karl Marx wrote presciently about globalization in the *Communist Manifesto*:

> The need of a constantly expanding market for its products chases the bourgeois over the whole surface of the globe. It must nestle everywhere, settle everywhere, establish connections everywhere. The bourgeois has through its exploitation of the world market given a cosmopolitan character to production and consumption in every country. To the great chagrin of reactionaries, it has drawn from under the feet of industry the national ground on which it stood. All old-established national industries have been destroyed or are daily being destroyed. They are dislodged by new industries whose introduction becomes a life and death question for all civilized nations; by industries that no longer work up indigenous raw material, but raw material drawn from the remotest zones; industries whose products are consumed, not only at home, but in every quarter of the globe. In place of the old wants, satisfied by the production of the country, we find new wants, requiring for their satisfaction the products of distant lands and climes. In place of the old local and national seclusion and self-sufficiency, we have intercourse in every direction, universal inter-dependence of nations. . . . The bourgeois, by the rapid improvement of all instruments of production, by the immensely facilitated means of communication, draws all nations, even the most barbarian, into civilization. The cheap prices of its commodities are the heavy artillery with which it batters down all Chinese walls, with which it forces the barbarians' intensely obstinate hatred of foreigners to capitulate. It compels them to introduce what it calls civilization into their midst, i.e., to become bourgeois like themselves. In a word, it creates a world after its own image.

In *Globalization: A Very Short Introduction*, Manfred Steger describes globalization as a process that brings about a state he calls "globality." Globality is "characterized by the existence of global economic, political, cultural, and environmental interconnections and flows that make many of the currently existing borders and boundaries irrelevant." Let us consider some of the ways in which globalization brings about globality.

The World Trade Organization is perhaps the most visible force for economic globalization. The WTO claims that its "overriding purpose is to help trade flow as freely as possible—so long as there are no undesirable side-effects—because this is important for economic development and well-being." (A visit to the WTO website is instructive.) The WTO helps trade flow freely by seeking to open markets among member states and by settling trade disputes. It is not clear how to interpret the qualification "so long as there are no undesirable side-effects." Negative side-effects of free trade (trade where national boundaries are largely irrelevant) is the key question for globalized economics. Among the possible negative side-effects of free trade is its effect on the world's poor. Does free trade help them, or do the benefits accrue mainly to the developed nations?

Apologists for free markets claim that a "rising tide raises all the boats," but whether this is true is a deeply contested matter. And what kinds of side-effects is the WTO prepared to count as "undesirable"? What about loss of indigenous cultures, the end of local sustainable agriculture, or damage to the environment? To what extent, in other words, does the WTO consider non-economic values in its calculation of undesirable side-effects of free trade?

Globalization might not make political boundaries completely irrelevant, but it weakens national sovereignty because trade arrangements with others reduce political authority at home. Political leaders are bound by trade agreements. Multinational corporations and international non-governmental agencies (NGOs) such as Oxfam International, Amnesty International, and Greenpeace also reduce national sovereignty. By focusing worldwide attention on the activities in a particular country, NGOs can influence political events there.

Culturally, one worry is that a globalized world will be blandly uniform—McDonald's restaurants everywhere, all serving up the same insipid, unhealthful food; fashion and other cultural norms determined by Western media (read: Hollywood); a world where local variations in food, music, entertainment, art, and all other aspects of local culture struggle against the leveling effects of powerful outside influences. Languages are among the most varied and richest aspects of culture. Will linguistic variations also slowly disappear in a globalized world?

English dominates science, commerce, and transportation around the world, but this is not the English of great poetry and literary sophistication. Rather, it is a flat, simplistic form of English that facilitates communication called "globish." A 2006 *New York Times* article compared a Globish Gettysburg Address to its eloquent original. See what you make of the two versions below.

Original

> Fourscore and seven years ago our fathers brought forth on this continent a new nation, conceived in liberty and dedicated to the proposition that all men are created equal. Now we are engaged in a great civil war, testing whether that nation or any nation so conceived and so dedicated can long endure. We are met on a great battlefield of that war. We have come to dedicate a portion of that field as a final resting place for those who here gave their lives that that nation might live. It is altogether fitting and proper that we should do this. . . .

Globish

> Eighty-seven years ago our fathers brought to this land a new nation, formed in liberty and committed to the proposition that all men are created equal. Now we are involved in a great civil war, testing whether that nation or any nation so born and so committed can long live. We are met on a great battlefield of that war. We have come to give a small piece of that field as a final resting place for those who here gave their lives that that nation might live. It is completely fitting and right that we should do this. . . .

The Globish Gettysburg Address gets the point across, but it is uninspired. This is the worry that many people have about the effects of globalization on all aspects of culture, not just language. Flat, one-dimensional language might be symptomatic of a larger enervation of human creativity and cultural sophistication.

Finally, the environment. A globalized world must deal with globalized environmental problems. Environmental degradation from globalization is one of the starkest problems we face. Polluted air and water do not respect national boundaries, as global warming makes clear. To make matters worse, those who will suffer the most from global warming had the least to do with creating it. People in the wealthy industrialized world can take steps to mitigate its worst effects, such as investing in dykes and levies, and using more energy to cool their homes and irrigate crops. By contrast, the poor of the world will suffer to a far greater extent from changing weather patterns and disruptions in their way of life.

Global climate change is a real phenomenon caused by human activity, so it is something for which we can bear responsibility. (That we are the cause has been incontrovertibly established by the IPCC—the Intergovernmental Panel on Climate Change—which received the 2007 Nobel Prize for peace along with Al Gore.) Clearly, humanity must do something about this problem, but international discussion is thwarted by an inability to figure out what would count as a fair distribution of responsibility. Thus questions about atmospheric emissions become a matter for moral philosophy.

When thinking about fairness, we can appeal to principles that look backward or to principles that look forward. The most obvious backward-looking principle of fairness says that whoever broke something should fix it. Because the developed countries of the world "broke" the atmosphere by emitting disproportionate amounts of carbon dioxide and other pollutants, it seems that they should bear the brunt of fixing it. This is politically and economically unrealistic to expect. However an obvious forward-looking principle of fairness is equality; each person has a right to an equal share of the atmosphere to use as an emissions waste "sink." Scientific calculation could determine how much total CO_2 the atmosphere can safely accommodate from human activity; dividing that by the number of people in the world would yield an equal per capita amount of CO_2 emissions. Many refinements will have to be made (What about population growth? What about emissions trading?), but the fundamental fairness of the equal per capita solution to CO_2 emissions is its most salient feature.

READINGS ON GLOBAL ETHICS

Peter Singer, from *One World*

See Singer's biographical note in Chapter 14. One World *is Singer's recent contribution to a fast-growing and vitally important area of practical moral philosophy called global ethics. In global ethics we examine the moral aspects of topics that are global in scope, such as human rights, world poverty, war and humanitarian intervention, global environmental issues, and the global economy. As we find ourselves increasingly interconnected worldwide, the myriad moral questions of globalization press ever more urgently upon us.*

Reprinted here is a section from One World *wherein Singer examines four charges that critics level against the World Trade Organization: The WTO places economic values over all others, the WTO erodes national sovereignty, the WTO is undemocratic, and the WTO benefits primarily the rich. Singer finds the first three charges accurate, but the accuracy of the most important fourth charge has not been demonstrated.*

Critical Reading Questions

1. According to Singer, why is it important to distinguish between inequality and whether the poor have become worse off from trade liberalization?
2. What is absolute poverty?
3. Is there a causal link between poverty and economic globalization, according to Singer?
4. In what ways does Singer think the WTO can do a better job managing economic globalization?
5. How should we understand political legitimacy, according to Singer? In his view, what is the relationship between political legitimacy and trade?

ONE WORLD

Peter Singer

TAKING FROM THE POOR TO GIVE TO THE RICH

Against the charge that the WTO is a kind of Robin Hood in reverse, President George W. Bush echoed the line taken by most advocates of global free trade when he said in a speech at the World Bank: "Those who protest free trade are no friends of the poor. Those who protest free trade seek to deny them their best hope for escaping poverty."[29] How much truth is there in the claim that free trade, as promoted by the WTO, has helped the world's poorest people?

Although the WTO's critics all agree that the trade body has done more to help huge global corporations than to help the poor, the facts are not easy to sort out, and on some aspects of this question, leading opponents of the WTO do not speak with one voice. Within the covers of a single volume published by the International Forum on Globalization, Walden Bello and Vandana Shiva, based respectively in Thailand and India, say that the rich nations do not offer a level playing field to the poor nations, and so free trade does not benefit the South, while Anuradha Mittal, of the U.S. group Food First, tries to arouse the opposition of Americans to free trade by showing that free trade between the United States, Mexico, and Canada has caused hundreds of thousands of U.S. jobs to shift to Mexico and Canada.[30] Since Mexico is a much poorer country than the United States, any transfer of work from the United States to Mexico can be expected to raise the income of people who are, on average, much less well off than those U.S. workers who lose their jobs. Those who favor reducing poverty globally, rather than only in their own country, should see this as a good thing.

Another relevant question is whether free trade means cheaper goods, and whether this is good for the poor. Vandana Shiva, one of the best-known WTO opponents from one of the less developed countries, writes that the liberalization of trade in India means that more food is exported, and as a result "food prices have doubled and the poor have had to cut their consumption in half." To anyone familiar with poverty in India *before* trade liberalization, it is difficult to believe that India's poor would be able to survive at all if they had to cut their food consumption in half, so such claims may well provoke skepticism. That skepticism is not allayed when one reads, on the very next page, that Indian farmers have lost markets and mills have had to close, because "cheap, subsidized imports of soybeans are dumped on the Indian market . . . thus worsening the country's balance of payments situation."[31] If the lowering of trade barriers has meant that soybeans are now cheaper than they were before, it is strange that this same lowering of trade barriers should have caused food prices as a whole to double. Moreover the large quantities of food that Shiva claims are exported because of trade liberalization should have improved the country's balance of payments. There may be an explanation of such apparently conflicting claims, but if there is, Shiva does not offer it.

In trying to assess the impact of recent trade reforms, it is useful to distinguish two questions:

- Has *inequality* increased during the period of global economic liberalization?
- Have the poor become worse off?

The questions are distinct, because it would be possible for the situation of the poor to improve, in absolute terms—they might eat better, have safer water and greater access to education and health care, and so on—while the situation of the rich improves even more, so that the absolute dollar gap in income and wealth between the rich and the poor is greater than it was when the poor were worse off. (In what follows, unless otherwise specified, I will use "rich" and "poor" to refer to people on high and low incomes, respectively, rather than those with great or small assets. Of course, those with a high income often tend to have a lot of assets, and vice versa. But the correlation is not perfect.) We will also, of course, need to ask whether the changes that can be observed are the result of economic globalization, or merely happen to have coincided with it.

We can begin by describing the present state of poverty in the world. One commonly cited figure, derived from development reports issued by the World Bank and the United Nations, is that of a global population of more than 6 billion, about one-fifth, or 1.2 billion, live on less than $1 per day, and nearly half, or 2.8 billion, live on less than $2 per day. Awful as this sounds, these figures, quoted without further explanation, can be misleading—in the sense of giving the impression that the world's poorest people are not as impoverished as they really are. For we may think to ourselves: the purchasing power of one U.S. dollar in, say, Ethiopia, is vastly greater than the purchasing power of one U.S. dollar in New York. So perhaps these people, though poor, are not as desperately poor as we might imagine? In fact, the figures already take the difference in purchasing power into account. The World Bank's international poverty line—below which these 1.2 billion people fall—is defined as "$1.08 1993 PPP US$" per day, and "PPP" stands for "purchasing power parity." Hence the purchasing power of the daily income of someone right on the World

Bank's international poverty line is equivalent to what one could have purchased in the United States in 1993 for $1.08. Granted, there has been some inflation in the United States since 1993, so if we were to express this sum in terms of what can be purchased in the United States in 2000, the figure would rise to $1.28. If we are interested in the actual income of someone living on the poverty line in one of the world's poorest countries—how much their annual earnings would amount to, if they changed them into $US at prevailing exchange rates—we would have to divide this sum by about 4 to take into account the greater purchasing power of $US1 in these countries, as compared with market exchange rates. That yields an actual income of about 32 cents per day. And this figure, remember, is the poverty line itself, in other words, the *upper* bound of a fifth of the world's population. The *average* income of these 1.2 billion people is about 30 percent less, which makes it about 23 cents in U.S. currency at market exchange rates, or the purchasing power equivalent of 92 cents in U.S. currency in the year 2000.[32]

It is not surprising that of these 1.2 billion people, about 826 million lack adequate nutrition, more than 850 million are illiterate, and almost all lack access to even the most basic sanitation. In rich countries, less than one child in a hundred dies before the age of five; in the poorest countries, one in five does. That is 30,000 young children dying every day from preventable causes. Life expectancy in rich nations averages 77, whereas in sub-Saharan Africa it is 48.[33]

This is absolute poverty, which has been described as "a condition of life so characterized by malnutrition, illiteracy, disease, squalid surroundings, high infant mortality and low life expectancy as to be beneath any reasonable definition of human decency."[34] In contrast the average per capita income of the world's wealthiest nations (which contain less than 15 percent of the world's population) is $27,500. This 15 percent of the population divides among itself almost 80 percent of the wealth that the world produces, whereas the assets of the poorest 46 percent of the world's population amount to just 1.25 percent of the world's wealth.[35] The 1999 *Human Development Report* provided an oft-quoted symbol of the far extremities of inequality in the distribution of the world's wealth when it noted that the assets of the world's richest three individuals exceeded the combined Gross National Products of all of the least developed countries, with a population totaling 600 million people.[36]

It is commonly said that inequality between the world's richest and poorest countries has increased during the period in which world trade has increased. Even a 1999 study published by the WTO accepts this view, stating flatly: "It is an empirical fact that the income gap between poor and rich countries has increased in recent decades."[37] According to the widely quoted 1999 *Human Development Report,* in 1820 the fifth of the world's population living in the world's richest countries collectively received three times the combined income of the fifth of the world's population living in the poorest countries. A century later this ratio had increased to 11 to 1. By 1960 it was 30 to 1; by 1990, 60 to 1; and by 1997, 74 to 1.[38] These figures suggest not only an increasing gap between rich nations and poor nations, but an increasing rate of growth in this gap, which grew at an annual rate of 1.66 percent between 1820 and 1960, but between 1990 and 1997 grew at an annual rate of 3 percent.

The 1999 *Human Development Report* figures need to be treated with caution, however, because they are based on comparing incomes at market exchange rates. As we have seen, a given unit of currency may purchase four times as much in a poor country as it could purchase in a rich one, if converted at market exchange rates. When Arne Melchior, Kjetil Telle, and Henrik Wiig, investigating the impact of globalization on inequality for the Norwegian Ministry of Foreign Affairs, adjusted incomes for purchasing power they found that between the 1960s and 1997 there was a continuous decrease in the gap between the average income of the richest nations containing a third of the world's population and the average income of the poorest nations containing a third of the world's population. There was also a small but steady decrease in the gap between the average income of the richest countries containing a fifth of the world's population, and the average income in the poorest countries containing a fifth of the world's population. On the other hand there was an increase in the gap between the average income in the richest countries containing a tenth of the world's population and the poorest countries containing a tenth of the world's population. The reason for the difference between the different sets of comparisons is that in the last three decades the fastest-growing developing countries have not been among the very poorest. Average income in China has grown rapidly and this explains most of the reduction in inequality between the top and bottom thirds. The 2001 *Human Development Report* acknowledged that the Norwegian researchers had got it right, accepting the need to base international comparisons of living standards on purchasing power parity and reporting that on this basis, the ratio of the average income of the richest nations containing a fifth of the world's population to the average income of the poorest nations containing a fifth of the world's population had fallen between 1970 and 1997, from 15 to 1 to 13 to 1, although in the case of the richest 10 percent of nations and the poorest 10 percent of nations, the ratio had grown from 19 to 1 to 27 to 1.[39]

There is, however, a problem even with these figures. As the cumbersome language of the previous paragraph indicates, they compare the average income in rich nations with the average income in poor nations. They are not comparisons of the richest tenth, fifth, or third of the world's population with the poorest tenth, fifth, or third. Obviously, there are some poor people in rich nations, and a few very rich people in poor nations, and when we compare national averages, these intrastate differences could mask the real differences between the world's richest and poorest people. Ideally, we should look at individual household income, rather than national averages. Branko Milanovic, a researcher at the World Bank, has attempted to do this, but the data are much more difficult to obtain. He has compared individual household incomes for two years, 1988 and 1993, and found a sharp increase in inequality between the income of the richest fifth and the poorest fifth of the world's population during these five years.[40] The main reason his results differ from those of Melchior, Telle, and Wiig is that income in urban areas of countries like China and India has risen much faster than income in rural areas. Using national average incomes compresses these urban/rural differences into a single figure. On the other hand, a comparison between just two time-points is not enough to establish a clear trend.

To sum up, although we have quite good data on national per capita average income, that data—on which Melchior, Telle, and Wiig base their study—cannot give us the answer to the right question: Has global income inequality increased? Milanovic, on the other hand, asks the right question, but doesn't have enough data to answer it. As he himself puts it, on the basis of the research he has done so far:

It is impossible to aver whether inequality is really increasing or whether we see just a temporary spike, or indeed whether the change in the coefficients is statistically significant—bearing in mind numerous and serious data problems.[41]

What really matters? Suppose that the changes Melchior, Telle, and Wiig found hold good for individual incomes, as well as national average incomes. If we are concerned about inequality, should we be pleased to learn that the top and bottom thirds—67 percent of the world's population—have, on average, more equal incomes, if at the same time the top and bottom tenths, amounting to 20 percent of the world's population, have grown even further apart? Different people may have different intuitions about this, but from a broadly utilitarian point of view, these apparently baffling questions do not really raise anything of fundamental importance. Inequality is not significant in itself. It matters because of the impact it has on welfare. We could argue about whether we should be equally concerned with promoting the welfare of all members of society, or whether we should give some kind of priority to promoting the welfare of society's poorest members, but whatever we decide, what matters is people's welfare, and not the size of the gap between rich and poor. Sometimes greater inequality will mean a decrease in overall welfare. There is some evidence that inequality hampers economic growth.[42] Inequality can also undermine the self-esteem of those on the lower levels of society and make them feel worse off than they would be if they were living on the same income in a more egalitarian society. Sometimes, however, inequality does not

matter so greatly. For those who are desperately struggling to get enough to eat and to house and clothe their children, perhaps the need to keep up with one's neighbors is less significant than it is for those who have no difficulty in meeting their basic needs. For people near the bare minimum on which they can survive, a small addition to their income may make a large difference to their welfare, even if their neighbors' incomes grow by much more in dollar terms. So the more important issue about the opening up of world trade may be whether it has made the world's poor worse off than they would otherwise have been, not relative to the rich, but in absolute terms.

Have the poor really become worse off during the globalization era? On this question the 1997 *Human Development Report* struck a positive note, indicating that poverty has fallen more in the past fifty years than in the previous 500.[43] But the 1999 *Human Development Report* painted a much gloomier picture, showing that on a per capita basis, the Gross Domestic Product of the world's least-developed countries declined by more than 10 percent between 1990 and 1997, from $277 to $245 per annum. Most of these countries are in sub-Saharan Africa, and for that region in general, poverty appears to have increased in recent years, with per capita GDP falling during the same 1990–1997 period from an average per annum of $542 to $518.[44] The 2001 *Human Development Report* combines both the positive and the negative, balancing the 1 percent fall in the already low average incomes in sub-Saharan Africa over the period 1975 to 1999 with the overall rise—almost a doubling—of average incomes in developing countries during the same period. Melchior, Telle, and Wiig paint a similar picture, showing that the average income in the poorest nations containing one-fifth of the world's population more than doubled, when adjusted for purchasing power, between 1965 to 1998, rising from $US551 to $US1137; but in 16 of the world's poorest countries—12 of them in sub-Saharan Africa—average per capita income has fallen. Because of its population size, China's economic improvement plays an important part in the increase in average income in the developing countries.[45]

Income is only one indicator of well-being, and it is helpful to consider others. Life expectancy is obviously an important one. Between 1962 and 1997 average global life expectancy at birth increased from 55 to 66.6 years. Moreover the biggest gain in life expectancy has been in the developing nations, so there has also been a significant decrease in the inequality of life expectancy between nations. In 1960 the average life expectancy for developing countries was only 60 percent of that in the industrial nations. By 1993, it was 82 percent.[46] (But note that, as with income, these figures are national averages, which mask within-country differences that mean greater global differences between individuals.) Life expectancy rose sharply in all regions in the period up to 1987; subsequently it rose much more slowly in Africa, where AIDS has caused life expectancy to fall in some countries, and it has also fallen in Eastern Europe, reflecting the impact of increased poverty following the end of communism.

Food is the most basic need of all, and hence the extent to which people lack it is a crude but useful measure of deprivation. According to the Food and Agriculture Organization, the number of people who are undernourished fell from 960 million in 1969–1971 to 790 million in 1995–1997. This decrease may seem like very modest progress over a quarter of a century, but taking into account the growth in world population during this period, it means that the proportion of people who are undernourished has fallen from 37 percent to 18 percent.[47]

Each year the United Nations Development Program reports on each country's progress in terms of a composite measure called the Human Development Index, based on a combination of indicators for income, life expectancy, and education. The Human Development Index scores for the developing countries, and also for the least developed countries, considered separately, have risen consistently between 1960 and 1993, suggesting that the world's poorer people have become better off overall in terms of income, life expectancy, and the amount of education they receive.[48]

Globally, the World Bank estimates that the number of people living below the international poverty line has risen slightly since 1987.[49] But should the increase in absolute numbers be taken as a sign that poverty is getting worse, or the decrease in the proportion of the population

who are poor as a sign that things are improving? One could argue either way. Life below the poverty line is so lacking in the basic necessities for a decent life that it is a bad thing that anyone has to subsist in these conditions. Yet if human life, when some minimum requirements are satisfied, is a good thing—and it takes a serious pessimist to deny that—then we should be pleased that there are more human beings living above the poverty line, and the diminishing fraction of the total population forced to live below that line can be seen as a good thing. To go further into the choice between these differing value judgments would lead us into deep philosophical issues and take us far from the themes of this book, so here it will be enough merely to note that both views have something to be said for them. We can then move on to our final question: Is there a causal link between poverty and economic globalization?[50]

On theoretical grounds, as we have seen, there is some reason to believe that open markets and free trade should increase economic welfare as a whole. The theory finds some support in an Organization for Economic Cooperation and Development (OECD) study showing that when corporations go into foreign countries, they generally pay more than the national average wage.[51] But information about average wages does not alleviate concerns about poverty, as long as inequality is increasing. We have seen that whether global inequality has increased during the era of expanding world trade is still highly contentious. We don't have the household income data we would need to get a well-grounded answer. Since a correlation does not show a causal connection, even if we had all the data we needed on trends in global income distribution, and even if these data showed rising inequality and poverty, it would still be difficult to judge whether economic globalization has contributed to any increase that might have occurred in economic inequality and in the number of people living in poverty. Consider, as illustrating the difficulty of the problem, the following three expert opinions.

Peter Lindert and Jeffrey Williamson have studied the connection between inequality and globalization for the National Bureau of Economic Research, in Cambridge, Massachusetts. They are among those who accept that as the global economy has become more integrated over the past two centuries, so too economic inequality between nations has increased. In their view, however, globalization has not brought about this widening income gap. On the contrary, without globalization the rise in inequality would have been greater still. Their figures indicate that in Third World countries between 1973 and 1992, per capita Gross Domestic Product rose fastest in those countries strongly open to trade, rose more slowly in countries moderately open to trade, and actually fell in countries that were hostile to trade. They summarize their conclusion by saying that "world incomes would still be unequal under complete global integration, as they are in any large integrated national economy. But they would be less unequal in a fully integrated world economy than in one fully segmented."[52]

World Bank researchers Mattias Lundberg and Lyn Squire used a sample of 38 countries to assess the impact of openness to global trade on economic gains for different sections of the population. They found that globalization benefits the majority, but its burden falls on the poorest 40 percent, for whom openness leads to a fall in economic growth. They conclude: "At least in the short run, globalization appears to increase poverty and inequality."[53]

The Norwegian team of Melchior, Telle, and Wiig hold, as we have seen, that when measured in particular ways, income inequality has decreased during the era of more open world trade. But they do not think that the data permit one to conclude that globalization reduces inequality. It is difficult to disentangle the impact of technological change from the impact of globalization, as the two have occurred in tandem—and are indeed interrelated. There is some evidence that technological change increases inequality between highly skilled workers, who can make use of new technologies, and unskilled workers, whose labor the new technologies may make redundant. Political changes are also important. There is a clear connection between the collapse of communism and the decline in average income and even in life expectancy in much of Eastern Europe during the 1990s, and in some countries in sub-Saharan Africa the lack of a stable and effective government can make progress impossible.[54] (The disastrous situation

of the Congo, which by 2001 was probably the world's poorest nation, is in large part the outcome of prolonged conflict there.[55])

With so many different ways of assessing inequality, and so many different findings, what is the ordinary citizen to think? No evidence that I have found enables me to form a clear view about the overall impact of economic globalization on the poor. Most likely, it has helped some to escape poverty and thrown others deeper into it; but whether it has helped more people than it has harmed and whether it has caused more good to those it has helped than it has brought misery to those it has harmed is something that, without better data, we just cannot know.

Judgment

We have now considered the four charges commonly made against the WTO. We found that, first, the WTO does, through its use of the product/process rule and its very narrow interpretation of Article XX, place economic considerations ahead of concerns for other issues, such as environmental protection and animal welfare, that arise from how the product is made. If the human rights of the workers were violated in the process of making the product, this would presumably be treated in a similar manner, if a complaint were made. Second, while the WTO does not violate national sovereignty in any formal sense, the operations of the WTO do in practice reduce the scope of national sovereignty. The WTO's defense to this charge, that the governments of member-nations have voluntarily opted for this curtailment, is weakened by the surprising interpretation its Appellate Body has given to Article XX; but even if this were not the case, and the member-nations had fully understood how the treaty they were signing would operate, it would still be the case that WTO membership curtails national sovereignty in the sense that, in the real world, it is often hard to leave the WTO and as long as it remains a member, a country's power to make some important decisions is eroded. Third, the WTO is undemocratic both in theory and practice, firstly because a procedure requiring unanimous consent to any change is not a form of democracy, secondly because the dispute panels and the Appellate Body are not responsible to either the majority of members or the majority of the planet's adult population, and thirdly because the organization is disproportionately influenced by the major trading powers. On the fourth, and arguably most important charge against the WTO, however, that it makes the rich richer and the poor poorer, the verdict has to be: not proven. The available evidence is insufficient to convict either globalization or the WTO of the charge.

This assessment of the charges against the WTO is based on the organization's actions up to the time of the 2001 ministerial meeting at Doha, the first WTO ministerial meeting since the protests in Seattle. The declarations agreed to at that meeting display a new concern for the interests of developing countries, including the world's poorest countries, and a willingness to consider other values as a constraint on what had hitherto been the overriding value of free trade. It will be several years before we know whether these declarations were merely good public relations or a sign of a substantial change in the thinking of the WTO that will make a real difference.

Can Do Better?

In the *Communist Manifesto,* Karl Marx described the impact of the capitalist class in terms that might today be applied to the WTO:

It has resolved personal worth into exchange value, and in place of the numberless indefeasible chartered freedoms, has set up that single, unconscionable freedom—Free Trade. . . . All fixed, fast-frozen relations, with their train of ancient and venerable prejudices and opinions are swept away, all new-formed ones become antiquated before they can ossify. All that is solid melts into air, all that is holy is profaned.[56]

Defenders of the WTO would reject loaded words like "unconscionable" but might otherwise accept this account of what they are seeking to achieve. That free trade is a goal of overriding importance is implicit in the decisions of the WTO dispute panels. They would also agree that a global free market will sweep away "ancient and venerable prejudices" and they would see this as a good thing, because such prejudices restrict the use of individual creativity that brings benefits both to the innovative producer and to the consumers who can choose to take advantage of it.

Whether we accept or reject the claim that economic globalization is a good thing, we can still ask if there are ways of making it work better, or at least less badly. Even those who accept the general argument for the economic benefits of a global free market should ask themselves how well a global free market can work in the absence of any global authority to set minimum standards on issues like child labor, worker safety, the right to form a union, and environmental and animal welfare protection.

According to standard economic models, if various assumptions hold—including the assumptions that people always act fully rationally and on the basis of perfect information—free trade within a single, well-governed nation can be expected to create a state of affairs that is "Pareto efficient"—in other words, a state of affairs where no one's welfare can be improved without reducing the welfare of at least one other person. This is because the government will have legislated so that the private costs of production are brought into line with their costs to society overall. A corporation that pollutes a river into which it discharges wastes will be made to clean it up and to compensate those who have been harmed. Thus the costs of keeping the environment clean become part of the costs of production—in economic jargon, they are "internalized"—and producers who try to save money by not cleaning up their wastes gain no economic advantages over their competitors. But when we consider global free trade in the absence of any global authority to regulate pollution, or any civil law that provides remedies to the victims of pollution, the situation is different. A national government may have little interest in forcing a producer to internalize damage done to the global environment, for example to the oceans or the atmosphere or to stocks of cetaceans, fish, or migrating birds. Even though all nations share the global environment, the "tragedy of the commons" rules here, and a nation may benefit more by allowing its fishing fleet to catch as much as it can than by restraining the fleet so that the fleets of other nations can catch more. Thus, judged strictly in economic terms, without global environmental protection there is no reason to expect free trade to be Pareto efficient, let alone to maximize overall welfare.

Even if we ignore goods that belong to no nation, and focus on the quality of life in each nation, since governments are imperfect, unconstrained globalization is likely to lead to economic inefficiencies. If a ruling elite does not care about the working classes, or about the people of a particular region of its territory, it may not take into account the cost to them of air or water pollution, or for that matter of being forced to work long hours for little pay. Countries governed by such elites can then out-compete countries that provide some minimal conditions for their workers and, as Herman Daly puts it, "more of world production shifts to countries that do the poorest job of counting costs—a sure recipe for reducing the efficiency of global production."[57] The result is that the nexus between human welfare and the growth of the global economy, incomplete at the best of times, will be further eroded.

Significantly, the desirability of uniform global environmental and labor standards is a point on which critics of the WTO from the poorer countries often differ with labor and environmental activists from the rich countries. The fear is that the rich countries will use high standards to keep out goods from the poor countries. Vandana Shiva claims "social clauses make bed-fellows of Northern trade unions and their corporations to jointly police and undermine social movements in the South."[58] There is no doubt that this could happen, but what is the alternative? Various measures could be taken to give developing countries more time to adjust, but in the end, just as national laws and regulations were eventually seen as essential to prevent the inhuman harshness of nineteenth century laissez-faire capitalism in the industrialized nations, so instituting global standards is the only way to prevent an equally inhuman form of uncontrolled global capitalism. The WTO accepts this idea, at least in theory. At its 1996 Ministerial meeting in Singapore, the WTO ministers renewed an earlier commitment "to the observance of internationally recognized core labor standards" and affirmed its support for the International Labor Organization as the body to set these standards. In Doha in 2001 the ministers reaffirmed that declaration and noted the "work under way in the International Labor Organization (ILO) on the social dimension of globalization."[59] Unfortunately nothing concrete had happened in the five years between those statements.

The WTO has up to now been dominated by neoliberal economic thinking. With some signs that the WTO is willing to re-think this approach, it is possible to imagine a reformed WTO in which the overwhelming commitment to free trade is replaced by a commitment to more fundamental goals. The WTO could then become a tool for pursuing these objectives. There are even clauses in the GATT agreement that could become the basis for affirmative action in trade, designed to help the least developed nations. In article XXXVI (3) the contracting parties agree that there is a "need for positive efforts designed to ensure that less-developed contracting parties secure a share in the growth in international trade commensurate with the needs of their economic development."[60] Under the present WTO regime, such clauses have been nice-sounding words with no practical impact. Far from making positive efforts to help the less-developed nations, the rich nations, especially the United States and the European Union, have failed to do even their fair share of reducing their own trade barriers in those areas that would do most good for the less developed nations. As *The Economist*—usually an avid supporter of the WTO—has reported, "Rich countries cut their tariffs by less in the Uruguay Round than poor ones did. Since then they have found new ways to close their markets."[61] The *New York Times* has said that several protectionist measures in the richest countries "mock those countries' rhetorical support for free trade."[62] Rich countries impose tariffs on manufactured goods from poor countries that are, according to one study, four times as high as those they impose on imports from other rich countries.[63] The WTO itself has pointed out that the rich nations subsidize their agricultural producers at a rate of $1 billion a day, or more than six times the level of development aid they give to poor nations.[64]

As we have already noted, there were signs at the November 2001 WTO meeting that the criticisms of the WTO are having some effect. If the WTO begins to take seriously GATT articles like XXXVI (3), we could in time come to see the WTO as a platform from which a policy of laissez-faire in global trade could be replaced by a more democratically controlled system of regulation that promotes minimum standards for environmental protection, worker safety, union rights, and animal welfare. But if the WTO cannot respond to these influences, it would be best for its scope to be curtailed by a body willing to take on the challenges of setting global environmental and social standards and finding ways of making them stick.

Trade, Legitimacy, and Democracy

We tend to think of trade as something politically neutral. In trading with a country, governments do not think that they are taking an ethical stand. They often trade with countries while disapproving of their regimes. In extreme cases, this neutrality breaks down. Many corporations and some governments recognized that doing business with South Africa under apartheid raised serious moral questions. Normally, however, governments keep the question of whether they should trade with a country separate from the question of whether they approve of its government. The United States has attacked China for its human rights record while at the same time expanding its trade with China. But sometimes trading with a country implies an ethical judgment. Many trade deals are done with governments. This is especially likely to be the case when transnational corporations make arrangements with the governments of developing countries to explore for oil and minerals, to cut timber, to fish, or to build big hotels and develop tourist complexes. Nigeria, for example, gets more than $6 billion a year, or about a quarter of its Gross Domestic Product, from selling oil. When multinational corporations like Shell trade with governments like those that Nigeria has had for most of the past thirty years—that is, military dictatorships—they are implicitly accepting the government's right to sell the resources that lie within its borders. What gives a government the moral right to sell the resources of the country over which it rules?[65]

The same question can be asked about international borrowing privileges. Corrupt dictators are allowed to borrow money from foreign countries or international lending bodies, and if they should happen to be overthrown, then the next government is seen as obliged by the signature of its predecessor to repay the loan. Should it refuse to do so, it will be excluded from international financial institutions and suffer adverse consequences. No questions are asked by the lenders about whether this or that dictator is entitled to borrow in the name of his or her country. Effective control of a territory is seen as being enough to obviate any inquiry into how that person came by that degree of control.

Both the conventional moral view, and the view taken in international law, is that once a government is recognized as legitimate, that legitimacy automatically confers the right to trade in the country's resources. The plausibility of this answer rests in the assertion that the government that is doing the trading is "legitimate." That sounds like a term that expresses an ethical judgment about the right of the government to hold power. If this were so, then the answer to the challenge to the government's right to trade in the country's resources would be: a government that satisfies certain ethical standards regarding its claim to rule has the right to trade in the resources of the country over which it rules. But in fact that is not what is usually meant by calling a government "legitimate." The standard view has long been that the recognition of a government as legitimate has nothing to do with how that government came to power, or for that matter with how it governs. "The Law of Nations prescribes no rules as regards the kind of head a State may have," wrote Lassa Oppenheim in his influential 1905 text on international law, and he added that every state is "naturally" free to adopt any constitution "according to its discretion."[66] The sole test is whether it is in effective control of the territory. More recently Roth has put it this way:

In such a conception, the international system regards ruling apparatuses as self-sufficient sources of authority—or rather deems their authority to derive from their characteristic ability to secure the acquiescence of their populaces, by whatever means . . . a government is recognized simply because its existence is a fact of life.[67]

International bodies, including the United Nations and the World Trade Organization, use this concept of legitimacy when they accept governments as the representatives of member nations.

The dominance of this conception makes alternatives seem unrealistic. There is, however, an alternative view with strong ethical credentials. In November 1792, in the wake of the French National Convention's declaration of a republic, Thomas Jefferson, then U.S. Secretary of State, wrote to the representative of the United States in France: "It accords with our principles to acknowledge any government to be rightful which is formed by the will of the people, substantially declared."[68] Now it is true that we cannot assume, from this statement, that Jefferson also intended the converse: that a government that cannot show that it has been formed by the declared will of the people is not rightfully the government of the nation. There may well be other grounds on which a government could be considered legitimate, perhaps by ruling unopposed for a long period without employing repressive measures to stifle dissent. The Jeffersonian principle does seem to imply, however, that some governments would *not* be regarded as legitimate—for example, one that had seized power by force of arms, dismissed democratically elected rulers, and killed those who spoke out against this way of doing things.

The claim that there is a fundamental human right to take part in deciding who governs us provides one reason for denying the legitimacy of a government that cannot show that it represents the will of the people. We could reach the same conclusion by arguing, on consequentialist grounds, that democratic governments can be expected to have more concern for the people over whom they rule than governments that do not answer, at regular intervals, to an electorate. In international law, this view of legitimacy has been gathering support in recent years, although it could not yet be said to be the majority view. In support of it, its defenders can point to many international documents, beginning with the opening words of the United Nations Charter, "We the peoples." The signatories of the Charter apparently regarded themselves as representatives of, and deriving their authority from, the peoples they governed. Next comes the Universal Declaration of Human Rights, which in Article 21 (3) states:

The will of the people shall be the basis of the authority of government; this will shall be expressed in periodic and genuine elections which shall be by universal and equal suffrage and shall be held by secret vote or by equivalent free voting procedures.

The Universal Declaration of Human Rights is not a treaty with explicit legal force, but the International Covenant on Civil and Political Rights is. Its first article states:

All peoples have the right of self-determination. By virtue of that right they freely determine their political status and freely pursue their economic, social and cultural development.

In the second article, the parties to the Covenant undertake to ensure that each individual in its territory has the rights it contains "without distinction of any kind, such as race, color, sex, language, religion, political or other opinion, national or social origin, property, birth or other status." The inclusion of "political or other opinion" is important here, since Article 25 reads:

Every citizen shall have the right and the opportunity, without any of the distinctions mentioned in article 2 and without unreasonable restrictions:
(a) To take part in the conduct of public affairs, directly or through freely chosen representatives;
(b) To vote and to be elected at genuine periodic elections which shall be by universal and equal suffrage and shall be held by secret ballot, guaranteeing the free expression of the will of the electors.

If we were to take these statements seriously, we would have to develop an entirely new concept of legitimate government, with far-reaching implications not only for trade but also for issues like the use of military intervention for humanitarian purposes, a topic to which I shall turn in the next chapter. But how would we decide when a government is sufficiently democratic to be recognized as legitimate? During the counting and recounting of votes in the United States presidential election in November 2000, jokes circulated to the effect that the United Nations was about to send in a team of observers to ensure that the elections were fair and democratic. The jokes had a serious point to make. Put aside the many allegations of irregularities in voting and counting and the refusal of the United States Supreme Court to allow a proper count of all votes. Forget about the fact that candidates must raise hundreds of millions of dollars to have any chance of success, thus ensuring that the rich have far more influence on the political process than the poor. Even without any of those blemishes, the use of the electoral college, rather than the popular vote, to elect the president of the United States gives greater value to the votes of people living in states with small populations than to those living in states with large populations, and hence fails the basic "one vote, one value" requirement of democracy, and the "equal suffrage" stipulation of Article 25 (b) of the Universal Declaration of Human Rights. Nevertheless, the evident imperfections of democracy in the United States are not of the kind that should lead us to withdraw recognition of the legitimacy of the U.S. government. A minimalist concept of democracy is needed, for otherwise there will be few legitimate governments left. It may be useful to distinguish between governments that, although not democratic, can claim a traditional, long-standing authority that enables them to rule with the apparent acquiescence of the population, and without severe restrictions on basic civil liberties, and other regimes that, having seized power by force, use repressive measures to maintain themselves in power. A traditional absolute monarchy might be an example of the first form of government; a military regime that has come to power through a successful coup, does not hold free elections, and kills or jails its opponents is an example of the second.

Even if we focus only on those governments that gain power by force and hold it through repression of opposition, accepting the democratic concept of sovereignty would make a huge difference to the way we conduct world affairs. With regard to trade issues, we can imagine that an internationally respected body would appoint a tribunal consisting of judges and experts to scrutinize the credentials of each government on a regular basis. If a government could not, over time, satisfy the tribunal that its legitimacy stemmed from the support of its people, it would not be accepted as having the right to sell its country's resources, any more than a robber who overpowers you and takes your watch would be recognized as entitled to sell it. For a private citizen to buy that watch, knowing or reasonably suspecting it to be

stolen, is to commit the crime of receiving stolen goods. Under a minimalist democratic concept of sovereignty, it would similarly be a crime under international law for anyone to receive goods stolen from a nation by those who have no claim to sovereignty other than the fact that they exercise superior force.

Far-reaching as they are, such suggestions are gaining increasing recognition. At the Summit of the Americas meeting held in Quebec City in April 2001, the leaders of 34 American nations agreed that "any unconstitutional alteration or interruption of the democratic order in a state of the hemisphere constitutes an insurmountable obstacle to the participation of that state's government in the Summit of the Americas process." This means that a country that ceases to be a democracy cannot take part in the continuing talks on the free trade pact that the Summit planned, nor receive support from major international institutions like the Inter-American Development Bank.[69] In other words, democracy takes precedence over free trade, and the perceived benefits of participation in the proposed free trade agreement provide an incentive for all the nations of the Americas to maintain democratic institutions.

Though most leaders present at the Summit of the Americas, including President George W. Bush, are strong defenders of free trade and of the WTO, there is a potential conflict between the vision implicit in their Quebec City agreement and that of the WTO. The leaders of the nations of the Americas envision a kind of club of democratic nations, who trade with each other, assist each other in various ways, and deny these benefits to undemocratic outsiders or to any democracies that fall into the hands of dictators. In contrast the rules of the WTO do not allow its member nations to refuse to trade with other members because they are not democratic. If the WTO should realize its vision of a global free trade zone, regional free trade agreements would become irrelevant, and there would be no way in which trade sanctions could encourage democracy.

In Europe the lure of entry into the European Union is already encouraging democracy and support for basic human rights. For the former communist nations of Central and Eastern Europe, membership in the European Union is an extremely desirable goal, one that is likely to bring with it stability and prosperity. The European Union is a free trade zone, but it is much more than that. It has criteria for admission that include a democratic form of government and basic human rights guarantees.[70] Implicitly, by refusing to accept nations that fail to meet these standards, the European Union puts democracy and human rights ahead of free trade. As a result, those Central and Eastern European nations that are plausible candidates for membership are gradually bringing their laws in line with the minimum standards required by the European Union.

It is not only in Europe and the Americas that there are moves to strengthen and encourage democracy. In Africa, there has been increasing acceptance of the monitoring of elections by international observers, and the Organization of African Unity has now monitored elections in 39 countries.[71] At the inaugural meeting of the Community of Democracies in Warsaw in June 2000, representatives of the governments of 106 countries signed the *Warsaw Declaration*, recognizing "the universality of democratic values," and agreeing to "collaborate on democracy-related issues in existing international and regional institutions, forming coalitions and caucuses to support resolutions and other international activities aimed at the promotion of democratic governance" in order to "create an external environment conducive to democratic development."[72] Here too democracy is seen as a great value, to be promoted through international collaboration. A trade pact between democracies, like that proposed for the Americas, would be a powerful means of promoting the value of democracy. So too would be a blacklist of illegitimate governments with no color of entitlement to rule, and with whom there is therefore no ethical basis for doing business. Corporations that wished to be perceived, not as the receivers of stolen goods, but as respectable global citizens and as supporters of democracy, might then be deterred from entering into agreements with these governments. This result would deny dictators the resources they need for buying weapons, paying their supporters, and boosting their bank balances in Switzerland. Obtaining power by ways that do not confer legitimacy would become just a little less attractive, and the prospects of an illegitimate government staying in power would be slightly reduced. Though the reduced prospects of development might be seen as a cost incurred not only by the illegitimate government but also by the people of the country, such development is, at best, a mixed blessing, and is often very damaging to the local people. For example, Shell's use of oil rights under the regime of the former Nigerian dictator General Sani Abacha was highly detrimental to the Ogoni people who lived above the oil fields. It can also be argued that it was, on balance, bad for Nigeria as a whole. In a study of the impact of extractive industries on the poor, Michael Ross, a political scientist at the University of California, Los Angeles, found that the living standards and quality of life experienced by the general population in countries dependent on selling minerals and oil are much lower than one would expect them to be, given the countries' per capita income. Mineral dependence correlated strongly with high levels of poverty and with unusually high levels of corruption, authoritarian government, military spending, and civil war. Ross's findings are in accord with those of an earlier influential study of natural resources and economic growth by Jeffrey Sachs and Andrew Warner.[73]

Consistently with such studies, we may think it is no coincidence that Nigeria has over the last 30 years had a preponderance of military governments, one of the world's highest levels of corruption, and enormous revenue from the sale of oil. Control of such vast wealth is a constant temptation for generals and others who have the means to overthrow civilian governments and then divert some of the wealth into their own pockets. If overthrowing the government did not bring with it control of the oil revenues, the temptation to do so would be that much less.[74]

A refusal to accept a dictatorial government as entitled to sell off the resources of the country over which it rules is not the same as the imposition of a total trade boycott on that country. Such boycotts can be very harmful to individual citizens in the country boycotted. Renewable resources, like agricultural produce and manufactured goods, might still be traded under private agreements. But when a corporation or a nation accepts the right of dictators to sell their country's non-renewable natural resources, it is accepting the dictators' claims to legitimate authority over those resources. This is not a neutral act, but one that requires ethical justification. In the rare case in which the dictatorship's record indicates that the money will be used to benefit the entire nation, that justification may be available, despite the absence of democracy. When, however, corporations can see that the money they are paying for a country's natural resources will be used primarily to enrich its dictator and enable him or her to buy more arms to consolidate his or her rule, there is no ethical justification for dealing with the dictator. The old-growth forests, oil, and minerals should be left alone, awaiting a government that has legitimate authority to sell them.

Questions for Discussion

1. How should we measure human well-being?
2. When is a government legitimate? How is that relevant to whether other countries ought to trade with that government?
3. Is moral reform of international commerce hopeless?

Thomas Pogge, "World Poverty and Human Rights"

Thomas Pogge is a professor of philosophy at Columbia University. His book with the same title as his article reprinted here is a deeply informed and carefully researched exploration of global justice. According to Pogge, we inflict severe poverty on the world's poor. If Pogge is right, we are morally responsible for their plight in a more profound way than we ever imagined.

Critical Reading Questions

1. What would it take to overcome severe global poverty?
2. According to Pogge, are we entitled to our share of the world's product?
3. How has the radical inequality between the haves and have-nots of the world evolved?
4. What does Pogge mean by "fictional history"? How is that relevant to his case?
5. What three notions of harm does Pogge discuss?
6. What does Pogge think our attitude should be toward illegitimate governments of resource-rich countries?

WORLD POVERTY AND HUMAN RIGHTS

Thomas Pogge

Despite a high and growing global average income, billions of human beings are still condemned to life-long severe poverty, with all its attendant evils of low life expectancy, social exclusion, ill health, illiteracy, dependency, and effective enslavement. The annual death toll from poverty-related causes is around 18 million, or one-third of all human deaths, which adds up to approximately 270 million deaths since the end of the Cold War.[1]

This problem is hardly unsolvable, in spite of its magnitude. Though constituting 44 percent of the world's population, the 2,735 million people the World Bank counts as living below its more generous $2 per day international poverty line consume only 1.3 percent of the global product, and would need just 1 percent more to escape poverty so defined.[2] The high-income countries, with 955 million citizens, by contrast, have about 81 percent of the global product.[3] With our average per capita income nearly 180 times greater than that of the poor (at market exchange rates), we could eradicate severe poverty worldwide if we chose to try—in fact, we could have eradicated it decades ago.

Citizens of the rich countries are, however, conditioned to downplay the severity and persistence of world poverty and to think of it as an occasion for minor charitable assistance. Thanks in part to the rationalizations dispensed by our economists, most of us believe that severe poverty and its persistence are due exclusively to local causes. Few realize that severe poverty is an ongoing harm we inflict upon the global poor. If more of us understood the true magnitude of the problem of poverty and our causal involvement in it, we might do what is necessary to eradicate it.

That world poverty is an ongoing harm *we* inflict seems completely incredible to most citizens of the affluent countries. We call it tragic that the basic human rights of so many remain unfulfilled, and are willing to admit that we should do more to help. But it is unthinkable to us that we are actively responsible for this catastrophe. If we

[1] World Health Organization, *World Health Report 2004* (Geneva: WHO, 2004), Annex Table 2; available at www.who.int/whr/2004.

[2] For detailed income poverty figures, see Shaohua Chen and Martin Ravallion, "How Have the World's Poorest Fared since the Early 1980s?" *World Bank Research Observe* 19, no. 2 (2004), p. 153; also available at wbro.oupjournals.org/cgi/content/abstract/19/2/141(repoting 2001 data). Ravllion and Chen have managed the World Bank's income poverty assessments for well over a decade. My estimate of the poors' share of the global product is justified in Thomas

W. Pogge, "The First UN Millennium Development Goal: A Cause for Celebration?" *Journal of Human Development 5*, no. 3 (2004), p. 387. For a methodological critique of the World Bank's poverty statistics, see "The First UN Millennium Development Goal," pp. 381-85, based on my joint work with Sanjay G. Reddy, "How *Not* to Count the Poor"; available at www.socialanalysis.org.

[3] World Bank, *World Development Report 2003* (New York: Oxford University Press, 2003), p. 235 (giving data for 2001).

Ethics & International Affairs 19, no. 1 (2005).

were, then we, civilized and sophisticated denizens of the developed countries, would be guilty of the largest crime against humanity ever committed, the death toll of which exceeds, every week, that of the recent tsunami and, every three years, that of World War II, the concentration camps and gulags included. What could be more preposterous?

But think about the unthinkable for a moment. Are there steps the affluent countries could take to reduce severe poverty abroad? It seems very likely that there are, given the enormous inequalities in income and wealth already mentioned. The common assumption, however, is that reducing severe poverty abroad at the expense of our own affluence would be generous on our part, not something we owe, and that our failure to do this is thus at most a lack of generosity that does not make us morally responsible for the continued deprivation of the poor.

I deny this popular assumption. I deny that the 955 million citizens of the affluent countries are morally entitled to their 81 percent of the global product in the face of three times as many people mired in severe poverty. Is this denial really so preposterous that one need not consider the arguments in its support? Does not the radical inequality between our wealth and their dire need at least put the burden on us to show why we should be morally entitled to so much while they have so little? In *World Poverty and Human Rights*,[4] I dispute the popular assumption by showing that the usual ways of justifying our great advantage fail. My argument poses three mutually independent challenges.

ACTUAL HISTORY

Many believe that the radical inequality we face can be justified by reference to how it evolved, for example through differences in diligence, culture, and social institutions, soil, climate, or fortune. I challenge this sort of justification by invoking the common and very violent history through which the present radical inequality accumulated. Much of it was built up in the colonial era, when today's affluent countries ruled today's poor regions of the world:

[4]Thomas W. Pogge, *World Poverty and Human Rights: Cosmopolitan Responsibilities and Reforms* (Cambridge: Polity Press, 2002). All in-text citation references are to this book.

trading their people like cattle, destroying their political institutions and cultures, taking their lands and natural resources, and forcing products and customs upon them. I recount these historical facts specifically for readers who believe that even the most radical inequality is morally justifiable if it evolved in a benign way. Such readers disagree about the conditions a historical process must meet for it to justify such vast inequalities in life chances. But I can bypass these disagreements because the actual historical crimes were so horrendous, diverse, and consequential that no historical entitlement conception could credibly support the view that our common history was sufficiently benign to justify today's huge inequality in starting places.

Challenges such as this are often dismissed with the lazy response that we cannot be held responsible for what others did long ago. This response is true but irrelevant. We indeed cannot inherit responsibility for our forefathers' sins. But how then can we plausibly claim the *fruits* of their sins? How can we have been entitled to the great head start our countries enjoyed going into the postcolonial period, which has allowed us to dominate and shape the world? And how can we be entitled to the huge advantages over the global poor we consequently enjoy from birth? The historical path from which our exceptional affluence arose greatly weakens our moral claim to it—certainly in the face of those whom the same historical process has delivered into conditions of acute deprivation. They, the global poor, have a much stronger moral claim to that 1 percent of the global product they need to meet their basic needs than we affluent have to take 81 rather than 80 percent for ourselves. Thus, I write, "A morally deeply tarnished history must not be allowed to result in *radical inequality*" (p. 203).

FICTIONAL HISTORIES

Since my first challenge addressed adherents of historical entitlement conceptions of justice, it may leave others unmoved. These others may believe that it is permissible to uphold any economic distribution, no matter how skewed, if merely it *could* have come about on a morally acceptable path. They insist that we are entitled to keep and defend what we possess, even at the cost of millions of deaths each year, unless there is conclusive proof that, without the horrors of the European conquests, severe poverty worldwide would be substantially less today.

Now, *any* distribution, however unequal, *could* be the outcome of a sequence of voluntary bets or gambles. Appeal to such a fictional history would "justify" anything and would thus be wholly implausible. John Locke does much better, holding that a fictional history can justify the status quo only if the changes in holdings and social rules it involves are ones that all participants could have rationally agreed to. He also holds that in a state of nature persons would be entitled to a proportional share of the world's natural resources. Whoever deprives others of "enough and as good"—either through unilateral appropriations or through instituional arrangements, such as a radically inegalitarian property regime—harms them in violation of a *negative* duty. For Locke, the justice of any institutional order thus depends on whether the worst-off under it are at least as well off as people would be in a state of nature with a proportional resource share.[5] This baseline is imprecise, to be sure, but it suffices for my second challenge: however one may want to imagine a state of nature among human beings on this planet, one could not realistically conceive it as involving suffering and early deaths on the scale we are witnessing today. Only a thoroughly organized state of civilization can produce such horrendous misery and sustain an enduring poverty death toll of 18 million annually. The existing distribution is then morally unacceptable on Lockean grounds insofar as, I point out, "the better-off enjoy significant advantages in the use of a single natural resource base from whose benefits the worse-off are largely, and without compensation, excluded" (p. 202).

The attempt to justify today's coercively upheld radical inequality by appeal to some morally acceptable *fictional* historical process that *might* have led to it thus fails as well. On Locke's permissive account, a small elite may appropriate all of the huge cooperative surplus produced by modern social organization. But this elite must not enlarge its share even further

by reducing the poor *below* the state-of-nature baseline to capture *more* than the entire cooperative surplus. The citizens and governments of the affluent states are violating this negative duty when we, in collaboration with the ruling cliques of many poor countries, coercively exclude the global poor from a proportional resource share and any equivalent substitute.

PRESENT GLOBAL INSTITUTIONAL ARRANGEMENTS

A third way of thinking about the justice of a radical inequality involves reflection on the institutional rules that give rise to it. Using this approach, one can justify an economic order and the distribution it produces (irrespective of historical considerations) by comparing them to feasible alternative institutional schemes and the distributional profiles they would produce. Many broadly consequentialist and contractualist conceptions of justice exemplify this approach. They differ in how they characterize the relevant affected parties (groups, persons, time slices of persons, and so on), in the metric they employ for measuring how well off such parties are (in terms of social primary goods, capabilities, welfare, and so forth), and in how they aggregate such information about wellbeing into an overall assessment (for example, by averaging, or in some egalitarian, prioritarian, or sufficientarian way). These conceptions consequently disagree about how economic institutions should be best shaped under modern conditions. But I can bypass such disagreements insofar as these conceptions agree that an economic order is unjust when it—like the systems of serfdom and forced labor prevailing in feudal Russia or France—foreseeably and avoidably gives rise to massive and severe human rights deficits. My third challenge, addressed to adherents of broadly consequentialist and contractualist conceptions of justice, is that we are preserving our great economic advantages by imposing a global economic order that is unjust in view of the massive and avoidable deprivations it foreseeably reproduces: "There is a shared institutional order that is shaped by the better-off and imposed on the worse-off," I contend. "This institutional order is implicated in the reproduction of radical inequality in that there is a feasible institutional alternative under which

[5]For a fuller reading of Locke's argument, see Pogge, *World Poverty and Human Rights*, ch. 5.

such severe and extensive poverty would not persist. The radical inequality cannot be traced to extra-social factors (such as genetic handicaps or natural disasters) which, as such, affect different human beings differentially" (p. 199).

THREE NOTIONS OF HARM

These three challenges converge on the conclusion that the global poor have a compelling moral claim to some of our affluence and that we, by denying them what they are morally entitled to and urgently need, are actively contributing to their deprivations. Still, these challenges are addressed to different audiences and thus appeal to diverse and mutually inconsistent moral conceptions.

They also deploy different notions of harm. In most ordinary contexts, the word "harm" is understood in a historical sense, either diachronically or subjunctively: someone is harmed when she is rendered worse off than she was at some earlier time, or than she would have been had some earlier arrangements continued undisturbed. My first two challenges conceive harm in this ordinary way, and then conceive justice, at least partly, in terms of harm: we are behaving unjustly toward the global poor by imposing on them the lasting effects of historical crimes, or by holding them below any credible state-of-nature baseline. But my third challenge does not conceive justice and injustice in terms of an independently specified notion of harm. Rather, it relates the concepts of *harm* and *justice* in the opposite way, conceiving harm in terms of an independently specified conception of social justice: we are *harming* the global poor if and insofar as we collaborate in imposing an *unjust* global institutional order upon them. And this institutional order is definitely unjust if and insofar as it foreseeably perpetuates large-scale human rights deficits that would be reasonably avoidable through feasible institutional modifications.[6]

The third challenge is empirically more demanding than the other two. It requires me to substantiate three claims: Global institutional arrangements are causally implicated in the reproduction of massive severe poverty. Governments of our affluent countries bear primary responsibility for these global institutional arrangements and can foresee their detrimental effects. And many citizens of these affluent countries bear responsibility for the global institutional arrangements their governments have negotiated in their names.

TWO MAIN INNOVATIONS

In defending these three claims, my view on these more empirical matters is as oddly perpendicular to the usual empirical debates as my diagnosis of our moral relation to the problem of world poverty is to the usual moral debates.

The usual *moral* debates concern the stringency of our moral duties to help the poor abroad. Most of us believe that these duties are rather feeble, meaning that it isn't very wrong of us to give no help at all. Against this popular view, some (Peter Singer, Henry Shue, Peter Unger) have argued that our positive duties are quite stringent and quite demanding; and others (such as Liam Murphy) have defended an intermediate view according to which our positive duties, insofar as they are quite stringent, are not very demanding. Leaving this whole debate to one side, I focus on what it ignores: our moral duties not to harm. We do, of course, have positive duties to rescue people from life-threatening poverty. But it can be misleading to focus on them when more stringent negative duties are also in play: duties not to expose people to life-threatening poverty and duties to shield them from harms for which we would be actively responsible.

The usual *empirical* debates concern how developing countries should design their economic institutions and policies in order to reduce severe poverty within their borders. The received wisdom (often pointing to Hong Kong and, lately, China) is that they should opt for free and open markets with a minimum in taxes

[6]One might say that the existing global order is not unjust if the only feasible institutional modifications that could substantially reduce the offensive deprivations would be extremely costly in terms of culture, say, or the natural environment. I preempt such objections by inserting the word "reasonably." Broadly consequentialist and contractualist conceptions of justice agree that an institutional order that foreseeably gives rise to massive severe deprivations is

unjust if there are feasible institutional modifications that foreseeably would greatly reduce these deprivations without adding other harms of comparable magnitude.

and regulations so as to attract investment and to stimulate growth. But some influential economists call for extensive government investment in education, health care, and infrastructure (as illustrated by the example of the Indian state of Kerala), or for some protectionist measures to "incubate" fledgling niche industries until they become internationally competitive (as illustrated by the example of South Korea). Leaving these debates to one side, I focus once more on what is typically ignored: the role that the design of the *global* institutional order plays in the persistence of severe poverty.

Thanks to the inattention of our economists, many believe that the existing global institutional order plays no role in the persistence of severe poverty, but rather that national differences are the key factors. Such "explanatory nationalism" (p. 139ff.) appears justified by the dramatic performance differentials among developing countries, with poverty rapidly disappearing in some and increasing in others. Cases of the latter kind usually display plenty of incompetence, corruption, and oppression by ruling elites, which seem to give us all the explanation we need to understand why severe poverty persists there.

But consider this analogy. Suppose there are great performance differentials among the students in a class, with some improving greatly while many others learn little or nothing. And suppose the latter students do not do their readings and skip many classes. This case surely shows that local, student-specific factors play a role in explaining academic success. But it decidedly *fails* to show that global factors (the quality of teaching, textbooks, classroom, and so forth) play no such role. A better teacher might well greatly improve the performance of the class by eliciting stronger student interest in the subject and hence better attendance and preparation.

Once we break free from explanatory nationalism, global factors relevant to the persistence of severe poverty are easy to find. In the WTO negotiations, the affluent countries insisted on continued and asymmetrical protections of their markets through tariffs, quotas, anti-dumping duties, export credits, and huge subsidies to domestic producers. Such protectionism provides a compelling illustration of the hypocrisy of the rich states that insist and command that

their own exports be received with open markets (pp. 15–20). And it greatly impairs export opportunities for the very poorest countries and regions. If the rich countries scrapped their protectionist barriers against imports from poor countries, the populations of the latter would benefit greatly: hundreds of millions would escape unemployment, wage levels would rise substantially, and incoming export revenues would be higher by hundreds of billions of dollars each year.

The same rich states also insist that their intellectual property rights—ever-expanding in scope and duration—must be vigorously enforced in the poor countries. Music and software, production processes, words, seeds, biological species, and drugs—for all these, and more, rents must be paid to the corporations of the rich countries as a condition for (still multiply restricted) access to their markets. Millions would be saved from diseases and death if generic producers could freely manufacture and market life-saving drugs in the poor countries.[7]

While charging billions for their intellectual property, the rich countries pay nothing for the externalities they impose through their vastly disproportional contributions to global pollution and resource depletion. The global poor benefit least, if at all, from polluting activities, and also are least able to protect themselves from the impact such pollution has on their health and on their natural environment (such as flooding due to rising sea levels). It is true, of course, that we pay for the vast quantities of natural resources we import. But such payments cannot make up for the price effects of our inordinate consumption, which restrict the consumption possibilities of the global poor as well as the development possibilities of the poorer countries and regions (in comparison to the opportunities our countries could take advantage of at a comparable stage of economic development).

More important, the payments we make for resource imports go to the rulers of the resource-rich countries, with no concern about whether they are democratically elected or at least minimally attentive to the needs of the people they

[7]See Thomas W. Pogge, "Human Rights and Global Health," *Metaphilosophy* 36, nos. 1–2 (2005), pp. 182–209.

rule. It is on the basis of effective power alone that we recognize any such ruler as entitled to sell us the resources of "his" country and to borrow, undertake treaty commitments, and buy arms in its name. These international resources, borrowing, treaty, and arms privileges we extend to such rulers are quite advantageous to them, providing them with the money and arms they need to stay in power—often with great brutality and negligible popular support. These privileges are also quite convenient to us, securing our resource imports from poor countries irrespective of who may rule them and how badly. But these privileges have devastating effects on the global poor by enabling corrupt rulers to oppress them, to exclude them from the benefits of their countries' natural resources, and to saddle them with huge debts and onerous treaty obligations. By substantially augmenting the perks of governmental power, these same privileges also greatly strengthen the incentives to attempt to take power by force, thereby fostering coups, civil wars, and interstate wars in the poor countries and regions—especially in Africa, which has many desperately poor but resource-rich countries, where the resource sector constitutes a large part of the gross domestic product.

Reflection on the popular view that severe poverty persists in many poor countries because they govern themselves so poorly shows, then, that it is evidence not for but against explanatory nationalism. The populations of most of the countries in which severe poverty persists or increases do not "govern themselves" poorly, but *are* very poorly governed, and much against their will. They are helplessly exposed to such "government" because the rich states recognize their rulers as entitled to rule on the basis of effective power alone. We pay these rulers for their people's resources, often advancing them large sums against the collateral of future exports, and we eagerly sell them the advanced weaponry on which their continued rule all too often depends. Yes, severe poverty is fueled by local misrule. But such local misrule is fueled, in turn, by global rules that we impose and from which we benefit greatly.

Once this causal nexus between our global institutional order and the persistence of severe poverty is understood, the injustice of that order, and of our imposition of it, becomes visible: "What entitles a small global elite—the citizens of the rich countries *and* the holders of political and economic power in the resource-rich developing countries—to enforce a global property scheme under which we may claim the world's natural resources for ourselves and can distribute these among ourselves on mutually agreeable terms?" I ask. "How, for instance, can our ever so free and fair agreements with tyrants give us property rights in crude oil, thereby dispossessing the local population and the rest of humankind?" (p. 142).

Questions for Discussion

1. How do countries acquire the right to trade their resources on the international market?
2. Do a little research into the gold market, the diamond market, or the market of any other international commodity to see whether Pogge is right.
3. If Pogge is right about our role in inflicting the harm of poverty, what should we do?

CHAPTER 17

Feminist Ethics

HARD QUESTION: ARE WOMEN FROM VENUS AND MEN FROM MARS?

Do women have a different moral experience than men? Do they conceive of themselves as moral beings in a different way than men? And are women inclined to regard different factors as relevant to the resolution of moral quandaries than men? In one sense these are straightforward empirical questions, but we must be careful how we describe any differences: Is one better than the other or are they equally good, just different? If there are differences in moral experience, they will be rather subtle, since men and women inhabit the same moral universe. Moral considerations used by men are comprehensible to women, and vice versa. Women just might tend to emphasize one kind of consideration and men another, so the idea that men are from Mars and women from Venus overstates things considerably. Moreover, differences in moral orientation will be statistical. That is, it is not as though all men think a certain way and all women another. Any differences are likely to be differences of "style" that loosely track gender. Some men might use a more feminine style of moral deliberation, whereas some women might use a more masculine style, and any particular man or woman can vacillate between the two, depending on the issue.

Having said all of that, what are the facts? Do men and women have different moral outlooks? In 1982 Carol Gilligan, a developmental psychologist at Harvard University, published an important book titled *In a Different Voice*. She claimed to have empirically identified a woman's perspective on morality. If true, this is a discovery with far-reaching practical and theoretical implications. According to Gilligan, in many accounts of moral development women repeatedly and systematically appear to be deficient. What is the probable explanation for the alleged moral deficiency of women? Are women in fact morally deficient, or is it more likely that the developmental theories were biased toward men? If the theories are biased and if the instruments designed to test the theories are perversely self-perpetuating of that bias, then it is no wonder that women come out looking bad.

Consider Freud's view that girls define themselves negatively with respect to you know what. Boys, on the other hand, struggle to overcome their attraction to their mothers and subsequent castration anxiety by adopting their fathers' moral sense; this resolution of the Oedipal complex produces a strong superego, where moral conscience resides. Girls undergo no such resolution, finding themselves instead continually competing with their mothers for their father's attention. Freud concludes that women "show less sense of justice than men, that they are less ready to submit to the great exigencies of life, that they are more often influenced in their judgments by feelings of affection or hostility." All because no penis!

Freud's assessment of women, even if true, is immediately interpreted as moral weakness because moral deliberation is supposed to require impartial assessment based on principle. According to Freud, women are mired in emotion and cannot reason very well about abstract principles of justice. Similar negative interpretations of women's moral experience, claims Gilligan, influenced standard theories of psychological development. Women routinely come out as less morally developed than men because they emphasize "feelings of affection" and maintenance of personal relationships rather than impartial judgments based on morality.

The idea that women are morally undeveloped was further "corroborated" by the influential work of Lawrence Kohlberg, also a moral psychologist at Harvard. Kohlberg defined six stages of moral development, beginning with simple reward and punishment, where "avoidance of punishment and unquestioning deference to power are valued in their own right," progressing through various levels of abstraction, integration, and generalization, culminating in something vaguely like Kant's moral outlook, where "right is defined by the decision of conscience in accord with self-chosen ethical principles appealing to logical comprehensiveness, universality, and consistency."

By asking children a series of hypothetical questions, such as whether it would be okay to steal a drug for someone who needed it to live, Kohlberg showed that as their thinking matured, children moved from stage to stage. Indeed, moral maturation consists in appealing to increasingly abstract and universal principles to resolve conflicts. The problem is that Kohlberg's scale of moral development was devised by talking only to boys. When he subsequently asked girls the same questions, they typically failed to ascend the scale as high as boys, often getting "stuck" around stage 3, where "good behavior is that which pleases or helps others and is approved by them." Rather than calling into doubt the instrument used to measure moral development, Kohlberg's work, like that of so many other theorists, was taken to confirm that women are not particularly good moral deliberators. Aristotle notoriously placed women in the category with slaves, children, and animals—that is, beings with diminished capacities for rational thought. And Kohlberg's findings seemed to support that ancient prejudice.

Children on a school playground, notes Gilligan, give insight into gender-based moral orientation. Boys frequently play competitive games, handling the disputes that inevitably break out by appeal to rules and thereby developing skills at applying principles of fairness impartially. Girls, on the other hand, typically play noncompetitive, "turn-taking" games where one's gain is not another's loss. Disputes among girls are less likely to erupt, and when they do, "rather than elaborating a system of rules for resolving disputes, girls subordinated the continuation of the game to continuation of relationships." Considerations such as these lead Gilligan to speculate that men are oriented to a morality of justice and women to a morality of care. She writes,

> When one begins with the study of women and derives developmental constructs from their lives, the outline of a moral conception different from that described by Freud, Piaget, or Kohlberg begins to emerge and informs a different description of development. In this conception, the moral problem arises from conflicting responsibilities rather than from competing rights and requires for its resolution a mode of thinking that is contextual and narrative rather than formal and abstract. This conception of morality as concerned with the activity of care centers moral development around the understanding of responsibility and relationships, just as the conception of morality as fairness ties moral development to the understanding of rights and rules.

Let us allow the empirical findings: Men are oriented to the administration of rules, women to maintaining relationships (although Gilligan's data have been criticized for being too limited to support her sweeping claims). This is an interesting finding, but can it give us a unique sort of gender-based ethics, feminist ethics? The mere fact that women have a different moral orientation than men is not enough to ground feminist ethics, since women's moral perspective might be distorted by oppression and discrimination. Why should women's moral experience have theoretical significance over the moral experience of any group that has been discriminated against, such as blacks, gays, or people with disabilities?

The case for a distinctively feminist ethics will rest on the inability of traditional moral theory to accommodate women's moral experience, which must be taken seriously, not simply explained away as a distortion resulting from oppression and discrimination. For were Gilligan-type studies to show an empirically discernible moral orientation for blacks or Jews, we would probably try to explain that away as a result of discrimination, rather than appealing to some peculiarly black or Jewish ethics. If women's moral orientation can be similarly explained away, then there is no distinctively feminist ethics. However, if it cannot, then it is time to suspect that the moral theories are male-biased. Thus the theoretical task to establish a special moral perspective—whether it is for women or gays or blacks or what have you—is to show that an empirically identifiable moral orientation is somehow intrinsic to a group, not the result of external factors, such as widespread discrimination, subordination, or (for that matter) privilege and elevated social status.

FEMINIST ETHICS AND MORAL PHILOSOPHY

There is no one feminist ethics but rather a number of views that make a similar gender-based criticism of traditional moral philosophy. The standard theories of moral philosophy, such as those we have studied in this text—utilitarianism,

Kantianism, contract ethics, natural law, and virtue ethics—are allegedly biased toward men. Although the philosophers who construct and elaborate these theories claim to speak for all of humanity everywhere and for all time, the work is largely done by men ("clerics, misogynists, and puritan bachelors," according feminist Annette Baier), so there is at least a prima facie reason to be suspicious that the theories overlook a woman's perspective. Feminist ethical views are united in holding that there is an identifiable women's moral perspective that has been systematically denigrated or ignored in moral thought. This, perhaps more than anything else, defines feminist ethics: the claim that women have a particular orientation to moral questions that is not captured by traditional theories.

One could deny that women have a unique moral orientation and perhaps still be a feminist of sorts insofar as one thought that women ought to have the same advantages and opportunities in life as men. "Equality feminism" would then be distinct from "difference feminism," the claim that women do have a unique moral outlook. Equality feminism is no challenge to traditional moral thinking, since it requires only the consistent application of ordinary moral principles (such as impartiality and equal consideration and worth) to women, rather than a whole new moral theory. However, if the moral experience of women is fundamentally different from that of men, and if (as argued above) the difference cannot be explained away as the historical effect of discrimination, then traditional moral thinking will be biased because it illegitimately enshrines a male moral perspective; women's moral perspective will have no voice.

Consider how traditional moral philosophy might be male-biased. If we accept Gilligan's findings, women are concerned to maintain personal relationships. Personal relationships are intimate and particular, so this is incompatible with the impartiality and universality that define standard moral theory. Think of close, small-scale personal relationships, such as those in a family. How do moral theories conceive of the relationships between parents and children? Parents are supposed to care for their children not because of duty (Kant) or because doing so will make the world better (utilitarianism) or because that was the bargain (contract ethics) or because doing so is a human excellence (virtue ethics) or because it is natural (natural law ethics), but simply because parents love their children. Caring for children for some other reason distorts the loving and intimate bond.

We might think that because intimate relationships are not very well captured by standard moral theory, perhaps they are not moral relationships. But this won't do. We are talking about contexts in which people can harm or benefit one another, thus affecting their "human predicament." This is sufficient to make a question a moral one (see Chapter 1). The question for philosophical ethics is whether concerns about care, intimacy, partiality, and the like—alleged to be the bulk of women's moral experience—can be explained with the conceptual resources of standard moral theory or whether those theories are indeed skewed toward male moral thought.

On the face of it, it does not look promising for traditional moral theory. Utilitarian concern with maximizing universal good from the perspective of an impartial, benevolent spectator seems woefully incapable of acknowledging the importance of intimate relationships—and certainly not for the reason that those relationships contribute to universal happiness. Kant's icy view of duty-bound action based solely on rational principles independent of emotional commitment or inclination seems bizarrely inappropriate for intimate settings where love or other feelings of attachment constitute the relationship. Contractarian ethics, based as it is on rational agents bargaining for mutual benefit, seems fine for market relationships, but it is perversely inappropriate for relationships where self-sacrifice is freely done for the good of another. Natural law might make room for intimate relationships as a fundamental human good. However, because the theory is traditionally linked to a patriarchal God who makes women's subordination in family life a "natural inclination," many feminists will have problems with natural law ethics. Virtue ethics is perhaps best able to accommodate women's moral experience, because caring would be a virtue for anyone to have. But virtue ethics often emphasizes "male" virtues such as autonomy, independence, will, and courage at the expense of "female" virtues such as community, sharing, dependency, and considerateness.

According to proponents of difference feminism, an irreducible feminist ethics can be constructed out of concern for relationships, partiality, and intimacy—features of women's moral experience that cannot easily be accommodated by moral theories that emphasize autonomy, impartiality, and universality. Whether this can be done remains to be seen, but feminist thinkers have nonetheless identified a significant problem in our conception of morality.

READINGS ON FEMINIST ETHICS

Nel Noddings, from *Caring: A Feminine Approach to Ethics and Moral Education*

Nel Noddings is professor emerita of education at Stanford University. Her influential book from which our selection is taken was published in 1984. It built on Carol Gilligan's work describing a female moral orientation and helped to establish the ethics of care as distinctively feminist. Whether care is the basis of a unique ethical system is in dispute, even among some feminists who think the concept of mothering is more fundamental. In a caring relationship, Nodding distinguishes the "one-caring" from the "cared-for," noting that a caring relationship requires some kind of reciprocity between the people involved. This puts theoretical limitations on the scope of caring relationships. Noddings writes, "I am not obligated to care for starving children in Africa, because there is no way for this caring to be completed in the other unless I abandon the caring to which I am obligated." Our dealings with animals, plants, and nature are similarly circumscribed.

Critical Reading Questions

1. How is ethical caring related to natural caring?
2. What is the obligation to care, according to Noddings?
3. How does an ethics of care deal with abortion, according to Noddings?
4. How does an ethics of care speak about right and wrong?
5. In what way is an ethics of care tough?

AN ETHIC OF CARING

Nel Noddings

FROM NATURAL TO ETHICAL CARING

David Hume long ago contended that morality is founded upon and rooted in feeling—that the "final sentence" on matters of morality, "that which renders morality an active virtue"—". . . this final sentence depends on some internal sense or feeling, which nature has made universal in the whole species. For what else can have an influence of this nature?"[1]

What is the nature of this feeling that is "universal in the whole species"? I want to suggest that morality as an "active virtue" requires two feelings and not just one. The first is the sentiment of natural caring. There can be no ethical sentiment without the initial, enabling sentiment. In situations where we act on behalf of the other because we want to do so, we are acting in accord with natural caring. A mother's caretaking efforts in behalf of her child are not usually considered ethical but natural. Even maternal animals take care of their offspring, and we do not credit them with ethical behavior.

The second sentiment occurs in response to a remembrance of the first. Nietzsche speaks of love and memory in the context of Christian love and Eros, but what he says may safely be taken out of context to illustrate the point I wish to make here:

There is something so ambiguous and suggestive about the word love, something that speaks to memory and to hope, that even the lowest intelligence and the coldest heart still feel something of the glimmer of this word. The cleverest woman and the most vulgar man recall the relatively least selfish moments of their whole life, even if Eros has taken only a low flight with them.[2]

This memory of our own best moments of caring and being cared for sweeps over us as a feeling—as an "I must"—in response to the plight of the other and our conflicting desire to serve our own interests. There is a transfer of feeling analogous to transfer of learning. In the intellectual domain, when I read a certain kind of mathematical puzzle, I may react by thinking, "That is like the sailors, monkey, and coconuts problem," and then, "Diophantine equations" or "modulo arithmetic" or "congruences." Similarly, when I encounter an other and feel the natural pang conflicted with my own desires—"I must—I do not want to"—I recognize the feeling and remember what has followed it in my own best moments. I have a picture of those moments in which I was cared for and in which I cared, and I may reach toward this memory and guide my conduct by it if I wish to do so.

Recognizing that ethical caring requires an effort that is not needed in natural caring does not commit us to a position that elevates ethical caring over natural caring. Kant has identified the ethical with that which is done out of duty and not out of love, and that distinction in itself seems right. But an ethic built on caring strives to maintain the caring attitude and is thus dependent upon, and not superior to, natural caring. The source of ethical behavior is, then, in twin sentiments—one that feels directly for the other and one that feels for and with that best self, who may accept and sustain the initial feeling rather than reject it.

We shall discuss the ethical ideal, that vision of best self, in some depth. When we commit ourselves to obey the "I must" even at its weakest and most fleeting, we are under the guidance of this ideal. It is not just any picture. Rather, it is our best picture of ourselves caring and being cared for. It may even be colored by acquaintance with one superior to us in caring, but, as I shall describe it, it is both constrained and attainable. It is limited by what we have already done and by what we are capable of, and it does not idealize the impossible so that we may escape into ideal abstraction.

Now, clearly, in pointing to Hume's "active virtue" and to an ethical ideal as the source of ethical behavior, I seem to be advocating an ethic of virtue. This is certainly true in part. Many philosophers recognize the need for a discussion of virtue as the energizing factor in moral behavior, even when they have given their best intellectual effort to a careful explication of their positions on obligation and justification.[3] When we discuss the ethical ideal, we shall be talking about "virtue," but we shall not let "virtue" dissipate into "the virtues" described in abstract categories. The holy man living abstemiously on top of the mountain, praying thrice daily, and denying himself human intercourse may display "virtues," but they are not the virtues of one-caring. The virtue described by the ethical ideal of one-caring is built up in relation. It reaches out to the other and grows in response to the other.

Since our discussion of virtue will be embedded in an exploration of moral activity we might do well to start by asking whether or under what circumstances we are obliged to respond to the initial "I must." Does it make sense to say that I am obliged to heed that which comes to me as obligation?

OBLIGATION

There are moments for all of us when we care quite naturally. We just do care; no ethical effort is required. "Want" and "ought" are indistinguishable in such cases. I want to do what I or others might judge I ought to do. But can there be a "demand" to care? There can be, surely, no demand for the initial impulse that arises as a feeling, an inner voice saying "I must do something," in response to the need of the cared-for. This impulse arises naturally, at least occasionally, in the absence of pathology. We cannot demand that one have this impulse, but we shrink from one who never has it. One who never feels the pain of another, who never confesses the internal "I must" that is so familiar to most of us, is beyond our normal pattern of understanding. Her case is pathological, and we avoid her.

But even if I feel the initial "I must," I may reject it. I may reject it instantaneously by shifting from "I must do something" to "Something must be done," and removing myself from the set of possible agents through whom the action should be accomplished. I may reject it because I feel that there is nothing I can do. If I do either of these things without reflection upon what I might do in behalf of the cared-for, then I do not care. Caring requires me to respond to the initial impulse with an act of commitment: I commit myself either to overt action on behalf of the cared-for (I pick up my crying infant) or I commit myself to thinking about what I might do. In the latter case, as we have seen, I may or may not act overtly in behalf of the cared-for. I may abstain from action if I believe that anything I might do would tend to work against the best interests of the cared-for. But the test of my caring is not wholly in how things turn out; the primary test lies in an examination of what I considered, how fully I received the other, and whether the free pursuit of his projects is partly a result of the completion of my caring in him.

But am I obliged to embrace the "I must"? In this form, the question is a bit odd, for the "I must" carries obligation with it. It comes to us as obligation. But accepting and affirming the "I must" are different from feeling it, and these responses are what I am pointing to when I ask whether I am obliged to embrace the "I must." The question nags at us; it is a question that has been asked, in a variety of forms, over and over by moralists and moral theorists. Usually, the question arises as part of the broader question of justification. We ask something of the sort: Why must I (or should I) do what suggests itself to reason as "right" or as needing to be done for the sake of some other? We might prefer to supplement "reason" with "and/or feeling." This question is, of course, not the only thorny question in moral theory, but it is one that has plagued theorists who see clearly that there is no way to derive an "I ought" statement from a chain of facts. I may agree readily that "things would be better"—that is, that a certain state of affairs commonly agreed to be desirable might be attained—if a certain chain of events were to take place. But there is still nothing in this intellectual chain that can produce the "I ought." I may choose to remain an observer on the scene.

Now I am suggesting that the "I must" arises directly and prior to consideration of what it is that I might do. The initial feeling is the "I must." When it comes to me indistinguishable from the "I want," I proceed easily as one-caring. But often it comes to me conflicted. It may be barely perceptible, and it may be followed almost simultaneously by resistance. When someone asks me to get something for him or merely asks for my attention, the "I must" may be lost in a clamor of resistance. Now a second sentiment is required if I am to behave as one-caring. I care about myself as one-caring and, although I do not care naturally for the person who has asked something of me—at least not at this moment—I feel the genuine moral sentiment, the "I ought," that sensibility to which I have committed myself.

Let me try to make plausible my contention that the moral imperative arises directly.[4] And, of course, I must try to explain how caring and what I am calling the "moral imperative" are related. When my infant cries in the night, I not only feel that I must do something but I want to do something. Because I love this child, because I am bonded to him, I want to remove his pain as I would want to remove my own. The "I must" is not a dutiful imperative but one that accompanies the "I want." If I were tied to a chair, for example, and wanted desperately to get free, I might say as I struggled, "I must do something; I must get out of these bonds." But this "must" is not yet the moral or ethical "ought." It is a "must" born of desire.

The most intimate situations of caring are, thus, natural. I do not feel that taking care of my own child is "moral" but, rather, natural. A woman who allows her own child to die of neglect is often considered sick rather than immoral; that is, we feel that either she or the situation into which she has been thrust must be pathological. Otherwise, the impulse to respond, to nurture the living infant, is overwhelming. We share the impulse with other creatures in the animal kingdom. Whether we want to consider this response as "instinctive" is problematic, because certain patterns of response may be implied by the term and because suspension of reflective consciousness seems also to be implied (and I am not suggesting that we have no choice), but I have no difficulty in considering it as innate. Indeed, I am claiming that the impulse to act in behalf of the present other is itself innate. It lies latent in each of us, awaiting gradual development in a succession of caring relations. I am suggesting that our inclination toward and interest in morality derives from caring. In caring, we accept the natural impulse to act on behalf of the present other. We are engrossed in the other. We have received him and feel his pain or happiness, but we are not compelled by this impulse. We have a choice; we may accept what we feel, or we may reject it. If we have a strong desire to be moral, we will not reject it, and this strong desire to be moral is derived, reflectively, from the more fundamental and natural desire to be and to remain related. To reject the feeling when it arises is either to be in an internal state of imbalance or to contribute willfully to the diminution of the ethical ideal.

But suppose in a particular case that the "I must" does not arise, or that it whispers faintly and disappears, leaving distrust, repugnance, or hate. Why, then, should I behave morally toward the object of my dislike? Why should I not accept feelings other than those characteristic of caring and, thus, achieve an internal state of balance through hate, anger, or malice?

The answer to this is, I think, that the genuine moral sentiment (our second sentiment) arises from an evaluation of the caring relation as good, as better than, superior to, other forms of relatedness. I feel the moral "I must" when I recognize that my response will either enhance or diminish my ethical ideal. It will serve either to increase or decrease the likelihood of genuine caring. My response affects me as one-caring. In a given situation with someone I am not fond of, I may be able to find all sorts of reasons why I should not respond to his need. I may be too busy. He may be undiscerning. The matter may be, on objective analysis, unimportant. But, before I decide, I must turn away from this analytic chain of thought and back to the concrete situation. Here is this person with this perceived need to which is attached this importance. I must put justification aside temporarily. Shall I respond?

How do I feel as a duality about the "I" who will not respond?

I am obliged, then, to accept the initial "I must" when it occurs and even to fetch it out of recalcitrant slumber when it fails to awake spontaneously.[5] The source of my obligation is the value I place on the relatedness of caring. This value itself arises as a product of actual caring and being cared-for and my reflection on the goodness of these concrete caring situations.

Now, what sort of "goodness" is it that attaches to the caring relation? It cannot be a fully moral goodness, for we have already described forms of caring that are natural and require no moral effort. But it cannot be a fully nonmoral goodness either, for it would then join a class of goods many of which are widely separated from the moral good. It is, perhaps, properly described as a "premoral good," one that lies in a region with the moral good and shades over into it. We cannot always decide with certainty whether our caring response is natural or ethical. Indeed, the decision to respond ethically as one-caring may cause the lowering of barriers that previously prevented reception of the other, and natural caring may follow.

I have identified the source of our obligation and have said that we are obligated to accept, and even to call forth, the feeling "I must." But what exactly must I do? Can my obligation be set forth in a list or hierarchy of principles? So far, it seems that I am obligated to maintain an attitude and, thus, to meet the other as one-caring and, at the same time, to increase my own virtue as one-caring. If I am advocating an ethic of virtue, do not all the usual dangers lie in wait: hypocrisy, self-righteousness, withdrawal from the public domain? We shall discuss these dangers as the idea of an ethical ideal is developed more fully.

Let me say here, however, why it seems preferable to place an ethical ideal above principle as a guide to moral action. It has been traditional in moral philosophy to insist that moral principles must be, by their very nature as moral principles, universifiable. If I am obligated to do X under certain conditions, then under sufficiently similar conditions you also are obligated to do X. But the principle of universifiability seems to depend, as Nietzsche

pointed out, on a concept of "sameness."[6] In order to accept the principle, we should have to establish that human predicaments exhibit sufficient sameness, and this we cannot do without abstracting away from concrete situations those qualities that seem to reveal the sameness. In doing this, we often lose the very qualities or factors that gave rise to the moral question in the situation. That condition which makes the situation different and thereby induces genuine moral puzzlement cannot be satisfied by the application of principles developed in situations of sameness.

This does not mean that we cannot receive any guidance from an attempt to discover principles that seem to be universifiable. We can, under this sort of plan, arrive at the doctrine of "prima facie duty" described by W. D. Ross.[7] Ross himself, however, admits that this doctrine yields no real guidance for moral conduct in concrete situations. It guides us in abstract moral thinking; it tells us, theoretically, what to do, "all other things being equal." But other things are rarely if ever equal. A and B, struggling with a moral decision, are two different persons with different factual histories, different projects and aspirations, and different ideals. It may indeed be right, morally right, for A to do X and B to do not-X. We may, that is, connect "right" and "wrong" to faithfulness to the ethical ideal. This does not cast us into relativism, because the ideal contains at its heart a component that is universal: Maintenance of the caring relation.

Before turning to a discussion of "right" and "wrong" and their usefulness in an ethic of caring, we might try to clear up the problem earlier mentioned as a danger in any ethic of virtue: the temptation to withdraw from the public domain. It is a real danger. Even though we rejected the sort of virtue exhibited by the hermit-monk on the mountaintop, that rejection may have been one of personal choice. It still remains possible that an ethic of caring is compatible with the monk's choice, and that such an ethic even induces withdrawal. We are not going to be able to divide cases clearly. The monk who withdraws only to serve God is clearly under the guidance of an ethic that differs fundamentally from the ethic of caring. The source of his ethic is not the source of ours, and he might deny that any form of human relatedness could be a source for moral behavior. But if, when another intrudes upon his privacy, he receives the other as one-caring, we cannot charge him with violating our ethic. Further, as we saw in our discussion of the one-caring, there is a legitimate dread of the proximate stranger—of that person who may ask more than we feel able to give. We saw there that we cannot care for everyone. Caring itself is reduced to mere talk about caring when we attempt to do so. We must acknowledge, then, that an ethic of caring implies a limit on our obligation.

Our obligation is limited and delimited by relation. We are never free, in the human domain, to abandon our preparedness to care; but, practically, if we are meeting those in our inner circles adequately as ones-caring and receiving those linked to our inner circles by formal chains of relation, we shall limit the calls upon our obligation quite naturally. We are not obliged to summon the "I must" if there is no possibility of completion in the other. I am not obliged to care for starving children in Africa, because there is no way for this caring to be completed in the other unless I abandon the caring to which I am obligated. I may still choose to do something in the direction of caring, but I am not obliged to do so. When we discuss our obligation to animals, we shall see that this is even more sharply limited by relation. We cannot refuse obligation in human affairs by merely refusing to enter relation; we are, by virtue of our mutual humanity, already and perpetually in potential relation. Instead, we limit our obligation by examining the possibility of completion. In connection with animals, however, we may find it possible to refuse relation itself on the grounds of a species-specific impossibility of any form of reciprocity in caring.

Now, this is very important, and we should try to say clearly what governs our obligation. On the basis of what has been developed so far, there seem to be two criteria: the existence of or potential for present relation, and the dynamic potential for growth in relation, including the potential for increased reciprocity and, perhaps, mutuality. The first criterion establishes an absolute obligation and the second serves to put our obligations into an order of priority.

If the other toward whom we shall act is capable of responding as cared-for and there are no objective conditions that prevent our receiving this response—if, that is, our caring can be completed in the other—then we must meet that other as one-caring. If we do not care naturally, we must call upon our capacity for ethical caring. When we are in relation or when the other has addressed us, we must respond as one-caring. The imperative in relation is categorical. When relation has not yet been established, or when it may properly be refused (when no formal chain or natural circle is present), the imperative is more like that of the hypothetical: I must if I wish to (or am able to) move into relation.

The second criterion asks us to look at the nature of potential relation and, especially, at the capacity of the cared-for to respond. The potential for response in animals, for example, is nearly static; they cannot respond in mutuality, nor can the nature of their response change substantially. But a child's potential for increased response is enormous. If the possibility of relation is dynamic—if the relation may clearly grow with respect to reciprocity—then the possibility and degree of my obligation also grows. If response is imminent, so also is my obligation. This criterion will help us to distinguish between our obligation to members of the nonhuman animal world and, say, the human fetus. We must keep in mind, however, that the second criterion binds us in proportion to the probability of increased response and to the imminence of that response. Relation itself is fundamental in obligation.

I shall give an example of thinking guided by these criteria, but let us pause for a moment and ask what it is we are trying to accomplish. I am working deliberately toward criteria that will preserve our deepest and most tender human feelings. The caring of mother for child, of human adult for human infant, elicits the tenderest feelings in most of us. Indeed, for many women, this feeling of nurturance lies at the very heart of what we assess as good. A philosophical position that has difficulty distinguishing between our obligation to human infants and, say, pigs is in some difficulty straight off. It violates our most deeply cherished feeling about human goodness. This violation does not, of course, make the position logically wrong, but it suggests that especially strong grounds will be needed to support it. In the absence of such strong grounds—and I shall argue in a later chapter that they are absent—we might prefer to establish a position that captures rather than denies our basic feelings. We might observe that man (in contrast to woman) has continually turned away from his inner self and feeling in pursuit of both science and ethics. With respect to strict science, this turning outward may be defensible; with respect to ethics, it has been disastrous.

Now, let's consider an example: the problem of abortion. Operating under the guidance of an ethic of caring, we are not likely to find abortion in general either right or wrong. We shall have to inquire into individual cases. An incipient embryo is an information speck—a set of controlling instructions for a future human being. Many of these specks are created and flushed away without their creators' awareness. From the view developed here, the information speck is an information speck; it has no given sanctity. There should be no concern over the waste of "human tissue," since nature herself is wildly prolific, even profligate.[8] The one-caring is concerned not with human tissue but with human consciousness—with pain, delight, hope, fear, entreaty, and response.

But suppose the information speck is mine, and I am aware of it. This child-to-be is the product of love between a man deeply cared-for and me. Will the child have his eyes or mine? His stature or mine? Our joint love of mathematics or his love of mechanics or my love of language? This is not just an information speck; it is endowed with prior love and current knowledge. It is sacred, but I—humbly, not presumptuously—confer sacredness upon it. I cannot, will not destroy it. It is joined to loved others through formal chains of caring. It is linked to the inner circle in a clearly defined way. I might wish that I were not pregnant, but I cannot destroy this known and potentially loved person-to-be. There is already relation albeit indirect and formal. My decision is an ethical one born of natural caring.

But suppose, now, that my beloved child has grown up; it is she who is pregnant and considering abortion. She is not sure of the love between herself and the man. She is miserably worried about her economic and emotional future. I might like to convey sanctity on this information speck; but I am not God—only mother to this suffering cared-for. It is she who is conscious and in pain, and I as one-caring move to relieve the pain. This information speck is an information speck and that is all. There is no formal relation, given the breakdown between husband and wife, and with the embryo, there is no present relation; the possibility of future relation—while not absent, surely—is uncertain. But what of this possibility for growing response? Must we not consider it? We must indeed. As the embryo becomes a fetus and, growing daily, becomes more nearly capable of response as cared-for, our obligation grows from a nagging uncertainty—an "I must if I wish"—to an utter conviction that we must meet this small other as one-caring.

If we try to formalize what has been expressed in the concrete situations described so far, we arrive at a legal approach to abortion very like that of the Supreme Court: abortions should be freely available in the first trimester, subject to medical determination in the second trimester, and banned in the third, when the fetus is viable. A woman under the guidance of our ethic would be likely to recognize the growing possibility of relation; the potential is clearly dynamic. Further, many women recognize the relation as established when the fetus begins to move about. It is not a question of when life begins but of when relation begins.

But what if relation is never established? Suppose the child is born and the mother admits no sense of relatedness. May she commit infanticide? One who asks such questions misinterprets the concept of relatedness that I have been struggling to describe. Since the infant, even the near-natal fetus, is capable of relation—of the sweetest and most unselfconscious reciprocity—one who encounters the infant is obligated to meet it as one-caring. Both parts of this claim are essential; it is not only the child's capability to respond but also the encounter that induces obligation. There must exist the possibility for our caring to be completed in the other. If the mother does not care naturally, then she must summon ethical caring to support her as one-caring. She may not ethically ignore the child's cry to live.

The one-caring, in considering abortion as in all other matters, cares first for the one in immediate pain or peril. She might suggest a brief and direct form of counseling in which a young expectant mother could come to grips with her feelings. If the incipient child has been sanctified by its mother, every effort must be made to help the two to achieve a stable and hopeful life together; if it has not, it should be removed swiftly and mercifully with all loving attention to the woman, the conscious patient. Between these two clear reactions is a possible confused one: the young woman is not sure how she feels. The one-caring probes gently to see what has been considered, raising questions and retreating when the questions obviously have been considered and are now causing great pain. Is such a view "unprincipled"? If it is, it is boldly so; it is at least connected with the world as it is, at its best and at its worst, and it requires that we—in espousing a "best"—stand ready to actualize that preferred condition. The decision for or against abortion must be made by those directly involved in the concrete situation, but it need not be made alone. The one-caring cannot require everyone to behave as she would in a particular situation. Rather, when she dares to say, "I think you should do X," she adds, also, "Can I help you?" The one under her gaze is under her support and not her judgment.

One under the guidance of an ethic of caring is tempted to retreat to a manageable world. Her public life is limited by her insistence upon meeting the other as one-caring. So long as this is possible, she may reach outward and enlarge her circles of caring. When this reaching out destroys or drastically reduces her actual caring, she retreats and renews her contact with those who address her. If the retreat becomes a flight, an avoidance of the call to care, her ethical ideal is diminished. Similarly, if the retreat is away from human beings and toward other objects of caring—ideas, animals, humanity-at-large, God—her ethical ideal is virtually shattered. This is not a judgment, for we can understand and sympathize with one who makes such a choice. It is more in the nature of a perception: we see clearly what has been lost in the choice.

Our ethic of caring—which we might have called a "feminine ethic"—begins to look a bit mean in contrast to the masculine ethics of universal love or universal justice. But universal love is illusion. Under the illusion, some young people retreat to the church to worship that which they cannot actualize; some write lovely poetry extolling universal love; and some, in terrible disillusion, kill to establish the very principles which should have entreated them not to kill. Thus are lost both principles and persons.

RIGHT AND WRONG

How are we to make judgments of right and wrong under this ethic? First, it is important to understand that we are not primarily interested in judging but, rather, in heightening moral perception and sensitivity. But "right" and "wrong" can be useful.

Suppose a mother observes her young child pulling the kitten's tail or picking it up by the ears. She may exclaim, "Oh, no, it is not nice to hurt the kitty," or, "You must not hurt the kitty." Or she may simply say, "Stop. See—you are hurting the kitty," and she may then take the kitten in her own hands and show the child how to handle it. She holds the kitten gently, stroking it, and saying, "See? Ah, ah, kitty, nice kitty. . . ." What the mother is supposing in this interaction is that the realization that his act is hurting the kitten, supplemented by the knowledge of how to avoid inflicting hurt, will suffice to change the child's behavior. If she believes this, she has no need for the statement, "It is wrong to hurt the kitty." She is not threatening sanctions but drawing dual attention to a matter of fact (the hurting) and her own commitment (I will not hurt). Beyond this, she is supposing that her child, well-cared-for himself, does not want to inflict pain.

Now, I am not claiming through use of this illustration that moral statements are mere expressions of approval or disapproval, although they do serve an expressive function. A. J. Ayer, who did make a claim of this sort before modifying his position somewhat, uses an illustration very like the one just given to support an emotivist position.[9] But even if it were possible to take a purely analytic stance with respect to moral theory, as Ayer suggests he has done, that is certainly not what I intend to do. One who labels moral statements as expressions of approval or disapproval, and takes the matter to be finished with that, misses the very heart of morality. He misses the commitment to behave in a fashion compatible with caring. Thus he misses both feeling and content. I may, after all, express my approval or disapproval on matters that are not moral. Thus it is clear that when I make a moral judgment I am doing more than simply expressing approval or disapproval. I am both expressing my own commitment to behave in a way compatible with caring and appealing to the hearer to consider what he is doing. I may say first to a child, "Oh! Don't hurt the kitty!" And I may then add, "It is wrong to hurt the kitty." The word is not necessary, strictly speaking, but I may find it useful.

What do I mean by this? I certainly mean to express my own commitment, and I show this best by daily example. But I may mean to say more than this. I may explain to the child that not only do I feel this way but that our family does, that our community does, that our culture does. Here I must be very careful. Our community may say one thing and do quite another. Such contradiction is even more likely at the level of "our culture." But I express myself doubly in words and in acts, and I may search out examples in the larger culture to convince the child that significant others do feel this way. The one-caring is careful to distinguish between acts that violate caring, acts that she herself holds wrong, and those acts that "some people" hold to be wrong. She need not be condescending in this instruction. She is herself so reluctant to universalize beyond the demands of caring that she cannot say, "It is wrong," to everything that is illegal, church-forbidden, or contrary to a prevailing etiquette. But she can raise the question, attempt to justify the alien view, express her own objections, and support the child in his own exploration.

Emotivists are partly right, I think, when they suggest that we might effectively substitute a statement describing the fact or event that triggers our feeling or attitude for statements such as "It is wrong to do X." When I say to my child, "It is wrong to hurt the kitty," I mean (if I am not threatening sanctions) to inform him that he is hurting the kitten and, further, that I believe that if he perceives he is doing so, he will stop. I am counting on his gradually developing ability to feel pain in the other to induce a decision to stop. To say, "It is wrong to cause pain needlessly," contributes nothing by way of knowledge and can hardly be thought likely to change the attitude or behavior of one who might ask, "Why is it wrong?" If I say to someone, "You are hurting the cat," and he replies, "I know it—so what? I like hurting cats," I feel "zero at the bone." Saying to him, "It is wrong to hurt cats," adds little unless I intend to threaten sanctions. If I mean to equate "It is wrong to hurt cats" with "There will be a sure and specific punishment for hurting cats," then it would be more honest to say this. One either feels a sort of pain in response to the pain of others, or one does not feel it. If he does feel it, he does not need to be told that causing pain is wrong. If he does not feel it in a particular case, he may remember the feeling—as one remembers the sweetness of love on hearing a certain piece of music—and allow himself to be moved by this remembrance of feeling. For one who feels nothing, directly or by remembrance, we must prescribe re-education or exile. Thus, at the foundation of moral behavior—as we have already pointed out—is feeling or sentiment. But, further, there is commitment to remain open to that feeling, to remember it, and to put one's thinking in its service. It is the particular commitment underlying genuine expressions of moral judgment—as well as the special content—that the emotivist misses.

The one-caring, clearly, applies "right" and "wrong" most confidently to her own decisions. This does not, as we have insisted before, make her a relativist. The caring attitude that lies at the heart of all ethical behavior is universal. As the mother in chapter two, who had to decide whether or not to leave her sick child, decided on the basis of a caring evaluation of the conditions and feelings of those involved, so in general the one-caring evaluates her own acts with respect to how faithfully they conform to what is known and felt through the receptivity of caring. But she also uses "right" and "wrong" instructively and respectfully to refer to the judgments of significant others. If she agrees because the matter at hand can be assessed in light of caring, she adds her personal commitment and example; if she has doubts—because the rule appealed to seems irrelevant or ambiguous in the light of caring—she still acknowledges the judgment but adds her own dissent or demurrer. Her eye is on the ethical development of the cared-for and, as she herself withholds judgment until she has heard the "whole story," she wants the cared-for to encounter others, receive them, and reflect on what he has received. Principles and rules are among the beliefs he will receive, and she wants him to consider these in the light of caring.

But is this all we can say about right and wrong? Is there not a firm foundation in morality for our legal judgments? Surely, we must be allowed to say, for example, that stealing is wrong and is, therefore, properly forbidden by law. Because it is so often wrong—and so easily demonstrated to be wrong—under an ethic of caring, we may accede that such a law has its roots *partly* in morality. We may legally punish one who has stolen, but we may not pass moral judgment on him until we know why he stole. An ethic of caring is likely to be stricter in its judgment, but more supportive and corrective in following up its judgment, than ethics otherwise grounded. For the one-caring, stealing is almost always wrong:

Ms. A talks with her young son. *But, Mother,* the boy pleads, *suppose I want to make you happy and I steal something you want from a big chain store. I haven't hurt anyone, have I? Yes, you have,* responds his mother, and she points to the predicament of the store managers who may be accused of poor stewardship and to the higher prices suffered by their neighbors. *Well, suppose I steal from a rich, rich person? He can replace what I take easily, and . . . Wait,* says Ms. A. *Is someone suffering? Are you stealing to relieve that suffering, and will you make certain that what you steal is used to relieve it? . . . But can't I steal to make someone happy?* her son persists. Slowly, patiently, Ms. A explains the position of one-caring. *Each one* who comes under our gaze must be met as one-caring. When I want to please X and I turn toward Y as a means for satisfying my desire to please X, I must now meet Y as one-caring. I do not judge him for being rich—for treasuring what I, perhaps, regard with indifference. I may not cause him pain by taking or destroying what he possesses. *But what if I steal from a bad guy—someone who stole to get what he has?* Ms. A smiles at her young son, struggling to avoid his ethical responsibility: *Unless he is an immediate threat to you or someone else, you must meet him, too, as one-caring.*

The lessons in "right" and "wrong" are hard lessons—not swiftly accomplished by setting up as an objective the learning of some principle. We do not say: It is wrong to steal. Rather, we consider why it was wrong or may be wrong in this case to steal. We do not say: It is wrong to kill. By setting up such a principle, we also imply its exceptions, and then we may too easily act on authorized exceptions. The one-caring wants to consider, and wants her child to consider, the act itself in full context. She will send him into the world skeptical, vulnerable, courageous, disobedient, and tenderly receptive. The "world" may not depend upon him to obey its rules or fulfill its wishes, but you, the individual he encounters, may depend upon him to meet you as one-caring.

THE PROBLEM OF JUSTIFICATION

Since I have chided the emotivist for not digging beneath the expressive layer of moral sentiment to the nature of the feeling itself and the commitment to act in accord with the feeling, one might ask whether I should not dig beneath the commitment. Why should I be committed to not causing pain? Now, clearly, in one sense, I cannot answer this better than we already have. When the "Why?" refers to motivation, we have seen that the one-caring receives the other and acts in the other's behalf as she would for herself; that is, she acts with a similar motive energy. Further, I have claimed that, when natural caring fails, the motive energy in behalf of the other can be summoned out of caring for the ethical self. We have discussed both natural caring and ethical caring. Ethical caring, as I have described it, depends not upon rule or principle but upon the development of an ideal self. It does not depend upon just any ideal of self, but the ideal developed in congruence with one's best remembrance of caring and being cared-for.

So far, in recommending the ethical ideal as a guide to ethical conduct, I have suggested that traditional approaches to the problem of justification are mistaken. When the ethical theorist asks, "Why should I behave thus-and-so?" his question is likely to be aimed at justification rather than motivation and at a logic that resides outside the person. He is asking for reasons of the sort we expect to find in logical demonstration. He may expect us to claim that moral judgments can be tested as claims to facts can be tested, or that moral judgments are derived from divine commandment, or that moral truths are intuitively apprehended. Once started on this line of discussion, we may find ourselves arguing abstractly about the status of relativism and absolutism, egoism and altruism, and a host of other positions that, I shall claim, are largely irrelevant to moral conduct. They are matters of considerable intellectual interest, but they are distractions if our primary interest is in ethical conduct.

Moral statements cannot be justified in the way that statements of fact can be justified. They are not truths. They are derived not from facts or principles but from the caring attitude. Indeed, we might say that moral statements come out of the moral view or attitude, which, as I have described it, is the rational attitude built upon natural caring. When we put it this way, we see that there can be no justification for taking the moral viewpoint—that in truth, the moral viewpoint is prior to any notion of justification.

But there is another difficulty in answering the request for justification. Consideration of problems of justification requires us to concentrate on moral judgments, on moral statements. Hence we are led to an exploration of the language and reasoning used to discuss moral conduct and away from an assessment of the concrete events in which we must choose whether and how to behave morally. Indeed, we are often led far beyond what we feel and intuitively judge to be right in a search for some simple and absolute guide to moral goodness.

For an ethic of caring, the problem of justification is not concentrated upon justified action in general. We are not "justified"—we are *obligated*—to do what is required to maintain and enhance caring. We must "justify" not-caring; that is, we must explain why, in the interest of caring for ourselves as ethical selves or in the interest of others for whom we care, we may behave as ones-not-caring toward this particular other. In a related problem, we must justify doing what this other would not have us do to him as part of our genuine effort to care for him. But even in these cases, an ethic of caring does not emphasize justification.

As one-caring, I am not seeking justification for my action; I am not standing alone before some tribunal. What I seek is completion in the other—the sense of being cared-for and, I hope, the renewed commitment of the cared-for to turn about and act as one-caring in the circles and chains within which he is defined. Thus, I am not justified but somehow fulfilled and completed in my own life and in the lives of those I have thus influenced.

It sounds all very nice, says my male colleague, but can you claim to be doing "ethics"? After all, ethics is the study of justified action. . . . Ah, yes. But, after "after-all," I am a woman, and I was not party to that definition. Shall we say then that I am talking about "how to meet the other morally"? Is this part of ethics? Is ethics part of this?

WOMEN AND MORALITY: VIRTUE

Many of us in education are keenly aware of the distortion that results from undue emphasis on moral judgments and justification. Lawrence Kohlberg's theory, for example, is widely held to be a model for moral education, but it is actually only a hierarchical description of moral reasoning.[10] It is well known, further, that the description may not be accurate. In particular, the fact that women seem often to be "stuck" at stage three might call the accuracy of the description into question. But perhaps the description is accurate within the domain of morality conceived as moral justification. If it is, we might well explore the possibility that feminine nonconformity to the Kohlberg model counts against the justification/judgment paradigm and not against women as moral thinkers.

Women, perhaps the majority of women, prefer to discuss moral problems in terms of concrete situations. They approach moral problems not as intellectual problems to be solved by abstract reasoning but as concrete human problems to be lived and to be solved in living. Their approach is founded in caring. Carol Gilligan describes the approach:

> . . . women not only define themselves in a context of human relationship but also judge themselves in terms of their ability to care. Woman's place in man's life cycle has been that of nurturer, caretaker, and helpmate, the weaver of those networks of relationships on which she in turn relies.[11]

Faced with a hypothetical moral dilemma, women often ask for more information. It is not the case, certainly, that women cannot arrange principles hierarchically and derive conclusions logically. It is more likely that they see this process as peripheral to or even irrelevant to moral conduct. They want more information, I think, in order to form a picture. Ideally, they need to talk to the participants, to see their eyes and facial expressions, to size up the whole situation. Moral decisions are, after all, made in situations; they are qualitatively different from the solution of geometry problems. Women, like act-deontologists in general, give reasons for their acts, but the reasons point to feelings, needs, situational conditions, and their sense of personal ideal rather than universal principles and their application.

As we have seen, caring is not in itself a virtue. The genuine ethical commitment to maintain oneself as caring gives rise to the development and exercise of virtues, but these must be assessed in the context of caring situations. It is not, for example, patience itself that is a virtue but patience with respect to some infirmity of a particular cared-for or patience in instructing a concrete cared-for that is virtuous. We must not reify virtues and turn our caring toward them. If we do this, our ethic turns inward and is even less useful than an ethic of principles, which at least remains indirectly in contact with the acts we are assessing. The fulfillment of virtue is both in me and in the other.

A consideration of caring and an ethic built upon it give new meaning to what Kohlberg assesses as "stage three" morality. At this stage, persons behave morally in order to be thought of—or to think of themselves as—"good boys" or "good girls." Clearly, it makes a difference whether one chooses to be good or to be thought of as good. One who chooses to be good may not be "stuck," as Kohlberg suggests, in a stage of moral reasoning. Rather, she may have chosen an alternative route to moral conduct. . . .

THE TOUGHNESS OF CARING

An ethic built on caring is thought by some to be tenderminded. It does involve construction of an ideal from the fact and memory of tenderness. The ethical sentiment itself requires a prior natural sentiment of caring and a willingness to sustain tenderness. But there is no assumption of innate human goodness and, when we move to the construction of a philosophy of education, we shall find enormous differences between the view developed here and that of those who find the child innately good. I shall not claim that the child is "innately wise and good," or that the aim of life is happiness, or that all will be well with the child if we resist interfering in its intellectual and moral life.[15] We have memories of caring, of tenderness, and these lead us to a vision of what is good—a state that is good-in-itself and a commitment to sustain and enhance that good (the desire and commitment to be moral). But we have other memories as well, and we have other desires. An ethic of caring takes into account these other tendencies and desires; it is precisely because the tendency to treat each other well is so fragile that we must strive so consistently to care.

Far from being romantic, an ethic of caring is practical, made for this earth. Its toughness is disclosed in a variety of features, the most important of which I shall try to describe briefly here.

First, since caring is a relation, an ethic built on it is naturally other-regarding. Since I am defined in relation, I do not sacrifice myself when I move toward the other as one-caring. Caring is, thus, both self-serving and other-serving. Willard Gaylin describes it as necessary to the survival of the species: "If one's frame of reference focuses on the individual, caring seems self-sacrificing. But if the focus is on the group, on the species, it is the ultimate self-serving device—the sine qua non of survival."[16]

Clearly, this is so. But while I am drawn to the other, while I am instinctively called to nurture and protect, I am also the initiator and chooser of my acts. I may act in accordance with that which is good in my deepest nature, or I may seek to avoid it—either by forsaking relation or by trying to transform that which is feeling and action into that which is all propositional talk and principle. If I suppose, for example, that I am somehow alone and totally responsible for either the apprehension or creation of moral principles, I may find myself in some difficulty when it comes to caring for myself. If moral principles govern my conduct with respect to others, if I must always regard the other in order to be moral, how can I properly meet my own needs and desires? How can I, morally, care for myself?

An ethic of caring is a tough ethic. It does not separate self and other in caring, although, of course, it identifies the special contribution of the one-caring and the cared-for in caring. In contrast to some forms of agapism, for example, it has no problem in advocating a deep and steady caring for self. In a discussion of other-regarding forms of agapism, Gene Outka considers the case of a woman tied to a demanding parent. He explores the possibility of her finding justification for leaving in an assessment of the greatest good for all concerned, and he properly recommends that her own interests be included. In discussing the insistence of some agapists on entirely other-regarding justification, he explores the possibility of her breaking away "to become a medical doctor," thereby satisfying the need for multilateral other-interests.[17] The one-caring throws up her hands at such casting about for reasons. She needs no special justification to care for herself for, if she is not supported and cared-for, she may be entirely lost as one-caring. If caring is to be maintained, clearly, the one-caring must be maintained. She must be strong, courageous, and capable of joy.

When we looked at the one-caring in conflict (e.g., Mr. Jones and his mother), we saw that he or she can be overwhelmed by cares and burdens. The ethical responsibility of the one-caring is to look clear-eyed on what is happening to her ideal and how well she is meeting it. She sees herself, perhaps, as caring lovingly for her parent. But perhaps he is cantankerous, ungrateful, rude, and even dirty. She sees herself becoming impatient, grouchy, tired, and filled with self-pity. She can stay and live by an honestly diminished ideal—"I am a tired, grouchy, pitiful caretaker of my old father"—or she can free herself to whatever degree she must to remain minimally but actually caring. The ethical self does not live partitioned off from the rest of the person. Thinking guided by caring does not seek to justify a way out by means of a litany of predicted "goods," but it seeks a way to remain one-caring and, if at all possible, to enhance the ethical ideal. In such a quest, there is no way to disregard the self, or to remain impartial, or to adopt the stance of a disinterested observer.

Pursuit of the ethical ideal demands impassioned and realistic commitment.

We see still another reason for accepting constraints on our ethical ideals. When we accept honestly our loves, our innate ferocity, our capacity for hate, we may use all this as information in building the safeguards and alarms that must be part of the ideal. We know better what we must work toward, what we must prevent, and the conditions under which we are lost as ones-caring. Instead of hiding from our natural impulses and pretending that we can achieve goodness through lofty abstractions, we accept what is there—all of it—and use what we have already assessed as good to control that which is not-good.

Caring preserves both the group and the individual and, as we have already seen, it limits our obligation so that it may realistically be met. It will not allow us to be distracted by visions of universal love, perfect justice, or a world unified under principle. It does not say, "Thou shalt not kill," and then seek other principles under which killing is, after all, justified. If the other is a clear and immediate danger to me or to my cared-fors, I must stop him, and I might need to kill him. But I cannot kill in the name of principle or justice. I must meet this other—even this evil other—as one-caring so long as caring itself is not endangered by my doing so. I must, for example, oppose capital punishment. I do not begin by saying, "Capital punishment is wrong." Thus I do not fall into the trap of having to supply reasons for its wrongness that will be endlessly disputed at a logical level. I do not say, "Life is sacred," for I cannot name a source of sacredness. I may point to the irrevocability of the decision, but this is not in itself decisive, even for me, because in many cases the decision would be just and I could not regret the demise of the condemned. (I have, after all, confessed my own ferocity; in the heat of emotion, I might have torn him to shreds if I had caught him molesting my child.)

My concern is for the ethical ideal, for my own ethical ideal and for whatever part of it others in my community may share. Ideally, another human being should be able to request, with expectation of positive response, my help and comfort. If I am not blinded by fear, or rage, or hatred, I should reach out as one-caring to the proximate stranger who entreats my help. This is the ideal one-caring creates. I should be able to respond to the condemned man's entreaty, "Help me." We must ask, then, after the effects of capital punishment on jurors, on judges, on jailers, on wardens, on newspersons "covering" the execution, on ministers visiting the condemned, on citizens affirming the sentence, on doctors certifying first that the condemned is well enough to be executed and second that he is dead. What effects have capital punishment on the ethical ideals of the participants? For me, if I had to participate, the ethical ideal would be diminished. Diminished. The ideal itself would be diminished. My act would either be wrong or barely right—right in a depleted sense. I might, indeed, participate ethically—rightly—in an execution but only at the cost of revising my ethical ideal downward. If I do not revise it and still participate, then my act is wrong, and I am a hypocrite and unethical. It is the difference between "I don't believe in killing, but . . ." and "I did not believe in killing cold-bloodedly, but now I see that I must and for these reasons." In the latter case, I may retain my ethicality, but at considerable cost. My ideal must forever carry with it not only what I would be but what I am and have been. There is no unbridgeable chasm between what I am and what I will be. I build the bridge to my future self, and this is why I oppose capital punishment. I do not want to kill if other options are open to me, and I do not want to ask others in the community to do what may diminish their own ethical ideals.

While I must not kill in obedience to law or principle, I may not, either, refuse to kill in obedience to principle. To remain one-caring, I might have to kill. Consider the case of a woman who kills her sleeping husband. Under most circumstances, the one-caring would judge such an act wrong. It violates the very possibility of caring for the husband. But as she hears how the husband abused his wife and children, about the fear with which the woman lived, about the past efforts to solve the problem legally, the one-caring revises her judgment. The jury finds the woman not guilty by reason of an extenuated self-defense. The one-caring finds her ethical, but under the guidance of a sadly diminished ethical ideal. The

woman has behaved in the only way she found open to protect herself and her children and, thus, she has behaved in accord with the current vision of herself as one-caring. But what a horrible vision! She is now one-who-has-killed once and who would not kill again, and never again simply one who would not kill. The test of ultimate blame or blamelessness, under an ethic of caring, lies in how the ethical ideal was diminished. Did the agent choose the degraded vision out of greed, cruelty, or personal interest? Or was she driven to it by unscrupulous others who made caring impossible to sustain?

We see that our own ethicality is not entirely "up to us." Like Winston in *Nineteen Eighty-Four*, we are fragile; we depend upon each other even for our own goodness. This recognition casts some doubt on Immanuel Kant's position:

It is contradictory to say that I make another person's *perfection* my end and consider myself obliged to promote this. For the *perfection* of another man, as a person, consists precisely of *his own* power to adopt his end in accordance with his own concept of duty; and it is self-contradictory to demand that I do (make it my duty to do) what only the other person himself can do.[18]

In one sense, we agree fully with Kant. We cannot define another's perfection; we, as ones-caring, will not even define the principles by which he should live, nor can we prescribe the particular acts he should perform to meet that perfection. But we must be exquisitely sensitive to that ideal of perfection and, in the absence of a repugnance overwhelming to one-caring, we must as ones-caring act to promote that ideal. As parents and educators, we have perhaps no single greater or higher duty than this.

The duty to enhance the ethical ideal, the commitment to caring, invokes a duty to promote skepticism and noninstitutional affiliation. In a deep sense, no institution or nation can be ethical. It cannot meet the other as one-caring or as one trying to care. It can only capture in general terms what particular ones-caring would like to have done in well-described situations. Laws, manifestos, and proclamations are not, on this account, either empty or useless; but they are limited, and they may support immoral as well as moral actions. Only the individual can be truly called to ethical behavior, and the individual can never give way to encapsulated moral guides, although she may safely accept them in ordinary, untroubled times.

Everything depends, then, upon the will to be good, to remain in caring relation to the other. How may we help ourselves and each other to sustain this will?

Questions for Discussion

1. Is Noddings correct to claim that reciprocity is necessary for an ethics of care? What does this imply about caring for plants or animals or strangers far away?
2. Is care ethics relativistic?
3. Is natural care different from ethical care? What is Noddings's view? Is she right?
4. Can we wrongly care? What would that imply for an ethics of care?

Virginia Held, from *Moral Theory From a Feminist Perspective*

Virginia Held is a professor of philosophy at the City University of New York. Her work is widely known and influential among contemporary philosophers, feminist and nonfeminist alike. Held takes the parent-child relationship as morally fundamental, but unlike Noddings, she is unwilling to base an entire ethical system on care alone, because "an ethic of care, essential as a component of morality and perhaps even as a framework, seems deficient if taken as an exclusive preoccupation or one which fails to make room for justice." Instead, Held opts for different moral orientations in different domains: care in the private realm, justice in the public. How different realms are to be reconciled in cases of conflict is not clear.

Critical Reading Questions

1. Why, according to Held, is feminist moral theory needed?
2. What is the moral experience of women, in Held's view?
3. Why does Held believe women's moral experience should figure in moral theory?
4. What is Held's criticism of conceiving of ethics as primarily about moral knowledge?
5. What is the moral significance of giving birth, according to Held?
6. How new is feminist moral inquiry, according to Held?

MORAL THEORY FROM A FEMINIST PERSPECTIVE

Virginia Held

In previous chapters I have discussed the method by which feminist moral inquiry might best proceed, with special attention to concepts that feminists have begun to transform: reason and emotion, the public and the private, the concept of the self. I turn now to some recommendations that feminist moral theory might offer. But first a word about the search for theory.

THE NEED FOR FEMINIST MORAL THEORY

The claim that feminism requires a transformation of moral theory predictably encounters not only hostility but honest skepticism.[1] Skeptics wonder whether there is or can be such a thing as a distinctively feminist moral theory. They doubt that it could be more valid than, say, Marxist mathematics or Communist physics, since they imagine that the validity or truth of a theory should not depend on political outlook or gender. They may acknowledge that traditional principles of fairness or equality must be applied to women in ways that have not been applied in the past, but they disagree that the principles or the theories in which they are embedded need to be transformed. Many feminists respond that the likelihood of feminist moral theory being different from nonfeminist moral theory is at least as substantial as that Marxist social theory differs from the social theory of, say, traditional liberalism. And if feminism will change our views of almost everything, as many think it will, feminist moral theory might even be as different from nonfeminist moral theory as has all or most theory been different since Copernicus, Darwin, and Freud—who of course also built on their pasts.[2]

To those who draw analogies between moral theory and mathematics,[3] the suggestion that feminist moral theory might legitimately differ from nonfeminist moral theory would presumably be as suspect as the notion that there is a distinctively feminist mathematics. But to many of us, the analogy between moral theory and mathematics is much more suspect than the idea of feminist moral theory.

At the very least, we need theories to deal with what is already known about the differing experiences and approaches of women and men in dealing with moral problems. We already have a wealth of personal experience, of literary and reportorial accounts of women's experience, and of social scientific attention to the experience of women. And we already have evidence, from the work of Carol Gilligan and others, that girls and women tend to approach at least some moral problems in ways characteristically different from the ways boys and men do.[4]

In the 1960s and 1970s, the psychologist Lawrence Kohlberg concluded that in their moral development, children go through various stages during which they approach moral problems in characteristic ways.[5] From an early stage of worrying about whether they are likely to get caught and punished, they progress to a final stage, not reached by everyone, in which they decide what to do on the basis of universal moral principles and how to act out of respect for these principles. When further empirical studies were made using these stages as a basis of interpretation, some showed that girls do not progress as fast as boys.

Carol Gilligan, who had worked with Kohlberg, became suspicious of the claim that girls are less morally advanced than boys. She pointed out that the studies leading to Kohlberg's interpretation of moral development in terms of "stages" and to his conclusions about what to count as "progress" were based entirely on studies of boys. Kohlberg, following Piaget, had merely assumed the development of children could be understood by considering boys only. Gilligan found that girls and women seemed to approach moral problems differently and to speak in "a different voice." Whether it is a defective voice or just a different voice or perhaps even a better voice remains an open question.

Kohlberg's final stage bears a remarkable resemblance to Kantian morality. In the view of Gilligan and many feminist moral philosophers, when one listens to the moral reasoning of women, one can discern ways of interpreting moral problems and of organizing possible responses to them that are different from any of the established moral approaches, including Kohlberg's. Women seem to be more concerned with context, and we seem to rely less on abstract rules.

Some psychologists dispute the empirical claim that men and women score differently on Kohlberg's scale, showing that when education and occupation are similar, so are the scores.[6] But such findings fail to consider that the scale itself has been constructed from a masculine point of view, and that those who score equally with men may simply have been socialized to think the way men do.

Gilligan and various feminist moral theorists now speak of two main perspectives in the interpretation of moral problems: the "justice perspective" and the "care perspective." The justice perspective emphasizes universal moral principles and individual conscience. The care perspective pays more attention to people's needs and to the relations between actual people; it considers how these relations can be kept in good condition or repaired if damaged. On traditional moral theories, girls and women have been thought to be less morally advanced than boys and men; on feminist theories it might be boys and men who are morally slower because of their underdeveloped capacities for relatedness and for caring about others.[7]

Empirical studies have shown that females are significantly more inclined than males to cite compassion and sympathy as reasons for their moral positions.[8] We need theories to assess such differences as these and the others discussed, if they do indeed exist, and to consider whether and how, for instance, justice and care can be combined, or if not, whether and how they are incompatible. Feminist moral theorists are exploring these issues.

Gilligan finds that among the two-thirds of the men and women who focus on one perspective or the other, about half the women adopt the perspective of justice, and half the perspective of care; among the men who focus, nearly all focus on justice. She draws our attention to the fact that "if women were eliminated from the research sample, care focus in moral reasoning would virtually disappear."[9] Since women have been virtually ignored in the construction of traditional moral theory, it is not altogether surprising that moralities focusing on justice or abstract rules have often been imagined to be the only true moralities. Children, Gilligan and others find, seem to use both the approaches of justice and of care; the divergence develops as boys gradually give up "caring." Some girls join them. Whether this represents genuine moral development or learning the ways of male-dominated societies is obviously an important question; philosophical positions that merely assume the superiority of the moral thinking of men and of male experience fail to address it.

Also of interest are the observed differences of approach to moral problems evident when persons are dealing with an actual problem rather than thinking about a hypothetical one. The hypothetical problem studied by Kohlberg—whether Heinz should steal a drug to save his dying wife—is obviously a very different kind of problem from the real one faced by the women studied by Gilligan—whether or not to have an abortion. But even when two groups are asked about what seems to be the same problem, they may interpret it to a different degree as real or as hypothetical, and this difference too should be studied for its possible significance. In one study of college students facing an actual problem of civil disobedience (whether or not to participate in a sit-in) many used forms of reasoning rated higher on Kohlberg's scale in comparison with their reasoning about hypothetical dilemmas. On the other hand, many students whose actions were inconsistent with their ideologies used forms of reasoning rated lower on Kohlberg's scale for the actual problem compared with the hypothetical ones.[10]

Of course we need theory to understand whether the differences between women and men in approaching moral problems are historically and culturally determined and to what extent they result from more permanent aspects of femaleness and maleness.[11] This theory, while necessarily philosophical as well as largely empirical, will not be specifically moral. Still, even if such questions could be settled, we would need moral theory to evaluate the differences or lack of differences and to decide on the kind of moral theory compatible with feminist commitments to pay attention to the experience of women.

Traditionally, the experience of women has been located to a large extent in the context of the family. In recent centuries the family has been thought of as a private domain distinct not only from the public domain of the polis, but also from the domains of production and the marketplace. Women (and men) certainly need to develop moral inquiries appropriate to the context of mothering and of family relations, rather than accepting the application to this context of theories developed for the marketplace or the polis or dismissing family issues as outside morality because governed by "natural sentiments." We can certainly show that mothering requires moral decisions and guidelines and that these must often be different from those that now seem suitable for various other domains of activity. But we need to do more. We need to consider whether distinctively feminist moral theories, suitable for the contexts in which the experience of women has been or will continue to be located, are better moral theories than those already available and better for other domains as well.

Sara Ruddick was among the first of contemporary philosophers to discuss some of the considerations that arise in the context of mothering. She has argued that mothering calls forth "maternal thinking," which is different from the thinking arising in other contexts. "Maternal practice," she wrote, responds "to the historical reality of a biological child in a particular social world"; she sees humility and cheerfulness as values which emerge from the practice of mothering. These should not be confused with self-effacement and destructive denial, "their degenerative forms."[12]

If such valuations emerge from mothering, and if on reflection they are endorsed as evaluations appropriate to mothering, we can assert that the moral understanding of persons who mother, and not only their attitudes and activities, is different from that of persons who do not mother, because such values are the values of a distinct practice. And if we acknowledge that a mothering context is an appropriate one in which to explore moral values—an acknowledgment only prejudice could lead us to deny—then paying attention to this context, as feminist moral philosophy does, can lead to different moral theories than ignoring it.

EXPERIENCE AND MORAL INQUIRY

The experience of women so far has been distinctively different from the experience of men. We need a theory about how to count the experience of women. It is not obvious that it should count equally in the construction or validation of moral theory. Merely surveying the moral views of women is not necessarily going to lead to better moral theories. On the views of rationality that emerged in Greek thought and were developed in the Western philosophical tradition, Reason was associated with the public domain, from which women were largely excluded.[13] If the development of adequate moral theory would be best based on experience in the public domain, the experience of women would be less relevant to the development of adequate moral theory. But that the public domain is the appropriate locus for the development of moral theory is among the tacit assumptions of existing moral theory being effectively challenged by feminist scholars. We cannot escape the need for theory in confronting these issues.

We need to take a stand on what moral experience is. Moral experience, as I understand it, is the experience of consciously choosing, of voluntarily accepting or rejecting, of willingly approving or disapproving, of living with these choices, of acting and of living with these actions and their outcomes. Action and feeling are as much a part of experience as is perception. Then we need to take a stand on whether the moral experience of women is as valid a source or test of moral theory as is the experience of men—and to consider whether it may be more valid.

Engaging in the process of moral inquiry is surely as open to women as it is to men, though the domains where the process may be engaged in have been open to men and women in different ways. Women have had fewer occasions to experience for themselves the moral problems of governing, leading, exercising power over others (except children), and engaging in physically violent conflict. Men, on the other hand, have had fewer occasions for experiencing the moral problems of family life and of relations between adults and children. Though vast amounts of moral experience are open to all human beings who make the effort to become conscientious moral inquirers, the contexts in which experience is obtained may make a difference.

The insights offered by and the reliability of women's experience in engaging in the process of moral inquiry should be presumed to be as valid as in the case of men. To take a given moral theory such as a Kantian one and to decide that those who fail to develop toward it are deficient is obviously to impose a theory on experience, rather than letting experience affect the fate of theories, moral and other than moral. We can assert that as long as women and men experience different problems and as long as differences of approach to moral problems are apparent, moral theory ought to reflect the experience of women as fully as it reflects the experience of men. Men ought not to have the privileged position of having their experience count for more. If anything, their privileged position in society should make their experience more suspect rather than more worthy of counting, for they have good reasons to rationalize their privileged positions by moral arguments that will obscure or purport to justify these privileges.[14]

If the differing approaches to morality that seem to be displayed by women and men are the result of historical conditions, we could suppose that in nonsexist societies the differences would disappear, and at that point the experience of either gender would more adequately substitute for the experience of the other. But since we can hardly imagine what nonsexist society would be like, we can say that we need feminist moral theory to contribute to its development, and we need feminist moral theory to deal with the regions of experience that have been central to women, yet neglected by traditional moral theory.

If the differences between men and women in confronting moral problems are due to biological factors that will continue to provide women and men with different experiences, the experience of women should still count for at least as much as the experience of men. There is no justification on biological grounds for discounting the experience of women as deficient or underdeveloped. Biological "moral inferiority" makes no sense.

The available empirical evidence of differences in the ways women and men approach moral issues is sometimes thought to be based on reportage and interpretation rather than on something more "hard" and "scientific."[15] Clearly this evaluation does not undermine the claim that we need feminist moral theory. But even if the differences turn out to be insignificant, we will still need feminist moral theory to make the moral claim that women themselves are of equal worth as human beings. Moral equality has to be based on moral claims, and since the devaluation of women has been a constant in human society as so far developed and has been accepted by those holding a wide variety of traditional moral theories, feminist moral theory will continue to be needed to provide the basis for women's claims to equality.

MOTHERING AND MARKETS

When we bring the experience of women fully into the domain of moral consciousness, we can see that the most central and fundamental social relation is that between mother or mothering person and child. It is mothering persons and children who turn biological entities into human social entities through their interactions. It is mothers and mothering persons who create children and construct with and for the child the human social reality of the child. The child's understanding of language and of symbols and of all that they create and make real occurs through cooperation between child and caretakers. Mothering persons and children thus produce and create the most basic elements of human culture. The development of language and the creation within and for each person of a human social reality thus seems utterly central to human society.

It is often argued that art and industry and government create new human reality while mothering merely reproduces human beings and their cultures and social structures. But in reality mothering persons change culture and social reality by creating the kinds of persons who can continue to transform themselves and their surroundings. And to create new and better persons is surely as creative as to construct new and better objects or institutions.

The familiar myth is that the original and creative achievements of the great men of history have been the result of the special talents within themselves which they developed. Or it has been thought that the bold and historic achievements of the masses have been the result of the social forces they brought into being. What is done in the sphere of government or production is seen as innovative, while what is done within the family is seen as the mere reproduction of people and forms. But just as bodies do not spring into being unaided and fully formed, neither do imaginations, personalities, or minds. New persons are created within families, in relations between mothering persons and children. And these relations are central not only to existing society but to its development.

In contrast, contractual relations, instead of being central or fundamental to society and morality, appear to be limited relations appropriate only for quite particular regions of human activity.[16] The relation of exchange between buyer and seller has often been taken as the model of all human interactions. Most of the social contract tradition has seen this relation as fundamental to law and political authority as well as to economic activity. And various contemporary moral philosophers believe that even morality itself should be based on the contractual relation.[17] The marketplace relation has become so firmly entrenched in our normative theories that it is rarely questioned as a proper foundation for recommendations extending far beyond the marketplace itself. Much moral thinking, then, is built on the concept of rational economic man. Relations between human beings are seen as justified, when they serve the self-interested goals of rational contractors.

In the society imagined in the model based on assumptions about rational economic man, connections between people become no more than instrumental. Nancy Hartsock effectively characterizes the worldview of these assumptions, and she shows how misguided it is to suppose that the relation between buyer and seller can serve as a model for all human relations: "The paradigmatic connections between people," on this view of the social world, "are instrumental or extrinsic and conflictual, and in a world populated by these isolated individuals, relations of competition and domination come to be substitutes for a more substantial and encompassing community."[18]

If instead we recognized the centrality of the relation between mothering person and child, the competition and desire for domination often thought of as characteristic of "human nature" would appear as a particular and limited connection suitable only, if at all, for a restricted marketplace. Such a relation of conflict and competition could be seen to be unacceptable for establishing the social trust on which public institutions must rest or for upholding the bonds on which caring, regard, friendship, or love, must be based.

A feminist approach to moral theory leads us to ask whether morality should not make room first of all for the human experience reflected in the social bond between mothering person and child and for the human projects of nurturing and of growth apparent for both persons in the relation. In comparison with this, the transactions of the marketplace seem peripheral, the authority of weapons and the laws they uphold beside the point. Clearly, the social map would be fundamentally altered by adoption of the point of view of feminist morality. Instead of seeing the relation between mothering person and child as peripheral and anomalous, and rational exchange as central, we might reverse the location of the "heart" or "foundation" or "core" of society. Relations between mothering persons and the future shapers of social reality would seem central, while the transient exchanges of rational calculators would seem relatively trivial. Social relations would be seen as dynamic rather than as fixed-point exchanges. And assumptions that human beings are equally capable of entering or not entering into the contractual relations taken to characterize social relations generally would be seen for the distortions they are. Though human mothers can, in an ultimate existentialist sense, do other than give birth, their choices to do so or not are usually highly constrained. And children, even human children, cannot choose at all whether to be born.

Perhaps no human relations should be thought of as paradigmatic for all the others. Relations between mothering persons and children can become oppressive for both, and relations between equals who can enter or not enter into agreements may seem attractive in contrast. But no mapping of the social and moral landscape can possibly be satisfactory if it does not adequately take into account and provide appropriate guidance for relations between mothering persons and children.

Suggestions have been made by some feminists that friendship rather than mothering should be the central category to be contrasted with rational contracting.[19] On the one hand this is appealing, since for many, friendship is a more satisfactory relationship, because based on choice, than are many family relationships. On the other hand, it weakens the contrast, since many friendships approach contractual relations in ways that the relation between mother and infant cannot. And we should not suppose that morality is somehow more relevant to satisfactory, chosen relationships than to unsatisfactory ones not chosen. To do so is to assume what we may be trying to show to be problematic.

When some male philosophers turn to friendship in this way, more often it seems to be part of a tradition of denying the significance of whatever it is in which they cannot participate. Giving birth is the foremost example, as they focus on giving birth to works of the mind or products of industry while overlooking the giving of birth to actual children. When feminist philosophers (who can be male) turn to friendship it is because they are skeptical that such a relation as that between parent and child—one not chosen—is capable of grounding any morality. But the very fact that it is not chosen is part of what makes it so important as an alternative

to be considered. It requires us not to ignore the biological component but then to consider whether various contexts of human experience previously thought of in terms of voluntarily chosen relations do not actually resemble more nearly, instead, the circumstances, clearly not made by choice, of the family. We need to decide what to do and what to try to feel in any of the circumstances we find ourselves in. And devising an ethical theory that enables us to see this in connection with family relationships may help us to deal with relations in the wider world, where the members of impoverished societies have not chosen their circumstances and where models of social contracts—or friendships—freely entered into seem to be of so little help in deciding what to do here and now.

BETWEEN THE SELF AND THE UNIVERSAL

Feminist approaches to moral theory often direct our attention to the domain between the self (the ego, the self-interested individual) on the one hand, and the universal (everyone, others in general) on the other. Traditionally, ethics has attended to these abstract or extreme alternatives but has neglected the intermediate region of family relations and relations of friendship, and felt sympathy and concern for particular other human beings. As Larry Blum has shown, "Contemporary moral philosophy in the Anglo-American tradition has paid little attention to [the] morally significant phenomena" of sympathy, compassion, human concern, and friendship.[20] The same is true of nonfeminist moral philosophy other than Anglo-American.

Standard moral philosophy has sometimes construed personal relationships as aspects of the self-interested feelings of individuals, as when a person might favor those he loves over those distant because it satisfies his own desires to do so. Or it has let others who are close stand in for the universal "other," as when the conflict between self and others might be resolved into something like "enlightened self-interest" or "acting out of respect for the moral law" and seeing this as what should guide us in our relations with those close, particular others with whom we interact.

Neither of these approaches is satisfactory. The region of "particular others" is a distinct domain where the "others" with whom we are interrelated are not valued merely in terms of our own interests and preferences, yet are not the "all others" of a universal point of view. They are particular flesh-and-blood others for whom we have actual feelings in our guts and in our skin, not the others of rational constructs and universal principles.

Relations can be evaluated as good or bad, and this can be a different question from how good or bad they are for the individuals in them. Evaluating relations as harmonious, say, or stressful will depend on aspects of what can be understood only if we look at relations between persons. To focus on either self-interested individuals or the totality of all persons is to miss the qualities of actual relations between actual human beings.

Owen Flanagan and Jonathan Adler provide useful criticism of what they see as Kohlberg's "adequacy thesis"—the assumption that the more formal the moral reasoning the better.[21] But they themselves continue to construe the tension in ethics as that between the particular self and the universal, ignoring the domain of particular others in relations with one another.

Mothering is, of course, not the only context in which the salient moral problems concern relations between particular others rather than conflicts between egoistic self and universal moral laws; all actual human contexts may be more like this than like those depicted by Hobbes or Kant. But the context of mothering may be the best in which to make explicit why familiar moral theories are so deficient in offering guidance for action and feeling. And the variety of contexts within mothering, with the different excellences appropriate for dealing with infants or with young children or with adolescents, provide rich sources of insight for moral inquiry.

The feelings so characteristic of mothering—that there are too many demands on us, that we cannot do everything we ought to do—are highly instructive.[22] They give rise to different problems from those of universal rule versus self-interest. They require us to weight the claims of one self-other relation against the claims of other self-other relations, to try to bring about some harmony between them, to see the issues in an actual temporal context, and to act rather than merely reflect.

For instance, we have limited resources for caring. We cannot care for everyone or do everything that a caring approach suggests. We need moral guidelines for ordering our priorities. Though the hunger of our own children comes before the hunger of children we do not know, the hunger of children in Africa ought to come before some of the expensive amusements we may feel like providing for our own children. These are moral problems calling to some extent for principled answers. But we have to figure out what we ought to do in the actual context of buying groceries, cooking meals, refusing the requests of our children for the latest toy they have seen advertised on TV, and sending money to Oxfam. The context is one of real action, not of ideal thought.

PRINCIPLES AND PARTICULARS

When we take the context of mothering as central for moral theory rather than as peripheral, we run the risk of excessively discounting other contexts. It is a commendable risk, given the enormously more prevalent one of excessively discounting mothering. But I think that the attack on principles has sometimes been carried too far by critics of traditional moral theory. Nel Noddings, for instance, writes that "To say, 'It is wrong to cause pain needlessly,' contributes nothing by way of knowledge and can hardly be thought likely to change the attitude or behavior of one who might ask, 'Why is it wrong?' . . . Ethical caring . . . depends not upon rule or principle" but upon the development of a self "in congruence with one's best remembrance of caring and being cared-for."[23]

We should not forget that an absence of principles can be an invitation to capriciousness. Caring may be a weak defense against arbitrary decisions, and the person cared for may find the relation more satisfactory in various respects if both persons, but especially the person caring, are guided to some extent by principles concerning obligations and rights. To argue that no two cases are ever alike is to invite moral chaos. Furthermore, for one person to be in a position of caretaker means that that person has the power to withhold care, leaving the other without it. The person cared for is usually in a position of vulnerability. The moral significance of this needs to be addressed along with other aspects of the caring relation. Principles may remind a giver of care to avoid being capricious or domineering. While most of the moral problems involved in mothering contexts may deal with issues above and beyond the moral minimums that can be covered by principles concerning rights and obligations, that does not mean that these minimums can be dispensed with altogether.

Noddings's discussion is unsatisfactory also in dealing with certain types of questions, including those about economic justice. Such issues cry out for relevant principles. Though caring may be needed to motivate us to act on such principles, the principles are not expendable. Noddings questions the concern people may have for starving persons in distant countries, because she sees universal love and universal justice as masculine illusions. She refrains from judging that the rich deserve less or the poor more, because giving care to individuals cannot yield such judgments. But this may amount to taking a specific economic stratification as given, rather than as the appropriate object of critical scrutiny that it should be. It may lead to accepting that the rich will care for the rich, and the poor for the poor, with the gap between them, however unjustifiably wide, remaining what it is. Some important moral issues seem beyond the reach of an ethic of caring, once caring leads us, perhaps through empathy, to be concerned with them.

On ethical views that renounce all principles as excessively abstract, we might have few arguments to uphold the equality of women. After all, as parents can care for children recognized as weaker, less knowledgeable, less capable, and with appropriately restricted rights, so men could care for women deemed inferior in every way. On a view that ethics could satisfactorily be founded on caring alone, men could care for women considered undeserving of equal rights in all the significant areas in which women have been struggling to have our equality recognized. So an ethic of care, essential as a component of morality and perhaps even as a framework, seems deficient if taken as an exclusive preoccupation or one which fails to make room for justice.

The aspect of the attack on principles that seems entirely correct is the view that not all ethical problems can be solved by appeal to one or a very few simple principles. It is often argued that all more particular moral rules or principles can be derived from such underlying ones as the Categorical Imperative or the Principle of Utility, and that these can be applied to all moral problems. The call for an ethic of care may be a call, in which I join, for a more pluralistic view of ethics, recognizing that we need a division of moral labor employing different moral approaches for different domains, at least for the time being. Satisfactory intermediate principles for areas such as those of international affairs or family relations cannot be derived from simple universal principles but only in conjunction with experience within the domains in question.

Attention to particular others will always require us to respect the particularity of the context and to arrive at solutions to moral problems which will not give moral principles more weight than their due. This is true for what has been thought of as the public realm as well as for what has been thought of as the private one. But we will continue to need some principles. We will need principles concerning relations, not only concerning the actions of individuals, as we will need evaluations of kinds of relations, not only of the character traits of individuals.

KNOWLEDGE OR ACTION

A shortcoming of most standard moral theory is that it construes ethics too much in terms of knowledge, or of trying to get a true picture about what we ought to do. This traditional tendency has been carried on in recent years both by those who deny that ethics can amount to knowledge and by those who assert that indeed ethics is capable of acquiring and accumulating knowledge.[24]

Construing ethics as primarily a matter of knowledge lets us lose touch with the issue of motivation and with the connection in ethics between thought and action. It leaves unaddressed the question, Even if I know what I ought to do, why should I do it? It assumes that knowledge will motivate action, but as soon as we recognize a capacity of the will to defy the dictates of reason or the counsels of knowledge, we are left with the gap between knowledge and action unfilled by theories that see ethics as a branch of objective knowledge. A recognition such as Sara Ruddick and others provide—that thought arises out of practice—can mitigate this difficulty. But we may wish not to limit the concept of thought to what interests produce.

In recognizing the component of feeling and relatedness between self and particular others, we address motivation as an inherent part of the inquiry. Caring between parent and child is a good example. We should not glamorize parental care. Many mothers and fathers exercise power over children in ways characteristic of domination; others fail to care adequately for their children. But when the relation between mothering person and child is as it should be, the caretaker does not care for the child (nor the child for the caretaker) because of universal moral rules. The love and concern one feels for the child already motivate much of what one does and much of what one concludes one ought to do. This is not to say that morality is irrelevant. One must still decide what one ought to do. But the process of addressing the moral questions in mothering and of trying to arrive at answers one can find acceptable involves acting and feeling, not just thinking. And neither egoism nor a morality of universal rules will be of much help.

If we pay attention to the region of particular others in actual contexts, problems of motivation are likely to be incorporated into the inquiry. Ethics will be seen as a question of action and feeling: How ought I to act and to try to feel toward these particular others, and how ought they to act and to try to feel toward me in view of the relation we are in? Answers are sought not in moral judgments comparable to the true statements of a branch of science but in recommendations about how to act and to try to feel and in deciding whether to accept or reject (in action and feeling) these recommendations. Accepting and rejecting are appropriately connected with the actual experience of acting and feeling.

Furthermore, we focus on relations between persons rather than construing moral problems simply as issues for us as isolated individuals making decisions among a range of options. We are partly constituted by the relations we are in, and we cannot adequately understand our moral situation only in terms of individuals and their problems. We need to find moral guidance for the evaluation and shaping of relations.

A number of nonfeminist moral philosophers have expressed objections to the claims of a universal, impersonal moral standpoint. They have pointed out that considerations of what is best from an impersonal standpoint seem to rule out much that seems morally permissible and important to us. As Michael Slote summarizes these positions, "Common sense . . . presumably permits each agent to give some preference to his own concerns, projects, and commitments even when that prevents him from producing the objectively best state(s) of affairs he is capable of bringing about and thus from acting as impersonal benevolence would prefer."[25]

While these discussions have offered useful criticism of an ethic of universal rules, especially utilitarian rules, they have done so largely in terms of individual preferences. Conceptually, they have not moved far beyond traditional arguments between the defenders of egoistic claims versus the defenders of universal claims. The alternatives to impersonal benevolence are seen as the concerns, projects, or commitments of individuals as separate entities. Slote himself discusses our preferences for benefiting others as well as ourselves, but he still interprets the problem in terms of the preferences of ourselves as theoretically isolable individuals. And all such discussions have been confined to the realm of possible moral knowledge without addressing the problem of whether moral knowledge would translate into moral practice.

A feminist focus on evaluating and guiding relations among persons would be quite different from these discussions of the preferences of either individuals in isolation or of all persons in general. And it would move beyond the mere picturing of moral issues.

Considerable philosophical attention has been paid in recent years to the notions of virtue and vice, as distinct from those of the right and the good and their contraries. In virtue theory, in contrast to theories about objective moral knowledge, motivation may be built into moral precepts, since the precepts of virtue theory concern the kinds of persons we ought to admire and the traits of character that ought to be culti-vated.[26] The virtues are usually seen as arising in or as connected to various practices, which are practices composed of actions. Here the connec-tion between morality and action is not lost. But the practices to which attention has so far been paid by nonfeminist virtue theorists have not included the practice of mothering. Attention to the practices involved in bringing up children might greatly improve these theories. Further, all such theories need to address the problem of finding grounds on which to decide how exist-ing practices ought to be changed. If one holds that imagined alternatives can arise from within a practice, it is not clear how such a position dif-fers from, or whether it should rather resemble, a theory that appeals to some point of view out-side any given practice from which to evaluate the practice.

We should be careful not to confine moral inquiry to anything that can only be conducted within an existing social practice.[27] The his-tory of existing social practices is overwhelm-ingly patriarchal, and even human mothering, engaged in primarily by women, is suspect as an existing practice because of the extent to which it is embedded in male-dominated cultures and societies. The practice of moral inquiry itself is practice enough within which to define the virtues and vices, and this practice includes theories about relatively independent moral principles and values.

The contexts to which feminist moral theory pays attention are especially suitable for illus-trating our claims about moral inquiry and for developing methods of moral inquiry that will be conducive not only to moral knowledge or understanding, but to the moral action of which morality itself must be composed or in which, at the very least, morality must be reflected.

Noddings does not lose sight of the issue of motivation. She offers a helpful account of how children learn to be moral and of how mother-ing persons shape this learning. But the conclu-sion need not be that moral principles and rules have little significance for morality. Rather we can see how action and feeling ought to inform the choice of principles as well as of practices and projects. Caring should not replace thought, nor should thought be a mere instrument of caring. Reflective choice and caring action are both needed for the development of adequate moralities.

BIRTH AND VALUING

To a large extent the activity of mothering is as open to men as to women. Possibly fathers could come to be as emotionally close, or as close through caretaking, to children as mothers are. The experience of relatedness, of respon-sibility for the growth and empowerment of new life, and of responsiveness to particular others will have to be incorporated into moral theory if moral theory is to be adequate. At present in this domain it is primarily the experi-ence of women (and of children) which has not been sufficiently reflected in moral theory and which ought to be so reflected. But this is not to say that it must remain experience available mainly to women. If men were to come to share fully and equitably in the care of all persons who need care—especially children, the sick, the old—the moral values that now arise for women in the context of caring might well arise as fully for men.

There are some experiences, however, that are open to women and not open to men: men-struating, having an abortion, giving birth, suckling. We need to consider their possible sig-nificance or lack of significance for moral expe-rience and theory. Here I will consider only one kind of experience not open to men but of great importance to women: the experience of giving birth or of deciding not to while being capable of doing so, or of identifying, as a woman, with those who give birth.

Birthing, of course, is a social as well as a personal or biological event. It takes place in a social context structured by attitudes and arrangements which deeply affect how women experience it—whether it will be accepted as "natural," whether it will be welcomed and cel-ebrated, or whether it will be fraught with fear or shame. But I wish in this brief discussion to focus on the conscious awareness women can have of what we are doing in giving birth, on the specifically personal and biological aspects of human birthing, and on the possible signifi-cance of these for moral experience.

Women are the persons who create other human beings. Women are responsible for the existence of new persons in ways far more fundamental than men are. We have in the past needed to call attention to the extent to which women do not control our capacity to give birth and to this extent are not responsible for its results. We have been under extreme economic and social pressure to engage in sexual intercourse, to marry, to have children. Legal permission to undergo abortion is a restricted and still threatened capacity. When the choice not to give birth requires grave risk to life, health, or well-being, or requires suicide, we should be careful not to misrepresent the situation of women when we speak of a woman's "choice" to become a mother, or of how she "could have done other" than have a child, or that "since she chose to become a mother, she is responsible for her child," and so forth. Still, in an ultimate sense, women are responsible for giving birth, and choices concerning it are increasingly uncoerced.

It does not follow at all that because women are responsible for creating human beings we should be held responsible by society for caring for them, either alone, primarily, or even at all. The two kinds of responsibility should not be confused. Women have every reason to be angry at men who refuse to take responsibility for their share of the events of pregnancy and birth or for the care children require. Because we have for so long wanted to increase the extent to which men would recognize their responsibilities for causing pregnancy and would share in the long years of care needed to bring the child of a mother and a father to independence, we have tended to emphasize the ways in which the responsibilities for creating a new human being are equal between women and men. The fact remains that it is women and not men who give birth to children. Men produce sperm and women produce babies, and the difference is very great. Excellent arguments can be made that boys and men suffer "womb envy", for indeed, men lack a wondrous capacity which women possess. To overcome the pernicious aspects of the womb envy she describes, Eva Kittay argues that boys should be taught that their "procreative contribution" is of equal importance. But while boys should certainly be told the truth, the truth may remain that, as she elsewhere states, "there is the . . . awesome quality of creation itself—the transmutation performed by the parturient woman."[28]

Of all the human capacities, it is probably the capacity to create new human beings that is most worth celebrating. It is to be expected that a woman would care and feel concern for a child she has created as the child grows and develops and as she feels responsible for having given the child life through giving birth. But it is more than what we might expect. It is, perhaps, justifiable in certain ways unique to women.

It might be thought that responsibility for the life of the child also lies with those who refrain from infanticide, and infanticide is as open to men as to women. But the killing of a child once the child has been born and is capable of life with different caretakers than the person who is responsible for having given birth to the child would be a quite different experience, and I am concerned in this discussion with the possible moral significance of creating life in the first place.

As suggested by Marcia Baron in correspondence, it might also be thought that those, including the father, who refrain from killing the mother, or from forcing her to have an abortion, are also responsible in some much more distant way for not preventing the birth of the child. But unless the distinctions between suicide and murder, and between having an abortion and forcing a woman to have an abortion against her will, are collapsed completely, the issues would be very different. To refrain from murdering a woman is not at all the same as deciding not to kill oneself. And to decide not to force someone else to have an abortion is very different from deciding not to have an abortion when one could. The person capable of giving birth who decides not to prevent the birth is the person responsible, in the sense of 'responsible' I am discussing, for creating another human being. And to give life is not the same as to refrain from ending it.

Whether there is or is not a significant difference between killing a person or letting that person die, where the person already has life, is yet another question. If one wishes to draw an analogy between taking life and giving life, the analogy, if it can be drawn at all, might be between the question of killing or letting die, on the one hand, and "natural" or "induced" childbirth on the other.

Perhaps there is a tendency to want to approve of or to justify what one has decided or done with respect to giving life. In giving birth to a particular child, perhaps women have a natural tendency to approve of the birth, to believe that the child ought to have been born. Perhaps this inclines women who give birth and those who identify with such women to believe whatever may follow from this, such as that the child is entitled to care, and that feelings of love for the child are appropriate and justified. The conscious awareness that one has created a new human being may provide women with an inclination to value the child and to have hope for the child's future. If in her view the child ought to have been born, a woman may feel that the world ought to be such as to be hospitable to the child. And if the child ought to have been born, the child ought to grow into an admirable human adult. The child's life has, and should continue to have, value that is recognized.

Consider next the phenomenon of sacrifice. In giving birth, women suffer severe pain for the sake of new life. Having suffered for the child in giving the child life, women may have a natural tendency to value what pain has been endured for. As often pointed out in connection with war, there is a tendency in people to feel that because sacrifices have been made, the sacrifice should have been "worth it," and, if necessary, other things ought to be done so that the sacrifice "shall not have been in vain." There may be comparable tendencies for those who have suffered to give birth to hold that the pain was for the good reason of creating a new life that is valuable and that will be valued.

Certainly this is not to say that there is anything good or noble about suffering or that merely because people want to believe that what they suffered for was worthwhile, it was. A vast amount of human suffering has been in vain and should have been avoided. The point is that once suffering has already occurred and the "price" (if we resort to such calculations) has already been paid, it will be worse if the result is a further cost, and better if the result is a clear benefit that can make the price, when it was necessary for the result, validly "worth it." The suffering of the mother who has given birth will more easily have been truly worthwhile

if the child's life has value. The chance for the suffering that has already occurred to be outweighed by future happiness is much greater if the child is valued by the society and the family into which it is born. To say that the mother's suffering has been worthwhile because the child is a valuable and valued human being can be a valid judgment. If her suffering has yielded nothing but further suffering and a being of no value, it may truly have been in vain. Anyone could agree with these judgments. But the person who has already undergone the suffering has a special reason to recognize that the child is valuable and to want the child to be valued so that the suffering she has already borne will have been truly worthwhile.

These arguments can be repeated for the burdens of work and anxiety normally expended in bringing up a child. Those who have already borne these burdens have special reasons to see the resulting grown human being for whom they were necessary as valuable and as valued. Traditionally, the burden of childbirth borne by women has been added to very greatly by the burdens of child rearing. But of course the burdens of child rearing could easily be shared fully by men, as they have been by women other than natural mothers, and the extent of these cares may greatly outweigh the suffering of childbirth itself. This does not mean that giving birth is incidental.

In exploring the values involved in birth and mothering, we need to develop views which do not exclude women who do not give birth.[29] For some women, a decision against bearing children is easy, for others it is consuming. The decision is often affected by a tendency to value the potential child to a degree comparable to that experienced by potential mothers. Knowing how much care the child would deserve and how much care she would want to give the child, a woman who relinquishes the prospect of motherhood often recognizes how much she is giving up. For such reasons the choice may be very difficult, and a woman can feel overwhelming ambivalence about pursuing a career that is hostile to women who try to combine it with motherhood.

Since men, then, do not give birth, and do not experience the responsibility for, the pain in, or the momentousness of childbirth, they lack the particular motives to value the child that may rest on this capacity and this fact. Of course it is open to men to identify with women far more than they have in the past. And of course many other motives to value a child are open to both parents, to caretakers of either gender and to those who are not parents, but the motives discussed, and others arising from giving birth, may be morally significant. Perhaps the decisions and sacrifices involved in bringing up a child are more affecting than those normally experienced in giving birth to a child. So the possibility for men to acquire such motives through child care may outweigh any long-term differences in motivation between women and men. But it might yet remain that the person responsible for giving birth would continue to have a greater sense of responsibility for how the child develops and stronger feelings of care and concern for the child.

That adoptive parents can feel as great concern for and attachment to their children as can biological parents may indicate that the biological components in valuing children are relatively modest in importance. But to the extent that biological components are significant, as according to some theories they must be, they affect women and men in different ways.

MORALITY AND HUMAN TENDENCIES

So far I have been describing possible feelings rather than attaching any moral value to them. That children are valued does not mean they are valuable, and if mothers have a natural tendency to value children, it does not follow that we ought to. But if feelings are taken to be relevant to moral theory, the feelings of valuing the child, like the feelings of empathy for other persons in pain, may be of moral significance.

To the extent that a moral theory takes natural male tendencies into account, it would at least be reasonable to take natural female tendencies into account. Traditional moral theories often assume that people are motivated by the pursuit of self-interest or by a desire to satisfy their preferences, and then many such theories go on to suppose that it is legitimate for individuals to maximize self-interest, or satisfy their preferences, within certain constraints based on the equal rights of others. If it can be shown that the tendency to want to pursue individual

self-interest is a stronger tendency among men than among women, this would certainly be relevant to an evaluation of such theory. And if it could be shown that a tendency to value children and to desire to foster the developing capabilities of the particular others for whom we care is a stronger tendency among women than among men, this too would be relevant in evaluating moral theories.

It is still different to assert that women have a tendency to value children and that we ought to. Noddings speaks often of the "natural" caring of mothers for children.[30] I do not intend to deal here with the disputed empirical question of whether there is or is not a strong natural tendency for mothers to love our children. Sara Ruddick's rich description of the ambivalent feelings mothers experience may be more relevant: "What we are pleased to call 'mother-love' is intermixed with hate, sorrow, impatience, resentment, and despair; thought-provoking ambivalence is a hallmark of mothering."[31] And I am not claiming that natural mothers have more talent for or greater skills in raising children than have others, including men.

What I am exploring, rather, are the possible "reasons" for mothers to value children, reasons that might be different for mothers and potential mothers than they would be for anyone else asking the question, Why should we value human beings? And it does seem that certain possible reasons for valuing actual living human beings are present for mothers, and for those who identify with mothers, in ways that are different from what they would be for others. The reason, if it is one, that the child should be valued because I have suffered to give the child life is different from the reason, if it is one, that the child should be valued because someone unlike me suffered to give the child life. And both these reasons are different from the reason, if it is one, that the child should be valued because the continued existence of the child satisfies a preference of a parent or because the child is a bearer of universal rights or has the capacity to experience pleasure.

Many moral theories, and fields dependent on them, employ such assumptions as that increasing the utility of individuals is a good thing to do. But if one asks *why* it is a good thing to increase utility, or satisfy desire, or produce

348

pleasure, or *why* doing so counts as a good reason for something, the question is very difficult to answer. It is often taken as a basic assumption for which no *further* reason can be given. It may rest (unsatisfactorily) on some such claim as that people seek pleasure; or it may rest on the claim that we can recognize pleasure as having intrinsic value. But if women start with different assumptions and recognize different values as much weightier, that would certainly be of importance to ethics.

We might take it as one of our assumptions that the survival of children has priority over most other moral considerations. A number of feminists have independently declared their rejection of the Abraham myth.[32] We do not approve the sacrifice of actual children out of religious duty or moral abstraction: reasons to value the actual life of the born seem better reasons than reasons justifying the sacrifice of such life.[33] This outlook can be especially poignant in the context of struggles to achieve greater justice for oppressed groups. Women are sometimes criticized by more militant group members for a reluctance to sacrifice the well-being of children to the needs of the movement; they may respond that it is the children the movement is for, not the reverse. Feminist positions may reflect an accordance of priority to caring for particular others over abstract principle. From the perspective of much moral theory, a tendency to take such a stand is a deficiency of women. But from a perspective of what is needed for twenty-first century global responsibility, it may suggest a superior morality.

It is of utmost importance to create good relations of care and concern and trust between ourselves and our children, and to create the cultural expressions, social arrangements, and environmental conditions in which children will be valued and well cared for. All these are more important than maximizing individual utilities or fulfilling purely abstract moral norms. The moral theories compatible with these starting positions are likely to be very different from traditional and contemporary nonfeminist moral theories.

In discussing ways in which a feminist approach to morality differs from a Kantian one, Annette Baier writes, "Where Kant concludes—'so much the worse for women,' we can conclude—'so much the worse for the male fixation on the special skill of drafting legislation, for the bureaucratic mentality of rule worship, and for the male exaggeration of the importance of independence over mutual interdependence.'"[34] Only feminist moral theory can offer satisfactory evaluations of such suggestions because only feminist moral theory can adequately reflect the alternatives to traditional and nonfeminist moral theory that the experience of women requires.

Traditional moral theory provides us with two alternatives: survival of self or duty to all mankind. We see the central priority of survival of the self powerfully argued in Hobbes, and we see the priority of obligation to the universal persuasively argued in Kant. These are the positions which have preoccupied much of the debate in traditional and nonfeminist moral theory ever since.

Feminist moral theory, in contrast, will, I believe, develop around the priority of the flourishing of children in favorable environments. The flourishing of children requires survival, but not of any self in isolation—whether of child or caretaker—and not at the sacrifice of any self. It does concern obligation to humankind, but not to an abstract universal. It should not pit the well-being of one's own children against the well-being of others, justifying conflict and favoritism. On the other hand, it can recognize that if the children who depend on or are touched by our care do not flourish, we have not contributed what we should have to the flourishing of children.

HOW NEW IS FEMINIST INQUIRY?

Is there anything really new about feminist moral inquiry, and will the theory that results be different from nonfeminist moral theory? The argument that there is nothing significantly new here asserts that if one looks at other parts of the various traditions in ethics than the ones on which I have focused, one can already find what feminists are saying and that what feminists are now proposing has been said before (and, it may be implied, said better). On the split between reason and emotion and the devaluation of emotion, for instance, it has been argued that Aristotle's emphasis on habit and practice in the development of morality, rather than on mere rational assent, is close to what feminists are arguing. Or it is claimed that Hume's reliance on emotion—on fellow-feeling and not being indifferent to the pain of others—as the foundation of morality already provides what feminists seek.

On the public/private distinction and the devaluation of the household, it can be pointed out that there is another tradition than the one I will emphasize: the tradition of Machiavelli, according to which one can be guided by morality in one's private dealings with family and friends, but in public, political life, "dirty hands" are inevitable and morality irrelevant. "You must realize this," Machiavelli said, "that a prince, and especially a new prince, cannot observe all those things which give men a reputation for virtue, because in order to maintain his state he is often forced to act in defiance of good faith, of charity, of kindness, of religion."[35] Isn't this, some ask, close to what feminists are saying?

Finally, on the concept of the self, feminists certainly have not been the first to criticize the atomistic, isolated self of liberal political and of much moral theory. Communitarians have long since done so. Marxists have said that the atomistic, individualistic self is not the human self but the bourgeois self. They have argued that the egoistic drives that such theorists as Hobbes and Locke assumed to be inherent in human nature are not inherent but rather are promoted by capitalism and transcendable through socialism. The self of liberal theory is thus defective, on the Marxist view, and should be replaced by a conception of the self as socially constituted. So again, it is argued that what feminists are asserting is a version of such critiques rather than anything new.

My response is that none of the nonfeminist theorists cited as having said before, or said better, what feminists are saying, has paid remotely adequate attention to the experience of women. They have not considered their alternatives from the points of view of women, and they have not listened to the voices of women expressing our thoughts, our feelings, our concerns. And these omissions make a difference.

For instance, the activity of mothering has been almost totally absent in all nonfeminist moral theorizing. Until Sara Ruddick wrote her paper "Maternal Thinking," there has been virtually no philosophical recognition that mothers *think,* that there are characteristic standards for *reasoning* in this activity, and that one can discern *moral values* being striven for and expressed in this practice.[36] On the few occasions in which mothering had been noticed, it had been evaluated in terms of the aims and projects of men, as with Locke and Rousseau, or its values had been seen as threatening to the "higher" values sought by men, as with Hegel. The whole area of relations between parents and children was characteristically conceptualized as belonging to the natural, empirical given, rather than to the domain of morality. But how could this be? The practice of mothering involves almost constant moral concern and deliberation. To characterize this large domain of human experience as irrelevant to the construction of moral theory is highly unlikely to have had no significant distorting effect on the shaping of moral theory.

Nor has there been any remotely adequate attention to other aspects of women's experience, such as friendship among women or life in women's communities. Or to the enormous *problems* women face *as women:* the problems of domestic violence, for instance, or of rape.[37] If "humanity" is recognized as including women on a par with men, then thinking about domestic violence should occupy as much theoretical space as should thinking about the kinds of personal security—the freedom to travel the highway unattacked, for instance, or the security of one's personal property—to which so much legal and political and moral theory has been devoted.[38] So even though there is, of course, a background on which feminists can draw, when feminists pay attention in *central* ways to the experience of women, we are doing something which has not been done before.

Moralities that do take adequate account of the experience of women will be unlike any traditional moralities, or their nonfeminist critiques, for they will combine theory and practice for an enormous but almost wholly neglected range of human experience. The virtues and practices and feelings upheld by the ethics of Aristotle and Hume uphold traditions mired in patriarchy. The "dirty hands" of men in public life can be matched by the moral impurities of domestic privilege and tyranny. If we look at Marxist criticisms of the tradition of liberal individualism, we find that they too accept a gender division of labor in the household as "natural," and they too pay almost no attention to the experience of women as women rather than as workers or nonworkers. Activity is divided between production and reproduction, and it is production only that is seen as transformative. And the "social self" of most communitarians, while offering helpful criticisms of the atomistic self of the liberal tradition, is still not the "relational self" of feminist theory. It provides a weak basis for oppressed members of actual communities to break away from and out of the traditions that contribute so much to their oppression.

We can conclude, I think, that feminist inquiry is offering something quite new and that feminist morality is different from pre-feminist and nonfeminist morality. Even if the theories feminists will come to espouse turn out to resemble traditional theories—this may be unlikely, but even if it should be the case—the theories would be different in the sense that they would have been applied to and tested in a whole new and very large domain of human experience—the experience of women. These theories would have been developed on the basis of this whole new domain of experience and would have to have been found satisfactory for it. If a traditional theory does turn out to meet these requirements, it will be different from what it was before in having been seen to be applicable to all this new territory, and it could be judged to be, itself, feminist theory as well as traditional theory.

A primary aim of feminism is to end the oppression of women. This involves upsetting the primacy of the male in thought and in soci-ety. All agree that the achievement of such an objective would have to count as enormous change. Surely the changes in moral theory will have to be comparably profound.

Questions for Discussion

1. Could there be a distinctive feminist morality? What would it look like?
2. Can traditional moral theory accommodate women's moral orientation, or are those theories irredeemably male-biased?
3. Are Held's criticisms of Noddings's ethics of care appropriate? How might Noddings respond?
4. Might a distinctively feminist ethics tend to subordinate rather than liberate women?
5. What is a bias? What is morally objectionable about biases?

CHAPTER 18

Metaethics

HARD QUESTION: COULD I HAVE DONE OTHER THAN I DID?

In **metaethics** we step back from particular moral theories such as Kantianism or utilitarianism, and from various practical issues like abortion or war, to reflect on the nature of moral inquiry itself. Indeed, thinking about moral theories and practical ethical questions leads one quite naturally to metaethics. We shall consider two important metaethical topics: moral responsibility and the metaphysical status of moral judgments.

MORAL RESPONSIBILITY

Only persons can be morally responsible. This may sound like a significant claim, but it is not, since part of what it means to be a person is being the proper object of praise or blame. Holding people morally responsible is an important way to assess their actions; they are worthy of praise or blame, as distinct from organisms that are merely caused to behave as they do. Moral responsibility thus suggests that persons have a special kind of control over their behavior that makes such assessments intelligible. In some crucial and hard-to-define sense, they are the authors of their actions.

   Moral responsibility is different from causal responsibility, although praise or blame sometimes depends on causal responsibility. Consider the nurse who mistakenly kills a patient because the medicine bottles were mislabeled at the factory. The nurse caused the patient's death, but the nurse is not morally responsible because the outcome was neither intended nor the result of negligence or any professional lapse. Causal responsibility means merely that one caused an event; moral responsibility requires that one caused it by design, or, in the case of negligence or omission, that one's failure to act allowed something to happen for which one is morally responsible.

Causal responsibility is hard to trace because causal chains can become complicated, until "contributing factors" make it impossible to locate a single cause. Tire failure was the immediate cause of the accident, but underinflation caused the tires to heat up; pneumonia was the immediate cause of death, but the patient's weakness following an operation allowed the virus to establish itself in the first place. Among the densely interwoven causal chains that constitute the natural world, we focus on those causal factors that are of interest to us in a particular situation.

Moral responsibility requires free choice. What does that mean? This innocent question quickly propels us into one of the most difficult areas of metaethics, if not all of philosophy: how to understand human freedom. One way to conceive of human freedom is as the ability to do other than one did. Imagine selecting apple pie for dessert. If it was available, could you have taken blueberry pie instead? One is inclined to say that if you had wanted blueberry, you could have picked it, but you decided to take apple. But could you have chosen blueberry even if everything had been the same up to the moment you decided to pick apple? Saying that you could have chosen otherwise if things had been different—specifically, if you had wanted blueberry instead—is not at issue. Up until the moment you decided, could things have gone either way?

Freedom, understood as the ability to do other than one did, means that the conditions preceding one's choice do not determine it, so given *exactly* the same antecedent conditions, one could still have chosen otherwise. This position is called **libertarianism,** and it expresses our conviction that our futures are truly open because we are free.

Think for a moment how mysterious libertarian freedom is. The world, at least as we understand it on the level of ordinary physical objects, operates by causal necessity. All events are caused by previous events. The roof collapsed because the supporting beams were weakened, which was caused by termites, an abundance of which was caused, let us say, by changing weather patterns, which was caused by global warming, which is caused by . . . an exhaustive causal analysis of a single event would take us back to the start of the universe with the Big Bang. (We are not supposed to ask what caused that!) Scientists describe the regular patterns of causal connections among events, known as the laws of nature. For example, ice melts because heat absorbed by the constituent water molecules overcomes the bonds between them, just as jiggling a structure of tiny balls held together with tape will break the adhesive, allowing them to roll around. This explanation for how ice melts is mechanical and depends only on causal interactions among molecules. Scientific explanation for any phenomenon will have this same basic form. No occult forces, intention, purpose, magic, agency (divine or otherwise), or anything of the sort—just causal interactions in accordance with the laws of nature, which are themselves generalizations of causal regularities. Thus science explains the workings of the world.

How do we fit into this scientific conception of reality? According to the libertarian, when we exercise our freedom, we function in a manner independent of causal necessity. We may be part of nature, but not completely so. Despite the fact that we have bodies made of flesh and blood, and brains that operate according to the (causal) principles of neurochemistry, somehow we are not consumed by the causal necessity that drives everything else. Herein lies our freedom, the ability to do other than we did irrespective of the conditions that obtained prior to our initial choice, or so the libertarian maintains. Given the entire history of the universe up to the exact point that you chose apple pie, you could have chosen blueberry instead. How this could be is a mystery.

It is no help to point out that physicists tell us that causal necessity breaks down at the subatomic level. The apparent randomness of some subatomic events is not freedom, even if physicists are right that those events are not causally determined. Freedom is not the mere absence of causal necessity; metaphysically free actions are neither caused nor random. As for the apparent randomness of subatomic events, it seems as likely that physicists do not understand what causes those events as that they are purely random, since purely random events would be as hard to comprehend as free ones. Purely random events would just happen—for no reason whatsoever. Nothing brought them about. Events can seem random to us, but that might be just because we do not know enough. The movement of gas molecules, for instance, might seem random, but we suppose that each particle is where it is because of causal factors too minute and too complicated for us to ascertain.

If moral responsibility requires freedom in the sense of the ability to do otherwise, where doing otherwise does not mean, trivially, doing otherwise if one had wanted otherwise, then it looks bad for moral responsibility. It is hard to see how that condition could ever be met. If all events are determined by previous events in accordance with the laws of nature, then we cannot do other than we did. So we cannot be morally responsible for anything. Libertarians recoil in horror, and rightly so, because causal determinism seemingly erases human freedom and with it moral responsibility. Praise and blame would be inappropriate responses to what people do (even though we would be determined to have those reactions), because in a sense people don't really "do" anything; they are just temporary swirls of particles in the immense causal nexus that is the world. Human agency is extinguished, and along with it all intelligible moral attribution. Since we *are* morally responsible, libertarians sometimes reason, causal determinism must be false.

The inference that since we are morally responsible, causal determinism must be false can be stood on its head. "Hard determinists" agree that freedom should be interpreted as the ability to do other than one did. But whereas libertarians think that we are free (and hence that causal determinism is false), hard determinists think that because causal determinism is true, we are not free; libertarian freedom is an illusion.

Libertarians and hard determinists agree that human freedom is the capacity to do other than one did, which is incompatible with causal determinism. So they are called **incompatibilists.** The choice (if we can call it that!) between libertarianism and hard determinism is difficult. We can either give up on moral responsibility because libertarian freedom is incompatible with causal determinism, or we can keep moral responsibility at the cost of an utterly mysterious ability to do other than we did. But recall that we arrived in this awkward position by starting with a particular conception of freedom. There is another way to understand freedom. Freedom can mean doing what one wants, or acting voluntarily, instead of doing other than one did, as the incompatibilists understand it.

How is freedom that is conceived as doing as one wants different from freedom in the incompatibilist's sense? Doing as you want is compatible with determinism. If causal determinism is true, then your wants are determined too, just like any other event in the universe. If your wants then move you, you are free in the sense of not being hindered, for you are caused to move by your wants. This position is called **compatibilism** because it claims that freedom, properly understood, is compatible with causal determinism. You are not free when causes other than your real or genuine wants (such as addictions, compulsions, chemical imbalances, hypnotism, brain tumors, and the like) motivate you. The compatibilist project is to explain how we can be free and morally responsible in all the ways that are important to understanding ourselves, while at the same time acknowledging the truth of causal determinism. It is a daunting task but considering the alternatives, perhaps a necessary one.

The basic problem with compatibilism is that we have to give up on libertarian freedom, our stubbornly unshakeable sense that we could have done other than we did, and speak instead of acting in accordance with our wants. Moral responsibility still requires freedom, just as we thought all along, but acting freely now means acting voluntarily, which means moved by one's wants, which are themselves causally necessitated. Remember, compatibilists want it both ways: You are free *and* all events are causally determined. This means that freedom will have to mean something different from what the libertarian has in mind. It also means that in a certain sense, I am a spectator on my life, since I am no longer an agent, in the sense of being the sole originator of action. Causal chains flow through me, certain of them are designated as my wants, and I am free when they are causally efficacious. But I do not initiate action, in the sense of being the sole originator of it. Decisions happen in me because of other events; I do not generate them *de novo*.

Compatibilists use ordinary moral concepts that seemingly presuppose libertarian agency, such as culpability, regret, intention, will, shame, and the like, but they reinterpret these ideas to reflect a different sense of freedom from what the libertarian means. This amounts to a sweeping conceptual reorientation of moral responsibility. It is as though religious ideas such as sin, sacred, grace, and salvation were reinterpreted and used by atheists; they don't quite mean what they did before. Compatibilism avoids the problems of incompatibilism, but it creates new ones of its own.

MORAL REALISM

Consider the following moral judgments: "Abortion is immoral." "Mary was right to apologize." "You ought to be more considerate." Are they true, false, or neither?

According to one line of thought, moral pronouncements are not propositions and are therefore neither true nor false. The general name for this view is **non-cognitivism.** As the name suggests, moral judgments do not involve an intellectual apprehension of something. A particular kind of non-cognitivism called **emotivism** holds that moral judgments are simply expressions of feeling. When stuck with a pin, one might cry "Ouch!!" But nothing is asserted; yelling "ouch!" is merely a linguistic manifestation of pain, much like jumping or whimpering. As linguistic creatures we have acquired a new form of squirming.

This emotivist analysis can be extended to more complicated mental states, such as emotions. Saying "I love you," according to the emotivist, is not a report of love but a linguistic manifestation of love, just like an increased pulse rate, inability to concentrate, and dilated pupils. And just as dilated pupils are neither true nor false, neither is saying, "I love you." Such an utterance may seem like an assertion, but it is not.

According to the emotive theory of ethics, the same applies to moral judgments. Moral judgments are mere linguistic expressions of emotions; as linguistic behavior they neither assert nor deny anything. Despite appearances to the contrary, to say "Capital punishment is immoral" is the same as twisting up one's face in disgust at the thought of capital punishment. Neither asserts anything; both are pure emotional expressions of disgust, one facial, the other linguistic.

Moral pronouncements might also influence the feelings of others. As creatures we are naturally attuned to the emotional states of those around us, so it is not absurd to suppose that expressions of emotion, linguistic or otherwise, can cause others to feel similarly.

Emotivism and other forms of non-cognitivism dominated metaethics for much of the twentieth century. This is one reason why many philosophers, at least until recently, were reluctant to discuss real-world moral questions. If moral judgments are non-cognitive, then philosophers have nothing to contribute because there is nothing to figure out. Yet actual moral discourse bears little resemblance to what non-cognitivism says about it. When we reflect on a moral issue, it certainly seems as though we are trying to figure something out. We say that we want to know the truth of the matter, and we can assess reasons for and against alternative solutions.

If non-cognitivism is true, then moral discourse is mere rhetoric. For non-cognitivists the goal of moral discourse is persuasion, not determination of a rationally defensible moral position. So anything that persuades will count as a reason, even if persuasion is non-rational. Pointing out to white racists that a particular policy discriminates against blacks will then count as a reason in favor of the policy because that information will elicit a positive attitude from them. But a reason cannot be any consideration that produces assent; good reasons must be rationally connected to what they are reasons for, and whether a consideration is rationally connected to what it is allegedly a reason for is not a psychological matter. Non-cognitivism is inadequate because it cannot account for the role of reason in moral discourse.

Cognitivism, by contrast, is the view that moral pronouncements are genuine propositions; they are either true or false. Unlike non-cognitivism, cognitivism does justice to ordinary moral discourse insofar as it seems to be genuinely propositional. However, it is possible to acknowledge this but to remain skeptical about the status of ethics. Even if moral discourse is fully propositional, it might be that all moral propositions are false! As famously expressed by the Oxford philosopher J. L. Mackie, ethics might be an "error theory." Consider religious discourse by analogy. "God loves me," "After death, souls will be reunited with their maker," and similar pronouncements really are propositions and are thus either true or false. This would be religious cognitivism. The believer, of course, thinks that some religious propositions are true. An error theorist, by contrast, holds that all of them are false. If God does not exist and if there are no souls, then the religious statements above are false. An error theory of ethics works the same way. Ethical pronouncements are genuine propositions, but all of them are false because there are no moral facts by virtue of which those propositions could be true.

Why have philosophers devised such elaborate theories about ethics? Unlike ordinary propositions whose truth or falsity can be verified by checking facts, the alleged truth of moral propositions cannot be similarly verified. We can verify that the library closes at 5 p.m. by calling; we can verify that today is Friday by checking the calendar, we can verify that water boils at 212° F, and so on. There are facts to which we can appeal in order to determine the truth or falsity of the statements at issue. But how do we verify moral propositions?

One traditional answer is intuition. We are alleged to apprehend moral facts via a moral sense, by analogy with other forms of sense perception used to apprehend ordinary non-moral facts. The problem with intuitionism is not just that our intuitions might differ, although that is serious enough, but that the moral facts alleged to be apprehended by intuition must be very unusual, not the everyday non-moral facts with which we are familiar. Moral facts would seem to be special non-natural facts. Appeal by intuition to non-natural facts makes many philosophers nervous, and rightly so. What are non-natural facts and why should we accept as authoritative the deliverances of intuition, whether our own or someone else's, when it is just as likely that what seems intuitively obvious to us is the result of cultural conditioning, rather than contact with a mysterious non-natural fact? The persistent worry with intuitionism is that we are unconsciously seeking external justification for our own biases and preferences. Positing strange moral facts accessible only by intuition—and perhaps only by the intuitions of those "properly" attuned—is a highly controversial metaethical position.

At issue is whether there are objective moral facts that hold independent of our theorizing about them and that justify, in the sense of "make true," at least some of our moral propositions. **Moral realists** say there are such facts; **moral anti-realists** deny it. We have already seen some background to the debate: non-cognitivists are moral anti-realists, as are error theorists; intuitionists are moral realists. The challenge for contemporary moral realists is to explain the moral facts by virtue of which at least some moral propositions are true, without falling into the obscurantist metaphysics of intuitionism.

READINGS FOR METAETHICS

Thomas Nagel, "Moral Luck"

Thomas Nagel is a professor of philosophy at New York University and one of the most influential contemporary philosophers in the world. He has contributed significantly to moral philosophy and the philosophy of mind, and he has brought sharp insights to neglected topics, as in his celebrated philosophical discussions on sexual perversion, death, and war.

In "Moral Luck," a modern classic, Nagel considers the role of luck in moral responsibility. We think that people are responsible only for what is under their control, but it turns out that very little is under their control. We judge the reckless driver more severely if he kills a pedestrian than if not, "[b]ut whether a reckless driver hits a pedestrian depends on the presence of the pedestrian at the point where he recklessly passes a red light." And that is not up to the reckless driver. Similar considerations apply to one's character and to the trials and temptations one encounters in life. The control required for moral responsibility vanishes when we subtract from what someone does, anything that merely happens. Nagel argues that a compatibilist response to this problem is inadequate, because "something in the idea of agency is incompatible with actions being events, or people being things. But as the external determinants of what someone has done are gradually exposed . . . it gradually becomes clear that actions are events and people things."

Critical Reading Questions

1. Why does Nagel think that Kant's view about moral risk is wrong?
2. What is the "fundamental problem about moral responsibility to which we possess no satisfactory solution"?
3. What is moral luck?
4. What are the four ways in which the natural objects of moral assessment are disturbingly subject to luck?
5. What worries does Nagel express about compatibilism?
6. What point of view do we adopt when we evaluate others morally?
7. What is the difference between internal and external points of view, and how are they relevant to moral luck?

MORAL LUCK

Thomas Nagel

Kant believed that good or bad luck should influence neither our moral judgment of a person and his actions, nor his moral assessment of himself.

The good will is not good because of what it effects or accomplishes or because of its adequacy to achieve some proposed end; it is good only because of its willing, i.e., it is good of itself. And, regarded for itself, it is to be esteemed incomparably higher than anything which could be brought about by it in favor of any inclination or even of the sum total of all inclinations. Even if it should happen that, by a particularly unfortunate fate or by the niggardly provision of a stepmotherly nature, this will should be wholly lacking in power to accomplish its purpose, and if even the greatest effort should not avail it to achieve anything of its end, and if there remained only the good will (not as a mere wish but as the summoning of all the means in our power), it would sparkle like a jewel in its own right, as something that had its full worth in itself. Usefulness or fruitlessness can neither diminish nor augment this worth.[1]

He would presumably have said the same about a bad will: whether it accomplishes its evil purposes is morally irrelevant. And a course of action that would be condemned if it had a bad outcome cannot be vindicated if by luck it turns out well. There cannot be moral risk. This view seems to be wrong, but it arises in response to a fundamental problem about moral responsibility to which we possess no satisfactory solution.

The problem develops out of the ordinary conditions of moral judgment. Prior to reflection it is intuitively plausible that people cannot be morally assessed for what is not their fault, or for what is due to factors beyond their control.

Such judgment is different from the evaluation of something as a good or bad thing, or state of affairs. The latter may be present in addition to moral judgment, but when we blame someone for his actions we are not merely saying it is bad that they happened, or bad that he exists: we are judging *him,* saying he is bad, which is different from his being a bad thing. This kind of judgment takes only a certain kind of object. Without being able to explain exactly why, we feel that the appropriateness of moral assessment is easily undermined by the discovery that the act or attribute, no matter how good or bad, is not under the person's control. While other evaluations remain, this one seems to lose its footing. So a clear absence of control, produced by involuntary movement, physical force, or ignorance of the circumstances, excuses what is done from moral judgment. But what we do depends in many more ways than these on what is not under our control—what is not produced by a good or a bad will, in Kant's phrase. And external influences in this broader range are not usually thought to excuse what is done from moral judgment, positive or negative.

Let me give a few examples, beginning with the type of case Kant has in mind. Whether we succeed or fail in what we try to do nearly always depends to some extent on factors beyond our control. This is true of murder, altruism, revolution, the sacrifice of certain interests for the sake of others—almost any morally important act. What has been done, and what is morally judged, is partly determined by external factors. However jewel-like the goodwill may be in its own right, there is a

359

morally significant difference between rescuing someone from a burning building and dropping him from a twelfth-story window while trying to rescue him. Similarly, there is a morally significant difference between reckless driving and manslaughter. But whether a reckless driver hits a pedestrian depends on the presence of the pedestrian at the point where he recklessly passes a red light. What we do is also limited by the opportunities and choices with which we are faced, and these are largely determined by factors beyond our control. Someone who was an officer in a concentration camp might have led a quiet and harmless life if the Nazis had never come to power in Germany. And someone who led a quiet and harmless life in Argentina might have become an officer in a concentration camp if he had not left Germany for business reasons in 1930.

I shall say more later about these and other examples. I introduce them here to illustrate a general point. Where a significant aspect of what someone does depends on factors beyond his control, yet we continue to treat him in that respect as an object of moral judgment, it can be called moral luck. Such luck can be good or bad. And the problem posed by this phenomenon, which led Kant to deny its possibility, is that the broad range of external influences here identified seems on close examination to undermine moral assessment as surely as does the narrower range of familiar excusing conditions. If the condition of control is consistently applied, it threatens to erode most of the moral assessments we find it natural to make. The things for which people are morally judged are determined in more ways than we at first realize by what is beyond their control. And when the seemingly natural requirement of fault or responsibility is applied in light of these facts, it leaves few prereflective moral judgments intact. Ultimately, nothing or almost nothing about what a person does seems to be under his control.

Why not conclude, then, that the condition of control is false—that it is an initially plausible hypothesis refuted by clear counter examples? One could in that case look instead for a more refined condition which picked out the *kinds* of lack of control that really undermine certain moral judgments, without yielding the unacceptable conclusion derived from the broader

condition, that most or all ordinary moral judgments are illegitimate.

What rules out this escape is that we are dealing not with a theoretical conjecture but with a philosophical problem. The condition of control does not suggest itself merely as a generalization from certain clear cases. It seems *correct* in the further cases to which it is extended beyond the original set. When we undermine moral assessment by considering new ways in which control is absent, we are not just discovering what *would* follow given the general hypothesis, but are actually being persuaded that in itself the absence of control is relevant in these cases too. The erosion of moral judgment emerges not as the absurd consequence of an over-simple theory, but as a natural consequence of the ordinary idea of moral assessment, when it is applied in view of a more complete and precise account of the facts. It would therefore be a mistake in argue from the unacceptability of the conclusions in the need for a different account of the conditions of moral responsibility. The view that moral luck is paradoxical is not a *mistake*, ethical or logical, but a perception of one of the ways in which the intuitively acceptable conditions of moral judgment threaten to undermine it all.

It resembles the situation in another area of philosophy, the theory of knowledge. There too conditions which seem perfectly natural, and which grow out of the ordinary procedures for challenging and defending claims to knowledge, threaten to undermine all such claims if consistently applied. Most skeptical arguments have this quality: they do not depend on the imposition of arbitrarily stringent standards of knowledge, arrived at by misunderstanding, but appear to grow inevitably from the consistent application of ordinary standards. There is a substantive parallel as well, for epistemological skepticism arises from consideration of the respects in which our beliefs and their relation to reality depend on factors beyond our control. External and internal causes produce our beliefs. We may subject these processes to scrutiny in an effort to avoid error, but our conclusions at this next level also result, in part, from influences which we do not control directly. The same will be true no matter how far we carry the investigation. Our beliefs are always, ultimately, due to factors outside our control, and the impossibility of encompassing those factors without being at the mercy of others leads us to doubt whether we know anything. It looks as though, if any of our beliefs are true, it is pure biological luck rather than knowledge.

Moral luck is like this because while there are various respects in which the natural objects of moral assessment are out of our control or influenced by what is out of our control, we cannot reflect on these facts without losing our grip on the judgments.

There are roughly four ways in which the natural objects of moral assessment are disturbingly subject to luck. One is the phenomenon of constitutive luck—the kind of person you are, where this is not just a question of what you deliberately do, but of your inclinations, capacities, and temperament. Another category is luck in one's circumstances—the kind of problems and situations one faces. The other two have to do with the causes and effects of action: luck in how one is determined by antecedent circumstances, and luck in the way one's actions and projects turn out. All of them present a common problem. They are all opposed by the idea that one cannot be more culpable or estimable for anything than one is for that fraction of it which is under one's control. It seems irrational to take or dispense credit or blame for matters over which a person has no control, or for their influence on results over which he has partial control. Such things may create the conditions for action, but action can be judged only to the extent that it goes beyond these conditions and does not just result from them.

Let us first consider luck, good and bad, in the way things turn out. Kant, in the above-quoted passage, has one example of this in mind, but the category covers a wide range. It includes the truck driver who accidentally runs over a child, the artist who abandons his wife and five children to devote himself to painting,[2] and other cases in which the possibilities of success and failure are even greater. The driver, if he is entirely without fault, will feel terrible about his role in the event, but will not have to reproach himself. Therefore this example of agent-regret[3] is not yet a case of *moral* bad luck. However, if the driver was guilty of even a minor degree of negligence—failing to have his brakes checked

recently, for example—then if that negligence contributes to the death of the child, he will not merely feel terrible. He will blame himself for the death. And what makes this an example of moral luck is that he would have to blame himself only slightly for the negligence itself if no situation arose which required him to brake suddenly and violently to avoid hitting a child. Yet the *negligence* is the same in both cases, and the driver has no control over whether a child will run into his path.

The same is true at higher levels of negligence. If someone has had too much to drink and his car swerves onto the sidewalk, he can count himself morally lucky if there are no pedestrians in its path. If there were, he would be to blame for their deaths, and would probably be prosecuted for manslaughter. But if he hurts no one, although his recklessness is exactly the same, he is guilty of a far less serious legal offense and will certainly reproach himself and be reproached by others much less severely. To take another legal example, the penalty for attempted murder is less than that for successful murder—however similar the intentions and motives of the assailant may be in the two cases. His degree of culpability can depend, it would seem, on whether the victim happened to be wearing a bullet-proof vest, or whether a bird flew into the path of the bullet—matters beyond his control.

Finally, there are cases of decision under uncertainty—common in public and in private life. Anna Karenina goes off with Vronsky, Gauguin leaves his family, Chamberlain signs the Munich agreement, the Decembrists persuade the troops under their command to revolt against the czar, the American colonies declare their independence from Britain, you introduce two people in an attempt at match-making. It is tempting in all such cases to feel that some decision must be possible, in the light of what is known at the time, which will make reproach unsuitable no matter how things turn out. But this is not true; when someone acts in such ways he takes his life, or his moral position, into his hands, because how things turn out determines what he has done. It is possible *also* to assess the decision from the point of view of what could be known at the time, but this is not the end of the story. If the Decembrists had succeeded in overthrowing Nicholas I in 1825 and establishing a constitutional regime, they would be heroes. As it is, not only did they fail and pay for it, but they bore some responsibility for the terrible punishments meted out to the troops who had been persuaded to follow them. If the American Revolution had been a bloody failure resulting in greater repression, then Jefferson, Franklin and Washington would still have made a noble attempt, and might not even have regretted it on their way to the scaffold, but they would also have had to blame themselves for what they had helped to bring on their compatriots. (Perhaps peaceful efforts at reform would eventually have succeeded.) If Hitler had not overrun Europe and exterminated millions, but instead had died of a heart attack after occupying the Sudetenland, Chamberlain's action at Munich would still have utterly betrayed the Czechs, but it would not be the great moral disaster that has made his name a household word.

In many cases of difficult choice the outcome cannot be foreseen with certainty. One kind of assessment of the choice is possible in advance, but another kind must await the outcome, because the outcome determines what has been done. The same degree of culpability or estimability in intention, motive, or concern is compatible with a wide range of judgments, positive or negative, depending on what happened beyond the point of decision. The *mens rea* which could have existed in the absence of any consequences does not exhaust the grounds of moral judgment. Actual results influence culpability or esteem in a large class of unquestionably ethical cases ranging from negligence through political choice.

That these are genuine moral judgments rather than expressions of temporary attitude is evident from the fact that one can say *in advance* how the moral verdict will depend on the results. If one negligently leaves the bath running with the baby in it, one will realize, as one bounds up the stairs toward the bathroom, that if the baby has drowned one has done something awful, whereas if it has not one has merely been careless. Someone who launches a violent revolution against an authoritarian regime knows that if he fails he will be responsible for much suffering that is in vain, but if he succeeds he will be justified by the outcome. I do not mean that *any* action can be retro actively justified by history. Certain things are so bad in themselves, or so risky, that no results can make them all right. Nevertheless, when moral judgment does depend on the outcome, it is objective and timeless and not dependent on a change of standpoint produced by success or failure. The judgment after the fact follows from an hypothetical judgment that can be made beforehand, and it can be made as easily by someone else as by the agent.

From the point of view which makes responsibility dependent on control, all this seems absurd. How is it possible to be more or less culpable depending on whether a child gets into the path of one's car, or a bird into the path of one's bullet? Perhaps it is true that what is done depends on more than the agent's state of mind or intention. The problem then is, why is it not irrational to base moral assessment on what people do, in this broad sense? It amounts to holding them responsible for the contributions of fate as well as for their own—provided they have made some contribution to begin with. If we look at cases of negligence or attempt, the pattern seems to be that overall culpability corresponds to the product of mental or intentional fault and the seriousness of the outcome. Cases of decision under uncertainty are less easily explained in this way, for it seems that the overall judgment can even shift from positive to negative depending on the outcome. But here too it seems rational to subtract the effects of occurrences subsequent to the choice, that were merely possible at the time, and concentrate moral assessment on the actual decision in light of the probabilities. If the object of moral judgment is the *person*, then to hold him accountable for what he has done in the broader sense is akin to strict liability, which may have its legal uses but seems irrational as a moral position.

The result of such a line of thought is to pare down each act to its morally essential core, an inner act of pure will assessed by motive and intention. Adam Smith advocates such a position in *The Theory of Moral Sentiments*, but notes that it runs contrary to our actual judgments.

But how well soever we may seem to be persuaded of the truth of this equitable maxim, when we consider it after this manner, in abstract, yet when we come to particular cases, the actual consequences which happen to proceed from any action, have a very great effect upon our sentiments concerning its merit or demerit, and almost always either enhance or diminish our sense of both. Scarce, in any one instance, perhaps, will our sentiments be found, after examination, to be entirely regulated by this rule, which we all acknowledge ought entirely to regulate them.[4]

Joel Feinberg points out further that restricting the domain of moral responsibility to the inner world will not immunize it to luck. Factors beyond the agent's control, like a coughing fit, can interfere with his decisions as surely as they can with the path of a bullet from his gun.[5] Nevertheless the tendency to cut down the scope of moral assessment is pervasive, and does not limit itself to the influence of effects. It attempts to isolate the will from the other direction, so to speak, by separating out constitutive luck. Let us consider that next.

Kant was particularly insistent on the moral irrelevance of qualities of temperament and personality that are not under the control of the will. Such qualities as sympathy or coldness might provide the background against which obedience to moral requirements is more or less difficult, but they could not be objects of moral assessment themselves, and might well interfere with confident assessment of its proper object—the determination of the will by the motive of duty. This rules out moral judgment of many of the virtues and vices, which are states of character that influence choice but are certainly not exhausted by dispositions to act deliberately in certain ways. A person may be greedy, envious, cowardly, cold, ungenerous, unkind, vain, or conceited, but *behave* perfectly by a monumental effort of will. To possess these vices is to be unable to help having certain feelings under certain circumstances, and to have strong spontaneous impulses to act badly. Even if one controls the impulses, one still has the vice. An envious person hates the greater success of others. He can be morally condemned as envious even if he congratulates them cordially and does nothing to denigrate or spoil their success. Conceit, likewise, need not be displayed. It is fully present in someone who cannot help

dwelling with secret satisfaction on the superiority of his own achievements, talents, beauty, intelligence, or virtue. To some extent such a quality may be the product of earlier choices; to some extent it may be amenable to change by current actions. But it is largely a matter of constitutive bad fortune. Yet people are morally condemned for such qualities, and esteemed for others equally beyond control of the will: they are assessed for what they are *like*.

To Kant this seems incoherent because virtue is enjoined on everyone and therefore must in principle be possible for everyone. It may be easier for some than for others, but it must be possible to achieve it by making the right choices, against whatever temperamental background.[6] One may want to have a generous spirit, or regret not having one, but it makes no sense to condemn oneself or anyone else for a quality which is not within the control of the will. Condemnation implies that you should not be like that, not that it is unfortunate that you are.

Nevertheless, Kant's conclusion remains intuitively unacceptable. We may be persuaded that these moral judgments are irrational, but they reappear involuntarily as soon as the argument is over. This is the pattern throughout the subject.

The third category to consider is luck in one's circumstances, and I shall mention it briefly. The things we are called upon to do, the moral tests we face, are importantly determined by factors beyond our control. It may be true of someone that in a dangerous situation he would behave in a cowardly or heroic fashion, but if the situation never arises, he will never have the chance to distinguish or disgrace himself in this way, and his moral record will be different.

A conspicuous example of this is political. Ordinary citizens of Nazi Germany had an opportunity to behave heroically by opposing the regime. They also had an opportunity to behave badly, and most of them are culpable for having failed this test. But it is a test to which the citizens of other countries were not subjected, with the result that even if they, or some of them, would have behaved as badly as the Germans in like circumstances, they simply did not and therefore are not similarly culpable. Here again one is morally at the mercy of fate, and it may seem irrational upon reflection, but our ordinary moral attitudes would be unrecognizable without it. We judge people for what they actually do or fail to do, not just for what they would have done if circumstances had been different.[7]

This form of moral determination by the actual is also paradoxical, but we can begin to see how deep in the concept of responsibility the paradox is embedded. A person can be morally responsible only for what he does; but what he does results from a great deal that he does not do; therefore he is not morally responsible for what he is and is not responsible for. (This is not a contradiction, but it is a paradox.)

It should be obvious that there is a connection between these problems about responsibility and control and an even more familiar problem, that of freedom of the will. That is the last type of moral luck I want to take up, though I can do no more within the scope of this essay than indicate its connection with the other types.

If one cannot be responsible for consequences of one's acts due to factors beyond one's control, or for antecedents of one's acts that are properties of temperament not subject to one's will, or for the circumstances that pose one's moral choices, then how can one be responsible even for the stripped-down acts of the will itself, if *they* are the product of antecedent circumstances outside of the will's control?

The area of genuine agency, and therefore of legitimate moral judgment, seems to shrink under this scrutiny to an extensionless point. Everything seems to result from the combined influence of factors, antecedent and posterior to action, that are not within the agent's control. Since he cannot be responsible for them, he cannot be responsible for their results though it may remain possible to take up the aesthetic or other evaluative analogues of the moral attitudes that are thus displaced.

It is also possible, of course, to brazen it out and refuse to accept the results, which indeed seem unacceptable as soon as we stop thinking about the arguments. Admittedly, if certain surrounding circumstances had been different, then no unfortunate consequences would have followed from a wicked intention, and no seriously culpable act would have been performed; but since the circumstances were *not* different,

and the agent *in fact* succeeded in perpetrating a particularly cruel murder, *that* is what he did, and that is what he is responsible for. Similarly, we may admit that if certain antecedent circumstances had been different, the agent would never have developed into the sort of person who would do such a thing; but since he *did* develop (as the inevitable result of those antecedent circumstances) into the sort of swine he is, and into the person who committed such a murder, *that* is what he is blameable for. In both cases one is responsible for what one actually does—even if what one actually does depends in important ways on what is not within one's control. This compatibilist account of our moral judgments would leave room for the ordinary conditions of responsibility—the absence of coercion, ignorance, or involuntary movement—as part of the determination of what someone has done—but it is understood not to exclude the influence of a great deal that he has not done.

The only thing wrong with this solution is its failure to explain how skeptical problems arise. For they arise not from the imposition of an arbitrary external requirement, but from the nature of moral judgment itself. Something in the ordinary idea of what someone does must explain how it can seem necessary to subtract from it anything that merely happens—even though the ultimate consequence of such subtraction is that nothing remains. And something in the ordinary idea of knowledge must explain why it seems to be undermined by any influences on belief not within the control of the subject—so that knowledge seems impossible without an impossible foundation in autonomous reason. But let us leave epistemology aside and concentrate on action, character, and moral assessment.

The problem arises, I believe, because the self which acts and is the object of moral judgment is threatened with dissolution by the absorption of its acts and impulses into the class of events. Moral judgment of a person is judgment not of what happens to him, but of him. It does not say merely that a certain event or state of affairs is fortunate or unfortunate or even terrible. It is not an evaluation of a state of the world, or of an individual as part of the world. We are not thinking just that it would be better if he were different, or did not exist, or had not done some of the things he has done. We are judging *him,* rather than his existence or characteristics. The effect of concentrating on the influence of what is not under his control is to make this responsible self seem to disappear, swallowed up by the order of mere events.

What, however, do we have in mind that a person must *be* to be the object of these moral attitudes? While the concept of agency is easily undermined, it is very difficult to give it a positive characterization. That is familiar from the literature on Free Will.

I believe that in a sense the problem has no solution, because something in the idea of agency is incompatible with actions being events, or people being things. But as the external determinants of what someone has done are gradually exposed, in their effect on consequences, character, and choice itself, it becomes gradually clear that actions are events and people things. Eventually nothing remains which can be ascribed to the responsible self, and we are left with nothing but a portion of the larger sequence of events, which can be deplored or celebrated, but not blamed or praised.

Though I cannot define the idea of the active self that is thus undermined, it is possible to say something about its sources. There is a close connection between our feelings about ourselves and our feelings about others. Guilt and indignation, shame and contempt, pride and admiration are internal and external sides of the same moral attitudes. We are unable to view ourselves simply as portions of the world, and from inside we have a rough idea of the boundary between what is us and what is not, what we do and what happens to us, what is our personality and what is an accidental handicap. We apply the same essentially internal conception of the self to others. About ourselves we feel pride, shame, guilt, remorse—and agent-regret. We do not regard our actions and our characters merely as fortunate or unfortunate episodes—though they may also be that. We cannot *simply* take an external evaluative view of ourselves—of what we most essentially are and what we do. And this remains true even when we have seen that we are not responsible for our own existence, or our nature, or the choices we have to make, or the circumstances that give our acts the consequences they have. Those acts remain ours and we remain ourselves, despite the persuasiveness of the reasons that seem to argue us out of existence.

It is this internal view that we extend to others in moral judgment—when we judge *them* rather than their desirability or utility. We extend to others the refusal to limit ourselves to external evaluation, and we accord to them selves like our own. But in both cases this comes up against the brutal inclusion of humans and everything about them in a world from which they cannot be separated and of which they are nothing but contents. The external view forces itself on us at the same time that we resist it. One way this occurs is through the gradual erosion of what we do by the subtraction of what happens.

The inclusion of consequences in the conception of what we have done is an acknowledgment that we are parts of the world, but the paradoxical character of moral luck which emerges from this acknowledgment shows that we are unable to operate with such a view, for it leaves us with no one to be. The same thing is revealed in the appearance that determinism obliterates responsibility. Once we see an aspect of what we or someone else does as something that happens, we lose our grip on the idea that it has been done and that we can judge the doer and not just the happening. This explains why the absence of determinism is no more hospitable to the concept of agency than is its presence—a point that has been noticed often. Either way the act is viewed externally, as part of the course of events.

The problem of moral luck cannot be understood without an account of the internal conception of agency and its special connection with the moral attitudes as opposed to other types of value. I do not have such an account. The degree to which the problem has a solution can be determined only by seeing whether in some degree the incompatibility between this conception and the various ways in which we do not control what we do is only apparent. I have nothing to offer on that topic either. But it is not enough to say merely that our basic moral attitudes toward ourselves and others are determined by what is actual; for they are also threatened by the sources of that actually, and by the external view of action which forces itself on us when we see how everything we do belongs to a world that we have not created.

NOTES

1. *Foundations of the Metaphysics of Morals*, first section, third paragraph.
2. Such a case, modelled on the life of Gauguin, is discussed by Bernard Williams in "Moral Luck" *Proceedings of the Aristotelian Society*, supplementary vol. L (1976), 115–35 (to which the original version of this essay was a reply). He points out that though success or failure cannot be predicted in advance, Gauguin's most basic retrospective feelings about the decision will be determined by the development of his talent. My disagreement with Williams is that his account fails to explain why such retrospective attitudes can be called moral. If success does not permit Gauguin to justify himself to others, but still determines his most basic feelings, that shows only that his most basic feelings need not be moral. It does not show that morality is subject to luck. If the retrospective judgment were moral, it would imply the truth of a hypothetical judgment made in advance, of the form "If I leave my family and become a great painter, I will be justified by success; if I don't become a great painter, the act will be unforgivable."
3. Williams' term (*ibid.*).
4. Pt II, sect. 3, Introduction, para. 5.
5. "Problematic Responsibility in Law and Morals," in Joel Feinberg, *Doing and Deserving* (Princeton: Princeton University Press, 1970).
6. "If nature has put little sympathy in the heart of a man, and if he, though an honest man, is by temperament cold and indifferent to the sufferings of others, perhaps because he is provided with special gifts of patience and fortitude and expects or even requires that others should have the same—and such a man would certainly not be the meanest product of nature—would not he find in himself a source from which to give himself a far higher worth than he could have got by having a good-natured temperament?" (*Foundations of the Metaphysics of Morals*, first section, eleventh paragraph).
7. Circumstantial luck can extend to aspects of the situation other than individual behavior. For example, during the Vietnam War even U.S. citizens who had opposed their country's actions vigorously from the start often felt compromised by its crimes. Here they were not even responsible; there was probably nothing they could do to stop what was happening, so the feeling of being implicated may seem unintelligible. But it is nearly impossible to view the crimes of one's own country in the same way that one views the crimes of another country, no matter how equal one's lack of power to stop them in the two cases. One *is* a citizen of one of them, and has a connection with its actions (even if only through taxes that cannot be withheld)—that one does not have with the other's. This makes it possible to be ashamed of one's country, and to feel a victim of moral bad luck that one was an American in the 1960s.

Questions for Discussion

1. Should unsuccessful murderers be less harshly judged than successful ones? Can we distinguish between moral assessments of persons and their actions?
2. In what aspects of our lives are we lucky or unlucky?
3. What is the relationship between moral luck and moral responsibility?

J. L. Mackie, "The Subjectivity of Values"

J. L. Mackie (1917–1982) was a prominent philosopher at Oxford University. Our selection is from his celebrated book Ethics: Inventing Right and Wrong, *wherein Mackie argues that cognitivism, not non-cognitivism, is the proper way to conceive of moral judgments. However, all moral propositions are false. Mackie presents two arguments for thinking that there are no moral facts; the first argument is the argument from moral disagreement. Mackie claims that the best interpretation of moral disagreement is that "the actual variations in the moral codes are more readily explained by the hypothesis that they reflect ways of life than by the hypothesis that they express perceptions, most of them seriously inadequate and badly distorted of objective values." (Mackie evidently assumes that there is moral disagreement; but see the section in Chapter 1 on moral relativism, where this is questioned.) The second argument against moral objectivity is the argument from queerness—the idea that if there were moral facts, they would have to be facts of a very peculiar sort. Mackie also gives us a perceptive account of why we are mistakenly inclined to think that moral judgments reflect an objective moral reality.*

Critical Reading Questions

1. What does Mackie mean by moral subjectivism?
2. How is his view clarified by the difference between hypothetical and categorical imperatives?
3. What is an error theory?
4. What is the argument from relativity and what is it supposed to show?
5. What is the argument from queerness and what is it supposed to show?
6. What is the pathetic fallacy? How is it relevant to morality?

THE SUBJECTIVITY OF VALUES

J. L. Mackie

MORAL SCEPTICISM

There are no objective values. This is a bald statement of the thesis of this chapter, but before arguing for it I shall try to clarify and restrict it in ways that may meet some objections and prevent some misunderstanding.

The statement of this thesis is liable to provoke one of three very different reactions. Some will think it not merely false but pernicious; they will see it as a threat to morality and to everything else that is worthwhile, and they will find the presenting of such a thesis in what purports to be a book on ethics paradoxical or even outrageous. Others will regard it as a trivial truth, almost too obvious to be worth mentioning, and certainly too plain to be worth much argument. Others again will say that it is meaningless or empty, that no real issue is raised by the question whether values are or are not part of the fabric of the world. But, precisely because there can be these three different reactions, much more needs to be said.

The claim that values are not objective, are not part of the fabric of the world, is meant to include not only moral goodness, which might be most naturally equated with moral value, but also other things that could be more loosely called moral values or disvalues—rightness and wrongness, duty, obligation, an action's being rotten and contemptible, and so on. It also includes non-moral values, notably aesthetic ones, beauty and various kinds of artistic merit. I shall not discuss these explicitly, but clearly much the same considerations apply to aesthetic and to moral values, and there would be at least some initial implausibility in a view that gave the one a different status from the other.

Since it is with moral values that I am primarily concerned, the view I am adopting may be called moral scepticism. But this name is likely to be misunderstood: 'moral scepticism' might also be used as a name for either of two first order views, or perhaps for an incoherent mixture of the two. A moral sceptic might be the sort of person who says 'All this talk of morality is tripe,' who rejects morality and will take no notice of it. Such a person may be literally rejecting all moral judgements; he is more likely to be making moral judgements of his own, expressing a positive moral condemnation of all that conventionally passes for morality; or he may be confusing these two logically incompatible views, and saying that he rejects all morality, while he is in fact rejecting only a particular morality that is current in the society in which he has grown up. But I am not at present concerned with the merits or faults of such a position. These are first order moral views, positive or negative: the person who adopts either of them is taking a certain practical, normative, stand. By contrast, what I am discussing is a second order view, a view about the status of moral values and the nature of moral valuing, about where and how they fit into the world. These first and second order views are not merely distinct but completely independent: one could be a second order moral sceptic without being a first order one, or again the other way round. A man could hold strong moral views, and indeed ones whose content was thoroughly conventional, while believing that they were simply attitudes and policies with regard to conduct that he and other people held. Conversely, a man could reject all established morality while believing it to be an objective truth that it was evil or corrupt.

With another sort of misunderstanding moral scepticism would seem not so much pernicious as absurd. How could anyone deny that there is a difference between a kind action and a cruel one, or that a coward and a brave man behave differently in the face of danger? Of course, this is undeniable; but it is not to the point. The kinds of behaviour to which moral values and disvalues are ascribed are indeed part of the furniture of the world, and so are the natural, descriptive, differences between them; but not, perhaps, their differences in value. It is a hard fact that cruel actions differ from kind ones, and hence that we can learn, as in fact we all do, to distinguish them fairly well in practice, and to use the words 'cruel' and 'kind' with fairly clear descriptive meanings; but is it an equally hard fact that actions which are cruel in such a descriptive sense are to be condemned? The present issue is with regard to the objectivity specifically of value, not with regard to the objectivity of those natural, factual, differences on the basis of which differing values are assigned.

SUBJECTIVISM

Another name often used, as an alternative to 'moral scepticism', for the view I am discussing is 'subjectivism'. But this too has more than one meaning. Moral subjectivism too could be a first order, normative, view, namely that everyone really ought to do whatever he thinks he should. This plainly is a (systematic) first order view; on examination it soon ceases to be plausible, but that is beside the point, for it is quite independent of the second order thesis at present under consideration. What is more confusing is that different second order views compete for the name 'subjectivism'. Several of these are doctrines about the meaning of moral terms and moral statements. What is often called moral subjectivism is the doctrine that, for example, 'This action is right' *means* 'I approve of this action', or more generally that moral judgements are equivalent to reports of the speaker's own feelings or attitudes. But the view I am now discussing is to be distinguished in two vital respects

from any such doctrine as this. First, what I have called moral scepticism is a negative doctrine, not a positive one: it says what there isn't, not what there is. It says that there do not exist entities or relations of a certain kind, objective values or requirements, which many people have believed to exist. Of course, the moral sceptic cannot leave it at that. If his position is to be at all plausible, he must give some account of how other people have fallen into what he regards as an error, and this account will have to include some positive suggestions about how values fail to be objective, about what has been mistaken for, or has led to false beliefs about, objective values. But this will be a development of his theory, not its core: its core is the negation. Secondly, what I have called moral scepticism is an ontological thesis, not a linguistic or conceptual one. It is not, like the other doctrine often called moral subjectivism, a view about the meanings of moral statements. Again, no doubt, if it is to be at all plausible, it will have to give some account of their meanings, and I shall say something about this [in a later section of the original work.] But this too will be a development of the theory, not its core.

It is true that those who have accepted the moral subjectivism which is the doctrine that moral judgements are equivalent to reports of the speaker's own feelings or attitudes have usually presupposed what I am calling moral scepticism. It is because they have assumed that there are no objective values that they have looked elsewhere for an analysis of what moral statements might mean, and have settled upon subjective reports. Indeed, if all our moral statements were such subjective reports, it would follow that, at least so far as we are aware, there are no objective moral values. If we were aware of them, we would say something about them. In this sense this sort of subjectivism entails moral scepticism. But the converse entailment does not hold. The denial that there are objective values does not commit one to any particular view about what moral statements mean, and certainly not to the view that they are equivalent to subjective reports. No doubt if moral values are not objective they are in some very broad sense subjective, and for this reason I would accept 'moral subjectivism' as an alternative name to 'moral scepticism'.

But subjectivism in this broad sense must be distinguished from the specific doctrine about meaning referred to above. Neither name is altogether satisfactory: we simply have to guard against the (different) misinterpretations which each may suggest.

[. . .]

HYPOTHETICAL AND CATEGORICAL IMPERATIVES

We may make this issue clearer by referring to Kant's distinction between hypothetical and categorical imperatives, though what he called imperatives are more naturally expressed as 'ought'-statements than in the imperative mood. 'If you want X, do Y' (or 'You ought to do Y') will be a hypothetical imperative if it is based on the supposed fact that Y is, in the circumstances, the only (or the best) available means to X, that is, on a causal relation between Y and X. The reason for doing Y lies in its causal connection with the desired end, X; the oughtness is contingent upon the desire. But 'You ought to do Y' will be a categorical imperative if you ought to do Y irrespective of any such desire for any end to which Y would contribute, if the oughtness is not thus contingent upon any desire.

[. . .]

A categorical imperative, then, would express a reason for acting which was unconditional in the sense of not being contingent upon any present desire of the agent to whose satisfaction the recommended action would contribute as a means—or more directly: 'You ought to dance', if the implied reason is just that you want to dance or like dancing, is still a hypothetical imperative. Now Kant himself held that moral judgements are categorical imperatives, or perhaps are all applications of one categorical imperative, and it can plausibly be maintained at least that many moral judgements contain a categorically imperative element. So far as ethics is concerned, my thesis that there are no objective values is specifically the denial that any such categorically imperative element is objectively valid. The objective values which I am denying would be action-directing absolutely, not contingently (in the way indicated) upon the agent's desires and inclinations.

[. . .]

THE CLAIM TO OBJECTIVITY

If I have succeeded in specifying precisely enough the moral values whose objectivity I am denying, my thesis may now seem to be trivially true. Of course, some will say, valuing, preferring, choosing, recommending, rejecting, condemning, and so on, are human activities, and there is no need to look for values that are prior to and logically independent of all such activities. There may be widespread agreement in valuing, and particular value-judgements are not in general arbitrary or isolated: they typically cohere with others, or can be criticized if they do not, reasons can be given for them, and so on: but if all that the subjectivist is maintaining is that desires, ends, purposes, and the like figure somewhere in the system of reasons, and that no ends or purposes are objective as opposed to being merely inter-subjective, then this may be conceded without much fuss.

But I do not think that this should be conceded so easily. As I have said, the main tradition of European moral philosophy includes the contrary claim, that there are objective values of just the sort I have denied. I have referred already [in the original work] to Plato, Kant, and Sidgwick. Kant in particular holds that the categorical imperative is not only categorical and imperative but objectively so: though a rational being gives the moral law to himself, the law that he thus makes is determinate and necessary. Aristotle begins the *Nicomachean Ethics* by saying that the good is that at which all things aim, and that ethics is part of a science which he calls 'politics', whose goal is not knowledge but practice; yet he does not doubt that there can be *knowledge* of what is the good for man, nor, once he has identified this as well-being or happiness, *eudaimonia*, that it can be known, rationally determined, in what happiness consists; and it is plain that he thinks that this happiness is intrinsically desirable, not good simply because it is desired. The rationalist Samuel Clarke holds that

these eternal and necessary differences of things make it *fit and reasonable* for creatures so to act . . . even separate from the consideration of these rules being the *positive will* or *command of God*; and also antecedent to any respect or regard, expectation or apprehension, of any *particular private and personal advantage or disadvantage, reward or punishment*, either present or future . . .

Even the sentimentalist Hutcheson defines moral goodness as 'some quality apprehended in actions, which procures approbation . . .', while saying that the moral sense by which we perceive virtue and vice has been given to us (by the Author of nature) to direct our actions. Hume indeed was on the other side, but he is still a witness to the dominance of the objectivist tradition, since he claims that when we 'see that the distinction of vice and virtue is not founded merely on the relations of objects, nor is perceiv'd by reason', this 'wou'd subvert all the vulgar systems of morality'. And Richard Price insists that right and wrong are 'real characters of actions', not 'qualities of our minds', and are perceived by the understanding; he criticizes the notion of moral sense on the ground that it would make virtue an affair of taste, and moral right and wrong "nothing in the objects themselves"; he rejects Hutcheson's view because (perhaps mistakenly) he sees it as collapsing into Hume's.

But this objectivism about values is not only a feature of the philosophical tradition. It has also a firm basis in ordinary thought, and even in the meanings of moral terms. No doubt it was an extravagance for Moore to say that 'good' is the name of a non-natural quality, but it would not be so far wrong to say that in moral contexts it is used as if it were the name of a supposed non-natural quality, where the description "non-natural" leaves room for the peculiar evaluative, prescriptive, intrinsically action-guiding aspects of this supposed quality. This point can be illustrated by reflection on the conflicts and swings of opinion in recent years between non-cognitivist and naturalist views about the central, basic, meanings of ethical terms. If we reject the view that it is the function of such terms to introduce objective values into discourse about conduct and choices of action, there seem to be two main alternative types of account. One (which has importantly different subdivisions) is that they conventionally express either attitudes which the speaker purports to adopt towards whatever it is that he characterizes morally, or prescriptions or recommendations, subject perhaps to the logical constraint of universalizability. Different views of this type share the central thesis that ethical terms have, at least partly and primarily, some sort of

non-cognitive, non-descriptive, meaning. Views of the other type hold that they are descriptive in meaning, but descriptive of natural features, partly of such features as everyone, even the non-cognitivist, would recognize as distinguishing kind actions from cruel ones, courage from cowardice, politeness from rudeness, and so on, and partly (though these two overlap) of relations between the actions and some human wants, satisfactions, and the like. I believe that views of both these types capture part of the truth. Each approach can account for the fact that moral judgements are action-guiding or practical. Yet each gains much of its plausibility from the felt inadequacy of the other. It is a very natural reaction to any non-cognitive analysis of ethical terms to protest that there is more to ethics than this, something more external to the maker of moral judgements, more authoritative over both him and those of or to whom he speaks, and this reaction is likely to persist even when full allowance has been made for the logical, formal, constraints of full-blooded prescriptivity and universalizability. Ethics, we are inclined to believe, is more a matter of knowledge and less a matter of decision than any non-cognitive analysis allows. And of course naturalism satisfies this demand. It will not be a matter of choice or decision whether an action is cruel or unjust or imprudent or whether it is likely to produce more distress than pleasure. But in satisfying this demand, it introduces a converse deficiency. On a naturalist analysis, moral judgements can be practical, but their practicality is wholly relative to desires or possible satisfactions of the person or persons whose actions are to be guided; but moral judgements seem to say more than this. This view leaves out the categorical quality of moral requirements. In fact both naturalist and non-cognitive analyses leave out the apparent authority of ethics, the one by excluding the categorically imperative aspect, the other the claim to objective validity or truth. The ordinary user of moral language means to say something about whatever it is that he characterizes morally, for example a possible action, as it is in itself, or would be if it were realized, and not about, or even simply expressive of, his, or anyone else's, attitude or relation to it. But the something he wants to say is not purely descriptive, certainly not inert, but something that involves a call for action or for the refraining from action, and one that is absolute, not contingent upon any desire or preference or policy or choice, his own or anyone else's. Someone in a state of moral perplexity, wondering whether it would be wrong for him to engage, say, in research related to bacteriological warfare, wants to arrive at some judgement about this concrete case, his doing this work at this time in these actual circumstances; his relevant characteristics will be part of the subject of the judgement, but no relation between him and the proposed action will be part of the predicate. The question is not, for example, whether he really wants to do this work, whether it will satisfy or dissatisfy him, whether he will in the long run have a pro-attitude towards it, or even whether this is an action of a sort that he can happily and sincerely recommend in all relevantly similar cases. Nor is he even wondering just whether to recommend such action in all relevantly similar cases. He wants to know whether this course of action would be wrong in itself. Something like this is the everyday objectivist concept of which talk about non-natural qualities is a philosopher's reconstruction.

The prevalence of this tendency to objectify values—and not only moral ones—is confirmed by a pattern of thinking that we find in existentialists and those influenced by them. The denial of objective values can carry with it an extreme emotional reaction, a feeling that nothing matters at all, that life has lost its purpose. Of course this does not follow; the lack of objective values is not a good reason for abandoning subjective concern or for ceasing to want anything. But the abandonment of a belief in objective values can cause, at least temporarily, a decay of subjective concern and sense of purpose. That it does so is evidence that the people in whom this reaction occurs have been tending to objectify their concerns and purposes, have been giving them a fictitious external authority. A claim to objectivity has been so strongly associated with their subjective concerns and purposes that the collapse of the former seems to undermine the latter as well.

This view, that conceptual analysis would reveal a claim to objectivity, is sometimes dramatically confirmed by philosophers who are officially on the other side. Bertrand Russell, for example, says that 'ethical propositions should be expressed in the optative mood, not in the indicative'; he defends himself effectively against the charge of inconsistency in both holding ultimate ethical valuations to be subjective and expressing emphatic opinions on ethical questions. Yet at the end he admits:

Certainly there *seems* to be something more. Suppose, for example, that some one were to advocate the introduction of bull-fighting in this country. In opposing the proposal, I should *feel*, not only that I was expressing my desires, but that my desires in the matter are *right*, whatever that may mean. As a matter of argument, I can, I think, show that I am not guilty of any logical inconsistency in holding to the above interpretation of ethics and at the same time expressing strong ethical preferences. But in feeling I am not satisfied.

But he concludes, reasonably enough, with the remark: 'I can only say that, while my own opinions as to ethics do not satisfy me, other people's satisfy me still less.'

I conclude, then, that ordinary moral judgements include a claim to objectivity, an assumption that there are objective values in just the sense in which I am concerned to deny this. And I do not think it is going too far to say that this assumption has been incorporated in the basic, conventional, meanings of moral terms. Any analysis of the meanings of moral terms which omits this claim to objective, intrinsic, prescriptivity is to that extent incomplete; and this is true of any non-cognitive analysis, any naturalist one, and any combination of the two.

If second order ethics were confined, then, to linguistic and conceptual analysis, it ought to conclude that moral values at least are objective: that they are so is part of what our ordinary moral statements mean: the traditional moral concepts of the ordinary man as well as of the main line of western philosophers are concepts of objective value. But it is precisely for this reason that linguistic and conceptual analysis is not enough. The claim to objectivity, however ingrained in our language and thought, is not self-validating. It can and should be questioned. But the denial of objective values will have to be put forward not as the result of an analytic approach, but as an 'error theory', a theory that although most people in making moral judgements implicitly claim, among other things, to be pointing to something objectively prescriptive, these claims are all false. It is this that makes the name 'moral scepticism' appropriate.

But since this is an error theory, since it goes against assumptions ingrained in our thought and built into some of the ways in which language is used, since it conflicts with what is sometimes called common sense, it needs very solid support. It is not something we can accept lightly or casually and then quietly pass on. If we are to adopt this view, we must argue explicitly for it. Traditionally it has been supported by arguments of two main kinds, which I shall call the argument from relativity and the argument from queerness, but these can, as I shall show, be supplemented in several ways.

THE ARGUMENT FROM RELATIVITY

The argument from relativity has as its premiss the well-known variation in moral codes from one society to another and from one period to another, and also the differences in moral beliefs between different groups and classes within a complex community. Such variation is in itself merely a truth of descriptive morality, a fact of anthropology which entails neither first order nor second order ethical views. Yet it may indirectly support second order subjectivism: radical differences between first order moral judgements make it difficult to treat those judgements as apprehensions of objective truths. But it is not the mere occurrence of disagreements that tells against the objectivity of values. Disagreement on questions in history or biology or cosmology does not show that there are no objective issues in these fields for investigators to disagree about. But such scientific disagreement results from speculative inferences or explanatory hypotheses based on inadequate evidence, and it is hardly plausible to interpret moral disagreement in the same way. Disagreement about moral codes seems to reflect people's adherence to and participation in different ways of life. The causal connection seems to be mainly that way round: it is that people approve of monogamy because they participate in a monogamous way of life rather than that they participate in a monogamous

way of life because they approve of monogamy. Of course, the standards may be an idealization of the way of life from which they arise: the monogamy in which people participate may be less complete, less rigid, than that of which it leads them to approve. This is not to say that moral judgements are purely conventional. Of course there have been and are moral heretics and moral reformers, people who have turned against the established rules and practices of their own communities for moral reasons, and often for moral reasons that we would endorse. But this can usually be understood as the extension, in ways which, though new and unconventional, seemed to them to be required for consistency, of rules to which they already adhered as arising out of an existing way of life. In short, the argument from relativity has some force simply because the actual variations in the moral codes are more readily explained by the hypothesis that they reflect ways of life than by the hypothesis that they express perceptions, most of them seriously inadequate and badly distorted, of objective values.

But there is a well-known counter to this argument from relativity, namely to say that the items for which objective validity is in the first place to be claimed are not specific moral rules or codes but very general basic principles which are recognized at least implicitly to some extent in all society—such principles as provide the foundations of what Sidgwick has called different methods of ethics: the principle of universalizability, perhaps, or the rule that one ought to conform to the specific rules of any way of life in which one takes part, from which one profits, and on which one relies, or some utilitarian principle of doing what tends, or seems likely, to promote the general happiness. It is easy to show that such general principles, married with differing concrete circumstances, different existing social patterns or different preferences, will beget different specific moral rules; and there is some plausibility in the claim that the specific rules thus generated will vary from community to community or from group to group in close agreement with the actual variations in accepted codes.

The argument from relativity can be only partly countered in this way. To take this line the moral objectivist has to stay that it is only in these principles that the objective moral character attaches immediately to its descriptively specified ground or subject: other moral judgements are objectively valid or true, but only derivatively and contingently—if things had been otherwise, quite different sorts of actions would have been right. And despite the prominence in recent philosophical ethics of universalization, utilitarian principles, and the like, these are very far from constituting the whole of what is actually affirmed as basic in ordinary moral thought. Much of this is concerned rather with what Hare calls "ideals" or, less kindly, 'fanaticism'. That is, people judge that some things are good or right, and others are bad or wrong, not because—or at any rate not only because—they exemplify some general principle for which widespread implicit acceptance could be claimed, but because something about those things arouses certain responses immediately in them, though they would arouse radically and irresolvably different responses in others. 'Moral sense' or 'intuition' is an initially more plausible description of what supplies many of our basic moral judgements than 'reason'. With regard to all these starting points of moral thinking the argument from relativity remains in full force.

THE ARGUMENT FROM QUEERNESS

Even more important, however, and certainly more generally applicable, is the argument from queerness. This has two parts, one metaphysical, the other epistemological. If there were objective values, then they would be entities or qualities or relations of a very strange sort, utterly different from anything else in the universe. Correspondingly, if we were aware of them, it would have to be by some special faculty of moral perception or intuition, utterly different from our ordinary ways of knowing everything else. These points were recognized by Moore when he spoke of non-natural qualities, and by the intuitionists in their talk about a 'faculty of moral intuition'. Intuitionism has long been out of favour, and it is indeed easy to point out its implausibilities. What is not so often stressed, but is more important, is that the central thesis of intuitionism is one to which any objectivist view of values is in the

end committed: intuitionism merely makes unpalatably plain what other forms of objectivism wrap up. Of course the suggestion that moral judgements are made or moral problems solved by just sitting down and having an ethical intuition is a travesty of actual moral thinking. But, however complex the real process, it will require (if it is to yield authoritatively prescriptive conclusions) some input of this distinctive sort, either premises or forms of argument or both. When we ask the awkward question, how we can be aware of this authoritative prescriptivity, of the truth of these distinctively ethical premises or of the cogency of this distinctively ethical pattern of reasoning, none of our ordinary accounts of sensory perception or introspection or the framing and confirming of explanatory hypotheses or inference or logical construction or conceptual analysis, or any combination of these, will provide a satisfactory answer; 'a special sort of intuition' is a lame answer, but it is the one to which the clear-headed objectivist is compelled to resort.

Indeed, the best move for the moral objectivist is not to evade this issue, but to look for companions in guilt. For example, Richard Price argues that it is not moral knowledge alone that such an empiricism as those of Locke and Hume is unable to account for, but also our knowledge and even our ideas of essence, number, identity, diversity, solidity, inertia, substance, the necessary existence and infinite extension of time and space, necessity and possibility in general, power, and causation. If the understanding, which Price defines as the faculty within us that discerns truth, is also a source of new simple ideas of so many other sorts, may it not also be a power of immediately perceiving right and wrong, which yet are real characters of actions?

This is an important counter to the argument from queerness. The only adequate reply to it would be to show how, on empiricist foundations, we can construct an account of the ideas and beliefs and knowledge that we have of all these matters. I cannot even begin to do that here, though I have undertaken some parts of the task elsewhere. I can only state my belief that satisfactory accounts of most of these can be given in empirical terms. If some supposed metaphysical necessities or essences resist such treatment, then they too should be included, along with objective values, among the targets of the argument from queerness.

This queerness does not consist simply in the fact that ethical statements are 'unverifiable'. Although logical positivism with its verifiability theory of descriptive meaning gave an impetus to non-cognitive accounts of ethics, it is not only logical positivists but also empiricists of a much more liberal sort who should find objective values hard to accommodate. Indeed, I would not only reject the verifiability principle but also deny the conclusion commonly drawn from it, that moral judgements lack descriptive meaning. The assertion that there are objective values or intrinsically prescriptive entities or features of some kind, which ordinary moral judgements presuppose, is, I hold, not meaningless but false.

Plato's Forms give a dramatic picture of what objective values would have to be. The Form of the Good is such that knowledge of it provides the knower with both a direction and an overriding motive; something's being good both tells the person who knows this to pursue it and makes him pursue it. An objective good would be sought by anyone who was acquainted with it, not because of any contingent fact that this person, or every person, is so constituted that he desires this end, but just because the end has to-be-pursuedness somehow built into it. Similarly, if there were objective principles of right and wrong, any wrong (possible) course of action would have not-to-be-doneness somehow built into it. Or we should have something like Clarke's necessary relations of fitness between situations and actions, so that a situation would have a demand for such-and-such an action somehow built into it.

The need for an argument of this sort can be brought out by reflection on Hume's argument that 'reason'—in which at this stage he includes all sorts of knowing as well as reasoning—can never be an 'influencing motive of the will'. Someone might object that Hume has argued unfairly from the lack of influencing power (not contingent upon desires) in ordinary objects of knowledge and ordinary reasoning, and might maintain that values differ from natural objects precisely in their power, when known, automatically to influence the will. To this Hume could, and would need to, reply that this objection involves the postulating of value-entities or value-features of quite a different order from anything else with which we are acquainted, and of a corresponding faculty with which to detect them. That is, he would have to supplement his explicit argument with what I have called the argument from queerness.

Another way of bringing out this queerness is to ask, about anything that is supposed to have some objective moral quality, how this is linked with its natural features. What is the connection between the natural fact that an action is a piece of deliberate cruelty—say, causing pain just for fun—and the moral fact that it is wrong? It cannot be an entailment, a logical or semantic necessity. Yet it is not merely that the two features occur together. The wrongness must somehow be 'consequential' or 'supervenient'; it is wrong because it is a piece of deliberate cruelty. But just what *in the world* is signified by this 'because'? And how do we know the relation that it signifies, if this is something more than such actions being socially condemned, and condemned by us too, perhaps through our having absorbed attitudes from our social environment? It is not even sufficient to postulate a faculty which 'sees' the wrongness: something must be postulated which can see at once the natural features that constitute the cruelty, and the wrongness, and the mysterious consequential link between the two. Alternatively, the intuition required might be the perception that wrongness is a higher order property belonging to certain natural properties; but what is this belonging of properties to other properties, and how can we discern it? How much simpler and more comprehensible the situation would be if we could replace the moral quality with some sort of subjective response which could be causally related to the detection of the natural features on which the supposed quality is said to be consequential.

It may be thought that the argument from queerness is given an unfair start if we thus relate it to what are admittedly among the wilder products of philosophical fancy—Platonic Forms, non-natural qualities, self-evident relations of fitness, faculties of intuition, and the like. Is it equally forceful if applied to the terms in which everyday moral judgements are more likely to be expressed—though still, as has been argued [in the original work], with a claim to objectivity—'you must do this', 'you can't do that', 'obligation', 'unjust', 'rotten', 'disgraceful', 'mean', or talk about good reasons for or against possible actions? Admittedly not; but that is because the objective prescriptivity, the element a claim for whose authoritativeness is embedded in ordinary moral thought and language, is not yet isolated in these forms of speech, but is presented along with relations to desires and feelings, reasoning about the means to desired ends, inter-personal demands, the injustice which consists in the violation of what are in the context the accepted standards of merit, the psychological constituents of meanness, and so on. There is nothing queer about any of these, and under cover of them the claim for moral authority may pass unnoticed. But if I am right in arguing that it is ordinarily there, and is therefore very likely to be incorporated almost automatically in philosophical accounts of ethics which systematize our ordinary thought even in such apparently innocent terms as these, it needs to be examined, and for this purpose it needs to be isolated and exposed as it is by the less cautious philosophical reconstructions.

PATTERNS OF OBJECTIFICATION

Considerations of these kinds suggest that it is in the end less paradoxical to reject than to retain the common-sense belief in the objectivity of moral values, provided that we can explain how this belief, if it is false, has become established and is so resistant to criticisms. This proviso is not difficult to satisfy.

On a subjectivist view, the supposedly objective values will be based in fact upon attitudes which the person has who takes himself to be recognizing and responding to those values. If we admit what Hume calls the mind's 'propensity to spread itself on external objects', we can understand the supposed objectivity of moral qualities as arising from what we can call the projection or objectification of moral attitudes. This would be analogous to what is called the 'pathetic fallacy', the tendency to read our feelings into their objects. If a fungus, say, fills us with disgust, we may be inclined to ascribe to the fungus itself a non-natural quality of foulness. But in moral contexts there is more than this propensity at work. Moral attitudes themselves are at least partly social in origin: socially established—and socially necessary—patterns of behaviour put pressure on individuals, and each individual tends to internalize these pressures and to join in requiring these patterns of behaviour of himself and of others. The attitudes that are objectified into moral values have indeed an external source, though not the one assigned to them by the belief in their absolute authority. Moreover, there are motives that would support objectification. We need morality to regulate interpersonal relations, to control some of the ways in which people behave towards one another, often in opposition to contrary inclinations. We therefore want our moral judgements to be authoritative for other agents as well as for ourselves: objective validity would give them the authority required. Aesthetic values are logically in the same position as moral ones; much the same metaphysical and epistemological considerations apply to them. But aesthetic values are less strongly objectified than moral ones; their subjective status, and an 'error theory' with regard to such claims to objectivity as are incorporated in aesthetic judgements, will be more readily accepted, just because the motives for their objectification are less compelling.

But it would be misleading to think of the objectification of moral values as primarily the projection of feelings, as in the pathetic fallacy. More important are wants and demands. As Hobbes says, 'whatsoever is the object of any man's Appetite or Desire, that is it, which he for his part calleth *Good*'; and certainly both the adjective 'good' and the noun 'goods' are used in non-moral contexts of things because they are such as to satisfy desires. We get the notion of something's being objectively good, or having intrinsic value, by reversing the direction of dependence here, by making the desire depend upon the goodness, instead of the goodness on the desire. And this is aided by the fact that the desired thing will indeed have features that make it desired, that enable it to arouse a desire or that make it such as to satisfy some desire that is already there. It is fairly easy to confuse the way in which a thing's desirability is indeed objective with its having in our sense objective value. The fact that the word 'good' serves as one of our main moral terms is a trace of this pattern of objectification.

[. . .]

Another way of explaining the objectification of moral values is to say that ethics is a system of law from which the legislator has been removed. This might have been derived either from the positive law of a state or from a supposed system of divine law. There can be no doubt that some features of modern European moral concepts are traceable to the theological ethics of Christianity. The stress on quasi-imperative notions, on what ought to be done or on what is wrong in a sense that is close to that of 'forbidden', are surely relics of divine commands. Admittedly, the central ethical concepts for Plato and Aristotle also are in a broad sense prescriptive or intrinsically action-guiding, but in concentrating rather on 'good' than on 'ought' they show that their moral thought is an objectification of the desired and the satisfying rather than of the commanded. Elizabeth Anscombe has argued that modern, non-Aristotelian, concepts of *moral* obligation, *moral* duty, of what is *morally* right and wrong, and of the *moral* sense of 'ought' are survivals outside the framework of thought that made them really intelligible, namely the belief in divine law. She infers that 'ought' has 'become a word of mere mesmeric force', with only a 'delusive appearance of content', and that we would do better to discard such terms and concepts altogether, and go back to Aristotelian ones.

There is much to be said for this view. But while we can explain some distinctive features of modern moral philosophy in this way, it would be a mistake to see the whole problem of the claim to objective prescriptivity as merely local and unnecessary, as a post-operative complication of a society from which a dominant system of theistic belief has recently been rather hastily excised. As Cudworth and Clarke and Price, for example, show, even those who still admit divine commands, or the positive law of God, may believe moral values to have an independent objective but still action-guiding authority. Responding to Plato's *Euthyphro* dilemma, they believe that God commands what he commands because it is in itself good or right, not that it is good or right merely because and in that he commands it. Otherwise God himself could not be called good. Price asks, 'What can be more preposterous, than to make the Deity nothing but will; and to exalt this on the ruins of all his attributes?' The apparent objectivity of moral value is a widespread phenomenon which has more than one source: the persistence of a belief in something like divine law when the belief in the divine legislator has faded out is only one factor among others. There are several different patterns of objectification, all of which have left characteristic traces in our actual moral concepts and moral language.

Questions for Discussion

1. What do we mean when we say that something is wrong?
2. Is Mackie right to claim that objective values would have to be queer?
3. Is the objectivity of rationality and its role in moral deliberation inconsistent with Mackie's claims about the subjectivity of morality?

CHAPTER 19

Challenges to Ethics

HARD QUESTION: WHY BE MORAL?

What a strange question! This is a question of a very different sort than trying to determine what morality requires of us in a particular situation. It is asking why we should care about morality at all. Morality sometimes demands that we forgo an advantage to ourselves for the sake of others. Why should we ever do that?

It might seem that the question is ill-formed, since in asking why we *should* care about morality, it appears that morality is presupposed, just as rationality is presupposed when we ask, "Why be rational?" A justification for rationality presupposes rationality because giving reasons for rationality is being rational. So if we understand "Why be moral?" as asking for a moral justification to be moral, then it is just like "Why be rational?" But we do not have to interpret it that way. We can interpret the question as asking for grounds for adopting the moral point of view—that is, the point of view that takes the interests of others seriously.

The moral point of view requires us to see ourselves and our own concerns as the perspectives and concerns of just one person among many; our own well-being does not automatically trump that of others. Selflessness is not required, but morality does require that we recognize other people (more broadly, other beings or "moral patients") with interests comparable to our own and worthy of our attention. In asking "Why be moral?" we are asking why we should adopt that perspective on matters, since other perspectives could be adopted. Economics might say one thing, aesthetics another, immediate self-interest a third. So why should we adopt the perspective of morality?

Asking why *we* should be moral is different from asking why *I* should be moral. "Why should *we* be moral?" can be easily answered. As Thomas Hobbes told us (see Chapter 4), life in the state of nature—a condition outside of morality—is "solitary, poor, nasty, brutish, and short." Morality makes social living possible, and we all benefit from that; it "ameliorates the human predicament" (Chapter 1). Fine, but why should *I* adopt the moral point of view? Better for me to reap the benefits of social living without having to suffer any of the restraints that morality imposes. Morality is great for others, but not for me. I might prefer to be a "free rider."

In response, pointing out that it is unfair for me to expect others to follow the rules of morality but to excuse myself assumes that I have already adopted morality. Unfairness cannot be a reason for why *I* should be moral if I am wondering why I should adopt the moral point of view in the first place. I want *others* to be moral because that is to my benefit. What I want to know is why I too should be moral. Of course, I realize that if I appear immoral I won't reap the benefits of everyone else following morality, so I will disguise my motivation from them. I will follow morality only insofar as it serves my interests, and I will act immorally when that serves my interests. If I am clever, I will do just fine.

Could someone live like that? Actually, many people do; they are called psychopaths (*psycho*, soul + *pathy*, suffer, disease). Psychopaths live among us; they can be ruthless business executives, manipulative politicians, difficult co-workers, and charming seducers. Psychopathy is a social disorder characterized by a stunning lack of empathy. In *Without Conscience*, clinical psychologist Robert Hare developed a widely used Psychopathy Checklist to identify psychopaths. His insights into psychopathy came from working with prisoners, but he is quick to note that not all criminals are psychopaths and, more chillingly, most psychopaths are not criminals. In 1993 Hare estimated that there were two million psychopaths in North America; undoubtedly there are many more now. The key symptoms of psychopathy on Hare's checklist are glib superficiality, grandiosity, lack of remorse or guilt, lack of empathy, deceitful and manipulative, emotionally shallow, impulsive. Psychopaths typically have an audacious self-confidence, disarming charm, and an uncanny ability to manipulate others, often causing great harm. Their emotional impoverishment and moral indifference are incomprehensible to the rest of us.

A rational and intellectually sophisticated psychopath might seem like a straw man imagined just for philosophical discussions. However, the facts about psychopathy suggest that such individuals are not entirely fictitious. Let's consider how making the case for morality to an intellectually sophisticated psychopath might unfold.

AMORALISM

Amoralism is the rejection of morality. Amoralists should not be confused with immoralists, since the latter acknowledge wrongdoing but do it anyway, whereas amoralists reject morality entirely. The psychopath is a kind of amoralist.

In her essay "Morality as a System of Hypothetical Imperatives," the distinguished American philosopher Philippa Foot claims that "the man who rejects morality because he sees no reason to obey its rules can be convicted of villainy but not of inconsistency." That is the philosophical challenge: Is the psychopath irrational? Many have thought so. The traditional answer to "Why be moral?" is that morality is in one's self-interest. Because the psychopath wants to promote his own interests, adopting the moral point of view will achieve his ends; rejecting morality will not. So he is not being consistent according to his own ends. This answer requires more thought.

"Self-interest" answers to "Why be moral?" can take different forms, but they share a common defect: If morality can fail to promote one's self-interest, then there is no reason to be moral. Unless morality is somehow necessarily linked to one's interest, it could fail to promote that self-interest. So our commitment to morality is then tenuous at best and depends on whether it is to our benefit. And is it? How could morality benefit one?

Plato and Aristotle, among others, argue that a moral life will make one happy. That is how morality is supposed to benefit us. We have already seen (Chapter 5) that the ancients understand happiness broadly as human fulfillment. So their position is that only a moral life can be truly fulfilling for a human being. This means that even if one is miserable living according to the requirements of morality, one is fulfilled nevertheless, and therefore "happy" according to their understanding of that term.

Would rational psychopaths have to agree that morality is necessary for fulfillment? We need a full account of human fulfillment and an explanation of how morality is a necessary component of it. Why can't psychopaths simply reject morality as necessary to their happiness? Perhaps morality is necessary for non-psychopaths to lead full truly happy lives, but psychopaths can object that there is no reason to foist that understanding of happiness on them. Alternatively, they could even agree that happiness is fulfillment but maintain that psychopath fulfillment is different from non-psychopath fulfillment.

Despite the etymology of the term *psychopath*, psychopaths might deny that they are sick or defective. They are different, to be sure, but that does not easily translate into defective. They could concede that there is a "natural" sentiment among many human beings to care for one another, but how do we know that it is good to have that propensity in the first place? We might also have a natural propensity to hate strangers or to quickly take offense at others. So the mere fact that a sentiment is "natural" is not a good reason to think that it ought to be followed or that anyone without it is defective. The same could hold for moral sentiments, such as empathy or care. Moreover, psychopaths can claim that they are glad others have moral sentiments, because it makes their lives easier when others are moral.

Psychopaths might even say that *we* are the ones duped by morality, since a clear-eyed assessment of our situation shows a pathetic willingness to subordinate our own interests to the interests of others. That willingness has been carefully cultivated by powerful forces of enculturation to ensure the greater social good, but at our individual expense. In the end, morality is a form of fascism, for it subordinates individual happiness to the general good. Only a chump would agree to do that, they could say. Unless we make it true by definition, it seems that morality is not necessary for happiness, understood broadly as fulfillment or narrowly as pleasure. Indeed, morality is often at odds with our own pleasure.

We might try a different tack to justify morality as self-interest by appealing to God: We should be moral because God will punish us if we are not. Since it is clearly in our interest to be rewarded by God, or at least not punished by God, we had better be moral. This justification for morality obviously depends on the existence of a particular sort of God, a God who takes an active interest in our affairs. One does not even have to be a psychopath to question that. Moreover, since morality is independent of God (see Chapter 1), in this view God would be a sort of external enforcer of morality; he would threaten us with cosmic sanctions if we do not follow the rules. This might compel moral behavior even among psychopaths, but it could not compel assent. Psychopaths would not embrace morality; they would just realize that they could never get away with being immoral. No inconsistency here. They would be like bank robbers encountering a heavily guarded bank. They want to rob it but can never find the opportunity to do so. They are still bank robbers at heart; the only difference between them and actual bank robbers is the vigilance of the guards.

It seems that the psychopath can consistently evade justifications for morality that appeal to self-interest. Maybe the psychopath can be convicted of inconsistency this way: Rationality requires us to treat like cases alike, because if we treated like cases differently, we would want to know why, since the cases are alike. We are inconsistent or are biased or act without good reason if we treat similar cases differently. Professors, for example, are supposed to give the same grades to equally good (or equally bad) work; to give different grades to similar work is irrational, at least without some further explanation. Perhaps one student overcame greater obstacles than another or made a greater effort or something of the sort, although there is a serious question whether such factors are relevant. Our sense is that, other things being equal (*ceteris paribus* in Latin), equal work merits equal grades.

Psychopaths seemingly violate the "Treat likes alike" requirement of rationality, because they acknowledge that other people have interests too but consistently choose to place their own interests above those of others. Psychopaths treat their own interests as more important for no reason other than the fact that they are their own, which is no reason at all, since everyone can say the same about his or her own interests. Some philosophers think that this argument is successful; psychopaths can be convicted of inconsistency because they regard their own interests as more important than comparable interests of others. They are treating similar cases differently and that is irrational. Or so it seems.

The psychopath can agree that rationality requires us to treat like cases alike, but he can disagree that his interests are like those of others. He can claim that his interests are objectively more important, so he is justified in favoring his own. The challenge, of course, is for the psychopath to show that his interests really are more important than those of anyone else. Asserting it does not make it so. Does he love life more than other people, does he feel more deeply, are his projects more meaningful than those of other people? The answer is "no," so ordinary psychopaths can be convicted of inconsistency by this argument. But this argument does not hold against any conceivable psychopath. What I have in mind is the sort of character celebrated by the great nineteenth-century philosopher Friedrich Nietzsche—the "Superman," a new form of person who is alleged to be "beyond good and evil" (see the reading from Nietzsche for this chapter).

As Nietzsche sees it, traditional morality is a life-denying attitude created by slaves (those who are burdened by life) to protect themselves from the powerful (those who are courageous and noble enough to live fully, unencumbered by the sickly enervations and apprehensions of the weak). "Supposing that the abused, the oppressed, the suffering, the unemancipated, the weary, and those uncertain of themselves should moralize, what will be the common element in their moral estimates?" Common, according to Nietzsche, will be a herd-like mentality of protection, concern for others, tender sentiments, and the like. Slave morality—everyday morality—is the kiss of death to those capable of a higher and more robust existence, because "life is *essentially* appropriation, injury, conquest of the strange and weak, suppression, severity, obtrusion of peculiar forms, incorporation, and at the very least, putting it mildest, exploitation." By opposing what is essential to life, morality opposes life. "Egoism belongs to the essence of a noble soul," Nietzsche avers.

Nietzsche's Superman certainly sounds like a psychopath, but if Nietzsche is correct about the nature of morality, then his Superman really does lead a better or more fulfilled life than the enslaved. His psychopathic Superman could argue that his interests are not comparable to the interests of others; his really do come first. And if he is right, then the rest of us must agree! We should be prepared to subordinate our interests to those of persons capable of a higher mode of life. At issue are profound matters of equality among human interests (not to mention the interests of other beings). Can we ever say that one person's interests are simply more important than comparable interests of another? Relative to a Nietzschean Superman, our interests could be compared to the interests of a brain-damaged person. Is it more worthy for one of us to flourish than for a brain-damaged person to realize his or her tragic and unfortunately low potential? If we say yes, then we agree with Nietzsche; if we say no, then we must explain why all interests are equally worthy of fulfillment.

READINGS ON CHALLENGES TO MORALITY

Plato, from *Republic*

Plato (c. 428–347 BCE) is probably the most influential philosopher of all time. As the twentieth-century philosopher and mathematician Alfred North Whitehead famously quipped, "The safest general characterization of the European philosophical tradition is that it consists of a series of footnotes to Plato." Many philosophers agree with that assessment.

The Republic, *one of Plato's most beloved dialogues, explores the nature of justice and how it may be cultivated in the individual and in the State. By justice, Plato means what we mean by morality or righteousness. In the scene reprinted here, Socrates (as a tribute to his esteemed mentor, Plato always features Socrates in his dialogues) engages Glaucon and Adeimantus, two young supporters of morality who are nonetheless puzzled by amoralist objections. They ask Socrates to defend morality as valuable in itself, since if morality is useful merely as a means to an end, it can be abandoned if it no longer serves that end. Socrates' answer occupies the remainder of the dialogue.*

He argues that the just individual, like the just State, flourishes because of an internal structure that makes injustice impossible.

Critical Reading Questions

1. What does the Ring of Gyges story demonstrate?
2. What two lives does Adeimantus sketch for Socrates?
3. According to Adeimantus, what account should we take of the gods knowing our evil actions?

THE IMMORALIST'S CHALLENGE

Plato

When I said this, I thought I had done with the discussion, but it turned out to have been only a prelude. Glaucon showed his characteristic courage on this occasion too and refused to accept Thrasymachus' abandonment of the argument. Socrates, he said, do you want to seem to have persuaded us that it is better in every way to be just than unjust, or do you want truly to convince us of this?

I want truly to convince you, I said, if I can.

Well, then, you certainly aren't doing what you want. Tell me, do you think there is a kind of good we welcome, not because we desire what comes from it, but because we welcome it for its own sake—joy, for example, and all the harmless pleasures that have no results beyond the joy of having them?

Certainly, I think there are such things.

And is there a kind of good we like for its own sake and also for the sake of what comes from it—knowing, for example, and seeing and being healthy? We welcome such things, I suppose, on both counts.

Yes.

And do you also see a third kind of good, such as physical training,[1] medical treatment when sick, medicine itself, and the other ways of making money? We'd say that these are onerous but beneficial to us, and we wouldn't choose them for their own sakes, but for the sake of the rewards and other things that come from them.

There is also this third kind. But what of it?

Where do you put justice?

I myself put it among the finest goods, as something to be valued by anyone who is going to be blessed with happiness, both because of itself and because of what comes from it.

That isn't most people's opinion. They'd say that justice belongs to the onerous kind, and is to be practiced for the sake of the rewards and popularity that come from a reputation for justice, but is to be avoided because of itself as something burdensome.

I know that's the general opinion. Thrasymachus faulted justice on these grounds a moment ago and praised injustice, but it seems that I'm a slow learner.

Come, then, and listen to me as well, and see whether you still have that problem, for I think that Thrasymachus gave up before he had, to, charmed by you as if he were a snake. But I'm not yet satisfied by the argument on either side. I want to know what justice and injustice are and what power each itself has when it's by itself in the soul. I want to leave out of account their rewards and what comes from each of them. So, if you agree, I'll renew the argument of Thrasymachus. First, I'll state what kind of thing people consider justice to be and what its origins are. Second, I'll argue that all who practice it do so unwillingly, as something necessary, not as something good. Third, I'll argue that they have good reason to act as they do, for the life of an unjust person is, they say, much better than that of a just one.

It isn't, Socrates, that I believe any of that myself. I'm perplexed, indeed, and my ears are deafened listening to Thrasymachus and countless others. But I've yet to hear anyone defend justice in the way I want, proving that it is better than injustice. I want to hear it praised *by itself,* and I think that I'm most likely to hear this from you. Therefore, I'm going to speak at length in praise of the unjust life, and in doing so I'll show you the way I want to hear you praising justice and denouncing injustice. But see whether you want me to do that or not.

I want that most of all. Indeed, what subject could someone with any understanding enjoy discussing more often?

Excellent. Then let's discuss the first subject I mentioned—what justice is and what its origins are.

They say that to do injustice is naturally good and to suffer injustice bad, but that the badness of suffering it so far exceeds the goodness of doing it that those who have done and suffered injustice and tasted both, but who lack the power to do it and avoid suffering it, decide that it is profitable to come to an agreement with each other neither to do injustice nor to suffer it. As a result, they begin to make laws and covenants, and what the law commands they call lawful and just. This, they say, is the origin and essence of justice. It is intermediate between the best and the worst. The best is to do injustice without paying the penalty; the worst is to suffer it without being able to take revenge. Justice is a mean between these two extremes. People value it not as a good but because they are too weak to do injustice with impunity. Someone who has the power to do this, however, and is a true man wouldn't make an agreement with anyone not to do injustice in order not to suffer it. For him that would be madness. This is the nature of justice, according to the argument, Socrates, and these are its natural origins.

We can see most clearly that those who practice justice do it unwillingly and because they lack the power to do injustice, if in our thoughts we grant to a just and an unjust person the freedom to do whatever they like. We can then follow both of them and see where their desires would lead. And we'll catch the just person red-handed travelling the same road as the unjust. The reason for this is the desire to outdo others and get more and more.[2] This is what anyone's nature naturally pursues as good, but nature is forced by law into the perversion of treating fairness with respect.

The freedom I mentioned would be most easily realized if both people had the power they say the ancestor of Gyges of Lydia possessed.

The story goes that he was a shepherd in the service of the ruler of Lydia. There was a violent thunderstorm, and an earthquake broke open the ground and created a chasm at the place where he was tending his sheep. Seeing this, he was filled with amazement and went down into it. And there, in addition to many other wonders of which we're told, he saw a hollow bronze horse. There were windowlike openings in it, and, peeping in, he saw a corpse, which seemed to be of more than human size, wearing nothing but a gold ring on its finger. He took the ring and came out of the chasm. He wore the ring at the usual monthly meeting that reported to the king on the state of the flocks. And as he was sitting among the others, he happened to turn the setting of the ring towards himself to the inside of his hand. When he did this, he became invisible to those sitting near him, and they went on talking as if he had gone. He wondered at this, and, fingering the ring, he turned the setting outwards again and became visible. So he experimented with the ring to test whether it indeed had this power—and it did. If he turned the setting inward, he became invisible; if he turned it outward, he became visible again. When he realized this, he at once arranged to become one of the messengers sent to report to the king. And when he arrived there, he seduced the king's wife, attacked the king with her help, killed him, and took over the kingdom.

Let's suppose, then, that there were two such rings, one worn by a just and the other by an unjust person. Now, no one, it seems, would be so incorruptible that he would stay on the path of justice or stay away from other people's property, when he could take whatever he wanted from the market-place with impunity, go into people's houses and have sex with anyone he wished, kill or release from prison anyone he wished, and do all the other things that would make him like a god among humans. Rather his actions would be in no way different from those of an unjust person, and both would follow the same path. This, some would say, is a great proof that one is never just willingly but only when compelled to be. No one believes justice to be a good when it is kept private, since, wherever either person thinks he can do injustice with impunity, he does it. Indeed, every man believes that injustice is far more profitable to himself than justice. And any exponent of this argument will say he's right, for someone who didn't want to do injustice, given this sort of opportunity, and who didn't touch other people's property would be thought wretched and stupid by everyone aware of the situation, though, of course, they'd praise him in public, deceiving each other for fear of suffering injustice. So much for my second topic.

As for the choice between the lives we're discussing, we'll be able to make a correct judgment about that only if we separate the most just and the most unjust. Otherwise we won't be able to do it. Here's the separation I have in mind. We'll subtract nothing from the injustice of an unjust person and nothing from the justice of a just one, but we'll take each to be complete in his own way of life. First, therefore, we must suppose that an unjust person will act as clever craftsmen do: A first-rate captain or doctor, for example, knows the difference between what his craft can and can't do. He attempts the first but lets the second go by, and if he happens to slip, he can put things right. In the same way, an unjust person's successful attempts at injustice must remain undetected, if he is to be fully unjust. Anyone who is caught should be thought inept, for the extreme of injustice is to be believed to be just without being just. And our completely unjust person must be given complete injustice; nothing may be subtracted from it. We must allow that, while doing the greatest injustice, he has nonetheless provided himself with the greatest reputation for justice. If he happens to make a slip, he must be able to put it right. If any of his unjust activities should be discovered, he must be able to speak persuasively or to use force. And if force is needed, he must have the help of courage and strength and of the substantial wealth and friends with which he has provided himself.

Having hypothesized such a person, let's now in our argument put beside him a just man, who is simple and noble and who, as Aeschylus says, doesn't want to be believed to be good but to be so.[3] We must take away his reputation, for a reputation for justice would bring him honor and rewards, so that it wouldn't be clear whether he is just for the sake of justice itself or for the sake of those honors and rewards. We must strip him of everything except justice and make his situation the opposite of an unjust person's. Though he does no injustice, he must have the

greatest reputation for it, so that his justice may be tested fullstrength and not diluted by wrongdoing and what comes from it. Let him stay like that unchanged until he dies—just, but all his life believed to be unjust. In this way, both will reach the extremes, the one of justice and the other of injustice, and we'll be able to judge which of them is happier.

Whew! Glaucon, I said, how vigorously you've scoured each of the men for our competition, just as you would a pair of statues for an art competition.

I do the best I can, he replied. Since the two are as I've described, in any case, it shouldn't be difficult to complete the account of the kind of life that awaits each of them, but it must be done. And if what I say sounds crude, Socrates, remember that it isn't I who speak but those who praise injustice at the expense of justice. They'll say that a just person in such circumstances will be whipped, stretched on a rack, chained, blinded with fire, and, at the end, when he has suffered every kind of evil, he'll be impaled, and will realize then that one shouldn't want to be just but to be believed to be just. Indeed, Aeschylus' words are far more correctly applied to unjust people than to just ones, for the supporters of injustice will say that a really unjust person, having a way of life based on the truth about things and not living in accordance with opinion, doesn't want simply to be believed to be unjust but actually to be so—

Harvesting a deep furrow in his mind,
Where wise counsels propagate.

He rules his city because of his reputation for justice; he marries into any family he wishes; he gives his children in marriage to anyone he wishes; he has contracts and partnerships with anyone he wants; and besides benefiting himself in all these ways, he profits because he has no scruples about doing injustice. In any contest, public or private, he's the winner and outdoes[4] his enemies. And by outdoing them, he becomes wealthy, benefiting his friends and harming his enemies. He makes adequate sacrifices to the gods and sets up magnificent offerings to them. He takes better care of the gods, therefore, (and, indeed, of the human beings he's fond of) than a just person does. Hence it's likely that the gods, in turn, will take better care of him than of a just person. That's what they say, Socrates, that gods and humans provide a better life for unjust people than for just ones.

When Glaucon had said this, I had it in mind to respond, but his brother Adeimantus intervened: You surely don't think that the position has been adequately stated?

Why not? I said.

The most important thing to say hasn't been said yet.

Well, then, I replied, a man's brother must stand by him, as the saying goes.[5] If Glaucon has omitted something, you must help him. Yet what he has said is enough to throw me to the canvas and make me unable to come to the aid of justice.

Nonsense, he said. Hear what more I have to say, for we should also fully explore the arguments that are opposed to the ones Glaucon gave, the ones that praise justice and find fault with injustice, so that what I take to be his intention may be clearer.

When fathers speak to their sons, they say that one must be just, as do all the others who have charge of anyone. But they don't praise justice itself, only the high reputations it leads to and the consequences of being thought to be just, such as the public offices, marriages, and other things Glaucon listed. But they elaborate even further on the consequences of reputation. By bringing in the esteem of the gods, they are able to talk about the abundant good things that they themselves and the noble Hesiod and Homer say that the gods give to the pious,[6] for Hesiod says that the gods make the oak trees

Bear acorns at the top and bees in the middle
And make fleecy sheep heavy laden with wool

for the just, and tells of many other good things akin to these. And Homer is similar:

When a good king, in his piety,
Upholds justice, the black earth bears
Wheat and barley for him, and his trees are
heavy with fruit.
His sheep bear lambs unfailingly, and the sea
yields up its fish.

Musaeus and his son make the gods give the just more headstrong goods than these.[7] In their stories, they lead the just to Hades, seat them on couches, provide them with a symposium of pious people, crown them with wreaths, and make them spend all their time drinking—as if they thought drunkenness was the finest wage of virtue. Others stretch even further the wages that virtue receives from the gods, for they say that someone who is pious and keeps his promises leaves his children's children and a whole race behind him. In these and other similar ways, they praise justice. They bury the impious and unjust in mud in Hades; force them to carry water in a sieve; bring them into bad repute while they're still alive, and all those penalties that Glaucon gave to the just person they give to the unjust. But they have nothing else to say. This, then, is the way people praise justice and find fault with injustice.

Besides this, Socrates, consider another form of argument about justice and injustice employed both by private individuals and by poets. All go on repeating with one voice that justice and moderation are fine things, but hard and onerous, while licentiousness and injustice are sweet and easy to acquire and are shameful only in opinion and law. They add that unjust deeds are for the most part more profitable than just ones, and, whether in public or private, they willingly honor vicious people who have wealth and other types of power and declare them to be happy. But they dishonor and disregard the weak and the poor, even though they agree that they are better than the others.

But the most wonderful of all these arguments concerns what they have to say about the gods and virtue. They say that the gods, too, assign misfortune and a bad life to many good people, and the opposite fate to their opposites. Begging priests and prophets frequent the doors of the rich and persuade them that they possess a god-given power founded on sacrifices and incantations. If the rich person or any of his ancestors has committed an injustice, they can fix it with pleasant rituals. Moreover, if he wishes to injure some enemy, then, at little expense, he'll be able to harm just and unjust alike, for by means of spells and enchantments they can persuade the gods to serve them. And the poets are brought forward as witnesses to all these accounts. Some harp on the ease of vice, as follows:

Vice in abundance is easy to get;
The road is smooth and begins beside you,
But the gods have put sweat between us and virtue,

and a road that is long, rough, and steep.[8] Others quote Homer to bear witness that the gods can be influenced by humans, since he said:

The gods themselves can be swayed by prayer,
And with sacrifices and soothing promises,
Incense and libations, human beings turn
them from their purpose
When someone has transgressed and sinned.[9]

And they present a noisy throng of books by Musaeus and Orpheus, offspring as they say of Selene and the Muses, in accordance with which they perform their rituals.[10] And they persuade not only individuals but whole cities that the unjust deeds of the living or the dead can be absolved or purified through sacrifices and pleasant games. These initiations, as they call them, free people from punishment hereafter, while a terrible fate awaits the uninitiated.

When all such sayings about the attitudes of gods and humans to virtue and vice are so often repeated, Socrates, what effect do you suppose they have on the souls of young people? I mean those who are clever and are able to flit from one of these sayings to another, so to speak, and gather from them an impression of what sort of person he should be and of how best to travel the road of life. He would surely ask himself Pindar's question, "Should I by justice or by crooked deceit scale this high wall and live my life guarded and secure?" And he'll answer: "The various sayings suggest that there is no advantage in my being just if I'm not also thought just, while the troubles and penalties of being just are apparent. But they tell me that an unjust person, who has secured for himself a reputation for justice, lives the life of a god. Since, then, 'opinion forcibly overcomes truth' and 'controls happiness,' as the wise men say, I must surely turn entirely to it.[11] I should create a facade of illusory virtue around me to deceive those who come near, but keep behind it the greedy and crafty fox of the wise Archilochus."[12]

"But surely," someone will object, "it isn't easy for vice to remain always hidden." We'll reply that nothing great is easy. And, in any case, if we're to be happy, we must follow the path indicated in these accounts. To remain undiscovered we'll form secret societies and political clubs. And there are teachers of persuasion to make us clever in dealing with assemblies and law courts. Therefore, using persuasion in one place and force in another, we'll outdo others[13] without paying a penalty.

"What about the gods? Surely, we can't hide from them or use violent force against them!" Well, if the gods don't exist or don't concern themselves with human affairs, why should we worry at all about hiding from them? If they do exist and do concern themselves with us, we've learned all we know about them from the laws and the poets who give their genealogies—nowhere else. But these are the very people who tell us that the gods can be persuaded and influenced by sacrifices, gentle prayers, and offerings. Hence, we should believe them on both matters or neither. If we believe them, we should be unjust and offer sacrifices from the fruits of our injustice. If we are just, our only gain is not to be punished by the gods, since we lose the profits of injustice. But if we are unjust, we get the profits of our crimes and transgressions and afterwards persuade the gods by prayer and escape without punishment.

"But in Hades won't we pay the penalty for crimes committed here, either ourselves or our children's children?" "My friend," the young man will say as he does his calculation, "mystery rites have great power and the gods have great power of absolution. The greatest cities tell us this, as do those children of the gods who have become poets and prohets."

Why, then, should we still choose justice over the greatest injustice? Many eminent authorities agree that, if we practice such injustice with a false façade, we'll do well at the hands of gods and humans, living and dying as we've a mind to. So, given all that has been said, Socrates, how is it possible for anyone of any power—whether of mind, wealth, body, or birth—to be willing to honor justice and not laugh aloud when he hears it praised? Indeed, if anyone can show that what we've said is false and has adequate knowledge that justice is best, he'll surely be full not of anger but of forgiveness for the unjust. He knows that, apart from someone of godlike character who is disgusted by injustice or one who has gained knowledge and avoids injustice for that reason, no one is just willingly. Through cowardice or old age or some other weakness, people do indeed object to injustice. But it's obvious that they do so only because they lack the power to do injustice, for the first of them to acquire it is the first to do as much injustice as he can.

And all of this has no other cause than the one that led Glaucon and me to say to you: "Socrates, of all of you who claim to praise justice, from the original heroes of old whose words survive, to the men of the present day, not one has ever blamed injustice or praised justice except by mentioning the reputations, honors, and rewards that are their consequences. No one has ever adequately described what each itself does of its own power by its presence in the soul of the person who possesses it, even if it remains hidden from gods and humans. No one, whether in poetry or in private conversations, has adequately argued that injustice is the worst thing a soul can have in it and that justice is the greatest good. If you had treated the subject in this way and persuaded us from youth, we wouldn't now be guarding against one another's injustices, but each would be his own best guardian, afraid that by doing injustice he'd be living with the worst thing possible."

Thrasymachus or anyone else might say what we've said, Socrates, or maybe even more, in discussing justice and injustice—crudely inverting their powers, in my opinion. And, frankly, it's because I want to hear the opposite from you that I speak with all the force I can muster. So don't merely give us a theoretical argument that justice is stronger than injustice, but tell us what each itself does, because of its own powers, to someone who possesses it, that makes injustice bad and justice good. Follow Glaucon's advice, and don't take reputations into account, for if you don't deprive justice and injustice of their true reputations and attach false ones to them, we'll say that you are not praising them but their reputations and that you're encouraging us to be unjust in secret. In that case, we'll say that you agree with Thrasymachus that justice is the good of another, the advantage of the stronger, while injustice is one's own advantage and profit, though not the advantage of the weaker.

You agree that justice is one of the greatest goods, the ones that are worth getting for the sake of what comes from them, but much more

so for their own sake, such as seeing, hearing, knowing, being healthy, and all other goods that are fruitful by their own nature and not simply because of reputation. Therefore, praise justice as a good of that kind, explaining how—because of its very self—it benefits its possessors and how injustice harms them. Leave wages and reputations for others to praise.

Others would satisfy me if they praised justice and blamed injustice in that way, extolling the wages of one and denigrating those of the other. But you, unless you order me to be satisfied, wouldn't, for you've spent your whole life investigating this and nothing else. Don't, then, give us only a theoretical argument that justice is stronger than injustice, but show what effect each has because of itself on the person who has it—the one for good and the other for bad—whether it remains hidden from gods and human beings or not.

NOTES

1. "Music" or "music and poetry" and "physical training" are more transliterations than translations of *mousikē* and *gymnastikē*, which have no English equivalents. It is clear from Plato's discussion, for example, that *mousikē* includes poetry and stories, as well as music proper, and that *gymnastikē* includes dance and training in warfare, as well as what we call physical training. The aims of *mousikē* and *gymnastikē* are characterized at 522a. For further discussion see F.A.G. Beck, *Greek Education 430–350 B.C.* (London: Methuen, 1964).
2. *Pleonexian*. See 343e n. 18.
3. In *Seven Against Thebes*, 592–94, it is said of Amphiaraus that "he did not wish to be believed to be the best but to be it." The passage continues with the words Glaucon quotes below at 362a–b.
4. *pleonektein*. See 343e n. 18.
5. See Homer, *Odyssey* 16.97–98.
6. The two quotations which follow are from Hesiod, *Works and Days* 332–33, and Homer, *Odyssey* 19.109.
7. Musaeus was a legendary poet closely associated with the mystery religion of Orphism.
8. *Works and Days* 287–89, with minor alterations.
9. *Iliad* 9.497–501, with minor alterations.
10. It is not clear whether Orpheus was a real person or a mythical figure. His fame in Greek myth rests on the poems in which the doctrines of the Orphic religion are set forth. These are discussed in W. Burkert, *Greek Religion* (Cambridge: Harvard University Press, 1985). Musaeus was a mythical singer closely related to Orpheus. Selene is the Moon.
11. The quotation is attributed to Simonides, whom Polemarchus cites in Book I.
12. Archilochus of Paros (c. 756–16 B.C.), was an iambic and elegiac poet who composed a famous fable about the fox and the hedgehog.
13. *Pleonektountes*. See 343e n. 18.

Discussion Questions

1. How would you act if you could do whatever you wanted without suffering any penalty?
2. Are immoral people unhappy?
3. Why be moral?

Frederich Nietzsche, Selections from *Beyond Good and Evil*

Nietzsche (1844–1900) produced some of most strikingly original and disturbingly insightful philosophical works of the nineteenth century. In addition to Beyond Good and Evil, *from which our selection is taken,* The Gay Science, On the Genealogy of Morals, The Will to Power, *and* Thus Spake Zarathustra *are among his better known writings. Nietzsche is thought by many to have defined modernity with his startling proclamation "God is dead!" thus abandoning us to lives of self-definition. For with the death of God, Nietzsche reasoned, there are no universal normative standards to which we must conform. Rather than seeking protection in absurd myths born of weakness, such as "the dogma of human equality," Nietzsche looks hopefully toward a brave new world with the emergence of different people, "those who give themselves the law, those who create themselves!" (*The Gay Science, 335*).

Critical Reading Questions

1. How does Nietzsche contrast "master-morality" with "slave-morality"?
2. What is the "Will to Power"? How is it relevant to Nietzsche's position?
3. What does Nietzsche mean when he says that the morality of the noble is "self-glorification"?

NIETZSCHE, SELECTIONS FROM
BEYOND GOOD AND EVIL

Frederich Nietzshe

257

Every elevation of the type "man," has hitherto been the work of an aristocratic society—and so will it always be—a society believing in a long scale of gradations of rank and differences of worth among human beings, and requiring slavery in some form or other. Without the *pathos of distance,* such as grows out of the incarnated difference of classes, out of the constant outlooking and downlooking of the ruling caste on subordinates and instruments, and out of their equally constant practice of obeying and commanding, of keeping down and keeping at a distance—that other more mysterious pathos could never have arisen, the longing for an ever new widening of distance within the soul itself, the formation of ever higher, rarer, further, more extended, more comprehensive states, in short, just the elevation of the type "man," the continued "self-surmounting of man," to use a moral formula in a supermoral sense. To be sure, one must not resign oneself to any humanitarian illusions about the history of the origin of an aristocratic society (that is to say, of the preliminary condition for the elevation of the type "man"): the truth is hard. Let us acknowledge unprejudicedly how every higher civilisation hitherto has *originated!* Men with a still natural nature, barbarians in every terrible sense of the word, men of prey, still in possession of unbroken strength of will and desire for power, threw themselves upon weaker, more moral, more peaceful races (perhaps trading or cattle-rearing communities), or upon old mellow civilisations in which the final vital force was flickering out in brilliant fireworks of wit and depravity. At the commencement, the noble caste was always the barbarian caste: their superiority did not consist first of all in their physical, but in their psychical power—they were more *complete* men (which at every point also implies the same as "more complete beasts").

258

Corruption—as the indication that anarchy threatens to break out among the instincts, and that the foundation of the emotions, called "life," is convulsed—is something radically different according to the organisation in which it manifests itself. When, for instance, an aristocracy like that of France at the beginning of the Revolution, flung away its privileges with sublime disgust and sacrificed itself to an excess of its moral sentiments, it was corruption:—it was really only the closing act of the corruption which had existed for centuries, by virtue of which that aristocracy had abdicated step by step its lordly prerogatives and lowered itself to a *function* of royalty (in the end even to its decoration and parade-dress). The essential thing, however, in a good and healthy aristocracy is that it should *not* regard itself as a function either of the kingship or the commonwealth, but as the *significance* and highest justification thereof—that it should therefore accept with a good conscience the sacrifice of a legion of individuals, who, *for its sake,* must be suppressed and reduced to imperfect men, to slaves and instruments. Its fundamental belief must be precisely that society is *not* allowed to exist for its own sake, but only as a foundation and scaffolding, by means of which a select class of beings may be able to elevate themselves to their higher duties, and in general to a higher *existence:* like those sun-seeking climbing plants in Java—they are called *Sipo Matador,*—which encircle an oak so long and so often with their arms, until at last, high above it, but supported by it, they can unfold their tops in the open light, and exhibit their happiness.

259

To refrain mutually from injury, from violence, from exploitation, and put one's will on a par with that of others: this may result in a certain rough sense in good conduct among individuals when the necessary conditions are given (namely, the actual similarity of the individuals in amount of force and degree of worth, and their co-relation within one organisation). As soon, however, as one wished to take this principle more generally, and if possible even as *the fundamental principle of society,* it would immediately disclose what it really is—namely, a Will to the *denial* of life, a principle of dissolution and decay. Here one must think profoundly to the very basis and resist all sentimental weakness: life itself is *essentially* appropriation, injury, conquest of the strange and weak, suppression, severity, obtrusion of peculiar forms, incorporation, and at the least, putting it mildest, exploitation;—but why should one for ever use precisely these words on which for ages a disparaging purpose has been stamped? Even the organisation within which, as was previously supposed, the individuals treat each other as equal—it takes place in every healthy aristocracy—must itself, if it be a living and not a dying organisation, do all that towards other bodies, which the individuals within it refrain from doing to each other: it will have to be the incarnated Will to Power, it will endeavour to grow, to gain ground, attract to itself and acquire ascendency—not owing to any morality or immorality, but because it *lives,* and because life *is* precisely Will to Power. On no point, however, is the ordinary consciousness of Europeans more unwilling to be corrected than on this matter; people now rave everywhere, even under the guise of science, about coming conditions of society in which "the exploiting character" is to be absent:—that sounds to my ears as if they promised to invent a mode of life which should refrain from all organic functions. "Exploitation" does not belong to a depraved, or imperfect and primitive society: it belongs to the *nature* of the living being as a primary organic function; it is a consequence of the intrinsic Will to Power, which is precisely the Will to Life.—Granting that as a theory this is a novelty—as a reality it is the *fundamental fact* of all history: let us be so far honest towards ourselves!

260

In a tour through the many finer and coarser moralities which have hitherto prevailed or still prevail on the earth, I found certain traits recurring regularly together and connected with one another, until finally two primary types revealed themselves to me, and a radical distinction was brought to light. There is *master-morality* and *slave-morality;*—I would at once add, however, that in all higher and mixed civilisations, there are also attempts at the reconciliation of the two moralities; but one finds still oftener the confusion and mutual misunderstanding of them, indeed, sometimes their close juxtaposition—even in the same man, within one soul. The distinctions of moral values have either originated in a ruling caste, pleasantly conscious of being different from the ruled—or among the ruled class, the slaves and dependents of all sorts. In the first case, when it is the rulers who determine the conception "good," it is the exalted, proud disposition which is regarded as the distinguishing feature, and that which determines the order of rank. The noble type of man separates from himself the beings in whom the opposite of this exalted, proud disposition displays itself: he despises them. Let it at once be noted that in this first kind of morality the antithesis "good" and "bad" mean practically the same as "noble" and "despicable";—the antithesis "good" and "*evil*" is of a different origin. The cowardly, the timid, the insignificant, and those thinking merely of narrow utility are despised; moreover, also, the distrustful, with their constrained glances, the self-abasing, the dog-like kind of men who let themselves be abused, the mendicant flatterers, and above all the liars:—it is a fundamental belief of all aristocrats that the common people are untruthful. "We truthful ones"—the nobility in ancient Greece called themselves. It is obvious that everywhere the

392

designations of moral value were at first applied to *men*, and were only derivatively and at a later period applied to *actions*; it is a gross mistake, therefore, when historians of morals start with questions like, "Why have sympathetic actions been praised?" The noble type of man regards *himself* as a determiner of values; he does not require to be approved of; he passes the judgment: "What is injurious to me is injurious in itself"; he knows that it is he himself only who confers honour on things; he is a *creator of values*. He honours whatever he recognises in himself: such morality is self-glorification. In the foreground there is the feeling of plenitude, of power, which seeks to overflow, the happiness of high tension, the consciousness of a wealth which would fain give and bestow:—the noble man also helps the unfortunate, but not—or scarcely—out of pity, but rather from an impulse generated by the superabundance of power. The noble man honours in himself the powerful one, him also who has power over himself, who knows how to speak and how to keep silence, who takes pleasure in subjecting himself to severity and hardness, and has reverence for all that is severe and hard. "Wotan placed a hard heart in my breast," says an old Scandinavian Saga: it is thus rightly expressed from the soul of a proud Viking. Such a type of man is even proud of *not* being made for sympathy; the hero of the Saga therefore adds warningly: "He who has not a hard heart when young, will never have one." The noble and brave who think thus are the furthest removed from the morality which sees precisely in sympathy, or in acting for the good of others, or in *désintéressement*, the characteristic of the moral; faith in oneself, pride in oneself, a radical enmity and irony towards "selflessness," belong as definitely to noble morality, as do a careless scorn and precaution in presence of sympathy and the "warm heart."—It is the powerful who *know* how to honour, it is their art, their domain for invention. The profound reverence for age and for tradition—all law rests on this double reverence—the belief and prejudice in favour of ancestors and unfavourable to newcomers, is typical in the morality of the powerful; and if, reversely, men of "modern ideas" believe almost instinctively in "progress" and the "future," and are more and more lacking in respect for old age, the ignoble origin of these "ideas" has complacently betrayed itself thereby. A morality of the ruling class, however, is more especially foreign and irritating to present-day taste in the sternness of its principle that one has duties only to one's equals; that one may act towards beings of a lower rank, towards all that is foreign, just as seems good to one, or "as the heart desires," and in any case "beyond good and evil": it is here that sympathy and similar sentiments can have a place. The ability and obligation to exercise prolonged gratitude and prolonged revenge—both only within the circle of equals—artfulness in retaliation, *raffinement* of the idea in friendship, a certain necessity to have enemies (as outlets for the emotions of envy, quarrelsomeness, arrogance—in fact, in order to be a good *friend*): all these are typical characteristics of the noble morality, which, as has been pointed out, is not the morality of "modern ideas," and is therefore at present difficult to realise, and also to unearth and disclose.—It is otherwise with the second type of morality, *slave-morality*. Supposing that the abused, the oppressed, the suffering, the unemancipated, the weary, and those uncertain of themselves, should moralise, what will be the common element in their moral estimates? Probably a pessimistic suspicion with regard to the entire situation of man will find expression, perhaps a condemnation of man, together with his situation. The slave has an unfavourable eye for the virtues of the powerful; he has a scepticism and distrust, a *refinement* of distrust of everything "good" that is there honoured—he would fain persuade himself that the very happiness there is not genuine. On the other hand, *those* qualities which serve to alleviate the existence of sufferers are brought into prominence and flooded with light; it is here that sympathy, the kind, helping hand, the warm heart, patience, diligence, humility, and friendliness attain to honour; for here these are the most useful qualities, and almost the only means of supporting the burden of existence. Slave-morality is essentially the morality of utility. Here is the seat of the origin of the famous antithesis "good" and "*evil*":—power and dangerousness are assumed to reside in the evil, a certain dreadfulness, subtlety, and strength, which do not admit of being despised. According to slave-morality, therefore,

393

the "evil" man arouses fear; according to master-morality, it is precisely the "good" man who arouses fear and seeks to arouse it, while the bad man is regarded as the despicable being. The contrast attains its maximum when, in accordance with the logical consequences of slave-morality, a shade of depreciation—it may be slight and well-intentioned—at last attaches itself even to the "good" man of this morality; because, according to the servile mode of thought, the good man must in any case be the *safe* man: he is good-natured, easily deceived, perhaps a little stupid, *un bonhomme*. Everywhere that slave-morality gains the ascendancy, language shows a tendency to approximate the significations of the words "good" and "stupid."—A last fundamental difference: the desire for *freedom*, the instinct for happiness and the refinements of the feeling of liberty belong as necessarily to slave-morals and morality, as artifice and enthusiasm in reverence and devotion are the regular symptoms of an aristocratic mode of thinking and estimating.—Hence we can understand without further detail why love *as a passion*—it is our European speciality—must absolutely be of noble origin; as is well known, its invention is due to the Provençal poet-cavaliers, those brilliant ingenious men of the "*gai saber*," to whom Europe owes so much, and almost owes itself.

265

At the risk of displeasing innocent ears, I submit that egoism belongs to the essence of a noble soul, I mean the unalterable belief that to a being such as "we," other beings must naturally be in subjection, and have to sacrifice themselves. The noble soul accepts the fact of his egoism without question, and also without consciousness of harshness, constraint, or arbitrariness therein, but rather as something that may have its basis in the primary law of things:—if he sought a designation for it he would say: "It is justice itself." He acknowledges under certain circumstances, which made him hesitate at first, that there are other equally privileged ones; as soon as he has settled this question of rank, he moves among those equals and equally privileged ones with the same assurance, as regards modesty and delicate respect, which he enjoys in intercourse with himself—in accordance with an innate heavenly mechanism which all the stars understand. It is an *additional* instance of his egoism, this artfulness and self-limitation in intercourse with his equals—every star is a similar egoist; he honours *himself* in them, and in the rights which he concedes to them, he has no doubt that the exchange of honours and rights, as the *essence* of all intercourse, belongs also to the natural condition of things. The noble soul gives as he takes, prompted by the passionate and sensitive instinct of requital, which is at the root of his nature. The notion of "favour" has, *inter pares*, neither significance nor good repute; there may be a sublime way of letting gifts as it were light upon one from above, and of drinking them thirstily like dew-drops; but for those arts and displays the noble soul has no aptitude. His egoism hinders him here: in general, he looks "aloft" unwillingly—he looks either *forward*, horizontally and deliberately, or downwards—*he knows that he is on a height.*

Discussion Questions

1. Is Nietzsche's view dangerous? Why?
2. How can we identify the new sort of person Nietzsche has in mind, one who can live "beyond good and evil"? Could there be such people?
3. Does the commitment to human equality have a rational basis?
4. What would a world of Nietzschean Supermen be like?

CHAPTER 20

Non-Western Ethics

HARD QUESTION: IS ETHICS THE SAME EVERYWHERE?

In 1972 Colin Turnbull, an anthropologist of near mythic stature in the field, published *The Mountain People,* an account of a very unusual tribe living in Uganda called the Ik. The creation of a national park forced the Ik to settle in a drought-prone mountainous area, disrupting their former way of life. What ensued is a horrific story of a people who live "beyond humanity."

According to Turnbull, the Ik lived in near-starvation conditions that stripped them of all that makes life coherent and meaningful. Emotional sensitivity, family relations, community solidarity, mutual concern, hope, love, and any sense of moral responsibility—all were gone. In their stead was a bizarre individualism where people did what they had to do to survive.

As Turnbull described it, the Ik society is one where the weak, the old, the young, and the sick are left to fend for themselves. Food is even snatched from their mouths by those with greater strength. Children are abandoned by their mothers after nursing for almost four years; the ones who survive band together in gangs in their search for food, evidently finding just enough for a portion of them to make it to adulthood—that is, age twelve or thirteen.

Cruelty and indifference to the suffering of others are apparently a source of amusement. Turnbull has numerous accounts of Ik laughing at those who, because of hunger-induced weakness, fall down and flail about on the ground trying to get up again. On other occasions "men would watch a child with eager anticipation as it crawled toward the fire, then burst into gay and happy laughter as it plunged a skinny hand into the coals. Such times were the few times when parental affection showed itself: a mother would glow with pleasure to hear such joy occasioned by her offspring, and pull it tenderly out of the fire" (112).

The Ik spent most of their time squatting passively on their mountainside scanning the horizon for telltale wisps of smoke indicating that someone was cooking something, and off they would dash in hope of sharing a meal. As a result, Ik would often eat game raw, quickly and privately, for fear of being forced to share their catch with the crowd that was sure to arrive if they tried to cook it.

Helping others, especially the old or weak, is frowned upon. For the Ik, the old and weak are already dead and so not worthy of assistance. Turnbull was surprised to be constantly reprimanded for "wasting" his food or medicine or tobacco on those unable to care for themselves.

The Mountain People is Turnbull's compelling account of living among the Ik for almost two years. His book is a modern classic, but what lesson can we learn from the Ik? "The Ik teach us," claimed Turnbull, "that our much vaunted human values are not inherent in humanity at all, but are associated only with a particular form of survival called society, and that all, even society itself, are luxuries that can be dispensed with. . . . If man has any greatness it is surely in his ability to maintain these values, clinging to them to an often very bitter end, even shortening an already pitifully short life rather than sacrificing his humanity. But that too involves a choice, and the Ik teach us that man can lose the will to make it" (294).

As Turnbull sees it, the Ik didn't choose to abandon their humanity, which includes their moral sense. It was even worse than that; they were so dispirited that they couldn't even make the choice to abandon it. They were bereft of it. But Turnbull's interpretation of the Ik as a people without morality is not the only one possible; perhaps the Ik have their own strange morality, or perhaps they even share aspects of our morality. How can we tell whether a society has a morality at all? And how can we tell what a society's morality is?

If the Ik really are a society, rather than just a loose collection of unfortunate individuals, then it might be difficult to claim that they have no morality at all, since morality makes social living possible. When emphasized, the lies, the stealing, the unwillingness to share, the lack of sexual prohibitions, the unwillingness to raise the young, and the indifference to death and suffering make it sound like there is no such thing as Ik *society*. Rather than a society, their condition instead resembles a Hobbesian state of nature (see Chapter 4).

On the other hand, perhaps there was just enough cohesion among the Ik for Turnbull to correctly say that they still formed a society, however rudimentary. Yet even minimal social structure suggests various norms and social expectations; otherwise, the Ik would not be a society at all. Ik social norms might be things like these: You should not waste resources by giving them to people who will die soon. You should try to eat unobserved, for otherwise you will have to share. Because children are a dangerous and unwanted burden, you are not required to care for them. You should not kill other Ik, but if they are trying to steal your food (which means that you will die), then it is permissible to kill. And so forth. With a little ingenuity, we could probably construct a set of norms that regulate Icean society.

What's more, with refinement, many of those norms actually start to look like some of our moral norms! Thankfully, we don't have to make the same awful choices as the Ik about daily survival, but is it absurd to suppose that giving food and other scarce resources to those who will die soon anyway is wasting it? And if women have no control over becoming pregnant, is it absurd to abandon one's children if caring for them will probably mean one's death? If there is not enough food to go around, should others be expected to share what little they have? And is it acceptable for them to take steps to avoid having to share it? After all, the Ik tried to eat game without lighting fires because decency would require them to share with anyone who showed up. The Ik start to look more and more like us, if we imagine ourselves faced with similar dire choices about everyday life. Do the Ik think that what they do is rationally defensible by appeal to principle? Do they regret some of their actions, claiming that harsh circumstances force them to make choices that they otherwise would not make?

We cannot definitively say that we and the Ik share broadly similar moral principles; perhaps they really do have no morality, as Turnbull suggests. It will require a lot more inquiry to determine whether the Ik have no morality, our morality, or a fundamentally different morality. The point, however, is that wherever people live in society, minor differences not withstanding, perhaps morality is broadly the same. At a minimum, that is a hypothesis that even the strange case of the Ik does not decisively refute.

TWO NON-WESTERN ETHICAL TRADITIONS: BUDDHISM AND CONFUCIANISM

Buddhist Ethics

The central figure of Buddhism, Gotama Siddartha (563–483 BCE), was a man, not a god; he is revered, not worshipped. Called the Buddha, which means "enlightened one," he is alleged to have figured out the path to enlightenment. It is possible for others to achieve "Buddha-hood," and indeed many have, though Gotama is thought by some Buddhists to be the most fully enlightened of all. This is in sharp contrast to Christianity, wherein the central figure of Jesus is regarded as divine and worshipped as such, and although his followers might aspire to become Christ-like, they can never achieve divinity, nor should they try.

As legend has it, Gotama was born into Indian aristocracy surrounded by luxury. He was intentionally sheltered because his parents had a premonition that someday he would abandon his family and the earthly pleasures most people desire for the hard life of a wandering religious ascetic. Of course, that is precisely what happened. On trips outside of his enclosed palace, the young prince Gotama saw old age, sickness, and death. According to a Pali version of Gotama's experience of the world outside his palace (Pali is the Indo-Aryan dialect of the earliest Buddhist documents),

> Now there arose in the mind of Gotama the Bodhisat, when he had gone to his place and was meditating in seclusion, this thought: Verily this world has fallen upon trouble—one is born, and grows old, and dies, and falls from one state, and springs up in another. And from this suffering, moreover, no one knows of

any way of escape, even from decay and death. O, when shall a way of escape from this suffering be made known—from decay and from death? ("The Legend of the Four Signs")

Thus began Gotama's quest for release from the sufferings of the world. He wandered with ascetics, praying, meditating, fasting, and engaging in every imaginable kind of self-denial in his search for enlightenment, but to no avail. The path of self-mortification led nowhere and Gotama abandoned it to reconsider.

Gotama's enlightenment purportedly came in a series of visions whereby he directly saw his innumerable past lives. Now the Buddha, Gotama also saw how to secure release from the cycle of rebirths (known as *samsara*) and the suffering that attends each life. The Buddha's fundamental insight on how to attain enlightenment or Nirvana (Buddhist "heaven") was explained by the Four Noble Truths (reprinted below), his first sermon, in which he converted his fellow ascetics to the path of enlightenment they had been seeking. The Four Noble Truths are Buddhism's core teachings, the many varieties of Buddhism notwithstanding; they are comparable to Christianity's Sermon on the Mount.

The Four Noble Truths express several metaphysical theses, with Buddhist ethics as an implication of them. Buddhists think that people are reborn, and not haphazardly but according to the law of karma. How one leads one's life determines how one will be reincarnated. Karma is not a system of reward and punishment administered by an intelligence who determines what one deserves; rather, karma is the wholly impersonal workings of things. The form that one's rebirth takes is simply a natural consequence of how one has lived. If one is stingy, for example, one is reborn poor; if one is angry, one is reborn ugly; if one harms others, one is reborn sickly; and so forth.

The fit between action and karmic consequence reflects a rough sort of natural justice. Metaphysically, stinginess in this life could have resulted in some other effect in a subsequent life, such as beauty or health, which suggests that even though karma is supposed to be wholly impersonal, it reflects our moral sense of how things ought to be. Nonetheless, the karmic consequences of one's actions are such that as one sows, so shall one reap (or, to use another cliché, what goes around comes around!). Moreover, there is no guarantee that one will be reborn as a person; evil deeds might return one as an animal, and especially evil deeds could return one as something else, such as an insect.

Buddhists deny that there is an essential or core "self" that persists through time. So what gets reborn? According to Buddhists, we are nothing but a bundle of experiences that are causally linked to one another. One thought leads to another thought, one desire causes another, a belief causes an intention, and so forth. There is no persisting substrate or core self that has those experiences. Think of a river. There is no such thing as the river itself; there is just an ever-changing flow of water. That is what we are supposed to be like. Reincarnation is a particular stream of consciousness flowing "through" sequential embodiments, depending on impersonal karmic laws. If someone does a serious wrong, the stream of consciousness that is currently embodied as that human being might then be deflected next into the embodiment of an insect.

It is not as though the insect would really be a person trapped in an insect's body thinking the thoughts of a person (as Gregor Samsa was in Kafka's

Metamorphosis). Rather, the stream of consciousness would be diminished to a bug's awareness (as the flow of a river can be constricted). On and on the stream of consciousness flows, suffering through embodiment after embodiment, as determined by karma (the law of consequences) until, guided by the Four Noble Truths, it reaches enlightenment, thus escaping *samsara* (the wheel of rebirth). For Buddhists, being born a human being is especially auspicious because that particular stream of consciousness is now poised to reach Nirvana. Nirvana is not a place; it is a condition of being. After Buddha reached enlightenment, he did not disappear; he lived and taught for forty years.

Buddhist conceptions of the self are in sharp contrast to Christianity's preoccupation with an eternal soul, a persisting real you. Much frustration in life, claim Buddhists, arises from mistaken conceptions of the self. Hence our desires to preserve ourselves or to act in ways that are focused on our selves all derive from the same mistaken view of ourselves. Clearly, egoism is a non-starter for Buddhists. *The Dhammapada* (an early compilation of Buddhist wisdom from the Pali canon) begins like this:

> All that we are is the result of what we have thought: it is founded on our thoughts, it is made up of our thoughts. If a man speaks or acts with an evil thought, pain follows him, as the wheel follows the foot of the ox that draws the carriage.

All that we are is the result of our prior thoughts; we are nothing but a system of floating thoughts. And the consequences of our thoughts determine our lives (karma!) with the inevitability of the cart wheel turning because the ox pulls it. They are yoked together.

Why should we want to escape the cycle of rebirths? This involves the first of the Four Noble Truths: Life is suffering. "Suffering" is how the Sanskrit word *dukkha* is translated. But dukkha is apparently a much richer concept than suffering, having to do with all things unsatisfactory. Linguists tell us that the term originally referred to the misalignment of cart wheels on an axel, such that they do not roll smoothly, they squeak, they jamb, they bind. And so it is with life; life is dukkha. In the First Noble Truth, the Buddha claimed, "Birth is dukkha; decay is dukkha; illness is dukkha; death is dukkha; presence of objects we hate is dukkha; separation from objects we love is dukkha; not to obtain what we desire is dukkha."

Consider the idea that not to obtain what we desire is dukkha. To desire something implies that one does not have it and unsatisfied desires are necessarily bad, so desire is a state of unease—dukkha. And the more we satisfy our desires, the more desires we create, desire upon desire, a pitiful condition. As expressed in the *Dhammapada*, "Beset with lust, men run about like a snared hare; held in fetters and bonds, they undergo pain for a long time, again and again." We live "like a monkey seeking fruit in the forest." Since, as Buddha explained in the Second Noble Truth, dukkha originates in our cravings, relinquishing our cravings is the way to overcome dukkha.

Buddhist ethics derives from the Fourth Noble Truth, or the Eightfold Path, which is also known as the Middle Way because it is a way of life between asceticism and an unreflective life of ordinary desires. The eight factors (see below) are arranged sequentially, just like a path, allegedly leading to the cessation of dukkha. Step 1, right view, refers to the metaphysics of rebirth and karma; step 2 refers to thought properly directed toward freedom and away from craving. Buddhist ethics flows from steps 3, 4, and 5: right speech, right action, and right livelihood. Right speech encourages us to eschew lies, slander, deception, gossip, and hateful and angry words. Right action forbids harm, and right livelihood forbids a life that causes suffering, such as being a butcher or soldier, and so is really an aspect of the previous step. Because the ethical steps are expressed so vacuously, endless interpretations are possible. Telling us to do "right action" is not very helpful. The other steps refer to ways of cultivating the mind and how to meditate.

The metaphysical peculiarities of rebirth and karma aside, if so much of ordinary life is dukkha, eliminating dukkha would seem to eliminate much of ordinary life. Buddhists, it would seem, cannot have strong passions or commitments or be outraged by atrocities; they must remain detached from the suffering of the world. Despite their reputation for compassion, Buddhists should remain indifferent to the homeless, the orphaned, and the poor, because the sad plight of those people is just the karmic result of misdeeds in a previous existence. Perhaps their suffering presents one with an opportunity to gain karmic merit by helping to reduce their suffering, but in the end their plight is a result of their own actions. Consuming desires are portrayed as bad because of their karmic effects, but what kind of commitment must a mother have to her child or a social reformer to justice? Courage requires strong allegiance to moral ideals and a willingness to risk what one holds dear for its sake. Buddhist disengagement from ordinary life stands in sharp contrast to the pressing concerns of the world. Their equanimity is achieved at the expense of much that seems worthy for a fully formed human character, or so it seems.

Confucianism

For many Americans, Confucius' name is forever linked to a genre of bad jokes that begin with 'Confucius says'. But Confucius (551–479 BCE) is the most influential sage in human history. His thoughts, recorded by his disciples in the *Analects,* or *Selected Sayings,* have affected more people over a greater period of time than those of any other world thinker. The legacy of Confucius can be compared to those of Socrates and Jesus combined.

Master Kung, or Kung Fu-tzu (Latinized as Confucius), lived during a time of great instability in China. Feudal kingdoms were constantly battling one another, and ordinary life was uncertain and hard. Confucius sought in vain to obtain an administrative position to implement his ideas for bringing peace and harmony to the land, wandering with a group of disciples from kingdom to kingdom. Evidently regarding himself as a failure, Confucius returned to his home district in northeast China to a quiet life of teaching. But many of his followers did get administrative appointments, and for millennia thereafter all such appointments required deep knowledge of Confucian teachings and classic Chinese literature. Literary scholars ruled the country, and the modern Chinese respect for education shows how profoundly Confucian ideals permeated Chinese culture.

Confucianism developed in complex ways after Confucius' time; we will focus exclusively on his sayings in the *Analects,* excerpts from which are reprinted below. As with all significant ancient texts, intense scholarly debate surrounds the authenticity and interpretation of the *Analects.* At first the *Analects* seems to be a disjointed collection of opaque aphorisms about rulers, people, and everyday behavior. It takes considerable effort to find any coherent themes, much less an argumentative structure for Confucius' ideas. But implicit arguments can be constructed to support the ideas buried in Confucius' pithy sayings, and with effort, themes emerge from seemingly random statements.

What did Confucius teach? The overriding theme is that individual rectitude and social obedience will achieve harmony between human life and a somewhat mysterious heavenly order. For Confucius, the turmoil of his time, known as the Warring States Period, was evidence that our lives are out of synch with a much larger world dynamic. Thus the way to restore order was to harmonize social and individual life to that larger order, as was alleged to have been the case during an earlier Chinese dynasty of peace and prosperity. Confucius thus looked to models for proper deportment in the stories, ritual, and culture of the time before social order collapsed. He regarded himself not as an innovator but as a conservative who sought to transmit to his troubled times the key to stability that society had known earlier.

Confucius' ideal society consists of rectified individuals, people who have cultivated the goodness of their characters or their "humanity." According to Chinese scholars these individuals have *ren,* the written character depicted as a combination of "person" and "two." Thus the perfected person, the Confucian Sage, knows how to get along with other people. We cultivate our humanity by observing ritual. Ritual is not meaningless formality for social interaction; for Confucius, ritual is the codified expression of *ren.* So by practicing ritual carefully and sincerely, we internalize *ren.* Ritual makes us aware of our proper deportment as parents, children, spouses, friends, and citizens, thereby establishing harmony in society. "The most precious fruit of Ritual is harmony" (*Analects* I.12).

Confucius thinks that as we perfect ourselves, our humanity will spread out in a ripple-like fashion to affect others, thus transforming the social order into a harmoniously functioning whole. The key to good society is good individuals. "Someone asked Confucius: 'Why aren't you in government?' The Master replied: the Book of History says: Honor your parents, simply honor your parents and make your brothers friends—this too is good government. That's really being in government, so why govern by serving in government?" (II.21).

Of course, those actually in government have a special responsibility. Confucius imagines wise, paternalistic rulers who govern by moral force, not by regulation and threats of punishment. They set an example of moral rectitude that will influence others. In a famous image, "The noble-minded have the integrity of the wind, and little people the integrity of grass. When the wind sweeps over grass, it bends" (XII.19). Or "In government, the secret is integrity. Use it and you'll be like the polestar: always dwelling in its proper place, the other stars turning reverently about it" (II.1).

Internalizing *ren* by observing ritual, a Confucian Sage now understands the Mandate from Heaven and so will "never impose on others what you would not choose for yourself" (XV.24). Confucius described his own path: "At fifteen I devoted myself to learning, and at thirty stood firm. At forty I had no doubts, and at fifty understood the Mandate of Heaven. At sixty I listened in effortless accord. And at seventy I followed the mind's passing fancies without overstepping any bounds" (II.4). At fifteen Confucius studied Chinese classics learning ritual so that at thirty he could act with propriety. At forty he moved from mere conformity with ritual to a deeper understanding of its significance by fifty. By sixty Confucius' will is so permeated by the Mandate from Heaven that at seventy there is no distinction between the two; Confucius' actions are now a natural expression of an inner perfected state. The Sage acts with humanity naturally and effortlessly; moral behavior is the spontaneous expression of the Sage's character, a character that is in harmony with the Mandate from Heaven. Thus is the Way of the Sages, exemplary human beings who lead by example.

Rather than being an innovative thinker, Confucius reminded the Chinese people of their own heritage articulated in their classic literature. The virtues of humility and social order are stressed, as well as deference to one's superiors, all rooted in the common decency of a negative version of the Golden Rule: "Never impose on others what you would not choose for yourself" (XV.25). However, such reverence for the past makes Confucius an easy target of criticism, especially now when the Chinese are struggling to negotiate a vibrant capitalist economy within a nominally communist state. Confucius' distain for profit ("The noble-minded are clear about duty. Little people are clear about profit." IV.16), means that the culture's commitment to Confucian ideals will be severely tested by modern life.

READINGS IN NON-WESTERN ETHICAL TRADITIONS

Buddhism, "The Four Noble Truths," from the *Dhammapada*

Disturbed by the pervasiveness of suffering in life, the Buddha sought to eliminate it by discovering its root cause in our mistaken cravings for permanence in a world where everything is subject to change. We can eliminate suffering, he claimed, only by relinquishing our attachments to things and conditions. This is accomplished by following the Eightfold Path of right ethical conduct and mental discipline. The Buddha's message has influenced countless people throughout the world for millennia.

Critical Reading Questions

1. What are the Four Noble Truths? What are the elements of the Eightfold Path?
2. What is the Middle Path?
3. What makes the Buddha awakened?
4. What does "thirst" mean? What role does it play in our lives?

TURNING THE WHEEL OF THE TEACHING
(Also known as The Four Noble Truths)

This is what I heard. The Fortunate One was once staying at Varanasi, in the deer park [9.1] at Isipatana. There he addressed the group of five mendicants [9.2] as follows.

"There are two extremes that are not to be embraced by a person who has set out on the path. Which two? The practice of clinging to sensory pleasure in sensory objects. This practice is lowly, common, ordinary, dishonorable, and unprofitable. And the practice of exhausting oneself with austerities. This practice is distressful, dishonorable, and unprofitable.

"Not tending toward either of these extremes, a *tathāgata* [9.3]—a person who has come to know reality—has completely awakened to the middle way [9.4]. The middle way engenders insight and understanding, and leads to calmness, to direct knowledge, to full awakening, to unbinding. So what is that middle way completely awakened to by a *tathāgata*? It is precisely this preeminent eight-component course [9.5]; namely, sound view, sound inclination, sound speech, sound action, sound livelihood, sound effort, sound awareness, and sound concentration. This is the middle way, realized by a *tathāgata,* which gives rise to vision and knowledge, and leads to calmness, to direct knowledge, to full awakening, to unbinding.

"Now, this is unease [9.6]. It is a preeminent reality [9.7]. Birth is unsettling, aging is unsettling, illness is unsettling, death is unsettling, association with what is displeasing is unsettling, separation from what is pleasing is unsettling, not getting what is wanted is unsettling. In short, the five existential functions subject to grasping [9.8] are unsettling.

"This is the origination of unease. It is a preeminent reality. It is this craving [9.9] that leads to further being, accompanied by passion and delight, seeking pleasure here and there. It is, namely, craving for sensual pleasures, craving for being, and craving for non-being.

"This is the cessation of unease [9.10]. It is a preeminent reality. It is the complete dissolution and cessation of precisely that thirst, the relinquishment and rejection of it, freedom from it, non-attachment to it.

"This is the way leading to the cessation of unease. It is a preeminent reality. It is this preeminent eight-component course; namely, sound view, sound inclination, sound speech, sound action, sound livelihood, sound effort, sound awareness, and sound concentration.

"When I realized *This is unease*, there arose in me vision, insight, discernment, knowledge, and clarity concerning things that have not been previously heard. When I realized *This unease is to be fully recognized*, there arose in me vision, insight, discernment, knowledge, and clarity concerning things that have not been previously heard. When I realized *This unease has been fully recognized*, there arose in me vision, insight, discernment, knowledge, and clarity concerning things that have not been previously heard.

"When I realized *This is the origin of unease*, there arose in me vision, insight, discernment, knowledge, and clarity concerning things that have not been previously heard. When I realized *The arising of unease is to be abandoned*, there arose in me vision, insight, discernment, knowledge, and clarity concerning things that have not been previously heard. When I realized *The arising of unease has been abandoned*, there arose in me vision, insight, discernment, knowledge, and clarity concerning things that have not been previously heard.

"When I realized *This is the cessation of unease,* there arose in me vision, insight, discernment, knowledge, and clarity concerning things that have not been previously heard. When I realized *The cessation of unease is to be realized,* there arose in me vision, insight, discernment, knowledge, and clarity concerning things that have not been previously heard. When I realized *The cessation of unease has been realized,* there arose in me vision, insight, discernment, knowledge, and clarity concerning things that have not been previously heard.

"When I realized *This is the path leading to the cessation of unease,* there arose in me vision, insight, discernment, knowledge, and clarity concerning things that have not been previously heard. When I realized *The path leading to the cessation of unease is to be cultivated,* there arose in me vision, insight, discernment, knowledge, and clarity concerning things that have not been previously heard. When I realized *The path leading to the cessation of unease has been cultivated,* there arose in me vision, insight, discernment, knowledge, and clarity concerning things that have not been previously heard.

"As long as [9.11] my insight and vision concerning these four preeminent realities just as they are, in their three sequences and twelve aspects [9.12], was not completely purified, I did not claim to have fully realized unsurpassed, complete awakening in this world with its resplendent beings, God, and death, with its seekers and priests, its supernatural beings and humans. But as soon as my insight and vision concerning these four preeminent realities just as they are was completely purified, then did I claim to have fully realized unsurpassed, complete awakening. The insight and vision arose in me: *Unwavering is my release; this is the final birth, there is now no further becoming.*"

That is what the Fortunate One said. Exalted, the group of five mendicants delighted at the words of the Fortunate One. And while this discourse was being spoken, there arose for the venerable Kondañña this dustless, stainless insight: *All that is subject to origination is subject to cessation.*

And when the Fortunate One had set in motion the wheel of teaching, the resplendent earth-dwelling beings cried out, "At Varanasi, in the deer park at Isipatana, the Fortunate One has set in motion the unexcelled wheel of the teaching, which cannot be stopped by any seeker or priest, any resplendent being, by God or death, or by anyone in the world!" Hearing the resplendent earth-dwelling beings' cry, resplendent beings throughout the cosmos cried out in the exact fashion.

Thus, at that moment, at that instant, at that second, the cry extended as far as the *brahm* realm, and this ten thousand–fold cosmos trembled, shook, and violently quaked, and an immeasurable, great radiance appeared in the cosmos, exceeding the brilliant majesty of the resplendent beings themselves.

Then the Fortunate One exclaimed this inspired utterance: "So you really know, Kondañña! So you really know!" And that is how the venerable Kondañña acquired the name Añña-Kondañña—Kondañña-Who-Knows [9.13].

Questions for Discussion

1. Assess the metaphysics of karma and rebirth. In what sense could "you" be reborn?
2. What kind of ethics can we derive from Buddhism?
3. Why should Buddhists be compassionate?
4. Sometimes Buddhism is criticized for being "negative." Is that a legitimate criticism?

Confucius, from the *Analects*

Confucius' sayings were collected as the Analects, *or* Selected Sayings, *by his disciples (or disciples of disciples) over one hundred years after his death, so their authenticity is often a matter of scholarly debate.*

Nevertheless, one can still get a glimpse of a character that has influenced more people throughout history than any other sage. A word of caution: Confucius' sayings are decidedly masculine; he regarded women as inferior beings, hardly capable of moral perfection. Like so many other great thinkers, such as Aristotle and Kant, he was unable to free himself entirely from his times. We should interpret Confucius to mean that all people are capable of undertaking the arduous path of a sage.

Critical Reading Questions

It is difficult to construct critical reading questions for this material. Try reading each aphorism and see whether you can decipher its meaning in light of our introductory discussion above.

THE ANALECTS

Confucius

Translated by David Hinton

I.3

The Master said: "Clever words and sanctimonious looks: in such people, Humanity is rare indeed."

I.8

The Master said: "If you're grave and thoughtful, people look to you with the veneration due a noble. And if you're learned, too, you're never inflexible.

"Above all else, be loyal and stand by your words. Never befriend those who are not kindred spirits. And when you're wrong, don't be afraid to change."

II.3

The Master said: "If you use government to show them the Way and punishment to keep them true, the people will grow evasive and lose all remorse. But if you use Integrity to show them the Way and Ritual to keep them true, they'll cultivate remorse and always see deeply into things."

II.11

The Master said: "If you can revive the ancient and use it to understand the modern, then you're worthy to be a teacher."

III.3

The Master said: "If you're human without Humanity, you know nothing of Ritual. If you're human without Humanity, you know nothing of music."

III.7

The Master said: "The noble-minded never contend. It's true that archery is a kind of contention. But even then, they bow and yield to each other when stepping up to the range. And when they step down, they toast each other. Even in contention, they retain their nobility."

III.26

The Master said: "Governing without generosity, Ritual without reverence, mourning without grief—how could I bear to see such things?"

IV.2

The Master said: "Without Humanity, you can't dwell in adversity for long, and you can't dwell in prosperity for long. If you're Humane, Humanity is your repose. And if you're wise, Humanity is your reward."

IV.5

The Master said: "Wealth and position—that's what people want. But if you enjoy wealth and position without following the Way, you'll never dwell at ease. Poverty and obscurity—that's what people despise. And if you endure poverty and obscurity without following the Way, you'll never get free.

"If you ignore Humanity, how will you gain praise and renown? The noble-minded don't forget Humanity for a single moment, not even in the crush of confusion and desperation."

IV.12

The Master said: "If profit guides your actions, there will be no end of resentment."

V.9

Tsai Yü slept in the daytime. The Master said: You can't carve much of anything from rotted wood. And you can't whitewash a wall of dung. So why bother scolding a person like Yü?

"In dealing with people," the Master added, "I once listened to their words, and then trusted them to do what they said. Now I listen to their words, and then watch what they do carefully. It was Yü that changed me."

VI.14

The Master said: "Meng Chih-fan[6] never boasts. When the army fled, he brought up the rear. Then when he was coming in through the gates, he spurred his horse on, saying *It wasn't courage that kept me behind. This horse just won't go any faster.*"

VII.12

The Master said: "If there were an honorable way to get rich, I'd do it, even if it meant being a stooge standing around with a whip. But there isn't an honorable way, so I just do what I like."

VII.16

The Master said: "Poor food and water for dinner, a bent arm for a pillow—that is where joy resides. For me, wealth and renown without honor are nothing but drifting clouds."

VIII.2

The Master said: "Reverence becomes tedium without Ritual and caution becomes timidity. Without Ritual, courage becomes recklessness, and truth becomes intolerance.

"When noble-minded leaders honor their parents, the people feel called to Humanity. And when leaders never forget old friends, the people live open and true."

XI.12

When Adept Lu asked about serving ghosts and spirits, the Master said: "You haven't learned to serve the living, so how could you serve ghosts?"

"Might I ask about death?"

"You don't understand life," the Master replied, "so how could you understand death?"

XII.2

Jan Yung asked about Humanity, and the Master said: "Go out into the world as if greeting a magnificent guest. Use the people as if offering a magnificent sacrifice. And never impose on others what you would not choose for yourself. Then, there will be no resentment among the people or the great families."

XII.11

Duke Ching[4] asked Confucius about governing, and Confucius said: "Ruler a ruler, minister a minister, father a father, son a son."

"How splendid!" exclaimed the Duke. "Truly, if the ruler isn't a ruler, the minister a minister, the father a father, and the son a son—then even if we had grain, how could we survive to eat it?"

XIII.3

Adept Lu said: "If the Lord of Wei wanted you to govern his country, what would you put first in importance?"

"The rectification of names," replied the Master: "Without a doubt."

XIII.13

The Master said: "Once you've rectified yourself, you can serve in government without difficulty. But if you haven't rectified yourself, how can you rectify the people?"

XIII.29

The Master said: "The people should be broadly educated by a wise teacher for seven years—then they can take up the weapons of war."

XIII.30

The Master said: "Sending people to war without educating them first: that is called *throwing the people away.*"

XV.2

Confucius left the next day.

In Ch'en, when supplies ran out, the disciples grew so weak they couldn't get to their feet. Adept Lu, his anger flaring, asked: "How is it the noble-minded must endure such privation?"

"If you're noble-minded, you're resolute in privation," the Master replied. "Little people get swept away."

XVI.8

Confucius said: "The noble-minded stand in awe of three things: the Mandate of Heaven, great men, and the words of a sage. Little people don't understand the Mandate of Heaven, so they aren't awed by it. They scorn great men, and they ridicule the words of a sage."

XVII.2

The Master said: "We're all the same by nature. It's living that makes us so different."

XVII.24

The Master said: "It's women and small-minded men that are impossible to nurture. If you're close and familiar with them, they lose all humility. If you keep your distance, they're full of resentment."

Questions for Discussion

1. What ethical paradigm emerges from the Confucian sayings?
2. What version of Western moral philosophy does Confucius' thought most closely resemble?
3. Do Confucius' ideas have relevance today?

Amartya Sen, "Human Rights and Asian Values"

Amartya Sen is Lamont University Professor and professor of economics and philosophy at Harvard University. He is a scholar of worldwide influence on matters of economics and public policy. He is particularly interested in economic and moral aspects of globalization. In "Human Rights and Asian Values," Sen examines the case for the presence of so-called Western values of individual freedom and tolerance in Asian culture. He shows that those values are not unique to Western thought; moreover, they did not emerge until fairly recently in Western thought.

Critical Reading Questions

1. What is the stereotype of Asian thought on individual freedom and political liberty? How is this alleged to be an aspect of Confucianism?
2. What criticisms does Sen make of the Asian stereotype?
3. Who are Ashoka, Kautilya, and Akbar, and what did each think, according to Sen? What is the significance of their views for Sen's position?
4. What is the basis for human rights, such as a right not to be tortured, according to Sen?
5. What does Sen mean when he says that there is no "grand dichotomy"?

HUMAN RIGHTS AND ASIAN VALUES

Amartya Sen

In 1776, just when the Declaration of Independence was being adopted in this country, Thomas Paine complained, in *Common Sense,* that Asia had "long expelled" freedom. In this lament, Paine saw Asia in company with much of the rest of the world (America, he hoped, would be different).

Freedom hath been hunted round the globe. Asia and Africa have long expelled her. Europe regards her as a stranger and England hath given her warning to depart.

For Paine, political freedom and democracy were valuable everywhere, even though they were being violated nearly everywhere too.

The violation of freedom and democracy in different parts of the world continues today, even if not as comprehensively as in Paine's time. There is a difference, though. A new class of arguments has emerged that denies the universal importance of these freedoms. The most prominent of these contentions is the claim that Asian values do not give freedom the same importance as it is accorded in the West. Given this difference in value systems, the argument runs, Asia must be faithful to its own system of political priorities.

Cultural and value differences between Asia and the West were stressed by several official delegations at the 1993 World Conference on Human Rights in Vienna. The foreign minister of Singapore warned that "universal recognition of the ideal of human rights can be harmful if universalism is used to deny or mask the reality of diversity."[1] The Chinese delegation played a leading role in emphasizing regional differences and in making sure that the prescriptive framework adopted in the declarations made

room for regional diversity. The spokesman for China's foreign ministry even put on record the proposition, apparently applicable in China and elsewhere, that "individuals must put the state's rights before their own."[2]

I shall examine the thesis that Asian values are less supportive of freedom and more concerned with order and discipline than are Western values, and that the claims of human rights in the areas of political and civil liberties are, therefore, less relevant in Asia than in the West. The defense of authoritarianism in Asia on grounds of the special nature of Asian values calls for historical scrutiny, to which I shall presently turn. But there is also a different line of justification that argues for authoritarian governance in the interest of economic development in Asia. Lee Kuan Yew, the former prime minister of Singapore and a great champion of "Asian values," has defended authoritarian arrangements on the ground of their alleged effectiveness in promoting economic success. I shall consider this argument before turning to historical issues.

ASIAN VALUES AND ECONOMIC DEVELOPMENT

Does authoritarianism really work so well? It is certainly true that some relatively authoritarian states (such as South Korea, Lee's own Singapore, and post-reform China) have had faster rates of economic growth than many less authoritarian

[1]Quoted in W. S. Wong, "The Real World of Human Rights" (mimeographed, 1993).

[2]Quoted in John F. Cooper, "Peking's Post-Tiananmen Foreign Policy: The Human Rights Factor," *Issues and Studies* 30 (October 1994): 69; see also Jack Donnelly, "Human Rights and Asian Values," paper presented at a workshop of the Carnegie Council's Human Rights Initiative, "Changing Conceptions of Human Rights in a Growing East Asia," in Hakone, Japan, June 23–25, 1995.

ones (including India, Costa Rica, and Jamaica). But the "Lee hypothesis" is, in fact, based on very selective information, rather than on any general statistical testing of the wide-ranging data that are available. We cannot take the high economic growth of China or South Korea in Asia as proof positive that authoritarianism does better in promoting economic growth, any more than we can draw the opposite conclusion on the basis of the fact that the fastest-growing country in Africa (and one of the fastest growers in the world) is Botswana, which has been a oasis of democracy in that unhappy continent. Much depends on the precise circumstances.

There is, in fact, little general evidence that authoritarian governance and the suppression of political and civil rights are really beneficial in encouraging economic development. The statistical picture is much more complex. Systematic empirical studies give no real support to the claim that there is a conflict between political rights and economic performance.[3] The directional linkage seems to depend on many other circumstances, and while some statistical investigations note a weakly negative relation, others find a strongly positive one. On balance, the hypothesis that there is no relation between the two in either direction is hard to reject. Since political liberty and individual freedom have importance of their own, the case for them remains untarnished.

There is also a more basic issue of research methodology here. We must not only look at statistical connections, we must also examine the causal processes that are involved in economic growth and development. The economic policies and circumstances that led to the economic

success of East Asian economies are by now reasonably well understood. While different empirical studies have varied in emphasis, there is by now a fairly well-accepted general list of "helpful policies," among them openness to competition, the use of international markets, a high level of literacy and school education, successful land reforms, and public provision of incentives for investment, exporting, and industrialization. There is nothing whatsoever to indicate that any of these policies is inconsistent with greater democracy and had to be sustained by the elements of authoritarianism that happened to be present in South Korea or Singapore or China.[4] The recent Indian experience also shows that what is needed for generating faster economic growth is a friendlier economic climate, rather than a harsher political system.

It is also important to look at the connection between political and civil rights, on the one hand, and the prevention of major disasters, on the other. Political and civil rights give people the opportunity to draw attention forcefully to general needs and to demand appropriate public action. The response of a government to acute suffering often depends on the pressure that is put on it, and this is where the exercise of political rights (voting, criticizing, protesting, and so on) can make a real difference. I have discussed elsewhere the remarkable fact that in the terrible history of famines in the world, no substantial famine has ever occurred in any independent and democratic country with a relatively free press.[5] Whether we look at famines in Sudan, Ethiopia, Somalia, or other countries with dictatorial regimes, or in the Soviet Union in the 1930s, or in China during the period 1958 to 1961 with the failure of the Great Leap Forward (when between 23 million and 30 million people died), or currently in North Korea, we do not find exceptions to this rule.[6]

[3]See, among other studies, Robert J. Barro and Jong-Wha Lee, "Losers and Winners in Economic Growth," Working Paper 4341, National Bureau of Economic Research (1993); Partha Dasgupta, *An Inquiry into Well-Being and Destitution* (Oxford: Clarendon Press, 1993); John Helliwell, "Empirical Linkages Between Democracy and Economic Growth," Working Paper 4066, National Bureau of Economic Research (1994); Surjit Bhalla, "Freedom and Economic Growth: A Vicious Circle?" presented at the Nobel Symposium in Uppsala on "Democracy's Victory and Crisis," August 1994; Adam Przeworski and Fernando Limongi, "Democracy and Development," presented at the Nobel Symposium in Uppsala cited above; Adam Przeworski et al., *Sustainable Democracy* (New York: Cambridge University Press, 1995); Robert J. Barro, *Getting It Right: Markets and Choices in a Free Society* (Cambridge, MA: MIT Press, 1996).

[4]On this see also my joint study with Jean Drèze, *Hunger and Public Action* (Oxford: Clarendon Press, 1989), Part III.

[5]Amartya Sen, "Development: Which Way Now?" *Economic Journal* 93 (1983) and *Resources, Values and Development* (Cambridge, MA: Harvard University Press, 1984, 1997); see also Drèze and Sen, *Hunger and Public Action*.

[6]Although Ireland was a part of democratic Britain during its famines of the 1840s, the extent of political dominance of London over the Irish was so strong and the social distance

While this connection is clearest in the case of famine prevention, the positive role of political and civil rights applies to the prevention of economic and social disasters in general. When things go fine and everything is routinely good, this role of democracy may not be badly missed. It comes into its own when things get fouled up, for one reason or another. Then the political incentives provided by democratic governance acquire great practical value. To concentrate only on economic incentives (such as the market system provides) while ignoring political incentives (such as democratic systems are equipped to provide) is to opt for a deeply unbalanced set of ground rules.

ASIA AS A UNIT

I turn now to the nature and relevance of Asian values. This is not an easy exercise, for various reasons. The size of Asia, where about 60 percent of the total world population lives, is itself a problem. What can we take to be the values of so vast a region, with such diversity? There are no quintessential values that apply to this immensely large and heterogeneous population, that differentiate Asians as a group from people in the rest of the world.

The temptation to see Asia as one unit reveals, in fact, a distinctly Eurocentric perspective. Indeed, the term "the Orient," which was widely used for a long time to mean essentially what Asia means today, referred to the direction of the rising sun. It requires a heroic generalization to see such a large group of people in terms of the positional view from the European side of the Bosporus.

In practice, the advocates of "Asian values" have tended to look primarily at East Asia as the region of particular applicability. The generalization about the contrast between the West and Asia often concentrates on the land to the east of Thailand, even though there is an even more ambitious claim that the rest of Asia is also rather "similar." For example, Lee Kuan Yew outlines "the fundamental difference between Western

concepts of society and government and East Asian concepts" by explaining, "When I say East Asians, I mean Korea, Japan, China, Vietnam, as distinct from Southeast Asia, which is a mix between the Sinic and the Indian, though Indian culture also emphasizes similar values."[7]

In fact, however, East Asia itself has much diversity, and there are many variations between Japan and China and Korea and other parts of East Asia. Various cultural influences from within and outside this region have affected human lives over the history of this rather large territory. These diverse influences still survive in a variety of ways. To illustrate, my copy of Houghton Mifflin's international *Almanac* describes the religions of the 124 million Japanese people in the following way: 112 million Shintoists and 93 million Buddhists. Buddist practices coexist with Shinto practices, often within the same person's religious makeup. Cultures and traditions overlap over wide regions such as East Asia and even within specific countries such as Japan or China or Korea, and attempts at generalization about Asian values (with forceful—often brutal—implications for masses of people in this region with diverse faiths, convictions, and commitments) cannot but be extremely crude. Even the 2.8 million people of Singapore have vast variations in their cultural and historical traditions, despite the fact that the conformism surrounding Singapore's political leadership and the official interpretation of Asian values is very powerful at this time.

FREEDOM, DEMOCRACY, AND TOLERANCE

The recognition of heterogeneity in Asian traditions does not, in any way, settle the issue of the presence or absence of a commitment to individual freedom and political liberty in Asian culture. It could be argued that the traditions extant in Asia differ among themselves, but nevertheless may share some common characteristics. It has been asserted, for example, that the treatment of elderly members of the family (such as aged parents) is more supportive in Asian countries than in the West. It is possible to argue about this claim, but there would be nothing very peculiar if similarities of this or

so great (well illustrated by Edmund Spenser's severely unfriendly description of the Irish as early as the sixteenth century) that the English rule of Ireland was, for all practical purposes, a colonial rule. The separation and independence of Ireland later on simply confirmed the nature of the division.

[7]Fareed Zakaria, "Culture Is Destiny: A Conversation with Lee Kuan Yew," *Foreign Affairs* 73 (March/April 1994): 113.

other kinds were to obtain across the diverse cultures of Asia: diversities need not apply to every field. The question that has to be asked, rather, is whether the Asian countries share the common feature of being skeptical of freedom and liberty, while emphasizing order and discipline. The advocates of Asian particularism often—explicitly or by implication—make this argument, which allows for heterogeneity within Asia, but asserts that there is a shared mistrust of the claims of liberal rights.

Authoritarian lines of reasoning often receive indirect backing from modes of thought in the West itself. There is clearly a tendency in the United States and Europe to assume, if only implicitly, the primacy of political freedom and democracy as a fundamental and ancient feature of Western culture—one not to be easily found in Asia. A contrast is drawn between the authoritarianism allegedly implicit in, say, Confucianism and the respect for individual liberty and autonomy allegedly deeply rooted in Western liberal culture. Western promoters of personal and political liberty in the non-Western world often see this as bringing Western values to Asia and Africa.

In all this, there is a substantial tendency to extrapolate backwards from the present. Values spread by the European Enlightenment and other relatively recent developments cannot be considered part of the long-term Western heritage, experienced in the West over millennia. Indeed, in answer to the question when and under what circumstances "the notion of individual liberty . . . first became explicit in the West," Isaiah Berlin has noted, "I have found no convincing evidence of any clear formulation of it in the ancient world."[8] This diagnosis has been disputed by Orlando Patterson, among others.[9] Patterson points to features in Western culture, particularly in Greece and Rome and in the tradition of Christianity, that indicate the presence of selective championing of individual liberty. The question that does not get adequately answered—indeed, it is scarcely even asked—is whether similar elements are absent in other cultures. Isaiah Berlin's thesis concerns

[8]Isaiah Berlin, *Four Essays on Liberty* (Oxford: Oxford University Press, 1969), xl.

[9]See Orlando Patterson, *Freedom*, Vol. I: *Freedom in the Making of Western Culture* (New York: Basic Books, 1991).

the notion of individual freedom as we now understand it, and the absence of "any clear formulation" of this can coexist with the support and advocacy of *selected components* of the comprehensive notion that makes up the contemporary idea of individual liberty as an entitlement of everyone. Such components do exist in the Greco-Roman world and in the world of Christian thought, but we have to examine whether these components are present elsewhere as well—that is, in non-Western cultures. We have to search for parts rather than the whole—both in the West and in Asia and elsewhere.

To illustrate this point, consider the idea that personal freedom for all is important for a good society. This claim can be seen as being composed of two distinct components, to wit, (1) *the value of personal freedom:* that personal freedom is important and should be guaranteed for those who "matter" in a good society, and (2) *equality of freedom:* that everyone matters and should have similar freedom. The two together entail that personal freedom should be guaranteed, on a shared basis, for all. Aristotle wrote much in support of the former proposition, but in his exclusion of women and slaves did little to defend the latter. Indeed, the championing of equality in this form is of quite recent origin. Even in a society stratified according to class and caste—such as the Mandarins and the Brahmins—freedom could be valued for the privileged, in much the same way freedom is valued for non-slave men in corresponding Greek conceptions of a good society.

Another useful distinction is between (1) *the value of toleration:* there must be toleration of diverse beliefs, commitments, and actions of different people, and (2) *equality of tolerance:* the toleration that is offered to some must be reasonably offered to all (except when tolerance of some will lead to intolerance for others). Again, arguments for some tolerance can be seen plentifully in earlier writings, without that tolerance being supplemented by equality of tolerance. The roots of modern democratic and liberal ideas can be sought in terms of constitutive elements, rather than as a whole.

ORDER AND CONFUCIANISM

As part of this analytical scrutiny, the question has to be asked whether these constitutive components can be seen in Asian writings in the way they can be found in Western thought. The presence of these components must not be confused with the absence of the opposite, namely ideas and doctrines that clearly *do not* emphasize freedom and tolerance. Championing of order and discipline can be found in Western classics as well as in Asian ones. Indeed; it is by no means clear to me that Confucius is more authoritarian in this respect than, say, Plato or St. Augustine. The real issue is not whether these non-freedom perspectives are *present* in Asian traditions, but whether the freedom-oriented perspectives are *absent* there.

This is where the diversity of Asian value systems becomes central, incorporating but transcending regional diversity. An obvious example is the role of Buddhism as a form of thought. In Buddhist tradition, great importance is attached to freedom, and the part of the earlier Indian theorizing to which Buddhist thoughts relate has much room for volition and free choice. Nobility of conduct has to be achieved in freedom, and even the ideas of liberation (such as *moksha*) have this feature. The presence of these elements in Buddhist thought does not obliterate the importance for Asia of ordered discipline emphasized by Confucianism, but it would be a mistake to take Confucianism to be the only tradition in Asia—indeed even in China. Since so much of the contemporary authoritarian interpretation of Asian values concentrates on Confucianism, this diversity is particularly worth emphasizing.

Indeed, the reading of Confucianism that is now standard among authoritarian champions of Asian values does less than justice to the variety within Confucius's own teachings, to which Simon Leys has recently drawn attention.[10] Confucius did not recommend blind allegiance to the state. When Zilu asks him "how to serve a prince," Confucius replies, "Tell him the truth even if it offends him."[11] Those in charge of censorship in Singapore or Beijing would take a very different view. Confucius is not averse to practical caution and tact, but does not forgo the recommendation to oppose a bad government.

"When the [good] way prevails in the state, speak boldly and act boldly. When the state has lost the way, act boldly and speak softly."[12]

Indeed, Confucius provides a clear pointer to the fact that the two pillars of the imagined edifice of Asian values, namely loyalty to family and obedience to the state, can be in severe conflict with each other. The governor of She told Confucius, "Among my people, there is a man of unbending integrity: when his father stole a sheep, he denounced him." To this Confucius replied, "Among my people, men of integrity do things differently: a father covers up for his son, a son covers up for his father, and there is integrity in what they do."[13]

Elias Canetti has pointed out that in understanding the teachings of Confucius, we have to examine not only what he says, but also what he does not say.[14] The subtlety involved in what is often called "the silence of Confucius" has certainly escaped the modern austere interpreters in their tendency to assume that what is not explicitly supported must be implicitly forbidden. It is not my contention that Confucius was a democrat, or a great champion of freedom and political dissent, but there is reason enough to question the monolithic authoritarian image of him that is presented by the contemporary advocates of Asian values.

FREEDOM AND TOLERANCE

If we shift our attention from China to the Indian subcontinent, we are in no particular danger of running into hard-to-interpret silence; it is difficult to outdo the Indian traditions of speaking at length and arguing endlessly in explicit and elaborate terms. India not only has the largest religious literature in the world, it also has by far the largest volume of atheistic and materialistic writings among the ancient civilizations. There is just a lot of literature of all kinds. The Indian epic *Mahabharata*, which is often compared with the *Iliad* or the *Odyssey*, is in fact seven times as long as the *Iliad* and *Odyssey* put together. In a well-known Bengali poem written in the

---

[10]Simon Leys, *The Analects of Confucius* (New York: Norton; 1997).

[11]Ibid., 14.22, p. 70.

[12]Ibid., 14.3, p. 66.

[13]Ibid., 13.18, p. 63.

[14]Elias Canetti, *The Conscience of Words* (New York: Seabury Press, 1979); see also Leys, *The Analects of Confucius*, xxx–xxxii.

nineteenth century by the religious and social leader Ram Mohan Ray, the real horror of death is described thus: "Just imagine how terrible it will be on the day you die,/Others will go on speaking, but you will not be able to respond."

This fondness for arguing, and for discussing things at leisure and at length, is itself somewhat in tension with the quiet order and discipline championed in the alleged Asian values. But in addition, the content of what has been written indicates a variety of views on freedom, tolerance, and equality. In many ways, the most interesting articulation of the need for tolerance on an egalitarian basis can be found in the writings of Emperor Ashoka, who in the third century B.C. commanded a larger Indian empire than any other Indian king in history (including the Moghuls, and even the Raj, if we leave out the native states that the British let be). He turned his attention in a big way to public ethics and enlightened politics after being horrified by the carnage he saw in his own victorious battle against the king of Kalinga (now Orissa). Ashoka converted to Buddhism and helped to make it a world religion by sending emissaries abroad with the Buddhist message. He also covered the country with stone inscriptions describing forms of good life and the nature of good government.

The inscriptions give a special importance to tolerance of diversity. For example, the edict (now numbered XII) at Erragudi puts the issue thus:

A man must not do reverence to his own sect or disparage that of another man without reason. Depreciation should be for specific reason only, because the sects of other people all deserve reverence for one reason or another.

By thus acting, a man exalts his own sect, and at the same time does service to the sects of other people. By acting contrariwise, a man hurts his own sect, and does disservice to the sects of other people. For he who does reverence to his own sect while disparaging the sects of others wholly from attachment to his own, with intent to enhance the splendour of his own sect, in reality by such conduct inflicts the severest injury on his own sect.[15]

These edicts from the third century B.C. emphasize the importance of tolerance, both in public policy by the government and in the behavior of citizens to each other.

On the domain and coverage of tolerance, Ashoka was a universalist and demanded this for all, including those whom he described as "forest people," the tribal population living in pre-agricultural economic formations. Condemning his own conduct before his conversion, Ashoka notes that in the war in Kalinga, "men and animals numbering one hundred and fifty thousands were carried away (captive) from that kingdom." He goes on to state that the slaughter or the taking of prisoners "of even a hundredth or thousandth part of all those people who were slain or died or were carried away (captive) at that time in Kalinga is now considered very deplorable [by him]." Indeed, he proceeds to assert that now he believes that even if a person should wrong him, that offense would be forgiven "if it is possible to forgive it." He describes the object of his government as "non-injury, restraint, impartiality, and mild behaviour" applied "to all creatures."[16]

Ashoka's championing of egalitarian and universal tolerance may appear un-Asian to some commentators, but his views are firmly rooted in lines of analysis already in vogue in intellectual circles in India in the three preceding centuries. It is interesting, however, to consider another author whose treatise on governance and political economy was also profoundly influential. I refer to Kautilya, the author of *Arthashastra*, which can be translated as the "economic science," though it is at least as much concerned with practical politics as with economics. Kautilya, a contemporary of Aristotle, lived in the fourth century B.C. and worked as a senior minister of Emperor Chandragupta Maurya, Emperor Ashoka's grandfather, who had established the large Maurya empire across the subcontinent.

Kautilya's writings are often cited as a proof that freedom and tolerance were not valued in the Indian classical tradition. Two aspects of the impressively detailed account of economics and politics to be found in *Arthashastra* might tend to suggest that there is no support there for a liberal democracy.

[15]Translation in Vincent A. Smith, *Asoka* (Delhi: S. Chand, 1964), pp. 170–71.

[16]*Asokan Studies*, pp. 34–35, edict XIII.

First, Kautilya is a consequentialist of quite a narrow kind. While the objectives of promoting the happiness of subjects and order in the kingdom are strongly backed up by detailed policy advice, he depicts the king as a benevolent autocrat, whose power is to be maximized through good organization. Thus, *Arthashastra* presents penetrating ideas and suggestions on such practical subjects as famine prevention and administrative effectiveness that remain relevant even today, more than two thousand years later; yet at the same time, it advises the king how to get his way, if necessary through the violation of freedom of his opponents and adversaries.

Second, Kautilya seems to attach little importance to political or economic equality, and his vision of good society is strongly stratified according to lines of class and caste. Even though the objective of promoting happiness, which is given an exalted position in the hierarchy of values, is applied to all, the other objectives have clearly inegalitarian form and content. There is an obligation to give the less fortunate members of the society the support that they need to escape misery and enjoy life— Kautilya specifically identifies as the duty of the king to "provide the orphans, the aged, the infirm, the afflicted, and the helpless with maintenance," along with providing "subsistence to helpless women when they are carrying and also to the [newborn] children they give birth to."[17] But recognizing that obligation is very far from valuing the freedom of these people to decide how to live—tolerating heterodoxy. Indeed, there is very little tolerance in Kautilya, except for the upper sections of the community.

What do we conclude from this? Certainly, Kautilya is no democrat, no egalitarian, no general promoter of everyone's freedom. And yet, when it comes to the characterization of what the most favored people—the upper classes— should get, freedom figures quite prominently. Denial of personal liberty of the upper classes (the so-called Arya) is seen as unacceptable. Indeed, regular penalties, some of them heavy, are specified for the taking of such adults or children in indenture, even though the slavery of the existing slaves is seen as perfectly acceptable.[18] To be sure, we do not find in Kautilya anything like the clear articulation that Aristotle provides of the importance of free exercise of capability. But the importance of freedom is clear enough in Kautilya as far as the upper classes are concerned. It contrasts with the governmental duties to the lower orders, which take the paternalistic form of state assistance for the avoidance of acute deprivation and misery. Still, insofar as a view of the good life emerges from all this, it is an ideal that is entirely consistent with a freedom-valuing ethical system. The domain of that concern is narrow, to be sure, confined to the upper groups of society, but this limitation is not wildly different from the Greek concern with free men as opposed to slaves or women.

I have been discussing in some detail the political ideas and practical reason presented by two forceful, but very different, expositors in India in the third and the fourth centuries B.C. because their ideas have influenced later Indian writings. I do not want to give the impression that all Indian political commentators took lines of approach similar to Ashoka's or Kautilya's. Quite the contrary. Many positions taken before and after Kautilya and Ashoka contradict their respective claims, just as others are more in line either with Ashoka or with Kautilya.

For example, the importance of tolerance— even the need for universality in this—is eloquently expressed in different media, such as Shudraka's drama, Akbar's political pronouncements, and Kabir's poetry, to name just a few examples. The presence of these contributions does not entail the absence of opposite arguments and recommendations. Rather, the point is that in their heterogeneity, Indian traditions contain a variety of views and reasonings, but they include, in different ways, arguments in favor of tolerance, in defense of freedom, and even, in the case of Ashoka, in support of equality at a very basic level.

AKBAR AND THE MOGHULS

Among the powerful expositors and practitioners of tolerance of diversity in India must be counted the great Moghul emperor Akbar, who

---

[17]*Kautilya's Arthasastra,* translated by R. Shama Sastry (Mysore: Mysore Printing and Publishing House, 8th edition, 1967), p. 47.

[18]See R. P. Kangle, *The Kautilya Arthasastra,* Part II (Bombay: University of Bombay, 1972), chapter 13, section 65, pp. 235–39.

reigned between 1556 and 1605. Again, we are not dealing with a democrat, but with a powerful king who emphasized the acceptability of diverse forms of social and religious behavior, and who accepted human rights of various kinds, including freedom of worship and religious practice. Such rights would not have been easily tolerated in parts of Europe in Akbar's time.

For example, as the year 1000 in the Muslim Hejira calendar was reached in 1591–92, there was excitement about it in Delhi and Agra (not unlike what is happening right now as the year 2000 in the Christian calendar approaches). Akbar issued various enactments at this juncture of history, and some of these focused on religious tolerance, including the following:

No man should be interfered with on account of religion, and anyone [is] to be allowed to go over to a religion he pleased.

If a Hindu, when a child or otherwise, had been made a Muslim against his will, he is to be allowed, if he pleased, to go back to the religion of his fathers.[19]

Again, the domain of tolerance, while religion-neutral, was not universal in other respects, including gender equality or equality between younger and older people. The enactment went on to argue for the forcible repatriation of a young Hindu woman to her father's family if she had abandoned it in pursuit of a Muslim lover. In the choice between supporting the young lovers and the young woman's Hindu father, old Akbar's sympathies are entirely with the father. Tolerance and equality at one level are combined with intolerance and inequality at another level, but the extent of general tolerance on matters of belief and practice is quite remarkable. It is interesting to note, especially in light of the hard sell of "Western liberalism," that while Akbar was making these pronouncements on religious tolerance, the Inquisition was in high gear in Europe.

THEORIES AND PRACTICE

It is important to recognize that many of these historical leaders in Asia not only emphasized the importance of freedom and tolerance, they also had clear theories as to why this was the appropriate thing to do. This applies very strongly to both Ashoka and Akbar. Since the Islamic tradition is sometimes seen as being monolithic, this is particularly important to emphasize in the case of Akbar. Akbar was, in fact, deeply interested in Hindu philosophy and culture, but also took much note of the beliefs and practices of other religions, including Christianity, Jainism, and the Parsee faith. In fact, he attempted to establish something of a synthetic religion for India—the Din Ilahi—drawing on the different faiths in the country.

There is an interesting contrast here between Ashoka's and Akbar's forms of religious tolerance. Both stood for religious tolerance by the state, and both argued for tolerance as a virtue to be practiced by all. But while Ashoka combined this with his own Buddhist pursuits (and tried to spread "enlightenment" at home and abroad), Akbar tried to combine the distinct religions of India, incorporating the "good points" of different religions. Akbar's court was filled with Hindu as well as Muslim intellectuals, artists, and musicians, and he tried in every way to be nonsectarian and symmetric in the treatment of his subjects.

It is also important to note that Akbar was by no means unique among the Moghul emperors in being tolerant. In many ways, the later Moghul emperor, the intolerant Aurangzeb, who violated many of what would be now seen as basic human rights of Hindus, was something of an exception.[20] But even Aurangzeb should be considered in his familial setting, not in isolation. None of his immediate family seems to have

[19]Translation from Vincent A. Smith, *Akbar: The Great Mogul* (Oxford: Clarendon Press, 1917), p. 257.

[20]The exponents of contemporary Hindu politics in India often try to deny the tolerant nature of much of Moghul rule. That tolerance was, however, handsomely acknowledged by Hindu leaders of an earlier vintage. For example, Sri Aurobindo, who established the famous ashram in Pondicherry, specifically identified this aspect of the Moghul rule (*The Spirit and Form of Indian Polity,* Calcutta: Arya Publishing House, 1947, pp. 86–89):

The Mussulman domination ceased very rapidly to be a foreign rule. . . . The Mogul empire was a great and magnificent construction and an immense amount of political genius and talent was employed in its creation and maintenance. It was as splendid, powerful and beneficent and, it may be added, in spite of Aurangzeb's fanatical zeal, infinitely more liberal and tolerant in religion than any medieval or contemporary European kingdom or empire.

shared Aurangzeb's intolerance. Dara Shikoh, his elder brother, was much involved with Hindu philosophy and had, with the help of some scholars, prepared a Persian translation of some of the *Upanishads,* the ancient texts dating from about the eighth century B.C. In fact, Dara Shikoh had much stronger claims to the Moghul throne than Aurangzeb, since he was the eldest and the favorite son of their father, Emperor Shah Jahan. Aurangzeb fought and killed Dara, and imprisoned their father for the rest of his life (leaving him, the builder of the Taj Mahal, to gaze at his creation in captivity, from a distance).

Aurangzeb's son, also called Akbar, rebelled against his father in 1681 and joined hands in this enterprise with the Hindu kingdoms in Rajasthan and later the Marathas (though Akbar's rebellion too was ultimately crushed by Aurangzeb). While fighting from Rajasthan, Akbar wrote to his father protesting his intolerance and vilification of his Hindu friends. The issue of tolerance of differences was indeed a subject of considerable discussion among the feuding parties. The father of the Maratha king, Raja Sambhaji, whom the young Akbar had joined, was no other than Shivaji, whom the present-day Hindu political activists treat as a superhero, and after whom the intolerant Hindu party Shiv Sena is named.

Shivaji himself took quite a tolerant view of religious differences. As the Moghul historian Khafi Khan, who was no admirer of Shivaji in other respects, reports:

[Shivaji] made it a rule that wherever his followers were plundering, they should do no harm to the mosques, the book of God, or the women of any one. Whenever a copy of the sacred Quran came into his hands, he treated it with respect, and gave it to some of his Mussalman followers.[21]

In fact, a very interesting letter to Aurangzeb on the subject of tolerance is attributed to Shivaji by some historians (such as Sir Jadunath Sarkar, the author of the classic *Shivaji and His Times,* published in 1919), though there are some doubts about this attribution (another possible author is Rana Raj Singh of Mewar/ Udaipur). No matter who among Aurangzeb's

contemporaries wrote this letter, the ideas engaged in it are interesting enough. The letter contrasts Aurangzeb's intolerance with the tolerant policies of earlier Moghuls (Akbar, Jahangir, Shah Jahan), and then says this:

If Your Majesty places any faith in those books by distinction called divine, you will there be instructed that God is the God of all mankind, not the God of Muslims alone. The Pagan and the Muslim are equally in His presence. . . . In fine, the tribute you demand from the Hindus is repugnant to justice.[22]

The subject of tolerance was indeed much discussed by many writers during this period of confrontation of religious traditions and the associated politics. One of the earliest writers on the subject of tolerance was the eleventh-century Iranian Alberuni, who came to India with the invading army of Sultan Mahmood of Ghazni and recorded his revulsion at the atrocities committed by the invaders. He proceeded to study Indian society, culture, religion, and intellectual pursuits (indeed his translations of Indian mathematical and astronomical treatises were quite influential in the Arab world, which in turn deeply influenced Western mathematics), but he also discussed the subject of intolerance of the unfamiliar.

In all manners and usages, [the Hindus] differ from us to such a degree as to frighten their children with us, with our dress, and our ways and customs, and as to declare us to be devil's breed, and our doings as the very opposite of all that is good and proper. By the bye, we must confess, in order to be just, that a similar depreciation of foreigners not only prevails among us and the Hindus, but is common to all nations towards each other.[23]

The point of discussing all this is to indicate the presence of conscious theorizing about tolerance and freedom in substantial and important parts of Asian tradition. We could consider many more illustrations of this phenomenon in writings from early Arabic, Chinese, Indian, and other cultures. As was argued earlier, the championing of democracy and political freedom in the modern sense cannot be found in

[21]*The Oxford History of India,* 4th edition, translated by Vincent Smith, edited by Percival Spear (London: Oxford University Press, 1974), p. 412.

[22]Ibid., pp. 417–18.

[23]*Alberuni's India,* translated by Edward C. Sachau, edited by Ainslie T. Embree (New York: Norton, 1971), Part I, Chapter I, p. 20.

the pre-Enlightenment tradition in any part of the world—the West or the East—so we have to look at the constituent components of this compound idea. The view that the basic ideas underlying freedom and rights in a tolerant society are "Western" notions, and somehow alien to Asia, is hard to make any sense of, even though that view has been championed by both Asian authoritarians and Western chauvinists.

INTERVENTION ACROSS NATIONAL BOUNDARIES

I want to turn now to a rather different issue, which is sometimes linked to the debate about the nature and reach of Asian values. The championing of Asian values is often associated with the need to resist Western hegemony. The linking of the two issues, which has occurred increasingly in recent years, uses the political force of anticolonialism to buttress the assault on basic political and civil rights in postcolonial Asia.

This linkage, though quite artificial, can be rhetorically very effective. For example, Lee Kuan Yew has emphasized the special nature of Asian values and has made powerful use of the general case for resisting Western hegemony to bolster the argument for Asian particularism. The rhetoric has extended to the apparently defiant declaration that Singapore is "not a client state of America."[24] That fact is certainly undeniable, and is an excellent reason for cheer, but the question that has to be asked is what the bearing of this fact is on the issue of human rights and political liberties in Singapore, or any other country in Asia.

The people whose political and other rights are involved in this debate are not citizens of the West, but of Asian countries. The fact that individual liberty and freedom may have been championed in Western writings and even by some Western political leaders can scarcely compromise the claim to liberty and freedom that people in Asia may otherwise have. As a matter of fact, one can grumble, with reason, that the political leaders of Western countries take far too *little* interest in issues of freedom in the rest of the world. There is plenty of evidence that the Western governments have, by

and large, tended to give priority to the interests of their own citizens engaged in commerce with the Asian countries and to the pressures generated by business groups to be on good terms with the ruling governments in Asia. It is not so much that there has been more bark than bite; there has in fact been very little barking either. What Chairman Mao had once described as a "paper tiger" has increasingly looked like a paper mouse.

But even if this had not been the case, and even if Western governments really had tried to promote political and civil rights in Asia, how could that possibly compromise the status of the rights of Asians? In this context, the idea of "human rights" has to be properly spelled out. In the most general form, the notion of human rights builds on our shared humanity. These rights are not derived from the citizenship of any country, or the membership of any nation, but taken as entitlements of every human being. They differ, thus, from constitutionally created rights guaranteed for specified people (such as, say, American or French citizens). For example, the human right of a person not to be tortured is independent of the country of which this person is a citizen and thus exists irrespective of what the government of that country—or any other—wants to do. A government can, of course, dispute a person's *legal* right not to be tortured, but that will not amount to disputing what must be seen as the person's *human* right not to be tortured.

Since the conception of human rights transcends local legislation and the citizenship of the person affected, it is not surprising that support for human rights can also come from anyone—whether or not she is a citizen of the same country as the person whose rights are threatened. A foreigner does not need the permission of a repressive government to try to help a person whose liberties are being violated. Indeed, in so far as human rights are seen as rights that any person has as a human being and not as a citizen of any particular country, the reach of the corresponding *duties* can also include any human being, irrespective of citizenship.

This basic recognition does not, of course, suggest that everyone must intervene constantly in protecting and helping others. That may be both ineffective and unsettling. There

[24]*International Herald Tribune,* June 13, 1995, p. 4.

is no escape from the need to employ practical reason in this field, any more than in any other field of deliberate human action. I have discussed elsewhere the nature of the necessary scrutiny, including the assessment of rights and their consequences.[25]

Ubiquitous interventionism is not particularly fruitful or attractive within a given country, or across national boundaries. There is no obligation to roam the four corners of the earth in search of liberties to protect. The claim is only that the barriers of nationality and citizenship do not preclude people from taking legitimate interest in the rights of others and even from assuming some duties related to them. The moral and political examination that is central to determining how one should act applies across national boundaries and not merely within each realm.

A CONCLUDING REMARK

The so-called Asian values that are invoked to justify authoritarianism are not especially Asian in any significant sense. Nor is it easy to see how they could be made into an Asian cause against the West, by the mere force of rhetoric. The people whose rights are being disputed are Asians, and no matter what the West's guilt may be (there are many skeletons in many cupboards across the world), the rights of the Asians can

[25] Amartya Sen, "Rights and Agency," *Philosophy and Public Affairs* 11 (1982); "Liberty and Social Choice," *Journal of Philosophy* 80 (January 1983); "Well-Being, Agency and Freedom: The Dewey Lectures 1984," *Journal of Philosophy* 82 (April 1985).

scarcely be compromised on those grounds. The case for liberty and political rights turns ultimately on their basic importance and on their instrumental role. This case is as strong in Asia as it is elsewhere.

I have disputed the usefulness of a grand contrast between Asian and European values. There is a lot we can learn from studies of values in Asia and Europe, but they do not support or sustain the thesis of a grand dichotomy. Contemporary ideas of political and personal liberty and rights have taken their present form relatively recently, and it is hard to see them as "traditional" commitments of Western cultures. There are important antecedents of those commitments in the form of the advocacy of tolerance and individual freedom, but those antecedents can be found plentifully in Asian as well as Western cultures.

The recognition of diversity within different cultures is extremely important in the contemporary world, since we are constantly bombarded by oversimple generalizations about "Western civilization," "Asian values," "African cultures," and so on. These unfounded readings of history and civilization are not only intellectually shallow, they also add to the divisiveness of the world in which we live.

Authoritarian readings of Asian values that are increasingly being championed in some quarters do not survive scrutiny. The thesis of a grand dichotomy between Asian values and European values adds little to our comprehension, and much to the confusion about the normative basis of freedom and democracy.

Questions for Discussion

1. Interpret Sen's claim that "the case for liberty and political rights turns ultimately on their basic importance and on their instrumental role."
2. Consider the idea of "Asian particularism." Is it a form of moral relativism? Is Sen a moral relativist?
3. What does Sen see as the basis for human rights?
4. Do different cultures have different moral traditions?

Etiquette and Ethics

The term *etiquette* comes from a French word for "ticket" that originally referred to an order issued to soldiers for food and lodging. Perhaps that archaic meaning is preserved in a very indirect sense, because proper etiquette is still regarded as something of a ticket, but to what? There are innumerable social settings where you are closely watched and judged on your deportment, such as job interviews, dinner with potential in-laws, and a round of golf with your boss. Even in less stressful settings, the social impact of your manners is a source of assessment; rightly or wrongly, people draw inferences about your character and form opinions of you based your observance of social customs. The ways in which you hold your fork, dress, open a door, shake hands, converse, look at someone, or sit down are small but significant indicators to those around you of the sort of person you are. The cues are often subtle and require extensive enculturation even to recognize and interpret, which suggests that the "ticket" in question with etiquette is admission to a particular class, subgroup, or community. It means that you know the rules of social intercourse—that you pass the test.

Insofar as proper etiquette simply consists of observing arbitrary social customs, the rules of deportment required to function in a particular social setting can be learned and practiced. A veritable cottage industry exists to teach the correct forms of behavior in foreign cultures to business people, diplomats, military leaders, politicians, and others for whom knowledge of such rules is important. A crash course in the etiquette of a foreign culture can never make one an insider, but it can probably steer one clear of the worst offenses against protocol—the kinds of social gaffs that can ruin business deals or strain international relations, since ignorance of them suggests little regard for what someone from that culture finds offensive, rude, or tasteless. Such ignorance can only be interpreted as a failure of respect. And even within our own culture, self-appointed "keepers of the flame" of civility write for the popular audience. Many people read Judith Miller, also known as "Miss Manners," one of several contemporary gurus of good taste. The desire for social acceptance—not to mention the rewards of social climbing—fuels a thriving market in civility training and advice.

But beneath the surface of the sometimes elaborate and seemingly arbitrary rules of protocol, there is a deeper significance to etiquette than learning how to maneuver within a culture or subgroup. Etiquette has several important connections to ethics, even though etiquette focuses on what is socially correct rather than on what is morally correct. One connection is basically utilitarian: When everyone observes the little rules that facilitate social interaction, everyone will benefit. We are happier when civil, polite, courteous, affable, and charming behavior is the norm. Not that we all excel in each of these areas, but to the extent that everyone makes a conscious effort not to fall below some minimal standard of civility, social interaction is facilitated and our communal level of happiness is higher than would otherwise be the case.

Another connection between etiquette and ethics turns on Kant's central idea of respect for persons. There is nothing more instructive (or humbling) than to imaginatively put yourself on the receiving end of your own uncivil behavior. Would you want others to behave that way toward you? Basic courtesy in the details of everyday interaction with others is readily interpreted, and properly so, as manifesting fundamental respect for the humanity of others. It involves more than saying "please" or "thank you," because these expressions can become utterly mechanical and annoyingly superficial, as when the benumbed cashier mumbles something about having a nice day. As an outward sign of respect, courtesy involves recognizing the other as a person, just like oneself, and treating the other with the respect and recognition that one expects for oneself.

Surprisingly, Kant did not see etiquette as a manifestation of respect for persons. For him etiquette—what he called social virtue—is merely a means of cultivating such respect. In his Lectures on Ethics, he said, "They [the rules of etiquette] relate to the pleasure and charm of social intercourse and to nothing more. But even though they are no virtues, they are a means of developing virtue. Courtesy and politeness make men gentle and refined and so lead to the practice of goodness in the small details of life" (*Lectures on Ethics*, 236). For Kant, then, the value of etiquette is purely instrumental; practicing the social virtues makes us more sensitive and hence more civil.

Kant may well be correct about the civilizing aspects of etiquette, but it seems shortsighted to stop there, since once we are civilized, how do we behave? Recall that for Kant (see Chapter 3) morality is a matter not of being moved by sentiment but of acting for the sake of universalizable principles. According to Kant, then, etiquette is useful in getting us to that position. Once there, we will still follow the rules of etiquette (which Kant seems to think are limited to "courtesy and politeness"), but we will follow them not simply because they are the rules of etiquette but because those rules manifest respect for persons. Our behavior toward others will not change, but the reason why we behave with courtesy and politeness will.

This suggests that someone can follow all the culturally expected rules of social deportment and do so for the wrong reason—if, for example, one does so merely to impress others or, as mentioned earlier, to pass some sort of test of social acceptance. In this case, one's observance of etiquette is utterly superficial and has no connection to ethics at all, because the motivation is not based on respect for persons.

Worse still, we can imagine twisted kinds of etiquette for morally objectionable practices, such as an etiquette observed among slave traders. Perhaps it was considered a breach of good form to undercut one's fellow slave traders by selling one's slaves below market value in order to gain a larger share of the market, or to sell them on Sunday or while other dealers are at lunch. Thus etiquette, in the minimal sense of socially correct behavior, has no intrinsic connection to ethics, since socially correct behavior might still be immoral. Following certain social expectations of courtesy and politeness may cause us to become moral, as Kant speculated. But once we become moral agents capable of acting for the sake of principle, we will behave in ways that will manifest respect for others. To the extent that various rules of social deportment are expressive of respect for others, we will follow them, not merely because they are social rules but because those rules, in this particular society, have a deeper foundation in a principle that is at the heart of Kant's conception of ethics.

There is yet another way to think about etiquette. Emily Post (1873–1960), whose name was synonymous with good manners and social refinement in her time, expressed it this way: "Manners are made up of trivialities of deportment which can be easily learned if one does not happen to know them; manner is personality—the outward manifestation of one's innate character and attitude toward life." In distinguishing between *manner* and *manners*, Post draws attention to a distinction between arbitrary social rules and the people who follow them. Her point is that one's moral character is manifested in how one behaves. A punctilious or rigidly mechanical observance of the rules for proper etiquette displays a character of a certain sort—perhaps someone who is unreflective, who lacks a natural grace, or who is uncomfortable relating to others in anything other than formulaic and strict, socially prescribed ways. In relating to others, however, our characters are constantly on display.

What Is Plagiarism and Why Is It Wrong?

Ethics can be baffling because we tend to focus on the most difficult and conflicted issues we can imagine, forgetting that there are many less controversial cases that are important too. Such cases remind us that ethics is discussable and amenable to reasoned investigation. Odds are you have encountered stern warnings about plagiarism in your student conduct code, from your college or university, and from your professors. But what is it and why is it wrong?

Despite the fact that plagiarism is vociferously and categorically condemned publicly, professors doggedly, sometimes even gleefully, go to inordinate lengths to pursue suspected cases of it, and accusations of plagiarism (not to mention convictions) alter lives and cast long shadows of doubt on personal integrity, plagiarism is a widespread phenomenon, especially now that the Internet makes it so easy (search engines also make it easy to detect). How widespread is a matter of dispute, since how it is defined will determine its prevalence. In a (June 28, 2001) *New York Times* article on Internet plagiarism, Professor Donald McCabe, who studies student plagiarism, said that approximately 50 percent of high school students and some 20 percent of college students have plagiarized. He attributed the lower rate among college students to their greater sense of purpose and to the more severe consequences of being convicted of plagiarizing in college. (In a subsequent article [September 3, 2003], Professor McCabe is again cited. According to his latest study, 38 percent of the undergraduate students surveyed report engaging in plagiarism in the past year. So much for Professor McCabe's earlier speculation about why college plagiarism is relatively low!)

Dictionaries trace *plagiarism* to the Latin, *plagium*, which means "to kidnap." Hence our modern sense of the term often having to do with stealing or theft—literary theft. A random search among the more than 651,000 websites on plagiarism confirms that theft is frequently mentioned as an important feature of plagiarism and that theft is evidently a large part of the explanation for plagiarism's moral seriousness in the minds of many people. Plagiarism is theft, and theft is wrong, so plagiarism is wrong. But this cannot be correct because someone can plagiarize and not steal. If your friend *gives* you a paper to submit under your name, your doing so would be plagiarism, but you would not have stolen anything.

The problem with plagiarism is not how you acquired the ideas but what you do with them. Submitting under your own name a paper that you did not write (we will focus on papers, though obviously one can also plagiarize art, music, data, etc.) is fraud. That is, you intend to deceive your professor into thinking that you generated the paper when you did not. What is wrong with that, you might ask? After all, presidents give speeches that they did not write, and they get credit for perceptive, well-crafted speeches. Yes, but no one expects presidents to write their own speeches, at least not anymore. The expectations are different in school. In school you are expected to do your own work because that is what school is all about; the educational mission is to cultivate individual skills—*your* ability to express yourself, to analyze ideas and arguments, and to comprehend the positions of others. Plagiarism thus strikes at the heart of education. That is why it is taken so seriously.

Of course, it is important to keep some perspective on the matter. Not all plagiarism is equally serious because not all fraud is equally serious. Push-up bras and embezzlement both work, when they work, by intentionally inducing false beliefs in others, but no one regards them as equally fraudulent. And if you think about it for a moment, the multiple-choice exam (that old warhorse of college education) employs fraud too, because it intentionally seeks to induce false beliefs in the minds of the test takers to distinguish between those who have a firm grasp of the material and those who do not. Although it is best to avoid plagiarism scrupulously, many of the admonitions in student conduct codes seem designed to scare, and they give the impression that plagiarism is a monolithic phenomenon, all of it equally grave.

If the only problem with plagiarism were that it subverts the educational mission so that the plagiarist does not get the education he or she claims to want, it would be hard to see why it is a serious moral issue. This point is sometimes expressed as "You are just cheating yourself." That is irrational because self-defeating puts plagiarism in the same category as deceiving your doctor about smoking; you come out worse off, but so what? This makes plagiarism stupid (which it is), but what makes it immoral? We can get a better grasp on the moral features of plagiarism if we concentrate on the context in which plagiarism occurs.

The professor–student relationship is contractual; each have certain rights and responsibilities in virtue of their respective positions. Students have a right to expect professors to be professionally competent, impartial, and intellectually engaged with the material of the course. Professors have responsibilities that correspond to these student rights: the responsibility to be professionally competent, impartial, and intellectually engaged with the material of the course. Similarly, professors have legitimate claims—rights—with regard to their students, among them the right to expect that the work the students submit for a course has not been plagiarized. Hence a student a responsibility not to plagiarize. By enrolling in a college or university, you have tacitly (often explicitly) agreed to the conditions of the contract between professor and student.

But why does a professor have a right to expect that the work you turn in is yours? The obvious answer is that you are being graded for it; you receive something of value (a grade) according to the quality of what you produce. The better you do, the better the grade you deserve. So in the end, grades are a matter of justice, and professors are supposed to give students grades that they deserve based on their performance in the class. If you submit plagiarized material, you do not deserve the good grade because you did not earn it. It is not a result of your intellectual effort, creativity, or insight.

The professor–student contract goes both ways; professors, not just students, can violate the agreement. A professor who fails to meet his or her responsibilities (and by extension the college that does little about it) no longer has a strong right to expect students to uphold their end of the bargain. In this sad state of affairs, it is the remarkable and self-motivated student who continues stoically in his or her studies, unaffected by the polluted educational surroundings, just as it is noble for the committed professor to continue to do his or her best to uphold academic integrity in the face of persistent and widespread student plagiarism. Clearly, neither state of affairs is desirable. Best is when both students and professors live up to the conditions of their agreement, and this is the educational atmosphere colleges should seek to foster.

Your professor is not the only one to whom you have promised not to plagiarize; you promised your fellow students that as well. You promised not to put them at a competitive disadvantage by plagiarizing. This was part of the agreement you made with the professor, since the professor has other students to grade, and grading is often a comparative judgment. Plagiarists also don't want others to plagiarize, because it makes their plagiarism ineffective if others do it too. Bank robbing and counterfeiting—indeed, probably all crimes for gain—presuppose that others do not engage in the same activity; otherwise, there is no benefit from the crime. The fact that the plagiarist does not want others to plagiarize exposes a deep problem with plagiarism: Why is it acceptable for the plagiarist to plagiarize but not for others to do so too? The answer "Then my plagiarized work will not help me" is no good, because everyone can say the same thing. Clearly, the plagiarist has no acceptable answer to the question, and this is an important reason to think that plagiarism is immoral. The immorality of plagiarism derives from the moral equality of people—the idea that from the moral point of view, none of us is special. We cannot expect others to follow the rules yet make arbitrary exceptions for ourselves. Plagiarism is immoral, then, because it is irrational, and not irrational in the simple, self-defeating way discussed above, but irrational because the plagiarist makes an exception for himself or herself when no such exception can be justified.

As a kind of fraud, plagiarism is dishonest. But why is honesty so important? We can approach the question of honesty in several ways. Perhaps the best is to consider honesty as a good character trait, a virtue or human excellence. The basic question is this: What kind of a person do you want to be?

Among the long list of character traits that we hope for and sometimes work to achieve will be honesty, at least honesty in those situations where honesty is desirable. Is the poker player honest? Is the diplomat? Complete brutal honesty in all situations at all times is neither good nor prudent. (When asked, do you tell the murderer where his intended victim can be found?) But even limiting ourselves to those situations where a sensible honesty is expected, why do we want to be honest? The familiar "Honesty is the best policy" comes to mind. Here we count the practical benefits of honesty: We will be trusted by others, and this will lead to good things; we will not have to worry about getting caught being dishonest, which can be a lot of work; and so on. But this approach misses a fundamental point: If you could be assured of getting away with being dishonest—plagiarizing a paper, for instance—why not do it? You could have the benefits of being thought honest while enjoying goods dishonestly acquired. Surely that is the best state of affairs.

The only way to respond to such a possibility is to consider your life from the "inside"—that is, to ponder what it is like to live a life of apparent probity but actual perfidy. Others might trust you, but you know that you are untrustworthy. You know that you do not deserve whatever benefits you illicitly achieved. The gap between your public image and your self-knowledge would probably produce a kind of self-loathing. Unfaithful marriage partners frequently suffer from a similar and apparently excruciating need to confess to their mates. Moreover, a life of illicit gains could not be a dignified one, for human dignity requires an integrated self that recognizes and takes responsibility for its actions—its accomplishments as well as its failures. Plagiarism is certainly not an accomplishment, unless you want to count "pulling it off" as one, in the way an accomplished art forger might delight in having his fakes accepted as originals. But the art forger at least has sophisticated artistic skills in which he can take pride. The plagiarist, by contrast, is not a brilliant essayist who mimics the style of others. The plagiarist simply presents the work of others as his own. The inner life of the plagiarist is unappealing, cut off as he is from authentic contact with others, unable to take genuine pride in his work and having to be content with appearances, all the while knowing the awful truth about himself. Perhaps such a life is possible, but it is hardly something to which one could reasonably aspire. The plagiarist knows that he is a fraud; this fills his heart with sadness as he hangs his head in shame.

Because plagiarism is fraud and fraud requires dishonesty, plagiarism requires dishonesty. And since dishonesty is intentional—one cannot be unintentionally dishonest—plagiarism is necessarily intentional. Yet student codes often distinguish between intentional and unintentional forms of plagiarism. For instance, the student code at my college states, "Whether intended or not, plagiarism is a serious offense against academic honesty." But if plagiarism is fraud it cannot be unintentional, because there cannot be unintentional intentions to deceive. Something has to give. Either not all forms of plagiarism are dishonest because not all forms require an intention to deceive, or, if plagiarism is necessarily an offense against academic honesty, then there cannot be unintentional forms of it because one cannot be unintentionally dishonest. Student conduct codes might find it easier to lump intentional and unintentional failures to cite sources together and call them all plagiarism, but then it makes no sense to condemn them all as dishonest.

How, you might ask, are we going to distinguish between intentional and unintentional failures to cite sources? Sometimes we can distinguish between intentional and unintentional failures to cite sources and sometimes we cannot. Any inquiry into culpability seeks to distinguish between intentional and unintentional acts; this is so for homicide, and it is no different for plagiarism. We simply have to make our best judgment based on the specific facts of each case.

Establishing intention is important for determining honesty or dishonesty, but intention to deceive is not the only basis on which to judge plagiarism. We can still strongly condemn unintentional failures to cite sources on grounds of negligence, not dishonesty. A negligent action need not be less serious just because it is unintentional. The drunk driver who kills someone is not exonerated simply because the killing was unintentional; the killing is seriously wrong irrespective of intention and is prosecuted accordingly. A similar case can be made for an unintentional failure to cite sources. Given that the accidental plagiarist *ought* to have known better, there is little excuse for a failure to cite sources. But when ought the accidental plagiarist to have known better? When he has been properly instructed about plagiarism and the college's policies regarding it. This is why it is so important for a college campus to cultivate a strong community ethos regarding plagiarism (through a sensible and widely promulgated student conduct code, constant reminders from professors, training in the proper documentation of sources, and discussions such as this one), because the plausibility of holding someone morally responsible for accidental or negligent plagiarism increases with the extent to which an individual should have known otherwise. So even though it is not very helpful to call both intentional and unintentional plagiarism violations of academic honesty, it still makes sense to regard "unintentional plagiarism" as a serious academic offense, given a proper institutional setting.

Our discussion of plagiarism gives us insight into the nature of moral inquiry. We have seen that an assessment of plagiarism is not just a matter of personal opinion, because we grounded the moral seriousness of plagiarism in the particulars of college life. It is not as though someone could agree with us that the purpose of college is the morally commendable one of cultivating various human excellences—intellectual, aesthetic, physical, and so on—but disagree that plagiarism subverts that aim. Nor could someone agree that plagiarism is a kind of fraud but doubt that in the proper context it is a serious moral failure. We have also seen that the moral grounds for assessing plagiarism involve consequences, duties, contracts, and character. Each of these features of commonsense moral assessment plays a key role in moral theories that we examine in this book. Moral inquiry requires a tough-minded willingness to pursue lines of questioning, even ones that go against received wisdom. The adequacy of our reasoning is our only authority.

Credits

Chapter 2: John Stuart Mill, *Utilitarianism*, The Library of Liberal Arts, Oskar Piest, ed. 1957, The Liberal Arts Press. pp. 10–16, 22–23, 44–48.

Chapter 3: Immanuel Kant, *Grounding for the Metaphysics of Morals*, James Ellington, trans. 3rd edition, 1993, Hackett Publishing Company, pp. 7–15, 30–36.

Chapter 4: Thomas Hobbes, from *The Leviathan*, Prometheus Books, 1988, Chapter 13, pp. 63–66, Chapter 14, pp. 66–73, Chapter 15, p. 74; John Rawls, from *A Theory of Justice*, pp. 11–16, 60–65, 1971, 1999, Harvard University Press.

Chapter 5: Aristotle, "The Nature of Virtue," pp. 1–5, 7–12, 15–29, from *Nichomachean Ethics*, second edition, trans. Terrence Irwin, Hackett Publishing Company, 1999.

Chapter 6: St. Thomas Aquinas, from *Summa Theologica*, in *basic Writings of St. Thomas Aquinas*, volume two, ed. Auton C. Pegis. Indianapolis: Hackett 1997, pp. 749–751.

Chapter 7: Judith Jarvis Thompson, "A Defense of Abortion," *Philosophy & Public Affairs*, vol 1, no. 1, 1971, Princeton University Press; Don Marquis, "An Argument that Abortion is Wrong," from *Ethics in Practice*, ed. Hugh LaFollette, pp. 91–102, 1997, Blackwell Publishers.

Chapter 8: Ann Garry, "Sex, Lies, and Pornography," from *Ethics in Practice*, Hugh LaFollette, 2nd edition, 2002, pp. 344–355, Blackwell Publishers; Burton Leiser, "Homosexuality and the 'Unnaturalness Argument'" in *Liberty, Justice and Morals: Contemporary Value Conflicts*, by permission of author.

Chapter 9: James Rachels, "Active and Passive Euthanasia," *New England Journal of Medicine*, 292, pp. 78–80, January 9, 1975; J. David Velleman, "A Right of Self-Termination?" *Ethics*, 109, April 1999, pp. 606–620. The University of Chicago.

Chapter 10: Hugo Bedau, "An Abolitionist's Survey of the Death Penalty in America Today," in *Debating the Death Penalty*, Hugo Bedau and Paul Cassell, eds., 2004, Oxford University Press, pp. 15–49; Louis Pojman, "Why the Death Penalty is Morally Permissible," same source, pp. 51–75.

Chapter 11: Jeff McMahan, "Innocence, Self-Defense and Killing in War," *Journal of Political Philosophy*, vol 2, no. 3, 1994, pp. 193–221; Michael Walzer, "Terrorism: A Critique of Excuses," from *Problems of International Justice*, Steven Luper-Foy, ed., Westview Press, 1988, pp. 237–247. By permission of author.

Chapter 12: Bernard Williams, "Toleration: An Impossible Virtue?" pp. 18–27 in *Toleration: An Elusive Virtue,* David Heyd, ed., 1996, Princeton University Press; T.M. Scanlon, "the Difficulty of Tolerance" same source, pp. 226–239.

Chapter 13: Jeffrie Murphy, "Forgiveness and Resentment," from *Forgiveness and Mercy,* Cambridge University Press, 1988. pp. 14–34; Norvin Richards, "Forgiveness," *Ethics,* vol. 99, issue 1 (Oct. 1988), 77–97. The University of Chicago Press.

Chapter 14: Peter Singer, from *Animal Liberation,* Avon Books, New York, 1977, pp. 1–9, 15–23; Carl Cohen, "A Critique of the Alleged Moral Basis of Vegetarianism" *The Nation,* vol 226, no. 17, May 6, 1978. By permission of author.

Chapter 15: J. Baird Callicott, "The Conceptual Foundations of the Land Ethic," from *Companion to A Sand County Almanac,* 1987, University of Wisconsin Press; William Baxter, from *People or Penguins: The Case for Optimal Pollution,* 1974, Columbia University Press, New York.

Chapter 16: Peter Singer, from *One World: The Ethics of Globalization,* 2004, 2nd edition. Yale University Press, pp. 77–105; Thomas Pogge, "World Poverty and Human Rights," *Ethics and International Affairs,* vol 19, no 1, 2005, pp. 1–7. Carnegie Council on Ethics and International Affairs.

Chapter 17: Nel Noddings, from *Caring: A Feminine Approach to Ethics and Moral Education,* pp. 79–97, 98–103. University of California Press, 1884; Virginia Held, from *Feminist Morality,* pp. 64–90, University of Chicago Press, 1993.

Chapter 18: J.L. Mackie, "The Subjectivity of Values," from *Inventing Right and Wrong,* pp. 15–18, 27–46. Penguin Books, New York, 1977; Thomas Nagel, "Moral Luck," *Proceedings of the Aristotelian Society,* vol 50, pp. 137–155, 1976.

Chapter 19: Plato, Ring of Gyges, from *The Republic,* pp. 496–502, Book II, 357A-367E, trans. G.M.A. Grube, revised by C.D.C. Reeve, Hackett Publishing Company, 1992; Frederich Nietzsche, from *Beyond Good and Evil,* trans Helen Zimmern, pp. 223–232, Prometheus Books, 1989.

Chapter 20: Buddhism, "Four Noble Truths" from *Basic Teachings of the Buddha,* Glenn Wallis, trans. Pp. 36–38, Modern Library (imprint of random House Publishing), 2007; Confucius, from *The Analects,* David Hinton, translator, Counterpoint New York, NY (member of Perseus Books Group) 1998. I.3, I.8, II.3, II.7, II.11, III.3, III.7, III.26, IV.2, IV. 5, IV.12, V.9, VI.14, VII.12, VII.16, VIII.2, XI.12, XII.2, XII.11, XIII.3, XIII.13, XIII.29,30, XV.2, XV.18, XVI.2, XVI.8, XVII.2, XVII.24; Amaryta Sen, "Human Rights and Asian Values," 16th Morgenthau Memorial Lecture, 1997, Carnegie Council of Ethics and International Affairs. 170 E. 64th St., New York, NY.